WRIGLEYVILLE

PETER GOLENBOCK

WRIGLEYVILLE

A Magical History Tour of the Chicago Cubs

ST. MARTIN'S PRESS ❧ NEW YORK

A NOTE ABOUT THE JACKET PHOTOMONTAGE

Wrigley Field was the last major league ballpark to install lights for night games. The "lights/no lights" debate raged for four years, and artist Scott Mutter joked that the only way night baseball would be played in Wrigley Field would be if the fans brought flashlights. After three seasons of working with a technique of photomontage, he illustrated his fantasy by transforming a June 1987 day game into this apparent night game. It was published as a poster in October 1987. The poster, now in its sixth press run, was called a "genuine classic" and was featured in newspapers and on television throughout the country, including *Sunday Morning with Charles Kuralt*. It is included in *Surrational Images,* a collection of Mutter's photomontages, and a 1997 calendar of the same title.

All photos © George Bruce

Design by Pei Koay

Library of Congress Cataloging-in-Publication Data

Golenbock, Peter.
    Wrigleyville : a magical history tour of the Chicago Cubs / by Peter Golenbock.
      p. cm.
    ISBN 0-312-14079-7
    1. Chicago Cubs (Baseball team)—History. I. Title.
GV875.C6G66 1996
796.357'64'0977311—dc20   95-26052
                                                CIP

First Edition: March 1996

10 9 8 7 6 5 4 3 2 1

Dedication

This book is dedicated to Studs Terkel, whose oral histories I have so greatly admired through the years. Using oral history, a writer can bring to the reader an immediacy rarely found in books in the writer's voice. In oral histories, the reader meets the participants, one by one. Studs's successes have inspired me to use this form for my team histories.

Also to Harry Caray, the last of a unique breed.

Through my childhood I had the privilege of being able to listen to Mel Allen and Red Barber. We can no longer listen to these talented sources of entertainment and inspiration do play by play, but thank heaven, we still have Harry, not only the voice of the Cubs but, thanks to cable television, the voice of the game of baseball itself.

For fifty years Harry has embraced the game of baseball. He never fails to remind us how wonderful, how thrilling, and most important, how much fun the game can be.

With every broadcast Harry Caray keeps alive baseball's spirit in the purest sense. True baseball fans everywhere thank you.

Folks marvel at the great throngs which attend important baseball matches. They really need not be wondered at. The spectators have mostly been players, and once the germ of baseball gets in their blood, they never get it out.

—ALBERT SPALDING, 1911

I took out a package of Spearmint and I stuck a rib in my throat. Always buy Wrigley's, I said, it lasts longer. Besides, they spend $5,000,000,963.00 a year for advertising. Gives people work. Keeps the subways clean.

—HENRY MILLER, *The Colossus of Maroussi*, 1941

Time is of the essence. The crowd and players
Are the same age always, but the man in the crowd
Is older every season. Come on, play ball!

—ROLFE HUMPHRIES

Contents

	Introduction	*xv*
	Acknowledgments	*xvii*
CHAPTER 1	Chikagou	*1*
CHAPTER 2	Albert Spalding	*6*
CHAPTER 3	Spalding's Revolution	*12*
CHAPTER 4	The Great Anson	*20*
CHAPTER 5	Mike Kelly	*29*
CHAPTER 6	Spalding's Dynasty	*36*
CHAPTER 7	World Series Failure	*49*
CHAPTER 8	Stars for Sale	*61*
CHAPTER 9	The Players Revolt	*71*
CHAPTER 10	Anson's Demise	*81*
CHAPTER 11	Al Spalding: Savior	*90*
CHAPTER 12	Selee's Genius	*94*
CHAPTER 13	The Cubs Grow Claws	*99*
CHAPTER 14	The Peerless Leader	*104*
CHAPTER 15	116–36	*111*
CHAPTER 16	A Fine Bunch of Stiffs	*119*
CHAPTER 17	World Champs	*124*
CHAPTER 18	The Warren Gill Affair	*128*
CHAPTER 19	September 23, 1908	*132*
CHAPTER 20	A Tie	*137*
CHAPTER 21	Four to Two	*142*
CHAPTER 22	Champs Again	*150*
CHAPTER 23	Continued Success	*154*
CHAPTER 24	Murphy's Law	*158*

CHAPTER 25	Charles Weeghman	*164*
CHAPTER 26	Hippo Loses a No-Hitter	*167*
CHAPTER 27	Transitions	*170*
CHAPTER 28	Tales from the Visiting Clubhouse	*182*
CHAPTER 29	Alex	*185*
CHAPTER 30	Marse Joe Arrives	*191*
CHAPTER 31	Mr. Wrigley	*199*
CHAPTER 32	A Powerhouse	*204*
CHAPTER 33	When Eight Runs Weren't Enough	*212*
CHAPTER 34	One Firing Too Many	*219*
CHAPTER 35	The Death of William Wrigley	*225*
CHAPTER 36	Scandal—and Victory	*229*
CHAPTER 37	The Mythical Called Shot	*234*
CHAPTER 38	The Death of William Veeck	*239*
CHAPTER 39	Philibuck	*245*
CHAPTER 40	Twenty-one in a Row	*250*
CHAPTER 41	Stan Hack Stands on Third	*256*
CHAPTER 42	The Home Run in the Gloaming	*258*
CHAPTER 43	Diz's Last Stand	*263*
CHAPTER 44	The Crazy World of PK Wrigley	*265*
CHAPTER 45	Wartime Ball	*280*
CHAPTER 46	The Workhorse	*287*
CHAPTER 47	Jolly Cholly	*294*
CHAPTER 48	Roomies	*302*
CHAPTER 49	The War Pennant	*305*
CHAPTER 50	The Depths	*313*
CHAPTER 51	The Minor Leagues	*325*
CHAPTER 52	Boyhood Memories	*334*
CHAPTER 53	Mr. Cub	*342*
CHAPTER 54	The Professor	*354*
CHAPTER 55	The Kid from Garlic Gulch	*358*
CHAPTER 56	The College of Coaches	*365*
CHAPTER 57	The Cornerstone	*375*
CHAPTER 58	Kenny Hubbs	*381*
CHAPTER 59	Leo	*384*
CHAPTER 60	Fergie	*393*
CHAPTER 61	Flying High in '69	*400*
CHAPTER 62	Freefall	*415*
CHAPTER 63	Leo's Demise	*421*
CHAPTER 64	Mad Dog and Bruce	*431*
CHAPTER 65	The Death of the Reserve Clause and PK Wrigley	*440*
CHAPTER 66	Big $$$, Low Morale	*443*
CHAPTER 67	Harry	*454*

CHAPTER 68	Dallas Green Takes Over	459
CHAPTER 69	The Red Baron	472
CHAPTER 70	So Close	480
CHAPTER 71	The Demise of Dallas	487
CHAPTER 72	Let There Be Lights	491
CHAPTER 73	Departures	493
CHAPTER 74	Semper Harry	497
	Bibliography	501
	Notes	505
	Index	525

List of Illustrations

Albert Spalding   *14*
Adrian Anson   *25*
Mike Kelly   *31*
John Clarkson   *45*
The 1884 Team   *54*
Billy Sunday   *89*
Frank Selee   *95*
Frank Chance   *105*
Mordecai Brown   *112*
Joe Tinker   *115*
John Evers   *116*
The 1906 Cubs   *124*
Charles Murphy   *158*
Hippo Vaughn   *169*
Alexander, Wrigley, and Killefer   *171*
Rabbit Maranville   *179*
Grover Cleveland Alexander   *187*
Joe McCarthy   *192*
Hack Wilson   *197*
William Wrigley   *200*
Woody English   *205*
Rogers Hornsby   *208*
Charlie Grimm   *230*
Babe Ruth and Phil Cavarretta   *249*
Grimm, Herman, Jurges, and English   *252*
Dizzy Dean   *260*

Gabby Hartnett	262
PK Wrigley	266
Bill Nicholson	285
Hank Borowy	307
Emil Verban	341
Ernie Banks	350
Lou Brock	373
Ron Santo	378
Ken Hubbs	383
Leo Durocher	386
Fergie Jenkins	397
Billy Williams	410
Randy Hundley	413
Bill Madlock	437
Dave Kingman	448
Bruce Sutter	450
Dallas Green	461
Ryne Sandberg	470
Rick Sutcliffe	474
Andre Dawson	488
Lee Smith	490
Greg Maddux	494
Harry Caray	499

Introduction

Wrigleyville, in addition to being the easygoing North Side neighborhood around the charming old Chicago ballpark, is so much more than that. It is a state of mind, harkening to a warm afternoon at Wrigley Field: the sun reddening the exposed backs of devoted bleacherites, the smell of peanuts, popcorn, and hot dogs in the air, the Cubs players on the grassy field below striving against whoever comes to town.

If visitors inside the ivy-coated park listen closely, they can summon the echoes of the past: the brogue of Mike Kelly, the deep voice of Joe McCarthy, the laughing banter of Gabby Hartnett, the feisty bark of Phil Cavarretta, the singsong joy emanating from Ernie Banks. If they close their eyes and look out onto that expanse of emerald green, they can see Hack Wilson lift high fly balls into the stands, recall Ron Santo clicking his heels after a win, and marvel at the flawless fielding of Ryne Sandberg.

From childhood forward, things happen to us, good and bad, but nothing bad has ever happened to us at a baseball game, even when our favorite player makes an error and the team loses a pennant on the final day of the season. This is especially true of Cubs fans, the purest, truest fans in America. Cubs fans have a Jobian view of life. Yes, Job was a Cubs fan. Didn't Job ask, "Why are you doing this to me, God?" Isn't this the refrain of all Cubs fans?

For Cubs fans, there are no bad Cubs ballplayers, only players trying to become more proficient; there are no bad Cubs teams, only teams that promise success in the future.

Cubs fans love the Cubs, warts and all, no questions asked. This quality is called faith.

Cubs fans have blindly and faithfully thrilled to their personal heroes, regardless of result. In the wonderful world of Wrigleyville, Paul Minner, Wayne Terwilliger, Roy Smalley, Bob Buhl, and Glen Hobbie were heroes to someone, someplace, the same way Shawon Dunston, Rey Sanchez, Jim Bullinger, and Turk Wendell have their rabid fans today. An outsider may see these players as flawed. To Cubs fans, they are family, to be accepted at whatever skill level they perform.

And when a truly talented player arrives: ecstasy. For Cubs fans, every Ernie Banks home run was a thrill. Every Phil Cavarretta or Billy Williams hit a joy. Every Fergie Jenkins victory a cause for celebration. When Rick Sutcliffe and Ryne Sandberg almost led the Cubs to the pennant in 1984, this sophisticated city almost lost its mind.

The goal of *Wrigleyville* is to allow the reader to experience what the ballplayers experienced while they played for the Chicago Cubs. Through the hallowed corridors of the various home ballparks through the years has passed a virtual Hall of Fame lineup in Chicago uniforms: Albert Spalding, Cap Anson, King Kelly, John Clarkson, Joe Tinker, Johnny Evers, Frank Chance, Rabbit Maranville, Grover Cleveland Alexander, Rogers Hornsby, Hack Wilson, Joe McCarthy, Kiki Cuyler, Dizzy Dean, Billy Herman, Frankie Frisch, Phil Cavarretta, Ernie Banks, Leo Durocher, Ron Santo, Fergie Jenkins, Billy Williams, Bruce Sutter, Andre Dawson, and Ryne Sandberg, just to name a few.

These are fascinating men in their own right, and through them and their teammates in Wrigleyville you will get to meet the greatest players and managers the game has ever known, including George and Harry Wright, Charles Comiskey, John McGraw, Christy Mathewson, Babe Ruth, Ty Cobb, Honus Wagner, Stan Musial, Robin Roberts, Johnny Vander Meer, Jackie Robinson, Willie Mays, Warren Spahn, Bob Gibson, Hank Aaron, Eddie Mathews, Pete Rose, and Mike Schmidt.

So many players. So many stories. So many memories.

The brilliant actor Rod Steiger once stated, "The greatest gift an artist can give is a warm, pleasant memory."

When I heard him say that, I nodded vigorously, for after all, these ballplayers are artists, and what they bring us game after game are thousands of warm, pleasant memories. In *Wrigleyville,* they have given us their personal stories that make the game of baseball so special.

As in life itself, here is more than a century's worth of great drama, joy and sadness, fulfillment and bitterness, frustration and exultation, from the players themselves. Through them you will see clearly that the essence of the game of baseball has not changed. What the owners faced then, they face now. What the players faced then, they face now.

The players were special then. They are special now.

For all you Cubs and baseball fans, here is a compilation of more than a hundred years of those warm, pleasant memories.

I sincerely hope that you enjoy this magical history tour.

Acknowledgments

This book has been a joy to research and write from start to finish. For that I have a legion of supporters to thank.

To Jay Acton, for coming up with the idea and selling it to George Witte, my esteemed editor at St. Martin's Press. To Neil and Dawn Reshen, my business managers, for their bulldogged support and encouragement. I love you both.

To the staffs of the public libraries in New York, Chicago, Tampa, and St. Petersburg, as well as to the librarians of the Chicago Historical Society. To Mark Rifkin, a copy editor of extraordinary ability. Thank you all.

To Bill Young, for pointing me in the right directions.

To my family: the lovely Rhonda, the wonderful Charlie, the bassetty Doris.

To Marty Appel for being kind enough to photocopy King Kelly's book and send it to me; to Paul Bauer, for lending me a copy of Johnny Evers's rare book.

To the late Ed Froelich: it was a privilege having known you. To Woody English and Phil Cavarretta, fine gentlemen, thanks for your many hours of recollections.

To Randy Hundley, for allowing me to come to your Cub fantasy camp to interview you and your teammates, Glenn Beckert, Gene Oliver, Ron Santo, and Ferguson Jenkins and allowing me to see the true nature of Cubworld.

Also my deep appreciation to former Cubs players Billy Jurges, the late Billy Herman, Bill Nicholson, Ken Raffensberger, Henry Wyse, Don Johnson, Lennie Merullo, Dewey Williams, the late Don Elston, childhood hero Jim Brosnan, Darold Knowles, Dickie Noles, Bruce Sutter, and Rick Sutcliffe.

To Cubs fans Paul and Ned Buchbinder, Jim Shapiro, and Bruce Ladd, and to Jack Wiers, my former announcing partner with the St. Petersburg Pelicans. You said Chicago was a great city. You were right.

To Al Spalding, Cap Anson, Mike Kelly, and Johnny Evers. Your books allowed me to succeed beyond my wildest dreams.

And finally, to the truest, purest fans in the world, the millions who love the Cubs, win or lose. The rest of society could learn a thing or two from your approach to life. This big fat book is for you.

When the Cubs win their next pennant, I'll be cheering too.

1

Chikagou

The Potawatomi called the place *Chikagou*. The word, according to local talk show interviewer Irv Kupcinet, means "anything powerful or great." Another famous Chicagoan, author Studs Terkel, says its meaning is less highfalutin. His translation: "city of the big smell."

This conundrum is typical, according to yet another local celebrity, writer Nelson Algren, who portrayed Chicago as a city of opposites and contradictions. Algren wrote, "Chicago . . . forever keeps two faces, one for winners and one for losers; one for hustlers and one for squares . . . One face for Go-Getters and one for Go-Get-It-Yourselfers . . . One for poets and one for promoters . . . One for early risers, one for evening hiders."

The city is a mix of the erudite and the profane, the respected and the feared, the admired and the reviled. It is the city of world-famed architects Louis Sullivan, Frank Lloyd Wright, and Mies van der Rohe. Ernest Hemingway and Hillary Clinton grew up in Oak Park. Carl Sandburg, Theodore Dreiser, Ben Hecht, Saul Bellow, and Richard Wright all lived in and around the city, as did others in Chicago's Writers Hall of Fame: Willa Cather, Vachel Lindsay, Sherwood Anderson, and Edgar Lee Masters, who at one time was a law partner of the esteemed Clarence Darrow, the city slicker at the Scopes trial.

Chicago has been home to reformers Jane Addams, Billy Sunday, Adlai Stevenson, and Eliot Ness as well as to world-class gangsters John Dillinger, Bugsy Moran, and Al Capone and the dangerous bartender Mickey Finn, whose drink could put you out for three days and nights.

Flo Ziegfeld and Mike Todd were Windy City inhabitants, as were Little Egypt, who created the hoochie-kootchie dance during the Columbian Exposition of 1893, and Sally Rand, who unveiled her fan dance at the Century of Progress Exposition in 1933. When Rand was prosecuted for lewdness, the presiding judge, who ruled in her favor, commented, "Would you put pants on a horse?"

The judge wasn't the only comedian in town. Steve Allen comes from Chicago, and famous members of the Second City comedy troupe—John and Jim Belushi, Dan Aykroyd, Bill Murray, and John Candy to name a few—either came from Chicago or formed emotional ties to the place.

Chikagou, an Indian town, was a dangerous place to live. Commerce consisted of trade in pelts, guns, furs, hatchets, blankets, and whiskey, with Indians the chief buyers. In 1832, Chikagou still had only 350 residents.

Then, on September 26, 1833, after years of massacres and skirmishes, western expansion fueled the desire of the Pilgrims' descendants to get rid of the perceived cause of the danger: the Indians. The U.S. government got tough. Seventy-six Indian chiefs from the Chippewa, Ottawa, and Potawatomi tribes were assembled to sign a peace treaty that ended all Indian claims to lands in Illinois territory. Under the treaty, the Indians would be given land west of the Mississippi. Shortly thereafter, Indians were seen no more around Chikagou town.

One eyewitness to the uneasy relationship between the White Man and the Potawatomi Indians was Adrian "Cap" Anson, who would later become a Chicago institution. Anson grew up in Marshalltown, Iowa, which was about 130 miles from Illinois across the far banks of the Mississippi. Anson, who was born in 1852, was about fifteen when the displaced Indians from around Chikagou gave him the scare of his young life.

ADRIAN ANSON: "I remember one little occurrence in which I was concerned those early days that impressed itself upon my memory in a very vivid fashion. . . .

"The Pottawattamics [sic] were to have a war dance at the little town of Marietta, some six or seven miles up the river, and of course we boys were determined to be on hand and take part in the festivities. There were some twelve or fifteen of us in the party and we enjoyed the show immensely, as was but natural. Had we all been content to look on and then go home peacefully there would have been no trouble, but what boys would act in such unboyish fashion? Not the boys of Marshalltown, at any rate. It was just our luck to run up against two drunken Indians riding on a single pony, and someone in the party, I don't know who, hit the pony and started him to bucking.

"Angrier Indians were never seen. With a whoop and a yell that went ringing across the prairies they started after us, and how we did leg it! How far some of the others ran I have no means of knowing but I know that I ran every foot of the way back to Marshalltown, nor did I stop until I was safe, as I thought, in my father's house.

"My troubles did not end there, however, for along in the darkest hours of the night I started from sleep and saw those two Indians, one standing at the head and one at the foot of the bed, and each of them armed with a tomahawk. That they had come to kill me I was certain, and that they would succeed in doing so seemed to me equally sure. I tried to scream but I could not. I was as powerless as a baby. I finally managed to move and as I did so I saw them vanish through the open door-way and disappear in the darkness."

Immediately following the evacuation of the Indians in 1833, Chicago began to grow. A year later 150 buildings were built. In 1847 the city's first industrial giant, Cyrus McCormick, opened his reaper plant.

The city began to bustle with the arrival of two groups of polar-opposite peoples: pious, decorous, beer-shunning Yankees from New England and beer-loving émigré Germans, who flowed from the East by stagecoach and by steamboat on the newly opened Erie Canal.

Early on, the battle for the heart and soul of Chicago was joined between the wets and the drys. The German community opened dozens of beer gardens. The English temperance bloc countered by charging that beer drinking was foreign and un-American.

In 1853 the Spiritual Bank opened, refusing to lend money to anyone who drank, smoked, or wanted money to pay gambling debts.

It became a political issue when two years later Mayor Levi Boone raised the liquor license fees six hundred percent. He ordered the saloons closed on Sunday. That first Sunday two hundred barkeeps were arrested.

A trial was held on April 21, 1855. A mob scene formed in the courtroom. A riot in the streets followed. After shooting began, the militia was called out.

When the first temperance organizations were founded, 2,000 of the 7,500 Chicago citizens signed up to battle sin. The battle between the drinkers and the temperance crusaders continues to this day.

Through the mid-1800s, Chicago industry boomed. Trains, boats, and the wireless turned Chicago into the Heart of the West. In 1859 the Galena and Ogden began laying rails. A few years later the Michigan Southern opened, followed by the Illinois Central. By the end of the next decade Chicago was the nation's most important rail center.

About the same time, the Illinois and Michigan Canal allowed travel from Chicago to New Orleans. Chicago would become the world's leading inland port, handling more traffic than the Panama Canal. When telegraph lines were strung as far as New York, Chicago became connected to the East Coast.

In 1850 the population was 30,000. By 1860, it was 93,000. That year the city hosted the Republican National Convention, starring Illinois's number one son, Abraham Lincoln. Republican Senator William Seward, who later helped the United States buy Alaska from the Russians, was the favorite for president, but he was considered a radical: He wanted to abolish slavery.

Chicago Tribune editor Joseph Medill feared that the Republicans could not beat Democrat Stephen Douglas unless a westerner was nominated. His choice was Lincoln, who was espousing a more moderate line on slavery. With Medill's support, Lincoln was nominated by the Republicans at the Chicago convention and was elected president. Five weeks later the Civil War began.

Like the rest of America, the city became torn. While most German Chicagoans supported the North, the other large group of immigrants, the Irish, were mostly Democrats who supported the Southerners and celebrated every rebel victory.

After Lincoln delivered his Emancipation Proclamation, Chicago's divisions intensified. Even the Democrats who had supported the war felt that Lincoln had betrayed them. The *Chicago Times* was so anti-Lincoln and anti-abolitionist that 20,000 protesters marched in front of the *Times* building. Union General Ambrose Burnside threatened to send troops to seize it.

As an indication of Chicago's divided yet passionate nature, when Lincoln was assassinated right after the end of the war, 125,000 pro-Lincoln Chicagoans turned out to see the funeral train on its way to the president's final resting place in Spring-field.

After the war Chicago's boom continued unabated. The Union Stockyards opened Christmas Day, 1865. Philip Armour, a Yankee packer who foresaw the end of the Civil War, that year sold pork "short" and cleared somewhere around a million dollars profit. After the war Armour moved to Chicago and along with Gustavus Swift started the city's huge meat-packing industry.

The Civil War also brought gaming to Chicago, as gambling dens sprung up on Randolph Street. Keno was very popular in Chicago during the war. By 1869, Chicago was described in the *St. Louis Democrat* as a town of "fast horses, faster men, falling houses, and fallen women." Chicago boasted just about everything: wealth, gambling, prostitution—everything but a baseball team. That year the Red Stockings of Cincinnati, the only recognized professional team in America, won all fifty-seven of their games. Their stars, Harry and George Wright, were famed throughout the land, and their success made other cities, including Chicago, insanely jealous.

The *Chicago Tribune* wrote an editorial calling for a baseball team in Chicago, "a representative club; an organization as great as her enterprise and wealth, one that will not allow the second-rate clubs of every village in the Northwest to carry away the honors in baseball."

To show that Chicago was serious about its baseball, leaders raised $20,000 to organize a strong team. They placed ads soliciting top-rated players. They built a ballpark on Lake Michigan. The Chicago team, called the White Stockings, was successful, talented enough in 1870 to defeat the legendary Cincinnati Red Stockings, whose ninety-two-game winning streak had been broken earlier by the Brooklyn Atlantics. The White Stockings became so popular that after the players returned from a road trip, one hundred thousand fans came out to cheer them.

The Red Stockings' loss to Chicago changed the history of the game. With that loss, the men controlling the Red Stockings' purse strings fired free-spending president A. B. Champion, a local lawyer and the brains behind one of baseball's legendary teams.

Champion had known how to build a team and how to keep his players happy. The moneymen knew only that Champion was spending too much money. Angry that their ballplayers were staying at the best hotels and riding to games in fancy carriages, the bean counters got rid of their most valuable employee and replaced him with a flunky whose primary job was to tighten the operating budget.

The Cincinnati stockholders became the first group of wealthy businessmen in the history of our National Pastime to learn just how easy it is to kill the Golden Goose. Their shortsightedness also demonstrated to the public that in baseball, management can care more about saving money than the won-loss record.

The results were catastrophic. At the end of the season Cincinnati's two best players, Harry and George Wright, whose one-year contracts had expired, left to sign with Boston. The dynasty in Cincinnati was over. Other disgruntled players also departed. A year later the franchise would fold. There would be no beans left to count.

When the Wrights quit, there was a shift of power from West to East, as Boston soon would become the reigning powerhouse.

On March 17, 1871, St. Patrick's Day, Chicago was one of eight cities represented when the National Association of Base Ball Players, the first organized baseball league, was founded at a meeting at Collier's Cafe on Broadway and Thirteenth Street in New York City. The other originals were Boston, Brooklyn, New York, Troy, and Philadelphia in the East and Cleveland, Fort Wayne, and Rockford along with the White Stockings in the West. Philadelphia had the best record that initial season.

Baseball games were rowdy affairs back in 1871. Ulysses S. Grant was president, and following the general's reputation, booze was imbibed freely across the land.

At amateur baseball games in the Chicago area it was common for a keg of beer and a dipper to be placed alongside third base. Any player who reached third was entitled to a dipperful of what Chicagoans called "the German disturber."

According to historian Fred Lieb, in the ballparks of the professional teams "liquor vendors went through the stands selling some of the potent illicit potions of the Grant Administration." Liquor selling was so prevalent "as to make scenes of drunkenness and riot of every day occurrence, not only among the spectators, but now and then in the ranks of the players themselves. Many games had fist fights, and almost every team had its 'lushers.'"

By 1871, Chicago had three hundred thousand residents, most of whom lived in two-story wooden houses. There had been little rain that year between July and October. Sunday the 8th of October was warm. Around nine at night flames began to flicker from the cow barn of Patrick and Catherine O'Leary on DeKoven Street. Twenty-four hours later, a raging inferno encompassing most of the city continued to burn. The new ballpark was reduced to ashes. Seventeen thousand homes were destroyed, and more than a hundred thousand people were left homeless. The Sons of Temperance from Urbana, a hundred miles to the south, expressed the sanctimonious belief that the fire was God's answer to Chicago's failure to close its saloons on Sunday.

Almost miraculously Chicago recovered from the disaster as the rest of America pitched in to help. Relief trains flowed into the city with goods for the desperate citizens. President Grant sent $1,000 of his own money.

The city furiously rebuilt itself. Wooden structures were forbidden in the business district. Soon iron buildings known as skyscrapers would make their first appearance in America.

From the ashes, the city became reborn. Potter Palmer made a fortune in the dry goods business and then sold out to Marshall Field, who got even richer. John Montgomery Ward, another dry goods merchant, prospered from his Chicago base, as did the team of Richard Sears and Alva Roebuck, who sold throughout the country by catalog. George Pullman based his railroad-car-building empire in Chicago.

Because of the Great Conflagration, the Chicago White Stockings had to finish the 1871 season on the road and did not field a team in 1872 and 1873. Chicagoans had to sit on the sidelines as the Boston team, led by George and Harry Wright, dominated the game.

Making Boston's success even less tolerable to Chicagoans was that its star pitcher, a youngster named Albert Spalding, was from Illinois. Discovered pitching for Rockford in 1867 by George Wright in a game against the powerful Washington club, Spalding in 1870 shocked the baseball world when, pitching for Chicago, he defeated Cincinnati. After hearing of that performance, Harry Wright signed him to play for Boston beginning in 1871. In five years Albert Spalding won 207 games for the Boston Red Stockings (the Wrights fled Cincinnati and took the nickname too), including an incredible 57–5 record in 1875.

In 1876, during America's centennial, momentous events were transpiring. On March 10, Alexander Graham Bell invented the telephone. On June 25, George Armstrong Custer was wiped out at the Little Bighorn. In August, in Deadwood in the Dakota Territory, Wild Bill Hickok was shot in the back while playing poker.

That same year Albert Spalding shocked the baseball world by deserting Boston and returning to his beloved Illinois to pitch for Chicago. Spalding would embark on a course that would make him rich and forever change the nature and the course of the game of baseball.

Mumsey's magazine once called Chicago "the city of the big idea." From this great city came the skyscraper, the refrigerator car, the mail-order store, the packing-house, and equally important, baseball's first professional league, the brainchild of Albert Goodwill Spalding.

2

Albert Spalding

Albert Goodwill Spalding, the George Washington of professional baseball, was born on September 2, 1850, in Rockford, Illinois. Even at a young age, the tall, raw-boned, powerfully built Spalding showed his genius on the mound and with a bat. A natural leader, he organized a group of teenagers into a team, defeating every opponent by large scores.

ALBERT SPALDING: "My association with the game of Base Ball began at Rockford, in 1865. As a school boy, I belonged to a club called the Pioneers. Since nobody in the team was over sixteen years of age, the title may have appeared to some as a misnomer; but it sounded all right. Most of us had heard our fathers spoken of as 'pioneers,' and we knew it could not mean anything bad. The Pioneers put up a pretty fair article of ball, for boys—if I do say it—and it was not long before we became ambitious. There were at Rockford at that time two amateur rival nines—the Forest Citys, just organized, and the Mercantiles. These played occasional matches, the Forest Citys having rather the better of the argument.

"Ross Barnes, afterwards to win fame on the diamond as one of the greatest second basemen of his time, and in my opinion one of the best all around players the game has produced, was a member of the Pioneers, and he and I conceived the idea that we could 'do' the Mercantiles, whose players were for the most part salesmen in the several stores of the city. A challenge was therefore sent; but the tradesmen at first regarded it as a joke; they were not in the game to play with children. However, after much insistence on our part, and some chaffing, perhaps, by members of the Forest Citys, the Mercantiles finally accepted. The game took place one fine day in the fall of 1865, with the Forest City players present and rooting good and hard for 'the kids.' The game resulted in a score of 26 to 2 in favor of the Pioneers.

"Call it science, skill, luck, or whatever you please, I had at that time, when only fifteen years old, acquired the knack of pitching winning ball, and in the game with the Mercantiles it was first recognized."

Rockford's Forest Citys team invited Spalding and Ross Barnes to join, arranging with the school principal to let them out of school early on game days. The head of Forest Citys also arranged for Spalding to earn $4 a week working at a local grocery store after school. With Spalding on the mound, Forest Citys became a powerhouse, and on July 25, 1867, his name first attracted national attention when at age seventeen he defeated the Washington Excelsior Club, victors over the legendary Cincinnati Red Stockings. Years later Spalding remembered the incredible upset with fondness:

ALBERT SPALDING: "I was the pitcher of the Forest City Club in this victory over the famous Nationals, and, as a lad of seventeen, experienced a severe case of stage fright when I found myself in the pitcher's box, facing such renowned players as George Wright, Norton, Berthrong, Fox, and others of the visiting team. It was the first big game before a large audience in which I had ever participated. The great reputations of the Eastern players and the extraordinary one-sided scores by which they had defeated [the other clubs] caused me to shudder at the contemplation of punishment my pitching was about to receive. A great lump arose in my throat, and my heart beat so like a trip-hammer that I imagined it could be heard by everyone on the grounds.

"I knew, also, that every player on the Rockford nine had an idea that their kid pitcher would surely become rattled and go to pieces as soon as the strong batters of the Nationals had opportunity to fall upon his delivery. They had good grounds for that fear. Every member of the team cautioned me to take my time and keep cool; but I was not so rattled but that I recognized the fact that everyone of them was so scared that none could speak above a whisper. The fact is, we were all frightened nearly to death, with possibly the exception of Bob Addy, who kept up his nerve and courage by 'joshing' the National players as they came to bat with his witticisms, which made him famous among ball players for many years."

Incredibly, after six innings Rockford Forest Citys led 24–18.

ALBERT SPALDING: "While the Forest Citys had by this time gotten pretty well settled and their stage fright had disappeared, yet none of us even then had the remotest idea that we were destined to win the game over such a famous antagonist. The thought or suggestion of such a thing at that stage would probably have thrown us into another mental spasm.

"At this psychological moment, Col. Frank Jones, President of the [Washington] National Club, rushed up to George Wright, who was about to take his position at the bat, and said, in a louder voice possibly than he intended:

"'Do you know, George, that this is the seventh inning and we are six runs behind?' You must discard your heavy bat and take a lighter one; for to lose this game would be to make our whole trip a failure.' Col. Jones' excited manner plainly indicated his anxiety.

"This incident inspired the Rockfords with confidence and determination, and for the first time we began to realize that victory was not only possible, but probable, and the playing of our whole team from that time forward was brilliant. I have always given Col. Jones credit for Rockford's victory.

"None but a ball player can understand how much of a factor little incidents of this kind are in a closely contested match."

At the end of the 1867 season Albert Spalding discovered the possibilities and pitfalls that lay ahead for a talented ballplayer. Rules under the National Association set down years earlier said that no player could be paid for playing ball, but for years teams had evaded the rule by hiring players for phantom jobs at a good salary, with the provision that they play on the ball club.

When young Al Spalding finished the 1867 season with Forest Citys, the Excelsiors of Chicago offered him ten times his salary to be a bill clerk for a wholesale grocer (and also to pitch for the Excelsiors) for a breathtaking $40 a week.

The rules demanded that ballplayers remain amateurs, and because Spalding realized that any money he was getting above the usual $5-a-week clerk pay had to be for playing ball, he had to wrestle with his conscience. How could he break the rule and still live with himself?

It is interesting to follow Spalding's thinking as he mulled his dilemma. He knew he was breaking the rules. But he also knew he was being offered a lot of money.

ALBERT SPALDING: "I was employed at the time at a very small salary in a Rockford grocery, whose proprietor affected to be quite proud of my efficiency as a pitcher—but who regularly 'docked' me when absent from the store. Therefore, when I was approached one day by a Chicago man with an offer of $40 per week to take a position as bill clerk with a wholesale grocery house of that city, with the understanding that my store duties would be nominal, and a chance given to play ball frequently, without affecting my salary to reduce it, I found no difficulty so far as my Rockford job was concerned in making up my mind as to what I ought to do.

"But there were other considerations that might not be so easily disposed of. I was a mere youth both in age and in experience. I dared not trust my own judgment as to what was best. My home was and had long been at Rockford, with my widowed mother. Ought I, just as I was becoming a man, to leave her whose tender care and fond affection had been so lavishly bestowed upon me through the years of my boyhood life? Would she approve of my going to a large city, with its dangers in the busy whirl, and its greater dangers in the temptations that so thickly abound?

"Moreover, what did this offer mean? That it meant separation from the Forest Citys Club was quite apparent, but that problem did not count; I could not afford to rest my business interests on a mere sentiment. But there was a moral side to the question which I might not ignore. Were my services worth the proffered salary? What did I know of the wholesale grocery business that I should be offered $40 per week as a bill clerk? Was I not being paid for my skill as a ball player rather than as an expert in the grocery trade? And, if so, would I not be violating at least the spirit of that rule of the National Association of Base Ball Players that forbade the payment of salaries to players.

"Again, from a mere business standpoint, would it be wise for me at my age to sever the relations that had been established at the home of my youth? All my acquaintances were at Rockford. Did not they constitute an asset with which I might not lightly part? All these, and many other questions, presented themselves to my mind, and I did what I would now advise any other boy to do in the circumstances. I carried the whole subject to my mother. I knew that she approved of my connection with the game of Base Ball as a pastime; but how she would view it as a vocation I was not sure at all.

"When I broached the subject I saw at once that it distressed her. She, far better than I, realized what it meant. The commercial aspect of the case, in making use of whatever skill I possessed as a ball player to gain a competence, made her shrink at first. She had looked upon the game as a means of health-giving exercise, and had rejoiced in it. She had followed the early victories of our club, and, like a loyal mother, had gloried in them. But, to make a business of ball playing? That was altogether different; it required consideration; perhaps advice.

"Finally, the problem reduced itself—as have so many problems in other Rockford households in the last half century and more—to an appeal to Rockford's grand Old Man, Hiram H. Waldo, to whom I here pay the homage of man's sincere tribute to man. I held him in honor in the days of my youth. I esteemed him in my early manhood, and now, in my maturer years, I count him as one of the noblest, purest, most unselfish men I have ever known.

"Mr. Waldo was at that time President of the Forest Citys Club, and yet we laid the severing of my connection with that organization before him, assured that his advice would be fair, honest, unbiased; as, indeed, it proved. I remember well how we received the announcement of the offer made to me to go to Chicago; how we placed before him the situation in all its bearings; how I rather earnestly pleaded the opportunity it presented for my advancement of life. He heard the case quite patiently and then said:

"'You know, my boy, that, as a citizen of Rockford, I don't want you to go; and perhaps, as President of the Forest Citys Club, I ought to urge you to stay; but, as a friend to whom you have come for advice, I must say to you, accept the offer and go; but,' he added, smiling, 'you needn't tell that I advised it.'

"And so, in the fall of 1867, I went to Chicago, ostensibly to accept a clerkship in a wholesale grocery, but really to become a member of the Chicago Excelsior Base Ball Club."

So much for Al Spalding's ironclad morality.

Spalding never did get to play a game for the Excelsiors. When he arrived in Chicago he learned that the wholesale house that was going to pay his salary had failed. A few days later he was back in Rockford, again playing for Forest Citys but now employed in the insurance office of A. N. Nicholds, secretary of the team. Spalding never did say whether Nicholds made him show up for work or not. He did, however, comment on the contract he signed with the Chicago Excelsiors. By 1867 the rule against taking money to play ball was so freely ignored or circumvented, he said, it no longer had any meaning.

* * *

ALBERT SPALDING: "As to the question of my agreeing to accept a semi-professional position on the Excelsior team of Chicago at a time when professionalism of every kind was 'tabu,' I have this to say: Although at this date there was no strictly professional club in existence—the Cincinnati Red Stockings not being organized as such until 1869—the rule prohibiting salaries was nevertheless a dead letter. Most clubs of prominence, all over the country, had players who were either directly or indirectly receiving financial advantage from the game. Some held positions like that proffered me; others were in the pay of individual lovers of the game. I believed that I foresaw the day soon coming when professional Base Ball playing would be recognized as legitimate everywhere. I was not able to understand how it could be right to pay an actor, or a singer, or an instrumentalist for entertaining the public, and wrong to pay a ball player for doing exactly the same thing in his way. I did not like the roundabout schemes that were being worked in all large cities to secure good players, by giving the nominal employment in stores, warehouses, etc. It seemed to me to be educating young men in a school of false pretense. I felt that the only right thing to do was to come out openly and honor the playing of the game as a legitimate avocation, and this position I have ever since consistently maintained."

Spalding continued to pitch and win for Rockford Forest Citys, earning national renown. In the five years Spalding pitched for them, Rockford won fifty-one of its sixty-five games, including a 12–5 victory in 1870 over the great Cincinnati Reds led by Harry Wright.

After that season Harry Wright raided the Forest Citys team, signing Spalding, Ross Barnes, and Fred Cone to play for the Boston Red Stockings. Wright wanted it kept quiet that he was paying Spalding to play ball. Wright feared that once it became known that players were getting paid to play ball, the class of player would drop. One general fear was that blacks, even former slaves, would be allowed to play.

Wrote Spalding, "Any sort of man could enter the ranks, 'regardless of race, creed or color or previous condition of servitude.'"

Another concern was that professionalism would increase the number of rowdies, drunkards, and deadbeats, both on the field and in the stands.

Wrote Spalding, "Somehow, it was felt that the game would lose in character if it departed from its original program, and they honestly deplored the proposed innovation."

Albert Spalding, who sought to lead the fight for professionalism, had no such reservations. When Harry Wright came to sign him to a contract, Spalding argued he was against the subterfuge of getting paid to be a clerk or a bank teller when in reality the money was for his ballplaying. The true arrangement, he said, should be brought out into the open.

ALBERT SPALDING: "In 1871 [Harry Wright] came to Rockford to secure the services of Roscoe Barnes, Fred Cone and myself for the Boston Club.

"The experiment [of professionalism] had not yet been tried in an Eastern city. Hence, when Wright came with his overtures to Barnes, Cone and myself, it was to join a club ostensibly amateur but really professional; for all were to receive good salaries. I knew, of course, that the manager of the Bostons felt exactly as I did with regard to the subject; but I could see that he was reluctant to break over the custom in vogue in New England and oppose the honest prejudice existing in that section and all over the East against professional Base Ball.

"However, I was inclined to be obstinate in my views of the matter. I had determined to enter Base Ball as a profession. I was neither ashamed of the game nor of my attachment to it. Mr. Wright was there offering us adequate cash inducements to play on the Boston team. We were willing to accept his offer. Why, then, go before the public under the false pretense of being amateurs? The assumption of non-professionalism would not deceive anybody. It was not possible that any could be found so simple as to believe that George and Harry Wright, Cal McVey and the rest were in the game merely for healthful or philanthropic reasons. Then why engage in duplicity?

"We went over the whole subject, thrashed it out in all its bearings, and finally agreed to come out openly and above-board as a professional organization. The result was even more gratifying than we had hoped. Opposition in the East faded rapidly away. Soon after the organization, in 1871, of the National Association of Professional Ball Players, professionalism was firmly rooted and established."

Thanks to Spalding, by 1873 the sham of amateurism among the top teams had dropped away. Unfortunately, the rise of professionalism did not help baseball's biggest problems disappear. It had been Al Spalding's hope that with the ragtag nature of amateurism gone, baseball would rid itself of the ugly elements connected with the game, especially the gamblers and their influence on too many of the players, and the drunks, both on and off the field. Spalding, who was aligned with the temperance bloc, rued the rowdiness that pervaded the game throughout his tenure playing in Boston.

ALBERT SPALDING: "The seasons of 1873 and 1874 had been characterized by an increase of the abuses and evils which the National Association of Professional Base Ball Players had inherited from the National Association of Amateur Base Ball Players. It may be possible that had the professional management been in control of affairs at the beginning of organized Base Ball things might have been different.

"Gambling, in all its features of pool selling, side betting, etc., was still openly engaged in. Not an important game was played on any grounds where pools on same were not sold. A few players, too, had become so corrupt that nobody could be certain as to whether the issue of any game in which these players participated would be determined on its merits. The occasional throwing of games was practiced by some, and no punishment meted out to the offenders.

"Liquor selling, either on the grounds or in close proximity thereto, was so general as to make scenes of drunkenness and riot of every day occurrence, not only among spectators, but now and then in the ranks of the players themselves.

"Many games had fist fights, and almost every team had its 'lushers.'

"A game characterized by such scenes, whose spectators consisted for the most part of gamblers, rowdies, and their natural associates, could not possibly attract honest men or decent women to its exhibitions. Consequently, the attendance fell away to such a degree that the season of 1875 closed with bankruptcy facing every professional club in the country."

*   *   *

The way Spalding saw it, merely changing the game from amateur to professional status was not enough to put the game on a firm footing for the future. According to what he wrote years later, the state of the game was so demoralizing to him that he considered quitting if things didn't get any better.

ALBERT SPALDING: "The abuses that had played havoc with the old association not only continued, but were rapidly increasing in numbers and strength under the new organization. It was not conceivable that the men who were depending upon the game as a means of obtaining a livelihood were desirous of deliberately wrecking it.

"All were agreed that the game must be reformed. But how?"

3

Spalding's Revolution

During his six years with Boston, Al Spalding was a dominating force. He pitched 301 games and won 241 of them, an average of 50 starts and 40 wins a year. In 1875 he started 63 games, winning 57, including 20 in a row. His fame was such that he was known as "Al Spalding, champion pitcher of the world." Said an article in the *St. Louis Dispatch*, "As a pitcher he has no superior, being very fast as well as very cunning." Wrote newspaperman Henry Chadwick in 1875, "In judgment, command of the ball, pluck, endurance, and nerve, in his position he has no superior. His forte in delivery is the success with which he disguises a change of pace from swift to medium, a great essential in successful pitching."

Al Spalding was also seen as a man of character. He neither drank nor smoked, and in five years in Boston, he never missed a game. Unlike some players who snubbed the young fans who flocked around them, Spalding talked with them, enjoying his celebrity and enhancing his already stellar image.

Wrote Henry Chadwick, "He has sense enough to know that fair and manly play, and honorable and faithful service, are at least as much the essential of a professional ballplayer as is still in the field and at the bat."

Spalding may have been a great and famous ballplayer, but it was his vision that made him a historical figure.

Al Spalding had far-reaching, ambitious plans, both for himself and for the game of baseball. His aspirations were far beyond the scope and imagination of the average businessman, never mind those of a ballplayer. Spalding, who was described by a close associate as "a schemer and promoter to his very core," had plans for himself that included ownership of a team and the proprietorship of a substantial sporting goods firm. For baseball, he envisioned a league of professional teams, nationwide in scope, run as a business to make money.

The other players spent their free time chasing women, drinking beer, and blowing everything they earned. While a ballplayer with Boston, Spalding spent his time away from the diamond educating himself to accomplish his goals, learning about the business of sports. He apprenticed under player-manager-mentor Harry Wright, who was only too happy to teach his star pitcher every facet of team management, both on and off the field.

Harry Wright, who was one of the star players of the Boston Red Stockings, was also the business manager of the team. In addition to his playing duties, Wright arranged for transportation, directed the ground crew, scheduled games, kept the books and handled all the advertising, payroll, and club expenses. In all these areas his assistant was Al Spalding.

Spalding admired and shared Wright's philosophies. Wright was a stickler for players being on time for practice, and he demanded they be in the best physical shape. Wright, who was religious, was against smoking and drinking as well as Sunday baseball. Spalding and Wright had great admiration for each other.

Harry Wright and his brother George also were in the sporting goods business. The Wrights allowed Spalding to work with them in that business as well. Spalding, who was as ruthless in business as he was on the mound, had designs in that direction, intending to start a competing firm in the Midwest, and to do it even better.

When the good-looking, persuasive Spalding set his mind to accomplishing a goal, he had the charm and the power of personality to succeed by getting others to help him carry out his plan. In 1874 he demonstrated that ability when he wanted to visit Europe. To attain that goal, he came up with the rationalization for the trip: to show the British that baseball was a superior game to cricket. The plan he finally set upon was to take two teams to England, including his Bostons, to play exhibition matches. He was a schemer all right. He convinced Henry Chadwick, the first nationally known baseball writer, to stress the need for bringing baseball to the Mother Country. The public supported the plan, and Spalding got the funding for his trip.

Despite unsurpassed personal success with Boston, Spalding saw events in terms of the big picture and the long term. In 1875, Spalding and Boston were at their most successful. The Red Stockings won every home game and lost only eight on the road. That year Spalding's personal record was 57–5. But Spalding saw his team's dominance as a negative, and he continually worried for the prosperity of the game, acutely aware that the lack of competition was badly hurting business. At the end of the season his concern was borne out when six of the thirteen teams dropped out of the league.

Other aspects of the game troubled him too. As the Christy Mathewson/Walter Johnson/Tom Seaver/Nolan Ryan of his day, Spalding fiercely protected his clean-cut image. He didn't like to go to saloons, believing drink to lessen his value as a player, and he continued to rue the corruption of the game by gamblers, whom he carefully avoided so as not to hurt his reputation. Baseball was being dragged down by corruption, Spalding believed. If things didn't change, Spalding vowed, he was going to quit the game entirely.

According to historian Robert Smith, Albert Spalding used to spend "most of his idle hours working out schemes for reforming the organized game." One of the problems, Spalding realized, was that since the first games in the 1840s the ballplayers were also the owners. Harry Wright had had great success running the Boston team, but Spalding saw him as the exception. As long as the ballplayers were running the business of baseball, Albert Spalding became convinced, the game was doomed to failure.

Albert Spalding

While himself still one of the players, Spalding concluded that for baseball to flourish, there had to be a demarcation between team owners and the players. It would be the job of the owner to run the business end of the game. The players could then concentrate on what they did best: perform.

In his autobiography, written in 1911, Spalding described how he and (unnamed) others had decided to change the system, whereby club owners would relieve "the players of all care and responsibility for the legitimate functions of management, require of them the very best performance of which they were capable, in the entertainment of the public, for which service they were to receive commensurate pay."

Spalding was being modest. He was the catalyst from the beginning. Albert Spalding's intention was for baseball to become professional in every way, a thriving business run by businessmen. That he succeeded and in a very short period of time is testament to his genius.

In 1875, Albert Spalding was the key participant in an event that ultimately would fulfill his vision for revamping the game. What he did was as shocking within baseball's small society as a coup against a government. Al Spalding and three of his teammates walked out on mentor Harry Wright, refused to honor their contracts, and announced that the following year they would play with the Chicago team.

And if anyone in the league objected, Spalding would start his own league—a professional league.

At the time Spalding and the three teammates made their move, no one was aware of Spalding's intentions. It is only through hindsight that one can watch Spalding boldly and brilliantly carry out his battle plan, as he ran roughshod over all opposition.

And then an odd thing happened: After he accomplished all his goals, starting the new league, owning a team, and becoming a sporting goods magnate, he did all he could to downplay his role. For the rest of his life, Spalding tried to cover up his role as revolutionary.

According to Spalding, it was not he but William Hulbert, a Chicagoan who made his money in the coal business and was a member of the Chicago Board of Trade, who was responsible for setting his grand scheme in motion.

ALBERT SPALDING: "I was greatly impressed by the personality of Mr. Hulbert at our first meeting, in Chicago, early in 1875. He seemed strong, forceful, self-reliant. I admired his businesslike way of considering things. I was sure that he was a man of tremendous energy—and courage. He told me of the interest of the game at Chicago in Base Ball; how that thousands of lovers of the game at Chicago were wild for a winning team, but couldn't get one; how she [Chicago] had been repeatedly robbed of her players, and, under Eastern control of the Professional Association, had no recourse. It seemed to me that he was more deeply chagrined at the insult to Chicago than over that city's failure to make a creditable representation in the game. I told him that I was quite familiar with the entire situation; that it was the same all over the West—no city had any show under the present regime; that the spirit of gambling and graft held possession of the sport everywhere; that the public was disgusted and wouldn't patronize the pastime, and, finally, that unless there was a new deal throughout, with a cleaning out of the gamblers, both in and outside the Base Ball profession, I for one, proposed to quit.

"We talked for quite a while upon the different phases of the situation, and then he said to me: 'Spalding, you've no business playing in Boston; you're a Western boy, and you belong right here. If you'll come to Chicago, I'll accept the Presidency of this Club, and we'll give those fellows a fight for their lives.'"

The way Spalding tells it, all William Hulbert wanted was for Spalding and Spalding alone to join him in Chicago. But such a move would not have been far-sighted or far-reaching enough for a man as ambitious as Al Spalding. If Spalding came to Chicago, he was going to do everything he could to make sure Chicago would end up a winner.

After assessing the Chicago club and discerning that "[Paul] Hines, [John] Glenn and [Johnny] Peters" were the only "strong players on the Chicago nine," Spalding said he determined that in order for Chicago to reign supreme, he would bring three of his best teammates on Boston with him, plus recruit two of the best players on the Philadelphia team as well.

Concerning his reply to Hulbert, Spalding wrote in his autobiography: "I gave him to understand that I was not averse to such a movement [from Boston to Chicago], and said that, if I did come, I would bring a team of pennant winners."

In midseason, June 1875, Albert Spalding secretly recruited three of the best everyday players on the Boston team, Jim "Deacon" White, his catcher; first baseman Cal McVey; and his childhood friend, second baseman Ross Barnes. He also recruited two Philadelphia stars, Adrian Anson, a top batsman whom Spalding had discovered and recruited to play with him during his 1874 trip to England, and third baseman Ezra Sutton. A dollar went a long way in those days. Anson signed with

Chicago after he was offered two hundred dollars more than he was getting in Boston.

All parties desperately wanted the signings to remain secret, but it wasn't long before rumors began to spread. One had Harry and George Wright coming to Chicago. Everyone involved denied this rumor.

About two weeks later the secret got out when an accurate report of Chicago's wholesale pirating appeared in the *Chicago Tribune*. The news created a sensation in Boston and Philadelphia and around the rest of the baseball world. Boston fans were especially angry, labeling their four stars as "filthy traitors" and "dirty seceders," a sobriquet left over from the Civil War period. It was, after all, only ten years since Appomattox.

Years later Al Spalding remembers what happened when he first learned that the news of his team switching had broken in Boston.

ALBERT SPALDING: "The Monday morning when the announcement appeared in the Boston papers it so happened that I, being out of the city, spending Sunday with some friends, did not read the papers, and I arrived at the grounds just in time to don my uniform and get onto the field in time to play in a game against the St. Louis team.

"I was alone in the dressing room, when Ross Barnes came in and said:

"'Well, you will get a chilly reception when you come on the field.'

"'What's the matter now?' I asked.

"'Why, don't you know?' said Barnes. 'Haven't you read the morning papers?'

"I replied that I had not, whereupon he continued:

"'The jig is up. The secret is out and H---'s to pay. McVey, White and I took to the woods early in the day and just arrived at the grounds a few minutes ago. Everybody seems to take it as a huge joke,' added Barnes, 'and we have treated it the same way, and have neither affirmed nor denied the rumor.'

"I knew that the Boston crowd would consider me the head devil in this sucession movement, so I made a clean breast of the whole affair, and turned the joke into a reality by announcing that the statement was absolutely true. We had been dubbed the 'Big Four,' and for the balance of that season were caricatured, ridiculed, and even accused of treason. Boys would follow us on the streets, shouting, 'Oh, you seceders; your White Stockings will get soiled,' and would hurl all kinds of facetious remarks at us."

Spalding accepted the barbs as coming to him, all the while pitching the best baseball of his life, winning 56 games. He felt it important to prove to the Boston fans that his new contract with Chicago for the 1876 season in no way impaired his ability to win for Boston in '75.

Spalding, though a moralist, apparently saw nothing immoral in his act of jumping the Boston club to feather his own nest in Chicago. His sights only on the future, Spalding never looked back. He later rationalized his act by saying that he and the other three jumpers really wanted to stay in Boston but once they had signed contracts with Chicago, and once William Hulbert had accepted the presidency and taken on financial responsibilities, they were obligated to keep their promise to jump teams. You can imagine how Harry Wright responded to that.

Spalding couldn't wait to get to Chicago to make a name for himself on the ball field in his home territory in the Midwest and to put the plans for his new sporting goods operation into business.

In addition to being named Chicago's team manager, it seems likely from later events that Spalding also received an ownership interest in the team, an equitable recompense for his jumping teams and bringing a group of all-stars with him. Immediately he was made a member of the Chicago White Stockings board of directors and named secretary of the Chicago Baseball Club.

Spalding had not come to Chicago just to better his lot as a player. He came to better his lot in life. After playing with Chicago only two seasons, Spalding in 1878 succeeded his stalking horse, William Hulbert, as president of the Chicago Club. When Hulbert died in 1882, Spalding succeeded him as owner.

The news that pitching star Al Spalding and the other five players were jumping to Chicago created a frenzy of angry protestation throughout the country wherever baseball was played. At the close of the 1875 season it was rumored in the papers that the Big Four and the Philly Two would be expelled for violating the rule against signing players in the middle of the season. For most players, the threat of such an expulsion would have been terrifying. For Albert Spalding, it was an opportunity to exercise his grand plan, under which each team would have two "interdependent divisions, the executive and the productive," with the former given absolute control over the latter. Under Spalding's new setup, the players were to become employees.

In his memoirs Spalding once again gives William Hulbert the credit for what came next.

ALBERT SPALDING: "I discussed this phase of the question [of expulsion] with Mr. Hulbert while visiting his home in Chicago in the fall of 1875. I probably exhibited some uneasiness on that subject, but Mr. Hulbert answered by assuring me that whatever happened Chicago would pay the salaries of her players in full. Chicago, he said, had been working for years to get a winning ball team, and now that she had finally secured one, he proposed that Chicago should have what was coming to her.

"William A. Hulbert was a typical Chicago man. He never spoke of what *he* would do, or what *his club* would do, but it was always what *Chicago* would do. 'I would rather be a lamp-post in Chicago than a millionaire in any other city,' was one of his frequent and characteristic expressions.

"In again referring, that same evening, to our possible expulsion, Mr. Hulbert said: 'Why, they can't expel you. They would not dare do it, for in the eyes of the public you six players are stronger than the whole Association.' For a few moments I noticed that he was engrossed in deep thought, when suddenly he rose from his chair and said:

"'Spalding, I have a new scheme. Let us anticipate the Eastern cusses and organize a new association before the March meeting, and then see who will do the expelling.'

"It was an inspiration. I shared his enthusiasm, and thus was a new association conceived, and out of it all came the National League of Professional Base Ball Clubs."

*   *   *

Historically, William Hulbert has been given the credit for organizing this new league. But if you look at Albert Spalding's grand plans and then follow the steps as they become reality, it seems far more likely that Spalding was the mastermind, with Hulbert, who saw the wisdom of what Spalding wanted to do, helping him carry out the plan. Spalding himself wrote that Hulbert had not been a reformer; rather, he was a raconteur who "loved all of the good things of life."

Once Spalding and Hulbert embraced the notion of starting a new, professional league, the next step was to draw up a constitution. Over the years Spalding had been concerned with baseball's ills, and this constitution methodically addressed each and every one of them.

Among those who counseled Spalding were Hulbert, Harry Wright, and Orick Bishop, an attorney who played with the St. Louis Unions in the 1860s.

A further indication that the ideas in the constitution came from Spalding, not Hulbert: After Spalding showed the finished document to Hulbert, he reported that Hulbert told him, "I don't think it can control the game for more than five years."

But Hulbert had underestimated the farsightedness and wisdom of Albert Spalding, whose constitution was as strong and binding on the game of baseball as the U.S. Constitution has been on the country. Spalding's document controlled the game intact for a century beginning in 1876 and ending in 1976, when the federal courts intervened to change one of Al Spalding's rules, overturning the legality of the reserve clause and allowing players freedom of movement.

Like the true robber baron that he turned out to be, Al Spalding wrote a constitution that created a monopoly, with teams in large cities (with a population of at least 75,000) controlling their respective markets.

His plan was to line up eight of the strongest franchises in the country (including his Chicago team) to form the National League of Base Ball Clubs. Under his plan each team would be organized by owners rather than players, who would have no elected representative to the board of directors and no voice in the conduct of the game's affairs.

Two financial objectives to maximize profits were gained through rules that demanded teams adhere to the schedules (any team that didn't finish a schedule would be expelled from the league) and that controlled player salaries by limiting their ability to switch teams, in effect barring all other players from doing as Spalding had done.

Spalding's constitution also included rules to make sure teams kept their schedule commitments and bans against Sunday games, unruly fans (umpires could throw them out), and gamblers being allowed inside stadiums. Dishonest players would be barred from baseball for life.

Everyone in baseball had feared the nefarious influence of gambling, and Spalding used this pervasive fear as a sledgehammer to convince owners of other clubs to adopt his new constitution on moral, if not financial, grounds.

Once the constitution was completed, Spalding's first bold move in December 1875 was to call a secret meeting in Louisville, where he and Hulbert, whom pioneer historian Fred Lieb described as "Albert Spalding's mouthpiece," enlisted three of the stronger Western teams, St. Louis, Cincinnati, and Louisville, to ratify his document and join his crusade to clean up the game.

Spalding picked the Western teams first because he knew they held a grudge against the Eastern teams, who were wealthier and often were able to outbid the Western teams for players. Sign up with my league, Spalding told the Western teams, and I will stop the Eastern teams from stealing your players. They did, quickly.

Spalding and Hulbert then sent notices to the presidents of four powerful Eastern teams, Philadelphia, Boston, Hartford, and Brooklyn, asking them to meet Hulbert in his suite at the Grand Central Hotel in New York on February 2, 1876.

According to Spalding, Hulbert locked them all in the room, lectured them about this new league, and pointed out the evils of gambling and the abuse of "revolving" from team to ream.

He praised the managers there, showed them the constitution, and, according to Spalding, everyone lined up like sheep to sign on the dotted line. As a sop to the Eastern bloc, Hulbert named Morgan Bulkeley of Hartford as the first National League president. After one year Bulkeley resigned, and Hulbert took over as president, serving until his death in 1882.

Long after the new league was organized, Spalding went out of his way to sing the praises of his loyal conspirator, William Hulbert.

ALBERT SPALDING: "There have been other forceful men at the head of our national organizations, men of high purpose, good judgment and fine executive ability. But in all the history of Base Ball no man has yet appeared who possessed in combination more of the essential attributes of a great leader and organizer of men than did William A. Hulbert."

Spalding, as we have seen, was again being modest. Hulbert, it is clear from everything that transpired, merely helped carry out Albert Spalding's grand design. Baseball's founding fathers realized this too, because William Hulbert didn't end up in Albert Spalding's other brainchild, the Baseball Hall of Fame in Cooperstown, New York, until 1995.

There was good reason why Spalding wanted William Hulbert to get the credit for starting the National League. Moralists cannot admit their own transgressions. If Spalding had admitted his true role, he would have had to confess that he had been responsible for stabbing his mentor and friend Harry Wright in the back when he and his teammates jumped teams.

He also would have had to admit publicly that he had learned the sporting goods business at Harry's knee with the express intention of using those secrets to set up a rival business that not only competed with his friend but soon was to control a substantial share of the market. Evidence of Spalding's duplicitous double dealing wasn't merely circumstantial. According to historian Robert Smith, Spalding, before leaving Boston, had made a secret deal with Harry Wright's business partner (named Mahn) to act as Mahn's agent in Chicago. Mahn had developed a baseball that was rubber covered, was tightly wound, had a double cover, and was more durable than the average ball. Under the agreement, Mahn was to supply Spalding's new store with baseballs.

Soon after Spalding arrived in Chicago, Spalding opened his sporting goods store with his brother, J. Walter, a bookkeeper with the Winnebago National Bank. In February 1876 the *Chicago Tribune* wrote about the opening of the Spaldings' store at 118 Randolph Street. It wrote, "It is [Spalding's] intention to open a large empor-ium in Chicago that will sell all kinds of baseball goods and turn his place into headquarters for the Western baseball clubs." In 1878, Spalding induced the Na-tional League to buy baseballs from him exclusively. Before the end of the century Spalding Bros. was to become the largest sporting goods store in the country. Harry Wright's company, Wright & Ditson, continued to do well, but Wright would have done far better without the fierce competition from his former teammate.

And so it appears that Al Spalding foisted the myth of the vision of William Hul-bert onto the public to conceal his own purposes. Thirty years later, he foisted the myth of the famed general, Abner Doubleday, who had had absolutely nothing to do with baseball but who, because of Spalding, became known as the game's founding father. Spalding wanted it known that baseball came from America, not England. To prove it, he chose Doubleday to be founder. As with everything he did, Spalding got his way.

The Professional Baseball Hall of Fame logically could have been placed in Chi-cago rather than Cooperstown. Perhaps it would have been had Al Spalding not been so modest about his role in putting baseball on firm financial ground. Despite his protestations, Albert Goodwill Spalding was the game's George Washington, the Father of Professional Baseball.

In 1876, the first year of the National League of Professional Baseball Clubs, Spalding's iron-fisted constitutional rules would benefit baseball greatly. On the field, his strong right arm would lead his Chicago team to the new league's first championship.

The impressive presence of Albert Spalding loomed over the game he first de-scribed as America's Pastime.

4

The Great Anson

After the hysterical press reported in mid-June 1875 that Chicago had signed six of the league's stars for the following season, the pressure on the six players to jump back to their original teams became intense.

The Boston president, Nathaniel Appolonio, topped the Chicago offers to the Big Four, but Spalding, the leader of the coup, kept the others in line.

The two Philadelphia players, Adrian Anson and Ezra Sutton, didn't have Spald-ing with them to ease their concerns. When the next spring Sutton refused to honor his contract, there wasn't much Spalding could do about it, but he made sure Adrian Anson, arguably the best hitter in the league, didn't renege too.

Spalding had a hold over Anson that he did not possess with Sutton. When Spald-ing was a boy pitching for Forest Citys of Rockford, Anson was playing for Marshalltown, Iowa. They had played against each other and instantly had de-veloped a strong mutual respect.

Anson in his autobiography described how even back then Spalding had sought to intimidate all who opposed him. Anson recalled that Forest Citys had been a far superior team to Marshalltown; after one game that Forest Citys had won by the score of 18–3, Spalding was furious that the score was so close. He and his Forest Citys teammates demanded a rematch, canceling the next scheduled game and staying overnight to play another game with Marshalltown.

According to Anson, in order to inflict a heavier beating on the Marshalltown up-starts, Spalding and Forest Citys underhandedly substituted a lively ball for the preferred Ryan, or dead ball. This time the final score was 35–5 in favor of Forest Citys.

During the game Anson got into a verbal tussle with Spalding. After the game Spalding decided he preferred to have Anson playing for him rather than against him, and later made him an offer to play for Forest Citys.

Eighteen-year-old Adrian Anson signed with Forest Citys for a salary of $65 a month. At the end of the season, with the Forest Citys team faltering financially, Anson signed with Philadelphia, where he played until 1876, when Spalding lured him to Chicago.

Philadelphia offered Anson five hundred dollars a year more than his contract called for in Chicago, but after Ezra Sutton's defection, Spalding pressured Anson against rebolting, arguing to Anson that once he signed his contract, he must be bound by it.

Anson, who was both religious and honorable, was torn. His wife did not want to leave her hometown of Philadelphia. She pleaded with him to stay, and Anson made two trips to Chicago to beg Spalding and William Hulbert to be freed from his con-tract, even offering to pay $1,000 severance.

But Spalding—in one of his first actions in the role of owner—bared his teeth and threatened Anson if he didn't honor the contract.

Though Anson believed he had acted wrongly by jumping the Philadelphia team and though he suffered inside for moving his wife from her family, his loyalty to and fear of Spalding won out. In March 1876 he showed up in Chicago for the first day of spring practice—but in street clothes. When his new teammates began throw-ing the ball around, he couldn't resist getting out there and playing catch.

"Now Anse," Spalding told him, "come tomorrow in uniform."

Anson did, and for the next twenty-three years he made his indelible mark on the history of Chicago sports.

All through the 1876 season the bitterest rivalry was between Chicago and Boston, whose fans could not forgive the Big Four for running out on them. Boston had been devastated by the defections, but it still had a strong team led by the Wright brothers, George and Harry, as well as stars John Morrill, A. J. Leonard, and Jim O'Rourke.

Years later Anson remembered the very first meeting between the teams in Boston.

CAP ANSON: "The first game that we played on the Boston grounds that season I re-member well, because of the enormous crowd that turned out to witness the contest. The advent of the Big Four in a new uniform was of course the attraction, and long before the hour set for calling the game had arrived the people were wending their way in steady streams toward the scene of action. Every kind of conveyance that could be used was pressed into service, from the lumbering stage coach that had been retired from active service, to the coach-and-four of the millionaire. Street cars were jammed to suffocation, and even seats in an express wagon were sold at a premium.

"It was Decoration Day, and therefore a holiday, and it seemed to me as if all Boston had determined to be present on that occasion. By hundreds and thousands they kept coming, and finally it was found necessary to close the gates in order to keep room enough in the grounds to play the game on. With the gates closed the crowd began to swarm over the fences, and the special policemen employed there had their hands more than full of trouble.

"The 'Big Four' were given a great ovation when they put in an appearance, and of course the whole team shared in the honors that were showered upon them. The game that followed was, as might have been expected, played under difficulties, but thanks to the excellent pitching of Spalding we won by the score of 5 to 1, and the Hubbites were sorer than ever over the 'Big Four's' defection."

Chicago, which won its first nine games of the season against Boston, had the best pitcher in the game in Al Spalding, and it featured their four all-star team jumpers, first baseman Cal McVey, who in 1876 hit .347; catcher Deacon White, who hit .343 the one year he played in Chicago; second baseman Ross Barnes, who hit .404 and led the league in doubles, triples, and runs scored; and the twenty-four-year-old phenom Adrian Anson, called Infant Anson, Baby Anson, and the Marshalltown Infant, even though he was large and bellicose. That year Anson batted .343 and impressed everyone with his powerful line drives.

In addition to his batsmanship, Anson initiated a practice in Chicago that soon became standard practice around the league. Anson stood along the third-base line, and as the runners came around third, he would yell directions to them such as "Run on, he'll throw wild." Thus, the third-base coach was born.

Led by the pitching and managing of Al Spalding, in 1876 the White Stockings won the championship that first National League season with a 52–14 record. Spalding won 47 of those games. As manager, Spalding earned a reputation for being a master of tactics and for his toughness on opposing players and the umpires, who never seemed to know the rules as well as he did. On the mound his specialties were the feinted throw to first (the move later would be deemed illegal, a balk) and the beanball, aimed at the batter's head.

In 1877, Al Spalding surprised the baseball world by stepping down as pitcher when he was at the peak of his fame. To replace him the team signed George Bradley, the star pitcher of the St. Louis team. Spalding, twenty-six, felt he was losing his effectiveness as a pitcher, so he played first base. The team finished 26–33 and finished fifth in the six-team league. That year Spalding learned firsthand what generations of managers would learn over the years: that the reputation of the manager correlates directly with the quality of the pitching staff. Minus his best pitcher (himself), Spalding's reputation for managerial brilliance suddenly disappeared. He was accused of being a poor manager.

If Spalding was guilty of anything, it was neglecting the ball club, as he spent a great deal of his time building his sporting goods business. He was hard at work generating ideas that would bring his company to the forefront of the sporting world.

Because he was the inspiration behind the founding of the National League, Spalding had immense power behind the scenes. One of his less successful ideas was that there be a different-colored uniform for each position. It was a brilliant suggestion for a man selling uniforms. Unfortunately, each team ended up looking like a hodgepodge circus team, and the experiment was abandoned after one season.

He was more successful in his scheme to sell baseballs. To maximize sales, Spalding determined that if he could become the exclusive supplier to the National League, then all the other league members and all the young boys around the country would flock to buy his brand of balls.

Until 1876 the home team had supplied the balls, which came in different weights and degrees of hardness. Spalding pushed for the National League to use a uniform ball, one lively enough to keep the customers awake. To accomplish his goal, he told league officials his company would supply the balls for free and even pay one dollar for every box of Spalding-brand balls used. In 1878, Spalding and the National League reached an agreement giving him the exclusive right to supply balls to the league. As a result, for one hundred years the Spalding company supplied baseballs to the major leagues, and around the country millions of youngsters played in their backyards and on the playgrounds using Spalding baseballs.

After Spalding outbid his friend Al Reach for rights to publish the *National League Guide*, which purported to list all the major league rules, one of the "official" rules Spalding wrote into the guide was that the Spalding ball had to be used in all National League games.

According to A. G. Mills, a friend of Spalding's, putting that "rule" in the book was "an unmitigated falsehood," evidence that Spalding's tactics showed "a disposition to use the League in any way he pleases to aid his money getting schemes." It was this ruthlessness, more than any other negative trait, that caused Spalding's enemies to seethe.

Albert Spalding's brilliant scheming to get rich within the confines of the game continued when during the 1877 season he decided he would popularize the use of gloves worn by fielders in order to add to his line of equipment.

The first glove had been worn by Doug Allison, the catcher for the Cincinnati Red Stockings. A saddle maker was said to have made it for him in 1869. The first glove Spalding ever saw was worn in 1875 by a first baseman named Waite from New Haven. Spalding had also wanted to wear one, but Waite took a terrible ribbing from the fans, who called him a "sissy," so Spalding waited until 1877—when he was prepared to market and sell gloves—to wear one himself.

When Spalding, now playing first base, decided to market the gloves, he wore ones that were black to make sure they were visible to the fans. He inserted a little padding, cut the fingers down to stubs, and wore one on each hand.

Because it was the great Al Spalding wearing the glove, no one said a word. That same year he began selling the Spalding glove at prices ranging from $1 for "medium quality" to $2.50 for "extra quality." His advertisements read: "No catcher or player subject to sore hands should be without a pair of these gloves." His glove business took off wildly.

That year Spalding also added a catcher's mask to his line. Fred Thayer, a Harvard player, had invented it, getting the idea from a fencing mask. Soon many of the catchers in the National League began wearing them. So did the catchers in every league in America.

A. G. Spalding & Bros. introduced sliding pads, which were a boon to base runners. He sold them to everyone, pros and amateurs.

He also began selling the *Spalding Score Book*. The new method of scoring, invented by Alexander Cartwright, soon became universal and is still used today.

Before the turn of the century Spalding also added to his wealth by embracing the sale and promotion of the newfangled personal transportation vehicle called the bicycle. He published a cycling guide and later cornered the market on bicycles as his pricing policies put other companies at a disadvantage until they had to sell out to him.

In only fifteen years A. G. Spalding & Bros. would swallow up most of the competition and then reorganize with a total capital stock of $4 million. Included in the new consolidation were Peck & Snyder; the A. J. Reach Company, once owned by his friend from Philadelphia; and Wright & Ditson, formerly owned by mentor Harry Wright. Over time Spalding became so rich that his relatives fought over his estate when he died.

In 1878, Albert Spalding retired from active ball. He was only twenty-six. Years afterward he told his son, Keith: "I knew that I was slipping before anybody else did, and that it was time for me to retire. When a batter hit a ball in my direction, I noticed that I had to move around to locate it, instead of just sticking out my hand and catching it."

His retirement was a shock to the baseball world. It wouldn't be for another 116 years (1994) that a similar retirement by a star Chicago baseball player would create such a commotion in the city.

Shortstop Bob Ferguson took Spalding's place as manager and captain. Under Ferguson the team finished fourth. Adrian Anson, who would replace Ferguson as manager the next year, described Ferguson as neither a "top-notcher" as a shortstop nor as a manager—"he not having the necessary control over the men that he had under him."

The next year, 1879, Spalding's favorite, Anson, moved to first base, where he would begin a run that over time would eventually gain him fame at the position as a defensive paragon. Anson played for twenty-two years, hit a lifetime .333, and was the first player to accumulate 3,000 hits. Though Anson was a free swinger who believed a bunt was a sissy thing to do, in 9,067 at bats Anson struck out only 294 times. At bat he could push hits to open spots, or if the situation dictated, he could swing away and hit the ball over the fence. On August 5 and 6, 1884, Anson hit five home runs in two consecutive games, a feat not matched until 1925, forty-one years later.

When it came to picking the right bat, Anson was a fanatic. An article in the *Cincinnati Enquirer* proves it:

> There are more loose timbers around the Chicago ball park and Spalding's store than it would take to start a good-sized lumberyard. In odd nooks and corners at the ball yard especially you will run onto an old log, a wagon tongue, or an old cart shaft.

Anson has either taken them there himself or has had them hauled in. They are timber for his bats. He never overlooks a good piece of wood, no matter where he is.

If he sees a well-seasoned and solid piece of wood in Galveston, New York, or San Francisco, he will ship it to Chicago. Someday, when he thinks of it again, he will haul it out and have it turned into a bat.

It has been stated that he has two hundred and seventy-six bats in the basement of his home but there are some who say the figure is closer to five hundred. He has them hung up like hams. His locker is always full of bats. He never permits anybody else to use any stick in his private stock.

As great a hitter as Anson was, it was as manager of the Chicago team that the martinet made his mark on the whole league.

Anson, who like Spalding had a fierce, win-at-all-costs nature, was a heavyset man who always spoke his mind regardless of the consequences.

His players were wary of his temper and were stung by his barbed criticism. Anson, who didn't believe players should rest after getting hurt, rarely allowed a day off for an injury. It wasn't manly, he said.

Chicago fans loved him. Around the league everyone else reviled him bitterly for his bellicose manner. When he thought he had been victimized by an umpire—or when he felt he could change a decision or gain an advantage for his team—he would bellow at the umpire unmercifully. According to historian Arthur Bartlett,

Adrian Anson

Anson's arguments with umpires were regular and famous, "often ending in a comprehensive summary of his views directed not only at the umpire but at the opposing team and the grandstand too." He was fined often for his battles with umpires, opponents, and even fans. Though he prided himself on his moral purity, his language was vile, but the Chicago fans loved the show he put on. In other towns fans tired of his tirades changed "Baby" Anson to "Crybaby" Anson.

From his position on the coaching line at third base (he was a notorious "coacher") Anson not only was one of the first to direct traffic, but he also figured out that it was a good spot from which to taunt, name-call, and deride the opposing players and the umpires. Anson was an intimidator, and no one was immune.

He also tended to anger fans around the league for his knack of being smarter than the opposition.

He was the first manager to figure out the system whereby one fielder would back up another. He was the first to coordinate the infield and outfield defense and the first to use a pitching rotation, though his staff in 1882 had only two pitchers.

CAP ANSON: "Unlike the majority of the clubs the Chicago Club did not have to depend upon the services of one first-class pitcher, but had two, both of whom were 'cracker-jacks,' and were therefore able to play them on alternate days instead of breaking them down or laming them by continued and arduous service."

Anson was the first to use signals to communicate with the batters, telling them to take or hit away, and he was the first to platoon. He rarely had his players bunt, calling the tactic a "baby act."

One of his ploys was to wait and see if the first two batters hit safely, in which case he would bat next. If they made out, he'd send someone else up, waiting to bat when there were runners on base. As a result of his ingenuity, the league passed a rule beginning in 1881 that the batting order had to be made up before the game.

Under the imaginative, devious, tyrannical dominance of Anson, who became known as Cap (for captain), Chicago dominated the National League during the first half of the 1880s, winning the championship in 1880, 1881, 1882, 1885, and 1886. During Cap's heyday and long beyond, Chicago fans didn't just love him, they worshiped him.

"During that time [Anson's] name became a household word, better known," according to historian Harold Seymour, than "that of any statesman or soldier of his time."

Anson, who was very opinionated and judgmental, prided himself on his great strength, moral purity, and honest dealing. He also was proud of his bigotry. Anson reflected the accepted prejudice of his time and place when in 1882 in an exhibition game against Toledo, he demanded that a black player be removed from the game because of his skin color.

Five years later Anson, who did not hide his "dislike for negroes," refused to let his White Stockings take the field if a black were to compete. Since racism ran rampant in all of America at the time, it was certainly easier and more politically correct to go along with Anson, the most popular player in the game, than stand up to him.

Anson did not limit his expressions of bigotry to blacks. In the schism in Chicago between the Germans and Irish, Anson wasn't averse to making disparaging comments against the Irish. He once joined with two clowns in a vaudeville skit to sing the song "We're Three Chubelin [Shoveling] Tipperary Turks." The Irish were made comic targets, as were the Jews, but Anson did not revile and shun them the way he did the blacks.

When John Montgomery Ward made a deal to bring pitcher George Stovey to the New York Giants, Anson drummed up support from other club owners to keep Stovey, and all other blacks, out of baseball. Irish and Jewish players got to compete, but the blacks didn't, not just because of Anson, but because of other powerful bigots, including National League team owners like Al Spalding.

Sol White, who was a star first baseman for the Philadelphia Giants Baseball Team in the black leagues at the turn of the century, was perplexed at Anson's bigotry. Neither he nor anyone else knew what was at the root of it, but White certainly knew that because of Anson, blacks effectively were barred from playing in the major leagues.

SOL WHITE (IN 1907): "The color line has been agitated by A. C. Anson, Captain of the Chicago National League team for years. As far back as 1882, Anson, with his team, landed in Toledo, O., to play an exhibition game with the American Association team. Walker, the colored catcher, was a member of the Toledos at the time. Anson at first absolutely refused to play his nine against Walker, the colored man, until he was told he could either play with Walker on the team or take his nine off the field. Anson in 1887 again refused to play the Newark Eastern League club with Stovey, the colored pitcher, in the box. Were it not for this same man Anson, there would have been a colored player in the National League in 1887. John M. Ward, of the New York club, was anxious to secure Geo. Stovey and arrangements were about completed for his transfer from the Newark club, when a howl was heard from Chicago to New York. Just why Adrian C. Anson, manager and captain of the Chicago National League Club, was so strongly opposed to colored players on white teams cannot be explained. His repugnant feeling, shown at every opportunity, toward colored ball players, was a source of comment throughout every league in the country, and his opposition, with his great popularity and power in base ball circles, hastened the exclusion of the black man from the white leagues."

Chicago, as it has been about most issues of importance, was split as to how blacks should be treated. Slavery had almost been legalized in Illinois in 1824. For many years there a black could not testify in court against a white. Before the Civil War, if a black couldn't prove he wasn't an escaped slave, he could be jailed, and if no one stood up for him, he would be sold at auction to recover the cost of his incarceration.

At the same time Chicago was a hot spot for the abolitionist movement. It had been an early and important stop on the Underground Railroad. The issue produced violence in 1837 when Illinoisans who favored the institution of slavery stormed the Alton office of newspaperman and abolitionist Elijah Lovejoy and murdered him. It was not until 1857 that an Illinois judge ruled that blacks were not chattel but individuals.

By 1888, the time of Al Spalding's world tour, blacks were treated poorly in America, and not just in the South. In Chicago they were segregated, forced to live in separate housing and eat in separate restaurants, and warned not to associate with whites on a day-to-day basis.

To some whites, like Anson and Spalding, blacks could be mascots or clowns, as long as they behaved themselves.

In his autobiography, Anson describes in vividly disturbing detail the relationship between Clarence Duval, a black who signed on with the White Stockings as the team mascot, and the White Stocking entourage, including Anson and Al Spalding. It is very clear from his writings that for Anson and the others, blacks existed to provide entertainment and amusement. Equal treatment was totally out of the question.

CAP ANSON: "[In Omaha,] we were met with another great reception [during the 1888 trip around the world.] Here Clarence Duval turned up, and thereby hangs a story. Clarence was a little darkey that I had met some time before while in Philadelphia, a singer and dancer of no mean ability, and a little coon whose skill in handling the baton would have put to the blush many a bandmaster of national reputation. I had togged him out in a suit of navy blue with brass buttons, at my own expense, and had engaged him as a mascot. He was an ungrateful little rascal, however, and deserted me for Mlle. Jarbeau, the actress, at New York, stage life evidently holding out more attractions for him than a life on the diamond.

"Tom Burns smuggled him into the carriage that day, tatterdemalion that he was, and when we reached the grounds he ordered us to dress ranks with all the assurance in the world, and, taking his place in front of the players as the band struck up a march, he gave such an exhibition as made the real drum major turn green with envy, while the crowd burst into a roar of laughter and cheered him to the echo.

"When, later in the day, I asked him where he had come from, he replied that Miss Jarbeau had given him his release that morning. I told him that he was on the black list and that we had no use for deserters in our business.

"'Spec's you's a' right, Cap'n,' he replied and then he added, with a woe-begone expression of countenance that would have brought tears of pity to the eyes of a mule: 'I'se done had a mighty ha'd time of et since I left all you uns.' I told him that he looked like it, but that he had deserved it all, and that we were done with him, and this nearly broke his heart. When I got back to the car I found the little 'coon' there, and ordered him out, but the boys interceded for him, raised a purse, in which I chipped in my share, of course, and I finally consented that he should accompany us as far as San Francisco, and farther, provided that he behaved himself.

"The little coon did not prove to be much of a mascot for Chicago that afternoon, as the All-Americans dropped to Ryan's slow left-handed delivery after the fifth inning, he having been a puzzle to them up to that time, and pounded him all over the field, they finally winning by the score of 12 to 2.

"That night we were off for Hastings, Neb., where we were scheduled to play the next day. Arriving there Clarence Duval was taken out, given a bath, against which he fought with tooth and nail, arrayed in a light checkered traveling suit with a hat to match, new underwear and linen, patent leather shoes and a cane. When he marched onto the field that afternoon he was the observed of all observers, and attracted so much attention from President Spalding, who had been absent on a trip to Kansas City, that it was at once decided to take him to Australia. The contract that he was made to sign was an ironclad one, and one that carried such horrible penalties with it in case of desertion that it was enough to scare the little darkey almost to death. When I looked him over that night on the train I told him that I should not be in the least surprised were he again to desert us at San Francisco, and especially if Miss Jarbeau should run across him.

"'Den dat's jest 'case you doan' know me,' he retorted; 'I specs dat if dat 'ooman sees me now,' and here he looked himself over admiringly, 'she's jes' say to me, "My gracious, Clarence, whar you been? Come right along wid me, my boy, an' doan't let me lose sight ob you no more." I know she'd just say dat.'"

"'What would you say then?' I asked."

"'What I say? Why, I jes' say, "Go on, white 'ooman, I don't know you now, an' I nebber did know you. No, sir, Mr. Anson, I'se done wid actresses de res' ob my nat-rel life, you heah me.'

"To my astonishment he kept his word, remaining with us all through the trip and returning with us to Chicago. Outside of his dancing and his power of mimicry he was, however, a 'no-account nigger,' and more than once did I wish that he had been left behind."

Anson described how "the mascot" taught the players craps, and Cap recounted hearing the cries of "come, seben, come eleben, what's de mattah wid you dice."

He described how Duval had bet he could jump with an umbrella from the rigging thirty feet above the deck. Fortunately, according to Anson, the players talked him out of it.

Anson's most telling commentary described an incident that occurred on the leg of the trip from Australia to Ceylon. When the steamship *Salier*'s waiters, none of whom was steeped in America's tradition of bigotry, perceived Duval to be of Indian royalty and treated him with great respect, it was Al Spalding himself who stepped in to teach the man a lesson for forgetting his place.

CAP ANSON: "Clarence Duval, our colored mascot, had been appreciated on the 'Alameda' at his true value, but on the 'Salier' for a time the waiters seemed to regard him as an Indian Prince, even going so far as to quarrel as to whom should wait on him. A word from Mr. Spalding whispered in the ear of the captain worked a change in his standing, however, and he was set to work during the meal hours pulling the punka rope which kept the big fans in motion, an occupation that he seemed to regard as being beneath his dignity, though his protests fell on deaf ears."

5

Mike Kelly

Albert Spalding and William Hulbert knew what they were doing when they put Adrian "Cap" Anson in charge of the team because not only was Anson a great player and manager, he was also a superior judge of baseball talent. In one of his most important moves to build a team that soon would dominate the National League, in 1880, Anson prevailed on his bosses to steal away from the Cincinnati team a flashy but headstrong young player by the name of Mike Kelly.

Kelly, the son of a Union soldier, had moved at age ten with his family when his father was transferred from Troy, New York, to Washington, D.C. After he moved to Paterson, New Jersey, Kelly as a teen was so good a ballplayer he founded and starred on a team called the Paterson Keystones. He caught his good friend, pitcher Jim McCormick, who would later join him in Chicago, where they became famous as the Keystone Battery.

In 1873, when he was only sixteen, Kelly caught and played the outfield for the famed Troy Haymakers. Five years later he joined the Cincinnati Buckeyes. A year later Cap Anson discovered him while traveling to California with an all-star team. They bickered for a week over salary.

MIKE KELLY: "Anson became a bit interested in my playing. He asked me if I would like to become a member of the Chicago club, and I replied that nothing would please me better. Anson wired President Hulbert, and he replied, 'Get Kelly by all means.' For two weeks Anson and I struggled before signing the contract. Anson wanted me for $100 less than my price. We met every day and talked the thing over. Anson was obstinate; so was I. Anson came into my room one day and said, 'Well, Kel, are you going to sign?'

"'No, sir,' I replied, 'not unless you give me the money I want. I am not at all particular to become a member of the Chicago nine, and unless I get the money I want, I would just as soon go somewhere else.'

"Anson looked at me, shrugged his shoulders, and said that I would be sorry by-and-by. I told him that I could stand it, if he could. As a matter of fact, it was the dream and ambition of my life to become a member of the Chicago club. I knew it meant lots of hard work, and I also knew that if I was a member of the club, and could play ball at all, Anson would be the one to give me a chance. He was always willing to push a young fellow ahead. He didn't know what professional jealousy meant. Well, I wasn't anxious that he should know that I wanted to go to Chicago. If he did, he would get me at his own price, just as sure as fate. So I remained indifferent. For several days I kept away from Anson. Finally, I was gathering my things and was about to start for home. Anson came up into my room. 'Well, are you ready to sign, Kelly?'

"'Quite ready, Mr. Anson, providing, of course, you pay me what I think is fair.'

"'Well, all right, my boy, you can have it. Put your name on the contract.'

"I did so, and in less than no time I was a member of the Chicago Base Ball Club."

Mike Kelly joined the Chicago team in 1880 and for seven years was the greatest player of the nineteenth century, the engine that drove the Chicago machine, winner of five championships in the next seven years. A tall, muscular, handsome Irishman with a stylish mustache, Kelly was a multitalented player who could field, throw, hit, hit for power, run the bases, and leave the field with the prettiest woman in the stands.

How good was he? John McGraw, whose career stretched from before the turn of the century until 1932, picked him as the best catcher he had ever seen. Players who lived long enough to see Ty Cobb, Honus Wagner, Babe Ruth, Tris Speaker, and even Joe DiMaggio have said that Kelly was the best player of them all. Hugh Duffy, who was a rookie in 1888 and whose Hall of Fame career in the majors, first as a player and then as a coach, lasted until his death in 1954, was one of them. When Duffy once was asked to compare Honus Wagner and Nap Lajoie, two of the greatest players of the 1910s, Duffy instead chose Kelly as the best:

HUGH DUFFY: "I think that a pitcher would rather face Wagner than Lajoie, but it's my opinion that Mike Kelly was the greatest player ever to put on a uniform. There never was a player so outstanding, despite his many limitations. Mike had a wonderful head. He was not a fast runner, yet he was the best base runner the game ever knew. A wonderful light went out when he was lost to the game. No one ever put as much life and snap into a game as he did. He was a winning ballplayer, and he infused his spirit into every man who played with him."

Tommy McCarthy, a Hall of Fame outfielder for Boston (among other teams) during the nineteenth century, agreed.

TOMMY MCCARTHY: "King Kel was the greatest player I ever knew. He was better than [Buck] Ewing, [Charlie] Bennett, and [Charlie] Ganzel [three outstanding turn-of-the-century catchers]. He had the most baseball brains, and invented new rules. He wasn't so very fast, but he was a great slider."

Connie Mack, who played against Kelly in the 1880s and lived to manage the Philadelphia Athletics through the 1950 season, compared Kelly to Ty Cobb.

One time in 1888, when Mack was catching for Washington, manager Ted Sullivan ordered pitcher Hank O'Day not to walk Kelly. But Kelly was a superb batsman, and after working the count to 3–2, he fouled off four straight pitches, then walked. Kelly stole second on Mack and then went to third on a short fly to center

Mike Kelly

field. With the infield in, Kelly broke to the plate on a grounder right to the short-stop. He looked like a sure out when the throw beat him home, but Kelly fooled Mack with a feint and then made a curving slide to touch the plate with his hand.

CONNIE MACK: "Like Cobb, Kelly never gave an infielder or catcher anything more than the tip of his toe to tag. He had all of Ty's stuff—the fadeaway, fallaway, and hook slides, and a few so distinctively his own that others could not copy them."

According to baseball historian Fred Lieb, Mike Kelly had as much hold on the baseball fans of the 1880s as Babe Ruth had during his heyday.

FRED LIEB: "To many, King Kelly and baseball were synonymous. Like Ruth, he burned the candle at both ends, and he could make headlines outside of the ball field. Kelly was all for wine, women, and song. Kelly gave Anse plenty of gray hair over his parties, as Babe Ruth did to Miller Huggins four decades later."

Like manager Anson, Kelly was crafty and extremely quick-witted. He studied the rules and was the author of many a scheme that gave the rule makers fits. He was one of the first catchers to use finger signals to his pitchers.

MIKE KELLY: "Unless I am very much mistaken, I was the first one to introduce signs to the pitcher. I did it in the games I caught, and it caught on right away. Before the season was over, many a base runner was caught because of those signs. But after a year the custom spread. In two years about every pitcher and catcher in the league were using signs. How a little thing does spread."

Kelly was the first catcher to throw his mask in the path of an incoming runner. Some credit him with the invention of the hit-and-run play. He taught his battery mate, John Clarkson, the necessity and the method of signaling the infielders what pitch he was going to throw. As an outfielder he was one of the first to back up plays in the infield and was the first player to demonstrate that it was possible to catch a line drive on the bounce in right field and still throw the runner out at first.

In addition to being a great athlete, Kelly had a personality the Chicago fans loved. He was totally fearless, at times reckless, and enjoyed showing up the opposition with his quick thinking and his hustle.

At one time he was the highest-paid player in the game, earning $3,000 a year with Chicago and later $5,000 a year with Boston. Throughout his career he added to his wealth by getting paid to do endorsements for streetcar companies, cigar firms, and other advertisers. His handsome Irish face looked down from billboards in big cities throughout the nation. Wherever he went, small boys and grown men would know him at a glance and run to touch him or just stay close for a moment to hear his voice.

Kelly was an outstanding fielder, who possessed a magnificent throwing arm, whether from behind the plate or from the outfield, but it was as a hitter that he earned his fame.

Kelly was so famous as a batter that Chicago columnist Eugene Field coined his swing "the Kelly swat," which, Field explained, was an Anglo-Saxon word meaning "sweat," so he used it to signify that which precipitated sweat.

"Swat on, most admirable paragon, swat on!" Field wrote. Which Kelly did.

His technique of sliding, copied by many, was called the Kelly Spread. Today it is called the hook slide. Kelly would throw his body away from the base and hook the bag with his foot. He could also slide headfirst.

Robert Smith, the baseball historian, recalled the effect that Kelly had on the fans when he came up to the plate and then got on base.

ROBERT SMITH: "Kelly at the plate never failed to bring a bubbling of cheers and delighted comment as spectators pointed him out to their neighbors, shouted his name, begged him to hit, laughed in ecstatic anticipation. Almost any sort of hit was enough to bring howls from the crowd, and it was often enough to put King Kel on base, for he could move like the wind.

"Once he stood on the base lines, his head erect, his wide shoulders thrown back, and a look of studied innocence on his face, the crowd had eyes for nothing else. With every pitch they begged him to be off; and when at last he did start for second, a roar would go up as if a dam had let go. Wildly the catcher would grab the ball in his thin gloves and fiercely he would speed it over the diamond to the waiting baseman. The baseman, catching the ball well ahead of Kelly's arrival, would bend grimly toward the looming figure of the big Irishman, ready to tag the first part of Kelly's body that offered. 'Slide,' the crowd would scream. 'Oh, slide, Kelly! Slide!' And Kelly never failed to slide. His great body would drop suddenly, almost as if he had been shot in full career. In a roaring spasm of dust he would pile into the base, his feet flicking like a clever boxer's hands until the baseman did not know whether it was morning, late afternoon or deepest midnight. While the baseman was reaching for one of Kelly's legs with the ball, the other would swing in from nowhere and safely hook the base."

Ball fans could never imagine what trick he would next pull on the opposition. In one game, Chicago was tied with Detroit with nobody out in the last of the ninth and Kelly the batter. He singled. The next batter, Ed (Ned) Williamson, walked. They then executed a double steal, Kelly sliding into third, Williamson into second.

After his slide into third, Kelly began picking himself up, clutching his arm, and howling as if in great pain. Play was suspended while Williamson ran over from second base to see if Kelly was OK.

"It's thrown out of joint, Ed," he announced loudly. "Take hold of it and pull on it. Easy now."

Then under his breath Kelly spoke quickly to Williamson.

"Keep hold of it, Ed. Nothing wrong with it. Get this, now. On the next pitch I'll start for home. I'll run slow so you can get around third and come in behind me. I want you to be right on my heels as I go into the plate. [Charlie] Bennett [the Detroit catcher] will try to tag me, and just as he does, I'll spread my legs apart. You dive through my legs for the plate. He can't tag both of us at the same time—one of us is sure to score."

It worked exactly as Kelly had planned it. Kelly slowly broke for home on the next pitch. The ball was tossed to catcher Charlie Bennett in plenty of time to tag out Kelly, but just as he approached the plate, he stopped short. As Bennett went to tag Kelly, Kelly spread his legs, and the dashing Williamson came sliding through his legs with the run that gave Chicago the victory.

In another game between Boston and Cleveland, late in Kelly's career when he was with the Red Sox, Jesse Burkett of Cleveland was on third base with two outs. The batter hit a ground ball to Boston's Herman Long at short, but the throw to first was too late to retire the runner. Burkett had started for home when Long made his throw, but as Burkett neared home, Kelly dropped his mitt as though the batter were out at first and the side was retired. Burkett stopped running and turned to take the field. Kelly then called for the ball, caught the throw from first baseman Tommy Tucker barehanded, and tagged Burkett.

Kelly outwitted not only the opposition but the umpires, who at times knew he was doing *something* against the rules but weren't able to catch him at it.

ROBERT SMITH: "Kelly had a better trick for the other corner of the diamond; the spectators who had seen him before would be clutching each other's arms by this time and hoarsely whispering: 'Wait until he comes to third! Wait, just wait!'

"There would be a hit, a long single to right, and Kelly would be off. Down toward third he would speed, watching over his shoulder meanwhile to see—well, not to see where the ball was, or what the other runner was doing, but simply to see where the solitary umpire was looking. Was he looking out to right, to see if the ball was fair? Or was he watching first base, to see what play might be there? Then Kelly would cut suddenly toward the plate, right past the pitcher's mound, amid a swelling uproar of laughter and cheers, and would pound into home plate without ever coming within fifteen feet of third base. 'Murder' the third baseman would yell; but the noise of the crowd would drown him utterly. And the bewildered umpire could do no more than harbor one more angry suspicion about Kelly.

"Kelly was more than a match for an umpire. He was weaned on the rule book and bred in craft. At a time when the rules permitted the sending in of a substitute 'at any point in the game' simply on notifying the umpire, Kelly jumped off the bench one day, shouted, 'Kelly now catching!' and caught a foul fly which the regular catcher could not possibly have come close to. When the umpire set out to protest, Kelly read him the rule that made this move legal.

"In a game at Chicago, in the twelfth inning, with the score tied, Kelly was patrolling right field. It was twilight; and unquestionably it was the last inning, if only they could bring it to an end. There were two outs and the bases were full. The batter laid into a pitch that sailed almost on a line to right field and disappeared in the dusk. Kelly leaped high in the air, grabbed with both hands, came down, and trotted toward the clubhouse.

"'Three out!' said the umpire. 'Game called on account of darkness.'

"When Kelly's teammates reached the clubhouse, he grinned happily at them. His hands were empty.

"'It went a mile over my head,' he said."

His feats seemed to come from tales from Baron Münchausen or Paul Bunyan.

HAROLD KAESE: "In an exhibition game played at Austin, Texas, Kelly hit a ball into the tall grass behind the right fielder. The right fielder couldn't find it, so Kelly ran out from first base and helped him look for it.

"'Well, I can't waste me time no longer,' said Kel at last, and he trotted in and touched second. From there he went out and circled the left fielder, then returned to third. He started for home, but the ball had been found, and he was trapped. There ensued a long rundown, but just as the third baseman yelled, 'I gotcher now, Kel,' the King replied, 'The hell yer have, me bucko,' and he took off for right field. With the third baseman pursuing him hotly, Kelly dashed through a gate in the fence and kept on running until he had reached the hotel. By then the third baseman had given up the chase, so Kelly did the only thing a sensible man could do under the circumstances. He sat down and had a drink."

Kelly reveled in the effect he had over the opposition's fans. One time playing right field in St. Louis on Queen Victoria's birthday in 1886, he told the fans in the bleachers, many of whom came from the Kerry Patch district: "So yer Kerry Patchers, eh? Well, this is the 24th of May. God save the Queen! I'm coming up yer way tonight and start an Orange lodge. I expect all of yez ter join up."

Kelly particularly enjoyed stirring up the Boston fans. Boston had never forgiven Spalding for jumping to Chicago and taking his three teammates with him, and during the 1880s it was Boston that gave Chicago the toughest competition. Kelly loved to pull one of his tricks in Boston and stir up the crowd.

MIKE KELLY: "How a Boston audience would shout and roar, with mingled feelings of anger and joy, when I would cut the third bag on my way home. It almost reminded one of hundreds of insane people let loose."

If Kelly had a weakness, it was his love of the bottle. Anson tried to watch him like a hawk, attempting to keep him from the bars and the adoring women, but Kelly, who was as raucous and profane as Anson was stolid and stodgy, often escaped his tail.

Anson one time early in his life had spent a night in jail for drunkenness. Ashamed, he swore off alcohol and tobacco and became a fervent temperance advocate. Anson would hand out a $100 fine to any player caught drinking beer. The whole time Kelly was with Chicago, the two battled. As great as Kelly was, Anson was convinced that he would have been still better sober.

Said Anson about Kelly, "Had he been possessed of good habits instead of bad there is no telling to what heights Kelly might have climbed, for a better fellow in some respects never wore a base-ball uniform."

According to Anson, when Kelly was "bowled up," as Anson put it, he sometimes misjudged fly balls. Even then, said Anson, he seldom missed by much. When he did miss, Kelly would shout, "By Gad, I made it hit me gloves, anyhow!"

What added greatly to Mike Kelly's reputation was not that he drank but that he made no secret of the fact that he drank hard. He admitted that he drank not for mild stimulation or to whet his appetite but to get good and drunk. When a reporter once asked Kelly if he drank while playing baseball, he replied, "It depends on the length of the game."

ROBERT SMITH: "[Kelly] knew how to enjoy every minute of his life, and, in the style of the great free spenders of the day, he took no thought of the morrow. His wealth, his strength, his stomach, his breath, or his kidneys he used each day as if they would all be restored brand-new in the morning. He was far from the type of man the writers and the moralists of the day held up as the American ideal. Yet he was precisely the type that American small boys would worship openly in the street, a man to make a person's heart beat faster to see, to hear about, or to stand next to in public."

Kelly was such an American hero that a lithograph showing him sliding into second base replaced Custer's Last Stand behind the bars of many saloons, and the enigmatic song "Slide, Kelly, Slide" rivaled "Casey at the Bat" in popularity, as phonograph records of it sold widely in the 1890s. It went:

> *Slide, Kelly, Slide!*
> *Your running's a disgrace!*
> *Slide, Kelly, Slide!*
> *Stay there, hold your base!*
> *If someone doesn't steal you,*
> *And your batting doesn't fail you,*
> *They'll take you to Australia!*
> *Slide, Kelly, Slide!*

6

Spalding's Dynasty

By 1880, under the leadership of William Hulbert and Albert Spalding, the Chicago team became a powerhouse, the envy of the entire country. Not only was the team a winner on the field, but because of Spalding's natural flair for promotion, publicity, and showmanship, the team came to represent what was classiest about professional baseball in the 1880s. He dressed his White Stockings in the finest uniforms, and on the road he picked the best hotels that would accept ballplayers. He hired white horses for his carriages when he could, and those carriages transported his team from the hotel to the ballpark and back.

Once at the park, Cap Anson would head a procession of players into the park and onto the field.

Recalled Mike Kelly, "We wore silk stockings and the best uniforms money could git. We had 'em whipped before we even threw a ball. We had 'em scared ter death."

The inspiration behind the Chicagoans was Anson, a martinet who trained his players hard and long. Mike Kelly recalled what manager Anson put them through during spring training.

MIKE KELLY: "You haven't any idea what Anson meant by training. He meant training in every sense of the word. Directly after a light breakfast he would accompany us to the park, where the morning exercises would begin. We would walk a mile or so, to get limbered up, so to speak. Then Anson would lead the procession, and we would indulge in a fifteen-mile dog-trot.

"He worked just as hard as the rest of us, and so we couldn't do any kicking. It wouldn't do any good, anyhow."

Kelly recalled when outfielder George "Piano Legs" Gore tried to use trickery to escape Anson's rigors.

MIKE KELLY: "George Gore didn't like the training, and he suggested that we escape for a couple of days, by feigning illness. There was some kind of sport going on down there, and we wanted very much to be present. We sent word down stairs in the morning that we were very ill, and wanted to be excused. Anson came up and looked at us.

"'You fellows don't look very well,' he said. 'I guess a big dose of hot ginger won't do you any harm.'

"It was pretty rough on us, but we had to do the ginger up. Then Anson went off, whistling a merry tune. We were in bed—in lavender—when Anson returned. 'Feel better?' he asked, and we replied, 'No.'

"That meant another dose of ginger. Well, we stood it, thinking of the sport. Just as we were going to leave the hotel in a carriage, Anson came up and said: 'Boys, I just felt a little ill myself, and thought I'd lay off this afternoon. But you both look healthy, and it braces me up. I guess the sport will get along without you both this afternoon. Come over to the park. We're going to have a little practice game over there.'

"We went with him. It was pretty hard to fool the old man."

Kelly, whose hustling style built his reputation, admired how often his manager gambled in order to win games.

MIKE KELLY: "Anson took more long chances to win a game of ball than any other captain I ever saw. He has tried and invented more schemes to win games than any player living. He will advise his men to steal bases, and will encourage them if they fail.

"'Never mind, old fellow,' he will say, 'you made a great bluff at it. You'll get it the next time, you bet.'"

Kelly attributed much of the team's success to Anson. He felt he knew why.

MIKE KELLY: "It's a comparatively easy matter to answer the question. He enthuses his followers. He doesn't demand it, but does ask politely that every man who steps on the field shall play ball from beginning to end. If his club is seven runs ahead in the last inning, he's going to have his men play as hard as if they were just seven behind. Anson has no favorites. He won't have any in his club. He treats all men alike. I was as near to him as any man who ever played ball in the White Stocking nine. Yet never did he show it, on or off the field. He treated me like the rest, never better, and once in a while a bit worse. When it was the latter, I thoroughly deserved it.

"Anson is the easiest captain in the league to get along with, if you mind your own business—the hardest, if you won't. He thoroughly believes in discipline.

"Sometimes he is apt to be harsh, but when he is it is with a man whom the other players think is the white-headed boy. He watches every point in the game. Nothing escapes him. He is working all the time for success, and, as a result, his men are bound to do the same thing.

"He never discourages a player, and when a young man comes into the club, he treats him like a younger son until the young man gets fresh, and then he is sat down on very, very hard. As a result, the players are always working hard to win the love of the old man. When they make a brilliant play, he is the first one to come forward and say something about it. When a poor play is made does he kick? Not at all. He simply tells the man who makes the error that mistakes will happen, but cautions him to try and be a little more careful.

"There isn't any doubt about his standing, at all. He is the greatest captain in the league."

Anson, who always was blunt in his player evaluations, knew his own worth. When he was once asked how he put his ball clubs together, he answered, "Round up the strongest men who can knock a baseball the farthest the most often, put yourself at first base, and win."

Anson's juggernaut won five championships in seven years, including his first three in 1880, 1881, and 1882 behind the pitching tandem of Larry Corcoran and Freddie Goldsmith. Corcoran, the only Chicago pitcher to throw three no-hitters, won 43 games his rookie season in 1880. Goldsmith was the first pitcher ever to throw a curve ball, even though Arthur "Candy" Cummings got credit for doing so. After a 21–3 record in 1880, Fred's curve ball won Chicago 24, 28, and 25 games starting in 1881.

It was a team of which Cap Anson was extremely proud.

CAP ANSON: "The team that brought the pennant back to Chicago in the early '80s was a rattling good organization of ball players, the 'fans' who remember them can testify, and while they were the cracks of that time, and perhaps as strong a team as the League had seen up to that date, yet they were not as strong either as a team or as individual ball players as the team that represented Chicago several years afterward. The secret of the club's success in those days lay in its team work, and in the fact that a goodly portion of the time was spent in studying and developing the fine points of the game, which long practice made them fairly perfect in. There were one or two weak spots in its make up, but so well did it perform as a whole that these weak spots were quite apt to be lost sight of when the time for summing up the result of the season's play had arrived.

"In its pitching department the team was particularly strong at that time as compared with some of the League clubs.

"Larry Corcoran, upon whose skill great reliance was placed, was at that time in the zenith of his glory as a twirler. He was a very little fellow, with an unusual amount of speed, and the endurance of an Indian pony. As a batter he was only fair, but as a fielder in his position he was remarkable, being as quick as a cat and as plucky as they made them.

"A sort of an all-around sport was Larry, and a boxer of no mean ability. I remember a set-to that he had one night in the old club house with Hugh Nichol, in which he all but knocked Hughey out, greatly to that gentleman's surprise, as he had fancied up to that time that he was Corcoran's master in the art of self-defense.

"Fred Goldsmith, the other pitcher, was a great big, overgrown, good-natured boy, who was always just a-going to do things that he never did. He, too, came from the East, and was, I believe, pitching for the Tecumseh, Canada, Club when he signed with us.

"He was the possessor of a great slow ball and was always cool and good-natured. As a batsman he was only fair, and as a fielder decidedly careless. When it came to backing up a player 'Goldy' was never to be relied upon, and after the play was over and he was asked why he had not done so, he would reply, 'Oh, I'd a-bin thar ef I'd bin needed.' But in spite of this the fact remains that he was rarely on hand when he was needed, and many an overthrown ball found its way into the field that would have been stopped had he been backing up the basemen in the way that he should have done.

"His arm was gone when he left us, and if he played ball any afterward, it was only in desultory fashion. He tended bar in different places for a time, but finally settled down to the business of market gardening near Detroit, where, from all that I can learn, he is making a good living."

On April 10, 1882, as the National League was about to begin its seventh season William Hulbert, who was both president of the Chicago team and president of the league, died of heart failure in his Chicago home. Al Spalding, who owed so much to Hulbert, mourned his death, saying, "Will loved all of the good things of life." At the time of Hulbert's death, Spalding, the biggest stockholder in the White Stockings, procured the necessary financial backing and took over control of the team.

Mike Kelly, who thought of Hulbert as a noble man, also mourned him, calling him kindly, as softhearted as a child, bighearted, honest, and straightforward (everything he felt Spalding wasn't).

Hulbert died only a few weeks before the Chicago White Stockings began playing at their magnificent new ballpark called the Congress Street Grounds (later called West Side Park). It was a short walk from downtown Chicago and was the finest ballpark in the country. *Harper's* magazine called it "indisputably the finest in the world in respect of seating accommodations and conveniences."

It sat 10,000 fans, with 2,000 grandstand seats, 6,000 uncovered seats, and standing room for 2,000 more. To show how far ahead of the times he was, Spalding even had a row of eighteen private roof boxes that were "cozily draped with curtains to keep out wind and sun, and furnished with comfortable armchairs." Spalding's own private box was equipped with the newly popular telephone and a gong for when he desired service.

According to the *Harper's* article, this palatial ballpark employed forty-one uniformed attendants—seven ushers, six policemen, four ticket sellers, four gatekeepers, three groundskeepers, three cushion renters, six refreshment sellers, and eight musicians. (In 1893 it was torn down to make room for the site of the Columbian Exposition.)

It had facilities for cycling, track, and lawn tennis and featured a toilet with a private entrance for ladies. Like the Polo Grounds in New York, it was long and horseshoe-shaped. It was 560 feet to center, and its fences were only 216 down the foul lines. When in 1884 the ground rule was changed to allow balls hit over the short right-field fence to be called home runs and not doubles, Chicago's outstanding third baseman Ned Williamson hit 27 homers—the National League home run record until Babe Ruth of the Red Sox broke it thirty-five years later with 29.

In 1884, Fred Pfeffer hit 25, Abner Dalrymple 22, and Anson 21. The Chicago team set the record for homers in a season with 142, a milestone that wasn't reached until the New York Yankees hit 158 forty-three years later, with a lineup that featured the famed Murderer's Row.

Anson, a traditionalist, wasn't enamored with the park. Though his Chicago team hit a lot of home runs, this was still the dead ball era, and Anson, a conservative, saw that the short fences made his hit-and-run style of baseball obsolete.

CAP ANSON: "The only fault that could be found with the [grounds] were that they were too small, both for the crowds that thronged them when an important game was being played, and because of the fact that the fences interfered too often with the performance of the League's star batsmen."

The White Stockings of the 1880s were a team of large men. Seven of the players, including Kelly and Anson, stood over six feet tall. So did catcher Frank "Old Silver" Flint, infielder Ned Williamson, pitcher Fred Goldsmith, and outfielders George Gore and Abner Dalrymple.

Said Kelly, "All in all, it was the best ball team ever put together. That was the crowd that showed the way to all the others. They towered over all ball teams like Salvator's record dwarfs all the other race horses." (Salvator was the Secretariat of the 1880s.)

Chicago won the 1880 championship in a runaway, finishing fifteen games ahead of Providence, led by John Montgomery Ward. In 1881, Providence added the great Hoss Radbourn to its staff, but Chicago still won the championship by nine full games.

In 1882 the White Stockings started slowly and trailed Providence, only to win seventeen of their last eighteen games. To capture the 1882 championship, Chicago had to beat Providence, managed by Harry Wright, in a crucial three-game series toward the end of the season. As was his way, it was Mike Kelly who made the crucial play that propelled Chicago to victory.

MIKE KELLY: "Both the Wrights were confident that Chicago would drop three straight games to the Providence boys, and that they would win the championship. I wanted to bet Harry a new hat, but he wouldn't bet. The first game was the most hotly contested game of ball I ever played in. Every point was fought, and each man exerted every effort to have his side win. We, perhaps, had a little the best of it, in view of the fact that we were at home, and were sure to get the encouragement of the thousands of spectators who witnessed the game. The score in the last inning was four to three in favor of the Providence club. There was one man out when I scratched a hit. I got on first and was about to make an attempt to steal second, when [Tommy] Burns, who followed me, hit a hot grounder to [shortstop] George Wright. There was one player out, and if George ever got the ball to second it meant a double play, and that would settle the game. Instead of fielding the ball to the second baseman, he started for the bag himself. I never ran so hard in my life. I reached the bag a second before George, and then like a flash, he raised his arm to send the ball to first base, to cut off Burns. Somehow or other an accident occurred at that moment. My arm went up in the air, and it caught George on the shoulder. The result was, that when the ball left George's hand it went away over into the grand stand. I scored first, and Burns followed me a moment later. The cheers from a thousand enthusiastic spectators proved that the Chicago club had won the first great game. The next two were afterwards won by us, and in the ten games that followed with other clubs, Providence won but two.

"Harry Wright was the maddest man in Chicago when the series had finished, and he claimed that were it not for 'Kelly and his infernal tricks' the Providence club would have won the series and the championship. He swore that he would have revenge in the future. I saw him, and had quite a talk with him. I said, 'Mr. Wright, I have played ball for a number of years; I will do everything in the world to win a championship game of ball. That is what I am paid for. But during all the time I have played ball, I never hurt a player. I never spiked a man, never knocked a man down. I play ball to win, and if I have to employ a few subterfuges to win I cannot help it. I wouldn't willfully hurt George Wright, or any man in your club. But self-preservation is the law of nature. When I saw George raise his arm, I knew that if something didn't occur we would be defeated. I didn't think of George nor myself. I simply thought of the Chicago club.' Harry was smiling before I finished, and he was willing to forgive me. Instead of having revenge, he has been a good friend of mine since that date."

The year 1882 marked the inaugural season for a second major league, the American Association, a six-team league made up of four teams thrown out of the National League: Cincinnati, Louisville, St. Louis, and Philadelphia. The American Association had been started to compete with Al Spalding's powerful combine with an eye toward attracting customers through lower ticket prices (twenty-five cents rather than the National League's fifty cents) and through the sale of beer at the park, which was specifically forbidden in the National League.

Cincinnati had been thrown out of the National League in 1880 specifically for violating the ban against selling liquor in the park. Reds owner Justus Thorner wanted to sell J. G. Sohn & Co.'s best beer, and so after his ejection from the National League, he entered the American Association in 1882 and won the pennant that very first year.

Even though the two leagues were feuding, after the 1882 season Spalding and Thorner agreed among themselves that the winners of the two leagues would play two exhibition games on October 6 and 7.

The pitching star for Cincinnati was Will White, the brother of veteran star Jim "Deacon" White. Will White won 40 games that year with a 1.54 earned run average. Cincinnati's fielding star was second baseman John Alexander "Biddy" McPhee, who played in more than two thousand games for the Reds and nine times led the league in fielding, even though he fielded barehanded all but four years of his career.

The two games were pretty much ignored in Chicago, where the Reds were viewed as minor leaguers, but in Cincinnati, where fans had deeply resented their teams's ejection from the older league, feelings ran high against the Chicagoans. Reds fans were proud of White and McPhee, two churchgoing pillars of the community, and expressed their contempt for Anson, whom they viewed as a hothead, and for Kelly, who they felt was a cheat.

The first game was played in Cincinnati before 2,700 fans. The game, featuring Fred Goldsmith against Will White, was scoreless into the sixth inning when, with runners on first and third, Cincinnati scored a run on a hit to center that landed just in front of Chicago center fielder George Gore. When McPhee tripled, the Reds had two more runs. A wild pitch by Goldsmith made it 4–0.

Will White finished with an eight-hit shutout. The *Cincinnati Enquirer* teased Chicago in an editorial when it wrote, "Will White and his Lilliputian crew astonished the Chicagos, the champions of the League, the great, high-toned and only moral baseball show. . . ."

The second and final game of the series also was played in Cincinnati, and again Will White pitched, this time against a well-rested Larry Corcoran, who allowed Cincinnati only three hits. For this game 3,500 fans turned out to see the White Stockings score two runs in the first inning for the win, the first one scoring on one of Cap Anson's innovations, the hit-and-run play.

George Gore reached first base on an error. As White wound up to pitch to Ned Williamson, Gore ran for second. Both shortstop Chick Fulmer and second baseman McPhee ran to cover, thinking it an attempted steal. Williamson hit the ball to the spot vacated by McPhee, and Gore raced into third. Outfielder Harry Wheeler, perhaps rattled by the play, picked up the ball and threw it high over third, allowing Gore to score and Williamson to reach third. A ground ball by Anson scored Williamson.

More games were planned, but the president of the American Association, Denny McKnight, ordered the Reds to cease playing the enemy under threat of expulsion.

Two months later, the two leagues signed an agreement calling for each team to have an eleven-player reserve list, territorial rights, and a minimum player salary of $1,000.

The two-game series may not have lasted long enough to be called the first World Series, but it was the first time two teams from different leagues played each other, and as such it takes its rightful place in baseball history.

In 1883, Chicago continued to play well, but the team wasn't strong enough to stop Boston, led by Ezra Sutton, the infielder who had refused to join Chicago with Anson. The Chicago-Boston rivalry was closely followed by the entire sporting world. Gamblers fought to gain any edge possible. Mike Kelly described an encounter he had with a Boston gambler right after the first game of a key series with Boston late in the 1883 season.

MIKE KELLY: "This fellow came to me in the corridor of the United States Hotel [in Boston] the night after the first game.

"'Kelly,' he said, 'I have it on pretty good authority that Chicago is going to throw the championship to Boston this year. Is it so?'

"I looked at him for a moment, and thought perhaps that he was joking. I sized him up, and then said to him: 'You had better ask Anson. He knows more about it than I do.'

"'Look here, Kelly,' the fellow replied, 'what Anson knows in regard to this affair doesn't matter. You fellows can win it, if you want to. There isn't any doubt about that, in my mind. Now, I'm in this thing to make money, and I am willing to help you do the same. I understand that you are to catch in the coming games. If you will promise me that the Bostons will win, I will give you $2,500. You can fix the pitchers.'

"The proposition stunned me for a moment. Anson was in the office. I called him over, and told him what the man had said. He just stood there like a dummy, but looked as though he would like to be present somewhere else. I thought Anson would get mad but he didn't. He said, 'My friend, you cannot buy the Chicago club. There isn't money enough in Boston for that. Now, I will give you a straight tip. If we can win, we are going to. We're going to make the great fight of our lives. I heard, on the very best authority, tonight, that the Bostons were going to do the same thing. One thing I will admit. This week settles whether it will be Boston or Chicago, or Chicago and Boston. Good-night, sir. I'll play you a game of billiards, Kel.'

"The man looked as though he wished he were dead."

It was Mike Kelly's contention that the problem of gamblers wasn't nearly as great as baseball owners like Al Spalding and the press made it out to be.

MIKE KELLY: "A great many people in this lovely country of ours have an idea that the gamblers run base ball, and that a player can easily be bought, one way or the other. This is the most absurd idea imaginable. To be sure, there is more or less betting in every game which attracts sporting men. You will find this the case, from the third-class races at Clifton to the swell races of the Country Club. But on one thing I will risk everything I have in the world: there is no dishonesty about base ball, of the many players at present in the league, I am sure there is not one dishonest one. There may have been a few in the past. Let us thank God that there are none in the present, and hope that there won't be in the future."

He added, "This is the gospel truth."

Kelly recalled the strength of that 1883 Boston team and how four tough losses to Boston at the end of the season cost them the championship that year.

MIKE KELLY: "It takes just nine healthy, peaceable men, who are playing together, for each other and for the good of the club they work for, to win a game of ball.

"When the Chicago club came to Boston, at near the close of the season of 1883, we found the Bostons in this condition. The home club was playing a faultless game. They were in great trim. They were batting well, playing a great fielding game, ran bases in good shape, and had a get-there air of confidence which would demoralize almost any club. On the other hand, the Chicagos were pretty well broken up. 'Silver' Flint had a broken finger, and couldn't catch. I was also troubled with a broken finger, and every time I caught a ball it seemed as though my right hand would drop off. Neither Corcoran nor Goldsmith were in good condition, and they didn't pitch anywhere near the game they were capable of doing. Anson went in to catch, and so did Williamson. When we came to Boston, we had only ten games to play: four in Boston, three in Providence, and three in New York. We led the league by four games. We knew that if we finished in Boston all right, that we would make a strong fight for the pennant. Anson never encouraged the boys so in his life. But we had a good nine, in great condition, to oppose us, and we couldn't do impossible things.

". . . the Bostons played better and scored more runs. Boston deserved the honor. The boys won that pennant fairly and squarely. We accepted defeat like philosophers, and made up our minds to even things up at some future day. Well, the four games we lost at Boston demoralized us. We couldn't do anything with New York or Providence, and that settled it."

In 1884, Providence finally earned a championship behind its durable pitcher Hoss Radbourn, who recorded 60 wins and an earned run average of 1.38. Chicago finished fourth when Corcoran slipped and Goldsmith broke down.

By the middle of the 1884 season Anson could see that his two pitchers couldn't top Radbourn, and so toward the end of the season Anson added a replacement, "Handsome" John Clarkson, whom Anson once described as "a really great pitcher, in fact, the best that Chicago ever had."

One teammate, Billy Sunday, recalled Clarkson's greatness (and his questionable hygiene) in a book written in 1914.

BILLY SUNDAY: "He was as fine a pitcher as ever crawled into a uniform. There are some pitchers today, [Marty] O'Toole, [Chief] Bender, [Smokey Joe] Wood, [Christy] Mathewson, [Walter] Johnson, [Rube] Marquard, but I do not believe any one of them stood in the class with Clarkson.

"Cigarettes put him on the bum. When he'd taken a bath the water would be stained with nicotine.

"Oh, he could make 'em dance. He could throw overhand, and the ball would go down and up like that. He is the only man on earth I have seen do that. That ball would go by so fast that the batter could feel the thermometer drop two degrees as she whizzed by."

Clarkson was born July 1, 1861, in Cambridge, Massachusetts. He had two other Harvard-educated brothers, Arthur "Dad" and Walter, who also pitched in the major leagues.

Clarkson broke into pro baseball as a major leaguer with Worcester in 1882. The local boy was signed to boost attendance, but the team still folded at the end of the season, and he went to pitch for Saginaw in the Northwestern League. In the half year he pitched in 1884 he had ten shutouts, 399 strikeouts, and 45 walks.

Cap Anson saw him pitch for the Lumberjacks of Saginaw in a game in Grand Rapids, Michigan, and after the league folded in midseason he signed him for the price of a train ticket and lunch.

Clarkson, a control pitcher who featured a clever change of pace and a remarkable curve, studied hitters and pitched to their weaknesses. With strong fingers and wrists, he could spin a billiard ball so that it would make a complete circle on the table. He was noted for his acute memory, with which he remembered the strengths and weaknesses of the batters.

Mike Kelly, for one, had a deep appreciation of Clarkson's skill.

* * *

MIKE KELLY: "John Clarkson is the star pitcher of the Chicago club, and by many people is looked upon as the star pitcher of the league. Clarkson is a quiet, modest gentleman, and does less talking about base ball than any player in the country. He has all the essential qualifications necessary in the make-up of a great pitcher. He has a good long head, and knows how to use it. He has good judgment, and he displays it all at critical times. His command of the ball is simply wonderful. He has more curves and shoots than any pitcher in this country. There isn't a heavy batter in the league who likes to face Clarkson at a critical moment. He will keep them thinking, and the chances are ten to one that he will fool them on a deceptive ball."

Clarkson, like Kelly, became legendary in reputation. He reportedly was able to strike out batters by blinding them with his large, polished belt buckle, which he would employ to reflect the sun's rays into the opposing batter's eyes. Before the opposition would catch on and protest, Clarkson would have put out a number of unsuspecting players.

Clarkson was also the sort of competitor who hated to lose an argument when he knew he was right. During one game he thought play should have been called on account of darkness. To prove his point, he pitched a lemon instead of a baseball across the plate. Umpire Jack Kerins called it a strike. When the catcher showed him the lemon, the ump called the game.

Clarkson replaced Corcoran and Goldsmith in 1885, a year in which he pitched 68 complete games, threw 623 innings, and finished the year 53–16. He amassed ten shutouts and had a no-hitter against Providence and Radbourn, whom he defeated ten out of twelve times.

John Clarkson

After pitching Chicago to a pennant in 1885, he did it again in '86, with a 36–17 record, completing 50 of 55 starts. Cap Anson, who discovered him, recalled the strengths and weaknesses of his star pitcher.

CAP ANSON: "[Clarkson] was the possessor of a remarkable drop curve and fast overhand lifting speed, while his change of pace was most deceiving. He was peculiar in some things, however, and in order to get his best work you had to keep spurring him along, otherwise he was apt to let up, this being especially the case when the club was ahead and he saw what he thought was a chance to save himself. As a fielder he was very fair, and as a batsman above the average, so far as strength went, though not always to be depended upon as certain to land upon the ball."

But according to Anson, as Clarkson's success increased, he developed a terrible temper and had an extremely sensitive disposition. He would need constant praise. Adverse criticism caused him to sulk.

In addition to John Clarkson, who was elected into the Hall of Fame in 1963, Anson added pitcher Jim McCormick to the staff. The hard-drinking McCormick, who won fourteen straight from July through September, finished the 1885 season with 20 wins in 24 starts.

The White Stockings of 1885 also featured one of the great infields of its day, called the Stone Wall Infield, manned by four star-quality players, Ed Williamson at third, Tommy Burns at short, Fred Pfeffer at second, and Anson at first. The records show that the four made a lot of errors, but their assist, putout, and double play totals usually ranked high in the league.

Burns, at short, had been a star with Albany in the New York State League when Anson signed him to play in Chicago. As a rookie in 1880 he hit .309. A heady ballplayer, Burns was one of the few base runners who slid headfirst. Even though he was one of the few Chicago players who didn't drink, making him an Anson favorite, according to Fred Lieb, "Tommy had been one of Anson's hell raisers in Chicago, a roguish fellow who liked to play pranks on Cap and his teammates."

Ed Williamson, the best-fielding third baseman of his day, was the first player ever to hit three home runs in one game. Seven times Ed led the league in assists, four times in fielding average, twice in putouts, and twice in total chances.

The second baseman, Fred Pfeffer, was the best pivot man in the game, and he could cover more ground than anyone else. The glue of the Chicago infield, Mike Kelly called him "the greatest second baseman of them all." At bat he was a dangerous clutch hitter.

Both Williamson and Pfeffer, like a dozen other Chicago players, have been wrongly denied their place in the Hall of Fame. Both were rated highly by Cap Anson.

CAP ANSON: "Ed was, in my opinion, the greatest all-around ballplayer the country ever saw. He was a better-than-average batsman and one of the few that knew how to wait for a ball and get the one that he wanted before striking. He was a good third baseman, a good catcher and a man who could pitch more than fairly well, too, when the necessity for his doing so arose. Taking him all in all, I question if we shall ever see his like on a ball field again. He was injured some years later while the Chicago Club was making a trip around the world, and was never the same fellow afterward.

"Williamson was one of the most popular of the many players that the Chicago Club has had. A big, good-natured and good-hearted fellow, he numbered his friends by the hundreds, and his early death [in 1894, at the age of thirty-eight] was regretted by all who knew him. . . .

"Fred Pfeffer, who came from Louisville, Ky., was a ballplayer from the ground up, and as good a second baseman as there was in the profession, the only thing that I ever found to criticize in his play being a tendency to pose for the benefit of the occupants of the grand stand. He was a brilliant player, however, and as good a man in this position according to my estimate as any that ever held down the second bag. He was a high-salaried player and one that earned every cent that he received, being a hard worker and always to be relied upon. He was a neat dresser, and while not a teetotaler, never drank any more than he knew how to take care of. As a thrower, fielder and base runner he was in the first class, while as a batsman he was only fair."

Led by his team of stars, Anson's Chicago White Stockings were the talk of baseball fans across America.

CAP ANSON: "The team that brought the pennant back to Chicago in the years 1885 and 1886 was, in my estimation, not only the strongest team that I ever had under my management but, taken all in all, one of the strongest teams that has ever been gotten together in the history of the League, the position of left field, which was still being played by [Abner] Dalrymple being its only weak spot. The fact, however, that Dal was a terrific batter made up for a great many of his shortcomings in the field, which would scarcely have been overlooked so easily had it not been for his ability as a wielder of the ash. In its pitching department it was second in strength to none of its competitors and behind the bat were Flint and Kelly, both of whom were widely and favorably known. The outfield was, to say the least, equal to that of any of the other League clubs, and the infield that became famous as Chicago's stone wall, that name being given to it for the reasons that the only way that a ball could be gotten through it was to bat it so high that it was out of reach. The members of that famous infield were Williamson, Pfeffer, Burns and myself, and so long had we played together and so steadily had we practiced that there was scarcely a play made that we were not in readiness to meet. We had a system of signals that was almost perfect, and the moment that a ball was hit and we had noted its direction we knew just what to look for. We were up to all the tricks of the game, and better than all else we had the greatest confidence in each other.

"I had shifted the positions of Williamson and Burns and the former was now playing shortstop and the latter third base. At third base Burns was as good as the best of them, excelling at the blocking game, which he carried on in a style that was particularly his own and which was calculated to make a base-runner considerable trouble. At short Williamson was right in his element and in spite of his size he could cover as much ground in that position as any man that I have ever seen. While his throwing was of the rifle-shot order, it was yet easy to catch, as it seemed to come light to your hands, and this was also true of the balls thrown by Pfeffer and Burns, both of whom were very accurate in that line."

*   *   *

Johnny Evers, who himself would go down in baseball history as one of the finest infielders ever to play the game, in 1910 wrote a book that included chapters on his predecessors in Chicago and in which he praised the 1885–86 team for its skill and teamwork.

JOHNNY EVERS: "The Chicago team of 1880, which reached its fullest development five years later, was the pioneer of 'inside baseball,' and from that team came more original plays, now in common use, than from any other source. Those were the formative days of the modern game, and the players, [second baseman Joe] Quest, Anson, Kelly, Burns, Williamson, Gore, Flint, and Corcoran, were learning from each other while teaching others.

"But it really was with the coming of Pfeffer in 1883 that the team began to play 'inside baseball' coherently, both at bat and on the infield. A system of signaling, involving the catcher, shortstop, third and second baseman and pitcher, was invented, Anson for some reason being excluded from the team play. The marvelous success of the team was due more to intelligent team work, and the protecting of base runners by the batters than to the individual skill of the players, although that was great."

Evers (through his ghost, sportswriter Hugh Fullerton) recalled the innovations of this talented team, marveling at the brilliance of their ingenuity on the ball field. One of those plays the White Stockings called the Old Gag, the purpose of which was to tire out an unsuspecting pitcher on the base paths.

JOHNNY EVERS: "'The Old Gag,' a play christened and used by Anson's infield when Pfeffer and Burns and Williamson were helping invent plays, was one which taught the succeeding generations of players how a man caught between bases should be run down. With the White Stockings never more than three men were allowed in the play, and to the present time all managers direct their men to play it that way, one man chasing the runner down near the man guarding the base, and then tossing the ball to him and, when the baseman turns the runner back, the one who has been pursuing him, falls in to guard the base. Thus both avenues of escape are closed, and a fresh runner is always ready to pursue the tiring man. The White Stocking infield worked 'the Old Gag' to tire out pitchers of the opposing team and won many games through that alone. They would play to let the pitcher get a good start, and when they caught him between bases they ran him to a state of exhaustion, refusing to touch him until he surrendered from sheer weariness. They caught [Amos] Rusie once—but the big pitcher refused to run and throwing both hands above his head, trotted to the bench without waiting to be touched."

The 1885 pennant race came down to Chicago and New York, which featured the pitching of Smiling Mickey Welch and Tim Keefe and the hitting of first baseman Roger Connor, outfielder Orator Jim O'Rourke, and catcher Buck Ewing, all future Hall of Famers.

Chicago finished the season at 87–25. The Giants, another outstanding team, were 85–27. The pennant was settled in Chicago during a three-game series on September 30, October 1, and October 2. A lot was at stake. Betting on the games by spectators was widespread. Even the reporters couldn't resist.

CAP ANSON: "There were a good many funny stories told about those closing games between New York and Chicago. The admirers of the Giants came on to witness the games in force, and so certain were they that their pets would win that they wagered their money on the result in the most reckless fashion.

"Even the newspaper men who accompanied them on the trip caught the contagion. P. J. Donohue, of the *New York World*, since deceased, was one of the most reckless of these. He could see nothing in the race but New York, and no sooner had he struck the town than he began to hunt for someone who would take the Chicago end of the deal.

"About nine o'clock the night before the playing of the first game he appeared in the 'Inter Ocean' office and announced that he was looking for somebody who thought Chicago could win, as he wished to wager $100 on the result. He was accompanied by the sporting editor of that paper. The next night after the Giants had lost P. J. again appeared on the scene and announced his readiness to double up on the result of the second game. He was accommodated again, and again New York was the loser.

"Still a third time did P. J. appear with an offer to double up the whole thing on the result of the next game. This looked like a bad bet for the local man, but local pride induced him to make the wager. For the third time the Giants went down before the White Stockings, and that night P. J. was missing, but a day or two afterwards he turned up quite crestfallen, and had a draft on New York cashed in order that he might get back home again.

"Mr. Donohue was not the only man who went broke on the result, however. There was not a man on the delegation that accompanied the Giants that did not lose, and lose heavily on the games, which went a long ways toward illustrating the glorious uncertainties of baseball."

7

World Series Failure

The 1885 World Series was a curiosity, a traveling circus played between Chicago and the American Association champions, the St. Louis Browns, with games in Chicago, St. Louis, Pittsburgh, and Cincinnati. It was set up as a series of seven exhibition games by Spalding and Browns owner Chris Von der Ahe, with the winning team to get $1,000. While each owner put up $500—stakes akin to two professional gamblers playing nickel-and-dime poker—more money than that was bet among the players of the two teams, and far more by the fans.

St. Louis pitcher Parisian Bob Caruthers waved a roll of bills at Anson. "I'll bet you $1,000," he shouted, "that the Browns can easily beat your nine. And I'll put this money up as a forfeit."

Replied Chicago shortstop Ed Williamson, "We White Stockings stand ready to cover all bets the Brown Stockings wish to make."

Though it was just a series of exhibitions, pride was at stake, and the players were not friendly. Chicago, under Anson, was known for its rough tactics and for its abuse of umpires. St. Louis, led by Arlie Latham, called the Freshest Man on Earth, was another team with a reputation for rough play and foul language.

The National Leaguers strutted their superiority. Cap Anson, who with his teammates showed contempt for the upstart Browns and their "beer league," told one reporter he doubted that St. Louis could have finished fifth in the National League.

St. Louis was managed by one of baseball's legendary figures, Charles Comiskey, who like Al Spalding went from the playing field to become a club owner. Comiskey would later own the other team in Chicago, the one that would steal their name and be called the White Sox during the twentieth century.

In 1885, Comiskey, who like Anson encouraged aggressiveness and umpire baiting, managed the Browns to the pennant while also starring at first base. Comiskey, like Anson, was an innovator. It was Comiskey who dictated that the first baseman should play deep, allowing his second baseman to play deeper and closer to second base.

Comiskey also devised a new wrinkle to defensive strategy by insisting that when the first baseman had to range wide to field a grounder, the pitcher should cover first on the dead run and take the throw for the out. On balls hit to the outfield, Comiskey had his pitchers back up second, third, and even home plate.

Commented Johnny Evers, "Comiskey won pennants at St. Louis by his inventiveness and it is a remarkable thing that every team he ever has handled has had great fielding pitchers."

Leading the Browns team were pitchers Bobby Caruthers, who won 40 games that year, and Dave Foutz, who won 33, along with Latham, a third baseman who was one of the game's greatest base stealers, and outfielder Curt Welch, another speedster.

Though these were exhibition matches for small stakes, the games were hotly played. St. Louis was a commercial hub, the second-busiest railroad center. Budweiser, first marketed in 1876, was already the most popular beer in the Midwest. St. Louis was also the number one manufacturer of tobacco in the country.

With fifteen Chicago players splitting up the $1,000 in prize money (less than $70 a man), some of the Chicago players took the contests lightly. Some—including McCormick, Gore, Kelly, Williamson, and Dalrymple—did not consider these games part of the season, so they carried on like these were exhibitions, drinking heavily, frustrating Anson, and infuriating Spalding, who was pocketing the proceeds.

CAP ANSON: "The games were played after the regular season was over and after the players had in reality passed out of my control, and for that reason were not as amenable to the regular discipline as when the games for the League championship were going on."

The first game was played at the Congress Street Grounds before a crowd of 2,000 fans. St. Louis scored first on three errors, then Chicago tied it in the fourth on a Kelly single and two errors. St. Louis scored four runs on three singles and three more errors to take a 5–1 lead, and it stayed that way until the eighth when Chicago came to bat.

It was getting dark, and Caruthers made the mistake of rushing to get the inning in, walking George Gore. Kelly and Anson then singled to make the score 5–2. With two outs, Caruthers threw Pfeffer a pitch that the star infielder hit over the left-field fence to tie the game.

At the end of the inning the umpire called the game on account of darkness.

After the game Anson was furious. He hadn't liked the way they played, and he was sure that center fielder George Gore had been drinking before he arrived at the ballpark. He informed Gore that he would not be going to St. Louis. The fleet but weak-hitting Billy Sunday would play for him the rest of the way.

Anson in 1883 had discovered Sunday, who played outfield for the White Stockings, as a twenty-year-old youngster playing in an amateur tournament in his hometown of Marshalltown, Iowa. Sunday could run the hundred-yard dash in ten seconds flat, and he was the first to run the bases in fourteen seconds. His last year in the big leagues he stole 84 bases in 117 games. He once raced Arlie Latham, the fastest player in the American League, and won by fifteen feet.

Anson saw Sunday's breathtaking running ability and signed him immediately.

CAP ANSON: "It was the speed that he showed on that occasion that opened my eyes to his possibilities in the baseball playing line. He was, in my opinion, the fastest man afterwards on his feet in the profession, and one who could run the bases like a scared deer. The first thirteen times that he went to the bat after he began playing with the Chicagos he was struck out, but I was confident that he would yet make a ball player and hung onto him, cheering him up as best I could whenever he became discouraged. As a baserunner his judgment was at times faulty and he was altogether too daring, taking extreme chances because of the tremendous turn of speed that he possessed. He was a good fielder and a strong and accurate thrower, his weak point lying in his batting. The ball that he threw was a hard one to catch, however, it landing in the hands like a hunk of lead."

Chicago won Game 2, 5–4, in front of 3,000 fans in Sportsman's Park in St. Louis. The Browns had led 4–2 going into the top of the sixth and final inning. The crowd was upset because the umpire, Dave Sullivan, had made several calls that went against the home team.

Billy Sunday started off the sixth inning with a double, then went to third on a wild pitch. Kelly grounded to short, but umpire Sullivan was watching home to see whether Sunday would score, and when the shortstop threw to first, not home, the umpire had to guess, and he mistakenly called Kelly safe at first.

Comiskey and the St. Louis players began ranting. Comiskey told Sullivan that if he didn't change his call, he would take his team off the field. After fifteen minutes, Sullivan finally threatened Comiskey with a forfeit. Finally, the Browns returned to their positions.

With the score 4–3 in favor of the Browns, Anson came to the plate. Kelly stole second immediately, then Anson singled to knock in the tying run. After a force play at second, Fred Pfeffer stole second and went to third on a passed ball.

Chicago scored the winning run on another controversial play. Williamson grounded a ball into foul territory behind first base, but it began spinning, and by the time it was fielded it was in fair territory. Williamson, running all the way, was called safe by umpire Sullivan, who was again surrounded by Browns players, who claimed they had heard him holler that the ball was "foul." At the same time Pfeffer scored the go-ahead run.

When Comiskey argued that it was a foul ball and that Pfeffer should return to third, this time Sullivan went along, prompting Anson and Kelly to charge the beleaguered official.

Fearing them, Sullivan changed his mind again, and hundreds of rowdy, brawling spectators ran onto the field. The police raced to intervene, averting a brawl. The Chicago players were escorted off the field.

Later that evening Sullivan declared the game forfeited to Chicago. Comiskey, who declared that ball games were won on the field and not in hotel rooms, announced he would not abide by the decision.

So far the two teams had played two games, with one ending in a tie, the other in a forfeit.

The third game, again played in St. Louis, was won by the Browns, who refused to allow Sullivan to umpire again and selected as umpire Harry McCaffery, who officiated a 7–4 victory. Kelly and Dalrymple made costly errors on fly balls in the outfield, and Chicago generally played poorly.

Game 4, the final game in St. Louis, was delayed forty-five minutes because Anson decided he didn't want McCaffery umpiring again, and to accommodate him, a local fan in the stands was persuaded to umpire. It was a bad miscalculation on Anson's part in that the amateur ump, Harry Medart, decided every close call against Chicago and even called Chicago runners out when they clearly were safe.

In the fifth inning, with Tommy Burns on third base and pitcher Jim McCormick on first, the Browns catcher faked to first to pick off McCormick, then fired down to third in an attempt to catch Burns, who was standing on the bag. The fan-umpire, who probably hadn't seen the play, called Burns out.

With Chicago down by one run in the ninth inning and one out, the umpire skunked Chicago again. Burns reached base on an error, then McCormick was safe on another error when Comiskey dropped his pop fly. Before throwing the ball back to the pitcher, Comiskey tagged McCormick, who was standing on the base. Incredibly, Medart called him out. Anson had to keep McCormick from punching Medart. The mild-mannered Billy Sunday, doubling his fists, called the umpire a liar. It was King Kelly who stopped Sunday from hitting the man.

When the next batter, a seventeen-year-old amateur whom Anson was giving a look-see, made out, the game was over. St. Louis had been handed the win.

The sideshow next moved to Pittsburgh, where the series finally was afforded a professional umpire, John Kelly, one of the best in the game. The rest of the series proceeded smoothly with Kelly in control.

Before a sparse crowd of about 500, John Clarkson pitched a four-hitter and won easily. In Cincinnati, Chicago won again, behind a two-hitter by Jim McCormick.

After five games Chicago had two wins and St. Louis had two wins. The question: Did the forfeit count? If so, Chicago would be declared the victors.

But Anson, confident he had the better team, and Charles Comiskey, looking for another payday, agreed to ignore the forfeit. A sixth and final game would decide the champion.

When the mercurial John Clarkson showed up five minutes late (and in all probability drunk), Anson benched him and started Jim McCormick, who needed more rest as St. Louis pounded him and won 13–4. Where Clarkson was and why he was late no one knows. Apparently no reporter bothered to ask him, or else he didn't feel it anyone's business to know.

After the final loss, Al Spalding, a sore loser, expressed his fury at the result. He raved, "Does anyone suppose that if there had been so much as that at stake that I should have consented to the games being played in American Association cities, upon their grounds, and under the authority of their umpires?"

Their grounds? *Their* umpires? What was he talking about?

Though the baseball world regarded St. Louis as World Champions, Browns owner Chris Von der Ahe, who privately rejoiced at his team's victory, publicly declared that the forfeit should count and that the series was a tie, thereby cheating his own players out of the $1,000 prize money.

In 1886, Anson's bullies brought Chicago its fifth pennant in seven years. It still had the infield of Anson, Pfeffer, Burns, and Williamson. Clarkson and McCormick pitched, as did John "Jocko" Flynn, who was five foot six and weighed only 143 pounds. Flynn had a 24–6 record as a twenty-two-year-old rookie, but the next year he played one game in the outfield and then mysteriously vanished from the game.

The White Stockings were challenged for the league championship by Detroit, led by pitcher Lady Baldwin, called Lady because he didn't smoke or drink, much to the amusement of his boisterous opponents. Baldwin, however, was no pushover on the mound, winning 42 games with a 2.24 earned run average in 1886. At bat Detroit featured Big Dan Brouthers, a powerful, dangerous hitter, as well as outfielders Sam Thompson, a Hall of Famer, and Hardy Richardson, a lifetime .299 hitter who should be but isn't in the Hall. Legendary catcher Charlie Bennett was behind the plate.

Going into the final day of the season Chicago and Detroit were tied. Chicago defeated Boston while Detroit was losing two games to Charlie Ferguson, the fine pitcher for Harry Wright's Philadelphia team.

Mike Kelly remembered the Chicago-Detroit rivalry of 1886.

MIKE KELLY: "Perhaps the most exciting games of ball played in late years were the games between the Detroits and Chicagos, in the season of '86. [Jim] McCormick and I [from behind the plate] had won seventeen straight, successive victories, and the Detroit club had won eighteen straight on the home grounds. We went to Detroit, accompanied by hundreds of Chicago lovers of the game. They all carried new brooms; and even the little boy mascot of the Chicago club marched on the field with us with a big broom perched over his right shoulder. How the men from Chicago did cheer! What a tremendous noise the 'Hoosiers' did make! They cheered every player of the home club every time that they came to the bat. But McCormick was in great trim, and so were the members of the Chicago club. As a result, we won the first game. The men from Chicago were wild with enthusiasm. They coated the town of Detroit with paint of vermillion color. It was well they did, because on the next two games they didn't have a chance. The Detroit giants made a great race, and won both games."

The next three games between the two teams were held in Chicago. Five hundred Detroit fans showed up. Chicago won all three games.

Said Kelly, "It badly demoralized the Detroit players, and the lovers of the game went back to the Wolverine city, sadder, but wiser men."

Chicago won the final game in part by a circus catch made by outfielder Billy Sunday, who went on to become a nationally known evangelist after his baseball career ended in 1887.

BILLY SUNDAY: "That afternoon we played the old Detroit club. We were neck and neck for the championship. That club had [Sam] Thompson, [Hardy] Richardson, [Jack] Rowe, [Fred] Dunlap, [Ned] Hanlon and [Charlie] Bennett, and they could play ball.

"I was playing right field. Mike Kelly was catching and John G. Clarkson was pitching.

"We had two men out and they had a man on second and one on third and Bennett, their old catcher, was at bat. Charlie had three balls and two strikes on him. Charlie couldn't hit a high ball: but he could kill them when they went about his knee.

"I hollered to Clarkson and said: 'One more and we got 'em.'

"You know every pitcher puts a hole in the ground where he puts his foot when he is pitching. John stuck his foot in the hole and he went clean to the ground. John went clean down, and as he went to throw the ball his right foot slipped and the ball went low instead of high.

The 1884 Team: *(Top row, from left)* George Gore, Frank Flint, Adrian Anson, Elmer Sutcliffe, Mike Kelly, and Fred Pfeffer. *(Bottom row, from left)* Fred Goldsmith, Ed Williamson, Abner Dalrymple, Tom Burns, John Clarkson, and Billy Sunday.

"I saw Charlie swing hard and heard the bat hit the ball with a terrific boom. Bennett had smashed the ball on the nose. I saw the ball rise in the air and knew that it was going clear over my head.

"I could judge within ten feet of where the ball would light. I turned my back to the ball and ran.

"The field was crowded with people and I yelled, 'Stand back!' and that crowd opened as the Red Sea opened for the rod of Moses. I ran on, and as I ran I made a prayer; it wasn't theological, either, I tell you that. I said, 'God, if you ever helped mortal man, help me to get that ball, and you haven't very much time to make up your mind, either.' I ran and jumped over the bench and stopped.

"I thought I was close enough to catch it. I looked back and saw it was going over my head and I jumped and shoved out my left hand and the ball hit it and stuck. At the rate I was going the momentum carried me on and I fell under the feet of a team of horses. I jumped up with the ball in my hand. Up came Tom Johnson. Tom used to be mayor of Cleveland. He's dead now.

"'Here is $10, Bill. Buy yourself the best hat in Chicago. That catch won me $1,500. Tomorrow go and buy yourself the best suit of clothes you can find in Chicago.'

"An old Methodist minister said to me a few years ago, 'Why, William, you didn't take the $10, did you?' I said, 'You bet your life I did.'"

According to baseball writer Harold Kaese, after Philadelphia beat Detroit twice to give Chicago the championship, a grateful Cap Anson bought each Philadelphia player a suit of clothes.

CAP ANSON: "A notable incident of the campaign was the fact that in the closing month it lay entirely in the hands of the Philadelphia Club to decide whether the pennant was to go to Detroit or to Chicago.

"When Chicago left Philadelphia for Boston the last of September all Detroit was in a fever of excitement at the prospect of their club's success. The only question of interest was, 'Would they go through Philadelphia safely?' It was only when Harry Wright's pony League team captured the Detroits twice out of four games, one being drawn, that Chicago felt relief from anxiety as to the ultimate outcome of the pennant race. It was a gallant struggle by Philadelphia, and it made the close of the campaign season one of the most exciting on record.

"This was one of the hardest seasons I had ever gone through, and when it was over I felt that we were lucky, indeed, to have captured the pennant for the third successive time.

"It was a close race that season between Mike Kelly and myself for the batting honors of the League, and Michael beat me out by a narrow margin at the finish, his percentage being .388 as against .371, while Brouthers came third on the list with .370.

"That was the last season that the championship pennant was flown in Chicago up to the present writing [1900], and looking back at it now it seems to me an awful long time ago."

By 1886 the World Series had become a national phenomenon. Once again, the two champions from their respective leagues, Chicago and St. Louis, were facing one another. The recriminations from the '85 Series hadn't been forgotten, and the fans' interest in the series of games was heightened after Chris Von der Ahe of St. Louis challenged Albert Spalding, only to be scornfully turned down, then rechallenged by a vindictive Spalding but only on a winner-take-all basis.

This time it wasn't a measly grand at stake but rather a kingly $15,000, which made it the most followed sporting event in American history up to that point. As Robert Smith described it, it was "the talk of every ball fan between the Mississippi and the Atlantic Coast."

Spalding, who had taken the loss to the Browns badly in '85, wrote to Cap Anson and his players before the Series promising them a suit of clothes and half the gate receipts if the team won. This year, the players would have real incentive to win. The betting was that Chicago would not lose a single game.

The first game, played in Chicago, was marked by rowdyism and poor sportsmanship by the Chicago fans toward the Browns and their fans. At one point the Chicago newspaper reporters seated in the press box directed the heckling, proving even back then the difficulty of covering a team and not rooting for it. Pitcher John Clarkson rubbed salt into the Browns' psychic wounds by pitching a 6–0 runaway.

St. Louis star Bobby Caruthers, who was known to be suffering from a weak heart, played the outfield in the first game and went 0 for 4. Chicago fans taunted him with calls of "Bobby's got the heart disease bad."

The next day, again in Chicago, Caruthers took the mound and pitched a one-hitter. So much for his bad heart.

The loser in a 12–0 drubbing was Jim McCormick. After the Series a bitter Albert Spalding would complain that as they had the year before, too many of the players, especially McCormick, had gotten drunk too often during the Series. When McCormick pitched Game 2, said Spalding, he "was so thoroughly soused, he could not have struck out the batboy."

The papers were filled with reports that the Chicago players had been drinking heavily the night before and that this was the reason for their lopsided loss. Cap Anson and Fred Pfeffer angrily denied the reports. (Lying to the press is not a new practice.)

Because Chicago was so heavily favored, the experts figured that if the White Stocking players weren't drunk, then they had to be hippodroming (throwing the game) to prolong the Series and increase gate receipts. Rumors to that effect also began circulating in the papers.

Anson defended his players against the hippodroming charge. "I can tell you now positively that these games are for blood, every one of them."

The Browns' Caruthers, crowing about his dominant performance in Game 2, begged Chris Von der Ahe to let him start the next game despite the lack of rest. In the first inning he allowed two runs, and Chicago, behind John Clarkson, roughed him up for an 11–4 win.

Pitcher Jim McCormick was supposed to have started the game for Chicago, but before the game he was so drunk "he could not even find his way to the mound and had to be led away to safety." Before the third game Anson would announce that the team would have to play without McCormick, who, he said, had "rheumatism in his legs." The big pitcher wouldn't play in another game for Chicago.

The teams went by train to the city of St. Louis, where several Chicago players were seen in gambling halls on the morning of Game 4. The smart money continued to be on the White Sox.

Ten thousand fans filled the Sportsman Field grandstands for the game, which featured a disagreement in strategy between pitcher Clarkson and manager Anson. With two outs and runners on first and second, Clarkson wanted to walk batter Tip O'Neill intentionally. Anson ordered him not to do it, but the big pitcher willfully did it anyway.

Clarkson got two strikes on the next hitter, Bill Gleason, but Gleason then grounded a single between short and third, giving the Browns the lead.

Chicago lost the game when second baseman Fred Pfeffer dropped a pop-up with the bases loaded and then failed to make the force-out that should have led to a double play.

St. Louis won 8–5.

Based on their behavior that night, it's not impossible that the Chicago players, without Anson's knowledge, had bet on the Browns and thrown the game.

At the Lindell Hotel the evening after the game, according to writer Jerry Lansche, "the White Stockings, with the exception of Cap Anson, seemed strangely undisturbed by their loss. The team stood around smoking big black cigars, toasting each other with champagne, and joking with reporters. Clarkson was in especially good humor. Shortstop Ned Williamson smiled enigmatically and said, 'Yes, sir, they beat us today on the level.' King Kelly told funny stories to a group of friends."

When the charges of hippodroming resurfaced, Anson, who would have tossed any player throwing a game out of baseball for life, swore up and down that his team had lost fair and square. He got in a shouting match with a *St. Louis Post-Dispatch* reporter who asked how it was possible the White Stockings lost.

"Didn't you see it yourself?" Anson angrily retorted. "Wasn't you there?"

The reporter said he had been there.

"Well, then you know as much as I do about it," Anson said as testily as any modern-day manager to the reporter whose questions were getting under his skin.

The whispers of hippodroming became a shout when Anson started third baseman Ed Williamson on the mound for Game 5. McCormick had been sent home, and Clarkson needed another day's rest, so it should have been the turn of Jocko Flynn, the third fine Chicago starter. Perhaps Anson had discovered Flynn too drunk to pitch. Anson didn't reveal the true story to anyone. But the reporters saw this as a sign that Chicago wasn't trying to win the Series, and Anson took a pounding in the press when Williamson was beaten badly, 10–3, giving the Browns a three-to-two-game lead.

On October 23, a reporter for the *Chicago News* wrote: "Admitting that base ball is a business conducted for pecuniary profit, there still can be no palliation for the offense of brazenly giving away a game as the game was given away yesterday in St. Louis. . . . The hippodrome was so artistically played that there really was no inclination to cry out against it. . . . The champion League club, having in its membership such pitchers as Clarkson, McCormick, Flynn and [Mark "Fido"] Baldwin, disdained the services of all these gentlemen and put in the box the very estimable short stop of the nine. . . . We presume to say that if such a shameless face had been attempted here in Chicago the conspirators and co-conspirators would have been hooted off the field."

The final game was played, according to Robert Smith, "on a warm, cloudy day before a grandstand full of men in high-crowned derbies, plug hats, and odd little round cloth hats like the Rollo hats which in later years used to make small boys wretched on Sunday. There were ladies in the audience, too, and a heavy sprinkling of kids, both in the grandstand and on the bleaching boards, the uncovered benches which became known as bleachers. There was an endless murmur from the crowd, for there was plenty of wagering going on, and St. Louis was an hour or two away from triumph."

Al Spalding came to St. Louis to convince Von der Ahe to start the game early at two so they could get in the entire nine innings before it got dark. Von der Ahe, confident of victory, complied.

Chicago took a 3–0 lead into the seventh with Fred Pfeffer scoring all three runs. Until the seventh, St. Louis didn't have a hit against John Clarkson. St. Louis batting star Tip O'Neill, who walked, had been the only base runner.

First baseman Charles Comiskey singled to lead off the Browns eighth. Curt Welch, the speedy center fielder, bunted a Clarkson fastball and sped on to second when the throw to first was wild. Comiskey reached third. The crowd, standing, began to scream and stamp. When Clarkson retired the next two batters on fly outs, the noise abated.

The catcher, Doc Bushong, stepped to the plate. Clarkson, only a few pitches away from victory, walked him to load the bases. Bushong represented the tying run.

Arlie Latham, the craftiest bunter in the league and probably the Browns' best base runner, took his spot at the plate. Latham had annoyed the White Stockings all Series long with his constant stream of invective and bench jockeying.

On this day, according to Robert Smith, "Arlie was oddly silent, and some of the locals began to tell each other that he couldn't stand the ragging he had been getting from Anson, that he was obviously too sick to play, or that he had been ordered to keep quiet because of complaints about his noise."

Anson, who himself was renowned for his tart tongue, spent the game inveighing his batters to hit the ball to Latham at third. Anson bellowed: "Knock it down here! This is our puddin'! This is the weak spot."

As Arlie dug in, catcher Mike Kelly began complaining to the umpire.

"He's got a flat bat," Mike said. "He can't use that bat."

Arlie, an expert bunter, had whittled one side of his soft-wood bat until it was flat so that he could bunt with less danger of fouling off the pitch. Umpire Dickey Pearce examined the bat and sent Arlie back for another.

The crowd, deriding Anson, Kelly, and the umpire's decision to bar Latham's bat, began screaming, "Ten men," another way of saying Pearce was on Chicago's side.

Arlie stepped to the plate with his new bat, looked at the base runners, and yelled to Doc Bushong at first, "Stay there, Doc, and I'll bring you both in."

The crowd responded with glee.

Suddenly the skies opened, and the rains came. Charles Comiskey, the St. Louis captain, called time and asked for a delay. Anson, whose team was leading 3–1, didn't think a delay was warranted. Not wanting his pitcher, Clarkson, to have to sit and take the chance his arm would tighten, Anson raged at umpire Pearce to continue. The crowd, still angry that Kelly had made Latham get a new bat, began pouring onto the field, yelling at both the umpire and at Anson.

The ruckus on the field made Anson's protest moot, as the umpire had to call time while the police drove the miscreants back into the stands. When the rain stopped, the game resumed with the based loaded and Latham at bat.

Clarkson delivered, and Latham took strike one. When the fans began to grumble, the little shortstop stepped away from the plate and held up one hand.

"Don't get nervous, folks!" he called. "I'll bring them in."

Robert Smith described what happened next.

ROBERT SMITH: "[Clarkson] took his stance again and, as he did, his alert eye caught the sudden jerk of Mike Kelly's head, which signaled Clarkson to put the next pitch inside. The ball came down straight and fast. Arlie, ready for it, brought his bat around in a half-chopping motion and sent the ball on a line to the very spot where Dalrymple would have been standing if he had not been trying to 'play position' on Latham. Dal, a swift-footed fielder, sprinted for the ball, clutched wildly at it, felt it graze his finger tips, and then watched it skim off into the deep grass of far left field. He took after it, and Arlie sped around the base lines. The noise of the crowd seemed to drown all thought. Curt Welch scored. Men beat the wooden railing with their hands. Bushong scored. Ladies jumped to their seats, screaming, and fluttered their tiny handkerchiefs. Arlie pulled up on third.

"The score was tied. Men in curled-brim derbies moved earnestly about the stands to make new bets, to inform each other with solemn excitement that, by golly, that little Arlie Latham was the greatest, yes, absolutely the greatest baseball player in the country today."

That ended the scoring in the eighth, and no one scored in the ninth.

In the tenth inning the initial batter was Curt Welch, one of the best defensive outfielders of the time.

Welch had been one of the first to turn his back on the ball and run to the spot where he thought it was going to come down. He played very shallow and robbed many batters who hit Texas Leaguers, making headlong dives just beyond the infield.

The aggressive Welch was an umpire baiter perfect for the rowdy Browns. Vulgar and nearly illiterate, his heavy drinking caused him to retire prematurely in 1893 at age thirty-one. He died of alcoholism three years later in his hometown of East Liverpool, Ohio.

A great base stealer, Welch made it a habit of getting hit by pitched balls. On Clarkson's first pitch, the Browns outfielder placed himself in front of a medium-fast pitch and was waved down to first by umpire Pearce.

Cap Anson came charging in from first to remind Pearce, at the top of his lungs, that Welch made it a habit to get hit by pitches. Pearce, agreeing, called Welch back to the plate. Few in the stands argued.

Welch, given another chance, lined a single that whizzed past Clarkson's ear into center field. The crowd roared. The winning run was on base.

Dave Foutz, the right fielder, then hit a sharp ground ball to Ed Williamson at short, a ball that should have been an easy double play. But Williamson booted it, so the runners were safe on first and second.

The next man at bat was second baseman Yank Robinson. The crowd was roaring now. Every spectator was on his feet.

Robinson bunted and was thrown out at first as the two runners advanced. Second-guessers in the stands wanted to know why Comiskey had him bunt rather than allow him to hit away.

Doc Bushong, the St. Louis catcher, advanced to the plate. Mike Kelly picked up the bat that Robinson had just dropped. As Bushong came close, Mike dropped to his knees, in the manner of an acolyte proffering a sacrificial sword, and held out the bat to Bushong. The crowd laughed and yelled nervously as Bushong gravely accepted the club.

There was a moment of tense silence again. The game was on the line. Clarkson looked at the two runners and turned back to face Bushong. His arm came back slowly, then he snapped it hard and sent a high ball almost at Bushong's head. Bushong let it go. Ball one. Clarkson didn't want the St. Louis catcher hitting anything on the ground. Rather, he was throwing high in hopes of getting a pop-up.

As Clarkson started to wind up again, out of the corner of his eye he saw Curt Welch seeking to steal home. To give Kelly a better chance to tag the runner, Clarkson pitched the ball inside and high. But Clarkson miscalculated, throwing it *too* high.

Kelly jumped and made a grab for it, but the ball skipped off the top of his fingers and bounded off toward the fence.

The crowd screamed as Charles Comiskey, coaching at third, began trailing after Welch, who could have scored standing up but instead dramatically but unnecessarily hit the dirt, sliding across the plate with the winning run. Comiskey, pounding on past home, grabbed the ball on the carom off the backstop before Kelly could lay his hands on it, shoving it in his pocket for a souvenir.

Kelly, after shaking both fists in the air, flung his glove and mask high over the grandstand, cursing all the way to the dugout.

The Series was over. The St. Louis Browns were champions of the world.

Welch became famous for his (unnecessary) slide, which was called the $15,000 Slide, in that the winning team was supposed to take home the expected $15,000 in game receipts. (The actual total was $13,920.10.) According to what Arlie Latham told Robert Smith, what the public wasn't made aware of was that the players on both teams had agreed among themselves before the Series to split the money evenly no matter who won.

Nevertheless, there was disappointment and anger in the Chicago clubhouse after the game. The White Stockings criticized Abner Dalrymple for letting Latham's hit tie the score. One Chicago player was quoted blindly in the papers as saying, "Ryan or Gore would have smothered it." Said Spalding, who never forgave his left fielder, "Dal should have caught the ball." When Mike Kelly was asked about Spalding's assessment, he refused to criticize his teammate. "I don't know about his catching it," said Kelly.

Chris Von der Ahe wanted to play the seventh game as an exhibition in Cincinnati, but Spalding turned him down. "We know when we've had enough," he telegraphed Von der Ahe.

As for Anson, he was gracious in defeat, though he resented that some of his players had been drunk and caroused too much during the Series.

CAP ANSON: "We were beaten, and fairly beaten, but had some of the players taken as good care of themselves prior to these games as they were in the habit of doing when the League season was in full swim, I am inclined to believe that there might have been a different tale to tell."

Albert Spalding, who wasn't as forgiving as Anson, again was furious that his champions had lost. He knew he would have to listen to the taunts, like the comment in the *St. Louis Republican* that said, "Chicago should confine itself to the slaughter of hogs as a popular amusement" because "baseball seems to require more headwork." Spalding was in a rage that some of his players hadn't taken the games more seriously, and he was angry that as a result of the loss he hadn't made any money on the Series. When it was over, Spalding spited his players by adamantly refusing to pay their train fare from St. Louis back to Chicago. His players, who had bet on the games and lost, were so broke they were stranded in St. Louis. Browns owner Chris Von der Ahe magnanimously advanced them the money to get home.

By the time the 1887 season rolled around, Spalding vowed he would do something about this deplorable team of drinkers, rowdies, and whorers.

8

Stars for Sale

Chicago, from its founding, endured a clash of cultures, as the Germans and the Irish fought for their right to drink and party while the transplanted New England Puritans fought to impose their standards of piety and joylessness.

In 1872 there had been a brawl between the steady drinkers and the temperance reformers trying to stop them. The following year Mayor Joseph Medill, a friend of Al Spalding's, had aligned himself with the Law and Order League in order to get elected, and he succeeded in closing the saloons on Sundays.

Said historian Llody Lewis, "Wealth, the Protestant churches and the Yankee aristocracy backed the Sunday closing, a situation which prompted a spokesman for the masses to declare, 'We are not against the arrest of Sunday drunks, but we are against the dictation of men who go to church on Sundays with long faces and then go to the Board of Trade on Monday to swindle their colleagues out of many bushels of grain.'"

The seesaw swung back in 1879 when Chicago elected as mayor Carter Henry Harrison, who was a proponent of the institutions of drinking, gambling, and going to whorehouses, arguing that they were good for the local economy and general well-being of the populace.

Harrison, who was shot to death in 1893 by a disgruntled job seeker, was a realist. It was his belief that the citizenry would frequent those places, whether there was a law against it or not, and so he felt it made more sense to just let the people have their little pleasures. The workingman, Harrison felt, had the right to a glass of beer on Sunday.

His beliefs nicely fitted the burgeoning city, where the aim of every citizen was to "make money, next to spend it—how, where and when is nobody's business."

Chicago's red-light district was the Levee, called that because of the influence of southern gamblers. There were gambling houses, saloons, dance halls, pawnshops, and penny arcades. Within the borders of a few blocks were more than two hundred brothels. Freiberg's dance hall was the most notorious saloon. There was the Everleigh Club, an elegant mansion, and the Library, the Opium Den, and the House of All Nations.

Under Harrison's aegis Chicago had become the Gomorrah of the West.

One of the civic leaders who favored temperance was the owner of the Chicago Nationals, Albert Spalding. It was his belief that the heavy drinking of his players hurt their performance and worse, hurt the team's chances of victory. That his team had won five championships in seven years didn't seem to deter him from his beliefs.

During the 1886 season Spalding, who had been the league's watchdog of morality ever since he drew up the constitution in 1876, had decided there was too much drinking going on by the players, and he suggested that each of the National League clubs hire a detective agency to shadow players and submit weekly reports on their activities.

The purpose, said Spalding, was to expose the bad habits of the players in order to elevate their social standing. Spalding was sounding very much like Frances Willard, the head of the Women's Christian Temperance Movement, who had begun her nationwide efforts to prohibit the sale of liquor with a suggestion that Chicago women replace the wineglasses on their parlor tables with pledge books; in these, gentlemen callers were to pledge their abstinence.

To many Chicagoans, Frances Willard was a kook, a busybody who had no right to tell others how to live their lives. But Willard kept pushing until February 16, 1920, when she was able to spearhead the passage of the Eighteenth Amendment, prohibiting the sale of alcohol nationwide.

Spalding sought the same prohibition for all baseball players. He wanted them not to drink not only during the season but during the off-season as well.

Spalding's philosophy on the subject was expressed in the 1889 *Spalding Guide*. An editorial read: "The two great obstacles in the way of success of the majority of professional ball players are wine and women. The saloon and the brothel are the evils of the baseball world at the present day; and we see it practically exemplified in the failure of noted players to play up to the standard they are capable of were they to avoid these gross evils. And so it goes from one season to another, at the cost of the loss of thousands of dollars to clubs who blindly shut their eyes to the costly nature of intemperance and dissipation in their ranks."

After his team lost to St. Louis in the 1885 World Series, Spalding decided that before the 1886 season he would send his players to Hot Springs, Arkansas, as one reporter put it, "to boil out the alcoholic microbes." Spalding was intent on getting rid of the effect of "winter lushing."

Before heading south Spalding forced all his players, including some very heavy drinkers like Mike Kelly, John Clarkson, Jim McCormick, Ed Williamson, George Gore, and Frank Flint, to utter a pledge that they would abstain from drinking wine, beer, or liquor. Cap Anson, who was a prohibitionist like Spalding, administered the oath in Spalding's sporting goods store.

After it was clear some of his players had no intention of keeping their word, Spalding carried through on his proposal and hired a Pinkerton Agency detective to follow them.

Spalding was particularly concerned that Mike Kelly was a negative influence on the younger players, staying out late and drinking heavily. When Spalding talked to him about it, Kelly asked him, "What are you running here, a Sunday School or a baseball club?"

The Chicago team was at a crossroads. Anytime an owner begins telling his players how to conduct their private lives, the chances of the team achieving success drop precipitously. The Mike Kellys win pennants because they can hit and field. The Billy Sundays make for calm, inspirational clubhouse meetings, but if you can't hit your weight, what good are you?

Mike Kelly, the greatest baseball player of his day, didn't want any club owner telling him how to live his life. Neither did many of his teammates. Despite Spalding's warnings, half of the Chicago players continued to stay out late, get drunk, and party.

After Spalding's detective followed them, Spalding learned that seven of the fifteen players, in Spalding's words, "were too awful for patient considerations. The detective had followed them up and down Clark Street, all over the tenderloin district, through the whole roster of saloons and 'speakeasy' resorts. . . ."

Spalding called the seven players to task. All acted repentant except Kelly, who resented this intrusion on his privacy.

When he read in the Pinkerton report that he was cited drinking lemonade at three in the morning, he told Spalding, "It was straight whiskey. I never drank a lemonade at that hour in my life."

The detective had cost $175. Spalding rubbed it in by making the seven sinners split the bill at $25 each.

When the team was slumping during one stretch of the 1886 season, Kelly sarcastically told a *Boston Herald* reporter the reason for the lull was "too much temperance."

Kelly was infuriated by Spalding's spies. As the team was about to board a train for Detroit, Kelly noticed a man who was watching them. It could have been a fan or someone just curious, but Kelly, who wasn't taking any chances, decided that the man was a Pinkerton. He walked over to him and punched him hard. Then he boarded the train.

As bitter as Kelly felt about Spalding, the reverse was equally true. The public drunkenness of some of his key players during the 1886 World Series and the team's resulting loss to the St. Louis Browns had hardened Spalding's feelings against the drinkers.

Early in 1887, Spalding told the press, "The Chicago management will aim to secure the highest standard of baseball efficiency obtainable. In fighting the encroachments of drink upon the efficiency of individual players, we are simply striving to give our patrons the full measure of enterprise and satisfaction they are entitled to. No dollar of the stock in our Club is owned by a prohibitionist but we don't intend to again insult lovers of the game in this city or any other by allowing men who are full of beer and whiskey to go upon the diamond in the uniform of the Chicago Club."

When the team returned to Hot Springs during the spring of 1887, Anson kept them sober and celibate. Upon their return, Spalding forced them to play a six-game "championship" against the Browns. The White Stockings won four of the six games, but unfortunately for Spalding, no one paid any attention whatsoever to the results.

The moralistic, ascetic Spalding, rather than take delight in the success of his powerhouse, did what so many owners who anoint themselves Keepers of High Morality have done over the years—arrogantly traded away talented players because of perceived or real character flaws, only to seriously injure, if not doom, the ball club.

The player Spalding was most furious with, pitcher Jim McCormick, was the first to go. McCormick's sin was that he hadn't taken the novel interleague series seriously the previous fall. His contract had run only through the regular season, and he, like a number of the Chicago players, didn't feel obligated to stay in tip-top shape as he had done during the regular season. To him and the other drinkers, the series against the Browns was a frolic, a mere series of exhibitions, and if he wanted to get drunk, he felt that was up to him.

The rich and powerful Spalding didn't see it that way. In the spring of 1887, Spalding began his housecleaning by selling McCormick, his 31-game winner, along with his slugging left fielder, Abner Dalrymple, to Pittsburgh, a new franchise in the National League. Chicago fans were angry at the loss of their star pitcher and starting left fielder. McCormick had won 16 games in a row in '86. Dalrymple had batted only .233, but he could still hit with power.

McCormick was so disgusted with Spalding's treatment of him that at the end of the 1887 season, during which he pitched and won only 13 games for a mediocre Pittsburgh team, he announced he would retire from baseball and open a café in his hometown of Paterson, New Jersey. Jim McCormick thus became the first outstanding player to retire while still at the peak of his game. (He was the first to quit because he was angry at the way baseball management had treated him, but he certainly wouldn't be the last.)

The next of the miscreants Spalding sent packing was Chicago's star center fielder, George Gore. Over a fourteen-year career Gore hit .301. His 150 runs scored in 1886 for Chicago were irreplaceable. But Gore had gotten so drunk during the '85 Series that Anson had to replace him for the rest of the games, and in '86, Gore had gone 0 for 9 in the final two losses to St. Louis. Spalding finally decided he had had enough and sent Gore to the New York Giants.

In the spring of 1887, Spalding was facing a challenge from yet another problem player, his star, Mike Kelly. Kelly was a problem for several reasons. His drinking and womanizing was one consideration. Though Anson did everything he could to keep Kelly from going to bars during the season, he wasn't wholly successful. Their fighting over his extracurricular activities was a constant. One year Kelly had reported a month late and out of condition. Anson ordered him to get in shape, but Kelly sent word back to Anson that he was in a Turkish bath and could not come to the ballpark. Anson later learned he had been at the racetrack.

Anson, who never resented his players as Spalding did, always had a warm spot for his talented star.

CAP ANSON: "He was a whole-souled, genial fellow, with a host of friends, and but one enemy, that one being himself.

"Money slipped through Mike's fingers as water slips through the meshes of a fisherman's net, and he was as fond of whiskey as any representative of the Emerald Isle, but just the same he was a great ball player and one that became greater than he then was before ceasing to wear a Chicago uniform. He was as good a batter as anybody, and a great thrower, both from the catcher's position and from the field, more men being thrown out by him than by any other man that could be named. He was a good fielder when not bowled up, but when he was he sometimes failed to judge a fly ball correctly, though he would generally manage to get pretty close in under it. In such cases he would remark with a comical leer: 'By Gad, I made it hit me gloves, anyhow.'"

And yet, when Spalding asked Anson if he could spare Kelly, Anson didn't try to dissuade him.

"Sure, spare anybody," grunted Anson.

Robert Smith suggested another possible reason Spalding decided to sell Mike Kelly. It was said that his interest in the ladies was a reason for his departure. Wrote Smith, "No man as handsome and as free-spending as Mike Kelly could walk the streets of Chicago or enter its taverns without getting more than his share of attention from the girls—attention that Kelly never shunned."

Johnny Evers, commenting on the sale of Kelly and later John Clarkson, provided only the hint of possible scandal when he wrote in his biography in 1910 that "the cause of that sale never was made public, but the real reason was a woman, and the club was compelled to sell the men. . . ." Whatever Evers meant by that we can only guess.

Another reason Spalding and Kelly weren't getting along was that Kelly insisted that Spalding return all the money Kelly had been fined the year before. Kelly, the team's star, hated that Spalding had put detectives on him, that Spalding had been keeping tabs on his life off the field, and that Spalding had fined him. When Spalding refused to return the fines, Mike Kelly demanded to be traded.

MIKE KELLY: "At the close of the season of 1886, I had some trouble with the Chicago management. I felt that Messrs. Spalding & Co. had not treated me fairly. I told President Spalding as much when the season closed. He smiled and regarded it as a Kelly joke. He said he guessed when the next season came around he would have things so arranged that I would be a member of the Chicago club. I said to him:

"'President Spalding, at the close of the season I'm going up to Hyde Park, in New York, for the winter. My brother-in-law has a farm there. If I'm not a member of some other club next season, you will find that farming is good enough for me during the summer. I will not play again in the Chicago club, under any circumstances, and don't you forget it.'

"Well, I meant just what I said. After leaving Mr. Spalding, almost the first man I met was Nat Goodwin, the Boston actor. Nat and I were always great friends, and had been for several years. He was playing in Chicago at the time. He invited me around to his rooms in the Palmer House. Naturally enough, I told him of the conversation I had just had with Mr. Spalding. Goodwin heard it all, and then said:

"'Kel, don't play in Chicago. You stick to what you said.'

"'But where would be the best city for me to play?' I inquired.

"'The best city in the country for you to play ball, Kel, is in Boston. You hang out, and I will make an even bet that you will be a member of the Boston club next season.'

"We had quite a long conversation, and I promised Goodwin that if it could be arranged, I would gladly go to Boston the next season. I think that when Nat and his manager, George Floyd, reached Boston, they saw the Boston managers, and told them what I had said. I met Goodwin in New York in November, I think it was, and he told me it was all right. He said I would be in Boston next year, if money would buy my release.

"About the 1st of December, '86, I wrote from Hyde Park to Mr. Spalding. The newspapers had been saying some pretty hard things about me, and one or two of them printed interviews with Spalding, in which he said a number of things which were more than unfair. In this letter, I told him that I would not play in Chicago; that I never had been under any obligations to the club, as I had always worked hard for what I got. I wrote again, the latter part of the month, and in return I received a letter from President Spalding, in which he denied several interviews alleged to have come from him."

According to Kelly, the team he *really* wanted to play for was New York. He wrote, "In fact, I was offered $7,750 to get my release from Chicago, and a promise of $5,500 salary in the bargain."

Though Spalding had sold George Gore to New York, he would not send Kelly there. Instead, he made a deal with Boston to sell the star player for $10,000. As part of the agreement, Boston had to pay Kelly $5,000 as a bonus.

J. B. Billings, one of the Boston owners, coveted Kelly, who had led the league with a .388 average in 1886. Billings offered Spalding $5,000. Spalding demanded $10,000.

First, Spalding talked to Kelly. Would he agree to the sale to Boston? Kelly didn't like the idea. Horses were sold. So were dogs. But not ballplayers.

"You'll get more money," promised Spalding.

Kelly said, "If you can get me five thousand dollars, I don't care a damn if you sell me for a hundred thousand."

Billings met Kelly in Poughkeepsie on February 14, 1887. Accompanying Billings was Ted Sullivan, former Washington manager and the sports editor of the *Globe*.

Five minutes after they met, Billings asked Kelly to sign his contract. Kelly said he would if it was the price agreed, $5,000.

Sullivan, who was there, described what happened next.

TED SULLIVAN: "So, they began a philosophical discussion on the value of ballplayers. Mike sat in the corner of the reading room, and a tight-fitting Prince Albert coat set off his finely built athletic figure, while he told why 'diamonds cannot be bought with shoestrings.' He toyed with a diminutive cane and puffed a cigarette. For an hour and a half the discussion went on. But just before noon it came to an end. Mr. Billings had come here to sign Kelly and was not going away without doing so.

"The contract was drawn up for two thousand dollars, the limit, and then Mr. Billings said that the Boston club wanted a picture of their new player and would pay well [three thousand dollars] for it.

"'Well, I am with you,' said Kelly to Sullivan. And Billings tucked the contract away, saying heavily, 'Good things come high, but we must have them.'"

When asked about the sale, Spalding rationalized his foolhardy act by telling reporters, "Championship teams can't afford to stand pat, need remodeling to stay up."

Baseball history is filled with owners who care more about propriety and making money than they do about winning. Spalding was one of the first to deliberately dismantle a winning team for no good reason except moral outrage and personal pique. Spalding would own the Chicago team for another fifteen years and never win another pennant as the lives of these players would be altered and the hopes and dreams of his fans dashed—all in the name of temperance.

Cap Anson hadn't stopped Spalding from selling Kelly, but he fully understood the importance of the transaction. Anson was quick to note that even though Boston had acquired Kelly, his addition had failed to bring it the pennant. (Anson failed to note that in 1887, Kelly hit .322 and stole 84 bases for Boston. He also failed to note that Chicago didn't win it, either.)

CAP ANSON: "The sensation of the year was the sale of Mike Kelly to the Boston Club by the Chicago management for the sum of $10,000, the largest sum up to that time that had ever been paid for a ball player, and Mike himself benefitted by the transaction, as he received a salary nearly double that which he was paid when he wore a Chicago uniform.

"The result of the pennant race was a great disappointment to the Boston Club management, who, having acquired the services of 'the greatest player in the country,' that being the way they advertised Kelly, evidently thought that all they had to do was to reach out their hands for the championship emblem and take it. 'One swallow does not make a summer,' however, nor one ball player a whole team, as the Boston Club found out to its cost, the best that it could do being to finish in the fifth place."

Kelly's sale was baseball's biggest event since the Four Seceders (including Al Spalding) left Boston to play for Chicago in 1879. It also brought commercialism to baseball on a grand scale.

When Chicago sold Kelly, it enraged its fans so that Kelly felt called upon to issue a tearful statement to the effect that his heart was well-nigh broken. And it scandalized a certain portion of the public who saw it as one more example of the immoral "slave trade" that had begun in 1870 when two men named Craver and Bechtel were sold by the Philadelphia Athletics to the Centennial Club of the same town. The $10,000 paid for Kelly was ten times what the average man earned in a year. So incredible did the sum sound to the people who were paying twenty-five and fifty cents to see baseball games that the check was photographed and reproduced in the newspaper.

When Albert Spalding, president of the pennant-winning Chicago club, decided to accept Boston's unprecedented $10,000 offer for the twenty-nine-year-old slugger, Chicago fans were astonished, yet somewhat proud, for Mike Kelly, their hero, had truly commanded a "king's ransom." Still, it was not long before they were optimistically predicting a Chicago pennant without him, singing, to the tune of "Climbing up the Golden Stairs," the following lyrics:

> Arab Kelly's gone and left us,
>   Of his presence he's bereft us—
> Kelly of the diamond bold,
>   He's deserted us for Boston.
> Although Albert laid the cost on,
>   Ten thousand clear in Puritanic gold.
> We surely have the pity
>   Of every sister city,
> In our loss of Kell, the tricky and the bold.
>   But we've entered for the pennant.
> And we'll win—depend on it.
>   Notwithstanding Mike has left us in the cold.

After he was traded, Mike Kelly himself predicted that with Anson as manager Chicago could win with even a mediocre group of players.

"He can make nine poor players go on the field and make them play a stiffer game of ball than any man living. Anson, I really believe, can take nine raw men who never saw a ball game, and in two months he will make ball players of them."

But neither the lyric writer nor Kelly was right about Chicago winning in '87. Without McCormick, Dalrymple, Gore, and Kelly, Chicago failed to repeat. Chicago and Detroit were tied for first at the end of August, but by mid-September powerful Detroit began to pull away, as Chicago fell to third behind Philadelphia.

Only later Spalding was heard to admit, "I guess we got rid of Mike too soon."

The negative ramifications of the Sale of the Century didn't stop there. When Spalding engineered the deal that netted him $10,000 and earned for Kelly the grand but deserved salary of $5,000 for the season, Chicago's great pitcher, John Clarkson, became envious. In 1887, Clarkson was 38–21. He led the league in wins, and he completed 56 of his 59 games started. He was the best pitcher in the league, and he wanted a salary commensurate with his greatness.

Spalding, who early on had understood and propagated the National League's reserve clause, which was designed to keep player salaries low, found himself in a terrible bind, the same bind owners would find themselves in the century to come: When teams win pennants, the players want to be paid handsomely for their efforts. Unfortunately, like many owners after him, Spalding seemed more concerned with the payroll than with winning. He also was under the mistaken belief that it was his genius that made the team win, not the players' ability. For Spalding and owners like him afterward, players were interchangeable robots. When Clarkson demanded that Spalding make a deal for him that would double his salary as he did for Mike Kelly, Spalding figured he could dump Clarkson for a pile of dough and then replace him with a pitcher of equal ability. Spalding foolishly obliged him. Mike Kelly recalled that Clarkson himself had let it be known he wanted to return to his hometown in Boston!

MIKE KELLY: "Clarkson himself wanted to play in Boston, for several reasons. His wife and family lived in that city, and he was slightly homesick in Chicago.

"At the conclusion of last season, Clarkson informed Mr. Spalding that he would not play in Chicago next season. Mr. Spalding said that he certainly would, unless a sufficient amount of money was paid for his release. When Clarkson came to Boston, he told several of his friends that he did not care to play in Chicago. These friends so informed the Boston management, and it at once went to work to get his release, in an honest, honorable way."

In 1888, John Clarkson, as good as ever, won 33 games for Boston. Chicago finished second, nine games behind the New York Giants. By 1889, the Chicago team, unable to replace its great stars, slipped badly, falling to third place a full nineteen games behind New York. Boston, behind Clarkson's 49 wins, finished just a game out of first. After two more years of competitiveness, in 1892, Chicago would fall apart completely as Ned Hanlon's Baltimore Orioles would dominate the league until the end of the century.

Spalding's dismantling of his team ostensibly had been the result of his attempt to cleanse it of rotters and drinkers. But like the temperance movement itself, he failed. His new players, while not as talented as those he so cavalierly discarded, were devils in their own right.

Johnny Evers recalled the 1888 team in his autobiography. One of those newcomers, Tom Daly, who caught for Chicago in 1887 and 1888, was as troublesome as but less talented than the men Spalding had traded away.

JOHNNY EVERS: "Tom Daly added gray hairs to the heads of many managers. Nothing stopped Daly and few things ever caused him to hesitate. Mischief bubbled out of him. One hot summer day he was riding westward with the team when the train stopped at a small station. Standing on the platform was a farmer with a benign, fatherly expression and enough whiskers to stuff a chest protector. Daly, leaning from the car window, accosted the farmer most politely, engaged him in conversation regarding crops, the effect of the drought upon the corn, prices and the weather outlook. Just as the train started, Daly stretched out his hand. 'Well, good-bye,' he remarked and grasping the astonished farmer by the whiskers, he dragged him half the length of the platform."

Evers remembered the 1891 Chicago team that featured not only Daly but two other hell-raisers, Jimmy Ryan and Elmer Foster, who came close to dropping a half-empty keg of beer four stories onto the head of Anson. Despite Spalding's housecleaning, it was obvious the drinking and partying hadn't ended. It never would.

JOHNNY EVERS: "Every new man or reporter, who sojourned with the team risked not only limb but life.

"One spring the Chicago team had been disrupting Texas and the southwest on the pretense of training and reached Kansas City to finish the work of preparation for the season. On April 1, the day on which pay commenced, Anson announced his intention of fining any man he caught taking a drink or keeping late hours. The players did not fear Anson but they knew him well enough to realize that the first one caught, at least, would suffer heavy punishment and no one desired to be the first. That evening after the game not one player dared order even a bottle of beer sent to his room, and there was gloom all over the training camp.

"After supper an innocent reporter was busy in his room when Foster, Ryan and several others of the choice spirits of the team began to drop in, as if casually. When the meek scribe inquired what mischief was afoot, they told him to go on writing and not to get inquisitive. A short time later a porter wheeled an eight gallon keg of beer into the room, the reporter's papers were brushed off the table, he was informed he had written enough for the evening, the keg was tapped, and cards produced. The poker game lasted until long past midnight and the beer was consumed. Anson meantime was camping in a chair at the entrance of the hotel, keeping grim watch. Occasionally he would stalk back to the bar room to make certain none of his players dared take a drink.

"The party in the reporter's room was continued every night, while Anson congratulated himself that at last he had effectually curbed the rowdies on the team. One evening when the keg was partly empty and the poker game full, Foster wandered to the open window and looked down four stories.

"'Well, I declare,' he said in surprise. 'If there isn't Captain Anson seated by the doorway.' Picking up the keg, he dropped it out the window.

"The keg struck the sidewalk twenty feet from where Anson was seated, with a report like the discharge of a fourteen-inch gun. It bounded twenty feet and crashed down again upon the sidewalk, but by the time it struck again Anson had dived to safety. Anson never really obtained evidence enough to convict anyone, but he had an idea.

"'I know it was Ryan, Daly or Foster,' he said, 'but which one I'm not certain.'

"On that same trip the team was departing from a hotel when Foster, polite, apologetic and courteously embarrassed, drew Anson aside.

"'Captain,' he whispered, 'I regret exceedingly an unfortunate predicament into which I have been forced, as it compels me to ask a great favor.'

"'What is it, Foster?' inquired Captain Anson.

"'To tell the truth, Captain, I am a bit short, and—and—I wanted to ask you, as a great favor, if you will settle my laundry bill.'

"'Certainly, Foster, certainly,' replied Anson heartily as he strode to the desk. Foster hastily grabbed his hand baggage and disappeared as rapidly as possible from the hotel. When Anson received the bill he staggered. It read: 'To laundry, $42.55.' Foster had charged up extra meals, drinks and every other item as laundry."

9

The Players Revolt

In 1890 most of the National League ballplayers, angry over low pay, quit their teams and started their own league, called the Players League. The main reason they took this drastic step was that the owners, who took their cue from Albert Spalding, had left them no choice. Under Spalding's system, the players, who were barred from switching teams, were forced to accept a salary cap of $2,000 a year.

They couldn't move from team to team because of a rule passed in 1879 called the reserve clause. Ironically, it was passed to stop the wily and ruthless Spalding from raiding and stealing other teams' players. At first it was agreed by the owners that each team could reserve five of its best players. Once reserved, a player was barred from signing with any other team during the off-season, in effect making him the property of the club in perpetuity.

When the reserve clause was put into effect, its sole purpose was to prevent the rich owners from luring away the best players from the weaker teams. But it did not take the owners long to realize an additional bonanza: A reserved player had no leverage to make monetary demands. If the player refused his club's contract offer, he had no bargaining power because there could be no escape to a team that might be willing to pay him more. Take it or quit. Those were his two choices.

The owners reaped an added financial advantage from the reserve clause: It stabilized the franchises and made them, and their players, far more valuable. It was the existence of the reserve clause that enabled Spalding to sell Mike Kelly and John Clarkson for $10,000 each. Had the Boston ownership been concerned about the new players going elsewhere, it never would have paid so dearly.

Once the owners realized the benefits of the players' reserved status, they kept upping the number of players reserved until the number reached eleven (of fifteen) in 1883, when the National League, the American Association, and the Northwest League made a pact called the Tripartite Agreement that effectively stopped teams from signing the reserved players from other teams. With no bargaining power, players' salaries plummeted.

At first the reserved players, not understanding the economic consequences of their designation, were proud to be awarded such a special, exalted status.

Then when they discovered that such a reserved status made it impossible for them to negotiate with any other team, their ego gratification disappeared. In fact, the blatant unfairness of the system made them furious. In 1887 the reserve clause was written into the contract of every player, causing further dissension.

In 1884 there had been a minirevolt by a dozen of the National League players who were able to garner higher salaries by jumping to a new league, called the Union League. Unfortunately for the players, the new league failed after just one season, and the players were forced to return, their tails between their legs.

In 1885, Al Spalding, smarting from his losses in '84 caused by the competition from the upstart league, tightened the screws on the players by inaugurating a new cost-cutting move: The National League teams adopted a $2,000 salary cap for each player.

The owners realized they couldn't keep their stars at such a low salary level, so they found subterfuges to get around the cap. Mike Kelly's bonus from Boston, for example, was paid as a fee for a photo of him.

Though the system allowed the owners to pay high salaries when it suited them, the salary cap allowed them to keep the large majority of players at a subsistence level.

For many players the salary cap caused a severe hardship. Players often had to pay for two residences, one in their hometown, the other in the city where their team played. They had to dress fitting the stature of the public figures that they were. They had to support themselves on the road. For most, their expenses ate up most of their salary.

In the 1890s ballplayers often made a little money on the side by selling baseballs. Whenever possible a player would seize a ball and hide it in his uniform or perhaps in the grass. At the conclusion of the game it was an easy matter to sell it. Small boys customarily gathered at the park exits, waiting with money in hand for the players to emerge, knowing that some of them would have balls to sell.

An executive of the Detroit team complained bitterly about the practice, declaring, "It's unbelievable that ballplayers receiving two hundred dollars or more a month would crib balls to sell to the boys, but it is a fact that they do." Several Chicago players were arrested for incurring debts in different cities. Newspapers even suggested that higher salaries might keep such unpleasant incidents from occurring.

To make extra money, players also took part in games in the off-season.

One year after pitcher Clark Griffith had finished his regular season, a man from California approached him to play for a local team in the amateur championships. He offered Griffith good money to play. He also asked Griffith to get several other National League players to go with him.

They showed up wearing shabby uniforms to conceal their identity. When they arrived at the field before a huge crowd, they noticed that the other team was also manned by major leaguers.

"When they came into view," said Griffith, "the first man I saw was Jerry Denny, who played infield for New York. Behind him was Big Bill Brown, the Giants catcher. Then I saw Fred Carroll, and after him came several other professionals. In fact the other team had more and better ringers than we had. Naturally we forgot about making any bets."

All of the ringers for each team played the entire game, and not one of them gave an indication that he recognized the others, lest the whole plot explode and the pay be withheld. The game was a close one, but Griffith's side won, becoming the amateur champions of California.

Most important, everyone got paid.

In Chicago, Albert Spalding was making it even tougher on his players than most owners. Besides paying low wages, in 1887 he docked the players fifty cents for every day they played on the road to help defray his hotel expenses. Spalding also had a policy of refusing to pay players during periods when they were hurt and couldn't play.

Outfielder Ross Barnes, Spalding's former boyhood teammate, missed three months of the '77 season because of illness. Spalding deducted $1,000 from his $2,500 salary. Barnes sued, but the court ruled against him, saying he couldn't recover something he had never received.

During Spalding's 1888–89 tour of the world, Chicago's shortstop, Ed Williamson, considered one of the best in baseball history, injured his knee severely while sliding into third in a game in Paris.

CAP ANSON: "In Paris on March 8, 1889, it was in the second inning of the game that the famous 'stone wall' infield of the Chicagos was broken up through an injury received by Ed Williamson, from the effects of which he never fully recovered. He had taken his base on balls in the second inning and was trying to steal second base when he tripped and fell, tearing his knee cap on the sharp sand and gravel of which the playing surface was composed. He was taken by his wife, who was among the spectators, to his hotel, and it was thought that a few days of rest would see him all right again, but such did not prove to be the case, as he was still confined to his room in London when we sailed for home, and it was not until late in the season of 1889 that he was again able to report for duty."

The tour moved to London, where Williamson's knee was mis-set by a doctor. Spalding paid the $157 in medical bills while Williamson was in England, but once the tour was over, he refused to pay his star infielder another dime, either in medical bills or in salary.

In the meantime, the players were aware that baseball was becoming more and more profitable, that teams were building new, expensive stadiums, and attendance was climbing. In Chicago, for instance, Spalding had built a regal baseball stadium, with curtained boxes, push buttons, telephones, and cushioned seats. The players read in the papers that he had spent $1,800 just for paint.

The players also read of the talk of raising the ticket price from twenty-five cents to fifty cents, but they were aware there was no hint that the owners wanted to raise salaries as well.

By the 1887 season the players knew they had to do something. They formed an organization called the Brotherhood of Professional Base Ball Players, and the man they chose to speak for them was John Montgomery Ward, the captain and shortshop of the New York Giants.

All Ward was seeking was a fair break for the players. Ward said his intent was not to injure the owners, only to get rid of the reserve rule.

For Ward's efforts, Al Spalding and his supporters in the sporting press labeled and libeled Ward, calling him "greedy, self-seeking, a liar, a conniver, a corrupter of youth, and a breaker of contracts."

Before the 1888 season the players were threatening not to sign their contracts, to boycott if the salary cap was not lifted. The club owners, including Al Spalding, agreed to their demand, and so the players signed for the season.

The players' trust was misplaced. After the 1888 season the owners did indeed lift the cap, replacing it with a new salary scale that was even harsher on the majority of the players than the $2,000 limit. The plan was insidious in that it was designed to make the stars happier—they could earn as much as $2,500. The owners figured if they could get the stars to play, the others would have no choice but to go along. Under the new arrangement, the lesser players could make as little as $1,500 a year.

The players, outraged that they were "graded like so many cattle," appointed a committee to convince the owners that unless their pay was improved, they were going to strike.

In an attempt to compromise the position of John Montgomery Ward, Spalding invited the Giants star to accompany his White Stockings on their tour around the world during the winter of 1888–89. After the trip, Spalding promised him, they would sit down and talk things over.

The trip, which lasted from November 1888 to early April 1889, included stops in San Francisco; Honolulu; Auckland, New Zealand; and four cities in Australia. Spalding's troupe then headed through the Suez Canal to the Mediterranean Sea, playing in Colombo, Ceylon, and then in Giza, Egypt, in the shadow of the Great Pyramids. The tour continued on to Naples, Rome, and Florence, then to Paris and England.

Spalding, by taking Ward with him, was able to neutralize the persuasive player spokesman in the States. But Ward could, and did, spend much of his time during the trip indoctrinating the White Stockings and star opponents about the crisis in pay.

According to writer Fred Lieb, Philadelphia outfielder Jim Fogarty, spouting Ward's rhetoric, stated the players' position upon their return: "We've got to get more money out of this game. We attract the fans, but the owners pocket all the profits."

At the tour's end Ward demanded that Spalding meet with him as he had promised. Spalding refused. Ward, speaking for the players, continued to demand the repeal of the pay classification system. When the owners stalled, Ward felt he had no other choice but to declare war.

He helped organize the players into a union called the Brotherhood. The players then contacted wealthy men in their various cities to back them in a new league called the Players League.

Fifty-three percent of the National League players jumped to the new league. Among them future Hall of Famers, including Mike "King" Kelly, Dan Brouthers, Hoss Radbourn, Connie Mack, Hugh Duffy, Charlie Comiskey, Ed Delahanty, Roger Connor, Tim Keefe, Orator Jim O'Rourke, Buck Ewing, Jake Beckley, and Pud Galvin, felt strongly enough that the players were being treated unfairly that they defected from the National League.

In Chicago, where Spalding not only had paid his players poorly but had spied on them and constantly monitored their private lives, all but two players left for the new league, including Fred Pfeffer, Ed Williamson, George Van Haltren, John Tener, Jimmy Ryan, Hugh Duffey, Arlie Latham, and Duke Farrell.

The two players who stuck with Anson were Bull Anderson, a young pitcher, and third baseman Tommy Burns. Anson would reward Burns after his retirement for his loyalty by getting him a five-year contract to manage the Pittsburgh Pirates.

The defection of Hugh Duffy and George Van Haltren to the new league was most harmful to Chicago's future. Duffy signed with the Chicago Pirates of the Players League. After the league folded, he would play for the Boston Braves for many productive years. He retired in 1906 with a .328 average and 103 homers, an impressive total considering the era in which he played.

Van Haltren, who hit .309 for Chicago in 1889, jumped to Brooklyn in the Players League. After joining the Pittsburgh Pirates in 1893, he batted over .300 nine years in a row, the last eight seasons with the New York Giants. His career numbers read 2,532 hits and a .316 batting average. Like other outstanding Chicago players ignored through history, including Ed Williamson and Fred Pfeffer, Van Haltren belongs in the Hall of Fame.

The only famous player in the National League not to jump to the new league was Cap Anson, who stubbornly remained loyal to Spalding. When John Ward asked him to join the new league, Anson turned him down.

CAP ANSON: "It was a proposal that I declined with thanks, giving as my reason that the League had always treated me fairly and honestly up to that time, and that such being the case I could see no reason why I should leave them in an underhand manner. The truth of the matter is, that I felt bound in honor to stand by my friends, even if I sank with them, and at that time the skies did look remarkably dark and it was a question in my mind as to what would be the outcome."

Anson, who through his long career had been paid and treated by Spalding like the star player he had been, had never had to sell baseballs to make ends meet. Anson criticized the Chicago players who had "deserted" him as "men of low principle." Like Spalding, Anson could see only one motivation for the walkout: "Greed, for that was certainly the corner stone of the entire structure."

The blinded Anson could not see that it had been Spalding's greed, and that of the other owners—not that of the players, whose only goal was to make a decent living—that had prompted the organization of the Brotherhood.

In the battle for public opinion, given the choice between the richer, more powerful owners and the struggling players, the newspaper writers tended to side with the money and power. They too saw the owners, not the men who actually performed on the field, as the embodiment of the Game. The owners were the constants. Players came and went. The owners provided the writers with access, allowed them to ride with the team on the trains, even gave them food during road trips. Without the owners the writers had nothing.

The players badly needed to have their problems aired in the press. They needed the working writers, men who covered their games every day and who knew them, to provide fair, unbiased coverage as these athletes attempted to earn a living commensurate with their skill level. They didn't get it very often.

When the ballplayers took action, the sportswriters lined up almost en masse on the side of the owners and vilified the players. The very idea that ballplayers should dare complain about their living conditions drove many writers into a frenzy of flowered opprobrium. It is interesting to note that these writers didn't just attack the players' position, they viciously attacked them personally, calling them vile names as though the players had somehow offended them by their action.

Writer Oliver Hazard Perry Caylor of Cincinnati, for instance, charged that the Brotherhood players were "a few porcine professionals who in their selfishness and love of gold tried to destroy reserve rule."

Wrote another, "Not one professional baseball player out of ten is to be trusted to keep his word or even his bond where there is any pecuniary temptation."

Yet a third: "A more ungrateful set of people than the majority of professional ballplayers it would be hard to find. Low drunken knaves have too long been allowed to hold positions in professional base ball."

One writer threw up the image of the carnage brought on by the French Revolution.

"It is wonderful," he wrote, referring to the collective efforts of the players, "that these poor oppressed souls do not organize a procession under a red flag and go through the streets shouting 'bread or blood.' The noteworthy part is that the men who kicked the most against the reserve rule are men who have come up through the slums, who were street loafers and idlers before playing ball; the men whose ignorance and loaferism made them a burden on the community and would fall to the same level again were baseball wiped out tomorrow. There are two instances in which a reserve jumper cannot write an intelligible letter. . . ."

Only a few of the sportswriters, including Al Spink of the *Sporting News*, Tim Murnane of the *Boston Globe*, and Jacob Morse of *Baseball* magazine, sided with the players.

Henry Chadwick, Spalding's mouthpiece and the editor of his yearly guide, disowned the players as money grubbers and revolutionists, unfit to share the earth with men like Spalding, Cincinnati president John T. Brush, or Boston president A. H. Soden.

Spalding, meanwhile, was secretly making money on the new league. The Chicago owner, who had shown he could stab a friend in the back if it was worth it financially (as he had done to Harry Wright), had been one of the first men to start an employment agency for ballplayers. Spalding had agents around the country who watched out for young players and advised management on prospects. His firm, A. G. Spalding and Bros., established a baseball bureau, operating out of the Chicago, New York, and Denver stores, to assist players to find jobs at no cost.

Despite his strong enmity toward the Players League, Spalding had no qualms about *making* money from the rival league. His company hired an agent named Samuel Morton to represent players switching from one league to the other. It was Morton's job to contact team owners in the new league and find the players jobs. The company earned a fee for each placement.

When National League president A. G. Mills learned of Spalding's arrangement, he was furious. He gave Spalding a choice: Put Morton out of business or get out of baseball. Spalding sheepishly had to comply.

At the same time Spalding was a leader in the assault against the Players League. Spalding attempted to break the Brotherhood by trying to re-sign the star he had once traded away for being such a bad influence on the younger players—Mike Kelly. Spalding figured if he could get Kelly to return to the National League, other players would follow.

Spalding set up a meeting with Kelly in a hotel room and handed him a blank National League contract. He could fill in any number he wanted, Spalding told him. And as a bonus for selling out, Spalding handed Kelly a check for $10,000.

As inducements went, this one was rather substantial. And for a man who was always broke, no matter how well he was paid, the temptation for Kelly must have been great.

"I'm going to take a walk," Kelly told Spalding. He hurried out of the hotel room and down to the dark streets.

When Kelly came back, he looked grim.

"I can't go back on the boys," he said.

Spalding told Kelly he admired his position and lent his former player a thousand dollars.

John Montgomery Ward himself was offered a king's ransom of $12,000 to leave the Brotherhood and play with Washington in the National League. He too declined, helping the Brotherhood strike to continue.

Henry Chadwick had accused the Brotherhood players of having "a lack of moral character," but the courageous stand taken by Kelly and Ward certainly belied that accusation.

The Brotherhood held through the summer. A few players were won back by rumors that the Brotherhood was about to collapse. When in September rain ruined gate receipts for the month, Spalding sensed it was again time to act. He called for a peace conference.

Spalding needed to find out whether the players could afford to continue their league another season or not. At the meeting Spalding suggested that both sides reveal how they were faring. The players were asked to go first.

The naive players admitted to Spalding that they were $3 million in debt. Bolstered with the information, Spalding knew the players were in no position to negotiate a truce.

Without giving away his position, a straight-faced Spalding ended the meeting, calling for a return in a few days. At the second meeting Spalding arrogantly informed the players that no common ballplayer had any right to sit as an equal among businessmen such as him. There would be no further negotiations, he informed them.

He then offered the owners of the Players League teams the chance to sell their bankrupt clubs to the National League owners for ten cents on the dollar. Take it or risk getting nothing when the league folded, he told them.

Spalding purchased 60 percent of the stock of the Chicago Onions of the Players League for $18,000. For his investment he received the ballpark, the lease, the seats, the books, and the players, which he incorporated into his White Stockings team.

Some Players League owners were promised National League franchises—promises that weren't kept. One Players League owner who was promised "complete reimbursement" of all losses ended up with nothing.

An added and unexpected benefit to Spalding and the other National League owners from the Brotherhood War was the demise of the American Association after the 1891 season.

In 1891 four clubs of the struggling American Association joined the National League: St. Louis, Baltimore, Washington, and Louisville. The twelve-team National League was once again a monopoly. At the start of the season National League owners cut payrolls between 30 and 40 percent. Rosters were cut from fifteen to thirteen.

The players' revolt never would have happened had Spalding paid each player just a thousand dollars a year more than he allowed them. His total cost would have been another $15,000 and he would have saved himself the hundreds of thousands of dollars he lost during the disastrous competition with the Players League in 1890.

Like the owners after him, Spalding, who himself had once been a player, resented that he was so dependent on his players. If only he could have run his team without them.

As a result of the Brotherhood War, in the end it was the Chicago fans who suffered the most as the fortunes of their team sank. They did not recover for another decade and a half, well into the 1900s.

For the first few years after the strike the superior managerial skill of Cap Anson managed to hold the Chicago team together. Artistically, 1890 had been a disastrous season for everybody in the National League as a result of the mass defection of players. Anson, though, was able to fashion a better team of neophytes than most anyone else and finished second only to Brooklyn.

CAP ANSON: "The defection of Tener, Williamson, Ryan, Pfeffer and others left me with a comparatively green team on my hands, when the season of 1890 opened, but long before the season came to a close constant practice had made it one of the best teams in the League, as it proved by finishing in second place. Few people, however, appreciate the amount of work that was necessary to attain that result. It was hard work and plenty of it, and though some of the players objected to the amount of practice forced upon them, and the strict discipline that was enforced, yet they had to put up with it, as that was the only manner in which the necessary playing strength could be developed. I myself worked just as hard as they did. If we took a three-mile run, I was at their head setting the pace for them. I have never asked the men under my control to do anything that I was not willing to do myself, because it was just as necessary for me to be in good condition as it was for them.

"The only player left of the 'old reliables' was Tom Burns, who had also refused to affiliate with the Brotherhood.

"The rest of the team was composed of a lot of half-broken 'colts,' many of whom were newcomers to the League."

Indirectly, Albert Spalding's part in the Brotherhood War brought to an end his role as president of the Chicago team. The criticism by the loyal fans and in the press of his leadership—how could he have sold first Kelly and then Clarkson and then caused the defection of virtually his entire team to the Players League?—became so intense that in 1891 Spalding decided the heat of visibility was too great. Ostensibly stepping down, he appointed James A. Hart, who had helped run the American leg of his around-the-world tour, to be his front man. Spalding would continue to wield the power behind the team, but no longer would he have to take abuse from the press, fans, or his players or have to answer publicly for his actions. Hart would get paid for doing that.

Commenting on the huge payroll cuts for 1891, Hart sounded like Spalding, rationalizing to reporters that the cuts were "only the natural consequences of baseball history." He pointed out that "the same thing is done every day in other lines of business, only no talk is made of it."

Al Spalding refused to take back any of the departed veterans in 1891 after the Players League folded, so once again Anson had to play his youngsters. He would have won the pennant too, but in 1891 two Eastern teams, Boston and New York, cheated Chicago out of it. Everybody knew it. No one, however, could do anything about it.

Anson said Boston and New York did it because they didn't want his kids to win. A more plausible explanation might have been that the opposing players didn't want Chicago to win because they didn't want Spalding and that traitor Anson to have the pleasure of victory.

CAP ANSON: "[We] would have landed the pennant had it not been for the fact that the jealousy of the old players in the East engendered by the Brotherhood revolt would not allow a team of youngsters, many of whom were newcomers in the League, to carry off the honors, and a conspiracy was entered into whereby New York lost enough games to Boston to give the Beaneaters the pennant and to relegate us at the very last moment into the second place.

"We had the pennant won had it not been for the games that were dropped by the 'Giants' to the Boston Club, in order that the honors might not be carried off by a colt team.

"The race in 1891 was one of the closest in the history of the League. At the beginning of the closing week of the season's campaign Chicago was in the van by a percentage of victories of .628 to Boston's .615, which was apparently a winning lead and which would have been had not the New York organization made a present of its closing games to the Boston Club for the express purpose of throwing us down and keeping the pennant in the East. As it was, however, we finished head and head with the leaders, New York being third, Philadelphia fourth, Clevelend fifth, Brooklyn sixth, Cincinnati seventh and Pittsburgh eighth.

"As an excuse for the queer showing made by the 'Giants' in these Boston games it has been alleged that the team was in poor condition when it left the metropolis for the Hub to play this closing series, and that its true condition was kept a secret by the management, one writer going so far as to say that Manager [Buck] Ewing's brother John was at that time disabled by a sprained ankle, while Rusie was suffering from a bruised leg, and also that [Lew] Whistler had been playing at first base so well that Ewing thought he could afford to give Connor a day or two off, all of which may have been true, though I am free to confess right now that I do not believe it."

There well may have been another explanation for the Giants' throwing those last few games. At the time owners were allowed to own a piece of more than one franchise. One man, Arthur Soden, owned stock in both Boston and New York. Perhaps Soden had fixed it with Giants owner John Day to give Boston the pennant. Why? No one knows. The mystery has continued to this day.

Jim Hart, the Chicago team spokesman, publicly charged that New York Giants manager Jim Mutrie, on orders from owner John Day, didn't play Buck Ewing, Roger Connor, and pitching star Amos Rusie the last three games of the season against Boston.

Day, said Hart, wanted to ensure a pennant for Boston owner Soden, who also owned substantial stock in the Giants.

Said Hart: "Were I under indictment for murder, with the circumstantial evidence against me as strong as it appears to be against the New York Club, I should expect to be hanged."

Hart protested with the league. His protest was thrown out, much to his embarrassment, when it was revealed that Al Spalding owned more stock in the Giants than even Arthur Soden did!

After coming so close in 1891, the next year the fortunes of the Chicago team took a nosedive, as it finished a dismal seventh in the twelve-team league. Cap Anson had looked forward to the return of his veterans. Other owners had forgiven the jumpers and had taken them back. When Al Spalding stubbornly and vindictively refused to follow suit, Anson was left with a vastly inferior team.

CAP ANSON: "With the downfall of the Brotherhood and the consolidation of some of the leading clubs I naturally thought that the Chicago team would be strengthened very materially, but such was not the case. I did not even get my old players back, those of them that continued in the profession being scattered far and wide among the other League clubs, while others retired from the arena altogether. As a result it was a constant hustle on my part to secure new players, and I think I may easily say that the hardest years of my managerial experience were those that followed the revolt of the Brotherhood."

Anson hadn't lost his ability to discover talent. It's just that other teams seemed to be doing a better job of signing players than Chicago.

Early in 1890, Chicago was beaten on a three-hitter in what was a young Cleveland pitcher's first major league game. That night Anson looked up Cleveland secretary Hawley. They talked about the Players League war, about politics, and then just before leaving, Anson, trying to make it sound like an afterthought, said to Hawley, "Funny about that big rube of yours beating us today. He must have been shot full of luck, 'cause he don't know a damn thing about pitching. He's too green to do your club much good, but I believe if I taught him what I know I might make a pitcher out of him in a couple of years. He's not worth it now, but I am willing to give you $1,000 for him."

According to Fred Lieb, Hawley blew out a few mouthfuls of cigar smoke and said, "Cap, I believe you're an old faker. If my memory serves me correctly that big rube struck you out twice this afternoon. What's more he can do it again. And I'm sure if he's worth $1,000 to Chicago, he's worth that much to us. So, Cap, you keep your thousand, and we'll keep the rube."

The rube, who won 27 games that year, was Dentin True "Cy" Young. Before he was through, the big pitcher would win 511 games, the winningest pitcher in the history of the game.

When Chicago hit bottom, the team shed its name, the White Stockings. In 1892 it became instead (Anson's) White Colts, then (Anson's) Broncos, and in 1897, after Cap Anson's unceremonious firing, the team would become known as the Orphans.

10

Anson's Demise

Cap Anson couldn't have known it, but Albert Spalding's trip around the world during the winter of 1888–89 was the beginning of the end for him. As with his former star players, Mike Kelly and John Clarkson, the great Adrian Anson, for twenty-two years the anchor of the Chicago infield, learned one of baseball's saddest but most enduring lessons: No one is indispensable. It had been Anson himself who had impressed that fact upon Al Spalding, after the owner had asked him whether it would be OK to sell Kelly.

"Sure, spare anybody," Anson had said.

Anson had made two mistakes, one of his own design, the other not. By 1891 he was thirty-nine years old, long past the retirement age of most ballplayers. That was not his fault. Moreover, at his age, he was in better shape than most of his players, as Johnny Evers described in his autobiography.

JOHNNY EVERS: "Anson was one of the most tireless runners in the world, and training under him was a nightmare to his players. 'Anse' would drive his men for three hours in practice, then lead them in long runs, placing himself at the head of the procession and setting a steady, jogging pace. If he felt well the morning training was a Marathon route.

"One afternoon in New Orleans Anson ordered ten laps around the field after practice, which on the old grounds was nearly ten miles. The afternoon was hot, one of those wilting Southern spring days that sap the life out of men fresh from the rigors of Northern winter. The players fell into line, grumbling and scrowling. Back of left field a high board fence separated the ball grounds from one of the old cemeteries and near the foul line a board was off the fence. The first time the panting athletes passed the hole in the fence [Bill] Dahlen gave a quick glance to see if Anson was looking and dived head first through the gap into the cemetery. The others continued on around the lot, but on the second round [Bill] Lange, [Jim] Ryan, [Malachi] Kittredge and [George] Decker dived after Dahlen and joined him in the cemetery. The third trip saw the line dwindle to four followers, with Anson still leading. The fourth round only Anson and poor Bill Schriver, who had the bad luck to be directly behind his captain, plodding on, and on the next trip Schriver made the leap for life.

"Majestically alone, Anson toiled on while the onlookers writhed with delight. Perhaps their behavior aroused suspicion, or the absence of following footsteps attracted Cap's attention. He stopped, looked at the vacant field, a grim grin overspread his red face, and he resumed the jogging. Straight to that fence he plodded, and sticking his head through the hole, he beheld his team leaning against the above-ground tombs, smoking and laughing. Just for that he marshalled them into line again and, sitting the stand, watched them grimly until every man had completed ten rounds."

* * *

The mistake Cap Anson made during the around-the-world tour was to snub Jim Hart, whom Spalding had hired to manage the league all-stars against the White Stockings and to make the travel arrangements during the American leg of the world tour.

Spalding was so impressed with the job Hart had done that when the tour arrived in San Francisco he asked Anson and the other players to contribute money to buy Hart a pair of jeweled cuff links. Anson, who was angered that Hart, not he, had been in charge of the trip, felt that Hart was being paid handsomely enough for his work. In his customary honest and gruff way, Anson questioned Spalding as to why Hart deserved any more than his salary, and he refused to contribute.

When Spalding appointed Hart president of the team in 1891, Spalding took great pains to assure Anson that his reign as manager was not in jeopardy.

However, as Anson was to learn, team owners don't always keep their promises. Hart's resentment over Anson's snub had continued, and the relationship between the two men was strained from the start. Perhaps not by coincidence, that same year Hart arrived, Chicago sportswriters began hinting that the thirty-nine-year-old Anson was too old to continue as player-manager of the team.

On September 4, in a game in Boston, Anson, replying to the charge he was too old to play, walked onto the field wearing flowing white whiskers and long white hair. As if to tweak the writers, he insisted on wearing the costume throughout the game. When he came to bat for the first time, he told umpire Tom Lynch, "If the ball so much as ruffles these whiskers, I'm claimin' that I was hit by a pitched ball and taking my base."

Fortunately, the issue never came up.

By the fall of 1892, Anson was openly feuding with Hart, who vetoed his proposed deals and refused to back his disciplinary measures. It was rumored the New York Giants were looking for a manager (the rumor may have been started by Spalding, who also owned stock in the Giants), and Spalding tried to persuade Anson to take the job. The deal, however, never materialized. The proud Anson still felt bound to prove he could win another pennant in Chicago.

Anson kept hunting new colts—one of them was a new pitcher named Clark Griffith, who would win 20 games or more in six of the seven full seasons he played with Chicago—but Anson's teams continually finished out of the money.

CAP ANSON: "[The 1893 club] was a team of great promises and poor performances, and no one could possibly have felt more disappointed than I did when the end of the season found us in ninth place, the lowest place that Chicago Club had ever occupied in the pennant race since the formation of the League, a showing that was bad enough to bring tears to the eyes of an angel, let alone a team manager and captain."

Boston won again in 1893. Then Baltimore, led by Ned Hanlon and its famous group of Hall of Famers (John McGraw, Willie Keeler, Wilbert Robinson, Joe Kelley, Hughie Jennings, and Dan Brouthers), began its string of three straight championships from 1894 through 1896.

As Anson began his twenty-second season of big league play in 1897, an admiring fan who signed his name Hyder Ali wrote a long poem that first appeared in the *Sporting News*. Here are two verses:

How old is Anson? No one knows.
I saw him playing when a kid,
When I was wearing still short clothes,
And so my father's father did;
The oldest veterans of them all
As kids, saw Anson play baseball

How old is Anson? Ask the stars
That glisten in the hair of night
When day has drawn her golden bars
To shut the sunbeams from our sight;
The stars were present at his birth—
Were first to welcome him to earth.

That last year turned out to be one of Pop Anson's most trying as manager. At the start of the season he told his players, "We'll win the flag this year for sure, and I'm betting on it, boys."

Jim Hart, for his part, had had his fill of Anson. Before the season Hart, mocking Anson, predicted that the Chicago team would win the pennant "sometime in the next 1,500 years."

By 1897, Anson's bond with his players had deteriorated to the point that the manager began to wonder whether the players had conspired with Hart to get him fired.

CAP ANSON: "The team with which I started out in 1897 was certainly good enough to win the pennant with, or at least to finish right up in the front rank, and that it failed to do either of these things can only be explained by the fact that underhanded work looking toward my downfall was indulged in by some of the players, who were aided and abetted by President Hart, he refusing to enforce the fines levied by myself as manager and in that way belittling my authority and making it impossible to enforce the discipline necessary to making the team a success. The ringleader in this business was Jimmy Ryan, between whom and the Club's President the most perfect understanding seemed to exist, and for this underhanded work Ryan was rewarded by being made the team captain, a position that he was too unpopular with the players to hold, though it is generally thought he was allowed to draw the salary as per the agreement.

"Lack of discipline and insubordination began to show from the start. Fines were remitted in spite of all the protests that I could make, several members of the club being allowed to do about as they pleased. There could be only one result, as a matter of course, and that was poor ball playing. When the April campaign ended we were in the eleventh place. At the end of May we stood tenth. At the end of July we had climbed up to eighth, and at the end of August we were sixth, having then climbed into the first division. When the close of the season came, however, we had dropped back again to the ninth position, the margin between sixth and ninth places being a very small one."

At the end of the season Anson began reading newspaper rumors that he was on the way out. Al Spalding insisted Anson go to the winter meetings and make trades, which were then blocked by Spalding and Hart, "this action making my position a most humiliating one," said Anson.

While traveling together to England, Anson offered to buy the team from Spalding. According to Anson, Spalding told him he would sell it to him, but Anson never believed Spalding was serious.

Upon their return from England, Anson learned that he was out as manager and Tommy Burns, who had failed miserably in his one stint as manager of Pittsburgh, was in. When Anson was asked to resign, he refused, forcing Spalding to fire him.

None of this would have happened had not Jim Hart pushed Spalding to it. Hart had committed himself to hiring Burns as manager, and when Spalding waffled, Hart gave the owner a choice: him or Anson. Spalding, who needed Hart to run the team while he oversaw his sporting goods empire, picked Hart. Calling it a business decision, he reluctantly let Anson go.

In February 1898, Hart announced that Anson's contract would not be renewed, even though Spalding had promised Anson that the contract he signed in 1893 would run through the 1898 season.

Pop Anson's retirement was buried under breaking news concerning the coming Spanish-American War. With the USS *Maine* having blown up in Havana harbor about the same time, the retirement of a baseball player seemed far less important, and the attention it received was far less than it might have been during a more peaceful era.

To ease the pain of his firing (and his own guilty feelings about it), Spalding began a campaign to raise money for a testimonial dinner for Anson. It was estimated that $50,000 would be raised for Anson. But Anson stubbornly refused to be the object of what he characterized as charity.

"The public owes me nothing," he said, "and I am neither old nor a pauper. I can earn my own living as hitherto, and, moreover, I am by no means out of baseball."

When Anson was fired, his bitterness toward Al Spalding was compounded by the disappointment he felt after the multiyear contract he signed in 1889 didn't turn out to be as lucrative as he had expected.

In it Spalding had promised Anson 10 percent of the net profits of the club as long as he was manager. In 1890, because of the Brotherhood War, it amounted to nothing. Anson then learned that Spalding was putting the team's profits into building a new stadium on the West Side, meaning there would be no profit sharing for Anson, who never did get a penny of profit sharing from a contract that spanned almost nine years. According to Anson, neither Spalding nor Hart ever once opened their books to him, nor did they present him with any statement of finance, even after he made such a demand.

Said Anson, "It is a poor plan for any man not to look closely after his own business interests."

After Spalding told Anson he would sell him the team, then wouldn't, Anson's antagonism grew.

Anson accepted an offer from owner Andrew Freedman—who would soon become an enemy of Spalding's—to become the manager of the New York Giants. Anson kept the job three weeks and then quit because Freedman, who respected no man, would not give him the free hand he had demanded.

When Anson returned home, he tried to buy a Chicago team in the Western League (soon to be renamed the American League), but Spalding opposed him there too. Later Anson would say that Spalding had contacted all the men who might have financed Anson and warned them against it.

CAP ANSON: "After I had been released by the club Mr. Spalding still posed as my best friend, and the affection that Damon had for Pythias was not greater than that I bore for him. I had not then learned the full nature of his duplicity, nor was it until some time later that it dawned on me."

Later Anson would blame Spalding for all his disappointments. Like so many star baseball players after him, Adrian Anson discovered he wasn't much good at anything else in life. One venture after another ended badly. Upon his retirement Anson opened an ice rink that failed because it wasn't a very cold winter. He then bottled ginger beer, a business that failed because, said Anson, "There was a flaw in the formula somewhere." Also, the caps tended to explode off the bottles. "It was the liveliest ginger beer ever placed on the market," he said.

He opened a ritzy pool parlor, but it went under, and after its collapse he tried unsuccessfully to persuade John Wanamaker to back him in a venture to manufacture baseballs and compete with Spalding. Anson served one term as city clerk in Chicago but lost a bid for reelection.

He entered vaudeville. Anson had been bitten by the acting bug when he was with Chicago. During a road trip to New York he took the entire team to Broadway to see a few friends perform in a play called *A Parlor Match*. Before the curtain went up, he was invited backstage. Would he agree to a bit part? He was given the part of a foreman of a crew digging for treasure.

When Anson appeared onstage, one of the "workmen," instead of saying, "Good morning," shouted, "Good morning, Captain Anson." When the audience saw the famous ballplayer, it cheered boisterously. Anson became so flustered he forgot his line and ran off the stage.

After his retirement he took up acting again. He performed one skit with his two daughters that was written by Ring Lardner. He also had a feature role as part of the cast of a play called *The Runaway Colt*.

The climax of the play came when the hero (Anson) hit a home run, dashed off into the wings to the right of the stage on his way to first base, circled behind the curtain, and reappeared from the opposite wings to slide into home plate.

The actor playing the part of the opposing catcher would receive the ball from somewhere up above and thrust it at the sliding Anson, whereupon the umpire would cry dramatically, "You're safe!" and the final curtain would descend.

One afternoon Anson ran into umpire Tim Hurst.

"Tim," said Cap, "there's nothing on earth like this stage business. You oughta get into it. Why don't you come over tonight and play the umpire part, just for one performance?"

Tim agreed, and that evening Hurst either forgot where he was or decided to play a practical joke on Anson. As Anson came sliding into the plate on the stage, umpire Hurst bent forward tensely, saw the ball arrive, saw the catcher slap it on the runner, and just as the curtain started to come down, cried: "YER OUT!"

The audience went crazy!

Anson was part of a slapstick vaudeville routine that required him to wear green whiskers, receive squirts of soapy water in the face, have buckets emptied upon him from above, and participate in snatching his fellow actors through a trapdoor. Between these antics, he and the other actors did a short hoedown and sang a song entitled "We're Ten Chubelin [Shoveling] Tipperary Turks."

In 1910, Anson appeared in theaters in small New England towns where crowds cheered him. He was still in vaudeville in 1921 at the age of sixty-nine. On April 14, 1922, he died in Chicago. His funeral was one of the largest ever given an American athlete.

To the end Anson still held great bitterness over the way Spalding had mistreated him. Looking back, considering all he had done for Spalding and seeing how little he felt he got in return, on some level Anson, who had been so critical of the Brotherhood players, later rued not having joined them.

CAP ANSON: "Base-ball as at present conducted is a gigantic monopoly, intolerant of opposition and run on a grab-all-that-there-is-in-sight policy that is alienating its friends and disgusting the very public that has so long and cheerfully given to it the support that it has withheld from other forms of amusement."

And yet, despite the bitterness, Cap Anson fared far better after his retirement than some of Chicago's star players, including his two $10,000 teammates, Mike Kelly and John Clarkson, both of whom died tragic, early deaths.

Kelly played for Boston for three rousing years before falling to the effects of his drinking. Giving him the new nickname King his first year with his new team, the Boston fans, who were predominantly Irish, embraced this son of Ireland to their bosoms, presenting him with a $12,000 house—paid in full—and with a carriage driven by two white horses. Some days the fans would unhitch the horses and pull Kelly to the park themselves.

As befitting his fame, Kelly dressed the part of Boston's hero, wearing tailored suits, ascots, high hats and black patent-leather shoes. According to Jerry Lansche, "He was often accompanied at night by a Japanese valet and a monkey."

By 1889, however, Kelly was spending so much money on the high life that during his years in Boston, despite a substantial salary, he never received a paycheck. According to George Tuohey, who wrote a book on the Braves in 1897, each week the treasurer collected canceled receipts but never handed Kelly money. According to Tuohey, it wasn't long before Kelly's house was mortgaged to the hilt.

Without the watchful eye of Cap Anson to moderate his behavior, Kelly's drinking was getting him in serious trouble. One time Kelly held up an exhibition game while he drank beer with disreputable characters in the stands. At other times he became so drunk before a game that he would be unable to play. Before a crucial game against Cleveland late in the 1889 season, Kelly was not in the dugout before the game. Boston lost 7–1.

HAROLD KAESE: "This was the day Boston lost the pennant, and also, what a way to lose it! Captain Mike Kelly could not play because of 'a jollification during last night with several theatrical friends.' The great King could only sit on the bench in a light overcoat, and he did not sit there long as he got thrown out of the game for calling the umpire a crook.

"'You're bound to do the Bostons out of the championship,' Kelly said to Umpire McQuaid, who asked police to put him out of the park. As one of the Cleveland policemen put a billy club over Kelly's head, one of the Cleveland players protested."

According to Tim Murnane of the *Boston Globe*, he overheard the policeman say, "We've heard of this chap and think he's a disgrace to the business."

He was released outside the park. Manager Jim Hart (the same Jim Hart who would become Chicago president in 1891 had managed Boston in 1889) bought Kelly a ticket so he could get back in, but the police refused to allow him in anyway.

Anson commented on Kelly's demise: "He played good ball for a time, but his bad habits soon caused his downfall . . . for baseball and booze will not mix any better than will oil and water. The last time that I ever saw him was at an Eastern hotel barroom, and during the brief space of time that we conversed together he threw in enough whiskey to put an ordinary man under the table. . . ."

Before the 1893 season opened Boston loaned Kelly to the New York Giants but he had trouble with John Montgomery Ward and after twenty games was returned unwanted. He then took a job in Allentown in the Penn State League, where his name kept the ballparks jammed. However, his skills had diminished. He was making errors. The fans began booing him, and one day he refused to take the field for fear that the crowd would assault him.

After the 1894 season he tried vaudeville in New York, where the fans loved him as dearly as they had in Chicago and Boston. At the height of his fame, he had been paid a fat fee to take a cameo role as a minor character in a play called *The Tin Soldier*. He was "made up so his own grandmother wouldn't know him."

When the New York crowd finally did recognize him, a roar would go up, and the ushers suddenly would trot down the aisle carrying a large baseball made of flowers. The first time it happened, Kelly's voice left him, along with all recollection of his lines. The prompters had to almost shout in his ear before he picked them up and got the play going again.

After his career was over he returned to New York, where he hoped people would pay money to hear him recite "Casey at the Bat," but by this time the legend had been tarnished. He and John Kelly, the famed umpire, opened a saloon on Sixth Avenue.

On a boat to Boston, where he was to perform his vaudeville act, he contracted pneumonia. While he was being carried on a stretcher to Boston Emergency Hospital, he slipped off and fell to the floor.

"This is me last slide," Kelly whispered. And it was.

He died at Boston Emergency Hospital on November 8, 1894. Five thousand fans went to the Elks Hall to view his body. He was baseball's first hero, dead at the age of thirty-six. The twelve team owners raised $1,400 for his widow. He was interred in the Elks' lot in Mount Hope Cemetery in a pauper's grave.

* * *

The other $10,000 player, John Clarkson, died raving mad on February 4, 1909, at the age of forty-seven after spending a long period in an asylum.

After his sale to Boston, Clarkson continued his pitching mastery, winning 33, 49, 25, and 33 games before he hurt his arm. Boston sent him to Cleveland in the middle of the 1892 season for the last two and a half years of his illustrious career.

Clarkson became unbalanced during the winter of 1894 after he witnessed a train accident involving his friend, catcher Charlie Bennett.

The two had gone hunting, and after they were done, they rode together on the Santa Fe railroad from Kansas City to Williamsburg, Virginia. The train made a short stop at Wellesville, Kansas, where they disembarked so Bennett could make a phone call.

It was cold that day in January 1894 when the train began to start up again. Clarkson jumped up safely, but Bennett slipped on the icy platform and fell onto the track, where he was crushed under the ponderous wheels. Both his legs were severed. As the terrified Bennett waited for the medics to arrive, a horrified Clarkson cradled him in his arms.

Bennett, who survived the accident better than Clarkson despite the amputation of both legs, moved to Detroit and opened a pottery business. Clarkson, however, never recovered from the trauma. After his playing career ended following the 1894 season, he lived in Bay City, Michigan, and opened a cigar store, which he ran until 1906.

He then suffered a mental breakdown, was declared insane, and spent most of the rest of his life in a mental hospital. He was visiting relatives in Cambridge when he died of pneumonia.

Two of Anson's other well-known White Stockings, Ed Williamson and catcher Frank "Old Silver" Flint, also died badly. Their deaths were witnessed by Billy Sunday, who had left the Cincinnati team in 1891 to pursue his religious work with the YMCA in Chicago. Sunday went on to become the most famous evangelist of the nineteenth century.

BILLY SUNDAY: "Ed Williamson came back to Chicago and started a saloon on Dearborn Street. I would go through there giving tickets for the YMCA meetings and would talk with them and he would cry like a baby.

"I would get down and pray for him and would talk with him. When he died [in March 1894] they put him on the table and cut him open and took out his liver and it was so big it would not go in a candy bucket. Kidneys had shriveled until they were like two stones.

"Frank Flint, our old catcher, who caught for nineteen years, drew $3,200 a year on an average. He caught before they had chest protectors, masks and gloves. He caught bare-handed. Every bone in the ball of his hand was broken. You never saw such a hand as Frank had. Every bone in his face was broken, and his nose and cheek bones, and the shoulder and the ribs had all been broken. He got to drinking, his home was broken up and he went to the dogs.

"I've seen old Frank Flint sleeping on a table in a stale beer joint and I've turned my pockets inside out and said, 'you're welcome to it, old pal.' He drank on and on, and one day in winter he staggered out of a stale beer joint and stood on a corner, and was seized with a fit of coughing. The blood streamed out of his nose, mouth and eyes. Down the street came a wealthy woman. She took one look and said, 'My God, is that you, Frank?' and his wife came up and kissed him.

"She called two policemen and a cab and started with him to her boarding house. They broke all speed regulations. She called five of the best physicians and they listened to the beating of his heart, one, two, three, four, five, six, seven, eight, nine, ten, eleven, twelve, and the doctors said, 'He will be dead in about four hours.' She told them to tell him what they had told her. She said 'Frank, the end is near,' and he said, 'Send for Bill.'

"They telephoned me and I came. He said, 'There's nothing in the life of years ago I care for now. I can hear the bleachers cheer when I make a hit that wins the game. But there is nothing that can help me out now. Won't you say a few words over me, Bill?' He struggled as he had years ago on the diamond, when he tried to reach home, but the great Umpire of the universe yelled, 'You're out!' and waved him to the club house, and the great gladiator of the diamond was no more."

Cap Anson had outlived Kelly, Williamson, and Flint, who had all died by the time he wrote his book in 1900. Anson, who all his life had loved the game, mourned their deaths.

CAP ANSON: "Over the graves of three of them the grass has now been growing for many a year, and yet I can see them as plainly now as in the golden days of the summers long ago, when, greeted by the cheers of an admiring multitude, we all played

Billy Sunday

ball together. If it were possible for the dead to come back to us, how I should like once more to marshall the members of that championship team of 1884, 1885, and '86 together and march with them once more across the field while the cheers of the crowd rang in our ears."

11

Al Spalding: Savior

In 1901 the National League called on Albert Spalding, the one man powerful enough to save baseball from a grim fate that was sure to follow if devilish genius Andrew Freedman, owner of the New York Giants, wasn't stopped from becoming president of the league.

The sixty-one-year-old Spalding, by now looking like the wealthy aristocrat he had become, took up the challenge to stop Freedman, who had made millions in the insurance business with the strong backing of Boss Croker and Tammany Hall, the Democratic machine of New York City.

Freedman was one of those owners who cared not for the game of baseball but rather only for the profits he could make from the game. He had pretty much run the Giants into the ground because of his unbalanced nature and a stinginess toward his players that made Spalding's cheapness pale in comparison. Freedman had made Amos Rusie hold out a full season before the great pitcher took him to court to test the legality of the reserve clause. The other owners, fearing the result of losing the case, ponied up $3,000 to meet Rusie's salary demands.

In eight years, Freedman had had twelve managers. When Cap Anson managed those three weeks for Freedman, he discovered a man who would jump out of his box to yell at the umpires, the opposition, and even his own players.

Having put his Giants in the toilet, Freedman was threatening the same fate for the entire National League, running for the presidency on the platform of syndicated baseball. In other words, what Freedman wanted to do was have a select few men, including himself, who would own all the teams jointly. This syndicate could then move the players where they felt the gate needed them most.

Freedman, who was backed by three other National League teams—Boston, Cincinnati, and St. Louis—argued that under this system, the syndicate could control players' salaries and would be able to put the biggest stars in the biggest cities. "The least talented laborers," wrote Robert Smith, "[would be] dumped on the vineyards where the picking was poorest."

It was a plan designed by Philistines to kill everything that was great about baseball's competitive nature.

Freedman's bottom-line mentality had badly hurt the National League two years earlier. After the 1899 season he had recommended dropping four of the weaker teams, Cleveland, Washington, Baltimore, and Louisville, from the National League.

(The remaining eight teams, Chicago, Pittsburgh, St. Louis, New York, Brooklyn, Philadelphia, Cincinnati, and Boston, made up the National League until 1953, when Boston moved to Milwaukee.)

The move backfired badly when just a year later Ban Johnson, who had been planning to start a new league, took three of those franchises, Cleveland, Washington, and Baltimore, plus Detroit (rather than Louisville), to start the rival American League.

With Johnson choosing to ignore the reserve clause, the Americans had succeeded in luring 111 former National Leaguers to jump leagues as the inaugural 1901 American League season began.

When the National League met to elect its new president on December 11, 1901, Freedman came to the meeting having lined up four votes. Spalding also had four votes. The future of the game truly hung in the balance.

After four days and twenty-four more ballots, nothing had changed when Freedman and his three allies left the room for a caucus. Still seated in the room to make sure Spalding and his side didn't pull any funny stuff was Giants secretary Fred Knowles.

For a vote to be taken, there had to be a majority to form a quorum. After the four representatives left, Colonel John Rogers of Philadelphia, an ally of Spalding's, immediately called for a roll call. He ruled that Knowles, representing the Giants, was present, so the five teams in the roll call were enough for a vote to be taken.

Rogers, banging on his gavel, called for a vote. The four votes for Spalding were counted. Despite Knowles's protests, Rogers determined that there was no one in the room who had voted for Freedman. Spalding, he announced, was the new president.

Freedman was able to get an injunction to stop Spalding, but Al Spalding had very powerful friends, and he hired as his lawyer Thomas Reed, the former Speaker of the House of Representatives, to continue the battle. Reed advised him to leave New York, removing him from jurisdiction, and to act like the league president, legal or no.

Spalding's proceedings had been unethical and probably illegal, but the delay was enough to kill the syndication scheme of Freedman, who in March was ousted as owner of the Giants under a truce. The most important concession was that Freedman's syndicate idea was dead. As part of the deal John T. Brush would sell the Cincinnati Reds to August "Garry" Herrmann. Freedman would sell the Giants to Brush and get out of baseball. Spalding would step down as league president.

Before his departure, during his final season as owner, Freedman scored a coup for the National League when he brought the fiery John McGraw from the American League in midseason of 1902 to manage the Giants.

In 1902, Al Spalding sold his interest in Chicago to Jim Hart, retiring to Point Loma, California. His interest in the game remained strong, and he continued to insist in his *Official Baseball Guide* that baseball, which he commonly referred to as Our National Game, was purely an American invention untainted by the relationship to any foreign game, including the English games of cricket and rounders.

American purity was an important concept to Spalding. Baseball, wrote Spalding, was "the exponent of American courage, Confidence, Combativeness; American Dash, Discipline, Determination; American Energy, Eagerness, Enthusiasm; American Pluck, Persistency, Performance; American Spirit, Sagacity, Success; American Vim, Vigor, Virility."

For years his English-born editor at the *Spalding Guide*, pioneer sportswriter Henry Chadwick, had argued that baseball evolved from England, where they played cricket and rounders, which had four bases and seemed rather similar.

How, Spalding would counter, could it have come from "that asinine pastime" of rounders?

Spalding preferred the notion that the game came from One-O-Cat, which called for three players—a pitcher, a catcher, and a batter. There were only two bases, first and home, and the runner would shuttle back and forth. As more kids wanted to play, Spalding hypothesized, the kids added two more bases and stuck a kid in the middle of the square. This game was called Town Ball, he said, and baseball came from it, *not* rounders.

In 1905, after years of arguing with Chadwick—with whom he agreed on almost all other issues—Spalding decided he would appoint a panel of experts to settle the issue once and for all. Settle that it had come purely from American origins, that is.

Spalding appointed James E. Sullivan, the president of the American Sports Publishing Company, to do his research. ASPC was a subsidiary of Spalding's sporting goods firm. Sullivan later became head of the American Athletic Union, and each year the Sullivan Award is given to America's premier amateur athlete.

For his six-member panel he selected two senators, Morgan Bulkeley, who had been the initial National League president in 1876 but who had gone on to become a senator from Connecticut, and Arthur Gorman.

Two longtime business associates, A. J. Reach and George Wright, were named, as were the third and fourth presidents of the National League, A. G. Mills and N. E. Young.

According to Spalding, Sullivan spent two years collecting "evidence." The information convincing to Spalding ended up coming from an eighty-year-old mining engineer from Denver by the name of Abner Graves.

Here's the story Graves reportedly told Sullivan: Abner Doubleday, the Union general, invented the game "either the spring prior or following the 'Log Cabin and Hard Cider' campaign of General William H. Harrison for the presidency," i.e., in 1839.

Doubleday, said Graves, like him was then a student of Green's Select School in Cooperstown. The pupils of Otsego Academy and Green's Select School were playing Town Ball when "Doubleday drew a diamond on the grounds of the 'Phinney lot,' and sketched the positions of the eleven men."

The letter was the only one sent by Graves, the only proof on behalf of General Doubleday, known best for aiming the first Union gun in reply to the Confederate attack on Fort Sumter. He was then captain of artillery at the fort.

The only problem with the story was that when checked by historians, it was found that Doubleday wasn't even attending Green's Select School in 1839 when Graves said he was but was at West Point. In all the letters Doubleday wrote, moreover, not once did he ever mention the game of baseball.

There is one other connection that needed to be explained but never was. A. G. Mills, who as a Union officer was reported to have taken a ball and bat with him to army encampments along with his rifle and pistols, had known General Doubleday. Mills had been in charge of the military escort that served as a guard of honor when Doubleday's body lay in state in New York City Hall and for the subsequent burial in Arlington Cemetery.

And it was Mills who announced that Doubleday had invented baseball. Spalding quickly backed his findings.

Chadwick, perhaps knowing Graves's letter to be a phony or a forgery or a concoction from the imagination of Mills or Spalding or both, continued to insist the game came from rounders.

Where did Sullivan find this "Abner Graves"? Did Graves really exist? The most likely scenario: When Mills told Spalding about his good friend General Doubleday, Spalding decided a heroic Union general would be the perfect answer to the age-old question of who invented baseball.

These "findings" were announced in the 1908 *Spalding Guide*. According to Robert Smith, Al Spalding promoted the Doubleday legend and "pretended he really believed it though privately he thought it was nonsense."

Spalding wanted everyone to believe that an American general had invented baseball in 1839, and he succeeded. As all good baseball fans know, we ignore Alexander Cartwright, the man who *really* invented the rules for the game of baseball. Instead, we embrace the Doubleday legend. In 1939 the U.S. government printed a stamp commemorating the one hundredth anniversary of the founding of the game.

And if you wish to travel to the Baseball Hall of Fame, the town you'll visit is Cooperstown, New York, the home of novelist James Fenimore Cooper and the home of that brave general, A. G. Mills's old buddy, Abner Doubleday.

Long after Al Spalding sold his stake in the Chicago team in 1902, his influence continued to be felt. Because of that baseball cornerstone, the reserve clause, the players were still feeling underpaid in 1912 when an upstart league called the Federal League began operation.

Not vacillating from their disastrous salary policy that led to the Players League revolt in 1890, the baseball owners had continued to keep players' salaries as low as possible, and so with the advent of this new league, a significant number of players jumped ship to earn the salaries they felt they deserved, again costing the owners far more money than if they had just paid the players a decent, fair salary.

Al Spalding died on September 9, 1915. Three months later the Federal League folded, and everything returned to normal. The reserve clause that he had championed in 1876 continued in force one hundred years after its invention, when an arbitrator appointed by a court finally declared it null and void.

Once the owners lost that court case in 1976, it is interesting to note that as late as 1995 the baseball owners have sought to return to the days of Al Spalding's salary cap.

They never, ever learn.

12

Selee's Genius

Before a ball game one afternoon in 1898 or 1899, Tom Burns, the Chicago manager, was standing by the cage during batting practice.

"Push it off to right field," he ordered a batter who was starting to the plate.

"Why, you old gray-headed stiff, you hit .212 the last season you played," responded the player.

Chicago owner Jim Hart determined after an eighth-place finish in 1899 that Burns was not the manager he thought he would be. He replaced Burns with the undistinguished Tom Loftus, who did even worse, as Chicago finished tied for fifth in 1900 and then sixth in 1901 with a 53–86 record.

Hart, desperate for leadership, in 1902 hired a manager with a glittering past even though he quite likely was suffering from tuberculosis. The manager, Frank Selee, had been sickly when he left Boston at the end of the 1901 season. Sick or not, Hart wanted Selee, one of the greatest unsung managers in the history of the game.

In his twelve seasons with Boston, Selee's teams had finished in the first division nine times, winning five pennants. Hart hoped Selee could devise for Chicago a championship team it hadn't enjoyed since the 1880s.

Frank Selee (like Joe McCarthy, another outstanding Chicago manager) never played a single game in the major leagues. Born in Amherst, New Hampshire, he was a modest, retiring New Englander, the son of a Methodist clergyman. His home was in Truro on Cape Cod. He played as a pro in Waltham and Lawrence in 1884, then became manager in Haverill in 1885 in the New England League. He won the Northwestern League pennant with Oshkosh in 1887 and moved to Omaha in 1888, winning the pennant there in 1889.

In 1890, Boston lost ten of its most important players including King Kelly, who went over to the Boston Brotherhood team as manager and captain. Kelly led the team to the Brotherhood championship.

With the Boston Nationals in disarray, Selee took over as manager. Though he didn't look spectacular—he managed in street clothes, as did Connie Mack some years later—and he was taciturn and colorless, Selee was a shrewd judge of talent, discovering such outstanding players as Fred Tenney, Jimmy Collins, Chick Stahl, Ted Lewis, and Marty Bergen.

One of Selee's master strokes was bringing with him from Omaha a phenomenal talent named Kid Nichols, a pitcher who had speed, a rubber arm, and brains. Seven years in a row Nichols won 30 games or more. Selee also recruited two other Westerners, Herman "Dutch" Long of Kansas City and Robert Lincoln Lowe of Milwaukee. For many years Long was rated second only to Honus Wagner as a shortstop. Lowe was a star outfielder and second baseman.

Under Selee's management, Boston also procured Hugh Duffy and Tommy McCarthy, the Heavenly Twins. King Kelly's return was crucial in 1891 as Boston won the league championship.

Selee was quiet, courteous, and mild of manner. A gentleman among ruffians, he treated his players with respect.

FRANK SELEE: "If I make things pleasant for the players, they reciprocate. I want them to be temperate and live properly. I do not believe that men who are engaged in such exhilarating exercise should be kept in strait jackets all the time, but I expect them to be in condition to play. I do not want a man who cannot appreciate such treatment."

His outstanding infielder, Bobby Lowe, remembered Selee fondly.

BOBBY LOWE: "He was a good judge of players. He didn't bother with a lot of signals, but let his players figure out their own plays. He didn't blame them if they took a chance that failed. He believed in place-hitting, sacrifice-hitting, and stealing bases. He was wonderful with young players."

Selee's Boston teams won pennants for three straight years, in 1891, 1892, and 1893. His team didn't repeat in 1894 because of the train accident that crippled his star catcher, Charlie Bennett. The next two years Boston finished out of the running, then returned to championship form, winning pennants in 1897 and 1898.

One of Selee's great strengths was his ability to judge what position a player should play. For instance, in 1897, Fred Tenney had come up as a catcher. Selee made him a first baseman, and he became one of the best. Selee's team was led by

Frank Selee

four Hall of Famers, pitcher Kid Nichols, third baseman Jimmy Collins, and out-fielders Hugh Duffy and Billy Hamilton.

Selee's team fell apart when some of the good players jumped to the Boston Red Sox in the new American League in 1901. The Boston Nationals had slipped to a .500 record that year. At the end of the season Selee signed with Chicago and brought his star second baseman, Robert Lowe, with him.

Immediately after taking over the Chicago team Selee began shifting his young-sters around to form the nucleus of one of the most formidable teams in the history of the game.

One of his young players was Frank Chance, who had been noticed playing col-lege and semipro ball in California by Chicago player Big Bill Lange.

Selee's teams outthought and outhustled the opposition. To play for Selee, it helped if you were clever and brazen. Frank Chance was the embodiment of a Selee-trained player.

JOHNNY EVERS: "The real beginning of the Chicago Cubs was in March 1898 when a big, bow-legged, rather awkward young player come from the Pacific Coast to be tried as a catcher. Quiet, good-natured, rather retiring off the field, serious, and in deadly earnest while playing, honest and sincere in everything, Frank Leroy Chance reported at training quarters at West Baden, Indiana, carrying a bunch of gnarled and wrecked fingers at the end of each hand. Anyone who at that time had predicted that Chance was to become the leader of the greatest club ever organized would have earned a laugh. He had no experience except the little gained in the am-ateur games in California. He played with the Fresno High School team in 1893, for two years with Washington University at Irvington, Cal., and he participated in the great amateur tournament played between all the school teams of California, catch-ing for Fresno, which team finished close to Oakland and Stockton. Bill Lange, then with the Chicago club, saw Chance and recommended him for trial.

"While awkward and unfinished, pitchers who worked with him declared that Chance from the first showed his genius for leadership and great skill in handling pitchers and watching batters. His fearless recklessness brought him many injuries as a catcher and twice he was nearly killed."

Until Selee came to Chicago, Chance had been a catcher and an outfielder. In his first game, on April 29, 1898, Chance had caught ace pitcher Clark Griffith, who beat Louisville 16–2. Playing first base for Louisville that day was Honus Wagner, who would go on to star at shortstop for the Pittsburgh Pirates.

Chance, the son of a banker, had caught in Chicago under Tom Burns and then Tom Loftus. Selee felt that the team would be better served if Chance were moved to first base. Chance was reluctant to make the switch.

JOHNNY EVERS: "Frank Chance, the 'Peerless Leader' of the Chicago Cubs, was a catcher. He declared he could not play first base and refused to play there, threat-ening to retire from baseball when Manager Selee ordered him to that position. Even then he balked until Selee offered him an increased salary, when he reluctantly consented to make the attempt."

* * *

Selee's catcher, Johnny Kling, had joined Chicago in 1990. Like Chance, Kling was aggressive and smart, knew how to work pitchers, and had a rifle arm.

JOHNNY EVERS: "There was not much sign of promise of a championship team in Chicago then, for Hart, in spite of his theories, still had his old stars; and it was not until 1900 that the club, with all the scouts, its purchases and trades, made another rich strike. This lucky find was John Kling, who was born knowing baseball in Kansas City. He was manager, pitcher and first batter of the Schmeltzers from 1893 to 1895, when he went to Rockford, Ill., as a catcher and lasted one pay day, being released as a failure. Returning to Kansas City, he led the Schmeltzers three more years. In 1898 he joined Houston, under the name of Klein, and quit because the team would not pay him his salary. He again caught for the Schmeltzers until 1900, when he went to St. Joe's.

"Ted Sullivan, the veteran scout, went on a secret visit to St. Joseph to buy Sam Strang, later of Chicago and New York, and was so impressed with Kling that he also was purchased. Chicago secured the greatest catcher the game ever has known."

Before the arrival of Frank Selee, two of the team's cornerstones, Frank Chance and Johnny Kling, were in place. With the coming of Selee, two other building blocks, Jimmy Slagle and Joe Tinker, swiftly followed.

JOHNNY EVERS: "Selee and Hart reached an agreement as to the management in the fall of 1901, and Selee immediately laid plans to strengthen Chicago. His first step was a bit of strategy to secure [Jimmy] Slagle, who was wanted to lead the batting list.

"Slagle was a quiet, cool, left-handed batter with much patience and judgment. His career in baseball had been full of vicissitudes. He started playing with Clarion, Pa., in 1889, and afterward went to Ohio Wesleyan University at Delaware, where he played the outfield two seasons. In 1894 he signed with Franklin in the Iron and Oil League, then played with Omaha for one season; next went to Houston, where a scout discovered him and took him to Boston in the fall of 1896. Boston banished him to Grand Rapids, from which place he went to Kansas City. Pittsburgh bought him but before he played there he was traded to Washington, and when the National League was reduced to eight clubs in 1900 Slagle was sent to Philadelphia, where, in the greatest aggregation of batters ever organized, the little fellow led the list. He was sold to Boston in 1901, and near the end of the season broke a finger. Selee, having a scheme, sold him to Baltimore. The release to Baltimore was part of the plot to get him to Chicago, for as soon as Selee became manager of Chicago he brought Slagle back.

"That same spring Selee found the man to stop the gap at short stop which had existed for years. The man was Joe Tinker, who began playing ball with the John Taylors in Kansas City in 1896. He was so good even then that the next year Hagen's Tailors paid two dollars for him, and he helped that team win the city championship in 1898. Then he went to the Bruce Lumbers, with which team he met and conquered Kling's Schmeltzers. The next season Kling traded two uniforms and a bat for Tinker and brought him to the Schmeltzers, but in June he went to Parsons, Kans., and later in the summer to Coffeyville. Denver purchased him and tried him at second base, but he was so bad that he was sold quickly to John McCloskey, who was managing the Great Falls team. It happened that Great Falls was in financial straits, and needing money. McCloskey sold Tinker to Helena for $200 and Joe Marshall, saving the team and the league from bankruptcy. He was taken to Portland, Ore., in 1901, by Jack Grim. Playing third base, he helped win the pennant of the Northwest League. He played so well that scouts for both Cincinnati and Chicago bid for him. Jack McCarthy, who had been ill-treated by Cincinnati, advised Tinker to try Chicago and he joined the team as a third baseman."

Joe Tinker had been a third baseman, but Selee didn't want him there. Selee noted his range and his strong arm, and he battled the fierce youngster to move to shortstop.

JOHNNY EVERS: "Joe Tinker refused to play shortstop, insisting that he was a third baseman, and was persuaded with difficulty to try the position at which he became famous."

When his captain and his second baseman, Bobby Lowe, got hurt in the final weeks of the 1902 season Selee demanded an emergency replacement. The Chicago scout sent diminutive Johnny Evers, from Troy, New York, at the cost of only a few hundred dollars. Evers (Ee-vers, not Evv-ers) reported on Labor Day, 1902. He was nineteen years old and weighed 115 pounds. Some of the older players threatened not to take the field with him, fearing he would get hurt. Because of his size, a few of the veterans made the mistake of underestimating his toughness and character. In the end, of course, Evers had the last laugh.

JOHNNY EVERS: "As I climbed aboard [the team bus the first day he joined the Cubs] 'Jack' Taylor, the pitcher, looked me over very carefully and cut me to the quick with, 'He'll leave in a box car tonight.' He meant that I wouldn't do at all. Some years later, I must admit, it gave me great pleasure to still be with the Chicago club when Taylor was released, and I refreshed his memory by remarking, 'Well, I'm still here, Jack, and I see you're getting the gate.'"

Evers was a very tough Irishman who was dedicated to the game. He reportedly went to bed each night reading the baseball rule book and the *Sporting News*.

HUGH FULLERTON: "All there is to Evers is a bundle of nerves, a lot of woven wire muscles, and the quickest brain in baseball. He has invented and thought out more plays than any man of recent years. He went to second base to fill Lowe's place the first day he reached Chicago, played twenty-two games to the end of the season without an error, and became the baseball idol of Chicago."

At the time of Johnny Evers's arrival, Frank Chance was out with an injury. In 1901 Chance primarily had caught, appearing in fifty games in the outfield, 33 behind the plate, and only six times at first base. In 1902, Chance caught twenty-nine games and appeared at first base thirty-eight times. When the lanky Chance returned to the lineup on September 13, 1902, to play first base, it was the first game in which the combination of Tinker, Evers, and Chance appeared together. Two days later they made a double play against Cincinnati, the first of many twin-killings.

Frank Chance became Selee's regular first baseman in 1903, a year in which Chicago climbed to third place behind Fred Clarke's Pittsburgh Pirates and John McGraw's New York Giants. One of those three teams would win the National League pennant over the next ten years. It would take several more years for Chicago's time to come. Chance's transition from catcher to first base in 1903 was of crucial importance.

JOHNNY EVERS: "Prospects for getting a winning team improved, but luck deserted Selee's banner in 1903. However, a change was made which was of as much importance, possibly more, than anything before or since. Selee persuaded Chance after long resistance to play first base and transformed him into a great first baseman.

"With Chance, Evers and Tinker in position, the team began to be formidable."

13

The Cubs Grow Claws

With Cap Anson a faded memory, in 1898 the Chicago team needed a more appropriate nickname than the Orphans. Because new owner Jim Hart had signed so many young players, the team took on the name the Chicago Spuds.

These players matured, but at the start of the 1901 season many of the players jumped leagues for higher pay, as they had during the Brotherhood War of 1890. This time they fled into the arms of the new American League.

With Frank Selee now working his magic, the core of young stars, including Chance, Tinker, Slagle, and Kling, was beginning to make its mark. Aware that the 1902 team was composed of these exciting young players, Chicago rooters expressed an interest in giving the team a more appropriate nickname than the Spuds. They couldn't go back to the White Stockings—Chicago in the American League had purloined the name during the years when the Chicago Nationals were called the Orphans. One group of civic-minded Chicagoans insisted the team should have a name indicative of "bear-like strength and a playful disposition." The idea may originally have come from Charles Sensabaugh, editor of the sports department of the *Chicago Daily News*. During the 1900 season Sensabaugh was writing a headline, and neither Orphans nor Spuds would fit. He substituted Cubs.

On March 27, 1902, the new nickname began to appear regularly. It was an endearing moniker that stuck with the team for the rest of its illustrious history: the Chicago Cubs.

It would not be long before the Chicago Cubs would develop into the greatest team in the history of National League baseball.

The two men primarily responsible for completing this juggernaut were scout George Huff and Frank Chance. Huff, who was Frank Selee's best scout, was the baseball coach at the University of Illinois. Huff discovered and sent to Chicago pitcher Carl Lundgren, one of his own players. He also signed pitcher Ed Reulbach from Notre Dame after chasing him cross-country and recommended that the Cubs get outfielder Frank "Wildfire" Schulte and star utility man Solly Hofman.

And it was Chance who rounded out the team by lobbying owner Jim Hart to trade catcher Larry McLean and pitcher Jack Taylor to St. Louis for catcher Jack O'Neill and Mordecai Brown, a rookie pitcher with only four fingers on his pitching hand. Hart was glad to get rid of Taylor, whom he petulantly accused of throwing games during the first intercity exhibition series with the White Sox after the 1903 season.

Johnny Evers, who was quick-tempered and renowned as one of the quickest minds in the game, greatly admired Frank Chance's skills as manager and player. It is Evers (with the aid of Chicago sportswriter Hugh Fullerton) who has provided a step-by-step account of the construction of Frank Chance's Cubs.

JOHNNY EVERS: "Chance, although only advisor to Selee, at once assumed the task of building up the team. He seemed to know just what men he wanted, and how to get them, as well as the weaknesses of his own team. His first move was to get Mordecai Brown. The Omaha management, desiring to keep Brown, told Selee his arm was bad, but Chance declined to believe it. Chance had been watching Brown and wanted him, but was overruled and St. Louis filed prior claim and secured him— but only temporarily. Chance was persistent, and when Jack Taylor fell into disgrace after the loss of the city championship, a deal was arranged whereby Taylor and McLean [who never pitched in the majors] were given to St. Louis for Brown, who had not pitched well there.

"Perhaps the great luck the Chicago club ever had was in forming an alliance with George Huff, athletic director of the University of Illinois, for the association of Huff with the club as scout marked an era in the making of the championship team. Huff's first contribution to the team was Carl Lundgren, the University of Illinois pitcher who had twice won the Intercollegiate championship for the school. Lundgren was quiet, studious and the 'Human Icicle,' one of the most careful observers of batters ever found. He was of the type that studies three aces and a pair of tens for two minutes before calling—and studies a pair of deuces just as hard. When he calls, he wins, and he pitched wonderful ball for Chicago.

"Late [in 1904] Scout Huff discovered three more men of championship calibre. The story of Huff's work that season reads like a Sherlock Holmes adventure, especially the tale of his pursuit of three ghostly pitchers. The story properly begins three years earlier, when Ed Reulbach, a giant youngster, was pitching for Notre Dame, Indiana, University. Reulbach is as near a physically perfect man as possible. [He stood six one, weighing 190 pounds.] Huff had seen his terrific speed and wonderful curves in college games and set watch on him. The next year, while beating the underbrush for young players, Huff began to receive reports from Sedalia, Mo., of a pitcher named Lawson and finally went there to see him pitch. The day before he reached Sedalia, Lawson disappeared, leaving no trace or clue. Huff wanted a pitcher, needed him, and hurried to find Reulbach, but imagine his surprise when, immediately after the close of school, Reulbach disappeared as utterly as Lawson had done, leaving no trace.

"Then Huff began to receive reports from Montpelier, Vermont, of a young pitcher who was winning everything in the Green Mountain league and whose name was Sheldon. Huff disguised himself as an alderman and went to Montpelier to see the new prodigy perform. The mystery was solved—Sheldon, Lawson and Reulbach all were pitching and they were one man; all Reulbach under assorted names. Huff straightened out the tangle and returned to Chicago with one of the greatest modern pitchers.

"Hart had heard that [Harry] McChesney of Des Moines was worth having and sent Huff to observe. Huff reported McChesney only a fair ball player, but that [Solly] Hofman, short stop, was one of the greatest players in the country. Both were purchased and Chicago thus accidentally secured the best utility man of modern times. Hofman played every infield and outfield position for Chicago during three pennant-winning seasons, being so good a substitute that Chance could not afford to use him as a regular until 1909 when he went to center field. Two seasons he saved the pennant for Chicago by understudying every man of the team who was injured, playing almost to the standard of every man he replaced. In one week he played six positions on the infield, and outfield.

"Hofman came into baseball from the amateurs of St. Louis. He played with Smith Academy team for a time, then with semi-professional teams in St. Louis and finally got into the Trolley League, where he became a contract jumper. His contract with East St. Louis guaranteed him $8 a game when weather conditions permitted play. One day the sun was shining, the weather warm and everything favorable, but the Mississippi River had risen and flooded the grounds. Hofman contended that weather did not prevent the game and claimed his money. The management refused to pay and Hofman jumped to Belleville, where Barney Dreyfuss found him in 1903, and took him to Pittsburgh, but immediately released him to Des Moines where Huff discovered him.

"Huff made one more important discovery that season. McCarthy's legs were giving way, and an outfielder was needed. Huff went to Syracuse to see Magee. He telegraphed Selee to get [Frank] Schulte, a quiet, droll New York state boy, and Mike Mitchell. Both were secured, but Chicago offered Mitchell less money than he was getting at Syracuse. He was forced to accept the offer, but openly stated he would not give his best efforts for the club, and so was lost to Chicago, Cincinnati securing a great player. Schulte quickly developed into one of the best players in the National League.

"Schulte proved to be the man needed. In him Chance had found one of the rarest baseball treasures, a 'third batter.' The third batter in any team is the most important. He must hit long flies, hit hard, bunt and run, because ahead of him in a well constructed team are two batters who are on the team for their ability to 'get on' and the third man must be able either to move them up or hit them home.

"The team, after eighteen years of effort, was growing strong, but not steady. It fought hard for the pennant in 1905, but was beaten. Chicago at last had a contender in the pennant race.

"Selee was sick, and he did things he would not have done had he been well. Having a team almost complete, he was kept from wrecking it only by Chance. Selee wanted to release Slagle; he wanted to let Evers go; he was so anxious to get rid of Hofman that he refused to permit him to practice on the diamond with the other players."

* * *

Midway through the 1905 season, Selee's health broke down. His tuberculosis had made him irritable, too ill to continue as manager. Selee held an election to see who would replace him as manager. Selee's choice was Doc Casey, his third baseman. Evers, and most everyone else, opted for Frank Chance.

JOHNNY EVERS: "[By 1905] Selee was sick, and really unable to perform the duties of manager. His sickness forced him to rely more and more upon the judgment of Chance, who suddenly developed a genius for handling men. [Bobby] Lowe was out of the game and a captain was needed. Selee decided to try something unheard of; to submit the election of a captain to the vote of the players themselves. There were three candidates, none especially active. Selee's choice was Casey; Kling and Chance both had admirers among the men. The election was held in the club house, Selee actively exerting his influence for Casey, while some of the players were urging Chance as the veteran of the squad. The result of the vote was Chance, 11, Casey 4, Kling 2. Selee was dumbfounded and for a time annoyed, but events proved the players had made the wisest selection and the vote was the turning point in the career of Chance and in the development of the club."

When tuberculosis forced Selee to go to Colorado in August 1905, owner Jim Hart, in one of his last acts before selling the team that winter to Charles Murphy and Charles Taft, ratified the players' choice of Chance as Selee's successor.

Selee moved to Colorado, and despite his serious illness, continued to manage, leading the Pueblo team. In 1909 he died in Denver of consumption. He was forty-nine.

The Chicago team's new owner, C. Webb "Charlie" Murphy, like the American League czar Ban Johnson, began as a baseball writer from Cincinnati. There he met John Brush, and in 1905 he was Brush's press agent and secretary when Brush tipped him off that Jim Hart wanted to sell the Cubs. Murphy moved quickly. After securing an option to buy the team, he took the train to Cincinnati, where he succeeded in getting Charles P. Taft, half-brother of William Howard, later the President, to finance him, since he had only $15,000 of his own money. The purchase price was reported by the *Cincinnati Enquirer* to be $105,000. As part of the deal Frank Chance was given one hundred shares of stock.

After Murphy took over, during the winter of 1905–6 he and Chance completed the Cubs' building process, finishing the puzzle by adding outfielder Jimmy Sheckard, pitcher Orvie Overall, and the talented third baseman Harry Steinfeldt, one of the most famous trivia answers in the history of sports.

JOHNNY EVERS: "In the middle of the season Selee's illness forced him to surrender and Chance was chosen as manager. The big, awkward youngster who had joined the team at West Baden seven years earlier, suddenly showed himself a great baseball leader. The day he took charge of the team he said: 'We need pitchers, we must have a new third baseman, and a hitting outfielder before we can win the pennant.'

"[Doc] Casey was playing a fair third base and [Billy] Maloney was a sensational, if erratic, outfielder, and was the idol of the crowd. That winter the team was sold by Hart, who had spent so many years trying to create a winner, to C. Webb Murphy, who gave Chance absolute power as far as playing and getting players was concerned.

"Chance knew the men he wanted. He wanted four; and three of them he got. To get the first one he made one of the most spectacular deals ever recorded in baseball history. This man was James Sheckard, a brilliant, clever and much wanted outfielder who had disturbed the Brooklyn club by playing hop scotch with the American League during the war. Here the gossip of the club proved valuable. Sheckard was dissatisfied with Brooklyn, and Chance knew it. The Brooklyn management did not think Sheckard was giving his best services, but feared to trade a man who was popular with the spectators. The trade Chance made to get Sheckard stunned Chicago followers of the game. He gave Outfielders [Jack] McCarthy and Maloney, Third Baseman Casey and Pitcher Herbert [Buttons] Briggs, with $2,000 added. Chance was satisfied. His outfield was complete at last. He swung Schulte to right field, his natural position, put Sheckard in left, and with Slagle in center regarded the work as finished.

"Chance realized third base must be filled or his pennant hopes would filter away at that corner. He knew the man he wanted, Harry Steinfeldt, who was playing indifferent ball with Cincinnati. He was slow, a heavy hitter, a good fielder and a wonderful thrower. Again inside gossip directed Chance to a man while older managers, not closely in touch with players, listened to other stories. Chance knew Steinfeldt had played with him two winters in California, and knew also that internal dissentions were causing the trouble in the Cincinnati ranks. The Cincinnati club was anxious to trade Steinfeldt, but gossip among his enemies in Cincinnati had kept other clubs from bidding for the player. Chance asked Murphy to make a trade. Murphy went to Cincinnati, but the stories whispered to him sent him flying back to Chicago without the player. A few days later Murphy asked Chance: 'What third baseman can we get?'

"'Steinfeldt.'

"Murphy argued, but went to Cincinnati again and returned without the player, but with even more startling stories to tell Chance. 'Who shall we get?' he asked.

"'Steinfeldt.'

"So Murphy, still unconvinced, went to Cincinnati and traded [Jake] Weimer, a left-handed pitcher, for Steinfeldt.

"The team was complete at last. The day Steinfeldt signed, Chance remarked that if he could add a little pitching strength the team would win the pennant.

"Huff was sent in frantic search of the additional pitching strength and recommended Jack Pfiester, a big left-hander who, after a career extending all over America, was pitching for Omaha well and often. Pfiester had a non-reserve contract with Omaha, so he owned himself, and when Huff and Chance tried to get him they dealt with him direct and purchased him for $2,500. Still Chance was not content. He wanted another strong catcher to assist Kling and he traded for Pat Moran, who had for five years hit well and caught steady ball for Boston. Then he profited again by his knowledge of players and the inside gossip of teams. He knew Overall was a fine pitcher, and he knew that the reason Overall was not pitching well for Cincinnati was that he was being overworked and was weak. Chance had played with Overall in California, had attempted to buy him from Tacoma when Cincinnati secured him, and had kept constant watch on the giant young pitcher. He knew better than Manager [Ned] Hanlon of Cincinnati how to handle the man—and believed he could win. A deal was made—Chance giving [pitcher Bob] Wicker for Overall and $2,000, a deal which proved the joke of the season.

"The team was complete; finished in every detail and with the pitching staff working like machinery, it swept through the season of 1906 breaking all records, winning 116 games and losing only 36."

14

The Peerless Leader

By 1906, Frank Chance had molded the Cubs into his image, tough and smart. Chance was one of the rare men who didn't need baseball to make his living. He had attended Washington University, studied dentistry, and was playing ball on the side when he was recommended to the Cubs by Cap Anson. Chance was not colorful like John McGraw and he was not from New York like McGraw, so there wasn't much written about him in the national publications, but those who knew him talked first about his toughness and then about his smarts.

Toughness became part of his legend. At bat he insisted on crowding the plate. On a May 4, 1904, doubleheader he was hit by the pitcher three times in the first game, tying the major league record. In the second game he was hit twice more. Though he was hit in the head thirty-six times by pitched balls and finally had to have a brain operation, no pitcher ever succeeded in making him back away from the plate.

One time the ruthless Chance was able to exact his own brand of revenge against a pitcher who threw at him. After Jack Harper of Cincinnati hit Chance in the head with a pitch early in the 1906 season, the Cubs manager persuaded owner Charles Murphy to trade for Harper, who had won 23 games in 1904 and 10 games in 1905. When the pitcher arrived in Chicago, Chance cut his salary from the $4,500 he had been getting in Cincy to $1,500. Chance told Harper he could sign or quit.

After Harper signed, Chance kept him on the bench, refusing to pitch him. Harper appealed to the National Commission but lost. Defeated, Harper quit baseball.

And yet, despite all the times he was hit, Chance insisted that for a pitcher to win he had to be able to keep the opposing batters off the plate.

JOHNNY EVERS: "One of the Chicago pitchers, at the start of his career, was timid, and the batters kept encroaching upon the plate and hitting his curve ball. Chance instructed the pitcher to hit one batter in the first inning of every game he pitched until the batters were driven back. The pitcher followed orders and after he had pitched once against each opposing team the batters were driven back until he became a success."

At six feet and 188 pounds Chance had intimidating size, which he used to his advantage. He was also proficient with his fists. During the off-season he was a professional boxer, rated by a Boston paper as the best boxer of all major league players. (This certainly contributed to his brain injuries.) James J. Corbett, the heavyweight champ, once said that Chance was one of the best amateur fighters he had ever seen.

For the most part Chance didn't need to use his pugilistic skills. But "if two players didn't get along together, he'd knock their heads together," said catcher Jimmy Archer, who played with Chance beginning in 1909. Chance's word was law and ordinarily unquestioned.

One time Solly Hofman asked his manager if he could get married. It was mid-September, and Chance told him he could not marry until after the season was over. Hofman complied.

"I guess [fiancée] Miss Looker and I can wait," said Hofman. "She's as anxious to have the Cubs win as I am."

If a player did not comply with his wishes or did not show him the respect he felt he deserved, Chance acted swiftly and surely. One time Chance sent pitcher Chick Fraser home early from a road trip to get his arm in shape to pitch an important Sunday game. The team arrived home Sunday morning, and Chance discovered the pitcher hadn't shown up at the ballpark at all. He immediately wrote Fraser's unconditional release.

In 1913, when Chance was managing the New York Yankees, he discovered that first baseman Hal Chase was making fun of him. Chance was deaf in one ear, so when they were on the bench, Chase made sure he sat on Chance's deaf side, mimicking his manager's throaty commands and imitating his facial expressions, a pastime for which Hal had a real gift.

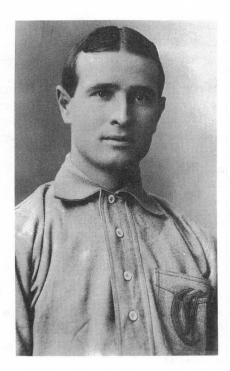

Frank Chance

When a player loyal to Chance told him what Hal had been up to, Chase very suddenly found himself traded away.

It was the rare player who offended Chance sufficiently to cause a fight. One time in Chicago, Chance became aware that Heinie Zimmerman was politicking with other players to form a clique against him.

"There's only one way to settle this," he told Zimmerman. "If you lick me, I'll resign as manager and maybe you'll get the job." Zimmerman, who later was thrown out of baseball for dishonesty, foolishly accepted Chance's challenge. The manager pummeled him.

Chance, moreover, was not averse to letting one of his players fight when it was called for. One time second baseman Dick Egan of Cincinnati got furious at Joe Tinker when Tinker executed a vicious slide into second. The two men had words, and Egan challenged Tinker to a fight, telling him that as "soon as this game's over I'm gonna knock your blank-blank-blank head off!"

Tinker accepted the challenge. Though hot-tempered, the Cubs shortstop cooled off rapidly, and by the time the game ended he had forgotten about the dispute. Not so Egan, who waited outside the dressing room and then went inside, only to find that Tinker had just departed.

"He's yellow!" cried Egan. "He's run out on me."

Frank Chance spoke up.

"Joe Tinker never ran away from a fight in his life. I'll get him for you."

Chance ran out onto the field and saw Tinker just passing second base, heading for the exit.

"Hey, Joe," yelled Chance, and Joe turned around just in time to see the bellicose Egan racing toward him, fists clenched.

According to writers Ira and H. Allen Smith, Tinker calmly removed his coat, and in a moment the battle was on inside a circle of ballplayers. It lasted perhaps five minutes; witnesses said few men ever took such a beating in that length of time as Egan got from Tinker. When it was over, Tinker's hair wasn't even ruffled, though unbiased witnesses said he did have to straighten his tie a little.

Chance's players respected him because he treated his players like adults. According to Jimmy Archer, the Cubs manager understood well the importance of allowing his players to blow off steam by having a few drinks. After home games, which were played at the old Cubs Park on Chicago's West Side, Chance would take the team to a saloon across the street called Biggio Brothers on the southwest corner of Polk and Lincoln Streets. He'd always buy the first drink. When a player had had enough, the bartenders knew to refuse to sell him any more drinks.

If the game was rained out, the booze was on the manager. Drinking would begin around three or three-thirty. According to Jimmy Archer, Chance had a rule that the players had to be out of the bar by a quarter to midnight!

JIMMY ARCHER: "When we'd get rained out, we'd be sitting around the clubhouse. Then Chance would come in. 'What have I got here, a Sunday school club?' he'd say. We'd all go to a saloon. You couldn't buy a drink. Chance would buy them all. Then at 11:45 [P.M.], he'd say, 'Drink up,' and we'd head for our rooms. You had to be—not in your hotel—but in your room by midnight. He insisted that every player be called at eight in the morning and if you weren't in the dining room by nine you didn't eat."

Chance also preferred his players to bet on the horses and play poker. He didn't agree with many of his fellow managers that betting on horses was demoralizing to baseball players. He once told a reporter, "I figure that a little bet now and then results in moderate excitement which, I really believe, helps to stir up mental activity."

According to Johnny Evers, poker also stirred up that "mental activity." Though he made sure the players didn't gamble for high stakes, Chance didn't trust a ballplayer who wasn't proficient at cards.

JOHNNY EVERS: "Chance never has dabbled in psychological experimentation on a scientific basis, but he can discover how rapidly a ball player thinks more quickly in a poker game than in any other way and thus saves the expense of carrying some player for months only to have him lose a game because his convolutions fail to revolve fast enough.

"Chance permits poker playing with a twenty-five-cent limit, but all games must stop by eleven o'clock. He stepped into a hotel room at midnight once and discovered five of his players and a newspaper man playing dollar limit. . . .

"'That will cost each of you $25,' he said quietly, 'not so much for playing as for deliberately disobeying the limit rule.'

"Every man in the game was a veteran.

"'I wouldn't mind you older players doing it,' Chance continued, 'but you're setting the worst kind of example to the young ones. As for you,' he added, turning to the reporter, 'I'll not give you a piece of news for a month.'

"'Can't I pay the fine and get the news?' inquired the reporter.

"'Sure, that will punish you and not the paper,' replied Chance.

"Later on, Chance was playing poker beyond the time limit and fined himself $25."

Chance, who came to the Cubs one year after the departure of Cap Anson, turned out to be as superior a player-manager as Anson had been. He played great defense in the field, and he was an outstanding base stealer for a man his size. Chance today still holds the Cubs single-season record for stolen bases with 67, set in 1903.

JIMMY ARCHER: "Chance was great on balls in the dirt. He'd step back to take them waist high or step into them. I never saw a better first baseman on the play. He wasn't fast, but he stole plenty of bases. He knew how to get the jump on the pitcher."

In one game against Cincinnati, Chance singled. Then, with one out, he stole second. Joe Tinker was next up; everybody expected him to hit away. Instead he laid down a bunt. Chance started running for third—but didn't stop. He kept right on going and slid safely into the plate, a remarkable display of skill, speed, and hustle.

As manager, Chance played the kind of baseball that exemplified the dead-ball-era game. His strategy was to manufacture the one run that would win the ball game. He was credited with inventing the delayed steal, though Johnny Evers refuted the claim. ("Kelly, Hamilton, Lange, O'Neill, Comiskey, Duffy, and many others used the play," said Evers.) Regardless, Chance relied on the steal and also the bunt, especially the sacrifice. His Cubs were also proficient at using the bunt as an offensive weapon. Johnny Evers recalled how the Cubs could execute the force bunt and also the bluff bunt.

JOHNNY EVERS: "The Chicago Cubs used the force bunt during all their championship term, pushing the ball, instead of bunting it dead, a short distance in front of the plate. Their success with the ball was marvelous.

"In one game at Philadelphia [Joe] Tinker made the bunt with two men on bases, pushing a slow roller toward short stop. [Mickey] Doolan was running to cover second base and the ball rolled clear onto the grass behind short stop, Tinker taking two bases.

"During the seasons of 1906 and 1907 [Jimmy] Sheckard used a bluff bunt which worked with great success. He bunted at the first ball pitched to him, and purposely missed it. Then he bluffed that he intended bunting again and, as the third baseman tore forward, Sheckard poked the ball over his head."

As a manager Chance expected his men to make the plays and not screw up. He forgave errors, just as long as the players tried. But nobody could last with him if he pulled boneheaded plays or didn't hustle. You had to be able to take direction and execute to play on Frank Chance's Cubs.

JIMMY ARCHER: "I was picking up a bat one day. I said to Chance, 'What do you want me to do?' He said, 'You're over 21. Go up there and see what you can do.' He didn't tell you what to do. If you made a mistake, he pointed it out later.

"He'd simply tell you to 'put em' [bunt] or 'send em' [hit and run]. With a tough pitcher, we'd bunt, bunt, bunt—every man—until we had him with his tongue out. Then we'd play for the big inning."

Chance wanted players who were continually thinking about the game.

JIMMY ARCHER: "No man can think for nine players. In our day, every player thought for himself. We'd talk baseball all the time. We'd go out for a beer after the game and we'd be talking about the other team. How to stop a guy who was hot. How to pitch to a certain player. We thought baseball and ate it too."

JOHNNY EVERS: "There was an odd play introduced on the Polo Grounds which was the result of a 'fanning match' [gab session] the previous evening. [New York Giant catcher Roger] Bresnahan and several of the Chicago players were discussing plays and arguing the chances of one umpire seeing everything that takes place, all conceding it to be impossible. A reporter who was present suggested that, when the one umpire was behind the plate and either a bunt or hit-and-run was attempted, the umpire always ran down into the diamond in front of the play in order to see a play either at first or second base, and that the catcher could, therefore, stop, trip or interfere with the batter without the slightest danger of being seen. Later in the evening, the reporter, meeting Kling, asked his opinion of the possibility of such a play.

"The following day, early in the game, Chicago had a runner on first base and the batter tried to sacrifice. Bresnahan cut in ahead of the runner, bumped him off his feet, and after the other runner had been forced at second the luckless batter was doubled at first base. Two innings later Kling did the same thing to a New York batter, tripping him so he was thrown out on a hit that probably would have been safe. Twice after that the catchers took advantage of the umpire and interfered with batters until the crowd was roaring with indignation. The play had one result—there were two umpires on the field the following day."

Once the game started Chance and the other Cubs watched the other team closely, looking to see if they could steal signals and then respond accordingly. One of the reasons the Cubs were so outstanding was that it was hard to outmaneuver the quick-thinking Frank Chance. The average fan couldn't see it, but on every pitch, the minds of the Cubs players were working hard. This was a *team*, a group of players working as a unit.

HUGH FULLERTON: "When [Cubs catcher Pat] Moran knelt down he put the index finger of his right hand straight down, then held it horizontally on the top of his mitt, Evers saw that Moran had signaled Reulbach to pitch a fast ball high and outside the plate. He rubbed his hand in the dirt, signaling Tinker, who patted his right hand upon his glove, replying he understood. Then Evers rested his hand upon his hip, signaling Sheckard, the outfield captain, what ball was to be pitched. Sheckard crept toward the spot where [Mike] Mitchell would hit that kind of a ball 95 out of 100 times. While Reulbach was 'winding up' swinging his arm to throw the ball, Evers called sharply to Chance (whose good ear is toward him), and Tinker called to Steinfeldt. While Reulbach's arm was swinging every man in the team was moving automatically toward right field, in full motion before Mitchell hit the ball.

"Every man on the team knew that if Reulbach pitched high, fast and outside, Mitchell would hit toward right field. The only chance Mitchell had to hit safe was to drive the ball over the head of the outfielders, or hit it on a line over 7 feet and less than 15 feet above the ground. If Reulbach had been ordered to pitch low and over the plate, or low and inside, or a slow ball, the team would have shifted exactly the opposite way."

Johnny Evers recalled a game against Cincinnati in which the Cubs knew every move the Reds were going to make.

JOHNNY EVERS: "In one game Evers and Kling analyzed and discovered every hit and run signal used by the Cincinnati club merely by their powers of observation. [John] Ganzel, then manager of the club, signaled entirely by words, and by close attention and listening for every unnatural phrase or expression the Cubs secured the entire code used by their opponents, and knew as well as Cincinnati players what Ganzel was ordering."

And then the Cubs were at bat, more brainwork was at work. With Frank Chance calling the shots, the Cubs had the advantage.

*   *   *

JOHNNY EVERS: "To show how closely the two teams watched each other, Cincinnati was playing Chicago with Frank Roth catching for the former team. Runners were on first and third. Roth signaled to the pitcher for a curve; Chance saw the signal and flashed a delayed double steal order. [Cincinnati second baseman Miller] Huggins caught that signal, the Reds switched positions rapidly, and Roth signaled for a pitch-out. The pitch-out was detected by [Chicago's third-base coach] Kane, and Chance signaled for a change. The result was the runners held their bases, and the pitcher wasted a ball. Roth signaled again, the infield changed, and Chance ordered the delayed steal. Roth was warned and ordered another pitch-out, but no sooner had he flashed that signal and Chance had ordered another wait, than Roth ordered a fast straight ball pitched, thinking to out-guess Chance. But as Roth changed his signal Chance, guessing he would do exactly that thing, signaled a hit and run, with the result that a base hit tore through the infield and broke up the game."

As a manager Chance had certain philosophies. He was a firm believer that a batter should take pitches, especially at the start of the game. Taking pitches, Chance believed, enabled a batter to familiarize himself with the pitcher. And after the at bat, the batter was expected to pass on his knowledge to the rest of the team. A batter who couldn't do that didn't last long on the Cubs.

JOHNNY EVERS: "Chance is a great believer in the waiting game, and insists upon his men trying out pitchers during the early innings of games, especially new and unfamiliar pitchers, believing that what each man discovers will help the succeeding batters.

"A few years ago the Chicago club purchased a player late in the season who was one of the great batters of the American Association. His hitting helped the team to win the pennant, yet Chance released him without even bringing him to Chicago to play the final games. The act surprised the followers of the Cubs and someone asked Chance why the man was released.

"'First ball hitter,' explained Chance."

Like many great managers, Frank Chance was a happy winner but a sore loser.

JIMMY ARCHER: "One time we won thirteen straight games, then lost the fourteenth in the tenth inning 2 to 1. He came in and threw his bat through the piano and threw all the tables out of the clubhouse. Nobody dared to speak to him for several days after that."

Few managers ever accepted defeat as reluctantly as Chance. One day he stamped blackly out of the park. The Cubs had left a lot of runners on base and lost.

After he arrived home Chance refused to eat dinner but just sat in the living room, glowering at the wall. His wife tried hard to comfort him, to no avail. She sat on the arm of his chair and stroked his hair.

"Don't worry, dear," she said. "You still have me."

"I know that," he grunted, "but many a time this afternoon I'd have traded you for a base hit."

15

116–36

When the 1906 season started, Chicago's new owner, Charles Murphy, said to Chance, "Frank, I think I've given you a pretty good team. McGraw says he'll win again, but you should give him a real fight."

Even Murphy didn't know how good a team the Cubs had become. Chance's men finished the 1906 season with 116 victories, a total that has never been equaled, not even by the New York Yankees at their best. At Cubs Park they were 56–21, and on the road their record was an even better 60–15. In August they won twenty-six and lost three. At the end of the season the Cubs won fifty of their last fifty-seven.

The 1906 Cubs finished a full twenty games ahead of McGraw and his second-place Giants.

In 1906 the Cubs had a solid offense. The team finished first in the league in batting average at .262.

During this dead-ball era the team's 20 home runs was second only to Brooklyn's 25. Occasionally the Cubs did erupt, as on June 7, 1906, when they beat the Giants, 19–0, beating Christy Mathewson, who allowed six runs in only one-third of an inning.

The great majority of games were low-scoring and decided by one run. Getting on, moving runners, stealing bases, getting the run home was the way the Cubs won. They stole 283 bases, best in the league, with Frank Chance himself leading the league with 57. Inevitably, the Cubs, who played for the one run that would win the ball game, would be victorious because it was especially difficult to score against them.

Frank Chance, like most great managers, built his team around pitching and defense. In 1906 his pitching staff had a team earned run average of 1.76. Mordecai Brown led the staff with a 26–6 record and a 1.04 ERA. Jack Pfiester finished 20–8 with a 1.56 ERA, followed by Ed Reulbach (19–4, 1.65) and Carl Lundgren (17–6, 2.21).

Jack Taylor, whom Murphy had gotten back from St. Louis in a trade on July 1, had been 8–9 with the Cards but was 12–3 with a 1.84 ERA with the Cubs. Orvie Overall was also 12–3 with a 1.88 ERA.

Brown, Pfiester, and Reulbach finished 1-2-3 in the league in earned run average. The Cubs staff threw 28 shutouts. Brown had ten by himself.

Brown, who was born with the name Mordecai Peter Centennial Brown, was elected into the Hall of Fame in 1949. The Centennial part of the name came from his having been born in 1876. In the papers he was referred to as Miner Brown because as a youth he had worked the coal mines of Indiana. His other nickname was Three-Finger Brown, a reference to an accident he had had at the age of seven while playing in the Nyesville, Indiana, wheat fields when he fell and caught his right hand in the whirling mechanism of a grain-cutter being operated by his older brother. Doctors had to amputate the index finger above his knuckle. They saved his pinky finger, though he no longer could use it. (And thus, even though he was called Three-Finger Brown, he actually had four fingers.)

During recovery, Brown fell while chasing a hog and broke the third and fourth fingers. His hand was a mangled mess.

Despite the disfigurement of his right hand, Brown, a side-armer, could still throw very hard. His curve devastated right-handed batters. After he spent his rookie year with the St. Louis Cardinals in 1903, the Cubs acquired him, and he became the cornerstone of the greatest of all National League teams.

One of Brown's teammates on the Cubs, Johnny Evers, recalled that it was because of the pitcher's deformed finger that he was able to get such great bite on his curve.

JOHNNY EVERS: "Mordecai Brown's 'hook' curve is the highest present development of the fast overhand curve pitch which breaks sharply down and outward. Brown probably owes much of his success to a feed chopper which cut off part of his right hand, leaving him without an index finger and with the middle finger bent at right angles at the first joint. Brown pitches the 'hook' overhand, releasing the ball at various points after his hand swings past his body. By the point at which he releases the ball he regulates the point at which it breaks in the air. He can make the ball either describe a wide fast arc, or by jerking his hand at the proper instant, make the ball go in almost a straight line, perhaps fifty feet, and then dart suddenly down and outward."

Another of Brown's teammates, catcher Jimmy Archer, recalled the remarkable control he possessed.

Mordecai Brown

JIMMY ARCHER: "Pitchers were pitchers in those days—not throwers. They knew the batters and they had wonderful control. I remember Mordecai Brown pitching five games in one week. They'd pitch double headers so they could get their turn at the team they knew they could beat.

"One time I was warming up Brown, and Bill Klem, the umpire, pushed me aside. He put a piece of paper the size of a half dollar on the ground. 'That's the only target that fellow needs to pitch to,' Klem said. And he was right."

After contributing 15 wins to the Cubs' cause in 1904 and 18 in 1905, beginning in 1906, Brown (his teammates, eschewing the other more colorful nicknames, called him Brownie) contributed six straight seasons of 20 victories or more (26, 20, 29, 27, 25, and 21). Most important, he had a knack for beating their bitter rivals, John McGraw and the New York Giants, and their ace pitcher, Christy Mathewson.

Al Bridwell, who played shortstop behind Mathewson from 1908 through the first half of the 1911 season, had great respect for Brown.

AL BRIDWELL: "Three-Fingered Brown, gee, he was one of the wonders of base-ball. What a tremendous pitcher he was. Just as good as Matty, in my book. Better, maybe. The two of them used to hook up all the time, and I think over the years Brown beat Matty way over half the time."

Bridwell was correct. Brown and Matty met a total of twenty-four times, and Brownie won thirteen times against the man reputed to be the best pitcher ever, including nine in a row from July 12, 1905, through October 8, 1908.

On defense the Cubs, led by the Steinfeldt, Tinker, Evers, and Chance infield, with Johnny Kling behind the plate, became the first team in history to commit fewer than two hundred errors in a season (194 in 1906).

Johnny Kling, nee Kline, was one of the best catchers of his day. Kling was a holler-type player generally called "the Jew" by his teammates. He was one of the first catchers to throw from a crouch, a skill he learned from Buddy Petway, who earned his own fame catching in the Negro Leagues. Before Kling did it most catchers would stand, stride, and throw. After Kling saw Petway just snap his wrist, Kling copied him, and so it was Kling who introduced the snap throw to the National League, where it soon became standard practice.

When Johnny Evers was asked to list the "great" players in 1910, his list included Ty Cobb, Honus Wagner, Tris Speaker, Christy Mathewson, Mordecai Brown, Pitts-burgh's Tommy Leach, and Kling. Of that group only Leach and Kling have not made the Hall of Fame. Both belong there.

According to Evers, not only was Kling expert at throwing out runners in key situations, but his ability to get umpires to call pitches his way made him one of the very best.

JOHNNY EVERS: "In this particular of catching runners in the crucial moments of games John Kling was the greatest in the business. His ability and his coolness in that style of play alone was enough to stamp him the best of catchers. Kling prob-ably did not catch as many runners in a season as some other catchers did, but he caught them always at the right moments, when they counted, and scores of games won by the Cubs during their championship career was due to that alone.

"Kling had a great advantage in having such an infield to throw to, but when Kling signaled his intention of throwing the others were so full of confidence that they executed the play with absolute certainty.

"Kling is a past master of the art of working umpires on balls and strikes, which is one of the duties of a catcher that is not suspected by the spectators. The importance of 'getting the corners' is realized by all players, and the catcher who gets this advantage is invaluable to his club.

"Kling's method was to be friendly with all umpires, siding with them, telling them they were right, and frequently whispering to them to be on the guard for a certain curve that was coming. He urged them not to pay attention to other players, and while never openly criticising umpires, he occasionally whispered that he thought the ball might have been over the corner."

With Kling behind the plate, Chance at first, and the others all thinking and analyzing every situation like baseball computers, rarely was there a team in the game's history that had such an advantage when it came to anticipation and execution. These Cubs simply outsmarted everybody else.

JOHNNY EVERS: "Late [one year] Boston presented a new outfielder who never had played in a major league before, and no one on the Chicago club knew him or ever had seen him play ball, yet they were perfectly familiar with him, his peculiarities, batting habits, and disposition. On the way to the grounds Brown and Reulbach, one of whom was to pitch, went minutely over that new man, analyzing his position at bat, the way he swung at a ball, the kind of ball he could hit, and what he could not, and exactly how fast he could reach first base. Steinfeldt was warned that the man was dangerous and a tricky bunter, and that he always bunted toward third. When the pitchers got through discussing the newcomer, Kling and Chance analyzed him as a base runner.

"'I think,' Kling remarked, 'we can catch that fellow a couple of times if he gets on base today. If he reaches second I'll pull off that delayed throw. Let Joe [Tinker] cover and Johnny [Evers] stall.'

"In the third inning of the game the unfortunate youngster reached second base on a hit and a sacrifice. On the first ball pitched to the next batter he raced up toward third. Kling motioned as if to throw, Tinker covered second base like a flash, and Evers stood still. The recruit at first made a jump toward second base, then seeing Kling had not thrown, he slowed down. Tinker, walking back past him, remarked, 'We'd have caught you that time, old pal, if the Jew had thrown.' For just one fatal trice the youngster turned his face to retort to Tinker's remark, and in that instant Kling threw. Evers met the ball at second base, jabbed it against the runner, and before he knew what had happened he was out. That man really caught the 'bus on the way to the ball grounds,' for the play was executed exactly as Kling planned."

Patrolling up the middle behind the pitcher—the heart of the Cubs defense—were two aggressive, talented battlers named Joe Tinker and Johnny Evers. Tinker, the

Joe Tinker

Cubs shortstop, was arrogant and carried a chip on his shoulder. He rarely said much but, if provoked, wouldn't hesitate to fight.

At bat Tinker was expert at working the pitcher for a base on balls, and every year with the Cubs he stole between twenty and forty-one bases. A lifetime .263 hitter, Tinker earned fame for his ability to hit Giants pitching star Christy Mathewson.

But it was on defense that he shone, solid, steady, making all the routine plays and often the spectacular ones. After one particularly impressive performance against the New York Giants, W. A. Phelon of the *Chicago Journal* wrote: "The fans saw the Cubs . . . put up a defense that was magnificent, and they saw Joe Tinker.

"Mr. Tinker was the whole works in several innings. It was his stop and throw to the plate that started a double play killing off the Giants with the bases full and runs sprouting like alfalfa in Pasadena. It was his superb pickup and hurl to first that beat [Al] Bridwell to the base by the eightieth of a step and saved another bundle of runs, and finally Joe delivered the goods with one of the greatest wallops ever scored on any field."

Tinker, however, said so little he was rarely quoted in the newspapers.

Evers, Tinker's keystone partner at second base, rarely shut up. He was the National League's equivalent of Ty Cobb, a brilliant player who was abusive and abrasive, someone prone to sarcasm and invective. His constant stream of heckling was so irritating that Frank Chance once admitted he would have preferred that Evers played the outfield.

Like Cobb, Evers was a sour, humorless character. He was appropriately nick-named the Crab. Like Cobb, he was not averse to sliding into a runner with spikes high. Like Cobb, he had a running feud with the umpires.

One time Evers got into an argument with umpire Bill Klem over a call. To settle the dispute, Evers said, "I will leave it to the league office."

"That suits me," replied Klem. "I'll see you at the office in the morning."

"I'll bet you five bucks you don't show up," Evers retorted.

"You're on," Klem spat.

Evers arrived at the headquarters, which was in Chicago, in the morning, but Klem failed to show up. In the days that followed, whenever Klem umpired a game played by the Cubs, every time he came to bat Evers would ask for his five dollars. Then he would obnoxiously draw a figure five with his bat in the dirt in front of home plate. In the field he would continually scream at Klem, and whenever he could get the umpire's attention, he would hold up his ungloved hand with the four fingers and thumb spread wide apart.

According to former Hall of Fame president Lee Allen, "The running battle was not concluded until one night when Evers cornered Klem in a smoking car on the ride from Chicago to Pittsburgh. This time Klem paid off. Evers wrote out a receipt and handed it to Klem, who then tore it into a thousand pieces."

*   *   *

John Evers

Evers plagued the opposition in so many ways. He was a superb sign stealer. Former Giants immortal Christy Mathewson recalled the time Evers learned the language of the deaf in order to steal the Giants' signs.

CHRISTY MATHEWSON: "In giving his signs from the bench to the players, McGraw depends on a gesture or catch word. When 'Dummy' Taylor, the deaf and dumb twirler, was with the club, all the players learned the deaf and dumb language. This medium was used for signing for a time, until smart ballplayers, like Evers and [Tommy] Leach, took up the study of it and became so proficient they could converse fluently on their fingers. But they were also great 'listeners' and we didn't discover for some time that this was how they were getting our signs. Thereafter we only used the language for social purposes.

"Evers and McGraw got into a conversation one day in the deaf and dumb language at long range and 'Johnny' Evers threw a finger out of joint replying to McGraw in a brilliant flash of repartee."

Evers had such a high energy level that for a time a great many baseball fans actually believed that he was charged by electricity. At the turn of the century electrical power was not fully understood by the public, and the unknowing sometimes gave it powers it did not in fact possess.

Fans would remark, "See old Johnny Evers out yonder? They say he's all charged up with a lotta 'lectricity buzzin' around in him. Wouldn't doubt it at all, at all."

According to Ira and H. Allen Smith, "One would have thought that Johnny Evers was an article turned out by Mr. Edison in his Jersey laboratory."

Evers himself was aware of the stories, and he helped them along and contributed to them. He announced one day that he did not want any of his admirers to give him any more watches; he said they were no good to him. The minute he started carrying a watch, he said, it ceased to give accurate time—the electrical currents in his body fouled up the mechanism.

At least one sportswriter took him seriously, for he wrote: "That just seems to indicate that there is something unusual—some special kind of energy currents—that you find in ballplayers who are exceptionally endowed with vim and liveliness."

The fanciful poet Ogden Nash once wrote an inventive four-liner about John Evers. As part of his "Line-up for Yesterday: An ABC of Baseball Immortals," he wrote:

> *E is for Evers,*
> *His jaw in advance;*
> *Never afraid*
> *To Tinker with Chance.*

The great irony of the Tinker-Evers partnership was that the two were so similar in nature that for many years they were at odds and spoke to each other only when absolutely necessary. Off the field they avoided each other, going their separate ways.

The dispute that caused the rift arose on September 13, 1905. The Cubs were playing an exhibition game in Bedford, Indiana. In the middle of the game, the spectators were surprised when Tinker and Evers began swinging at each other near second base. The fight was broken up, and no one wrote about it in the papers afterward.

According to Lee Allen, this was what happened:

LEE ALLEN: "The Cubs that day had dressed at a local hotel and were supposed to ride out to the ball park in hacks. Evers got into a hack by himself and drove off, leaving Tinker and several others on the sidewalk. Tinker was sore, and when he reached the field, he told Evers how he felt. They began jawing at each other in the early innings, one word led to another, and then they fought.

"The next day Joe went to Johnny and said, 'Look, Evers. If you and I talk to each other, we're only going to be fighting all the time. So don't talk to me, and I won't talk to you. You play your position and I'll play mine, and let it go at that.'

"'That suits me,' Evers said."

Despite their mutual disaffection, the two men nevertheless played side by side for most of eleven seasons. Their defensive wizardry led the Cubs to five pennants and two world championships. They knew each other so well that they could almost read each other's mind out on the field. They had a private signal for almost every move they planned to make, and they practiced and played together so constantly that sometimes the signals were almost superfluous. Their tactics could, and often did, disrupt whatever the opponents were planning. In the past with a runner on first and a steal situation coming up, the second baseman covered no matter who was at bat. Tinker and Evers changed that. They realized that a left-handed batter was more apt to pull the ball through the second-base hole, and so they worked out a system whereby if they suspected the other team was going to hit and run with a lefty at bat, they would silently gesture to each other, and Tinker would instead cover from his shortstop position. Evers would hold his ground, the batter would hit the ball right to him, and the Cubs would complete a double play, when any other team would find itself with runners on first and third.

According to Evers, he and Tinker devised another trick play that fooled opposing hitters and resulted in double plays.

JOHNNY EVERS: "Tinker and [I] plotted a play a few years ago that caught many men and furnished the spectators much joy. When a hit and run play is attempted and the batter hits a fly to the outfield, the base runner hearing the crack of the bat, must judge from actions of the fielders in front of him what has happened. When such a situation came up Tinker and [I] went through all the motions of trying to stop a grounder, or diving after a hit. The runner would fear being forced out at second and tear along under the impression the ball had gone through the infield. Sometimes he would be nearly to third base before the outfielder, catching the ball, would toss it to the first baseman and complete the double play. Sherwood Magee was caught three times in one season on the play, and finally in Philadelphia, the Cubs tried it again. Magee, not to be caught again, gave them a laugh and jogged back to first, whereupon Schulte dropped the ball, threw it to second, and Tinker fired it back to first, completing the double play."

It is very rare when ballplayers gain recognition for their defense. Only a handful of defensive stars in baseball history have ever been rewarded by a sporting public fixated on offensive statistics and the home run. But by the year 1908, Tinker and Evers had become known for their uncanny ability for making double plays at crucial moments in ball games. When the Chicago newspaper reporter Warren Brown checked into just how many Tinker to Evers to Chance (6-4-3) double plays there were, he found that during the four brightest years of their stardom, there were eight in 1906, seven in 1907, eight in 1908, and six in 1909, for a total of 29.

As for Evers to Tinker to Chance (4-6-3), in 1906 there were nine, in 1907 there were six, in 1908 they made eight, and in 1909 they made two, for a total of 25.

In all, the combination accounted for fifty-four twin-killings during those four seasons when they gained their renown.

"That's understandable," a veteran player explained to Charles Cleveland many years ago. "The ball was 'dead' and 'doctored' by the pitcher. The pitchers used to try to get the hitters to pop up to reduce the chance of error instead of making them hit it into the ground the way they do now."

The primary reasons Tinker and Evers (and Frank Chance) became so famous for making double plays were the ones they made in 1908 against the New York Giants. Poet Franklin P. Adams was a Giants fan, and after the Cubs and their double plays defeated the Giants too often for his emotional well-being, he was moved to write a poem he called "Baseball's Sad Lexicon." This poem, the most famous ever written about actual major leaguers, first appeared in July 1910 in the *New York Evening Mail.*

This is the poem that forever joined the three of them, and in 1946 the three brilliant infielders fittingly were enshrined together in baseball's Hall of Fame.

> *These are the saddest of possible words:*
> *"Tinker to Evers to Chance."*
> *Trio of bear cubs, and fleeter than birds,*
> *"Tinker and Evers and Chance."*
> *Ruthlessly pricking our gonfalon bubble,*
> *Making a Giant hit into a double—*
> *Words that are weighty with nothing but trouble:*
> *"Tinker to Evers to Chance."*

16

A Fine Bunch of Stiffs

For the first time in the short history of the World Series, the two teams came from the same city. During one week in mid-October 1906, Chicago was the sporting capital of the country.

Said an exuberant writer in the *Chicago Tribune,* "All the honors worth winning in the most sensational, record-breaking, and most financially successful season in baseball's history belong to Chicago, admittedly the greatest, most loyal, and enthusiastic baseball city in the world."

The West Side Cubs (or Spuds, as some writers continued to call them) had won 116 games. On the south side of town, the White Sox (or the more formal White Stockings) were champions of the American League, winning 93 games (thirty-two by shutout), seventeen by a young raw-boned spitball master named Ed Walsh.

Like the Cubs, the White Sox were an excellent defensive team, led by second baseman Frank "Bald Eagle" Isbell and first baseman Jiggs Donahue.

On offense the White Sox were one of the weakest-hitting teams ever to win a pennant, hitting only .230 as a team, with six homers all season. The regular outfield of Patsy Dougherty, manager Fielder Jones, and Eddie Hahn hit .233, .230, and .227, respectively. Third baseman Lee Tannehill hit .183. Catcher Billy Sullivan hit .214. The Sox finished last in the league in hits, home runs, and batting average. Writer Hugh Fullerton was the first to call this team the Hitless Wonders.

The White Sox lay mired in the second division until midseason, when the great pitching helped it to nineteen consecutive wins and the surprising pennant over the New York Highlanders. Commented Fred Lieb, "It must be admitted that [manager] Fielder [Jones] won his pennant with mirrors."

The meeting between the two Chicago teams created unprecedented national interest and a frenzied civil war in the city itself. Many of the city's Germans supported the Cubs with Schulte, Sheckard, Steinfeldt, Reulbach, Pfiester, Hofman, and Kling (a German Jew). The Irishers tended to support the White Sox, who featured Walsh, Donahue, Bill O'Neill, Dougherty, and Sullivan.

The White Sox were owned by Charles Comiskey, who in 1886 had played first base on the St. Louis Browns team that beat Cap Anson's Chicago team. Comiskey had played until 1894, when he became owner of the St. Paul team in the Western Association. The league changed its name to the American League in 1900, when Comiskey moved the team to Chicago. It was still a minor league team. Because Comiskey didn't want to anger the Cubs, he agreed not to use the word *Chicago* in the name and to set up his team in a small park at Thirty-ninth and Wentworth. The sportswriters called the new team the White Stockings, the name cast aside by the Cubs.

American League president Ban Johnson declared his league to be a major league in 1901, and that year the White Sox won the pennant. When White Sox owner Charles Comiskey challenged the Cubs to a series of postseason exhibitions, Cubs team owner James Hart refused to consider it. They first met in 1903, when the teams split two exhibitions. Hart was so incensed that his team had lost even a game to the upstart White Sox that he insisted that they had done so only because his pitcher, Jack Taylor, threw the game. Hart traded Taylor (along with Larry McLean) to St. Louis to get Mordecai Brown.

The Cubs, viewed as possibly the best team in the history of the game, were prohibitive 3–1 favorites to win the 1906 World Series. Adding to the woes of the White Sox was an injury to their star shortstop, George Davis, on the eve of the Series. His replacement was the unheralded utility man George Rohe. The consensus among Cubs fans was: "It's a joke to let the White Sox play in the same ball park as the Cubs."

When Hugh Fullerton of the *Chicago Tribune* picked the White Sox to win, his editor at first refused to print it, so ridiculous did it seem. But Fullerton believed that the Sox had the better pitching staff, and he went ahead with his prediction despite the protests from upstairs in the newsroom.

Another expert who viewed the White Sox as legitimate contenders was Giants manager John McGraw.

JOHN MCGRAW: "It's hitting that wins. They saw the White Sox won the flag without hitting, but I know better. Their grounds prevent anyone from hitting heavily, and as they played 77 games there, it made their averages look very small. On the road they hit as hard as anybody."

The demand for tickets was huge, despite the $3.50 price tag of a box seat. The Chicago Board of Trade became so worked up over the intercity series that they ordered thousands of tickets and organized a group that traveled to the ballparks en masse. The mobs gathered at the park gates in such crushing numbers that many ticket holders didn't get in. Those shut out were able to watch a re-creation of the games at the Auditorium Theater and the First Regiment Armory.

It was bitter cold when the Series began, so frigid that the fans inserted their programs under their collars to keep warm. Ed Walsh was supposed to start the first game for the Sox, but it was feared his spitball would freeze on the way to the plate, so White Sox pitcher Nick Altrock, a 20-game winner, was inserted in his place.

Mordecai Brown was sharp, striking out five in the first three innings. Altrock was equally good, and the game remained a scoreless tie through four innings.

Snowflakes began to fall. Many men kept warm in their bearskin coats.

In the fifth Brown faced George Rohe. The untried substitute had played at New Orleans in 1905; before the 1906 season White Sox owner Charles Comiskey had wanted to send him back there, but under the rules he had to be offered to the other major league teams first, and Giants manager John McGraw kept claiming him. McGraw didn't really want him, but at the time McGraw was feuding with the owner of the New Orleans team, and this was his way of getting back at him. As a result, Comiskey had to keep him on the White Sox all season long.

Rohe, who had six extra-base hits all year long, swung at a high fastball and tripled. He scored when Patsy Dougherty hit a ball back to Brown. On the throw home, catcher Johnny Kling tried to tag Rohe before he could catch the ball, and the runner was safe.

In the sixth Brown committed the sin of walking the leadoff batter, pitcher Altrock. Altrock was bunted to second and was later thrown out at home on a single by Fielder Jones, who slid safely into second. A passed ball by Kling, who didn't have a good day, let Jones get to third, and Jones scored the Sox's second run on Isbell's single to left.

Against Altrock, the Cubs could score only one run, on a walk, an infield single, a sacrifice bunt, and a wild pitch in the bottom of the sixth.

After the game, Cubs owner Murphy demonstrated his way with words when he commented on the opening-game loss.

"One swallow does not make a summer," he said. "I might add, one snow storm does not make a winter, but it keeps fans away from ballgames."

The Cubs fans considered the loss a fluke, and they became convinced of it when their team won the next game, 7–1, on a one-hitter by former Notre Damer Ed

Reulbach, who went on to lead the National League in winning percentage in 1907 and 1908. With Reulbach's victory, all of Cubdom, including federal judge Kenesaw Mountain Landis, taunted the White Sox fans with: "What league is it your team plays in?"

In the third game Cubs pitcher Jack Pfiester allowed the Hitless Wonders just four hits. Unfortunately, it wasn't quite good enough.

White Sox pitcher Ed Walsh, a coal miner until he left the mines to play pro baseball in 1902, gave up but two hits—and no runs. Walsh never would have gotten to the majors, except that his catcher on the mining team, Frank Burke, had signed with a team in Meriden, Connecticut. When the Meriden manager needed a pitcher, he asked Burke who his pitcher had been back in Pennsylvania. Burke told the manager that the kid, Walsh, was fast but wild and needed coaching. "Get him," said the manager. Burke sent for Walsh, and in his first game he struck out eleven. Two years later he was a mainstay with the White Sox.

In the sixth inning, with the score 0–0, Pfiester loaded the bases, and with two outs he faced George Rohe. Cubs catcher Johnny Kling began to taunt the White Sox hitter in an attempt to mislead him.

"So the lucky stiff is up again. I guess you're going to look for another high fast one. Busher, you don't get another pitch like that if the Series lasts until Christmas."

On the next pitch Pfiester threw a high hard one. Rohe wasn't fooled. He hit the ball deep down the left-field line. It took one hop into the crowd on the field and landed in the bleachers for what was then a ground-rule triple, scoring all three White Sox runs in what ended up a 3–0 shutout.

Mordecai Brown's two-hitter beat the White Sox 1–0 in Game 4, tying the Series at two games each. Brown was absolutely invincible, though it took a great play by the pitcher to complete the shutout. He had Fielder Jones on second with two outs in the ninth when first baseman Frank Isbell hit a hard line drive up the middle. Brown knocked it down, fell over, got up, and threw Isbell out to end the game. If he hadn't made the play, Jones surely would have scored to tie it up.

Johnny Evers's single had driven in Frank Chance in the seventh inning for the only run of the ball game.

At that point the White Sox were 11 for 113 for a .097 batting average. The fortunes of the Sox were brightened by the return to the lineup of George Davis, who replaced Lee Tannehill at short.

It was sunny and bright for Game 5, with 23,257 overflowing West Side Park, as at least that many were turned away. Among them was a friend of writer Joseph Kreuger, whom Kreuger called the Old Timer.

THE OLD TIMER: "When the gates were thrown open for the game, long lines that extended in every direction from the park, formed the wildest crush that was ever witnessed in the history of the classic. Crowds milled around the park all during the contest, following the play, by listening to those fortunate enough to be on the inside."

Two live bear cubs were brought into the ballpark as mascots. Many fans who couldn't get into the stadium gathered on the north side of the park and received reports of the game.

The White Sox scored a run in the first, but the Cubs came back and scored three runs against Ed Walsh. The roof then fell in on the Cubs.

After the fourth game White Sox manager Fielder Jones had ranted to his players about their lack of success hitting the ball. One of his targets was Frank Isbell. He told his second baseman, "Issy, you're a white-livered so-and-so. You're choked up to here—you have less guts than a gnat."

Against Reulbach, then Pfiester, then Overall, Isbell hit four doubles, scoring three times and driving in two runs. George Rohe added a double and two singles. Hits by George Davis drove Reulbach from the mound and then Pfiester. Davis, a switch-hitter, batted lefty against Big Ed and righty against Jack the Giant Killer. The Cubs added to the debacle by making six glaring errors. They lost 8–6.

Before the sixth game, played at the White Sox' South Side Park on a sunny and bright Sunday afternoon, a swarm of 19,249 filled the small arena. The gates were closed early to stem the flow of fans.

In the Cubs clubhouse before the game Frank Chance told his star pitcher, Mordecai Brown, "We're relying on you. You've got to keep us in this thing, so we can beat them in the seventh game."

But Brown had pitched all nine innings on Friday, and on this Sunday his arm hadn't recovered. All managers, even the great ones, sometimes forget that their stars are mere humans, and Chance was no exception.

Though Brown pitched with a tired arm, the White Sox might have been prevented from scoring three runs in the first inning if a local policeman, evidently a White Sox rooter, hadn't aided in his team's cause by jostling outfielder Frank Schulte as he was about to catch a fly ball that was heading into the throng of fans seated in right field on the grass.

According to Charles Dryden of the *Chicago Tribune*, the policeman gave Schulte a kick in the pants as he went back for the ball. There were two outs and two runners on base when the ball was hit. Schulte would have caught the ball had it not been for the policeman.

"Three runs scored where there should have been none," wrote Dryden.

In the second inning the White Sox would get four more runs. In one and a third innings, the great Mordecai Brown had allowed eight hits. Orval Overall, who should have started, came in and allowed one run the rest of the way but the damage had been done. When Cubs outfielder Frank Schulte grounded out to end the 8–3 game, the White Sox and their fans celebrated wildly.

"Thrilling almost as a battle scene was the invasion of the bleacherites upon the field at the close of the game," wrote Charles Dryden. Angry Cubs fans did their best to stop them, throwing scores of celebrators to the ground in frustration.

At the end of the Series, White Sox owner Charles Comiskey presented manager Fielder Jones with a check for $15,000. Each White Sox player received $1,874, as much as some made all season long. The players saw the money as a generous gift. Comiskey viewed it as a large part of their 1907 salary. The resultant dissension destroyed the White Sox team the following year.

The 1906 Series defeat rankled the Cubs players. According to writer Lee Smith, "Many of the Cubs had bet more on the games than their share of the receipts, and they were heartbroken."

M. BROWN. J. PFEISTER A. HOFMAN C.G. WILLIAMS O. OVERALL. E. REULBACH. J. KLING.
H. GESSLER. J. TAYLOR. H. STEINFELDT. J. MᶜCORMICK. F. CHANCE. J. SHECKARD. P. MORAN. F. SCHULTE.
C. LUNDGREN. T. WALSH. J. EVERS. J. SLAGLE. J. TINKER.

CHICAGO NATIONAL LEAGUE BALL CLUB 1906

The 1906 Cubs

When Frank Chance—called the Peerless Leader by *Chicago Tribune* sportswriter Charles Dryden following the 1906 season—gathered his players at the start of the following season, the Cubs skipper was still furious over losing to the White Sox.

Chance told them, "You're a fine bunch of stiffs. Maybe you so-and-sos have learned your lesson in overconfidence, and what happens when you underrate the other so-and-sos."

17

World Champs

The greatest team in the history of the Chicago Cubs continued its dominance during the 1907 season, as Frank Chance's team followed its 116-win season by winning 107 games, as the Cubs finished seventeen games ahead of the second-place Pittsburgh Pirates. Once again, the Cubs' pitching staff was awesome: Orval Overall was 23–8 with a 1.70 earned run average; Mordecai Brown was 20–6, 1.39; Carl Lundgren 18–7, 1.17; Jack Pfiester 15–9, with a league-leading 1.15 ERA; and Ed Reulbach was 17–4, 1.69. Thirty of the victories were shutouts.

The Cubs again led the league in fielding. Johnny Evers led all fielders with 500 assists. Joe Tinker had 390. Behind the plate Johnny Kling led the league with 499 putouts.

Frank Chance himself was the team's best hitter, at .293.

Over in the American League, the pennant winner was the surprising Detroit Tigers, managed by Hughie Jennings, who once played on the championship Baltimore Orioles alongside John McGraw. The Tigers, owned by William Yawkey, were led by a twenty-year-old lone wolf by the name of Ty Cobb.

Jennings became successful because unlike his predecessor, Bill Armour, who had used Cobb sparingly (in ninety-eight games) in 1906, Jennings gave Cobb a free reign, and the right fielder responded by winning the 1907 American League batting championship at .350. He led the league in stolen bases with 49, in RBIs with 119, and in hits with 212.

Cobb, the son of a Georgia state senator, was a vicious competitor who had no respect for anybody. When he was a rookie, his teammates disliked him so much they hazed and taunted him, knotting his clothes and breaking his bats. Their conclusion: "He's nuts."

A son of the Confederacy, Cobb was a virulent racist who once attacked a cleaning woman working in the hotel where he was staying because she was black. During a spring training feud with catcher Boss Schmidt, who once boxed Jack Johnson during an exhibition, the powerful Schmidt chose not to retaliate while the team was still training in the South for fear Cobb would recruit friends and lynch him. Once north, Schmidt beat him bloody on two separate occasions.

When Cobb first faced Cy Young, the winningest pitcher in the history of the game, he said to the veteran, "It's a wonder they wouldn't be carting you off to the Old Woman's Home. I guess they feel sorry for an old stiff like you, because you fought in the Civil War and they let you stay around."

Young, of course, threw at his head. The pitcher, who was not intimidated, replied, "All you Southerners are like that. My old man used to chase your pappy over the top of Lookout Mountain. It's too bad Sherman didn't do more to Georgia when he was down your way. He left too many corncobs lying around."

After Cobb dusted himself off, he had to have the last word. He said to Young, "Now, let's see your fast one. I could count the stitches on that last one coming in to the plate. I'll drive the next one down your throat, and they can cart you off to the G. A. R. cemetery."

Ty Cobb was a piece of work. But starting in 1907, the cocky Cobb won twelve batting titles in thirteen years and finished a long career with a .367 average, the best ever. When he retired in 1928 he was credited with stealing 892 bases, the most at the time.

Led by Cobb and Hall of Fame outfielder Wahoo Sam Crawford, the Tigers would win three consecutive pennants in 1907, 1908, and 1909.

The 1907 pennant came down to the Tigers and the Philadelphia A's. When the A's best pitcher, Albert "Chief" Bender, hurt his arm in late September, the Tigers snuck in by only one and a half games. The key game of the season was a 9–9 tie with the A's that was called after seventeen innings. Coming back from a six-run deficit, the Tigers were about to lose when Cobb hit a two-run home run in the ninth inning. With a week to go, the Tigers kept winning. When the A's lost a doubleheader to the lowly Washington Senators, Hughie Jennings and his Tigers became American League champs.

Perhaps mindful of the seventeen-inning tie with the A's, Tigers infielder Herman "Germany" Schaefer, representing the players, attended a pre-Series meeting of the

National Commission, baseball's ruling body. Schaefer knew the players were supposed to share in the gate receipts of the first four games. He wanted to know, "Is a tie game a legal game?" After a quick deliberation the commission decided that if there was a tie, the players would share in the profits from that game as well as four completed games.

The first game, played in Chicago, ended in a 3–3 tie.

The Tigers should have won the opener. Ahead 3–1 with one out in the ninth and the bases loaded, Tigers star pitcher Wild Bill Donovan (25–4, 2.19) induced Cubs outfielder Frank Schulte to ground out, scoring the second Cubs run. Now there were two outs, the Cubs down by a run.

Manager Chance sent in Del Howard to hit for Tinker, who had struck out all three times against Donovan. Howard swung and missed the first two curve balls. Donovan threw another one, and Howard again swung and missed, but Tigers catcher Charlie Schmidt couldn't catch it, and Steinfeldt scored the tying run from third.

The game continued for another three innings before it was called on account of darkness.

The National Commission pondered whether Schmidt and the players had pulled a fast one by allowing that ball to get past in order to tie the game and get money from an added game.

It was a coincidence, they decided, and no investigation was ordered. At the end of the Series, the commission ruled that in the future the players would get their money from the first four games, no matter how they ended.

Though Cobb was to be known as the greatest of all base stealers, in the 1907 Series it was the Cubs who gave the public a clinic on baserunning as they ran roughshod over the Tigers, stealing bases, as Fred Lieb put it, "like a merry-go-round whizzing around the diamond." In the five games the Cubs stole 18 bases. Leadoff man Jimmy Slagle stole six. Against Schmidt in the first game the Cubs stole seven bases alone.

Before Game 2, Jennings told his players, "Forget that tie. That's gone, and I don't want to hear any more about it. We didn't win it, but we didn't lose it."

But the Tigers, who had blown a sure victory in the opener, were so demoralized that they didn't win another game.

In the second game the Tigers tried a new catcher, Freddie Payne, against whom the Cubs stole five bases during a 3–1 victory.

The Cubs demonstrated their inside-baseball wizardry, scoring the winning runs in the fourth on a single by Joe Tinker, a sacrifice by pitcher Jack Pfiester, an infield single by Jimmy Slagle, a stolen base and a double by Jimmy Sheckard. They took a two-game lead when Ed Reulbach pitched a six-hitter in a 5–1 victory. To this point the heralded Cobb hadn't been a factor at all.

When the teams traveled to Detroit, the weather was cold and threatening. Before the game, manager Hughie Jennings was presented with a diamond-studded watch by an admirer and with a floral arrangement in the shape of a life-size tiger.

Frank Chance, a hard man, asked Jennings, "What are you going to do with that, Hughie? Eat it?"

"No, we'll ram it down your throats," said Jennings.

"Who, you and Cobb?" Chance taunted. "I thought you told me he was a hitter."

"He'll hit plenty before it's over."

"That's what you say."

Perhaps it was a coincidence that when Chance batted in the first inning Tigers pitcher Bill Donovan hit him in the left hand and broke his finger. Chance bandaged it and kept playing.

Ahead 2–1 in the seventh, the Cubs again put on a show of classic Frank Chance baseball when they scored three more runs without hitting the ball out of the infield.

There had been a rain delay in the fifth inning, and the ground was soft. Frank Chance decided to take advantage. Frank Schulte led off the seventh and beat out a bunt. Tinker bunted, and both runners were safe when Schulte beat Donovan's throw at second. Cubs pitcher Orval Overall sacrificed the runners over to second and third. Jimmy Slagle grounded to Tigers shortstop Charley O'Leary, who threw wide to the plate, allowing Schulte to score.

Jimmy Sheckard then bunted toward first—the push bunt was his specialty—and was safe when neither pitcher Donovan nor second baseman Schaefer covered first as first baseman Claude Rossman fielded the ball.

Chance forced Sheckard at second. From where he stood on first, Chance called for the double steal, and as the Tigers were trying to tag him out in the rundown, Slagle scored easily.

The Cubs were playing magnificent baseball. The Tigers didn't have a prayer.

In the final game, played in Detroit under severe weather conditions before a tiny crowd of only 7,370, everyone wondered whether Cubs owner Charles Murphy would order his Cubs to lose a game on purpose in order to return to Chicago, where 25,000 fans had already bought all the tickets for the next game.

It didn't happen that way. Chance selected his star, Mordecai Brown, to start. Brown told reporters, "To blazes to that crowd in Chicago tomorrow," said Brown. "I'll finish it today."

He shut out the toothless Tigers 2–0 on seven hits. Brown had fine control, walking only one. To stop the Cubs runners the Tigers tried a third catcher, Jimmy Archer, but he was no more successful than the other two, as the Cubs stole three more bases for a total of sixteen.

The Cubs were world champions, dominators of all they faced. In the five games Ty Cobb was held to four hits. The Tigers as a team hit .209.

The teams returned to Chicago to play an exhibition before the sellout crowd, adding $1,600 into the players' pool.

Because gate receipts were low, after the Series Tigers owner William Yawkey, a generous, kind man, gave his players $15,000 to split. Cubs owner Charles Murphy, fearing embarrassment if he didn't do something, offered his men $10,000. Each Cub thus earned a total of $2,250.

It was the last time any owner ever sweetened the pot.

Detroit drew so poorly during the Series, there was a movement to excise the team from the American League. League president Ban Johnson had dropped Buffalo and Baltimore when the American League was founded, and there was talk of doing away with Detroit and bringing back Buffalo. The nearby Cleveland franchise was suspected of leading the movement.

On October 31, 1907, the league decided to keep the status quo.

At the end of the year William Yawkey sold half his interest in the team to Frank Navin, and he became a silent partner. The Tigers players would learn there was a big difference between the two men.

In Chicago the players were lionized. "Cubs on Parade," a march two-step by H. R. Hempel, was dedicated to Chicago's 1907 world champions. A song called "Between You and Me," allegedly written by Johnny Evers and Joe Tinker, was referred to as "the catch of the season."

"Take Me Out to the Ball Game," baseball's anthem, was published in 1908. For Cubs fans that would be *the* year to remember.

18

The Warren Gill Affair

In 1906 and 1907 the Cubs clinched the National League pennant by August 1. In 1908, it would not be so easy. This year the Cubs started slowly. The year before a young utility player by the name of Heinie Zimmerman joined the team. A hothead, Zimmerman almost finished the career of Chicago's outstanding outfielder Jimmy Sheckard when he threw a bottle of ammonia at Sheckard, with the acidic liquid spilling into Sheckard's eyes and almost blinding him. Chance and some of his players then beat Zimmerman to a pulp. The manager never forgave Zimmerman, who was a troubling influence on the Cubs through the rest of Chance's tenure as manager.

NEW YORK GLOBE: "Just before the Cubs came East on their first trip it was announced that [Jimmy] Sheckard's eyesight was nearly ruined by the explosion of a bottle of ammonia in the Chicago clubhouse. About the same time Zimmerman was sent to a hospital. Some excuse was made for his dropping out of the game so suddenly.

"It has developed within the last few days that the injuries to Sheckard and Zimmerman were the result of a free-for-all fight in the Chicago clubhouse, in which Chance played a conspicuous part. According to our information, after a few hot words had been passed Zimmerman went at Sheckard. During the melee Sheckard threw something at Zimmerman.

"Angered by this style of attack, Zimmerman picked up a bottle of ammonia and hurled it at Sheckard. The bottle struck Sheckard in the forehead between the eyes. The force of the throw broke the bottle and the fluid streamed down Sheckard's face.

"Manager Chance, thoroughly enraged, buckled into Zimmerman, and the uproar continued. Chance is known for his fighting prowess, but it is claimed that Zimmerman stood his ground until Chance called on other players for help. Then, it is alleged, Zimmerman was borne to the floor by force of superior numbers, and while he was down he received such a beating it was necessary to cart him to the hospital for repairs. Afterward the players took sides on the matter and the affair created bad feeling all around.

"Sheckard and Zimmerman were out of the game for two or three weeks. That weakened the team, and when Schulte had to quit on account of illness the Cubs could not gain ground."

As late as mid-August, Chicago trailed star shortstop Honus Wagner and his Pittsburgh Pirates by six full games and McGraw's surprising Giants by three. That New York was in contention proved the managerial brilliance of McGraw. The year before the Giants had cut the salaries of many of the stars. Outfielder Mike Donlin sat out the entire season. Others played, but fumed, as the team finished fourth. McGraw, angry with their performance, got rid of most of them, keeping only Roger Bresnahan, Art Devlin, and Donlin. The rest were newcomers: Larry Doyle, Buck Herzog, Fred Snodgrass, and a young, inexperienced first baseman by the name of Fred Merkle.

Despite the Giants' youth, it took the heroics of Joe Tinker, who drove in the winning runs two days in a row against Christy Mathewson and Hooks Wiltse, to keep the Cubs as close as they were.

With four days left in August, the Giants came to town. With the Pirates doing a fade, it appeared likely that the pennant would come down to either Chicago or New York. In the opener left-hander Jack Pfiester (née Pfiestenberger), who in his first year with the Cubs shut out the Giants 19–0 and became known as 'Jack the Giant Killer,' continued his uncanny mastery over the New Yorkers, as the Cubs defense, led by Tinker and Evers, held the Giants to a single run.

The Cubs were creeping closer, and the city of Chicago continued its love affair with this exciting, irresistible team. When the New York press arrived in the city for the series, the widespread seriousness of Chicago's fandom was evident.

NEW YORK HERALD: "Chicago presents the spectacle of a great city positively raving over baseball. Everything else is forgotten—politics, business, home and family. At downtown bulletin boards, where the game was reproduced in miniature, crowds were estimated at 50,000.

"In offices tickers bringing bulletins absorbed all the attention. Grocers' boys and telephones conveyed the news of the great game to thousands of residences, for in Chicago women understand baseball and are as deeply interested as men. Hundreds of buildings in the vicinity of the ball park were black with spectators, while telegraph and telephone poles looked as though immense swarms of giant bugs had settled at their tops."

New York won the Saturday game, but the Cubs came back on Sunday when Mordecai Brown beat Mathewson 3–2, continuing his Matty-Can't-Beat-Me streak. The next day Pfiester the Giant Killer defeated the Giants 2–1, as a double play from Evers to Tinker to Chance killed the lone New York rally. William Kirk, a writer for the *New York American*, noted that "those double plays have done much to our boys here in Chicago."

By game's end the Giants were still in first, but the Cubs were only one half game out. Immediately after the Cubs recorded the final out of the game, the Chicago fans rioted in celebration.

NEW YORK WORLD: "After the game a cushion battle between 3,000 in the stands and 5,000 in the field raged for 15 minutes, during which many women were injured and their hats demolished. The police were powerless. In this way the crowd expressed its joy over the victory."

The race remained tight. The Cubs' next series was in Exposition Park in Pittsburgh. When those two teams met, it was war. Honus Wagner, the Pirates' Hall of Fame shortstop, recalled what it was like.

HONUS WAGNER: "We went into Chicago at a time when we were neck and neck, and the Cubs were especially rough on us, and I mean rough physically. We lost the series, two games out of three. We returned shortly afterward to Exposition Park for a series with Chicago. [Manager] Fred Clarke called a meeting in our clubhouse, and said: 'I'll give a fifty-dollar bonus to the player who can do the most damage to the Cubs.'

"One of our pitchers spoke up and asked whether he couldn't get in on the proposition. He suggested that after he'd get 'ahead' of the hitter, he'd start chucking at his head. After Clarke's offer, we all wore our longest spikes. And those who didn't have long ones filed the short ones down to a point. I'll tell you we were ready for them. That was managerial strategy in those days."

On October 4, the Pirates and the Cubs met.

JOHNNY EVERS: "Mordecai Brown was pitching for the Cubs and he'd shut out the Bucs three straight times earlier in the season. This day they hadn't scored off Brown again in nine innings, making it thirty-six frames he'd held them runless, but we couldn't get anything off Vic Willis either. In the tenth we got beat.

"Fred Clarke was on third, Wagner on second and [Doc] Gill on first with [Owen 'Chief'] Wilson at the plate."

Tommy Leach, the Pirates third baseman that day, recalled what happened next:

TOMMY LEACH: "We had the bases full and two out with the score tied in the tenth. Chief Wilson hit a clean single to center, and the winning run crossed the plate. Gill ran about halfway down to second and then started to run off the field. At the time, it was a common practice for players to dash for the clubhouse after the winning play had been made. Some of us older players on the bench saw what was going on, especially as we heard Evers and Tinker jabbering around second and calling for Artie Hofman, the Cub center fielder, to throw the ball to second base. We started running after Gill, to get him to retrace his steps and touch second, but in the meantime we noted that both of the umpires had walked off the field. They didn't see the play, and apparently were satisfied that Pittsburgh had won."

* * *

Evers, a devoted student of the game, knew that under the rules, the umpire should rule Gill out at second.

JOHNNY EVERS: "Gill didn't go to second. He ran off the field. I got the ball and hollered to [umpire] O'Day to look. He wouldn't. I stood on second and yelled that the run didn't count . . . that Gill was the third out, but Hank refused to listen. 'Clarke scored before the out could have been made,' he told manager Frank Chance and pushed his way to the dressing room.

"Ol' Hank was mad at me anyway for an argument we'd had in St. Louis a few weeks before and you could tell that his whole attitude was he'd be damned if that little squirt Evers was going to get him in another jam. But just the same he was a good umpire . . . if you didn't tell him so too often . . . and he realized later what had happened and in the long run we got the break when we needed it most in New York. As everybody knows, we couldn't have won the pennant if we hadn't."

E. I. Sanborn of the *Chicago Tribune* agreed with Evers that Gill should have been out. Wrote Sanborn the next day, "Everyone knows no run can count if the third out is made before the batsman reaches first, or if the third man out is forced out. Gill hadn't touched second base yet, and so Clarke's run could not have scored but for the fact O'Day took it for granted the game was over when Wilson's hit landed safe."

After the game Chicago owner Charles Webb Murphy made a formal protest to league president Harry Pulliam. In a letter Murphy argued: "Chicago claims Gill should have touched second base before he ran to the clubhouse, and will prove by affidavits of a number of persons that he failed to do so."

Said Murphy, "I do not expect the protest will be allowed, but it is certainly just, and should prove a strong argument in favor of the double-umpire system."

Murphy was right that the protest would not be allowed. Commented the *New York Globe* on September 9, "I think the baseball public prefers to see games settled on the field and not in this office."

Commented the *Sporting News*, "Chicago's protest was ill-advised and served only to afford the carping class of patrons an opportunity to question the integrity of the game."

The day the *New York Globe* article was published, giving the background of the play and what Evers did, the New York Giants were playing Brooklyn at the Polo Grounds. Neither John McGraw nor any of the other Giants apparently read or understood the import of the article, otherwise McGraw would have made sure that Giants runners reach the next base before heading for the dugout. Either that or McGraw was arrogant enough to believe that if the situation arose again, O'Day and Pulliam would rule the same way. And the situation would arise again.

The astute Fred Lieb commented, "It long has been a wonder that the crafty John McGraw, who never missed a trick on the diamond, did not call the [Gill] play to the attention of his players in a clubhouse discussion and warn them against such a contingency."

19

September 23, 1908

On September 21, 1908, after the two teams split a doubleheader, the Cubs trailed the Giants by three and a half games. Had the Cubs won both games, the lead would have been cut to one and a half games. But they didn't, and according to Johnny Evers, after losing a game they should have won, the players wanted to break training and get drunk. Chance refused to let them.

JOHNNY EVERS: "The race was close, and to Chicago even one defeat seemed to mean the loss of the pennant. The Chicago club had just finished a double header and lost one of the games in heart-breaking manner when it seemed won. New York had beaten Pittsburgh twice, and it appeared as if the results that day had decided the championship. The Cubs, returning to the hotel in carriages, were silent and down-hearted. Not a word was spoken for a long time. Suddenly Tinker remarked to Chance:

"'Well, Cap, I guess it's all off. Let's break training and make a good night of it.'

"For an instant Chance was silent. Then he said, 'No. We were good winners last year. Let's show them we are good losers and play the string out. We may win yet.'

"The following day Chicago won two games and New York lost two, and the Cubs were back in the race. When Tinker made the remark the team had twelve games to play, and by winning eleven of them, it tied New York for the championship and then won the deciding game."

On September 22, the Cubs beat the Giants in a doubleheader 4–3 and 2–1, as Orval Overall beat Red Ames and Mordecai Brown beat James "Doc" Crandall.

Before the first game McGraw ordered his rookie, the left-handed Rube Marquard, to warm up in the bullpen, with the right-handed Ames warming up under the stands. Before the second game he had Marquard and Joe McGinnity warming up and at the last minute brought Crandall out from under the stands.

McGraw was trying to catch Chance napping in the hopes the Cubs manager would pick alternate pitchers. Chortled the *Chicago News*, "Instead he got two beatings."

Commented the *New York World*, "The whole Chicago team is clever, machine-like, and game." The reporter added, "The only thing for McGraw to do to beat Chicago is to dig up a pitcher with only two fingers."

At this point the Giants led the Cubs by a game and a half. The Cubs had eleven more games to play. The Giants had seventeen, including eight with a mediocre Philadelphia team.

The race was very close, and everyone's nerves were on edge. In the final game of the Giants-Cubs series, Jack Pfiester started for the Cubs against Christy Mathewson. Crucial to what was to follow was that Hank O'Day was one of the umpires. (Bob Emslie was the other.)

O'Day had been a pitcher in the big leagues with connections to both Chicago and New York. He had grown up in Chicago, and in 1882 he pitched for the Spaldings, a semipro team sponsored by Al and his brother. O'Day pitched for Washington for three and a half years, and in 1889 he helped pitch the Giants to the pennant. After pitching for the New York Brotherhood League team, he umped his first game when one of the regular umpires didn't show up. Chicago was playing Cleveland. Chicago manger Cap Anson liked his work, and he retired as a player to pursue the career that would make him famous.

Twenty-five thousand fans packed the Polo Grounds in upper Manhattan to watch the archenemies, the Cubs and the Giants, fight it out for the pennant.

The Cubs took the lead in the fifth inning when Joe Tinker, Matty's nemesis, hit a line drive toward right fielder Mike Donlin. The Giants outfielder tried to make a shoe-string catch, but the ball hit in front of him and rolled past as Tinker circled the bases.

Today's ballplayers complain bitterly when reporters accurately report their failings. It was no different back in 1908. Consider two reports of the Donlin miss by these two anonymous writers from New York newspapers:

NEW YORK HERALD: "The ball went over second like a cannon shot and went skating through the grass in right center. Mike Donlin went over to stop it and tried to place his foot in its course, but failed, and the ball rolled to the ropes. Two or three ardent fans in a perfectly polite manner suggested to Mike that if he had stretched his anatomy on the greensward he might have stopped the ball and ended Tinker's wanderings on second base."

NEW YORK TIMES: "Mr. Tinker drives the ball out to right center for what would have been a two-bagger if you or I had made it, gentle reader—and this is no disparagement of the Tinker, for he is well seeming in our sight. As the ball approaches Master Donlin, this good man attempts to field it with his foot. It's a home run, all right, when you get down to scoring, but if this Donlin boy was our boy, we'd have sent him to bed without his supper, and ye mind that, Mike."

In the next inning the Giants tied the game as Buck Herzog beat out a slow roller to Steinfeldt at third and got to second when Harry made a bad throw to first. Donlin then made up for his fielding lapse by singling to score Herzog.

Going into the ninth, the score was 1–1. Jack Pfiester held the Giants despite having to pitch with a painful arm injury that prevented him from throwing his curve ball.

JOHNNY EVERS: "Pitching from angles consists in angling the ball from high overhand to the batter's knee, from the pitcher's knee to the batter's shoulder and from the limit of the outstretched arm to the outside corner of the plate. One of the best exhibitions of pitching by angles ever given was in the now famous game between Chicago and New York in September, 1908, in which Merkle forgot to touch second base. Pfiester had strained a ligament in his pitching arm, and a lump had formed on his forearm two inches high, the muscle bunching. He could not bend his arm, and to pitch a curve brought agony. He could pitch straight balls and he asked Chance to let him try, as he always had been successful against the Giants. During the game he pitched three curved balls, all to Donlin, and all when he had to retire Donlin on strikes to save the game. After each time he curved the ball he had to be helped to the bench, as he was nearly fainting. By changing the angles he kept New York from winning until the famous mixup in which Merkle figured."

Toward the end of his life, Johnny Evers, the Cubs second baseman, was asked by John P. Carmichael, author of one of the greatest oral histories in baseball literature, *My Greatest Day in Baseball*, what had been his most memorable day.

The contest he chose, this one, was the game that made Johnny Evers eternally famous. Evers picks up the narration as the ninth inning unfolded.

JOHNNY EVERS: "To show you what a pitcher's battle it was, Tinker handled fourteen chances that game and I had eleven which was as many as I had in any game all season. Matty set us down one-two-three in our half and New York put on a rally. With one out, [Art] Devlin singled and [Moose] McCormick slashed one right at me. It was just slow enough so the best Tinker and I could do was to get Devlin at second. Still there were two gone. Up came [Fred] Merkle. He was just a rookie at the time [he had seen limited play in 1907] and probably wouldn't have been playing if we hadn't had a southpaw working, but McGraw wanted to get as much right-handed hitting into his lineup as possible and anyway Fred Tenney had a bum ankle and could use extra rest, so Merkle was at first.

"Well, he singled and McCormick went to third. Al Bridwell was the next hitter and he singled to center. That's where the fun began."

Here's the way the *New York Times* reporter described what happened next: "McCormick trots home, the merry villagers flock on the field to worship the hollow where the Mathewson feet have pressed, and all of a sudden there is doings at second base."

Doings indeed. The instant McCormick's spikes hit home plate, the frenzied crowd headed for the field. Merkle, seeing the crazed New Yorkers heading his way, stopped running toward second and made a beeline for the dugout in an attempt to beat a retreat to safety. While the fans were carrying Mathewson on their shoulders, Evers began screaming for center fielder Solly Hofman to throw him the ball. Merkle had done the same thing Doc Gill had done two weeks earlier, and this time Evers was going to make sure umpire Hank O'Day saw that Merkle hadn't touched second and was out on a force play.

JOHNNY EVERS: "I had my eye on [Merkle], saw him stop, glance around at the fans pouring out of their seats, and start for the clubhouse beyond right field. Hofman's throw had gone over Tinker's head and rolled over to where Joe McGinnity, the Giant pitcher, was standing. Joe'd been coaching on third and he knew what was in our minds as Tinker and I raced for the ball. He got it first, but before he could get rid of the thing, Joe and I had him and we wrestled around there for what seemed to be five minutes.

"We grabbed for his hands to make sure he wouldn't heave the ball away but he broke loose and tossed it into the crowd."

McGinnity corroborated the part of the story about his throwing the ball into the crowd.

IRON JOE MCGINNITY: "I don't know where Evers got the ball that he used to claim the force-out but it wasn't the ball that Bridwell hit, because I flung that one out of sight."

But Evers recalled how he got the ball back once McGinnity threw it out toward the outfield.

JOHNNY EVERS: "I can see the fellow who caught it yet . . . a tall, stringy middle-aged gent with a brown bowler hat on. Steinfeldt and Floyd Kroh, a young pitcher we'd added to our staff during the summer, raced after him. 'Gimme the ball for just a minute,' Steinfeldt begged him. 'I'll bring it right back.' The guy wouldn't let go and suddenly Kroh solved the problem. He hit the customer right on top of that stiff hat, drove it down over his eyes and as the gent folded up, the ball fell free and Kroh got it. I was yelling and waving my hands out by second base and Tinker relayed it over to me and I stepped on the bag and made sure O'Day saw me.

"When the hit was made, the crowd surrounded the field, swarmed upon it. O'Day, remembering the Pittsburgh play, raced nearly to second base, saw Merkle turn and go to the club house, saw [me] with the ball on the base. 'The run doesn't count,' he said—just as the crowd swarmed over him. For two hundred feet he walked through a raging mob, telling them the run did not count, while they shrieked, struck at him, pulled him and threatened his life.

"As I said, he was waiting for that very play . . . he remembered the Pittsburgh game . . . and he said, 'The run does not count.' Then he walked away. But he made no attempt to continue the game in the confusion."

Wrote the *New York Herald*, "Rioting and wild disorder, in which spectators and players joined, causing a scene never witnessed in New York before, marked the conclusion at the Polo Grounds yesterday of the game between the Giants and Cubs."

When hundreds of drunk and angry Giants fans learned what Chance and the Cubs were trying to pull, they headed for the Chicago clubhouse, intent on revenge on the umpires and Frank Chance, the Cubs' leader.

Said the *New York World*, "The crowd, following [O'Day and Chance], jammed into the home bench, upsetting [Chicago owner] Charles Murphy, the groundkeeper, and stepping on McGraw's bulldog. They broke through the little door McGraw uses as [an] exit when banished and groped their way in the darkness over barrels, boxes and trap holes. The umpires finally reached their dressing room, but the riot outside continued.

"Chance was the target, and though he is a pugilist the crowd would have treated him harshly but for two fat policemen. Surrounded by them and some of his players,

the Chicago manager 'flying wedged' himself to the clubhouse. He was still bawling that he would protest the game and calling for O'Day."

Chance's complaint was that because the Giants fans had invaded the field and
prevented the continuation of the game, the Cubs should be declared winners by a
forfeit.

John Evers vividly remembered the raucous aftermath.

JOHNNY EVERS: "There was hell a-poppin'. Emslie refused to take a stand for or
against O'Day. 'I didn't see the play,' he insisted and that's all he'd say. Mathewson
and a couple of the Giants dashed for the clubhouse and tried to get Merkle back to
second, but I was standing there with the ball before they got him out the door. They
saw it was too late, although McGraw kept hollering that the Giants had won and the
fans, who only knew the Cubs were trying to pull some trick, gave us a good going
over. A couple of park 'fly cops' which McGraw had scattered around to 'protect' the
visiting players took a few pokes at Chance under the guise of keeping the crowd
back and there must have been five fist fights going on as we finally got out of there.

"Inside the clubhouse we made a horrible discovery. It was the custom of the club
in those days for some player, usually a pitcher, who was sure of not seeing service
during the game, to take charge of a bag in which we placed our money and valu-
ables for safekeeping while in uniform. [Pitcher Floyd "Rube"] Kroh had been the
man in charge this day and he'd left the bag near the bench while he went in pursuit
of the ball. Then he'd forgotten all about it, and of course it was gone when he tried
to find it. We lost about $200 in cash and $5,000 in jewelry."

When the umpires emerged in their dress clothes, Bob Emslie said he hadn't seen
anything. Hank O'Day shouted back over his shoulder, "Merkle didn't run to
second; the last run don't count; it's a tie game."

When Giants manager John McGraw began to protest with his customary vitriol,
O'Day told him if he didn't like the decision he could take it up with National
League president Harry C. Pulliam.

Though it was clear to Evers that umpire Hank O'Day's out call on Merkle was
the right one, Evers was aware enough to realize that O'Day could have saved himself a lot of grief by ignoring his plea to call Merkle out, as he had in the Gill game
two weeks earlier. That the umpire didn't was a testament to his integrity. In the
cosmic sense Evers was accurate when he said that O'Day's decision that day was
"one of the greatest examples of individual heroism the game has known." Evers
went on:

JOHNNY EVERS: "Even after New York claimed the game and the entire country
was aroused over the situation, O'Day could have ended the trouble with a word
and given New York the pennant. He knew the National League wanted New York
to win. He knew the Giants ought to have won, that the hit was clean and one that
deserved to bring home the winning run. Even when officers, politicians, men big
in baseball, urged him to say he had not seen the play, had not made a decision, he
stood firm. It was said O'Day would be mobbed if ever he went to the Polo Grounds
again, but when he next appeared he was greeted with cheers that showed the admiration of the fans for his courage."

20

A Tie

John McGraw and the Giants and the Giants' press and their fans had no intention of accepting Hank O'Day's ruling that Merkle was out at second base. After the game McGraw went so far as to insist that Merkle had actually touched second base. He told reporters, "As a matter of fact Merkle tells me he did reach and touch second. No Chicago player was on second base with the ball, anyway. It's a simple case of squeal! We won fair and square."

The next day in the *New York Sun* the Giants manager continued to assert that victory was theirs. Bullied McGraw, "The Chicago club can protest, of course, but they wouldn't have any grounds for a protest. The play in the ninth inning wasn't a question of interpretation of the rules, which is the only ground on which protest can be made. Emslie says he didn't see the play, and Merkle swears he touched the bag."

As for the New York press, the vitriol spewed by reporter Sam Crane in the *New York Evening Journal* against the Cubs reflected the feelings of all of Giantdom. Said Crane, "Directly after the argument on the field, which was brought about by Manager Chance and his fellow players developing the old yellow streak of claiming victories they can't win on the field, [Cubs owner Charles W.] Murphy saw his opportunity to make a claim for yesterday's game on a cowardly technicality. Manager Chance and his players in fact incited a riot, and but for the fortunate presence of hundreds of New York's 'finest' there would have been a serious riot."

Crane continued in this snit, "Merkle was on second with Mathewson, and as Evers, Tinker and Pfiester all rushed toward second, Matty, according to his own story, to which he will take an affidavit if such a ridiculous act is necessary, took Merkle by the arm and said, 'Come on to the clubhouse; we don't want to mix up in this,' and both Matty and Merkle left the base together."

But according to another New York reporter, Tom Meany, apparently John McGraw wasn't so sure Merkle had touched second. According to Meany, McGraw knew that after he appealed O'Day's decision there would be a hearing before the Board of Directors of the National League. If Merkle were asked whether he had touched second base, said Meany, McGraw wanted him to be able to say he had, and so the night after the game McGraw secreted Merkle at the Shelbourne Hotel in Brighton Beach and in the middle of the night had the youngster taken to the Polo Grounds, where he touched second base.

The next day the furious Giants appealed to league president Harry Pulliam. So did Chicago. Giants owner John T. Brush wanted O'Day's out call nullified, giving the Giants the victory. Chicago owner Charles Murphy demanded the Cubs be awarded the game by a forfeit.

E. I. Sanborn of the *Chicago Tribune* was one of those who called for the game to be forfeited to the Cubs because of the unruly nature of the milling crowd. Wrote Sanborn:

> If it had happened at any other's grounds than New York there is no question
> but that the umpire would have forfeited the game to the visiting club on ac-

count of the crowd's interference. Anywhere else an umpire would have been assured sufficient police protection to enable him to do his duty as prescribed by the rules without endangering the wholeness of his scalp. One hates to think what would have happened to O'Day in New York if he had remained and tried to make the Giants resume the game. New York fans have been taught by years of tolerating McGrawism that New York is a law unto itself in baseball."

During all the discussions concerning Merkle and Evers and whether the Giants first baseman had touched second base and whether he had needed to, the season continued.

In their final series of the season, played at the Polo Grounds, more people were turned away than got inside. In one game a man climbed up a telegraph pole just outside the fence and watched from there—until his legs tired and he fell to the ground and was killed. The ridge at Coogan's Bluff was lined with spectators. A dense crowd stood on the roof of the grandstand.

On Friday, September 25, the Giants shut out the Cubs 5–0 behind Hooks Wiltse. Giants fans took out all their anger on the visitors.

NEW YORK HERALD: "Every time Chance went to bat he was greeted with all sorts of names, and those greetings seemed to hang over the diamond in the humid atmosphere. As if attracted by the epithets hurled at Chance, ranging from 'yellow dog' through all the various stages of head, from 'pin head' to 'bone head,' a swarm of gnats came over the diamond like one of the plagues of Egypt. . . . Every time Chance was greeted with these pleasant titles his appearance reminded the 'rooters' of Hank O'Day, and he would be pounced on again with renewed vigor."

The Cubs left the Polo Grounds and moved east through Manhattan into Brooklyn. On Sunday, September 27, it was announced that Cubs starter Ed Reulbach would pitch both games of a doubleheader against the Dodgers.

Reulbach averaged 17 wins a year in his first eight seasons with the Cubs, but his whole career was overshadowed by Mordecai Brown, despite his many accomplishments. Reulbach was a workhorse, pitching one eighteen-inning game and a twenty-two-inning game his rookie season of 1905 at age twenty-two. His greatest game was the one-hitter he pitched against the White Sox in the 1906 World Series. In 1907 and 1908 he led the league in winning percentage. This year, 1908, he started 35 games, finished 25, and won 24. On this day Reulbach pitched two shutouts in the doubleheader. It was the first time any pitcher had ever accomplished such a feat.

The Cubs had six games left, the Giants eleven. On September 30, the Giants and Phils split behind Harry Coveleski. On Friday, October 2, the Giants and Phils split again. Coveleski, a coal miner like Mordecai Brown, beat the Giants for the second time in three days.

That evening league president Harry Pulliam upheld the tie in the Merkle game. He said if there was an appeal, it would be heard before the Board of Directors on October 5.

For eleven days both sides had been awaiting the decision. Giants fans had feared that Pulliam would declare a forfeit because of the crowd on the field. Cubs fans wanted the forfeit, not a tie. Instead, Pulliam backed his umpire. He ruled that O'Day had ruled Merkle out at second, leaving the game a tie. Said O'Day in his report, "The people had run out on the field. I did not ask to have the field cleared, as it was too dark to continue play." Pulliam said he was upholding the umpire on a question of fact. O'Day had ruled that the game had ended in a 1–1 tie. So it would stand. As neither club had an open date, Pulliam ruled that the contest would not be continued.

The decision angered everyone. According to an article in the *Boston Globe*, during one argument over President Pulliam's decision, George Brooks, a Giants fan, took a baseball bat and fractured the skull of Thomas Crocker, a Cubs fan.

Said the *Globe*, "During the resulting fight Brooks is said to have struck Crocker with the bat, after declaring, 'I'll show you how Mike Donlin makes a three-base hit.'"

The Giants dutifully appealed Pulliam's decision to the Board of Directors.

That same day the *New York Evening Journal* reported that Charles Murphy and Frank Chance had offered the Giants $50,000 for Christy Mathewson. It was a curious offer in the middle of this pennant fight. The question quickly became moot when the Giants said they would not sell Matty "at any price."

On Sunday, October 4, Harry Coveleski of the Phils continued his good work on behalf of the Cubs, beating Christy Mathewson and the Giants 3–2. It was Coveleski's third win over the Giants in a week. It would not be for another twelve years, as baseball was suffering through its infamous Black Sox scandal, that the public was to discover just how valiant and honest Coveleski had been.

After the 1919 World Series, Horace Fogel, who had owned the Phillies in 1908, corroborated the rumors that an emissary from the Giants had attempted to fix the last eight Philly-Giants games at the end of the season. Fogel's story was corroborated by Kitty Bransfield, the first baseman, and catcher Red Dooin. Dooin claimed that he, Bransfield, Mickey Doolan, Otto Knabe, Sherwood Magee, and other Philly players were offered more to throw their 1908 series games to the Giants than the White Sox were promised in 1919.

But the Phils played it straight, and time was running out for the Giants.

When the Cubs returned to Chicago, they discovered that the city had gone Cub crazy. On Monday, October 5, the Cubs hosted the Pittsburgh Pirates before the largest crowd ever to watch a baseball game anywhere in America, 30,247. The Cubs won 5–2. Mordecai Brown, the winner, drove in the winning run off Vic Willis.

Hugh Fullerton wrote a detailed description of the game and its aftermath in the *New York American*.

HUGH FULLERTON: "Piled in the immense stands were nearly 20,000 persons, and banked in immense solid masses around the great field, twenty deep, stood in an army.

"The game was grandly played. Chicago outplayed, outhit and outran the Pirates. They won the game on class and nerve, and demonstrated that they have the best ball team in the league.

"The defensive work of Chicago was grand, the stops of Evers and Tinker setting the crowd mad with applause. But for Chance was reserved the major honors, for in the eighth, by one of the most astounding plays ever made, he stopped the Pirates.

"Leach hit a fierce line drive straight over first, and it looked a sure double until Chance, with a running jump, shoved out one hand, turned backwards and clung to the ball. Against that kind of defensive work Pittsburgh had no chance."

Oddly, it was a decision by umpire Hank O'Day that gave the Cubs the game. With the bases loaded late in the game, Ed Abbaticchio hit a long fly ball down the left-field line. Fair, the Pirates win. Foul, the Cubs win. O'Day called it foul.

During the off-season a female fan sued the Pirates. She had been severely injured by the ball Abbaticchio had hit. She submitted as evidence her ticket stub. Witnesses attested to where she had sat. The location chart revealed that her seat had been in *fair* territory.

The revelations came too late to help either the Pirates or the Giants.

Hugh Fullerton recalled the emotion of the delirious Cubs fans when their heroes won the crucial ball game.

HUGH FULLERTON: ". . .[W]hen [Owen 'Chief'] Wilson hit a hard bounder straight at Tinker and the ball flashed to Evers on top of second, forcing [Alan] Storke, the crowd broke. With a roar like an ocean breaking a dike the thousands poured down in the battleground in the wildest, craziest demonstration of the year. Brown, carried aloft on the shoulders of admirers, was borne around and around. For 15 minutes the players, unable to escape to the clubhouse, were carried over the field, while the air was black with cushions, hundreds of men—women, too—hurling the cushions high in the air, throwing coats, screaming and flinging hats.

"But even then the demonstration was not over, and an hour after the game was done a thousand fans still waited outside the park. As Chance backed his automobile out, hundreds swarmed around him, cheering wildly. Evers escaped in a cab, with a hundred men trying to unhitch the horse and pull the cab themselves, and as for Brown, who tried to slip across to Joe's and wash the dust of battle from his throat, he found about 500 there waiting, each wanting to buy him a keg."

Chicago	98	55	.641	—
Pittsburgh	98	56	.636	1/2
New York	95	55	.633	1 1/2

On October 5, 1908, the Board of Directors of the National League met for eight hours with no intermission for dinner. They met at the Sinton Hotel in New York. Charlie Ebbets, the owner of the Brooklyn Dodgers, was appointed chairman of the meeting.

At the hearing umpire Bob Emslie backed his partner, O'Day.

Mr. Ebbets: "Why did you declare Merkle out?"

Mr. Emslie: "Because he failed to touch second base, and the ball was there and McGinnity was there and interfered with it, that is why."

Affidavits from Giants players, including Merkle, swore he touched second base. Both umpires Emslie and O'Day expressed their disgust at the blatant lies of the Giants.

Said umpire Emslie, "I would never have believed that men could swear to such statements as are made in some of the affidavits presented by the New York club. Several of these affidavits are absolutely false. It is a revelation to me that such documents could be obtained."

According to Jack Ryder in the *Cincinnati Enquirer*, O'Day also scoffed when the Giants' affidavits were read.

According to Johnny Evers, it was Ryder who helped sway the board to vote the way it did.

JOHNNY EVERS: "The Giants protested so vigorously and long that the board of directors finally had to settle matters. I'm not so sure they would have decided in our favor at that, but Jack Ryder, the old Cincinnati writer, who is dead now, broke into the meeting and delivered a helluva speech in our favor, claiming there was no choice but to play the game over and vowing that the league would make itself a laughingstock if it let the Giants get away with a pennant on a bonehead play."

The board met again the morning of Tuesday, October 6. In the afternoon the *New York Evening Journal* reported that two of the three directors had voted to reverse O'Day's decision and award the Merkle game to the Giants. A unanimous vote was needed for a reversal. The third member was George Dovey of Boston. The board, however, did not release its decision. On that day the Giants beat Boston 4–1. With the Cubs season over, the Giants still had one game remaining against the Boston Braves. If the Braves won, the whole thing would have been moot.

The *New York Globe* printed letters from Giants fans saying that if the National League cost their team the championship, they would immediately become American League fans.

In Chicago, the *Tribune* was offering prayers that the next day's Giants-Boston game be rained out, preventing them from finishing in a tie with the Cubs.

After the board made its decision to replay the Merkle game, it offered Giants owner John T. Brush and manager John McGraw a choice: If the Giants and Cubs finished in a tie, they could play a single game or the best out of five. Chicago owner Charles Murphy, who wanted the money a series would bring and also didn't want to have to risk everything on a game against Christy Mathewson, the best pitcher in baseball, had wanted to play the full five games. But McGraw cared more about winning than anything else, including the money. He had Mathewson. If it came to it, he would elect to play one game for the pennant.

Reflecting the feeling of Giants fans, reporter Sam Crane in the *New York Evening Journal* felt the Giants should refuse to play the playoff game.

Wrote Crane, "Charley Murphy and Barney Dreyfuss—bah and bah again. And Charley [sic] Ebbets, booh! and bah!!"

As for Murphy, he was disappointed he didn't get a forfeit. Said Murphy: "We will play them Thursday and we'll lick 'em too. We'll make it so decisive that no bone-headed base running can cast a shadow of doubt on the contest. We want to win the championship on the playing field. Manager Chance and his players are in good condition and will have no excuse if we fail to bring the third successive National League pennant to Chicago."

On Wednesday, October 7, the Giants rolled over Boston a third and final time. Joe Kelley, a teammate of McGraw's on the old Baltimore Orioles, managed the Braves. After three one-sided losses, all of Chicago accused Kelley of laying down against his old teammate.

For the first time in history the pennant race had ended in a tie.

The Giants owner, John T. Brush, not wishing to give credence to the rumor that the Giants would boycott the playoffs, quickly announced that the Giants would play.

This one-game playoff would be a true battle between West and East. It would be Tinker, Evers, Chance, and Brown against McGraw, Mathewson, and Donlin. The Teutonic Germans from Chicago were facing the Irishers from New York. (The hatred of one side for the other was made clear when the Polo Grounds burned a few years later. A brazier had overturned in the concession area, causing the fire. Giants fans blamed it on either the Bolsheviks or the Chicagoans.)

The players felt strong enmity for the Giants. Some of the feeling was because of McGraw, who the Cubs players knew was a conniver and a con man. Mordecai "Three-Finger" Brown, for instance, claimed McGraw tried to soften up a rival pitcher by hinting that a trade was in the works and he might join his club. McGraw's thinking was that if the pitcher thought he was coming to the Giants, he might not try as hard against them.

When McGraw tried that approach on Brown, the Cubs ace told him, "I'm pitching for the Cubs this afternoon and I'm going to show you just what a helluva pitcher you're dealing for."

Joe Tinker expressed how the players felt when he once said, "If you didn't honestly and furiously hate the Giants, you weren't a real Cub."

The coming showdown was going to be a war. Commented the *New York Herald*:

> Never before have two teams been tied at the end of a season. Never before has the race been so close. Never has it been necessary to play off the tie of six months' baseball in a single gigantic battle.
> That the game will be a struggle to the death is certain.

21

Four to Two

The Cubs players boarded the sleek Twentieth Century Limited supertrain at the Lake Shore Station as several hundred cheering fans saw them off. Team owner Charles Murphy, who had a reputation among the players for being tight with the dollar, paid an extra $11.75 per man to take the faster, ritzier train. Usually, the ride took twenty-eight hours. The Limited took ten hours less; Murphy wanted his boys as rested as possible.

Hostile New York fans had other ideas. When they learned in which midtown hotel the Cubs were staying, the Chicagoans were treated to a hint of the madness that was to come, as the Giants rooters, still bitter over the Merkle decision that cost them the 1908 pennant, stood outside the hotel through the night blaring horns and noise-makers in an attempt to keep the Cubs players from getting a good night's sleep.

The next day the Cubs kept a low profile in coming to the Polo Grounds. Like many in the throng, the Chicago players took the subway, unnoticed by the Giants fans who failed to recognize them in street garb.

A crowd estimated at 250,000 surged around the Polo Grounds in hopes of getting into the playoff game. Every vantage point was taken. A man hanging on to a pillar of the Eighth Avenue El high above the ground lost his balance and fell to his death. Police had to use clubs to keep others from taking his spot. One fan sitting in the bleachers either fell or was pushed from the top seat over the wall and fell to the ground. His right leg was broken. Recalled one observer:

> From the press box, the skyline was human heads. They were located on the grandstand, roofs, fences, 'L' structures, electric light poles and in the distance on smokestacks, chimneys, advertising signs and copings of apartment houses.
>
> On the viaduct, the Speedway and cliffs back of the grandstand there was practically a solid mass of people.
>
> There was something fascinating in watching the filling of the picture by the constantly growing inpour of people. Every possible vantage point, however precarious, came to have its human cluster. . . . And in the center of it all, in the middle foreground, the empty diamond.

At 12:45, two and a quarter hours before game time, the undermanned, over-whelmed police ordered the gates closed. Mounted police had to beat back those who didn't have tickets to get in. Though no one else would be allowed inside, speculators continued to sell tickets. The purchasers would then find their tickets worthless, and if they weren't timid, they'd return to find the seller. If the search was successful, a fistfight would ensue.

One of the spectators who arrived after the police barricaded the park was A. G. Spalding, who had come to see the game all the way from his home in California. Spalding had a season's pass and four box seats in his pocket, but when he arrived in a car at 1:30 with three friends, like everyone else he was refused entrance, even though he told police who he was. When fans learned he was in the car, they milled around his car, hoping he would be let in and they could push their way in behind him.

Spalding, unused to not getting his way, noticed that the police were opening a gate to let an ambulance enter. He drove his car nose to tail behind it, and as it drove inside, he followed. To the end, Al Spalding would not be denied.

Pitcher Mordecai Brown recalled the frenetic madness, the crush of fans, and the intensity of emotion before the game.

MORDECAI BROWN: "I want to tell you about this playoff game. It was played before what everybody said was the biggest crowd that had ever seen a baseball game. The whole city of New York, it seemed to us, was clear crazy with disappointment because we had taken that 'Merkle boner' game from the Giants. The

Polo Grounds quit selling tickets about 1 o'clock, and thousands who held tickets couldn't force their way through the street mobs to the entrances. The umpires were an hour getting into the park. By game time there were thousands on the field in front of the bleachers, the stands were jammed with people standing and sitting in aisles, and there were always little fights going on as ticket-holders tried to get their seats. The bluffs overhanging the Polo Grounds were black with people, as were the housetops. The elevated lines couldn't run for people who had climbed up and were sitting on the tracks.

"The police couldn't move them, and so the fire department came and tried driving them off with the hose, but they'd come back. Then the fire department had other work to do, for the mob outside the park set fire to the left-field fence and was all set to come bursting through as soon as the flames weakened the boards enough.

"Just before the game started the crowd did break down another part of the fence and the mounted police had to quit trampling the mob out in front of the park and come riding in to turn back this new drive. The crowds fought the police all the time, it seemed to us as we sat in our dugout. From the stands there was a steady roar of abuse. I never heard anybody or any set of men called as many foul names as the Giants' fans called us that day from the time we showed up til it was over."

Brown personally experienced the anger of the Giants fans. He had received hate mail and death threats. Though he desperately wanted to start this historic playoff game, manager Frank Chance selected a fresh Jack Pfiester over sending Brown to the mound on only two days' rest.

MORDECAI BROWN: "When manager Frank Chance led the Chicago Cub team into New York the morning of October 8, 1908, to meet the Giants that afternoon to settle a tie for the National League pennant, I had a half-dozen 'black hand' letters in my coat pocket. 'We'll kill you,' these letters said, 'if you pitch and beat the Giants.'

"Those letters and other threats had been reaching me ever since we had closed our regular season two days before in Pittsburgh.

"I'd shown the 'black hand' letters to manager Chance and owner Charles Murphy. 'Let me pitch,' I'd asked them, 'just to show those so-and-sos they can't win with threats.'

"Chance picked Jack Pfiester instead. Two weeks before, Pfiester had tangled with Christy Mathewson, McGraw's great pitcher, and had [tied] him on the play where young Fred Merkle, in failing to touch second on a hit, had made himself immortal for the 'boner' play. Since Mathewson had been rested through the series with Boston and would go against us in the playoff, Chance decided to follow the Pfiester-Mathewson pitching pattern of the 'boner' game. I had pitched just two days before as we won our final game of the schedule from Pittsburgh.

"Matter of fact, I had started or relieved in 11 of our last 14 games. Beyond that I'd been in 14 of our last 19 games as we came down the stretch hot after the championship.

"In our clubhouse meeting before the game, when Chance announced that Pfiester would pitch, we each picked out a New York player to work on. 'Call 'em everything in the book,' Chance told us. We didn't need much encouragement, either."

*   *   *

Things got uglier just prior to the game. The Polo Grounds were overcrowded, and the mob wanted blood. National League president Harry Pulliam needed a heavy police escort to reach his seat. Then, as the Cubs finally took the field, there weren't boos—just the hiss of real hatred.

When Frank Chance appeared on the field, the crowd began chanting, "Robber," "Bandit!" and "Quitter." Said the *New York Sun*, "Roars, hoots, hisses, and jeers are showered on him as he advances, but he smiles pleasantly as if the freedom of the city had been conferred on him." His smile faded when he was struck by a beer bottle in the neck, causing him to bleed profusely. Meanwhile, in right field, there arose a loud noise as the fence collapsed and thousands stampeded onto the grounds. The fire department turned their hoses on the rowdies. Every few minutes one of the gates would be slightly parted and another battered citizen would emerge to be conveyed to the West 153rd Street police station by a husky bluecoat.

It was decided not to wait until 3:00 P.M. to play the game, since the gates were closed and no one else was to be admitted. As Giants starter Christy Mathewson began warming up, two men, their arms locked, plunged seventy feet from the grandstand roof to the bleachers below. The men, dead, were carried away in blankets by police.

The rowdiness of the Giants fans wasn't the only thing concerning the Cubs players. In the Cubs dugout, the players were wary because they knew that Giants manager John McGraw was ruthless enough to try anything in order to win the game. They took seriously the rampant rumor that the Giants had bribed the umpires to throw the game the Giants' way.

JOHNNY EVERS: "On the afternoon that New York and Chicago played off their tie for the National League Championship of 1908, the rumor ran all over New York that the game was fixed for New York to win. Tinker was called from the Chicago bench an hour before the game and advised to save himself by betting on New York because the umpires were fixed, and offers to bet large sums were made at all saloons, and in the Polo Grounds itself on the strength of the rumor. When the Creamer case was exposed, months later, the probable origin of the rumor was revealed."

National League president Harry Pulliam investigated the rumors in December that someone connected with the Giants had attempted to bribe umpires Bill Klem and Johnny Johnstone to secure victory in the playoff game. The man put in charge of this "investigation" was Giants owner John T. Brush.

Umpire Bill Klem testified that shortly before the game was to begin, Giants physician Joseph Creamer, who had been hired as team doctor by John McGraw without Brush's knowledge, had approached him under the stands. According to Klem, Creamer, waving money, said, "Here's $2,500. It's yours if you will give all the close decisions to the Giants and see that they win sure. You know who is behind me and you needn't be afraid of anything. You will have a good job for the rest of your life."

Creamer, who had an excellent reputation, denied ever having spoken to Klem. Pulliam, however, believed Klem (who years later was inducted into the Hall of Fame), and the doctor was barred from all major league parks for life.

It wasn't the only Giants hanky-panky afoot. McGraw had cooked up a scheme to get Frank Chance thrown out of the game before it even began. Fred Snodgrass, a twenty-year-old kid sitting on the Giants bench that day, saw it all.

FRED SNODGRASS: "We tried to get Frank Chance thrown out of the game, but didn't succeed. Before the game we talked over in the clubhouse how in the world we could get Chance out of there. Matty was to pitch for us, and Frank always hit Matty pretty well. We felt if we could get him out, in some way, that we had a better chance of winning the play-off game and the pennant. Besides, we thought the pennant was ours by right, anyway. We thought the call on Merkle was a raw deal, and any means of redressing the grievance was legitimate.

"So it was cooked up that Joe McGinnity was to pick a fight with Chance early in the game. They were to have a knockdown, drag-out fight, Chance and McGinnity, and both would get thrown out of the game. Of course, we didn't need McGinnity, but they needed Chance. McGinnity did just what he was supposed to. He called Chance names on some pretext or other, stepped on his shoes, pushed him, actually spit on him. But Frank wouldn't fight. He was too smart."

MORDECAI BROWN: "We had just come out onto the field and were getting settled when Tom Needham, one of our utility men, came running up with the news that, back in the clubhouse he'd overheard Muggsy McGraw laying a plot to beat us. He said the plot was for McGraw to cut our batting practice to about four minutes instead of the regular ten, and then, if we protested to send his three toughest players, Turkey Mike Donlin, Iron Man McGinnity, and Cy Seymour charging out to pick a fight. The wild-eyed fans would riot and the blame would be put on us for starting it and the game would be forfeited to the Giants.

"Chance said to us, 'Cross 'em up. No matter when the bell rings to end practice, come right off the field. Don't give any excuse to quarrel.'

"We followed orders, but McGinnity tried to pick a fight with Chance anyway, and made a pass at him, but Husk stepped back, grinned and wouldn't fall for their little game."

Said the *New York Sun*, "At a quarter to three o'clock the real trouble begins. It is time."

Said W. J. Lampton in the *New York Times,* "Never before in the history of the game have there been so many to see a game who didn't see it."

Lampton described the fans sitting on the bluff waiting for the game to begin. He wrote, "After a while—two hours after a while—somebody in front announced the game had begun. A hush fell on the throng on Coogan's Bluff. Every breath was bated. Never in the history of the game had there been such a moment. It sounded like a pork packer's cheer for Upton Sinclair." (*The Jungle*, Sinclair's shocking exposé of the Chicago stockyards, had been published two years earlier.)

The playoff game of 1908 was one of the most fiercely fought in the history of the game of baseball. Against great odds, the Cubs achieved perhaps their greatest victory of all time. Hall of Fame pitcher Mordecai Brown recalled the day as the apex of his illustrious career.

* * *

MORDECAI BROWN: "Mathewson put us down quick in our first time at bat, but when the Giants came up with the sky splitting as the crowd screamed, Pfiester hit Fred Tenney [on the first pitch as a great roar filled the stadium], walked Buck Herzog [on four pitches], fanned Bresnahan [who did not bunt because McGraw didn't believe in using the sacrifice], but Kling dropped the third strike, and when Herzog broke for second, nailed him."

Kling's quick thinking was cited by Johnny Evers as one of the key plays in the game.

JOHNNY EVERS: "A throw of that kind made by Kling that caught Herzog off first base in the famous game between New York and Chicago when they played off their tie for the championship gave Chicago the pennant in 1908. Two men were on base, Bresnahan was striving to bunt. Kling caught the bunt signal, the ball was pitched out and like a flash Kling hurled the ball to Chance. Herzog was caught, hesitating eight feet from the bag and New York was stopped in the midst of a rally that ought to have netted half a dozen runs."

Despite Kling's play, the Giants scored the game's first run.

MORDECAI BROWN: "Turkey Mike Donlin doubled, scoring Tenney [Chance argued that the ball was foul as the crowd hooted] and out beyond center field a fireman fell off a telegraph pole and broke his neck. Pfiester walked Cy Seymour and then Chance motioned me to come in. [This was one of the great managerial strokes in Cubs history, a gutsy, decisive move by Frank Chance.] Two on base, two out. Our warmup pen was out in right center field so I had to push and shove my way through the crowd on the outfield grass.

"'Get the hell out of the way,' I bawled at 'em as I plowed through. 'Here's where you "black hand" guys get your chance. If I'm going to get killed I sure know that I'll die before a capacity crowd.'

"Arthur Devlin was up—a low-average hitter, great fielder but tough in the pinches. But I fanned him, and then you should have heard the names that flew around me as I walked to the bench.

"I was about as good that day as I ever was in my life. That year I had won 29 and, what with relief work, had been in 43 winning ball games.

"But in a way it was Husk Chance's day.

"That Chance had a stout heart in him. His first time at bat, it was in the second, the fans met him with a storm of hisses—not 'boos' like you hear in modern baseball—but the old, vicious hiss that comes from real hatred.

"Chance choked the hisses back down New York's throat by singling with a loud crack of the bat. The ball came back to Mathewson. He looked at Bresnahan behind the bat, then wheeled and threw to first, catching Chance off guard. Chance slid. Tenney came down with the ball. Umpire Bill Klem threw up his arm. Husk was out!

"Chance ripped and raved around, protesting. Most of us Cubs rushed out of the dugout. Solly Hofman called Klem so many names that Bill threw him out of the game.

"The stands behind us went into panic, they were so tickled and the roar was the wildest I ever heard when Matty went on to strike out Steinfeldt and Del Howard.

"Chance was grim when he came up again in the third. Tinker had led off the inning by tripling over Cy Seymour's head. We heard afterward that McGraw had warned Seymour that Tinker was apt to hit Mathewson hard, and to play away back. Seymour didn't."

The next day a sportswriter named Tad wrote in the *New York Evening Journal*, "Cy Seymour's wretched fielding yesterday was in a great measure responsible for the loss of the game." Here's how he described Tinker's triple:

TAD: "Tinker's fly to center should have been an easy out. It would have been had Seymour played the batter properly and it would have been caught had Seymour not misjudged it so badly. Instead of sprinting back and turning around, Seymour kept taking short backward steps. Finally he lunged at the ball and missed it altogether. The fans in centerfield moaned and after the game many of them said it was a play that any schoolboy fielder would have made. Then Cyrus groped about in the crowd and fielded the ball very slowly, allowing Tinker to get to third. Had this fly been caught chances are there would have been no runs in that inning, and the opportunity for a shut-out would have been splendid."

According to Johnny Evers, the acerbic Tad was not wrong—this was the play that cost the Giants the ball game.

JOHNNY EVERS: "Who lost the game? It was 'Cy' Seymour, but perhaps not a dozen of the 30,000 persons who witnessed the struggle know he did. New York had the game won until the third inning in which Tinker was Chicago's first batter. During the entire season Tinker had been hitting Mathewson hard, and the psychological effect of past performances has much to do with pitching and batting. Mathewson feared Tinker, and he signaled Seymour to play deep in center field. He was afraid that a long drive by Tinker might turn the tide of battle. Seymour saw the signal, but disregarded it, having an idea that Tinker would hit a low line fly, so he crept a few steps closer to the infield, instead of moving back. Matty dropped his famous 'fade away' over the plate, and Tinker drove a long, high, line fly to left center. Seymour made a desperate effort to reach the ball, but fell a few feet short, and the ball rolled to the crowd in the outfield for a three-base hit, and started a rally that gave Chicago the victory. If Seymour had played a deep field, as he was commanded to do, the probabilities are that New York would have won the pennant."

By the time Seymour threw the ball back in, Tinker was standing on third. A Cubs rally followed.

MORDECAI BROWN: "Kling singled Tinker home. I sacrificed Johnny to second. Sheckard flied out, Evers walked. Schulte doubled. We had Matty wobbling and then up came Chance, with the crowd howling. He answered them again with a double, and made it to second with a great slide that beat a great throw by Mike Donlin.

"Four runs.

"The Giants made their bid in the seventh. Art Devlin singled off me, so did Moose McCormick. I tried to pitch too carefully to Bridwell and walked him. There was sure bedlam in the air as McGraw took out Mathewson and sent up the kid, Larry Doyle, to hit. Doyle hit a high foul close to the stand and as Kling went to catch it, the fans sailed derby hats to confuse him—and bottles, papers, everything. But Kling had nerve and he caught it. [Second-guessed the *New York Tribune*, "It was strange that he should do so, for Matty is a strong batter, and Doyle has not faced an opposing pitcher in a big game since he was hurt weeks ago."]

"Every play, as I look back on it, was crucial. In the seventh after Tenney's fly had scored Devlin, Buck Herzog rifled one on the ground to left but Joe Tinker got one hand and one shin in front of it, blocked it, picked it up and just by a flash caught Herzog who made a wicked slide into first.

"In the ninth a big fight broke out in the stands and the game was held up until the police could throw in a cordon of bluecoats and stop it. It was as near a lunatic asylum as I ever saw. As a matter of fact the newspapers next day said seven men had been carted away, raving mad, from the park during the day. This was maybe exaggerated, but it doesn't sound impossible to anyone who was there that day."

New York could do nothing against the great Three-Finger Brown in the last two innings. Four pitched balls in the ninth disposed of Devlin, McCormick, and Bridwell as Chicago won the game and the pennant. For the third successive year the Chicago Cubs were National League champions, tying Pop Anson's record of three in a row in 1880, 1881, and 1882. At the end of the game, perhaps the greatest in Cubs history, the Cubs players were lucky to escape with their lives.

MORDECAI BROWN: "As the ninth ended with the Giants going out, one-two-three, we all ran for our lives, straight for the clubhouse with the pack at our heels. Some of our boys got caught by the mob and beaten up some. Tinker, Howard and Sheckard were struck. Chance was hurt most of all. A Giant fan hit him in the throat and Husk's voice was gone for a day or two of the World Series that followed. Pfiester got slashed on the shoulder by a knife.

"We made it to the dressing room and barricaded the door. Outside wild men were yelling for our blood—really. As the mob got bigger, the police came and formed a line across the door. We read the next day that the cops had to pull their revolvers to hold them back. I couldn't say as to that. We weren't sticking our heads out to see.

"As we changed clothes, too excited yet to put on one of those wild clubhouse pennant celebrations, the word came in that the Giants over in their dressing room were pretty low. We heard that old Cy Seymour was lying on the floor, in there, bawling like a baby about Tinker's triple.

"When it was safe we rode to our hotel in a patrol wagon, with two cops on the inside and four riding the running boards and the rear step. That night when we left for Detroit and the World Series we slipped out the back door and were escorted down the alley in back of our hotel by a swarm of policemen."

Back in Chicago, the *Tribune* had showed the game on the Electrical Baseball Board at Orchestra Hall for the benefit of the Tribune Hospital Fund. Seats were twenty-five cents, fifty cents, and $1 for boxes.

*   *   *

CHICAGO TRIBUNE: "In Orchestra Hall, a howling, shrieking, ball-mad crowd, wild in its enthusiasm, sometimes pleading, sometimes threatening, always 'pulling.' Through it all sat a handsome young woman whose eyes shone and cheeks flushed as the cheering increased, and who, when the Giants were retired at the close of the ninth, turned to the gray-haired woman by her side and said:

"'This is our anniversary day, Mother. He had to win. It's wonderful, isn't it?' and she laughed and cried at the same time.

"If the crowd had known that the wife of the great Cub leader was in their midst, Mrs. Frank Le Roy Chance would have been given an ovation that seldom falls to the lot of a woman.

"Another Cub wife was in the throng. With a party of friends Mrs. Joe Tinker sat only a few rows behind Mrs. Chance, madly waving a Cub banner.

"Upon leaving the building she shouted over and over:

"'Four to two, four to two.'"

Current Literature, a high-toned publication of the day, remarked in November 1908, "Had [Henry] Chadwick, who died a few months ago, lived until last month he would have seen a nation gone wild over the game, politicians forgetful of their campaigns, stockbrokers ignoring their tickets, well dressed women courting ruin for their gowns and more by the hundred risking their very lives in one mad scramble to see the closing games of the season. . . .

"Never has there been such a frenzied baseball year as the one that came to a close a few days ago."

22

Champs Again

The rift between Chicago and New York caused by the Merkle play and its aftermath never did heal. Until the day he died in 1934, manager John McGraw swore that his Giants had been robbed of the pennant. In the 1940s an aging Roger Bresnahan bitterly told *New York Times* writer Arthur Daley, "Johnny Evers hasn't completed the force-out on Merkle yet."

JOHNNY EVERS: "One day during the off season I ran into Roger Bresnahan, who caught Matty that afternoon, and the Giant catcher showed me a medal. It was one of 28 which John T. Brush, Giant owner, had struck off for each member of the team and showed a ballplayer with a bat in his hand and another throwing a ball and the inscription read: 'The Real Champions, 1908.'"

After winning that playoff game, Cubs owner Charles Murphy rubbed salt on the Giants' wounds. He was incensed at John McGraw's bellyaching that the Giants had been cheated out of the pennant. Said Murphy, referring to Fred Merkle's failure to run to second base on a ground ball, "We can't supply brains to the New York Club's dumb players."

For the second year in a row, the Cubs met Hughie Jennings's Detroit Tigers in the World Series. In 1908 only three American Leaguers had hit over .300, including league leader Ty Cobb at .324 and Tigers outfielder Sam Crawford at .311. (The third one, Doc Gessler of the Red Sox, hit .308.)

Like the Cubs, the Tigers won their pennant on the final day of the season. The race had been among four teams, the Tigers, the White Sox (led by Ed Walsh's 40–15 record), the Cleveland Naps (led by Napolean Lajoie and Addie Joss), and the St. Louis Browns (led by Rube Waddell). The Cleveland Naps could have won it had they swept their final two games. Instead they split, and thus the pennant came down to the winner of the Tigers–White Sox game on the last day. The Tigers' Wild Bill Donovan (18–7) pitched a two-hit shutout as Detroit won 7–0.

For the second year in a row, the Tigers were no match for Frank Chance's defensive machine. The Tigers came close to victory in the opening game in Detroit, when they led 6–5 in the ninth inning. Ed Summers, a rookie phenom with a 24–12 record, was one of the first knuckleball pitchers in baseball. The youngster entered the game in the third inning and seemed firmly in control. But there is always a risk when you pitch a rookie in the World Series: The pressure is very great, and rookies tend to make crucial mistakes under pressure. At the end Summers couldn't handle the strain.

Before Summers went out to pitch the ninth, Tigers manager Jennings told his pitcher, "You can do it, Eddie, just take your time."

After the youngster retired Johnny Evers, Frank Schulte beat out a slow roller to short. Then came the play that defeated Summers and the Tigers. Frank Chance hit another slow roller, this one back toward the pitcher. With the rain still falling, Summers raced in to make the play and slipped on the wet grass. Chance was credited with an infield hit.

Upset with himself, Summers allowed a short single to left by Harry Steinfeldt to load the bases. Solly Hofman then singled in two runs. When Joe Tinker and Johnny Kling singled, the Cubs had three more.

In all, the Cubs got six hits in a row off the rookie. The five ninth-inning runs he allowed gave the Cubs the first game, 10–6.

The second game was played in Chicago, where Cubs owner Charles Murphy infuriated his fans by raising World Series ticket prices considerably. Usually a team charged double the regular season price. Murphy charged five times as much. Adding to the fans' anger was the knowledge that somehow large blocks of tickets had been scooped up by speculators, who scalped them. The suspicion was that Murphy had made some extra money selling them to the ticket sellers. The fans rebelled.

Instead of the sellout crowd of 25,000 that was expected at West Side Park, only 17,760 came. Standing in mute testimony to the fans' anger were ropes stretched across the outfield to keep back the overflow—but no one was sitting behind them.

For seven innings Orval Overall and Will Bill Donovan dueled in a scoreless game.

With one out in the eighth, Solly Hofman beat out an infield hit, only Chicago's second hit. Donovan threw Joe Tinker a wide, slow pitch that the Cubs shortstop hit deep to right. It landed behind the outfield ropes in the right-field bleachers.

The ground rule was that hits behind the ropes were to be ground rule doubles. But umpire Bill Klem ruled that because there was no one sitting behind them, the hit was a home run. The Tigers argued loudly. Klem refused to abide by the ground rule.

"Why is it a homer?" asked Ty Cobb. "The ball dropped in the ropes in back of me, and that was to be two bases."

"That ground rule doesn't cover the bleachers when there is no overflow crowd," said Klem. "I've been calling balls that land in that bleacher home runs all season. And that rope out there don't change it."

"But that wasn't our agreement," said Jennings.

For fifteen minutes they argued. The home run call stood.

Donovan, unnerved, his arm stiff after the fifteen-minute delay, allowed four more hits and four more runs in what became a 6–1 loss.

In the third game Ty Cobb had four hits, and the Tigers beat Jack Pfiester 8–3 in the only game the Cubs would lose.

As the Series returned to Detroit, Tigers fans were confident that they had seen the real Tigers. They were expecting more of the same, but in the next game Cubs ace Mordecai Brown pitched a 3–0 shutout. The Tigers got only four hits; Cobb was blanked. The Cubs made no errors. The game took a short hour and thirty-five minutes.

In his autobiography Johnny Evers recalled the series of brilliant defensive plays that were characteristic of Frank Chance's flawless combine, an inspired defense that helped the Cubs win the fourth game and propelled them toward another championship.

JOHNNY EVERS: "Chicago had made two runs in the third inning and with Brown pitching, appeared to be winning easily until [Charley] O'Leary and [Sam] Crawford opened the fourth inning with line singles to left, putting runners on first and second, no one out, and Cobb, the best batter in the American league, at bat.

"O'Leary is fast, Crawford is extremely fast and Cobb is a natural bunter. Everyone knew Cobb intended to bunt, and that failure to retire him or one of the other runners probably meant victory for Detroit. Jennings sent Cobb to bat with instructions to bunt toward third base. They knew Brown intended to make the play to third base to force O'Leary, and O'Leary was signaled to take as much lead as possible and start running when the ball was pitched. Brown, past master in field generalship as well as execution[,] walked over to Steinfeldt at third base and said: 'Anchor yourself to that bag. The ball is coming here.' Kling signaled for a fast ball close in at the waist. It was his plan to have Cobb miss the ball on his first attempt to bunt and then by a quick throw to Tinker on second, to catch O'Leary off the base. Brown shook his head and signaled Kling his intention to pitch a curve ball low and on the outside corner of the plate. Cobb was hoping that Brown would pitch precisely that kind of a ball, and Brown knew that Cobb was hoping for it, and it was Brown's plan to force Cobb to do exactly what he was most anxious to do—to make a perfect bunt and toward third base. Brown pitched perfectly, and Cobb bunted perfectly, thirty feet toward third base and about five feet inside the foul line. As Brown pitched he went forward at top speed, 'following the ball through,' and he was in front of the ball when it bounded along. Still running he scooped the sphere, and whirling made a terrific throw straight to Steinfeldt, and O'Leary was forced out by fifteen feet on a seemingly impossible play, executed chiefly because Brown knew exactly what Cobb would do.

"Chance's magnificent machine was not through. Knowing that the failure of that play would 'rattle' the Tigers they instantly seized the psychological situation. Kling gave a quick signal for a fast inshoot across [Claude] Rossman's shoulders, and Brown, without waiting for Detroit to rally and plan a play, drove the ball fast and high. Rossman struck at the ball and missed it. Like a flash Kling hurled the sphere toward second base, Tinker met it at top speed, touched Crawford three feet from the base and standing still, and Detroit was beaten and in panic. An instant later as Rossman struck out, Kling threw to second, and Evers, leaping, stuck up one hand, dragged down the ball, and while descending touched Cobb as he slid. The big crowd, frenzied over the brilliant series of plays, and only half understanding them, cheered for five minutes."

By the last game, played in Detroit, the Cubs (and the bad weather) had demoralized not only the Tigers but their fans as well. Only 6,210 frozen fans attended, the poorest crowd in the history of the World Series. What they saw was a magnificent performance by Cubs pitcher Orval Overall, the big California curve ball specialist with the 1.92 earned run average.

Chicago scored a run in the first inning. With one out, Evers, Schulte, and Chance singled in succession.

The Tigers' one chance came in the first inning. Overall had to strike out four batters to end the threat.

After walking Matty McIntyre, Overall struck out Charley O'Leary. Sam Crawford singled, but Ty Cobb, who hit .368 and stole two bases in the Series, struck out. Claude Rossman swung for a third strike, but the pitch was wild, and Rossman was safe at first. The bases were loaded. Overall, who through the years was overshadowed by Mordecai Brown and Ed Reulbach on the Cubs staff, then struck out Germany Schaefer to end the threat.

JOHNNY EVERS: "There are many players, among them members of the Detroit team who faced him in the final game of the World Championship in 1908, who believe Overall's curve a more marvelous one [than Mordecai Brown's]. In that game the Chicago giant had one of the most remarkable curves ever pitched. At times the ball darted down two feet and struck the ground while the batters struck more than a foot over it.

"Overall pitches his curve with a wide, sweeping overhand swing, releasing the ball over the side of the index finger as his hand turns downward."

In the Cubs fifth Kling walked, was sacrificed to second by Overall, and scored on a double by Evers. That was all the scoring, as Overall and the Cubs won the finale 2–0. The big pitcher allowed just three hits and struck out ten as the Chicago Cubs became the first team in baseball history to win two world titles in a row.

After the game Jennings told his players, "Don't feel too badly about it. We were beaten again by a great team. A great team!"

The staff of Mordecai Brown, Ed Reulbach, Orval Overall, and Jack Pfiester had pitched the Cubs to three pennants and two consecutive world championships.

During those three years the four great pitchers won 232 games against 85 losses, a .732 winning percentage. Caught by Kling and backed by Tinker, Evers, and Chance, this was the very best team the National League ever offered.

But it was to be the Cubs' last world championship—ever.

FRED LIEB: "Could a soothsayer have told the happy Chicago fans what World Series cards fate would deal them in the next four [as of today nine] decades, they would have been more tempered in their gloating."

23

Continued Success

In 1909 the Cubs had another terrific season, winning 104 games while losing only 49, despite the absence of Johnny Kling, who held out all season in a salary dispute. This was five wins more than in 1908, but it still wasn't good enough as Fred Clarke's Pittsburgh Pirates, led by shortstop Honus Wagner, were so far ahead by Labor Day that there was no catching them. The Pirates went on to win 110 games and then beat the Detroit Tigers in the World Series.

The following year the Cubs again won 104 games, but in this season the Pirates tumbled precipitously, and the Cubs won the 1910 National League pennant by 13 games over John McGraw's Giants, their fourth pennant in five years. The Cubs went into first place on May 25 and stayed in front to the finish.

Despite being considered overwhelming favorites to defeat Connie Mack's Philadelphia A's in the 1910 World Series, the Cubs had suffered a crippling blow late in the season when their star second baseman, Johnny Evers, broke his leg sliding into home. An unnamed reporter for the popular *Literary Digest* recalled the string of unfortunate occurrences that plagued Evers that year.

LITERARY DIGEST: "It was in 1910, late in the season, that Luck commenced to wallop Evers and strive to knock him out. An automobile accident in which he was driving, and one of his best friends George McDonald, was killed, started it. Sickness, a run of nervous trouble, and then, late in the season, sliding to the plate in a game at Cincinnati, in a desperate effort to cinch the championship, Evers broke his leg. The bone snapped and protruded through the flesh. He was carried off the field, and in his suffering he grinned and waved his hand to me.

"A few weeks later a second blow fell. He was hobbling around on crutches, striving to aid the team, which without his services was going into a world series. He had invested all his money, every cent he had made, in the shoe business. His store in Troy, which he owned with one of his friends, was prosperous. On the strength of its earnings he had opened a huge shoe emporium in Chicago, using the credit of the Troy store to help establish the new one.

"The Chicago stock represented $50,000. He did not know that the trusted partner in Troy had been gambling until news came that the store was closed—and his partner gone. Investigation showed that the partner had gambled away the profits, the stock, and had incurred debts. The creditors at once seized the Chicago store. Evers was broke, in debt, the earnings of years swept away.

"I went to condole with him that evening. He grinned and told how sorry he was for his partner."

The aging Cubs faced the young but talented Philadelphia A's, a powerful team that finished fourteen and a half games ahead of the New York Highlanders and eighteen ahead of Detroit. The A's top pitcher was Colby Jack Coombs, who had a 31–9 record. Albert "Chief" Bender finished 23–5. Eddie Plank was 16–10, and spitballer Cy Morgan 18–12.

The A's also featured the $100,000 infield of veteran captain Harry Davis, Eddie Collins, Jack Barry, and Frank Baker. Second baseman Collins had led the league in stolen bases with 81. Cobb was behind him with 65.

It would take a stunning four games to one upset of the Cubs in this Series to show the baseball world that the A's were for real, and after Connie Mack's A's won pennants in 1911, 1913, and 1914, this club would be rated among the American League's best, as Bender, Plank, Home Run Baker, Eddie Collins, and Connie Mack all would be inducted into the Hall of Fame.

Colby Jack Coombs dominated the Series, winning Games 2, 3, and 5, a repeat of Christy Mathewson's iron-man performance of 1905.

Against A's pitching, the Cubs hit only .222, and it was clear to observers that Mordecai Brown, who lost two of the games, no longer was the same pitcher. His stamina was gone.

Commented an observer of the time known as the Old Timer, "The Cubs seemed to have lost the confidence and dash that was theirs in the days of 1906 to 1908."

The Cubs had grown old, seemingly overnight. Their time at the top had come to an end.

Chance's Cubs had another good year in 1911, winning 92 games, but they finished seven and a half games out of first because they were unable to catch McGraw's Giants, in part because Orval Overall retired, complaining of the way owner Charles Murphy was treating him. Overall stayed out of baseball for two years before making a brief comeback in the Pacific Coast League. In 1911 catcher Johnny Kling was traded away to the Boston Braves, and Johnny Evers had a nervous breakdown and played little.

The game had stopped being fun for manager Frank Chance.

JOHNNY EVERS: "One evening after Frank Chance had won two World Series Championships, he sat gloomily silent for a long time. The big, hearty, joyous boy who had come from California a dozen years before was battered, grizzled, careworn and weary. Still young, his fine face showed lines of care and worry and a few gray hairs streaked through his head. He was thirty-two and looked old. For a long time he sat musing. Then he looked up and smiled grimly.

"'This business is making a crab out of me,' he remarked."

*   *   *

Though the Cubs didn't win in 1911, the players were able to derive great pleasure whenever the team defeated the hated Giants. Years later, when Joe Tinker was asked about his finest moment as a Cubs player, he picked a game in 1911 when he single-handedly defeated Christy Mathewson and the Giants.

JOE TINKER: "My greatest day? You might know it was against the Giants. I think that goes for every Cub who played for 'Husk' Chance in those years on Chicago's West Side. I know it did for Johnny Evers and Miner Brown and I'm sure it would for Chance if he still was alive. [Chance died in 1924.]

"All of us have bright memories of World Series against the White Sox and Tigers and Athletics, but the games you play over and over, even after more than thirty years, were against the Giants and John McGraw. Chance and McGraw were born to battle on baseball fields.

"If you didn't honestly and furiously hate the Giants, you weren't a real Cub.

"I was in the famous game when Fred Merkle failed to touch second and then the playoff for the 1908 pennant when Chance and McGraw never were far from blows. I was in the lineup when we beat the Tigers in eight out of ten games in two World Series.

"But the game which gave me the greatest thrill was on August 7, 1911. That was the one in which I made four hits and stole home on Christy Mathewson, which is something a man tells his grandchildren or writes down in a book.

"The Cubs, with four pennants and two world championships in five seasons still were on top of the National League on that August day, but closer to a complete collapse than any of us knew. The old lineup was breaking. Young Vic Saier had taken Husk's job at first; Heinie Zimmerman was on third in place of Harry Steinfeldt and Jimmy Archer had replaced Johnny Kling back of the plate.

"I guess my memory of the game is made keener by the fact that two days before I'd had a terrific argument with Chance and had been suspended. On Saturday—that'd be August 5—we were playing Brooklyn and out in front 2–1 in the third. There was a strong wind blowing to left field and two were out and two on. The Dodger batter pumped one over my head. I went back and yelled to Jimmy Sheckard I'd take it. Well the wind blew the ball out and it dropped safe and two Dodgers scored.

"By the seventh we were ahead again, 4–3, and once more the Dodgers had two on and two out. At that time the wind had changed and was coming in from left field. When the batter popped another one over my head, Sheck started in and I didn't move. The wind drove the ball back toward the infield but I thought Jimmy would get it and let it alone. Jimmy couldn't reach the ball and two more runs scored.

"When I got back to the bench, Frank, his face red with fury, snarled, 'I'm damn sick and tired of you letting those flies drop.'

"I was just as mad because the Dodgers had scored, so I screamed right back, 'I'm sick and tired of you yelling at me.'

"Husk told me to turn in my uniform and fined me $150.

"Well, there was no game on Sunday and Charlie Murphy, he owned the Cubs, sent for me to come to his office. He said he wanted Frank and me to straighten things out and I said it would be all right with me.

"Now Monday also was an open day but the Giants were coming through and McGraw had agreed to stop off and play a postponed game. So Husk agreed to reinstate me for that game. Chance was a great guy and a square manager. And smart.

"Only two games out of first place and going into August the game looked like the spot for New York to pick up some ground. And McGraw had Matty ready to pitch. Chance countered with Brown, who always gave Matty a battle.

"There was a good crowd at the old West Side Park to see Matty and Brownie. The game was in an uproar before it was one minute old. Brownie hit John Devore in the head with his first pitch and they had to carry the Giant left fielder off the diamond.

"McGraw sent Red Murray in to run for Devore and Brownie was nervous. He passed Larry Doyle, and Fred Snodgrass singled to fill the bases. It looked for a minute as if Brownie wasn't going to last. Then Sheck took Beals Becker's low liner so fast that Murray had to stay on third. [Fred] Merkle slammed one hard at me and I could have forced Murray at the plate but I tossed the ball to Zim and he whipped it to Saier, and Snodgrass and Merkle were out by a mile.

"Sheckard opened our half with a triple on Matty's first pitch. And then Matty guessed wrong when Schulte's bunt didn't roll foul. Archer hit to Matty, and Sheck was run down but Schulte went all the way to third and then was nailed at the plate, trying to score on Zim's roller. You ran the bases and took the chances for Chance. Zim and Archer tried a double steal but [catcher Chief] Meyers broke it up easily and we were all square.

"I was up second in the next inning and hit a single to left and when Murray decided he'd throw to first, I went into second and scored on Saier's double to put us one run ahead.

"We got all tangled up in the fourth when the Giants tied the score. Schulte fumbled Becker's liner and Beals went clear to third and scored on Herzog's single. Then Brownie threw over first and Buck reached second and we were shaky again. But Meyers hit to me and I started a double play with young [Jim] Doyle, who was subbing for Evers, on the pivot and we got clear.

"Then we got two runs in the fourth, but I forget the details for the big moments of my greatest day were coming.

"In the sixth I hit off the left field fence for a triple. It might have been a homer inside the park except that Zim got a slow start off first and I had to pull up at third. I guess maybe Matty thought I was winded and would rest awhile. But I broke on his next pitch and scored standing up.

"Honestly, I believe that was one of the worst games Matty ever pitched. In the eighth, when Doyle sacrificed Zim to third, Matty scooped the ball with his bare hand and when Bob Emslie called Heinie safe, Christy was so mad he almost stopped the game.

"When I came up, Matty threw me one of those low, outside curves that almost sent me back to Kansas City before Frank made me change my batting style. I hit it for a long double to score Zim and Archer and that was the ball game. We won 8–6 and made fourteen hits off Big Six.

"And when we got back into the clubhouse, Chance came over to me with a big grin and said, 'Damn it, I ought to suspend you every day.'"

24

Murphy's Law

It is the rare team owner who can leave things alone, especially when the team is doing well. Charles Murphy, the owner of the Cubs, was not that rare owner.

For years Murphy had been a league irritant. As far back as 1906, Charlie Ebbets, the owner of the Brooklyn Dodgers, got the league to require that all parks install dressing rooms. At that time players in uniform would travel by horse-drawn carriage from their hotel to the ballpark, subjecting themselves to jeers and missiles of fans throughout their route. Charles Comiskey, the White Sox owner, applauded the end of the parades, saying he was "not in show business."

But Murphy announced he would defy the rule and transport his team any way he pleased. Moreover, he vowed, he would add bells to the horses and make the blankets on the horses even more elaborate. Against his will, he finally did install a clubhouse for the visiting teams, but the players complained it was unfit for use. Murphy accused the Cincinnati Reds players of twisting the doors from their lockers and throwing them outside. President Pulliam fined Murphy $25, and in 1909 the league passed a new rule, aimed at Murphy, banning carriage parades.

Murphy raised eyebrows in 1908 when he was accused of profiting from the sale of World Series tickets to speculators. After an investigation conducted by the National Commission, Murphy was severely criticized for his handling of the tickets, but no collusion with the scalpers was uncovered.

Charles Murphy

During that same World Series, Murphy infuriated the out-of-town writers by seating them in the back row of the grandstand. As a result, the writers organized into the Baseball Writers Association of America. They would never be given a bad seat again.

Murphy, an insufferable blowhard, believed in image over substance. In 1912 he glorified baseball as "a public benefactor, a friend of the anti-tuberculosis league since it brought people into the open air, and a beneficial influence on youth because of their emulation of big-league stars as models of conduct."

Through the years the other executives of the National League had grown tired of Murphy's penchant for trying to get around the rules and also for disparaging them in the newspapers.

In 1911, Murphy attempted to slip one of his players to the minors, only to see St. Louis manager Roger Bresnahan claim him, preventing Murphy from making the move. Murphy held it against Bresnahan, and later that season in the lobby of the Waldorf-Astoria Hotel, Murphy created a scene when he shouted across the room at Bresnahan, "You are a liar. I know the whole thing, and I've got something on you and will have you put out of the National League."

What Murphy was alluding to was his contention that during the 1911 season Bresnahan was helping out his old team, the Giants, by having his present team, the Cardinals, "take it easy" against them.

Bresnahan demanded that the league investigate Murphy, not because he himself needed the commission's protection against "windbags" like Murphy, but because "baseball did."

Nothing was done to Murphy at the time, but then later in the season the same charge against Bresnahan was made in the *Chicago Post* under the signature of Horace Fogel, the owner of the Philadelphia Phillies.

What the public didn't realize was that Charles P. Taft, the wealthy Cincinnatian and half-brother of William Howard Taft, had put up the money that enabled Murphy to take control of the Cubs, and that both Taft and Murphy had a financial stake in the Philadelphia Phillies, whose ballpark was owned by Mrs. Taft. Taft and Murphy had installed Horace Fogel as figurehead president of the Philadelphia team.

FRED LIEB: "Fogel, a former Philadelphia baseball writer, had no money of his own, and was sort of stooge-president for Charley Murphy, head of the Cubs, who had supplied the Philadelphia purchase money and controlled both clubs."

Not only did Fogel accuse Bresnahan of wrongdoing, he also accused National League president Thomas Lynch and the umpires of conniving to let the Giants win.

Lynch brought Fogel up on seven charges. He was convicted of five of them. Banned from sitting in on league meetings, Fogel was bought out by a backer.

Newspapermen knew Fogel was the scapegoat for the real culprit, Charles Murphy. When Fogel was ousted, they looked behind him to Murphy and G. F. Forman, the sports editor of the *Chicago Post*, who revealed that the article in his newspaper accusing Bresnahan and St. Louis of crookedness and signed by Fogel had in reality been written by Murphy.

Commented historian Harold Seymour, "Murphy turned out to be a growing trial to his fellow owners. [He] continued to act up until he became obnoxious to his colleagues."

Complained Garry Herrmann, president of the Cincinnati Reds, "He is continually trying to stir up trouble and strife and to cause hard feelings between the club owners of the two leagues."

Pittsburgh owner Barney Dreyfuss publicly called him a "rat" and a "sneak."

By the end of the 1912 season Murphy was feuding with his manager and first baseman, Frank Chance, whom Murphy once had called "the greatest manager in the past quarter century." But his manager was demanding a four-year contract, and Murphy was reluctant to give it to him.

Though the Cubs had won 91 games that year, the team finished third behind the Giants and Pirates. That the team had done as well as it had despite the appendicitis attack during spring training that killed starting third baseman Jimmy Doyle and the 5–6 record posted by Mordecai Brown was a testament to the Peerless Leader's managerial genius. If Chance had to put up with Murphy's interference and mouth, he wanted security and salary to make it worthwhile.

On September 28, 1912, while Chance was in the hospital undergoing an operation for a blood clot, Murphy attempted to undermine him when he denounced the Cubs players for drinking too much. He declared that the players would have to get along for the rest of the season without liquor.

Chance, who had been beaned often and suffered from terrible headaches, arose from his sickbed to defend his players as industrious and sober and to denounce Murphy.

A week later Chance wrote the following column in the *Chicago Tribune*, revealing that he had sold his interest in the team (he received $150,000 for his one-tenth interest) and appealing to the fans to support him.

FRANK CHANCE: "At the request of the *Chicago Tribune* I have consented to write articles about what may be my last series of games as manager of the Chicago Cubs. I hope for some reasons it won't be my last, but that is something I can't know now. Chicago has been good to me and I have tried to give the best I had to Chicago. I promised the gentleman who bought my one-tenth interest in the club that I would come back as manager if Mr. Murphy offered me a fair contract. I am ready to do so. It's up to Mr. Murphy. I have not resigned.

"The sporting editor told me the fans would want to know just what I thought of the chances of the Cubs against the White Sox. He said I ought to start my article right off with that, because it would give it what he called a good 'punch.' I always expect my own orders to be obeyed by my players, so here it is: I think the Cubs will beat the White Sox.

"Naturally that is what everyone would expect me to say. But I do expect to win. So do our players. We always feel that way. It is one of the reasons why we won four pennants. We expected to win the pennant this year. And I still think we would have won except for hard luck, the worst of which was the injury which put Archer out of the game. I knew all along that if anything happened to Archer we were gone. We cut the Giants' lead down from sixteen games to four games. Then just when we had them on the run we slumped ourselves and lost our chance.

"It was because we expected to win and never gave up fighting that we took the pennant in 1908. It was one of the greatest fights against handicaps ever made by a baseball club. I wouldn't give lead money for a ball club that didn't expect to win. A really game club should expect to win every game all season. It would be foolish to think so. But when it goes onto the field every day it should expect to win that particular one.

"I make these statements because I want the fans to know the Cubs.

"What we feel is what some of the regular baseball reporters call our 'fighting spirit.' The Cubs have just as much of that spirit now as ever."

As usual, Murphy got in the final word. During the ninth and final game of the Cubs–White Sox city exhibition series, the White Sox opened the game by scoring six runs in the first inning. Murphy was so furious he came down from his box seat to the bench and fired Chance as manager. Johnny Evers was named to succeed him. Murphy gave Evers the four-year contract he had refused to give Chance, paying him $10,000 a year.

Once Murphy announced that Chance would not be coming back in 1913, Chance gave vent to his feelings, charging that Murphy had refused to spend money on players or on the park and that he had refused to scout players in the better minor leagues as a way to keep his costs down.

Said Chance, "No manager can be a success without competent players, and some of these I have are anything but skilled. In all the time I have been with this club I have had to fight to get the players I wanted. Murphy has not spent one third as much for players as have other magnates. How can he expect to win championships without ballplayers?"

According to Chance, when he told Murphy what the other owners were spending for new players, Murphy told him, "If they want to be suckers and pay for it, they can, but I won't."

Before he left, Chance said that he had had to operate under Murphy's cheap reign for the past three years. He said his players often would complain to him of the low salaries Murphy was paying them. Chance revealed that in 1906, the year the Cubs won 116 games, he was making $5,500 when his less successful rivals John McGraw ($18,000 a year) and Fred Clarke ($10,000 a year) were making far more money than he was.

As a farewell statement, Chance brought up Murphy's often-made promise to build a new ballpark.

"I'll bet $1,000 he never does," said Chance.

Murphy in his own defense tried to tell everyone that Chance had resigned.

On December 15, 1912, Murphy's cost cutting continued when he began a sell-off of his high-priced stars, trading Joe Tinker to Cincinnati and in July 1913 trading Ed Reulbach to Brooklyn. His most criticized move was sending Mordecai Brown to the ignominy of the minor leagues.

Said Harold Seymour, "Ignoring the fact that these men had helped him toward very considerable profits and heedless of the deep attachment Chicago fans felt for them, he shed all sentiment and rid himself of some of these favorites."

Murphy's last player move as owner was the firing of Johnny Evers during the winter of 1913–14 even though Evers, his pitching staff decimated by Murphy's cost cutting, had done well to finish third with 88 wins in 1913.

According to Sam Weller in the *Chicago Tribune*, Evers and Murphy had had several run-ins, and only the success of the Cubs during the last six weeks of the season had kept Murphy from firing him. Wrote Weller, "Long before the season was over Evers had confided to some of his friends that he didn't feel sure of his job and in reality was manager in name only, because he dared make no move of any consequence without the sanction of Murphy. He explained that his financial condition compelled him to stick to the job, no matter how unpleasant it might be."

A few days before Murphy fired Evers, Murphy spoke to reporters. He told them, "Evers is a great ball player, but too impulsive to be a manager and a player at the same time." Murphy always viewed the intercity series with the White Sox as having the importance of the World Series. To the players, the series was merely an exhibition. But Murphy had fired Chance the year before for losing the series, and this year he again was using the series with the White Sox as the excuse to can his manager.

"We ought to have beaten the White Sox easily last fall, and would have licked them if the team had been properly handled," said Murphy. "Evers's bad judgment cost us the series. The worst case of bad judgment was in the fifth game, the one that [Joe] Benz pitched against us and won in eleven innings by a score of 2 to 0." Murphy then went on to explain the circumstances of the loss, Evers's failure to pinch-hit for the pitcher and pinch-run for a slow runner.

"We should never have been licked by the White Sox, and better handling of the team in the games would have won that series. [Sox manager Nixey] Callahan and [coach] Kid Gleason both said after the series was over that Evers could be thanked by the South Siders for giving them the big end of the purse."

What Murphy didn't understand was that Evers and his players had already played in 153 regular season games and they wanted to go home.

Said Weller, "It is doubtful if Evers knew of his impending discharge." During the fall Evers lived in Chicago and gave most of his time to the Cubs. When the Federal League became active late in December, Evers was dispatched about the country signing the Cubs before the "outlaws" could nab them. He journeyed beyond Fort Worth and down to Tampa. He was successful in signing Hippo Vaughn, Tommy Leach, Art Phelan, George Pearce, and perhaps two or three others. At the same time Murphy employed Hank O'Day to go to Chattanooga to sign Jimmy Johnston, the young outfielder.

When at the end of the season the Chicago Whales of the newly formed Federal League offered Evers a substantial raise over the $10,000 a year he was making in Chicago, the Cubs stalwart informed Murphy that unless he got more money, he would not play in the field for the Cubs.

Murphy, jumping at the chance to dump his long-term contract, took Evers's demand to be a resignation, and he gave Evers his ten days' notice, declaring him to be through.

At the same time Boston Braves owner James Gaffney saw the opportunity to obtain Evers, and he swapped Murphy second baseman Bill Sweeney for him. Evers balked, demanding he be made a free agent so he could make a deal for himself.

After Murphy fired Evers, he replaced him with former umpire Hank O'Day, the same man who had given the Cubs the 1908 pennant when he decided in their favor in the Merkle game. O'Day had managed the Reds in 1912 before he was fired at the end of the season.

Murphy, meanwhile, had underestimated how disapprovingly other National League executives viewed his dealings. Commented writer Lee Allen, "The reaction was electric, not only in Chicago but all over the National League, and it was demanded that something, at long last, be done to drive Murphy out of baseball."

The first move the league executives took was to make sure Johnny Evers remained happy in the National League. The Chicago Federals had already signed Joe Tinker and Mordecai Brown. They didn't want Evers going there also.

Evers was urged to sign with the Boston Braves. To get Evers to agree to go, the league paid him $25,000. The following year Evers, still a force, teamed with shortstop Rabbit Maranville to lead the Miracle Braves to the 1914 pennant.

When Evers was named the captain of the Braves, he told a reporter, "Anybody that comes to this ball club will either hustle with the rest of us, or we'll drive him off the team."

When Evers led the Boston Braves to the National League championship in 1914, sixteen and a half games ahead of the fourth-place Cubs, and Evers was named the Most Valuable Player in the league, one gloating Evers fan wrote:

> *Chubby Charlie from Chicago*
> *Must have made an awful squawk,*
> *When they named the Chalmers winner,*
> *Johnny Evers, Troy, New York.*

After making sure Evers was safely out of the clutches of the Federal League, the National League executives went out of their way to castigate Charles Murphy for the way he had treated his players.

For several years American League president Ban Johnson had been trying to get rid of Murphy, but now he had powerful company. The new National League president, John K. Tener, "requested" that Charles Taft buy out Murphy's interest. He did so, paying $503,500 for Murphy's 53 percent of the Cubs' stock.

Taft chose as the new president William Hale Thompson, Murphy's longtime assistant. Pittsburgh owner Barney Dreyfuss protested that making a virtual office boy a president was an insult to every club owner. Taft assured the owners he had bought all of Murphy's stock and convinced them to leave Thompson in there until he could sell the team.

When Murphy was forced out of baseball, the *Sporting Life* magazine printed the following poem, a vicious parody of Franklin P. Adams's classic poem.

> *Brought to the leash and smashed in the jaw,*
> *Evers to Tener to Taft.*
> *Hounded and hustled outside of the law,*
> *Evers to Tener to Taft.*
> *Torn from the Cubs and the glitter of gold,*
> *Stripped of the guerdons and glory untold,*
> *Kicked in the stomach and cut from the fold,*
> *Evers to Tener to Taft.*

25

Charles Weeghman

The other owners of the National League had good reason to be furious with Cubs owner Charles Murphy. Their league was under threat from a new challenge, the Federal League.

This new league had started in 1912 as a minor league called the United States League but folded after five weeks. The next year it had six teams, including Chicago, Pittsburgh, and St. Louis. In 1914 it added two teams and announced itself to be a major league.

Part of the National League competitive strategy was to keep its players from jumping to the newcomers. Murphy's actions were damaging the league. Because of his wholesale release of expensive players, the new league was able to feature former Cubs stars Joe Tinker, Mordecai Brown, and Ed Reulbach.

Murphy had traded Joe Tinker to Cincinnati in December 1912, and after an excellent season with the Reds during which the shortstop hit .317, Garry Herrmann of Cincinnati decided to deal him because he had been playing-manager and the Reds had finished seventh in 1913. In the winter of 1913–14, Brooklyn owner Charles Ebbets announced that he had purchased Tinker, exciting the Brooklyn fans who were looking forward to the prospect of watching the play of this famed star.

Ebbets told reporters that the deal provided for him to pay the Reds $15,000, with Tinker getting a $10,000 signing bonus.

A couple of days later the directors of the Reds challenged the right of Reds president Garry Herrmann to sell Tinker, demanding the deal be called off.

Ebbets, furious, vowed he would get Tinker. A deal was a deal.

The affair became complicated when Murphy, engaging in some blatant tampering, announced that he wanted Tinker back with the Cubs. Ebbets wired Murphy, "Have purchased the release of Joe Tinker. Please do not confer with him."

Murphy wired that he had no intention of doing anything with Tinker. Ebbets, who didn't believe or trust him, nevertheless sent a second telegram. Murphy again sent a "Who, me?" reply. In a third telegram Ebbets warned Murphy that he was going to call on the National Commission to punish him for his tampering.

Meanwhile, back in Chicago, Tinker told reporters he wanted to play in Chicago. In Cincinnati, Herrmann continued feuding with his directors. Ebbets demanded the Cincinnati directors uphold Herrmann's deal or fire him.

Reluctantly, they approved the deal. Ebbets paid the $15,000 and dispatched manager Wilbert Robinson to pay Tinker his $10,000. But by this time Tinker, tired of being a pawn, wired that he wanted more money.

When Robinson arrived in Chicago, he learned that Tinker had traveled to Indianapolis. Robbie was about to go there when he read the story in the Chicago papers that Tinker had signed with the Federal League. Charles Weeghman, the owner of the Chicago Whales, had signed Tinker as player-manager. There was nothing Robinson could do, so he returned to Brooklyn.

Tinker was the first of the star major leaguers to sign with the "outlaws."

Under Tinker's leadership, the Whales finished second and first during the two Federal League seasons.

Weeghman, who had made millions with his fifteen luncheon restaurants that dotted Chicago, almost landed Walter Johnson, the American League's top pitching attraction, as well. He offered the pitching great a $16,000 contract, $4,000 more than Washington, plus a $10,000 signing bonus. Senators owner Clark Griffith, who rarely had much spending money, went to Chicago to see White Sox owner Charles Comiskey.

"If Johnson signs with the Whales, how would you like to see him pitching on the north side and drawing away all your fans from the south side of Chicago?"

Comiskey gave Griffith $10,000. Walter Johnson stayed in Washington.

With the Whales, Charles Weeghman was regarded as a tough competitor who played rough when he had to. After he hired Joe Tinker and then Three-Finger Brown as players, he was barred from signing Philadelphia catcher Reindeer Bill Killefer after a court illogically ruled that the contract was voided on moral grounds, ruling that the Chicago Federal League team had come to court with "unclean hands."

A Philly fan chided Killefer with the following ditty:

> *Weeghman Weeghman Federal man*
> *Make me a contract as fast as you can,*
> *Pad it and sign it and make it O.K.*
> *And I'll go to the majors and ask for more pay.*

Opposed by baseball's establishment, Weeghman stepped up his fight. He decided it was time to retaliate. Before the Killefer decision, the Federals had agreed not to tamper with contracts. But since the American League and National League teams weren't respecting Federal League contracts, Weeghman declared war.

Weeghman had Joe Tinker send wires to major and minor league players all over the country: "You are invited to come to the Federal league quarters in Chicago and discuss terms. Even if you decide not to sign a contract, all your expenses will be paid by the Federal League."

Major league teams tried injunctions, but with little effect. Over the two-year period in which the league existed, it was able to sign 221 players—81 major leaguers and 140 minor leaguers.

In Chicago, Weeghman ran the most successful team in the Federal League in part because of his spectacular ballpark. In need of a place to play, he bought vacant land from the Chicago Lutheran Theological Seminary, in a busy residential district located inside an area bounded by North Clark Street, Waveland Avenue, Sheffield Avenue, and West Addison Street on the North Side of Chicago. The seminary had moved in 1910. The official address of his new ballpark was 1060 West Addison Street.

He hired architect Zachary Taylor Davis to build a $250,000 park that would be "an edifice of beauty," as Weeghman liked to call it. Davis, who had built Comiskey Park four years earlier, created a masterpiece. When Weeghman Park opened in 1914, it had 16,000 seats, including 2,000 ten-cent bleacher seats in right field. Since it was situated in the middle of a neighborhood, fans who couldn't afford to get in could stand on top of the El or on fence tops or even rooftops and watch the games over the left-field fence.

The one uncontrollable variable to playing ball in the new park was the unpredictable winds. If the wind blew off the lake, it became very difficult to hit the ball a long way. If it was blowing the other way, outfielders had to be careful not to let the ball soar over their heads.

The Chi Fed fans weren't put off by the wind. They saw that Weeghman Park was far larger and nicer than the dingy West Side Grounds where the mediocre Cubs were playing.

Weeghman's team also was a winner. The first year the Chi Feds, as they were called that first year, came in second. The next year Weeghman nicknamed his team the Whales. (He wanted to convey the idea that his team was *big*.) After the Whales won the 1915 Federal League pennant, Weeghman challenged the Cubs and White Sox to a three-cornered city series. When the other two teams refused, Weeghman declared his Whales the undisputed champions of Chicago.

From the start of the 1914 season the major league owners badly wanted to end the war with the Federal League. Everyone was losing a great deal of money. From August 1914 on, there was talk of peace. In September, Weeghman and Garry Herrmann, the owner of the Cincinnati Reds, met secretly, with rumors flying that Weeghman might be given the opportunity to buy the Chicago Cubs. No truce was declared, however. According to Herrmann, the Feds' demands were too great.

At the end of the 1915 season, the league's most powerful supporter, Robert Ward, died. The rest of the Federal League owners, losing big, wanted peace.

Talks continued through 1915. The one stumbling block was the suit before federal judge Kenesaw Mountain Landis. That year the Federal League had sued Organized Baseball, charging conspiracy, monopoly, and alleged violations of antitrust laws. Landis, who had a reputation for being a "trust buster," presided.

Quickly the Federal League owners learned that Landis was anything but a trust buster. Early on Landis asked the attorney for the Federal League: "Do you realize that a decision in this case may tear down the very foundations of this game, so loved by thousands, and do you realize the decision must also seriously affect both parties?" He told both sides that "any blows at the thing called baseball would be regarded by this court as a blow to a national institution."

It was no wonder the major league owners looked to him after the Black Sox scandal.

Landis took the case under advisement, stalled it for more than a year, and when it was agreed the league would fold, the case became moot. In December 1915, with the consent of both parties, Landis dismissed the suit. On December 22, 1915, the peace pact was signed in Cincinnati. Organized Baseball paid $600,000 in exchange for the dissolution of the Federal League, with two of the teams—the Chicago Whales and the St. Louis Federals—being absorbed into the major leagues.

Charles Weeghman and Harry Sinclair of Sinclair Oil were allowed to purchase the controlling interest in the Chicago Cubs and then merge the Cubs with the Whales and play in Weeghman's North Side ballpark.

Sinclair also got $10,000 a year for ten years to recoup his losses from his ownership in the Newark team. St. Louis businessman Phil Ball was allowed to buy the

St. Louis Browns and take over Sportsman Park. Major league teams paid Federal League team owners for their players. The total settlement cost the major league owners about $5 million.

One reason Charles Weeghman received such considerate treatment from the National League owners was that by buying the Cubs, the National League could finally eliminate the Charles Murphy–Charles P. Taft ownership team. Overnight Charles Weeghman became transformed in the Chicago press from an evil villain to a "sportsman" who no longer was reported to be in the game for the money but instead because of his love of the game.

Weeghman was granted the right to buy the Cubs in part because of his connections. He was a close friend of Monte Tennes's, a leading Chicago gambler, and also a friend of Arnold Rothstein, who owned a gambling establishment in New York called the Partridge Club and who later was accused of (but not charged with) being part of the fixing of the 1919 World Series. Rothstein was a partner in a poolroom with Giants manager John McGraw in New York. Charles Stoneham, the owner of the Giants, was a heavy gambler and a friend of Rothstein's. According to Bill Veeck Jr., Stoneham was also associated in a rum-running enterprise with Rothstein. Rothstein, Stoneham, and McGraw were all partners in a racetrack enterprise.

As late as 1921, a year after the Black Sox scandal revelations, Rothstein was showing up at the Polo Grounds and sitting in Stoneham's box. Stoneham's major source of interest was his brokerage business. His closest associate: Arnold Rothstein.

Charles Weeghman, despite his mobster ties, turned out to be an inspired baseball owner. It was he who initiated the practice of having stalls in back of the stands where fans could come and buy food rather than have vendors always annoy the customers by walking in front of them and blocking their view.

And in 1916 it was Weeghman, the first-year owner of the Chicago Cubs, who decided to allow fans to keep balls batted into the stands, though it was years before this policy was accepted in all parks.

And, of course, the most important decision Charles Weeghman made was to ignore the dire warnings that the Cubs would not be successful if he moved the team from the West Side Grounds to the North Side, where his park was spacious and new.

He was cocksure Cubs fans would flock to see the team once they laid eyes on beautiful Weeghman Park.

26

Hippo Loses a No-Hitter

One of the most unusual baseball games ever played was one between the Chicago Cubs and the Cincinnati Reds on May 2, 1917. The day was cold and bleak, so only 3,500 fans were present. On the mound for the Reds was Fred Toney, a 235-pound right-hander, and pitching for the Cubs was Jim "Hippo" Vaughn, a 220-pound left-hander.

Toney walked Cubs outfielder Cy Williams twice. Vaughn walked Reds third baseman Heinie Groh twice.

Reds outfielder Earle "Greasy" Neale (the Army football great) was safe on an error, but he was thrown out trying to steal second.

At the end of nine full innings these were the only men to reach base. No runs. No hits by either team.

With one out in the tenth, the Reds' Larry Kopf rolled a seeing-eye grounder between first baseman Fred Merkle and second baseman Larry Doyle into the outfield for the first hit of the game. After the second out, Hal Chase, the Cincy first baseman, lined a ball to right fielder Williams, who dropped it for an error. Kopf went to third. Vaughn should have been out of the inning.

The next batter, Jim Thorpe (the former Carlyle football great and Olympian), swung late on a Vaughn curve ball and hit it on the handle of the bat toward the mound. The ball took a high hop in front of the plate and Vaughn, realizing he wouldn't be able to throw out the lightning-fast Thorpe, faked out catcher Art Wilson when he threw home to try to get Kopf at the plate.

When the throw got past Wilson, Kopf scored the winning run. Thorpe was credited with a hit.

And so Vaughn, who had pitched a no-hitter over the regulation nine innings, lost the game 1–0, on two scratch hits in the tenth in one of baseball's greatest pitching duels on record. Years later, Vaughn never quite was able to forgive his catcher, Art Wilson, for the loss.

JIM "HIPPO" VAUGHN: "I don't believe there has been another game in the history of baseball like the one I'm going to talk about. It was between the Cubs and the Cincinnati Reds at Weeghman Park on May 2, 1917.

"The attendance that day was only about 3,500, but since then at least 10,000 people and maybe more have told me they saw that game. In fact, a couple of years ago a young lad rushed up and told me about it—said he was there. I asked him how old he was, and he said 23. Now—that game had been played 22 years before, so I said:

"'How did you go, in your mother's arms?'

"'Naw,' he said, 'my dad took me, but'—and he grinned a bit sheepishly—'I was pretty young.'

"Well—to get back to that game—it was the one where neither Fred Toney nor I allowed a hit for nine innings, but I lost out in the tenth. There didn't seem to be very much unusual about the game as it went along. I was just taking care of each batter as he came up there, that was all. And I didn't even notice what Toney was doing.

"As a matter of fact, I never ever spoke to Toney in the entire game—but I'll have to go back a little to explain that. When I broke into the big leagues with the Yankees in 1908, it was with such hard-boiled old-timers as Willie Keeler, Jack Chesbro, Jack Newton—a bunch of old heads. I learned my baseball from them.

"We never spoke to a player on another team on the field—there was none of this glad-handing and hello business. Why, if anyone on the other club ever spoke pleasantly to me, I thought he was framing on me. I didn't want 'em to speak to me at all.

"I'd always given Toney's team, Cincinnati, a fit, so this day they laid for me. One feature that seldom has been mentioned is the fact that there wasn't a left-

Hippo Vaughn

handed hitter in the Reds' lineup that day. They even took Edd Roush out of there to give 'em another right-handed hitter and an all-right-handed lineup.

"Another feature is this—after I'd got the first two men out in the first inning, Greasy Neale came up and hit a little looping fly just back of second base. The second baseman could have gotten it easy, but Cy Williams came in from center and made the catch. That was the only ball hit out of the infield off me until the tenth inning.

"Well, while we were having our 'outs' in the eighth inning, I was sitting on the bench. Remember how that old dugout was—with a partition in the middle cutting the bench in two? I was sitting on the end nearest the clubhouse. One of the fellows at the other end said, 'Come on, let's get a run off this guy.' Another one chimed in, 'Run, hell; we haven't even got a hit off 'im!' 'Well,' another chap chimed in, 'they haven't got a hit off Vaughn, either.'

"Well, I figured, 'If this is a no-hitter and only one more inning to go, I'm going to give it everything I've got to get through that inning.' And with the last three men in the batting order coming up, I really intended to get past them. I got [utility player Manuel] Cueto on a line fly to Charlie Deal at third and I got a third strike past [catcher Hap] Huhn. Then that big Toney came to bat.

"Remember how he used to hit—with that powerful, stiff-armed swing? Well, I gave him everything I had on that first pitch—and was careful to keep it inside. He took that big swing and missed. It looked like he might have hit it a mile, but he missed it with the handle of his bat.

"He missed the second one. And I made up my mind to give him everything I had on the next one. I pitched—he missed—and I'll never forget the great cheer that went up. But Toney went out and set us down too, and we went into the tenth inning. I knew I was tired, but I felt that I still had my stuff.

"[Third baseman Gus] Getz, the first man up, hit a pop fly which our catcher, Art Wilson, got in front of the plate. Then came the first hit of the game. Larry Kopf hit one into right center for a single. But Neale hit an easy fly to Williams in center and Hal Chase also hit a fly out that way. It was a hard hit ball, but not a line drive, and it was right at Williams. He got both hands on it—and dropped it. Any outfielder ordinarily would catch it easy. It was just a plain muff. Kopf got to third on that one, and Chase stole second.

"There's been a lot of discussion about the play that came up next—the one that lost the ball game. Indian Jim Thorpe, the famous old football player who was trying to make good in baseball, was at bat and he sent a swinging bunt toward third. I knew the minute it was hit that I couldn't get Thorpe at first. He was fast as a race horse. So I went over to the line, fielded the ball, and scooped it toward the plate. Kopf, running in, was right behind me and he stopped when he saw me make the throw to the plate. I didn't see him or I could have just turned around and tagged him out.

"Now, some of the writers said that Wilson didn't expect the throw. The truth is that Art just went paralyzed—just stood there with his hands at his sides staring at me. The ball hit him square on the chest protector—I'll never forget—it seemed to roll around there for a moment—and then dropped to the ground. The instant Kopf saw it drop, he streaked for the plate. But Wilson still stood there, paralyzed. I looked over my shoulder and saw Chase round third and start in too. So I said to Art:

"'Are you going to let him score too?'

"He woke up, grabbed the ball and tagged Chase out easily. But it was too late, the one big deciding run was in. Wilson cried like a baby after the game. He grabbed my hand and said, 'I just went out on you, Jim. I just went tight.'

"In the clubhouse afterward everybody was pretty sore. Charley Weeghman, the boss, stuck his head in the door and yelled, 'You're all a bunch of ————s.'

"But I wasn't sore. I'd just lost another ball game, that's all.

"I do remember this about it, though. After the game I told Fred Toney, 'You've got to pitch the kind of ball you did against me today to beat me from now on, Old Man.' He shook hands, but he looked at me kind of funny when I said that. He must have taken it as a bad omen. Anyway, he never did pitch that well against me again—and I don't believe he ever beat me again. We met a lot of times, and most of the games were close, but he'd licked me for the last time."

27

Transitions

Fortunes come and fortunes go. It was not long after Charles Weeghman bought the Cubs in 1916 that he and the rest of America began to suffer reversals brought on by a deepening national recession. Talk of war was hanging in the air. All of baseball was nervous. Would President Wilson stop play during wartime? Attendance was falling, and it was a time of belt tightening for baseball's owners. Soon Weeghman would be pinched badly enough to have to sell the team.

When Weeghman owned the Whales in the Federal League, he had been thwarted in his attempt to sign Philadelphia Phillies catcher Bill Killefer. Shortly after the 1917 season, a year in which the lackluster Cubs finished fifth under manager Fred Mitchell (who had been a coach for George Stallings and Boston's Miracle Braves in 1914), Weeghman was given the opportunity to buy Killefer—as well as the best pitcher in the National League, his famed batterymate, 30-game winner Grover Cleveland Alexander.

Weeghman had this once-in-a-lifetime chance because Alex had been notified by his draft board that it would not be long before he would be drafted into the service. The pitcher had demanded a $10,000 bonus from Phillies owner William Baker so that his girlfriend, Aimee Arrants, would be taken care of when he was off fighting the war. He knew he wasn't even making enough to take care of his mother when he went away.

Baker, fearing that Alexander would be killed and his investment wasted, chose expediency over risk, trading his workhorse without prior notice to the Cubs on December 17, 1917, for two mediocre players, pitcher Mike Prendergast and catcher Pickles Dillhoefer, and $60,000. Phillies fans and Alexander himself read with disbelief of the trade of the star pitcher who in just seven seasons had won 190 games, even though he pitched in the smallest park in the majors in Philadelphia. For three straight years his earned run average had been under 2.00. In 1915 it was 1.22.

On the mound Alex was a master. He studied the hitters and knew their habits. He pitched quickly and efficiently. On June 26, 1915, he threw only seventy-six pitches, an average of about eight an inning, to shut out Brooklyn 4–0. He often pitched games in less than an hour.

Alexander, Wrigley, and Killefer

In 1916 he won his twenty-ninth game in the first game of a doubleheader. He wanted to win 30, so he pitched the second game and won that too.

Phillies fans never forgave Bill Baker for selling Alexander nor for the way he ran his team. The Phillies were never the same after he sold Alexander. Baker was well-to-do, but after making his original investment, he put little of his money into the team. He tried to make the club carry itself, pay his president's salary, and pay off his notes. If he needed money, he knew which teams were willing to part with it for his top players. If the Phils didn't finish last, it was only because the Boston Braves did. When Bill Baker died on February 22, 1933, Phillies fans shed few tears.

After the trade, Alex demanded the same ten grand from the Cubs. Weeghman had been keeping himself afloat financially by selling some of his Cubs stock to minority partner William Wrigley, the founder of the Wrigley chewing gum company. It was left to Wrigley to get Alexander to agree to play for the Cubs.

Before spring training of 1918, Alexander and Wrigley arranged to play golf on a Pasadena, California, golf course, and during the round Wrigley met Alexander's demand, agreeing to send Alexander's wife $500 every other month for three years. If he was in the service longer than that, promised Wrigley, he would continue paying her until he came back. Alexander agreed to report to the Cubs. The agreement was never put in writing, but Wrigley kept his word.

In 1918, Alexander pitched three games for the Cubs, won two, and then went off to war. He would return the following year a changed man.

Though the Cubs lost Alexander's services, the league's best team, the New York Giants, lost out far worse. By midseason 1918, manager John McGraw had only three regulars and one starting pitcher remaining from his National League champs of the previous year.

The Cubs, led by three excellent pitchers, Hippo Vaughn (22–10, 1.74), Lefty Tyler (19–9, 2.00), and Claude Hendrix (19–7, 2.78), and by first baseman Fred Merkle (of all people), outfielder Max Flack, and catcher Killefer, won in 1918 not because they were so good but because many of the best players on the Giants were in the service. (The Cubs would win another pennant in 1945 during World War II under similar circumstances.)

Though a "Work or Fight" order halted all baseball right after Labor Day, the U.S. government permitted a World Series to be played right after the stoppage. The Cubs played the Boston Red Sox and the star pitcher-outfielder, Babe Ruth.

The plan of Cubs manager Fred Mitchell was to start left-handers Hippo Vaughn and George Tyler as often as possible to blunt the use of Boston's powerful left-handed batter, Ruth. Mitchell's problem was that there was nothing he could do to keep Ruth out of the lineup as a pitcher.

In the opener Ruth beat Vaughn 1–0. Cubs pitcher Lefty Tyler won the second game, also allowing only one run. The Red Sox' Carl Mays then beat the hard-luck Vaughn 2–1. Ruth won his second, 3–2, before Vaughn finally won a game, Game 5, a 3–0 shutout.

The two teams then went on strike. They foresaw that their World Series shares would be low, and they wanted to be assured that they weren't playing for nothing.

Going into the Series, John Tener promised $2,000 for winning players and $1,000 for losers. Because 1918 was the first year the league gave a portion of the World Series proceeds to players on the second-, third-, and fourth-place teams, the participants could see that their shares would be low indeed.

After the fifth game Les Mann of the Cubs and Harry Hooper of the Red Sox had gone to the members of the National Commission and asked that this money be given to them. They were rebuffed. The commissioners were told that the players would not play the next day.

The starting time for Game 5 was fast approaching, but the players hadn't appeared on the field. Former Boston mayor Honey Fitzgerald, fearing a riot, sent for police reinforcements. Commissioner Ban Johnson went to the clubhouses to plead with the players.

Johnson, who had drunk too much whiskey during the pregame ceremonies, staggered into the room to talk with Hooper.

"If you don't want to play, don't," Johnson said, "but Harry, you fellows are putting yourself in a very bad light with the fans. There are going to be wounded soldiers and sailors at the game today. With a war going on, and fellows fighting in France, what do you think the public will think of you ballplayers striking for more money?"

The players, seeing that further talks were hopeless, agreed to finish the Series. The game started an hour late.

Carl Mays of the Red Sox then beat Lefty Tyler 2–1 to win the world championship. In the third inning an error by Max Flack, the Cubs outfielder, allowed two unearned runs and cost the team the ball game.

In the 1918 Series, Ruth pitched 16 consecutive shutout innings, adding to the 13 $2/3$ straight goose eggs he had rung up during the Series against the New York Giants in 1916. His total of 29 $2/3$ would be a World Series record until Whitey Ford broke it with the Yankees in 1961 (with 32).

Because of the Cubs' lack of success against Ruth, the Boston pitcher was able to break Christy Mathewson's record of 28 scoreless World Series innings in a row. According to writer Warren Brown, it was one more reason why Giants fans hated the Cubs.

The 1918 Series would make a watershed for both the Red Sox and the Cubs. The players' share ended up $1,102.51 for each of the victorious Red Sox and $671.09 for each of the defeated Cubs.

The Red Sox, the winners in the Series, were owned by Harry Frazee, a theatrical promoter who lost all his money because of the recession and poor attendance during the Series. To keep afloat Frazee would sell pitchers Ruth, Bullet Joe Bush, Sad Sam Jones, and Carl Mays, plus catcher Wally Schang and shortstop Everett Scott, to the New York Yankees. The fall of the Red Sox would be swift and devastating.

The Cubs, the losers in the Series, would be resurrected by the talent and vision of one man, a chewing-gum magnate by the name of William Wrigley Jr.

William Wrigley, a self-made man, was born on September 30, 1861, in Philadelphia. He grew up there, the son of a man who owned a small soap factory. He began work in the factory stirring the bubbling vats with a paddle. His pay was $1.50 a week. When he was twelve, he convinced his father to let him go on the road as a salesman.

He would later boast, "I was a full-fledged long-pants traveling salesman before I was thirteen." He traveled from western Pennsylvania to northern New England. He sold scouring soap from a four-horse team with bells on the harness.

He once told his father, "I am about the best salesman who ever drew a breath. I could sell pianos to the armless men of Borneo."

William Wrigley had a genius in business: He never took no for an answer, and in the tactical war against competitors, he was smarter than everyone else.

He had something else too: an infectious joie de vivre. For years there hung a sign over his desk: "Nothing great was ever achieved without enthusiasm." Red-faced and beaming, he looked, said *Fortune* magazine, "like a jolly bartender, and he acted like a boy amazed and delighted with everything."

But under that sunny disposition, he could be cunning and ruthless. When competitors lowered their prices to undercut his father's scouring soap, William Wrigley countered in a novel, brilliant way: he immediately raised the price of his scouring soap from a nickel to a dime, then gave his dealers free baking soda as a premium for every box of soap they sold. Soon there was more of a demand for baking soda than soap.

When Wrigley added baking soda to his line, as a premium he gave his dealers free chewing gum. When the clamor for chewing gum grew, Wrigley decided not only to sell it but to manufacture it as well. In 1891, at the age of twenty-nine, he settled in Chicago with his wife and daughter. With a $5,000 check from his uncle and $32 in his pockets, he formed the William Wrigley Jr. Co.

One of the first William Wrigley products was a banana-flavored gum called You-canchu, which was sold as a "sure cure for dyspepsia and indigestion," as well as a "delicious confection."

To sell his gum, Wrigley decided upon a radical solution: massive advertising. Twice he spent $100,000 in advertising, with little results. But William Wrigley was a man who believed in himself and his ideas. Once William Wrigley made up his mind, he pushed ahead. His favorite saying was "A man's doubts and fears are his worst enemies."

Wrigley began a third advertising campaign that cost him $250,000, and this time profits rose dramatically. By 1907 sales totaled $2 million. His slogan was Tell 'Em Quick and Tell 'Em Often. By the mid-1910s, his company's profits soared, and he was becoming a rich man. World War I was to be a big boost to the profits of his company, as American soldiers taught Europeans the pleasures of chewing gum.

By the 1920s the William Wrigley Jr. Company had become an empire. Wrigley was spending $4 million a year on chewing-gum advertising while seeing his business triple during the decade.

Charles Weeghman, who bought the team from the Murphy-Taft regime, headed a consortium of minority owners including Wrigley that bought the team on January 20, 1916. Among Weeghman's other partners were William Walker, who was in the fish business, and meatpacker J. Ogden Armour, who had personally recruited Wrigley.

It had been William Wrigley's policy to keep large cash reserves and never to borrow money. As a result, he was usually in excellent financial shape whenever he invested.

Wrigley began his interest in the Cubs with a $50,000 investment, which he soon doubled. Though a club director, Wrigley had avoided any involvement with the team until 1917, when he persuaded Weeghman to send the team to California for spring training.

Weeghman, meanwhile, had spread himself too thin, investing in the movies and other ventures. Unable to raise capital, he continued borrowing money from William Wrigley, giving him Cubs stock as collateral. Though bank officers counseled Wrigley not to do it, the gum baron liked both Weeghman and baseball, so he went against their advice.

After the crash came in 1918, Weeghman was in deep financial trouble. In December 1918, William Wrigley attended his first stockholders' meeting. He presented Weeghman's resignation as club president. Manager Fred Mitchell was named president and a former Chicago sportswriter named Bill Veeck named vice president.

When Weeghman finally went under early in 1919, Wrigley received all his stock and found himself the holder of the largest voting block of stock in the Cubs.

In 1921, William Wrigley took over complete control of the Chicago franchise when he bought out the shares of the financially troubled Armour and then purchased a large block of stock from advertising magnate A. D. Lasker, a close friend who had disagreed with Wrigley's choices of Bill Veeck, manager Fred Mitchell, and his replacement, Johnny Evers.

Wrigley, tired of fighting with Lasker, ordered him to either sell him the team or buy him out. Lasker chose to sell. Wrigley allowed him to keep a hundred shares so he could stay on the board and keep his box seats.

Later that year Wrigley bought the Los Angeles Angels in the Pacific Coast League from John Powers, another businessman in financial difficulty. Powers wanted $100,000. Wrigley, who believed in fairness, offered $115,000, what he called his "buying price." Wrigley knew Powers badly needed to sell, and he didn't want to feel he was taking advantage of the man. He argued that if Powers had had an agent, the price would have been $115,000. Wrigley insisted on paying the higher price.

Baseball wasn't Wrigley's only large outside investment. In 1919 he purchased Catalina Island from the Banning Estate for $3.5 million in cash. He became sole owner of everything on the twenty-mile-long island, including the regal St. Catherine Hotel.

Catalina Island was a small fishing village that he dreamed of making into a "pleasure resort for persons of modest means." He spent $3 million more to bring fresh water to the town of Avalon from a river sixteen miles away. He rebuilt the sewer system. He spent another $2.5 million for a theater and a ballroom and paid $250,000 to build a ten-acre aviary.

In its heyday ten thousand visitors a day came to the island to experience its beauty.

Between 1920 and 1924, Wrigley spent $7.8 million to build his Chicago showpiece, the Wrigley Building. He put the bold skyscraper in a shabby neighborhood on Michigan Avenue near the Chicago River. He ordered the architects to build four enormous clocks, one on each side of the building's 400-foot tower, "so everybody within seeing distance in the Loop would turn to look to the Wrigley Building to find out what time it was." He coated the side of the building in white terra-cotta and had floodlights installed to shine on it at night. The building could be seen for miles. His farsightedness transformed the neighborhood and increased the value of his property many, many times over.

William Wrigley wasn't an ordinary mogul. He was a hard man to categorize. He hated organized religion. He would ask, "What form of superstition do you practice?" At the same time he was one of the first benevolent corporate dictators. He inaugurated the five-day workweek in 1924. He built a company lunchroom for his employees, devised life insurance schemes for them, and offered them stock-sharing plans. He would often talk about how employees should be treated as members of the family.

During the 1920s he also rebuilt the Chicago Cubs. William Wrigley was unlike most baseball owners. One of the things that made him different was that he insisted that the team be a winner. Another thing that made him different was that he was fascinated by the game of baseball even more than the business of it. He played hooky from the gum company to go to Wrigley Field.

It was William Wrigley who said, "Baseball is too much of a sport to be a business and too much of a business to be a sport." But William Wrigley was one owner who gleaned how to make it a great business. He knew how to make a lot of money from the game.

One policy that stood him in good stead was his insistence on paying his players top dollar. He did not believe in arm twisting during salary negotiations or in cutting salaries.

"I want a contented club, and no man whose salary has been clipped can be satisfied," he once said.

He was also smart enough to know that to be successful he had to hire someone who knew the game, then sit back and let that man make the decisions.

His most important decision concerned who he should pick to run the baseball operation. William Wrigley didn't know the first thing about running a major league team, and if he had wanted a shot at being competitive immediately, he should have hired a longtime baseball executive from another team to run the Cubs. That's what Colonel Jacob Ruppert of the New York Yankees did when he hired the brilliant Ed Barrow from the Boston Red Sox after the 1920 season. Wrigley didn't do that. Instead, William Wrigley picked a newspaper reporter, a man who knew no more about running a major league baseball team than any fan on the street.

Wrigley was reading the *Chicago American* soon after he took over the team when he became impressed by a series of well-thought-out but fiercely critical articles about the Cubs. The articles were written under the pseudonymous byline Bill Bailey. When Wrigley checked, he learned the articles were penned by a newspaperman named William Veeck. Mrs. Wrigley also liked Bailey's articles, and so Wrigley asked Veeck to have dinner with him and his wife at their home. During their conversation Veeck described the team by saying, "My infant son [Bill Veeck Jr.] could throw his bottle farther than the team can hit."

Said Wrigley, who immediately was attracted to the man's intelligence and passion, "If you're so smart, why don't you see if you can do a better job?"

In June 1919, Bill Veeck became president (and acted as general manager) of the Cubs, a post he held until October 5, 1933, when he died of leukemia. Though Wrigley had taken a risk in choosing for his chief operating officer a man with absolutely no experience, William Veeck turned out to be a solid selection. Veeck was no miracle worker. How could he have been? When he started he didn't know the talents of the players in the league. Under the leadership of the two novices—Wrigley and Veeck—for a decade the Cubs would stumble along, most often either in fourth or fifth place, unable to compete against the three dominant teams, the Giants, Cardinals, and Pirates.

In terms of advertising and marketing, however, no team featured a hipper ownership. Wrigley believed strongly in advertising, and during the 1920s his gum company was the nation's biggest advertiser. Both he and Veeck moreover believed in the power of that newfangled medium, radio.

Baseball owners understood how newspapers could help them promote the game. Papers had covered the games ever since an article on May 1, 1853, when the *New York Sunday Mercury* mentioned a game played on a barnstorming tour by the National Club of Washington. But most of the owners were afraid of radio. They feared that if they broadcast the games, the fans would stay home and listen rather than go to the ballpark.

The first radio broadcast was a re-creation of the Dempsey-Carpentier prizefight on July 2, 1921, by station WJZ in New York. That same year KDKA in Pittsburgh re-created a game between the Pirates and the Philadelphia Phils. In the fall the World Series between the New York Yankees and the New York Giants was broadcast. It was also re-created.

It wasn't until 1924 that famed announcer Graham McNamee broadcast live from the site. It was the exhibition doubleheader between John McGraw's Giants and the Washington Senators.

The idea for the Cubs to broadcast their games came from a woman named Judith Waller, the managing director of radio station WMAQ. In the spring of 1925 she suggested to William Wrigley that her station broadcast Cubs games. He was interested, and he consulted with Veeck, who looked at the phenomenon of radio and also drew a different conclusion from most owners: He believed that radio would introduce baseball to a whole new group of fans, including kids—baseball's future. When the Cubs announced they would broadcast some games in 1925, the other National League moguls told him they couldn't. Veeck threatened to play Cubs games against local teams and to broadcast these games.

"I'm going to broadcast," he told them.

The league reluctantly gave him approval. Veeck gave the broadcast rights for free to seven stations in the Chicago market. Johnny O'Hara and Bob Elson, the Old Commander, did the games. The embryonic stage of the Cubs phenomenon had begun.

"We'll tie up the entire city," Veeck predicted.

Though the 1925 Cubs were in disarray, Wrigley began to get letters from shut-ins, especially disabled veterans in hospitals. One dentist wrote that the broadcasts soothed his patients. Wrigley also noticed that on Sunday when the Cubs were playing at home, cars would begin arriving with license plates from Indiana, Michigan, and Wisconsin. The attractor: the radio broadcasts.

That year the Cubs tumbled to last place after William Veeck in midseason chose as his manager the wildest, drunkest, most rip-roaring wildman he could possibly have found: veteran shortstop Rabbit Maranville.

In the field Rabbit Maranville was a wizard. He played for twenty-three seasons, more than any other National League shortstop. He had unusually fast speed, great range, and sure hands, and he was quick releasing the ball. He was also a great entertainer. He pantomimed the mannerisms of the other players, and when he caught a pop-up, he did it with a basket catch, letting the ball reach his belt line before snaring it. The fans loved him all over the league.

FRED LIEB: "With the exception of the immortal Honus [Wagner], no shortstop ever could pack 'em in as did the playful New Englander. A five-foot, five-inch mite from Springfield, Mass., there never was any telling what the little guy would do, from pulling the hidden-ball trick to diving between the outstretched legs of the austere umpire, Hank O'Day, in making a steal of second. On another occasion when an argument was in progress over a disputed play, the tiny New Englander crept on all fours and, with elbows on the ground, rested his head on his hands, directly between the knees of the irate umpire."

He was nicknamed Rabbit, according to Harold Kaese, because one day as a youngster playing in New Bedford, Massachusetts, a little girl watched him bounce around in a pepper game and said, "You jump around just like a rabbit." Before that he had been known as Stumpy and Bunty.

Though baseball's Peter Pan might have been short in stature, in the field he was a giant. Along with another half-pint, teammate Johnny Evers, Maranville led the Boston Braves to their Miracle championship in 1914. In fact it was Maranville, well known for his high living, who started the team on its way to being known as the Miracle Braves.

After the team, which had been in last place during the season, won the 1914 pennant and swept the Philadelphia A's in the World Series, Maranville attended a church fair where he regaled a large Boston audience with the comment that the Braves had won the Series because of prayer. He and seven teammates, he explained, had agreed to attend holy communion each morning of the Series, and once in a "tough spot" they got together in the dugout and prayed silently that Evers would come through with a hit. And Hallelujah, praise the Lord, Evers did, said Maranville.

The fans loved him, owners and managers had trouble with him, and umpires hated him. As a rookie with Boston in 1912 he once took out a pair of glasses, polished them, and handed them to the umpire Bill Finneran.

Another time umpire Bob Hart cut himself in a fracas. Maranville offered to put iodine on his face. When he was done, the umpire looked like an Indian wearing warpaint.

Then there was the time his teammates locked him in his room on the twelfth floor. He was supposed to behave himself and get some rest. They were in another room playing cards when they looked out the window and saw him outside making faces at them from the narrow ledge.

Rabbit Maranville

In February 1921, after nine years with the Braves, Maranville was traded to the Pittsburgh Pirates, where he immediately sparked the Pirates to greater heights, a fine second-place finish. The Pirates were in the lead going into the end of August when they blew five straight to the Giants.

Pirates owner Barney Dreyfuss blamed losing the pennant on the antics of Maranville and Charlie Grimm, a young first baseman who played the banjo and sang. The two, plus outfielder George "Possum" Whitted and second baseman Cotton Tierney, formed a quartet. Whitted sang baritone, Grimm bass. They had an offer to tour the vaudeville circuit if the Pirates won. They didn't.

The four would sing in the batting cage before the games. One day the acerbic John McGraw chided, "You can't sing your way through this league."

Even though Maranville in 1921 hit .294 and handled 854 chances at shortstop and Grimm was excellent at first and hit .274, Dreyfuss hated that Grimm drank beer and Maranville whiskey and that they were pranksters. He also didn't like that Maranville was close with pitcher Chief Moses Yellowhorse, who himself drank too much.

During the season Pirates manager George Gibson ordered Yellowhorse not to drink—no booze, no beer. The pitcher, who would be gone from the league at the end of the 1922 season, was pitching into the seventh inning when he decided to take action. He stood on the mound and after the catcher gave the sign, just continued to stand there. The catcher put down another sign. The pitcher didn't move. Manager Gibson became angry and yelled at Grimm.

"Go over there and see what the hell is wrong," Gibson ordered.

Grimm went over and asked.

"I'll not throw the ball until I get a shot of liquor," the pitcher told him.

Grimm stood there. The catcher came out. Cotton Tierney joined the group, as did Maranville.

"He won't pitch unless he has a shot," Grimm told Maranville.

"It ain't a bad idea," Maranville said. "Anybody got one with him?"

According to Grimm, Maranville had a pint on him in the hip pocket of his uniform. With teammates surrounding him, the pitcher got his snort.

When the inning ended, Gibson asked Grimm what had been the problem.

"The guy's supporter was binding him," Grimm lied.

The three, Maranville, Grimm, and Yellowhorse, were rowdy, at times reckless. Later that year the team stayed at the Ansonia Hotel in New York, and during their visit Maranville and Yellowhorse played a little game, according to Grimm. They'd creep out on the ledge, fourteen stories above the street, to see which one could snare a pigeon first.

When Bill McKechnie took over as Pirates manager during the 1922 season, owner Barney Dreyfuss wanted to know what he was going to do to make his players behave. He told McKechnie, "I suppose you realize you have a couple of wild Indians on your club—[Yellowhorse] and that Irish Indian, Maranville."

McKechnie told Dreyfuss he intended to room with the two.

The first stop was New York, where the Pirates stayed at the Ansonia. Before the first game McKechnie warned the players against bootleg liquor and said he would enforce his midnight curfew.

McKechnie liked going to an early movie. That first night on the road he returned to the hotel about ten. When he arrived at the room and turned on the lights, he observed his two players in the bed snoring.

McKechnie started to undress. He opened the closet door and was almost knocked over as a flock of trapped pigeons flew into his face.

The two players had coaxed the pigeons from the balcony into the closet with popcorn.

"What goes on here, Rabbit?" the stern McKechnie wanted to know.

"Hey, Bill, don't open that other closet," Maranville told him. "Those pigeons that got out belong to the Chief. Mine are in that one over there!"

Another time Maranville was playing in Boston with the Pirates when he was fined $100 for drunk driving after playing flawlessly against the Braves.

When the Pirates returned home, his wife took him to task. He replied, "Just think how lucky you are, my dear. Most wives don't know where their husbands are on the road trips. But at least you knew that I was safe and sound in jail."

After the Pirates lost the 1924 pennant to the Giants, Dreyfuss blamed Charlie Grimm and Maranville and traded them to the Cubs during the winter of 1924–25.

Dreyfuss told Fred Lieb, "I got rid of my banjo players."

The pair didn't wait long to make an impression on their Cubs teammates. Bill Veeck, the son of William Veeck, recalled vividly the wild ways of Jolly Cholly and the Rabbit:

BILL VEECK: "The first drunken ballplayer I was really aware of was Rabbit Maranville. Maranville was always loaded.

"I first laid eyes on Maranville and Grimm on the golf course, the day they reported to spring training at Catalina, Mr. Wrigley's private island. Because of their reputation for high jinks and low humor, a photographer was posing them with Charlie lying flat on his back, a golf tee clenched between his teeth, and Rabbit holding a driver as if he were about to swing.

"The photographer said, 'OK. Good. Hold it.' Whereupon, Rabbit took a vicious swing and knocked the ball cleanly out of Charlie's teeth and over the photographer's head. Charlie arose, white as a sheet because, in case I have neglected to mention it, Rabbit had only played a few rounds of golf in his life.

"That was Rabbit Maranville. A little rascal to his dying day. A few days after he reported, he disappeared onto the mainland overnight—meditating or something—and returned to the island on the excursion boat. Upon disembarking, he snatched up a coal scuttle full of ashes, for he had learned that it was Ash Wednesday. Stationing himself at the entrance of the huge dining room of the St. Catherine Hotel, he dabbed ashes onto the foreheads of all the incoming guests. Regrettably, he was so loaded that he couldn't tell their foreheads from their elbows and he was flinging the ashes all over the place. The management had to serve the 100 meals all over again."

During the season, Maranville got into trouble with management when, from a high-floor window of the Hotel Buckingham in St. Louis, he dropped a paper laundry bag full of water in an attempt to brain Cubs secretary John Seys.

Another time the Rabbit dived into the outdoor fishpond of the Buckingham and surfaced with what looked like a goldfish in his mouth, much to the horror of the lady guests.

Said Charlie Grimm, "I always suspected it was a carrot."

The writer John Lardner included the Rabbit on his all-drinking team, along with King Kelly, Grover Cleveland Alexander, and other non-Cubs such as Babe Ruth, Pepper Martin, Ed Delahanty, Rube Waddell, Germany Schaefer, Art Shires, Rollie Hemsley, Phil Douglas, and Flint Rhem.

"In my day, friend," said Maranville, "I was the best right-and-left-handed rum hound in the country."

This was the man William Veeck chose to be the team's manager on July 7, 1925. According to Charlie Grimm, Maranville, who had no prior experience, apparently was hired out of the blue to be the Cubs manager.

CHARLIE GRIMM: "We were playing a game in Chicago, the last before we went on a road trip into the east. [Manager Bill] Killefer came to me before the game and said that he wanted to win that one more than he wanted anything else in the world. He said it was going to be his last ball game. He didn't tell me why, and I didn't ask him. We went out and won it, 1–0.

"When we arrived in New York, Bill Veeck called us all into a meeting in the ball room. I guess I had an idea what was coming off, but I'm sure no one else did, and least of all Maranville. Veeck told us that there was going to be a change in managers, and then called up the Rabbit, asking us to meet the new manager. This was the first intimation Maranville had of it, and he was just as surprised as the next one.

"As I look back now, I'm not sure whether Maranville was to be a fixture or whether he was just appointed to finish out the season."

Regardless, Maranville sealed his fate the very first night when on the train he celebrated his appointment by dousing ice water on his players at two in the morning as they slept in their Pullman berths. He rolled up the aisle with a bucket yelling, "There will be no sleeping on this club under Maranville management."

Rabbit was fired at the next opportunity—the next time owner William Wrigley saw him. On September 3, after eight weeks, he was canned. Making the trade for Maranville even more painful to the Cubs was the knowledge that pitcher Vic Aldridge, one of the players sent to the Pirates, had led Pittsburgh to the National League pennant.

According to Chicago reporter Warren Brown, Wrigley and Veeck pledged that never again would the Cubs suffer the indignity of finishing last.

It wouldn't be until the far-off dismal reign of Wrigley's strange son, Phil, that they would again.

Rabbit stopped drinking two years after losing his managerial job with the Cubs, and though he didn't manage again, he continued playing, with Brooklyn, St. Louis, and six more years with the Boston Braves, until 1935.

He died on January 5, 1954, at the age of sixty-two, only a few weeks before his election into the Hall of Fame.

28

Tales from the Visiting Clubhouse

Ed Froelich, a poor boy from the streets of Chicago, joined the Chicago Cubs in 1924. He was fourteen years old. His first job was visiting team batboy, work which allowed him to rub elbows with some of the legends of his day, especially two of the greatest competitors ever to wear spikes, New York Giants manager John McGraw and Pittsburgh Pirates third baseman Pie Traynor. Froelich later went to work for manager Joe McCarthy. After retiring from baseball, he achieved financial success with an orthopedic pillow of his own design. A bright, interesting man, I had the pleasure of interviewing him in 1982, four years before his death at age seventy-six. His remembrances of Cubdom in the 1920s were memorable, providing insight into a period few close to the ball club are left to recall.

ED FROELICH: "I was a baseball-crazy kid in the city of Chicago in the spring of 1924, and in those days everybody was poor, and I was particularly poor, so if I wanted to go to a ball game I would thumb a ride to Wrigley Field and then work in order to see the game. It wasn't like today when a parent hands a kid a $20 bill and the keys to the car and the gas-company credit card and says, 'Have a good time.' No, I thumbed a ride to the park, and when I got to the park I would wait until the game was over, and then they'd give you a big burlap sack and tell you to come back when it was filled with paper and trash left by the crowd. When the sack was full you'd be filthy dirty, and for that they'd give you a pass to the bleachers the next day.

"You could also get a pass for picking up pop bottles. In those days pop was sold in bottles until one day a fan hit Whitey Witt in the head with one in St. Louis, and then somebody decided they had better sell drinks in cups.

"Sometimes I would get lucky enough to turn stiles for the ticket taker, and by the second or third inning he would let you in. If I didn't do that, I'd sell scorecards and pencils. It was the days before the vendors were unionized.

"Later I became the megaphone holder for Pat Peiper, the Cubs' public address announcer. He had the most wonderful announcing voice I ever heard in a ballpark. He had a megaphone that was perhaps seven feet long, and it flared out at the end into a large circumference, and he needed someone to hold it on his head while he spoke. With that huge megaphone he could be heard throughout the entire ballpark.

"First, he would start with the megaphone pointed toward the press box, and he'd announce the complete lineups, and then he would turn and address the right-field stands along first base, just giving the batteries for the two teams, and he'd do the same thing along the left-field stands. That was a wonderful job, because you'd be down with him on the field while the game was going on.

"Before long, I became the batboy for the visiting teams. I was sixteen, and baseball meant everything to me. All I wanted was to be around baseball and baseball players.

"There were two requirements for the visiting batboy job. You had to come to the park with a clean shirt, and you had to keep your mouth shut on the bench. You couldn't say a word, especially if John McGraw and the Giants were in town. I remember the clubhouse man telling me, 'When McGraw is around, don't say a word, understand? If you have to cough, go in the runway.'

"I wanted the job so badly I used to come to the ballpark with my clean shirt wrapped in tissue paper.

"I can remember how stern John McGraw was. There was absolutely no margin of error with him.

"Oh, McGraw was such a tyrant! He had the twelve o'clock rule. You had better be inside your room when the trainer came around to check on you at midnight or it was an automatic fine. Don't tell him about traffic or that you were visiting your sick sister or anything like that. It was automatic. You were fined.

"I can remember on this particular night in Chicago, [future Hall of Famer] Bill Terry had been to the theater and for some reason was a few minutes late getting in, and he was turned in. Terry had tried to reach the hotel, tried to call McGraw, tried to reach the trainer, but he couldn't get through, and he wasn't in his room on time. He was fined. On top of that, McGraw benched him the next day. Terry was so mad he sat down on the bench and took his shoes off.

"It got to be the ninth inning with the Giants a couple of runs behind, and Grover Cleveland Alexander was pitching for the Cubs. There were a couple of men on base. McGraw said, 'You're the hitter, Terry.' Terry must have taken a full five minutes to lace up his cleats. He strolled over to the bat rack, found a bat, walked up the plate against Alexander, and hit one against the apartment buildings on the other side of Sheffield Avenue to win the game for the Giants.

"When Terry got back to the hotel—and these were the days of Prohibition— there was a case of real good genuine Canadian ale in his room. With a note: 'Your fine is rescinded.'

"Did you know that McGraw called every pitch? The pitcher had to look in the dugout before every single pitch for a sign from the bench. McGraw ran that ball game, and it didn't matter whether you were a rookie or a star.

"I can remember a conversation when Rogers Hornsby came over from the Braves to the Cubs in 1929. Sitting along the lockers in the Cubs dressing room were some pretty fair bats: Woody English, Hornsby, Hack Wilson, Kiki Cuyler, Riggs Stephenson. It was one of the greatest right-handed-hitting clubs in baseball history.

"Stephenson and Cuyler were looking at the newspaper studying the box scores from the day before, and Stephenson said, 'My gosh, look at this. Bill Terry went 5 for 5 in the first game of the doubleheader and 4 for 5 in the second. Nine for ten. That's a whole week's worth. I wonder what happened to him the other time up?'

"Cuyler said, 'Oh, he probably hit a blistering line drive right at somebody.'

"Stephenson said, 'I wonder if he's got to take signs hitting .410,' which is what he was hitting at the time.

"Hornsby was sitting a couple of lockers down, and he overheard them, and he said, 'You bet your ass he's taking signs. I don't care if he's hitting .810, if he's playing for McGraw, he's taking signs.' And that was the end of the conversation.

"One of the best teams around that time was the Pittsburgh Pirates, who won the pennant in 1927. The Pittsburgh team was rough and tough, a hell-bent-for-leather drinking crowd. The Waner brothers, Paul and Lloyd, were on that team, with Joe Harris on first base, George Grantham at second, and catching were Johnny Gooch and Earl Smith, Oil Smith, who may have been the toughest character of them all.

"Smith was the guy who when he was with the Giants picked McGraw up, stuck him up against the wall, and beat him up pretty badly. He was also the guy who was catching when [Boston Brave] Davey Bancroft slid to score a run, and Smith punched him in the face and knocked him out cold. He was a tough man, hard as nails. Nobody wanted to have anything to do with him. Nobody wanted to challenge him because he was so unpredictable. He'd hit you first and argue later. Earl Smith was a silent guy, had those cold, blue eyes, blond hair, and he'd always be chewing tobacco. He didn't mind taking a drink or two, either.

"The Pirates came into Chicago one time, and it was Prohibition days and the club was faltering a little at the time, and manager Donie Bush decided he would search everybody's suitcase. Everybody's suitcase was frisked, and Bush found whiskey in practically everybody's suitcase. Players would get good Canadian whiskey when they came to Chicago through Al Capone. Capone got the whiskey into the country inside cans of ham. You'd take a can opener and open up the ham can, and there inside would be a nice bottle of Canadian whiskey. Well, Donie Bush found ham cans in practically every suitcase. He didn't take their ham cans away, but he did fine them.

"The Pirates were something on the left side of their infield. Glenn Wright was the shortstop, and the third baseman was Pie Traynor, who was the greatest third baseman I ever saw. If you can picture Brooks Robinson with a much better bat, you've got Pie Traynor. In the field he played even with the bag. He made no concessions to the big powerful right-handers like Chick Hafey, Gabby Hartnett, Hack

Wilson, or Ernie Lombardi. And he used a glove with the palm completely cut out, like a lot of players did. He used his bare hand to catch the ball! And he could do all the things Brooks Robinson did: He was great at fielding balls over the bag, at diving to his left, and he was a wonder fielding swinging bunts. They used to say, 'The batter doubled to left, but Traynor threw him out at first.'

"Pie had one particular weakness. He couldn't hold a ball. The minute he'd catch it, he'd fire it over to first. The first baseman had better be alert because the ball was on its way as soon as it hit his glove.

"And Traynor was a wonderful hitter. After he retired, he became a manager, and if he had a weakness it was that he was too nice a person, too understanding. A fine man was Pie.

"During those years the Cubs were a bad team, always finished down in the race. I can remember when the teams like the Giants or the Pirates would come to town. I'd hear the visiting players talking, and somebody would say, 'Let's bear down here and see if we can win three out of four.' The guy would say, 'We're going to have to face Alexander one of the days, so let's bear down the other days.' They were more or less figuring old Alex was going to beat them, he was that good."

29

Alex

Rabbit Maranville wasn't the only drinker on the team. The Cubs' best pitcher, their workhorse, Grover Cleveland Alexander, came back from World War I in 1919 a ruined man, and he too drank heavily.

When Alexander left for Europe and the war, he had his drinking under control. Bills Wrigley and Veeck fully expected that when he returned, Alexander would be as dominating as ever. But during the fighting in Europe, Alexander suffered from shell shock.

In France, he had fought in the front lines as an artillery sergeant. The roar of the guns made him deaf in one ear. Within a few weeks of returning to the States, Alexander's wife, Aimee, discovered that the effects of the war had somehow caused him to have epileptic seizures. The disease haunted him, even striking him while he was on the pitcher's mound.

AIMEE ALEXANDER: "Sometimes a fit would strike him while he was out on the mound. He always carried a bottle of spirits of ammonia with him. They would have to carry him off the field. Some thought he was drunk. They would take him into the locker room, Alex would whiff the ammonia, fight to get control of himself, and then go right back out and pitch again.

"We were never certain when they were going to happen. Sometimes he'd get three or four in one month. Then he'd go months without anything happening. I remember once in Pittsburgh, I saw Alex signal the umpire suddenly and call time. I knew what was happening. He went into the dressing room for about fifteen minutes, came out again, and pitched the entire game. That takes a great deal of courage. They always left him so weak, and well, sort of helpless."

Alexander suffered from epilepsy throughout the remainder of his illustrious career.

PINKY WHITNEY (HIS TEAMMATE IN 1930): "Sometimes he'd have one of those spells out on the mound and we'd get around him and pull his tongue out. And then he'd get up and throw the next ball right through the middle of the plate."

When Alexander returned after the war, he suffered from another problem even more serious than epilepsy: alcoholism. The great pitcher lived every day in fear, and to make those fears tolerable, he drank heavily.

AIMEE ALEXANDER: "Alex always thought he could pitch better with a hangover, and maybe he could, at that. I did my best to keep him straight. When he was with me, he was all right. But then he'd wander off. Even so, he did pretty well as a pitcher, didn't he? I don't see any reason to hide the fact that he drank—everyone knows it."

And yet despite the twin curses of epilepsy and alcoholism, Grover Cleveland Alexander pitched in the major leagues a total of 20 seasons, compiling a record of 373 victories against only 208 losses, tied for third in wins in baseball history with Christy Mathewson behind Cy Young (511) and Walter Johnson (416). His 90 shutouts ranks him second in major league history behind Johnson's 110.

Alex's descent into alcoholism was made famous by actor Ronald Reagan, who played him in the 1952 movie *The Winning Team*.

As a youngster Cubs clubhouse boy Ed Froelich was fascinated by Alexander. With the Cubs the big pitcher wasn't as dominating as he had been before entering World War I, but during his seven seasons with Chicago, he continued to win regularly, winning 27 games in 1920 and 22 in 1923.

Ed Froelich had the opportunity to watch the great pitcher from up close during Alex's final years with the team.

ED FROELICH: "The most vivid memory I have of Grover Alexander is of him sitting in front of his locker watching the clock and waiting for exactly twenty minutes before game time. At twenty minutes to three his ritual would begin. Alex didn't believe in going to the trainer's room, and he would take a bottle of Sloan's liniment out of his locker and start pouring it onto his right shoulder and his pitching arm. He'd work and work and work until he had just the right degree of warmth, and then he'd go in and wash his hands and return to the stool in front of his locker. Then the other part of the ritual began.

"He'd light a Camel cigarette and sit there and smoke it, and that would consume about five minutes, and now it would be ten minutes to three, and he'd put on his undershirt, his uniform shirt, pick up his cap and his glove, and he'd start out for the field to warm up. He'd have less than ten minutes to get warm, and then he'd begin.

"Alex had a little white glove, and he'd wind up, put the ball in the glove, and throw. After he got the ball back from the catcher, he'd look about the crowd—take

Grover Cleveland Alexander

a survey—and then he'd spit into his glove, and with one finger he'd work the spit into his glove. He was stalling more than anything else, and then he'd throw another ball, and he'd repeat the procedure.

"I can remember one game when Alex was at the end of his career [in 1930], he was pitching for the Phillies, and Art Fletcher, who was a coach with the club, saw him warming up. Fletcher was a fiery guy who liked to win, a guy who liked to see everything done right, and Art shouted at Alexander, 'The game is going to start in a minute. When the hell are you going to throw hard?'

"Alex looked at Fletcher and said, 'When I get out there in the middle of the diamond, that's when.'

"It was nobody's business, really, to tell Alexander what to do. He won 373 games, third behind Cy Young and Walter Johnson. Who was going to criticize?

"But Alex always seemed so remote and distant. He wasn't an easy man to reach. Alex was a world apart really. On the mound he was so disdainful. He'd walk out there, and the first thing he'd do was kick the resin bag aside. He didn't believe in using a resin bag or wiping the brow or tugging at his belt or pulling up his pant leg. All that stuff was wasted motion, a lot of jazz.

"And he had such control. I remember hearing shortstop Jimmy Cooney ask him one day [with Chicago, in 1926], 'Hey Pete, with a man on first base, where do you want me to play Chick Hafey?'

"Alex said, 'Play for the double play.'

"Our second baseman, Sparky Adams, asked Alex where he should play with one on and Bill Terry coming to bat.

"Alex said, 'Play for the double play.'

"'But don't you want me to protect the hole?' Adams asked.

"Alex said, 'That's my job. Your job is to make the double play.'

"Oh, Alex could be sarcastic sometimes. We had a big, tall right-handed pitcher named Johnny Welch, who should have been a great pitcher but for some reason never was. Welch was about six foot four, tall and stringy, and he could throw. Except that he was a real handsome kid, and he had a hell of a singing voice, and he liked girls, and the girls liked him, and they kept him pretty occupied.

"In those days all the ballplayers wore Max Carey sliding pads. Carey had been the premier base stealer of the time, and he had invented a very good sliding pad, much like the hip pads you see in football. They prevented strawberries, but their drawback was that they got hot as hell out on the field, and as you sweated, they absorbed the sweat and became heavy so that as the years went on the players stopped wearing them. At any rate, at this time most of the players wore them, including a few of the pitchers.

"This particular day Johnny Welch was standing in front of a mirror in the clubhouse. He had put his Max Carey sliding pads on and had pulled up his pants, and he was standing there admiring himself when Alexander walked by.

"'What the hell are you looking at?' Alex asked Welch.

"'I'm looking to see how those sliding pads fit,' said Welch.

"'Sliding pads?' said Alex. 'What for?'

"'Oh, I guess to more or less fill out my pants more than anything else,' said Welch, who hadn't been pitching much.

"Alex said to him, 'If they ever put you in to pitch, you'd shit 'em full.'

"Alex had a particular fondness for catcher Gabby Hartnett. When Hartnett first came up [in 1922], Alex recognized his greatness. He went and asked manager Bill Killefer to let Hartnett catch him, and of course, the two became one of the greatest batteries in the history of the game.

"It was early in Hartnett's career, and the Cubs were playing the Cincinnati Reds. Pitching for the Reds was Carl Mays, the guy who killed Ray Chapman with a pitched ball only a few years earlier [in 1920]. Mays had a reputation for knocking down hitters, especially right-handers, and he was rough and mean.

"This day Hartnett came up, and Mays threw his underhand fastball that bore in on Hartnett and literally turned the peak of his cap around, that's how close it came to beaning him.

"Nobody said anything, but the next time Mays came up to bat, Alexander slowly walked off the mound and walked up to the plate.

"He said, 'Mays, I haven't made up my mind which eye I'm going to hit you in. Do you have a preference?'

"Mays pleaded with him. He told him the pitch to Hartnett he had wanted close, but not that close. He insisted the ball had slipped.

"'Please, Alex,' Mays said, 'please believe me.'

"Finally Alexander told him, 'I shouldn't believe you, but I'll give you the benefit of the doubt just this once.'

"And whenever Alexander pitched, Mays was careful not to throw too close to the Cubs batters.

"Another thing I remember about Alexander when he pitched was that he'd always be studying the wind. The wind was his ally. Alex was traded to the Cardinals in 1926, and the first time he came into Chicago he beat us 2–1, allowing three hits. In that game Hartnett hit four balls dead up against the left-field wall, balls that

Chick Hafey caught with his back right up against the wall. On any other day, those balls would have been on top of the apartment buildings across the street. On this day the wind had been blowing in so strongly from left they were only long outs.

"After the game Gabby was sitting in front of his locker feeling blue.

"'Imagine,' he said, 'I can't possibly hit a ball harder than the four I hit today, and all I got out of it was four outs.'

"Joe McCarthy wasn't standing too far away.

"'Don't feel too bad about it, Gabby,' he said. 'If the wind had been blowing in from center field, you'd have hit those balls to center field. If the wind had been blowing in from right, they would have gone to right.'

"And Hartnett, who had caught Alexander all those years, knew McCarthy was right.

"'I ought to know,' he said. 'I ought to know.'

"I remember another game in which Alexander was pitching for the Cardinals against us. We were getting ready to play, and Kiki Cuyler and Riggs Stephenson, who had adjacent lockers, were moaning over having to face him.

"Stephenson said, 'How do you try to hit him?'

"Cuyler, who over eighteen years hit better than .320, said, 'I don't really try. I gave up a long time ago. But just once before he quits pitching or before I quit playing, I'd like to get a strike I can hit. Every time I take a pitch, it's got an inch and a half of the plate, and if I swing at it, it's two inches outside. Just once I'd like to guess right.'

"Lew Fonseca was a rookie when he broke in with Cincinnati [in 1921], and the first time he faced Alexander he singled to left. No one was on base. The next time up no one was on, and he singled to center.

"The next time up there were two base runners. Fonseca told me, 'Alex struck me out so fast, I didn't even get settled in the batter's box.'

"Fonseca was walking back to the dugout, and he could see all the Cincinnati players laughing at him. When he got back to the bench Edd Roush put his arms around his shoulders and said, 'Son, that time you saw the real Alexander, not those other two times.'

"And of course, that was the way Alex pitched. You rarely saw his great stuff until it meant something. You'd see mediocre stuff, until he needed that extra.

"The umpires loved him because he was always around the plate. Catchers loved him. He was so easy to catch. And with Alex, you didn't have to call pitch-outs. When Hartnett first started to catch him, he said: 'Don't give me any pitch-out signs. I'll know when the guy is going. I'll take care of the pitch-outs.' Imagine that. And he was *very* difficult to run on. He didn't come way back with his arms, and he didn't have a high kick. He threw with a minimum of motion.

"I was saying that the umpires loved him because he was always around the plate, but that umpire better be doing a good job back there. I can remember quite a few occasions when Alex would stalk off that mound, storm all the way in to the umpire, and tell him off. If the umpire wasn't doing a good job, he'd let him know about it and let everyone else in the ballpark know too, because you could see what he was doing. Better not miss pitches on him.

"The one person who didn't like to see him pitch was the concessionaire. It was a Saturday before a Sunday game, and the concessionaire at Wrigley Field would always come to Joe McCarthy to ask him who was pitching so he could print up the scorecard for the next game. On this day McCarthy told him Alexander was pitching.

"He said, 'God almighty, Joe. Anybody but Alexander.'

"'What's wrong with him?' asked McCarthy.

"He said, 'Every time he pitches, it costs the ball club thousands of dollars. He pitches so quickly he's got 'em on the street in an hour and five minutes.'

"McCarthy said, 'I can't help it, Fred. Mr. Wrigley didn't hire me to make money for the concessionaire. He hired me to win ball games. It's Alexander's turn, and he's going to pitch.'

"I always got the impression that there was some deep sadness and remorse inside Alex. Maybe it was the epilepsy he suffered from. It may have been the war. He was never quite as great a pitcher as he had been before the war, and a lot of people say that when he came back, he was a heavy drinker.

"He always struck me as an introvert. He didn't seem to want to socialize, didn't do too much talking. If he went someplace, he went alone. He was a loner.

"In all the games I saw him pitch, I never saw him knocked out except one, and even then he wasn't taken out, but rather he walked off by himself. It was the weirdest thing you could possibly imagine.

"If you see a couple of Texas Leaguers in one inning, you think it's unusual. He was pitching for the Cubs against Cincinnati, and in this inning, there were six, and after the sixth one dropped in, a little looper that went over the shortstop's head with the bases loaded, Alexander stood in the center of the diamond, watched this thing fall in front of the left fielder, watched two more runs clatter across the plate, and without saying a word to anybody, he took his glove off, stuffed it in his pocket, and walked off the mound. He didn't wait for the manager, didn't wait for anybody, as much to say, 'This isn't my day.' I sat in the dugout and watched him shuffle off to the locker room.

"And you probably know, Alexander died in a gutter someplace. [He actually died in a hotel room in St. Paul, Nebraska.] After he left baseball, he pitched for the House of David team, and he was hired by a flea circus in New York. People would pay to see him.

"It didn't have to end that way. When he was in his heyday with the Cubs, Mr. Wrigley—that's William Wrigley Jr., the founder of the Wrigley fortune—wanted to do something for Alex.

"Alex was dabbling in insurance at the time, and Mr. Wrigley wanted to have Alex write a $1 million policy on his life. Alex would have gotten the commission on it, and that would have set him up for life.

"Mr. Wrigley set up a ten o'clock appointment with Alex, but as Alex was wont to do, he didn't keep it, and Mr. Wrigley washed out the deal. I guess Mr. Wrigley felt that if Alex didn't have the interest to show up, the hell with it. Alex could have used the money. It was a shame.

"I was talking with Joe McCarthy one day, just wondering out loud. I said, 'How good would Alexander have been if he wasn't that kind of a drinker?' McCarthy said, 'Who knows? Maybe he might not have been so good. Maybe that was one of the things that helped make him as good as he is.' He added, 'In the final analysis, how much better could he have been?'

"And when you stop to think about it, how much better could he have been?"

Chapter 30

Marse Joe Arrives

In 1926, William Veeck reached out for a new manager. He had no way of knowing it at the time, but his choice would turn out to be a brilliant one, perhaps the last great managerial find to be discovered by Cubs management.

The year before, Veeck had gone through three managers, including Maranville, who had been a disaster. Veeck knew the Cubs needed stability, and the man he selected, a career minor leaguer by the name of Joe McCarthy, at first seemed an odd choice. But Frank Selee, the molder of the Tinker-Evers-Chance Cubs, had also never played in the majors. To succeed, McCarthy would have to be able to choose winning players, mold a team in his image, and win over his players. Within his first year McCarthy would do all those things, and before his retirement in 1950, this unknown would be hailed as one of the greatest managers in baseball history.

Joe McCarthy was a boy who had grown up tough. His father, a contractor, was killed on the job when he was but three. To help feed his family, instead of going to high school McCarthy went to work in a textile mill. When he was a teenager he began playing semipro baseball on the sandlots of Philadelphia.

Though he never attended high school, Niagara College gave him a scholarship, and he went there for two years. He quit in 1906 to play pro ball.

For fifteen years he was a minor league player. The closest he came to the majors was signing to play in the Federal League for 1916 before it folded. In 1919 he became a player-manager but quit as a player in 1920 when he realized that performing both roles was hurting him in the eyes of his players.

During a game shortstop Jay Kirke made a bad throw to McCarthy, who was the second baseman. Kirke, a poor fielder, was leading the league in hitting.

"That's the dumbest play I ever saw in my life," said McCarthy. "Why didn't you give me the ball sooner?"

"Listen," Kirke replied, "what the hell right you got telling a .380 hitter how to play ball?"

Said McCarthy years later, "The trouble was, he was right. I was only hitting about .252 at the time. You couldn't blame Jay for figuring I had no right to be telling him off. A manager shouldn't play unless he's better than anybody else on the team."

McCarthy managed the Louisville Cardinals for seven years. Coincidentally, William Veeck had started his newspaper career at the *Courier-Journal* in Louisville, where McCarthy had managed the Cardinals since 1919, and after McCarthy's team won the American Association pennant in 1925, Veeck, on the recommendation of sportswriter John Foster, decided that McCarthy was his man. Veeck was taking a chance, picking an unknown, but as reporter Warren Brown said, you can do that when you're an eighth-place team.

When McCarthy first came to Chicago, he demonstrated a toughness and a singular aversion to losing. Said McCarthy when they hired him, "They tell me we don't look very good on paper. Well, we don't play on paper."

Joe McCarthy

As he expected, thirty-nine-year-old McCarthy faced opposition to his leadership from the veteran players, who soon were to learn how tough a man he was. According to Fred Lieb, when Grover Alexander arrived for spring training, he made the remark that he "wasn't going to be ordered around by a bush league manager." It was a pissing match Alexander surely thought he would win. He was very wrong. McCarthy was no lightweight.

From McCarthy's perspective, all he asked was that a player be ready when game time came. Alexander didn't always do that. McCarthy, a perfectionist and a martinet, let Alexander know who was in charge.

Early in spring training Alexander broke his ankle. While he was hospitalized, his teammates came to see him, but McCarthy never did. Alexander brooded. When Alexander left the hospital, McCarthy ordered him to make the trip from the team's hotel on Catalina Island to Wrigley Field in Los Angeles, where the Cubs played their exhibition games, even though Alexander wasn't playing and had to make the long, painful journey on crutches.

According to Alexander's wife, Aimee, no one had ever treated him so roughly.

When Alexander finally healed and went out to pitch, McCarthy called his pitches. Alexander resented the young manager tremendously.

In spring training the two fought for supremacy. Ed Froelich witnessed Alexander's contempt for McCarthy.

ED FROELICH: "I remember one spring, Joe McCarthy was managing the Cubs. He had a rule: The first swing around the league everyone had to report at 10 in the morning for meetings. If we won, he'd say, 'We'll do away with the meetings and report at 1. Until then, you report at 10.'

"So this particular day we were going to play the Cardinals. McCarthy was conducting the meeting, and Alex was in the back of the room, and it was cold outside and the radiator was hissing, and it was the only sound except for McCarthy's voice.

"Alex, as everyone knows, was a drinker, and the night before he hadn't gotten much sleep, and he was back there dozing. All of a sudden, from the back, came a noise that sounded like a branch cracking. Alex had snored. A few guys laughed.

"McCarthy had just finished saying, 'If Maranville gets on second, be sure you pitchers and catchers switch signs because he's pretty cagey, and he'll relay the sign to the hitter. He's good at that.'

"At that point Alex snored.

"McCarthy said, 'Alex, I know you've been in the league and you know all this stuff, but for the good of the club it would be a good idea if you stayed awake and paid a little attention to what's going on.'

"Alexander said, 'Joe, if I'm pitching and you look up and see that little piss-bottom Maranville on second base, don't lose any time. Just walk out there and take me out of the game, because you'll know I don't have my stuff.'"

JOE MCCARTHY: "Grover Cleveland Alexander was with the Cubs when I took over in 1926. He was getting along in years then but still quite a good pitcher. I had to get rid of him though. He didn't obey orders. Wouldn't get along with me. A fellow asked me one time if Alex followed the rules. 'Sure he did,' I said, 'but they were always Alex's rules.' So I had to let him go. St. Louis took him and he helped them win the pennant. That didn't bother me; he'd been with the Cubs the year before, and they had still finished last. If they finished last again, I'd rather it was without him. That's how I figured it. But he was a nice fellow. Alex was all right. Just couldn't keep to the rules, that's all."

Had McCarthy been a major league veteran he might have ignored Alexander's defiance and his bad habits. Had the manager been a major leaguer, Alex might not have challenged him. But McCarthy saw the tug-of-war between him and his star pitcher as a test: The winner would run the team, he knew. McCarthy, a perfectionist who never allowed his players to make mental mistakes, insisted they field their position, and he always wanted his players to put team considerations ahead of personal ones. Alexander wasn't doing that.

On June 22, 1926, McCarthy banished Grover Cleveland Alexander from Chicago, releasing him on waivers. Alexander's old catcher, Bill Killefer, had become a coach for the St. Louis Cardinals. Killefer convinced Cardinals manager Rogers Hornsby to sign him.

ROGERS HORNSBY: "In June of 1926 Joe McCarthy thought that Grover Cleveland Alexander was dissipated, drank too much and was finished as a major-league pitcher. Then too, Alex had suffered a broken ankle in spring training. They say McCarthy and Alexander didn't like each other.

"Even though Alex had been in a sanitorium at Dwight, Illinois, the winter before to try to quit drinking, I knew he still had a fast ball. Even if it was only half as good as it once was, it still was good. He had the greatest control I've ever seen. Could almost nick the corners of a soft-drink bottle cap. He won 30 games a season for three straight years while pitching for the Philadelphia Phillies in the smallest park in the big leagues. He once pitched four consecutive shut outs, including sixteen in one season; twice he won two games in one day.

"I was playing manager of the Cardinals, so I asked Branch Rickey, who was the general manager and had been the manager before me, to claim Alexander. I had heard of all those newspaper stories about Alex—that he carried a gin bottle more often than his glove—but I wanted him on my team. The Cardinals were in fourth place at the time, so that meant the four teams under us in the standings got a chance to pick him up for the $4,000 waiver price before we got him. All four teams figured he was washed up, or figured something, because none of them took him. We got him on June 22.

"Sports writers always exaggerated their stories about Alex's drinking episodes, and this is one of the reasons the Cubs put him on the waivers list in 1926. I always felt the stories weren't nearly as true as people made out. So did [Cards coach and Alexander's former teammate Bill] Killefer. That's one reason we got Alex for the cheapest price in baseball, $4,000, which helped the Cardinals win the pennant and the World Series. He stayed sober for me, although he wasn't one of those fellows who'd take an ax and break a beer barrel, or pour gin down a sink.

"But drinking bouts made good exciting stories and all the writers like to have exciting stories. Alex even thought one newspaper story about his drinking was exciting. He looked up one day and smirked, 'Good God, I was never as drunk as this fellow had to be who wrote this here story. You guys read this?'

"I consider Grover Cleveland Alexander the greatest pitcher who ever lived, righthanded or lefthanded, drunk or sober. He threw easily, but he had one of the fastest fast balls I ever saw. It sounds corny, I know, to say that old Alex could thread a needle. But he almost did.

"One time during spring training with the Cubs when the sports writers kept pestering Alex to say something exciting about his control, he decided to give them a demonstration. He warmed up with Bill Killefer, his old catcher. Killefer stood behind the plate with a gallon tomato can with the ends cut out of it. Alex warmed up for a good ten minutes, maybe fifteen, by throwing through the can. Never missed once.

"I knew Alex liked his highballs. He liked to go out and drink with his friends, and he had a lot of friends. But he never showed up drunk, and I don't think we could have won the National League pennant that year without him. The next year he won 21 games for the Cardinals, which certainly didn't look like he was finished as a pitcher, by any means."

The first time Alexander and the Cardinals faced Joe McCarthy's Cubs, he won the game 3–2.

After the game McCarthy, a bad loser, was sitting on the bench fuming as Alexander passed. The great pitcher looked the young manager in the eye, smiled, tipped his cap, and kept walking.

McCarthy didn't care how well Alexander was doing in St. Louis. His primary concern was instilling discipline and earning respect among his players, and by letting Alexander go, McCarthy had impressed on the rest of the players that he was in charge.

And from that first season Joe McCarthy, a master builder wherever he went, began to construct the type of team he would become famous for, a team with excellent pitching, good defense, and a lot of power.

Make no mistake about it—it wasn't William Wrigley or William Veeck who built this team, the heart of which would win three pennants. This was Joe McCarthy's team. Wrigley and Veeck should get credit for listening to McCarthy's advice and shelling out the money it took to buy the players he wanted.

Marse Joe, as he was called, built the Cubs by taking advantage of his knowledge of the American Association. When Cubs catcher Gabby Hartnett dropped a pop-up on the final day of the 1925 season, resulting in a loss, the Cubs finished the year with the worst record in the majors. As a result, the Cubs got first choice in the minor league draft. The player McCarthy wanted was Hack Wilson, the young slugger from the Giants organization.

McCarthy also drafted a talented prospect named Riggs Stephenson, and he directed the Cubs to acquire pitchers Charlie Root and Guy Bush. All would become Cub mainstays.

Years later McCarthy would brag about stealing Wilson, a future Hall of Famer, from the Giants.

JOE MCCARTHY: "Hack Wilson was a wonderful little fellow. Do you know how we got him? We stole him from the Giants. That's right. They had sent him to the minors and then forgotten to recall him. A clerical mistake. So he was unprotected when the draft came around. The Cubs had finished in the cellar the year before, so we had first pick. We took Wilson for $5,000. McGraw hit the ceiling when he heard about it. I don't think he ever got over it. Wilson led the league in home runs four out of the next five years."

In 1927 shortstop Woody English joined the team. A star at Toledo, the top Giants farm team, English was given the choice by manager Casey Stengel of whether he wanted to be sold to the Philadelphia A's, the Cleveland Indians, or the Cubs. The Giants didn't need him. They already had Travis Jackson at shortstop. Stengel steered him to the Cubs.

"Hack Wilson and Earl Webb are going to be going to the Cubs," said Stengel. The two had played with him in Toledo.

"Well, I'll go to the Cubs," said English, a star shortstop for a decade. Wrigley paid $50,000 and a couple of players for him, top dollar at the time.

Though McCarthy was a martinet, he was one of those managers who didn't care whether his players drank so long as they were obedient and didn't let their drinking hurt their play on the field. (Toward the end of his own career, McCarthy himself would be plagued by alcoholism.) As tough as McCarthy had been on the inebriate Alexander, he went easy on two young drinkers who were just as bad, Hack Wilson and Pat Malone. The difference: Wilson and Malone, who had played against McCarthy in the American Association, from the start respected him immensely.

Malone, who arrived in Chicago in 1928, had been a top prospect trying out for the Giants when John McGraw caught him partying late and released him to Toledo, where McCarthy grabbed him.

Lewis Robert Wilson, who was born in Elwood City, Pennsylvania, which was named in honor of the man who invented barbed wire, was the illegitimate son of a hard-drinking mill worker and a sixteen-year-old factory girl. His mother died when he was eight. His father was a drunk. He was raised by the owner of the boarding-house where he and his father lived.

Wilson, a rowdy, dropped out of school when he was sixteen (in the sixth grade) to work as a laborer pounding hot rivets with a sledgehammer at a locomotive works. Several years later he was playing pro ball in the Giants organization. After hitting .388 for Portsmouth in the Virginia League, in 1924 and 1925 he was a re-serve for John McGraw and his Giants. While there the short and stocky outfielder acquired his nickname, Hack. The Giants players noticed he looked like former Cubs outfielder Lawrence Miller, who had been called Hack because he looked like a professional wrestler named Hackenschmitt.

McGraw kept the kid at the start of the 1924 season, but the Giants were so deep in talent he had no place to play him. In 1925, McGraw sent him back to Toledo os-tensibly to learn the strike zone. When the Giants failed to protect him, McCarthy, who liked his power, nabbed him for the Cubs. When Wilson joined the team, he became a favorite of manager McCarthy's.

One of the great baseball stories was told during McCarthy and Wilson's first season with the Cubs. McCarthy saw that Wilson was in the habit of staying out all night carousing. Before one game McCarthy called the whole team together and told them he was going to conduct a scientific experiment.

He dropped a worm into a glass of water, and it wriggled wildly. Then he pulled it out and dropped it into a glass of whiskey. The worm died almost instantly.

McCarthy turned to Wilson and asked him, "What did you learn from that?"

"I guess," said Wilson, "it means that if I keep on drinking liquor, I ain't gonna have no worms!"

That 1926 season, Hack led the league with 21 home runs and the Cubs finished fourth. In 1927, McCarthy added shortstop Woody English and pitcher Hal Carlson. In 1928 he added pitcher Pat Malone and outfielder Kiki Cuyler, after the outfield star was put in the doghouse by manager Donie Bush in Pittsburgh.

By 1929, McCarthy had built a powerhouse.

When Joe McCarthy came to the Cubs, one of his favorites was young Ed Froe-lich. McCarthy made him first the Cubs clubhouse boy and later the trainer of whatever team he was managing, including the New York Yankees and the Boston Red Sox. Froelich remembered McCarthy's early Cubs team and what great char-acters Hack Wilson and Pat Malone were.

ED FROELICH: "Early in the 1926 season I went over to Joe McCarthy. It was his first year with the Cubs, and I happened to catch him going up to the clubhouse. I asked him if I could be the batboy for the Cubs. I was sixteen years old. I wanted the job because the Cub batboy wore a uniform.

"McCarthy said, 'Son, I'm sorry, but we already have a batboy.'

Hack Wilson

"I said, 'Well, he might get sick one day, and you might need another. It would be nice to have two, plus the bats are heavy.' They used to carry the bats in a stretcher-like contraption, and it took one person at each end to carry it. I told McCarthy that.

"He looked at me, and he started to laugh. 'You figured that out pretty good, didn't you?' he said. 'I'll tell you what. See me here tomorrow, and I'll let you know. I'll have to talk to Mr. Veeck about it.'

"I met McCarthy the next day, and he gave me the job. And I wouldn't have traded jobs with the president of the United States. But because I was an orphan, and because the two dollars a day I made as batboy didn't go very far in keeping oneself, and because Joe McCarthy had a heart of gold, he came up to me and said, 'I think it would be a good idea if you started to work in the dressing room and became the equipment man.'

"I started helping out the trainer, Doc Painter, and that was the start of my career. Still, I would have given anything if I could have been a ballplayer. But at sixteen I knew my limitations, and I decided that if I couldn't be a ballplayer, I was going to be around ballplayers.

"The Cubs were a nice bunch, but two players, Pat Malone and Hack Wilson, were wild enough to give their reputation to the entire Cubs team.

"Pat Malone was a big, strong, rough-tough character. On the mound he didn't hesitate to knock you down. When the visiting team came to Chicago, they would dread it, because the players knew they had to face Root, Bush, and Malone. Opposing players used to say, 'It's like going to the dentist,' because those three guys used to drill the batters so often.

"Malone was a stuff pitcher. He didn't have finesse, didn't nibble at the corners. He threw right down the middle of the plate and beat you with his good stuff.

"Joe McCarthy bought him from Minneapolis in the American Association in the spring of 1928 on a look-see basis. A lot of teams were bidding for him, but Minneapolis owner Mike Kelly was a longtime friend of McCarthy's, so he sold him to the Cubs for $25,000, with $10,000 down and another $15,000 if the Cubs decided to keep him after June 15. In those days you're talking about pretty good money.

"When June 15 rolled around, Malone's record was 0–8. The Cubs had to make a decision. McCarthy said, 'Buy him,' and he came down from the office to tell Pat they had just completed the sale with the Minneapolis club.

"Malone looked at him and said, 'Joe, all I can say is you people have to be nuttier than I am when you complete a sale for a guy who's 0 and 8.'

"McCarthy said, 'You're not going to stay that way, that I know,' and right afterward Malone won eleven in a row, lost one, and won seven more. He finished the season 18–13. The next year he was 22–10, and then he was 20–9, so in the three-year span he was 60–32.

"McCarthy hadn't let Malone's record fool him. McCarthy knew a good thing when he saw one.

"Pat was a guy with a wonderful sense of humor, and he was wonderful on the club, kept everyone loose.

"He and Hack Wilson were what you call kindred spirits. They gravitated to each other, two jolly guys who loved to have fun. They would bear down on the field, but when the game was over, they liked to have a few drinks and they liked to laugh.

"They were quite a pair. Someone once asked me about Pat, 'Does he drink?' The answer is about the same as the one Bob Lemon gave when someone asked him if he drank when he lost.

"Lem said, 'I drink when we lose, and I drink when we win, and I drink on off days.'

"Pat and Hack didn't pal around much at home because their wives were there. But on the road, with the wives back in Chicago, they were something. More than anything, they liked to be where there was some music and some drinking, and they liked to stay up late and have fun. If a stranger spoke out of turn, every once in a while there would be a fight.

"I remember one night the two were walking back to their rooms in the hotel, and they were minding their own business walking down the hall, and one or the other was laughing about something, 'Ha-ha-ha,' and as they walked by an open hotel room door, one of four guys playing cards mimicked the laugh.

"Pat and Hack looked at each other and said, 'Let's go back there and take care of those smart-asses.' They entered the room, and they filled it with uppercuts and pretty soon there was no more fight.

"Three of the four were out cold, and the fourth guy was standing up against the corner of the room while Malone was swinging away at him.

"Wilson came over and said, 'Why the hell do you keep hitting him for?'

"Malone said, 'He's still standing, isn't he?'

"Hack said, 'I knocked him out five minutes ago. Move the lamp, and he'll fall.' And Malone moved the lamp, and the guy slumped to the floor.

"It was a funny thing how people talked about the Cubs being a roistering bunch in those days. They weren't. Go down the roster: Gabby Hartnett, Charlie Grimm, Rogers Hornsby, Woody English, Riggs Stephenson, Kiki Cuyler. None of them were boisterous.

"But because of those two fellas, Pat and Hack, they gave the whole club an image it never lost."

31

Mr. Wrigley

William Wrigley Jr. had been part of a syndicate that bought the Cubs in 1916. By 1921 he was sole owner of the team. He and his son, Philip K., would own the Cubs until 1986, when it would be sold to the Chicago Tribune Corporation.

William Wrigley was an owner with unusual qualities. The most obvious was that he dearly loved the game and his players. Another was that in the tug between having to choose between viewing baseball as a sport and also as a business, William Wrigley always saw it first as a sport. That he was a man with deep feeling for the sport was evident in everything he said and did.

WILLIAM WRIGLEY [IN 1930]: "Outside of school hours, when I was a boy in Philadelphia, I worked for my father. This seemed to me a cruel conspiracy of the Fates. He was a kind man, but he belonged to a generation which was work-minded. Baseball was nothing to him. My work took me directly past the ball park of the Nationals. That was the trouble! I hadn't a chance in the world to get away to the ball game on any of the familiar alibis.

"The near relatives of my boy friends were buried regularly on ball-game days. No use to tell my employer of imaginary funerals in my family, for he was my father and had the death statistics of the family down to the minute. No other excuses worked. Moreover, he firmly refused to allow me to find another employer. Consequently, whenever I came to the ball park and heard the wild cheering within, I was in a state of rebellion.

"One day when the cheering was particularly wild inside the park, I resolved that same day I would own a ball team and a ball park. This is really how I came to get into baseball as an owner, for my interest in the game has never relaxed an instant from that moment to this. This incident also explains why I get a greater satisfaction out of this enterprise than any other in which I am interested.

"I'm not ashamed to confess that when the Cubs are playing in Chicago I refuse to make any business appointments which will interfere with my attendance at the games. In fact, I follow the team all over the country through the season and attend to my other business affairs outside of baseball hours. That's how well I love baseball. To me, it is the finest competitive sport in existence, and the fact that the American people spend annually close to $70 million for admission to baseball games [in 1930] indicates that they regard baseball as the great American game.

"The reasons for the supreme popularity of baseball are, it seems to me, obvious. It's an open game, every play being clearly exposed to the view of the spectators. In this particular it is in striking contrast to football. But the biggest element of

William Wrigley

fascination in baseball is due to the fact that a game is never over until the last man is out. One team may have everything its own way up to the last inning and then find victory turned into defeat by a fluke or a brilliant play. The popularity of baseball is not dependent upon others, institutional or even local spirit; it is inherent in the game itself.

"Still another reason why baseball holds the interest of millions of our people is that it can be followed closely and intelligently from an oral or printed description of the plays; millions of persons who cannot attend each game of the team in which they are most interested get a high degree of satisfaction from the broadcasts of the game which they do not see. Baseball broadcasting has become a godsend to shut-ins and those who are unable to follow my rule of not allowing business to interfere with baseball. It has millions of ardent and devoted fans who are seldom privileged to see a major-league game excepting through the eyes of imagination. A game which can inspire and hold this great absentee following certainly has a marvelous pulling power.

"Early in my experience as the owner of a major league ball team I said: 'Baseball is too much of a sport to be a business and too much of a business to be a sport.' Today that doesn't sound to me as being nearly so bright a wise crack as it did then. I've found baseball to be a whale of a business—but bigger and better as a sport than as a business! I draw larger dividends in fun and personal satisfaction from my ownership of the Chicago Cubs than I do in money—and it's profitable now.

"No man is qualified to make a genuine success of owning a big-league ball team who isn't in it because of his love for the game; he's sure to weaken in his support at some critical point of its development if his heart isn't in the sport. On the other hand, it is no undertaking for a man who hasn't practically unlimited financial resources at his command, regardless of how much he loves the game. If he regards it merely as a means of making money, he'd much better invest his time and capital in an enterprise strictly commercial in character.

"Operating a successful big-league ball team is radically different from running any commercial or industrial business, because you are dealing, 100 per cent, in and with human nature—and that's always a variable quantity. You can't standardize it either in players or patrons.

"The only product that the baseball business has to sell is good will. If you fail to furnish the kind of entertainment that results in general public good will, you're out of luck. There's a catch in this business at every turn, because you're playing with tricky, variable human nature, not inert physical commodities and mechanical methods."

After William Wrigley bought the Cubs, he began holding spring training on Catalina Island, twenty-four miles off the coast of California. Wrigley, who was immensely wealthy, owned the entire island. During the winter of 1926 the Cubs purchased the contract of shortstop Elwood "Woody" English from the Toledo Mud Hens, the top Giants farm team. In 1927, English first came to spring training as a twenty-year-old rookie. Among English's most vivid memories was his first trip to Catalina and its owner, William Wrigley.

WOODY ENGLISH: "For my first spring training to Catalina, I took the train from Columbus, Ohio, to Los Angeles, and then a two-hour boat ride to Catalina. William Wrigley owned the island, lock, stock and barrel, and everything on it except a few homes. He had a little bank. Everything belonged to Mr. Wrigley.

"Mr. Wrigley's home was up in a cliff, a beautiful, big estate, and he owned a nice big hotel there where the players stayed, and he had a bird aviary on the property, and there was a golf course. You couldn't see one flag from the tee. And he had a lot of quail, and they'd feed the quail every evening behind the big hotel. There were hundreds of those quail.

"We changed clothes in what we called the bathhouse down on the ocean there along the dock where the ships docked, and then we walked up maybe three blocks to the ballpark, and it had a nice fence around it, a huge place, though the stands weren't large. And I remember there were palm trees out by the fence.

"We didn't play a lot of exhibition games. There weren't too many teams training on the coast. The New York Giants were about the only team that came over there.

"I had never been to any place like that before. It seemed like I had always heard about Honolulu, Hawaii, and that's the first thing that entered my mind. The water was so clean and blue, and it really struck me. I thought, I must be in heaven.

"The team was owned by William Wrigley. Every family has to have a father, somebody who loves you and likes you and is good to you and is a little bit strict with you, but you know that he is for you all the way, right? Well, that's the way the players felt about William Wrigley. He would do anything for us. In fact, he'd come and ask you. I can remember him going to Charlie Grimm and saying, 'Charlie, everything going along smooth with you? Anything I can do, give me a call or come over and talk to me out here at the park.' He'd go around to all the guys and give the same message. You knew you had a friend in Mr. Wrigley.

"We used to get a new straw hat every spring and a new felt hat every fall, and you know what, he got us ringside seats at the Dempsey-Tunney fight in Wrigley. I was the kind of guy who pulled for Dempsey, so I'd have to say it *was* an awful long count.

"Mr. Wrigley was a fanatic about the beauty and cleanliness of the ballpark. Every year everything was painted and cleaned. The floors along the refreshment stand were so clean if you dropped a sandwich on the floor, you could pick it up and eat it. The toilets were immensely clean. There wasn't any dust on the seats. It was nice. But it was the only place—still is, I guess—that doesn't have any place to park cars.

"One time a businessman, one of Wrigley's friends from out of town, came to visit, a huge man. Wrigley's box was right behind home plate between third and home, and there were six chairs, three in front, three behind in each box. When this man went to sit down, he had a heck of a time. He was sitting part on one chair, part on the other. So Wrigley called the usher down, and he said, 'Take two chairs out of this box, and tomorrow take two chairs out of every box. We're going to make this more comfortable for the fans.'"

As batboy, then equipment manager, and finally trainer of the Chicago Cubs, Ed Froelich also was afforded an up-close view of the Cubs' remarkable owner.

Ed Froelich could see William Wrigley's love of the game every day when he came to his ballpark. Froelich was equally impressed with Wrigley's insistence that the ballpark, renamed Wrigley Field, be spotless and well maintained.

ED FROELICH: "The Cubs were Mr. Wrigley's pride and joy. It didn't make any difference what he had scheduled; if the Cubs were home, he would be at the ballpark. He'd show up with a flower in his lapel, step out of his great big imported car that would pull into the back, and he would walk in and take out his white handkerchief, and as he walked along to his seat, he would rub his white handkerchief along the hand railings, and even though there was a coal yard next door to the park, there had better not be any coal dust on the railings or he'd want to know why. Every box seat had to be cleaned by ushers before you sat down.

"Before every home stand a ground crew of twenty-two men would start at the very top row with big fire hoses, and they'd wash down every aisle and every seat. The park was always spotless. A lot of parks in those days used to lay off the ground crew when the team was on the road. Not Mr. Wrigley. They worked, whether the team was home or not. His theory was: How do you expect to keep good men if you're always laying them off? They'll find other jobs.

"Every spring the park would be painted stem to stern. Not every other year or third year like some parks. No sir. That park was his pride and joy.

"And it was Mr. Wrigley who was responsible for the ushering system that's in vogue today. Prior to his changing things, thugs were ushers. You'd walk in, and even if you had a seat near third base, if you didn't give the usher a tip, you'd sit down the left-field line.

"But one day a young fellow by the name of Andy Frain went to him and said, 'Mr. Wrigley, I would like to revolutionize the ushering system. I'd like to put decent young men in uniforms, train them, and I would see that their uniform didn't have any pockets.' And Mr. Wrigley gave Andy Frain the OK. He underwrote the whole experiment. Every day Frain came to work and had to fight the thugs. Every day he'd have a fistfight, and he didn't lose one. He'd come into the clubhouse early in the morning, and he might have a bloody nose or a split eyebrow, but you could bet your life that the guy he fought looked a hell of a lot worse. He'd come into the clubhouse and ask me, 'Can I use the shower, kid?' He'd put on a clean shirt or change to one that wasn't torn, and he'd continue about his business.

"Mr. Wrigley was a wonderful owner. It was such a vastly different thing than it is today. He was always conscious of his players. In the spring of the season when the straw hat season came in, there would be an envelope in everyone's locker with a ten-dollar bill to buy a straw hat. It was a small gesture, but he was showing his players he was thinking of them. Come the fall, there was another ten-dollar bill for a felt hat.

"And when the big hit plays came to Chicago, like the *Follies* or *Banjo Eyes*, Mr. Wrigley would tell McCarthy a week or two in advance that there were two tickets at the box office for everyone on the club Wednesday evening. The players and their wives and girlfriends would go, and everyone would have a great time.

"When Mr. Wrigley would come to the ballpark, he'd eat a hot dog to test it out. He'd eat the peanuts, which were roasted right at the park. He'd eat the popcorn, and he'd drink the lemonade, which was made fresh.

"One day the concessionaire came to Mr. Wrigley and said, 'The price of lemons has just gone through the roof. We can't use fresh lemon juice anymore.

"Mr. Wrigley said, 'Yes we can. We're known for our fresh lemonade in this ball-park, and that's the way it's going to be. I don't care what the price of lemons is.'

"And at the end of the home stand any food left over was taken to the poor-houses, given away to charity.

"During the summer if you stood out in front of Wrigley Field during the week, you could see that eighty percent of the people were women and children. Mr. Wrigley made the women into fans. On Fridays he let the women into the park for free. Twenty thousand of them would stream into the park until he finally had to put a limit on it.

"And what wonderful crowds flocked to Wrigley Field in those days. In the middle of the week they'd draw 54,000. Of course, the park was bigger then. The box seats were so narrow you had to sit with your neighbor's elbows in your ribs. To fit all those people, they had to throw ropes up across the outfield, and outside the stadium they had to call out the mounted police to keep the mob from storming the gates.

"What wonderful, glorious days they were. The Cubs were on the upswing, and they were the darlings of Chicago. On Ladies Day it was nothing for the women to bake fifteen or so of the biggest, most wonderful-looking cakes for the players. What are you going to do with so many cakes? We'd take them to the ground crew and tell them to take them to nursing homes or to the poor.

"Farmers used to come in and leave a box of the choicest tomatoes. A dairy farmer from the outskirts of Chicago would leave forty-eight bottles of this wonder-ful, wonderful Guernsey milk for the team every day.

"It was a wonderful era, the team was coming on, they were the darlings of Chi-cago, and every day was New Year's Eve."

32

A Powerhouse

In 1927, Woody English's rookie year, Joe McCarthy had molded a powerful lineup featuring Hack Wilson, Riggs Stephenson, outfielder Earl Webb, and their star catcher, Gabby Hartnett. The Cubs almost won the pennant before folding in September when pitcher Charlie Root's sore arm finished his season prematurely, but the Cubs' record improved to 85–68. The next year the team added the immensely likable Pat Malone and the vain loner Kiki Cuyler, and its '28 record jumped to 91–63, two games behind the New York Giants, four behind the pennant-winning St. Louis Cardinals. With Joe McCarthy at the helm the Cubs had become a team to be reckoned with.

WOODY ENGLISH: "After I came up to the Cubs in 1927, in June they traded away their starting shortstop, Jimmy Cooney. McCarthy told me, 'English, you're going to be the regular shortstop from now on.' Jimmy had some age on him [he was thirty-two]. He was a slick fielder but not much of an all-around athlete, couldn't run much.

"Oh, I liked Joe McCarthy. It was McCarthy who pushed the Cubs to get Earl Webb and Hack and me and Riggs Stephenson. He got a lot of players he had seen play in the American Association. Joe was very successful at Louisville. He won pennants down there.

"We'd have a meeting before every series with a new ball club, and he would have the pitcher and the catcher tell how they were going to pitch to every batter on that team. The whole club was in on it. The meetings were all baseball. There wasn't any monkey business about it. So we would understand where we were to play the hitters. I soon learned things, like how the Waner boys, left-handed batters, could run so you had to shorten up the distance a little bit. A guy like Ernie Lombardi [the Reds' powerful but plodding catcher], you could play left field and still throw him out.

"McCarthy was the kind of guy you respected. You wouldn't want to kid much with him. You had a deep respect for him. He was a nice guy, and we played ball for him. He was business. I think he treated everyone the same. If you made a good play or if you were playing good ball for him, he'd let you know that he appreciated what you were doing for him, and on the other hand, if you were doing something wrong, he'd try to correct you in a nice way. He didn't do it in front of the rest of the players. He wasn't that kind of guy.

"There was never any backtalk with McCarthy. No, no, no. You dared not. In other words, he was the boss.

"You have to remember that in nine out of ten years I played in Chicago [1927–36], the Cubs finished one, two, or three. The good teams, Pittsburgh, New York, St. Louis, and the Cubs, usually didn't beat the other contenders regularly. Whoever beat the tailenders the most would win the pennant. The only year we finished fourth was my first year up there, 1927. We were about five games in front going into our last eastern trip. At the end of the season we were over playing

Boston, and Charlie Root was complaining of a sore arm. That year we had the lead going into the last eastern trip. Root had a sore arm, and Mr. Wrigley said. 'No, don't pitch him any more. Let him take the rest of the season off to rest his arm.' See how Mr. Wrigley thought about everybody?

"The next year Pat Malone and Cuyler made us an even better club. Malone could throw that ball hard. Everybody seemed to like him; maybe it was because of his size [six feet, two hundred and thirty pounds] that you had to like him. I liked the guy real well.

"I can remember Pat liked to play practical jokes. In Cincinnati in old Crosley Field, the visiting clubhouse was kinda like a shanty. The home club had a little house where the players changed clothes down there and then the visiting club had another little house, and this day Pat Malone put one of them smoke bombs in Ernie Lombardi's car.

"Malone told us about it, so we were all out there on the porch, waiting for Lombardi, who dressed about as slow as he ran. I guess we had the whole darn team out there waiting. We knew what was going to happen, and he got into his car and that damn thing went off and the smoke rolled up and there were loud noises, and then he looked over and saw all of us guys standing there. He said, 'I can whip the guy that did that. If I knew which one it was . . .'

"Then we started kidding him, and he laughed. He took it real good.

"Cuyler was a lifetime .321 hitter and he could steal bases, and we were able to get him because he got in a feud with Donie Bush in Pittsburgh. There was a close play in a crucial game, and Cuyler didn't slide into second base. And that's why Donie got rid of Cuyler.

Woody English

"You know, Cuyler wasn't too popular with the players, either. He was a loner. There were several things about him that I could see where people wouldn't like him. For instance, he put suntan powder on his face to make it look like he was sunburned. And as good as he could throw, he never threw anybody out in a close game, and he never seemed to get the winning hit for the Cubs when I was there. He was an 'average' guy. He liked to get his average up. Probably didn't know who won the game, but he did all right. He could run. But I'd have to say he wasn't very popular with the majority of the players. He kept to himself. He liked to dance, and he'd go out, never palled around with a single player on the club. They didn't really dislike him, but he wasn't one of the boys.

"Funny Cuyler is in the Hall of Fame, and Riggs Stephenson isn't. Stephie was a nice fella, quiet. He was one great ballplayer. I really don't know why Stephenson isn't in the Hall of Fame. Well, one thing about him, he couldn't run very good, and he couldn't throw. When I'd play shortstop, I had to go farther out to Stephie. He was muscle-bound. He had been an all-American football player. That Cuyler had a heck of an arm, but he never threw anybody out.

"I'll tell you something about Riggs Stephenson. If the winning run was in scoring position where they couldn't walk him in the ninth inning, we'd put our gloves in our pockets and go up the runway to the clubhouse. That's what we thought of Riggs Stephenson. He would drive that winning run in time after time.

"Hartnett was so colorful. I liked Hartnett. I think he was the greatest catcher. I'm telling you that Hartnett threw the lightest ball, and hard. You could catch it almost with your bare hand. He was great, and he had color to him. He was a big, red-faced Irishman. When he was behind the plate, if there was a fast runner on first base, like Pepper Martin of the Cardinals, who usually stole a lot of bases, the pitcher would throw over there a couple times, and Hartnett would come right out in front of home plate, take his mask off, and say, 'Don't throw over there. Let him run. I'll throw him out by eight or ten feet.' Just so Martin could hear him. You could hear him all over the ballpark. A pop fly would go up by the stands, and Gabby would run over and yell out to the fans, 'I never dropped a pop fly in my life.' And he'd catch it. He was colorful. I liked him.

"In 1929, Gabby had a sore arm all that season, and I can tell you how that happened. Nobody ever knew about it. He did it shooting clay pigeons over in Lincoln Park in Chicago. The recoil from the gun shooting clay pigeons, that's what hurt his arm. They didn't want the news media to know about it. He liked to do that. So in July '29 we had to get Zack Taylor from the Braves to be our catcher. Zack was a nice guy, but compared to Hartnett, he wasn't much. His arm wasn't too strong. He was a nice receiver, but he wasn't a Hartnett.

"In 1928, Hack Wilson hit 31 homers and drove in 120 runs. He was five foot six and weighed 230 pounds, and he had a size five and a half shoe. And he used a long bat. He was a quiet farm boy from the country. He would talk about prizefights and sports of all kinds. The Black Hawks were a big thing in Chicago, ice hockey, and the football team, the Bears. He was a sports fan, and he knew Bronko Nagurski and Red Grange. We knew Red well. He was a real nice guy. Our trainer, Andy Lotshaw, trained the Bears too, for [George] Halas, so they came in in the fall of the year, and we got to know them pretty well."

*   *   *

At the end of the 1928 season one piece still was missing. Joe McCarthy was not satisfied with second baseman Freddie Maguire, another former Giants cast-off. William Wrigley was not satisfied his Cubs hadn't won a pennant. One intriguing player who could be had for a steep price was New York Giants second baseman Rogers Hornsby, the finest right-handed batter of all time (Ty Cobb, Babe Ruth, and Ted Williams were left-handed). Hornsby was a .358 lifetime hitter over a twenty-three-year career, including a five-year period (1921–25) during which he batted .402! Seven times he won the National League batting title.

Hornsby, a large man, was a vicious line-drive hitter, and he had power. One of the classic stories told about him came from Arthur Daley. According to the veteran *New York Times* writer, a rookie pitcher for the Brooklyn Dodgers was facing Hornsby for the first time. He asked Jack Fournier, the Dodgers first baseman, how to pitch to him.

"Just feed him inside pitches," said Fournier.

In his first confrontation the pitcher threw inside as instructed, and Hornsby hit a line drive so hard he almost took off the head of the third baseman.

"I thought you said his weakness was inside pitches," said the pitcher to the first baseman.

"I said nothing of the kind," said Fournier. "I just didn't want him hitting outside pitches on a line at me. I'm a married man with a family."

Hornsby once hit a line drive back at Art Nehf of the Giants. The ball caromed off his chest, leaving the name A. G. Spalding stenciled on his skin like a tattoo for a full week.

The lyrical Ogden Nash wrote about Hornsby in his "Line-up for Yesterday: An ABC of Baseball Immortals":

> *H is for Hornsby;*
> *When pitching to Rog,*
> *The pitcher would pitch,*
> *Then the pitcher would dodge.*

Experts said of him: His only weakness is base on balls.

LES BELL (A TEAMMATE ON THE CARDINALS): "Hornsby was the greatest right-handed hitter that ever lived, I can guarantee you that. Maybe even the greatest hitter, period. He had the finest coordination I ever saw. And confidence. He had that by a ton.

"There was another thing that Hornsby could do that a lot of people don't realize—he could run. When he was stretching out on a triple, he was a sight to see. If he had hit left-handed he probably would have hit .450. He was a streak going down the line.

"In '28 Hornsby led the league with .387. Paul Waner was chasing him most of the summer—I think Paul ended up around .370 or so. Anyway, toward the end of the year Pittsburgh came in for a series and the batting race was pretty close at the time. The papers made a big fuss over 'The Battle for the Batting Championship.' There wasn't much else to fuss over. Rog really went to town and got a carload of hits in the series while Waner didn't do too well. When it was over, Paul and Hornsby happened to be going back together through the runway underneath the stands to the clubhouse.

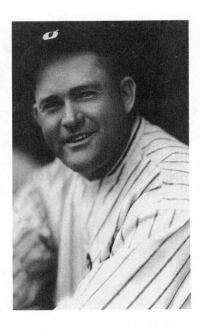

Rogers Hornsby

"'Well, Rog,' Paul said, 'it looks like you're gonna beat me.'

"Rog scowled at him and said, 'You didn't doubt for a minute that I would, did you?'"

But the unfortunate fact was that whoever got Hornsby's bat also got Hornsby. Outspoken and quick to criticize, he was a perpetual irritant on whatever team he played. He began as a St. Louis Cardinal in 1915; in 1923 he got into a fistfight with manager Branch Rickey. The next year Hornsby hit .424, the highest batting average of the twentieth century. It was then that William Veeck of the Cubs first attempted to buy him from Cards owner Sam Breadon for $300,000, the same price that Giants owner Charles Stoneham had offered. Breadon turned them down.

In May 1925, Branch Rickey was made the general manager, and Hornsby replaced him to become player-manager for the Cardinals. That year he hit .403; the next year he led his team to the 1926 pennant.

Through the 1926 season Hornsby fought with Rickey, demanding more say in player moves. When during the 1926 season he told off owner Sam Breadon and followed that by turning down a $50,000-a-year salary offer (he wanted a multiyear contract), he was traded to the New York Giants, where John McGraw was having legal problems caused by a bad land deal. When Hornsby came to the Giants for the 1927 season, McGraw told him he was to run the team whenever he was away.

Once when McGraw went to New York without telling anyone, the writers were upset that no one had told them.

"What difference does it make?" commented Hornsby. "Who the hell cares where he is?"

Another time in a game when McGraw was away Hornsby sharply criticized the play of third baseman Freddie Lindstrom.

"That's the way the Old Man taught me how to do it," said the third baseman.

"When I'm running this team," said Hornsby, "you do things the way I want them done."

Lindstrom, a decent man who was loyal to McGraw, told him, "Oh yeah? Listen to me, wise guy. Once you put down that bat of yours, you're a detriment to any ball club."

Later, after a game in which Hornsby was subbing for McGraw, Giants owner Charles Stoneham asked him why he didn't use a certain player to pinch-hit.

"Are you trying to tell me how to run this ball club?" snarled Hornsby.

"Why, no, I just thought . . ."

"I don't care what you thought, you ———. If you don't like the way I'm running the club, get somebody else to do it."

And so Stoneham did. At the end of his one season in New York it was bye-bye Hornsby, dealt to the hapless Boston Braves, owned by Judge Emil Fuchs. Hornsby was named captain there, and he constantly second-guessed his manager, Jack Slattery. By May, Slattery resigned. Hornsby became manager and led the league with a .387 average. The team finished seventh.

Hornsby's players disliked him immensely. He didn't care. One time he challenged several of them when he discovered them drunk.

He told them, "I don't smoke, drink or chew. I can hit to left, center and right. They call me a great player. If you live like I do, you can be great players too." Said Harold Kaese, "They did everything but yawn in his face."

On August 30, 1928, the Braves signed Hornsby to a six-year contract at $40,000 a year. Hornsby finally had his security. But Boston was practically bankrupt, and in September, when the Braves were in Chicago, Hornsby went to Judge Fuchs and told him, "Judge, what you need is a young club. Now, I have about one year left and could help Chicago. [He was right too. Though he remained in the league another nine years, he would have only two more truly productive years.] Why don't you let me make a deal for myself with Chicago? It would help everybody concerned."

ROGERS HORNSBY: "I really enjoyed playing for the Braves because the owner, Judge Emil Fuchs, was one of the nicest men I've ever met. When he told me that he had been offered five players and nearly $250,000 for me by the Chicago Cubs I strongly advised him to take it.

"'Look, Judge Fuchs,' I said, 'I can only play one position and those guys can play five a lot better than any five guys you have now. They can help the team more in the long run than me. Besides, you can get enough money to bail yourself out for a while.'"

Hornsby called Cubs president William Veeck, who then talked to Judge Fuchs and C. F. Adams, a Buffalo businessman who was on the Braves' board of directors. Veeck asked the Braves' directors what they wanted for Hornsby.

"Two hundred thousand and five players," said Adams.

Veeck called team owner William Wrigley long distance and advised Wrigley not to do it, that it was "a hundred thousand dollars and three players" too much.

Since the day he hired William Veeck, Wrigley had contented himself to be a fan, leaving the running of the club entirely to his president. But William Wrigley firmly believed that Rogers Hornsby could win the Cubs the pennant, and over Veeck's objections he approved the deal. Angry, Veeck resigned as president. It was only after Wrigley promised that he would never interfere again that he was able get Veeck to come back.

There was another downside to taking on the aging fourteen-year veteran. In 1927 a man named Frank Moore sued Hornsby for $70,075. He charged that Hornsby had lost that amount betting on horses through him over a three-month period and would not pay up.

Commissioner Kenesaw Landis suggested to Hornsby that he take up checkers or Parcheesi, but Hornsby refused, telling him, "Racing is legal. I don't do anything illegal."

His love of gambling on the horses never did stop.

To William Wrigley's credit, he was more interested in winning a pennant than making money, unlike many owners. To Joe McCarthy's credit, his primary interest was winning a pennant, not protecting his rear, like so many managers. Hornsby had managed before, and he had gotten managers fired before, and McCarthy had to know he was taking on a player who might threaten his leadership—no matter how good a hitter he might be.

Hornsby may have had a personality disorder and a gambling addiction, but he could hit like no one else could, and so Joe McCarthy wanted him anyway.

Against William Veeck's advice, Wrigley ordered Veeck to make the deal. Veeck told C. F. Adams, "He said to give it [the money and the five players] to you."

ROGERS HORNSBY: "I hated to leave the Braves, and feel Fuchs hated to trade me, but in November I went to the Cubs. The Braves got the check from the Cubs, plus pitchers Percy Jones, Bruce Cunningham, Harry Seibold, catcher Doc Legett and infielder Fred Maguire."

Rogers Hornsby joined the Cubs for the 1929 season. He told William Veeck that he wanted a roommate who didn't talk in his sleep, didn't snore, didn't get up early and didn't come in late, didn't whistle while shaving, and didn't keep gin in his room. The Cubs had just the player: Woody English, who was to perform with Hornsby admirably as the team's double play combination.

WOODY ENGLISH: "Before the 1929 season, we traded for Rogers Hornsby. He could hit! We didn't know anything about Hornsby, except he was a heck of a hitter and a heck of a ballpayer. We were glad he came. Winning the pennant was on everybody's mind all the time. We were tickled to death he came over there.

"When Hornsby came over to the Cubs, he was very particular who he wanted as a roommate. And they picked me. They knew his traits and his characteristics, and they knew I wasn't a rowdy. And besides, the shortstop and second baseman many times were roommates.

"We had a Victrola in those days, and we had a favorite tune that we played in the morning when we were getting dressed. I don't know the singer, probably someone we never heard of, an old-timer. We both liked it, not 'Coming Around the Mountain,' but something on that order. Every morning we'd have that tune going, especially during spring training on Catalina Island.

"He'd tell me about horse racing, and he talked about Texas. He was from there. And we talked baseball all the time. The first infield practice we had with him, it was out on Catalina Island. The ball was hit to him at second base, and he threw it to me, and God, that ball whizzed right by my ear a couple times, and he said, 'Hey, that's the way I throw that ball. You better learn how to catch them.' I thought, 'God almighty,' but that was all I needed to know.

"We'd practice, and he'd say, 'Woody, when the ball is hit to you at shortstop, don't throw it right at second base, throw it about eight inches or maybe a foot toward the pitcher's mound, and when they slide in there, Hornsby won't be anywhere near them. I throw that ball underneath my arm to first base.'

"We practiced where I was to throw that ball to him. You know how they slide in and take the second baseman and shortstop out of there? He was maybe four feet behind the pitcher when he delivered that ball.

"Hornsby liked me. He taught me quite a bit about hitting. I didn't weigh but 150 pounds. I choked the bat. He said, 'Woody, you stand closer to the plate. Stand about even with it, and if anything, one foot a little bit in front of the other. Then you'll get that curve ball before it snaps off too fast.'

"He said, 'Push the ball past the pitcher. You can run good. Make the pitcher cover first base, and you'll beat him over there nine times out of ten.'

"Rogers knew what was going on all the time. He knew the pitchers, how they were going to pitch to him. He outsmarted a lot of pitchers.

"As a hitter Hornsby stood as far back in the right-hand corner of the batter's box as he could, and he stepped directly toward home plate. He stood right on the back line and strode right toward the front of that plate, and he'd hit the ball wherever it was pitched. If it was pitched outside, he hit it that way. If it was thrown down the middle, he hit it up the middle. If it was inside, he'd pull it. Outside, he'd go the other way.

"We were playing an exhibition in Albuquerque, New Mexico, coming back from Catalina, against some college team. The ballpark we played in, the fences seemed like they were five miles away, and they said there had never been a ball hit over the fence right or left. The first time up, Hornsby hit one over the right-field fence, and a couple times up later he hit one over the left-field fence. He had the power. He was a good-sized man.

"He could hit, and listen, he could run all right. He did everything but catch a pop fly. One would go up, and he'd say, 'Come on, Wood.'

"I'll tell you one thing about Hornsby. He had a lot of guts. I remember there used to be a catcher with the St. Louis Browns, Rick Ferrell. We were playing an exhibition game in Texas, and Ferrell stepped on Charlie Grimm's foot at first base, did it on purpose. There was a lot of that stuff going on. The Browns had a catcher by the name of Pancho Snyder coaching at first base, and Hornsby was in our dugout on the first-base side, and he said, 'Hey, Snyder, let's cut out all this damn crap and you and I go out under the stands and see who's going to win this battle between the Cubs and the Browns.' Snyder didn't pay any attention to him. He didn't want to hear him.

"I never remember him ever reading anything, and I don't believe he ever went to a movie. Funny thing, the one thing he would read was the racing form. That racing really got him in trouble.

"I was single, and he used to come over to my hotel room. We lived three or four blocks from the ballpark. He would come over to my room in the morning and he'd call someone in St. Louis. I'd hear him say, 'What do you think about this horse?' or 'that horse?' And the guy would tell him. So he made a few bets here and there.

"One time we were walking to the ballpark from this hotel where I lived, and he had talked to this fella in St. Louis, got a tip on a horse, and so on the way to the park we went to the back of the Florsheim shoe store. Two Jewish boys ran the store and they booked horses in it, and we went in there. This was a block from the hotel where I stayed in. So Hornsby bet $500 on a horse. Sonny Stern was the name of the bookie.

"We're at the ballpark during the game, I was waiting for the throw to come down from the catcher, and Hornsby said, 'Woody, that horse won.' I said, 'How do you know?' He said, 'I got a way of knowing.' He said, 'I'll walk over with you after the game and get my money.' So we did, and Sonny Stern said, 'I couldn't lay your bet off, Rog. Nobody would take that big a bet to win.' Hornsby said, 'You took the bet, you should pay it off.' He said, 'No, I didn't get it laid off.' So Hornsby said, 'The first person who comes in here, whoever it is, if he says you should pay the bet off, will you pay it?' Sonny said, 'No, I can't pay it.' And he didn't.

"In 1929 we had a very powerful lineup. We had Hornsby, Gabby Hartnett, Hack Wilson, Riggs Stephenson, Kiki Cuyler. Kidding, we'd say, 'Let's get our eight runs early and then take it easy.' That's what we used to say.

"As long as I was with the Cubs, I don't think I got the steal sign ever. I could run good. I had 17 triples one year [1930]. Anytime you get 17 triples, you can move. But Joe McCarthy used to say to me, 'Don't try to steal a base. You got Cuyler and Wilson and Hornsby and Hartnett and Grimm behind you. They'll hit a fence, and you'll score easy from first base.' So I never got the darn steal sign.

"Oh, we had a great club, no question about that.

"By '29 we thought we were going to win, and of course, the Cubs hadn't been in the World Series for some time, and everyone was all hepped up.

"We sure had the power, didn't we?"

33

When Eight Runs Weren't Enough

The year 1929 should have been the greatest in the history of the Chicago Cubs. The Cubs were a rip-roaring success in every way. William Wrigley's gutsy $400,000 investment in talented players, Rogers Hornsby, Kiki Cuyler, Riggs Stephenson, and Woody English, paid off handsomely when the exciting, swaggering Chicago Cubs won the pennant in a walkaway.

This was a team with awesome right-handed power. First baseman Charlie Grimm was the one starting Cub to hit from the left side. From the right, Hornsby hit .380, with 39 home runs and 149 RBIs. Hack Wilson hit .345, with 39 homers and 159 RBIs, to lead the league; Riggs Stephenson hit .362, with 17 homers and 110 RBIs; and Kiki Cuyler hit .360, smote 15 home runs and drove in 102 runs. The hitting would have been even stronger had Gabby Hartnett not injured his arm skeet shooting.

On the mound Hack Wilson's running mate, Pat Malone, won 22 games. Charlie Root won 19, Guy Bush 18, Sheriff Blake 14, and Hal Carlson 11. In the field Hornsby led all second basemen with 547 assists and 106 double plays.

Joe McCarthy's team compiled a record of 98–54, winning the pennant by ten and a half games over Pittsburgh, as John McGraw's Giants finished a distant third.

Equally pleasing to William Wrigley, in 1929 the Cubs broke the major league attendance record, drawing 1,485,166 fans in a bandbox originally built during the days of the Federal League. And this record did not include the thousands of women who got in free. The previous record had been held by the 1927 Yankees. The Cubs would top the million mark five years in a row, from 1927 through 1931.

Wrigley had spent millions to make his chewing gum a national byword, and he believed the same sort of promotion could be used in baseball. He and William Veeck brought baseball into the homes with radio, made it attractive to women and children. As a result of his attention to cleanliness and hygiene at Wrigley Field, his Ladies Day crowds were huge. Wrigley was as proud of his success at attendance building as he was of the quality of his team.

WILLIAM WRIGLEY: "Not only are the admissions to Wrigley Field 1,000,000 more than they were when I bought the team, but that attendance has come to include all classes of people.

"When I entered upon my experience as a ball-club owner, back in 1916, the typical ball crowd was generally considered rather rough stuff. There was plenty of drinking, and the umpire who gave a decision which was resented by the home-town fans was in luck if he didn't receive a shower of pop bottles. The socially elect of our city did not then crowd the ticket lines. A ladies' day at that time would have been a joke—a target for the gibes of the sports writers and columnists.

"When, in 1919, I bought control of the Chicago Cubs, my ambition was not only to build up a winning team that would command the pride of Chicago fans but to make the game alluring to the large sections of the public not then baseball-minded.

"I held that no normal human being could remain indifferent to the allurements of baseball after being fully exposed to them. The problem was to induce the vast public then indifferent and uninterested to get acquainted with the game as played by stars.

"Improving the physical facilities for the enjoyment of the games seemed an obvious and simple means of accomplishing this purpose. The behavior of men is very sensitively influenced by their surroundings. Put a man accustomed to rough surroundings into a place which is not only clean but attractive, and instinctively he will at once improve his behavior to fit his environment. Again, persons used to refined surroundings will not voluntarily go to places for entertainment which offend their sense of cleanliness, comfort and decency.

"Therefore I spent $2,300,000 to make Wrigley Field clean, convenient, comfortable and attractive to the eye—a place in which any woman accustomed to refined surroundings would feel safe, comfortable and in a frame of mind to enjoy the game. The effect of these improved surroundings upon baseball patrons has been remarkable. Of course, other influences have had their effect also—among them, stricter discipline. But the improved atmosphere has been the strongest factor in transforming the boisterous crowd of the early days into an orderly and well-behaved assemblage. Undoubtedly the greatly increased attendance of women has played an important part in this improvement. But the statement calls for certain important amendments. It is easier to control a crowd of 100,000 men than of 10,000 women.

"In talking with William L. Veeck, president of the Chicago Cubs, about means of increasing the crop of baseball fans, the idea of giving a ladies' day at least once a week was developed. We then thought it a hot hunch—but we didn't know how hot until we saw it in action! Of course, the theory of handing out a lot of free admissions to ladies was that women are the best advertisers in the world for anything they like. Also they are instinctive bargain hunters.

"Admission to the major-league game at fifty cents to a dollar and a half is certainly a bargain in entertainment, and we relied upon the ladies to discover this fact and spread the good news to their women friends.

"There was another tactical advantage in selling baseball to the ladies. Thousands of men who would like to spend their Saturday or Sunday afternoons at a ball game stay away because their wives do not care for the game or think they don't because they haven't experienced its thrills. Doubling the attendance from families where husbands and wives wish to spend their holiday afternoons together was another consideration in starting ladies' day at Wrigley Field. It was simply an educational scheme to make the entire family baseball-minded.

"A bargain-day rush at a big State Street store is a tame event alongside a ladies' day at Wrigley Field. Telling the truth about the difficulties of controlling that crowd is difficult, for the truth sounds decidedly ungallant. There is no such thing as controlling these crowds of women besieging the admission booths. The ladies listen to a speech urging them to take their time and assuring them that each applicant will be accommodated; then they storm wickets, sweeping aside policemen and guards in a way to make men gasp and wonder how the phrase 'the gentler sex' ever originated. What they do to one another in the process of crashing the gate is astounding.

"If a big State Street store were to offer at fifty cents 5,000 pairs of the finest silk stockings made, the crush to get them would not, I think, exceed in intensity our ladies' day gate crash. One Friday, shortly after the gates were opened, and there were 45,000 spectators inside and thousands outside, an usher came upon a little old woman who was crying. He assured her that he would find her a seat somewhere.

"'I don't want a seat,' she sobbed. 'I want to get out. I came to visit my daughter, who lives near here. Before I knew it I was caught in this terrible mob and swept inside.' Women have actually brought oil stoves with them and camped in the early morning outside the gates in order to be sure to get seats. A coupon to a seat is a mere formality on ladies' day. Once a woman is in a seat, she's there to stay.

"However, the vigor of the battle is an eloquent testimonial to the intensity of woman's newly awakened passion for baseball. A Chicago newspaper recently printed these clever lines:

> *I saw a wounded baseball fan tottering down the street,*
> *Encased in bandages and tape, and bruised from head to feet;*
> *And as I called the ambulance, I heard the poor guy say:*
> *'I bought a seat in Wrigley Field, but it was ladies' day.'*

"This sudden and spectacular burst of feminine interest in baseball—sensational in both volume and intensity—swept us off our feet."

It had been eleven long years since the Chicago Cubs had won a pennant, and the prosperity that marked the 1920s continued to hold in October 1929. Everyone, it seemed, had money, and the Cubs' offices were flooded with demands for World Series tickets. They could have sold 200,000 of them. Clerks had to return half a million dollars to disappointed ticket seekers.

The team the Cubs had to face in the World Series was the Philadelphia A's, owned and managed by Connie Mack, now sixty-seven years old. It was Mack's seventh league championship, the first since 1914. Mack's A's had defeated Frank Chance and the 1910 Cubs.

The A's were led by four future Hall of Famers, first baseman Jimmie Foxx, out-fielder Al Simmons, catcher Mickey Cochrane, and manager Mack. Two more powerful teams never faced one another.

Mack knew that for the A's to win the World Series, he would have to be creative. He had two star pitchers, Lefty Grove and Rube Walberg, and both were left-handed. During the 1929 season only one left-hander, the Cardinals' Clarence Mitchell, a spitballer, had beaten the Cubs more than once. Mack knew that the Cubs were death against lefties. He decided to use his left-handed stars in relief.

Mack's right-handed pitchers included second-year man George Earnshaw (24–8, 3.28), John Picus Quinn (11–9, 3.97), nearing the end of a twenty-three-year career that had started in 1909, and thirty-five-year-old Howard Ehmke, a sidearm junk baller who couldn't break a pane of glass with his fastball.

In late August, Mack had called Ehmke into his office for the purpose of telling him he was through. Mack's intention was to give the fourteen-year veteran his un-conditional release.

CONNIE MACK: "He looked at me. 'Mr. Mack,' he said, 'I have always wanted to pitch in a World Series.' He lifted his arm. 'Mr. Mack,' he said, 'there is one great game left in this old arm.' That was what I wanted to hear. 'All right, Howard,' I told him. 'When we go west I want you to stay here. When the Cubs come in to play the Phillies, you watch them. Learn all you can about their hitters. Say nothing to any-body. You are my opening pitcher for the World Series."

As owner-manager, Connie Mack had the luxury of not having to face an owner who second-guessed him.

In the Cubs dugout Joe McCarthy knew well who was on the A's roster. Before the season was even over McCarthy knew the identity of Mack's opening day pitcher: Ehmke.

RED SMITH: "Ring Lardner was writing fiction and plays by 1929, but he had many friends in baseball after his years as a sportswriter. Joe McCarthy, the Cubs manager, was one.

"'I was chatting with Joe a little before the season ended,' Lardner said. 'I'm not afraid of Grove and Earnshaw,' he told me. 'We can hit speed. But they've got one guy over there I am afraid of. He's what I call a junk pitcher'—but Joe used an indelicate expression. 'His name,' he told me, 'is Howard Ehmke, and he's the sucker we're going to see in this Series.'"

The Cubs were not impressed when Mack announced that Ehmke would start the opener in Chicago.

WOODY ENGLISH: "We should have won the first game, hands down. Who would think a pitcher like him . . . ? Ehmke had scouted us for about a month, when he wasn't pitching, followed the Cubs around picking up our weaknesses. Ehmke had been a great pitcher, but he was supposed to have a bad arm, you know."

Ehmke's soft stuff kept the Cubs off balance. He allowed just one unearned run in Game 1, striking out Cuyler, Stephenson, Hornsby, Wilson, Hornsby again, then Wilson again, and Hartnett, until he had struck out 13, a World Series record. Even after Ehmke beat Charlie Root in the opener, the Cubs weren't much impressed.

ROGERS HORNSBY: "None of us figured on batting against Ehmke, who had a three-quarter side-arm delivery. Ehmke struck out 13 Cubs. He beat our best pitcher, Charlie Root, 3–1. It made Mr. Mack look like a smart gambler—he won.

"But Ehmke got the breaks and I'm not taking anything away from him when I say that. He could have been a bum just as easily. In the first inning we got a man on base when I came up. I hit a fair ball straight for the right-field bleachers, which certainly meant Ehmke was finished in this game.

"But the wind was blowing in off Lake Michigan, and the ball landed foul. Then I struck out and we didn't score. The next time we faced Ehmke we knocked him out in the fourth inning."

George Earnshaw started the second game for the A's, and when he gave up three runs in the fifth inning to trim the A's lead to 6–3, Mack brought in Lefty Grove, who shut out the Cubs the rest of the way. Pat Malone gave up a three-run homer to Foxx, and Hal Carlson allowed a two-run shot by Simmons in the loss.

After a travel day Mack made another unconventional move, starting Earnshaw a second game in a row. The move didn't pan out. Guy Bush beat the A's 3–1. The Cubs won when outfielder Hack Wilson made a fine running catch at the wall to rob Al Simmons of extra bases in the seventh. Wilson's heroics would be forgotten after the ignominy brought on by balls he would fail to catch the following day.

Game 4 was played in Philadelphia. Down two to one in games, the Cubs scored two runs in the fourth against John Quinn and added five more in the fifth with a barrage of hitting that was awesome to see. An eighth run in the seventh made the score Cubs 8, A's 0.

The A's came to bat in the seventh.

CONNIE MACK: "It was my intention at that stage of the game to send in substitutes for all the regulars at the start of the eighth inning. But when we came to bat in the seventh some odd things began happening. Al Simmons, the first man up for us, hit a home run which landed on the roof of the left-field stands, fair by just inches. If it had been foul—well, that doesn't matter now."

After Simmons homered, Jimmie Foxx singled. So did Bing Miller when Hack Wilson lost the ball in the sun. Then Jimmy Dykes singled, scoring Foxx. Joe Boley singled, and Miller scored. George Burns pinch-hit and popped out. Gabby Hartnett had missed most of the 1929 season with a bad arm. He was on the bench as the fatal seventh inning continued.

GABBY HARTNETT: "I was sitting beside Joe McCarthy, on the bench. Up to then, he wasn't worried much. We still had a big lead. But when Max Bishop got a hit and scored Dykes, making it 8 to 4, McCarthy chased Art Nehf out to pitch. Mule Haas was the hitter."

WARREN BROWN: "While Art Nehf was taking his warm-up pitches [in the seventh inning], one of the returns from catcher Zack Taylor was a trifle high. Art looked up, and as the blazing sun got in his eyes, he ducked hastily and the ball went on past him to be retrieved by one of the infielders.

"No one paid much attention to that—then. What if the sun is in a direct line from pitcher to catcher?"

GABBY HARTNETT: "[Haas] banged a kind of a line drive right out at Hack Wilson, in center. Hack never did see that ball in the sun. When he finally got it back, three more runs were in. Mickey Cochrane walked, and McCarthy sent Sheriff Blake in to pitch to Simmons, up for the second time. Simmons hit one. Then Foxx hit one and Cochrane scored the tying run.

"I was plenty excited, but I can still hear McCarthy asking no one in particular, 'What can I do?' But I didn't know, either. Pat Malone went in to pitch. He soaked Miller with a pitch, and the first thing we knew, Dykes unloaded a double, two runs scored, and it didn't matter much that Malone did fan the last two men. I never want to see anything like that again."

Wilson's teammates did not blame their center fielder. The Cubs chose others to shoulder the blame. Rogers Hornsby cited third baseman Norm McMillan. Woody English cited Riggs Stephenson.

ROGERS HORNSBY: "Two A's got on base, then Mule Haas hit a long drive to right center field, which is one of the worst places in the world to catch a ball. It's a bad sun spot. Hack Wilson, our center fielder, started in on the ball, then jumped back and saw the ball fall and roll for an inside-the-park home run that scored three runs. The Athletics went on to score 10 runs in that inning which was a record, and beat us 10–8. I've heard many stories about Hack's forgetting his sunglasses and losing the ball in the sun.

"But I don't think that's the truth. Wilson wasn't my favorite player. I didn't approve of the way he drank and broke training, but I still claim that too much blame was placed on him for that incident. People forget, I guess, that he led both teams in hitting in the Series with a .471 average.

"In my opinion Norm McMillan let two balls that he should have caught get through him for hits at third base. And if he had made those two plays the side would have been retired and there wouldn't have been any ball hit to Wilson."

WOODY ENGLISH: "On a ball hit to left field, Riggs Stephenson came in to play it off the fence instead of trying to catch it; he misjudged it and it hit in front of the fence. He kind of turned the wrong way. He could have caught it. It bounced in, and that resulted in some runs. And McCarthy changed pitchers pretty fast, kept bringing in new pitchers, and they kept hitting. I don't know, a base on balls here, a hit there. There were no errors. All hits and walks."

The bottom line was that whoever was responsible, instead of the Series being tied at two games apiece, the Cubs now trailed three games to one. After an off day because the Pennsylvania laws prevented baseball on Sunday, the Series resumed in Philadelphia with Pat Malone facing Howard Ehmke.

The Cubs knocked out Ehmke, a mystery no longer, in the fourth inning and were leading 2–0 in the ninth.

ROGERS HORNSBY: "Pat Malone, our pitcher, got pinch hitter Walter French out. Then Max Bishop singled. Haas hit a home run nobody could question—over the fence—and that tied up the ball game. Then after Mickey Cochrane made the second out, Simmons doubled. Jimmie Foxx was intentionally walked to get to Bing Miller. Miller hit a double to win the game—and the World Series—for the A's."

The best offensive team in Cubs history had lost, four games to just one.

WOODY ENGLISH: "It was the last game that hurt the worst, when Mule Haas hit the home run and Bing Miller doubled in a run. That was a tough game. The other [the fourth-game loss] was tough, with that big a lead, but it seemed like this one hit us harder.

"After we lost the final game it was pretty quiet in the clubhouse. We didn't have too much to say. Everyone was down, real bad."

Hack Wilson entered the clubhouse angry and silent. Joe McCarthy told sportswriters that it wasn't Wilson's fault.

"The poor kid simply lost the ball in the sun, and he didn't put the sun there."

McCarthy tried to console Wilson, but Wilson pushed him aside. Wrote one reporter, "There was fire in his eyes and who knows what was in his heart that minute . . . He seemed dazed as he stepped outside."

There the distraught outfielder met his four-year-old son. "Hello, Daddy." Wrote Sam Murphy in the *New York Sun*, "Hack picked up the child, kissed him, hugged him. His sturdy frame shook with emotion. He wept."

According to the Associated Press, when the Cubs' train returned to Chicago, "the big fellow forced his way out of a crowd of admirers with tears streaming down his face. 'Let me alone now, fellows,' he said as he choked and sobbed. 'I haven't anything to say except that I am heartbroken and that we did get some awful breaks.'"

Hack Wilson had hit .471 to lead both teams. He made several great catches in the field. But that fateful inning, when he lost two balls in the sun, is remembered more than all of his feats.

After the Series, said Warren Brown, "Everybody in Chicago was mad—and kept getting madder. Everybody had something to say—and said it."

The defeat in the 1929 World Series would lead to a rash decision by William Veeck, who blamed Joe McCarthy for the debacle. Veeck's decision would prove disastrous to the Cubs.

For the country, too, things soon would get much worse. Five days after the 1929 World Series ended, the stock market collapsed and the debilitating Great Depression began.

34

One Firing Too Many

The year 1930 started out wonderfully. The Cubs juggernaut continued unabated, with Hack Wilson, the media's goat of the '29 Series, driving in runs—and drawing fans—at an unprecedented rate. Friday, June 6, 1930, was Ladies Day, a promotion begun elsewhere at the turn of the century but perfected in Chicago. That day the Cubs set their all-time one-game attendance record at Wrigley Field when a mob of 51,556 fans, including 30,476 women guests of the Cubs, swept into the ballpark.

To get free tickets, the women had only to show up at the park and request a seat from the ticket seller. So many came in 1930 that the next year the Cubs changed the rules, limiting the available tickets to the upper deck and making the women write in for them.

Among Chicago's citizenry who came to Wrigley Field during this area of Prohibition was Al Capone, the head of the rackets. Capone had served a year in prison for carrying a gun without a permit, and soon after he got out he went to Wrigley Field.

WOODY ENGLISH: "Remember Al Capone? One day he came to see us play. He had a bodyguard on each side of him when he took his seat, and three more sitting behind him. We were taking infield practice, then batting practice, when the *Chicago Tribune* photographer came over, and he said to Gabby Hartnett, 'Would you mind having your picture taken with Capone?' Hartnett, you know that Irish face, he said, 'Sure.' So he went over, shook hands with Capone, and they snapped his picture, and the next morning it was in the *Tribune*, and the following day in every major league clubhouse a bulletin from Kenesaw M. Landis, 'No more fraternizing in all ballparks. The umpires will be seated in the stands to watch all your movements. If any fraternizing occurs, a stiff penalty will be assessed to you.' His shaking hands with Capone didn't go over with Landis at all."

When Landis scolded Hartnett for shaking hands with Capone, the Cubs catcher told the commissioner, "I go to his place of business. Why shouldn't he come to mine?"

What Capone and John Dillinger (who used to come to Wrigley Field and sit in the right-field bleachers dressed as a mailman) and thousands of other Chicagoans came to see was a team that could score runs by the bunches. The team hit .309 for the 1930 season and struck 171 home runs, nineteen more than the Babe Ruth–led New York Yankees.

Gabby Hartnett, back from his arm miseries, hit 37 homers and drove in 122 runs. Kiki Cuyler hit 13 homers and drove in 134 runs. But the Cubs star that year was the oft-ridiculed short hunk of muscle, Hack Wilson. The opposing bench jockeys called Wilson "Bastard." Because he was dark-skinned, it was reported they also called him racial names, including Caliban, after Shakespeare's savage and deformed slave. (That they could make references to Shakespeare was remarkable in itself.)

The sportswriters sometimes called Wilson the Boy with the Mountainous Chin. He was also called the Hardest Hitting Hydrant of All Time.

During spring training, 1930, Wilson would refer to the balls he missed in the Series, making jokes at his own expense. In the hotel dining room, Wilson pulled the window shade and asked the maître d' to dim the light so he wouldn't misjudge his soup.

Wilson might have looked like a fire hydrant with legs, but with a bat in his hands he terrorized National League pitching, hitting 56 home runs and driving in the most runs ever driven in by any player in a season in major league history: 190.

SPARKY ADAMS (A CARDINALS INFIELDER IN 1930): "Hack could hit a ball with his eyes shut, and he could hit it a long way. I have a mark on my shins yet. We played in to catch the man going home and he hit a line drive right at me. The grass was wet and it skidded and hit right on my shin. I didn't say nothin'. I picked the ball up and threw the guy out going home. But hurt? Oh boy!"

Wilson one time called his shot, as Babe Ruth was said to have done (but didn't really) a few years later.

Lloyd Waner of the Pirates lined a ball to center field. When Wilson fell down, the ball rolled to the wall for an inside-the-park homer. Back on the bench Wilson apologized to pitcher Sheriff Blake, who like him came from West Virginia.

Hack said, "Sheriff, it seems like things always happen to you that never have happened before. That belly-buster couldn't have occurred behind any other pitcher. But for your sake and for the pride of West Virginia, I'm going to get that home run back with a legitimate homer. And in this very inning."

Wilson, who had driven in two runs with a single and a third with a sacrifice fly, got up to the plate and homered to give Blake and the Cubs a 7–5 victory.

* * *

CHARLIE GRIMM: "He made the money for us, and never mind the two fly balls he lost in the sun in the 1929 World Series. He was vicious with the bat. The word would go along in the dugout when we needed runs. 'Let somebody get on base and give Hack another at bat.'"

His manager Joe McCarthy, who was slow to wax eloquent about his players, loved everything about Hack, including his toughness and his ability to both punch and hit.

On July 4, 1929, the Cubs were playing the Reds. Wilson charged into their dugout, and it took several men to restrain him. That night the Cubs and Reds were aboard the same train, and on the platform Wilson punched Reds pitcher Pete Donohue and knocked him to the ground. Wilson was suspended briefly.

Later that season he charged into the stands to silence an abusive fan, a milkman, who sued for $20,000 but lost.

McCarthy talked about Wilson's feistiness.

JOE McCARTHY: "Hack was small, but he was powerful. Wasn't afraid of anybody. There was a guy on the Cincinnati club that liked to ride him. One day in Chicago Hack couldn't stand it any longer and charged right into the Cincinnati dugout and began to maul him. Hack was a tough kid—don't worry about that— and he knew how to punch. He did a job on this fellow before they broke it up.

"That's the way it was with Hack. Good-natured as could be, but things seemed to happen to him. I guess people picked on him because he was small. They never did it twice, I can tell you.

"I never saw a guy win games the way he did that year. We never lost a game all year if he came up in the late innings with a chance to get a hit that would win it for us. . . . No tougher player lived than Hack Wilson."

Hack was afraid of no pitcher. In fact, his teammates hated it when Hack would rag an opposing pitcher before the game.

GABBY HARTNETT: "We had a little fellow named Clyde Beck on our club, years ago [from 1926 to 1930], when [Dazzy] Vance was tops. When Brooklyn was in town, Beck would come out on the field cautiously and peek around. If he saw Vance taking batting practice, which meant it was his turn to pitch, Beck would pick up his own bat and put it under the bench.

"Hack Wilson would come storming out on the field and start yelling at Vance, telling him what we were going to do to that 'broken-arm' delivery of his. I don't think Hack ever got a good foul off Vance, but that didn't stop him from trying, or yelling.

"Beck would walk over to Hack and ask him to please be quiet. I can still hear him saying: 'Please, Hack, I got to play today too.'"

Part of the Hack Wilson mystique was that like other Chicago Cubs heroes of the past, such as Mike Kelly and Grover Cleveland Alexander, Hack loved to drink. Though whiskey was illegal in 1930, Hack had great connections with bootleggers.

One year Wilson got arrested at a drinking party and another time at a speakeasy. When police entered the speakeasy, the wide-bodied Wilson tried climbing out the window headfirst and got stuck.

McCarthy, himself a drinker, didn't care a whit about Hack's drinking. When asked about it, McCarthy replied, "What am I supposed to do? Tell him to live a clean life and he'll hit better?"

Bill Veeck, the son of Cubs president William Veeck, was a young teenager when Hack was a Cub. Fabulous Bill, who later was known as something of a drinker himself, remembered the fun times he had with the Cubs star.

BILL VEECK: "Hack, one of the idols of my youth, was an oddly built, stocky little barrel of a man, with clothes hangers in his shoulders and watermelon in his gut. Below the waist he was so small that when I was twelve years old his shoes were too small for me. Hack was a warm and cheerful and full-blooded human being, well flavored by the malt and well seasoned by life. The fans in Chicago loved him whether he was hitting his home runs or misjudging fly balls. He had what is always defined as that indefinable something, that personal glow that warmed people to him from a distance of 500 feet—me included—and made him the most important person on the ball field.

"For years I found it impossible to look at any round outfielder who could hit a long ball without deciding that I had found myself another Hack Wilson. It took a long time before I got it through my thick head that you can no more manufacture colorful players like Hack Wilson than you can manufacture a colorful fan. They have to be authentic. There is nothing quite so phony as a phony phony.

"[One day] our trainer, Andy Lotshaw, had Hack in one of those big, high old tubs, sobering him up. In the tub with Hack was a 50-pound cake of ice. Well, what would you do if a 50-pound cake of ice jumped into your bathtub with you? You'd try to jump out, right? That was precisely what Hack was trying to do. Enthusiastically but not successfully. Every time Hack's head would bob up, Andy would shove it back down under the water and the cake of ice would come bobbing up. It was a fascinating sight, watching them bob in perfect rhythm, first Hack's head, then the ice, then Hack's head, then the ice.

"The date would be easy enough for any scholar to find. That afternoon Hack hit three home runs for the first and only time in his life. It was the same year that he hit fifty-six home runs, a National League record that still stands.

"Hack's only trouble was that he was overgenerous. He gave everything away he had. Always. His money, the shirt off his back—little things like that. Chicago was a toddling town in those days. Hack's drinking buddies, a rollicking crew of about two dozen Chicagoans, would wait for him after the game and they'd toddle over to the joints on the North Side and the West Side. Hack picked up every check. When he longed for the companionship of his teammates there were always a dozen or so heading out on the town. The players' favorite joint was the Hole in the Wall over in Cicero, a speakeasy which could easily be defined as the fallout shelter of the Prohibition era; it was the gangster hangout and that made it the safest place in town. At the core of the rollickers, in addition to Hack, was Pat Malone—a name to inspire any old Cub fan to hoist a mug of beer himself. Pat Malone was another of the perennial minor-leaguers. My father bought him cheap and he pitched us to a pennant. And, ah yes, there was—as I remember—a nonplaying member of this roistering crew of blessed memory, young Bill Veeck. By the time I was fifteen, I was getting around pretty good."

At the end of the 1930 season Hack Wilson was having a career year superior even to baseball's most famous slugger in its history, Babe Ruth. Here's how their numbers compared.

1930	BA	H	R	HR	RBI
Hack Wilson	.356	208	146	56	190
Babe Ruth	.359	186	150	49	153

After the 1930 season the Baseball Writers Association of America voted Wilson the Most Valuable Player of the National League ahead of Bill Terry (who hit .401) and Frankie Frisch (who led St. Louis to the pennant). Below is one of the tributes penned to Wilson. This one appeared in the *Sporting News*.

PITCHING to HACK

"How do you pitch to Wilson?"
      Asked the rookie up from the sticks.
"I'm up to learn the hitters,
      And know their little tricks."

"I'll tell ya," said the veteran,
      Who had pitched for many years,
"When ya dish up Hack yer fast one
      You'd better watch your ears.

"He'll drive that agate at ya'
      Like ya' never seen before.
He'll learn ya' in a jiffy
      Not to show him speed no more.

" 'N' then y'll try t'curve him,
      'N' he'll crash one off yer shins;
If ya' keep on throwin' hookers
      He'll tear off both yer pins.

" 'N' then ya' use yer change of pace,
      He might strike out on that;
'N' perhaps he'll ride the ball so far
      You don't know where it's at.

"I'll tell ya' son," the veteran said.
      "When ya' see that sawed-off squirt;
Jes' flip one towards th' platter
      'N' take care ya' don't get hurt."

At the end of the season Hack returned to his hometown of Martinsburg, West Virginia. An idolizing crowd, led by the mayor, met him at the railroad station with a brass band. The townsfolk gave him a big silver cup and a Buick.

Hack Wilson didn't know it at the time but events were conspiring to end his dominance. The first of these resulted from the failure of the Cubs to catch the St. Louis Cardinals at the end of the 1930 season. The pennant had come down to the wire, but Gabby Street's feisty Cards took the lead in mid-September, and when it became obvious that the Cubs couldn't catch them, owner William Wrigley and president William Veeck made one of the more detrimental decisions in the history of the franchise when they decided not to rehire manager Joe McCarthy for the 1931 season and to replace him with Rogers Hornsby, a great hitter but a man whose personality made him unfit to manage.

If William Wrigley had one negative trait as an owner, it was his penchant for churning managers. After Fred Mitchell, there was Evers, Killefer, Maranville, Gibson and then McCarthy. Wrigley's philosophy was to keep changing managers the way Lincoln had kept relieving generals until he found the one who could do the job—General Grant. But Wrigley had a General Grant in Joe McCarthy. [Like Grant, McCarthy drank. Hornsby didn't.] When he decided that Hornsby could do a better job than the man he had, Wrigley traded his Grant in for a Meade. It was as bad a judgment about baseball talent as William Wrigley would ever make.

When McCarthy heard the rumors and learned of Wrigley and Veeck's intentions, he quit as Cubs manager on September 30, 1930, with four games left in the season.

If either Wrigley or Veeck had felt strongly about keeping him, perhaps McCarthy would not have been let go, but each had his reason for not rehiring the sullen, autocratic McCarthy.

McCarthy and William Wrigley had crossed swords over a California outfielder named Lefty O'Doul. Wrigley had bought O'Doul from Salt Lake City for $15,000, but when O'Doul reported for spring training in 1926, McCarthy refused to consider him for the team and shipped him off to Hollywood in the Pacific Coast League.

In 1929, O'Doul, playing for the Philadelphia Phillies, led the National League in hitting with a .398 average. The next year he hit .383, twice hitting home runs at the end of the season to deny the Cubs the pennant, then (for Brooklyn) hit .336 and .368.

During Cubs-Phillies games, after a hit by the slugger, Wrigley reportedly would mutter, "Oh, that O'Doul . . . my O'Doul."

After the devastating loss in the 1929 World Series, Wrigley had another reason to fume. He was not alone, as William Veeck ("I want a man who can bring me a world championship") and a large segment of Cubs fans also felt the same way.

According to reporter Warren Brown, on the way to the training camp at Catalina in the spring of 1930, McCarthy confided in Brown that "he would not be with the Cubs after the current season, win, lose or draw."

Brown said he then told a friend of Colonel Jacob Ruppert, the owner of the New York Yankees, that McCarthy was available. Brown, who admired the Cubs manager, even traveled to the Ruppert Brewery and told the colonel himself. When Ruppert said he was interested, he went back and told McCarthy.

In late September, when word leaked that the manager was going to be replaced by Hornsby, McCarthy resigned from the Cubs. Wrigley and Veeck didn't try to stop him from leaving.

Said Wrigley, "I have always wanted a World Championship team, and I am not sure that Joe McCarthy is the man to give me that kind of a team."

Woody English, whose career flourished under McCarthy, felt the loss. So, he says, did the other players.

WOODY ENGLISH: "After the 1929 Series, it seemed that Mr. Wrigley blamed losing the Series on McCarthy. No facts came out to prove that, except that he got fired. I never heard a discussion about why Mr. Wrigley fired him, but I imagine it didn't take much to figure it out, losing two games in a row like we did in that World Series. Anyway, McCarthy was a great manager. I liked him. Like I told you, we respected the man. And when they fired him, there was a feeling like losing an old friend. We hated to see him leave, but like they say, that's the game."

The Cubs never did win another world championship, but Marse Joe McCarthy continued to prove his managerial greatness, winning eight pennants and seven world championships in sixteen seasons as manager of the New York Yankees.

Cubs Hall of Fame catcher Gabby Hartnett some years later described Joe McCarthy as the greatest manager he ever played for.

GABBY HARTNETT: "I think McCarthy knew more baseball than any other manager I ever saw in action or worked for. But that was only part of it. He knew how to handle men. He had understanding, and he was a great disciplinarian, while never losing his standing with all of us as a great guy. If there is a system to baseball, as there is to football, I'd say McCarthy's is best. At all events, I think his record comes close to proving it, doesn't it?"

35

The Death of William Wrigley

The Cubs didn't do as well in 1931 under new manager Rogers Hornsby as they had for Joe McCarthy the year before. The team finished third, seventeen games behind the speedy Gas House Gang of St. Louis. Keeping the Cubs from falling farther was the batting of Hornsby, who hit .331 with 16 homers and 90 RBIs. What wasn't evident in the standings was the enmity the players felt for their manager. They saw him as a cold-hearted loner, a great hitter perhaps but one who had nothing else to offer.

BILLY HERMAN: "I broke in with the Cubs under Hornsby in 1931. He ignored me completely, and I figured it was because I was a rookie. But then I saw he ignored everybody. He was a very cold man. He would stare at you with the coldest eyes I ever saw. If you did something wrong, he'd jump all over you. He was a perfectionist and had a very low tolerance for mistakes. He was one of the greatest hitters that ever lived—maybe the greatest—but he never talked hitting with us. He just expected you to go up there and do it. The best way to learn was from other players, sometimes on another team. You'd watch them, ask them questions. There was very little instruction given.

"Hornsby tried to have discipline on the club, but he had some bad actors and couldn't control them—fellows like Pat Malone and Hack Wilson. They'd get drunk and get into fights, and sometimes end up tossed in jail someplace. He'd fine them, but it didn't make any difference.

"Hornsby didn't smoke, didn't drink. And he wouldn't go to the movies or even read a newspaper because he said it was bad for the eyes. He wouldn't let you eat in the clubhouse, not even between games of a doubleheader. Couldn't even have a soft drink. He was the boss and there was nothing we could do about it.

"I'll tell you a funny thing about Hornsby though. He was against smoking and drinking, but he was a great gambler so you couldn't say that in being against smoking and drinking, Hornsby was being moralistic. It was a case of a manager imposing his own prejudices on the players, and I think a lot of managers are like that. Hell, I guess a lot of people are like that, period."

Hornsby, like most managers, had his favorites. Shortstop Woody English was one of them.

WOODY ENGLISH: "You know, I liked the guy, because see, he was so good to me, I couldn't help but like him, but a lot of players didn't like Rogers. He was a perfectionist. He expected everybody to be as good as he was. Like with Hartnett and Wilson. They'd go up and strike out with the bases full, and Hornsby would say, 'God, I don't believe he was even trying.' I'd go up and strike out with the bases full, and he'd say, 'You had a hell of a cut, Woody.' You know it was little things like that. [Pitcher] Lon Warneke didn't like him. Hartnett didn't like him. Neither did Hack Wilson.

"Hornsby was a loner. He didn't mix too good. He'd come in the clubhouse when he was manager, and he'd have a meeting. He had one belief: He would say, 'A major league pitcher, if he's a good one, can throw four out of five balls within six inches of where he wants to throw them.'

"Ned Garver [who pitched for Hornsby with the St. Louis Browns in 1952] was here in Newark [Ohio] playing golf. I went out to see him. I said, 'Ned, I want to ask you a question. How did you like Rogers Hornsby?' He said, 'He treated me fine, Woody, but he had to. I won about half his ball games.' I said, 'He was always good to me.' Ned said, 'How many guys on your ball club liked him?' I said, 'Maybe five.'

"One time we were playing in New York, I'll never forget this. It was all quiet, and somebody set a firecracker off in the stands—sounded like a gun—and Hornsby, geez, I could see him jerk up.

"I thought, 'My God, did somebody shoot Hornsby?'"

The player who suffered the most under Hornsby's rigid leadership was Hack Wilson. Once again the Cubs had a situation in which a manager who believed in temperance decided to bring to heel a star player who enjoyed drinking and carousing. From time to time Hornsby would punish Wilson by benching him. Hornsby also badly hurt the slugger's confidence by his insistence on making him take pitches on 2–0 and 3–1 counts.

HACK WILSON: "It just seemed that every time that situation came along, the pitcher would give me one that I thought I could have socked, and I had to take it. And that didn't help my temper or my confidence any."

A third factor contributed to the steep decline in Hack Wilson's productivity. The owners, concerned that the ball had become too lively, apparently did something to the baseball. The stitches were raised, giving the pitchers a better grip. Also, the ball was deadened.

WOODY ENGLISH: "In 1931 the owners decided the ballplayers were hitting too many home runs. We realized something was different in '31 almost from the start of the season. You hit balls like you always hit them, and they'd plunk, sound like they didn't have anything inside, just sawdust or something.

"Hack that year was hitting fly ball outs. The balls that used to carry into the stands were just long fly balls. Unless you were a line drive hitter, you suffered quite a bit. I don't know whether the American League had the same ball that year or not. We knew that our ball was a lot deader. You could tell when the ball was hit to you on the ground. The balls that used to be hit real sharp, now they came down on two or three big bounces to you. And so the premium was now on pitching and defense."

Scoring in the National League dropped 21 percent from 1930 to 1931. Al Lopez, who was a catcher with the Brooklyn Dodgers in 1931, recalled firsthand how the mushier baseball affected Wilson's hitting.

AL LOPEZ: "It killed Hack Wilson. Just murdered Hack Wilson. In 1930 Wilson hit 56 homers and hit .356 and drove in 190 runs. In '31 he hit 13 homers, .261 percentage, and 61 RBI. Was that because of the ball? No question about it. Hack was more of a right-center-field hitter in the Cubs' ballpark. When they came in with a dead ball it was just an easy fly ball."

On September 5, 1931, Wilson and Pat Malone hit the town after a loss in Cincinnati. They then went to the train station for the trip home to Chicago. Two sportswriters were on the platform, and Malone got into a fight with them.

Though Wilson was only a spectator, the Cubs suspended him for the rest of the season. On December 10, 1931, he and pitcher Bud Teachout were traded to St. Louis for pitcher Burleigh Grimes.

St. Louis general manager Branch Rickey, a notoriously low paymaster, wanted Wilson to sign a $7,500 contract, a 77 percent pay cut. Hack held out, and after a month, Rickey traded him to the Dodgers for a minor league pitcher and $45,000. Wilson signed with the Dodgers for $16,500.

When Wilson signed to play with Brooklyn in the winter of 1931–32, Joe McCarthy, his manager with the Cubs, came down from his home in Tonawanda, New York, outside Buffalo, for the ceremony.

"I wish I was going to play for you, Joe," Wilson told him.

"Shhh," the manager said. "Not so loud. I wouldn't want [Brooklyn manager] Max [Carey] to hear you—or me, either—because I wish you were too."

After the 1931 season sportswriter J. Roy Stockton visited Wilson at his home in Martinsburg, West Virginia. Wilson talked about his drop in productivity.

HACK WILSON: "It must have been a combination of things. Probably the ball had something to do with it, but it couldn't make that much difference. Then, possibly, I was trying too hard to live up to my new contract and my 1930 record. Even in the spring exhibition games I found myself fussing and swearing because I couldn't get hold of the ball. It wouldn't carry for me and I was missing more swings than usual. Naturally, after my good year of 1930, the fans were expecting me to do something every time I went to bat and even the spring exhibition crowds razzed me pretty hard. That bothered me and I kept on getting the old razzberries all year.

". . . Some people said I was a batting flop because I was carousing around too much. That was all wrong. I went out occasionally, but not as much as I did the year before, when I was hitting all those home runs. You have to do something for recreation, but I was in condition to play every day. They told me at Chicago that I'd have to quit this and that, but I'm not signing any pledges."

In 1932, Wilson hit 23 homers and drove in 123 runs with Brooklyn. While there he became part of the lore of the Daffiness Boys when, in 1933, during a visit to the mound by manager Carey, Wilson stood in the outfield badly hung over and dozing. When manager Max Carey removed pitcher Walter Beck, the pitcher became angry that he was being taken out of the game, and he petulantly threw the ball into the outfield, where it banged against the right-field Baker Bowl wall behind the daydreaming Wilson.

GLENN WRIGHT (THE DODGERS SHORTSTOP): "When [Wilson] heard the ball rattle off the fence, he hopped on it and fired a strike to second base. Then seeing no one running he came charging in to see what was going on. When he learned what had happened he was ready to murder Beck. I had to keep them apart. From that time on it was Boom-Boom Beck."

Wilson's drinking became worse until in 1934—only at age thirty-four—he was no longer productive. Wrote *Baseball* magazine, "Many a wiser man than Hack Wilson has drowned his sorrows in the flowing bowl." The Dodgers released him, and his life quickly went downhill. In 1938 his loyal wife, Virginia, divorced him as his drinking consumed him. He remarried, wandered from job to job, and wound up in Baltimore, where he died a pauper in 1948. He was forty-eight years old. Babe Ruth had died three months earlier.

Ruth's funeral was held in Yankee Stadium in front of many thousands of adoring fans.

When Hack Wilson died, his body lay unclaimed for three days. Ford Frick, the president of the National League, paid the $350 for the funeral, which was held in Baltimore and attended by about fifty mourners.

At a memorial service in Martinsburg ten months later Joe McCarthy told a crowd of about a thousand, "And may God rest his soul."

Wilson was elected to the Hall of Fame in 1979, where he is best remembered for his 190 RBIs in 1930. But he is also remembered for the ball Boom-Boom Beck threw in his direction and for the balls he lost in the sun in the 1929 World Series, a sad symbol of the Cubs' early frustration.

The year 1932 began with the sudden death on January 26 of William Wrigley in Phoenix, Arizona. The head Cub was seventy-nine years old. In his obituary there was a reference to his dying without having achieved his "fondest hope"—seeing his Cubs win a world championship. Surviving him, said the obituary, was a son, Philip K., and a daughter, Mrs. James Odfield. What it didn't say—and no one could know—was that after William Wrigley left the team to his eccentric son, he would run it into the ground.

The team William Wrigley built held a nucleus of players strong enough to win three more pennants (in 1932, 1935, and 1938). After that, nothing—except for a fluke pennant in 1945 won by the Cubs because most of the great players of the opposition were in the service during World War II. No one, not the players, not the fans, could have fully understood at that time what the death of William Wrigley would mean to the glorious history of the powerful Chicago Cubs. If they had, the period of mourning for William Wrigley would have continued to this day.

36

Scandal—and Victory

The pennant year of 1932 was marked by scandal. The veteran second baseman–manager, Rogers Hornsby, was fired for his gambling addiction, and the second-year shortstop, Billy Jurges, was shot in his hotel room by a jilted lover out for revenge.

Hornsby's most valuable asset was his bat, but when he severely injured an ankle sliding during spring training, the Cubs manager lost his best hitter—himself. Hornsby had predicted to Judge Emil Fuchs of the Boston Braves that his career soon would be on the decline, and he was right. In 1932 the great hitter was able to play in only nineteen games, batting a mere .224.

Without player Hornsby's bat, the team was left with only manager Hornsby's abrasive personality, and the grumblings about his treatment of the players as well as the pernicious nature of his gambling vice reached the front office. Judge Landis had investigated Hornsby and cleared him of wrongdoing—"gambling is legal," an unrepentant Hornsby reminded him—but when Cubs president William Veeck learned that Hornsby had borrowed $11,000 from Cubs players, Rogers was fired on August 2, 1932.

WOODY ENGLISH: "Hornsby had borrowed money from some of the ballplayers. He borrowed from me, borrowed from Guy Bush. I imagine Pat Malone was one.

They were pretty good friends. He said it was to pay his income tax, but it was gambling debts, and that was the main reason he got fired.

"I remember the day our traveling secretary, Bob Lewis, came down and fired Hornsby in Philadelphia. It rained that day, and we had a meeting. Charlie Grimm was made manager.

"Bob Lewis came up to me and said, 'Woody, did Hornsby borrow any money from you?' I said, 'Yeah, twelve hundred dollars, but he paid me back.'

"'Oh God,' Bob said, 'I'm glad of that. He's getting fired today.'"

The man William Veeck chose to replace him was first baseman Charlie Grimm, a talented ballplayer who loved baseball and entertained the players on the banjo. He was a major leaguer for twenty years, with the Cubs from 1925 to 1936. For nine consecutive seasons he led the first basemen in the league in fielding, and he had a lifetime batting average of .290. Three times he led the Cubs to pennants. Charlie Grimm has not been elected into the Hall of Fame, but based on his longevity and performance, he certainly belongs.

With the likable, affable, voluble Grimm at the helm, the days of Hornsby's criticism and cynicism were at an end. The Cubs players under Grimm once again were encouraged to have fun playing ball. Grimm, who was anything but, allowed the players some breathing room for the first time in a long time.

WOODY ENGLISH: "Charlie was my favorite of all managers to play for—as a man. Oh God, Jolly Cholly, they called him, and that hit it pretty good. He was always in a good humor. Everything was always all right.

Charlie Grimm

"We had a meeting, as I told you, the day they fired Hornsby and appointed Grimm manager. At the meeting Grimm made a speech, and he announced, 'Fellas, we got a chance to win this, a darn good chance. Everybody take good care of themselves.' Rollie Hemsley, our backup catcher, was sitting there. And Hemsley said, 'That's right. Let's all take good care of ourselves.'

"That very night at two o'clock in the morning, Bob Lewis and Grimm had to go over to Camden, New Jersey, and get Rollie out of jail. He had gotten drunk. He could only drink about two bottles of beer.

"We'd be sitting in the lobby after dinner in the hotel, and somebody would say, 'Let's go upstairs and play a little cards,' and Rollie would be sitting there, and we'd be playing cards about an hour, and here would come Hemsley, drunker than hell on about two bottles of beer! And he was a good little ballplayer. He could run. He was fast.

"Charlie was not the smartest manager, and he knew it. He depended on Hartnett, me, and Billy Herman. Grimm would usually ask Gabby if the pitcher was losing his stuff. 'What do you think?' and Hartnett would know. Gabby was a great catcher. Hartnett would tell him when to change pitchers."

With Hornsby's crabby presence gone and Grimm leading the cheers, the talented Cubs players began winning ball games. On the mound the foursome of Lon Warneke (22–6, 2.37), Guy Bush (19–11, 3.21), Pat Malone (15–17, 3.38) and Charlie Root (15–10, 3.58) helped the Cubs lead the league in earned run average. Others contributed as well.

In a year when the Cubs had to rely on pitching and defense, two young infielders named Billy—Herman and Jurges—formed the team's new double play combination, as Woody English moved over to third base. With Charlie Grimm at first, the Cubs had their finest infield since the days of Tinker, Evers, and Chance. Gabby Hartnett, a perennial all-star, was behind the plate.

A pennant seemed possible until it was jeopardized on July 6. The twenty-four-year-old Jurges's season and his life almost came to an end when Violet Valli, a showgirl who evidently wanted more out of her relationship with the ballplayer than he was willing to provide, entered room number 509 at the Carliss Hotel and shot him with a .25-caliber handgun, reportedly while she attempted suicide.

DICK BARTELL (WHO WAS PLAYING SHORT FOR THE PHILLIES IN 1932): "Billy Jurges was living at the Carliss Hotel in Chicago. Several of the single players lived there. He'd been going with a girl. Early one morning he was sleeping. There was a knock on the door. It was the girl. He got up and let her in. She sat on the edge of the bed and they started arguing. She wanted to get married, but he wasn't about to marry her and told her so. She asked him to get her a drink of water. He went into the bathroom and drank a glass of water and turned around and she was standing in the doorway with a gun and shot him in the stomach [and the derriere]."

"With Jurges out, the Pirates thought they had it won. But he came back at the end of the season and played in the series. When he was wounded, that's when the Cubs bought Mark Koenig. He played 33 games at short and hit .353. In a way you might say that young lady triggered all the historic events of the '32 series, including the Babe Ruth called shot that never happened."

* * *

WOODY ENGLISH: "I was living in the Sheraton. Billy was in the Carliss Hotel, just a block over from where I lived. I was walking toward the ballpark, and some guy said, 'Did you hear about Bill Jurges getting shot?' I said, 'Shot?' I was surprised. Anyway, it was pretty bad.

"He knew this girl. She was up in his room. She pointed a gun at him, and he put a hand up, and he got shot through the fat part of his hand and through the side of his stomach. He was lucky she didn't kill him.

"Later on, Bronko Nagurski, the football player, and a couple other Cubs ball-players including myself were over at a bowling alley, and somebody turned around and said, 'There's that girl that shot Jurges!' We ran out of there like a bullet! Everybody made a beeline out of that joint!

"I don't know whether he was joking. I never turned around to look."

Jurges refused to prosecute, and Miss Valli—a woman who sought financial gain from her notoriety long before Oprah Winfrey and *A Current Affair* made it fashionable—signed a contract to sing and dance in nightclubs.

By the time Jurges returned to the Cubs, Hornsby was gone, Grimm was in, and playing shortstop was Mark Koenig, whom William Veeck had purchased from the Detroit Tigers.

Koenig, a thirty-year-old veteran, had begun his career with the New York Yankees, playing with Babe Ruth and Lou Gehrig on three straight pennant-winning teams in 1926, '27, and '28.

With Koenig playing steadily at shortstop and batting .353 down the stretch, the Cubs won eighteen out of twenty games as they raced past the favored Pittsburgh Pirates and won the 1932 pennant by four games.

Their reward for victory was the opportunity to play against their old manager, Joe McCarthy, and perhaps the most powerful baseball team of all time, the Ruth-Gehrig New York Yankees.

The Cubs might have had a better chance if the Yankees had gone into the Series lackadaisical and overconfident. Instead, the Cubs enraged Yankees superstar Babe Ruth by refusing to vote former Yankee teammate Mark Koenig a full World Series share despite his important contributions to the team's pennant win. Because of the team's vote to give Koenig only a half share (he appeared in thirty-three games), his former teammates, Ruth and the New York Yankees, abused the Cubs players in the press and then took it out on the Cubs in the World Series, defeating them soundly in four straight one-sided games (12–6, 5–2, 7–5, and 13–6).

Woody English was in charge of the clubhouse meeting to decide how great a share each player would get. Rogers Hornsby, the manager most of the year, didn't even come up for a vote and got nothing. English recalled that most of the players wanted to give Koenig a full share. But if just one balked, he said, his veto was enough.

WOODY ENGLISH: "I was captain of the club. I held those meetings. You had to be a regular in order to vote, and if anyone objected to giving a player a full share, then he didn't get one. I can't even remember voting on Hornsby. I don't believe his name was even brought up. Most of us wanted to give Koenig a full share, but—I hate to name them—Billy Herman and Billy Jurges held out. We had quite a discussion about it, because Koenig really helped us. They wouldn't do it, because he came too late."

BILLY JURGES: "We figured he wasn't entitled to it. He did win the pennant for us, but he didn't play that many ball games, and he wasn't entitled to it. If we had to do it all over again, we'd probably give him a full share, but at that time we didn't think too much of it.

"We found out in the newspaper the Yankees were upset over us only giving Koenig a half share. They were saying we were tight. Babe Ruth was the guy who was popping off so much."

Woody English to this day defends the team's right to vote as they did. Judge Kenesaw Mountain Landis, he notes, backed them up.

WOODY ENGLISH: "I got called up to Judge Landis's office about that. I was at home after the Series was all over. His office called up and said, 'Judge Landis would like you to come up. He'd like to talk to you.' I said, 'Okay.'

"Judge Landis was a friend of mine. When I was captain of the Cubs, he was always sitting near home plate, and I always made it my business when I was taking up the lineup to go over and shake hands. He used to like that. 'Cause the fans would be watching, you know.

"He was in his apartment on the South Side of Chicago, in bed laid up with the flu. He said, 'Come in, Woody. I got the damn flu. Hand me one of them pills and get me a glass of water, will you?' I did.

"He said, 'Sit down, Woody,' and I did. 'I want to ask you a few questions.' He said, 'I want you to call up the Cubs office and get the exact date that Mark Koenig came to the Cubs.' So I called up, and I said, 'August 17.' He said, 'Now Woody, how many games did he play?' I said, 'Thirty, thirty-five maybe.' He said, 'How many did you play, Woody?' I said, 'I suppose, all of them.' [English played ninety-three games at third and thirty-eight at short.] He said, 'How many games did Mark Koenig win?' I said, 'I suppose three or four maybe. He got timely hits.' 'And how many did you win, Woody?' I said, 'I have no idea, but I must have helped win a couple of them, because we won the pennant.' He said, 'I guess you did.'

"He said, 'You played in almost all the games and got a full share. Mark Koenig played in thirty games and won three or four games.' He said, 'I think you treated him fairly. Now make your expense account out. Put down plenty for gas.' Gas was about fifteen cents a gallon. So I did."

The Cubs may have been within their rights to treat Koenig as they did, but perhaps they would have had a better time of it in the 1932 Series if the players had been more generous. The Yankees won all four games as Babe Ruth, Lou Gehrig, and Tony Lazzeri pounded Cubs pitching, leaving the defeated Cubs with the sobriquet of cheapskate ringing in their ears.

"They just had too much power for us," says Woody English. "Ruth and Gehrig. We couldn't compete with them in power. Every game we got beat pretty bad."

37

The Mythical Called Shot

Amid loud sniping between the scornful Babe Ruth and the stung Cubs players, there arose an incident that became part of baseball's legend. According to the leading sportswriter of the time, Grantland Rice, and famed columnist Westbrook Pegler, who were there that day, Babe Ruth pointed over the head of Cubs pitcher Charlie Root to the center-field bleachers before hitting the next pitch to the exact spot where he had pointed.

The incident took place in the fifth inning of Game 3 of the 1932 World Series.

If it is any consolation to Cubs fans, here is the solid evidence that the Called Shot by Babe Ruth never happened. And if anyone swears it did, well, he's not a Cubs fan—and he's wrong.

WOODY ENGLISH: "When we played the Yankees in the 1932 Series, we knew we were a good ball club. We didn't have the power like the Yankees did, but we thought we had better pitching than they did. Unfortunately, our pitchers didn't hold up too good.

"When the Series started, we were surprised when they came out in the paper the day before and called us the 'cheap' Chicago Cubs, 'penny-pinching' Cubs, and that's why we got on them from our dugout so badly. Babe Ruth especially was upset that we didn't give Mark Koenig a full share.

"So we were retaliating from what they said in the papers. When Ruth came up there, we really got on him, boy. Judge Landis was really upset by the profanity around the Cubs dugout.

"I didn't say anything. The others called him everything. It was too much for the fans sitting along the dugout.

"I remember in the third game Charlie Root was pitching for us. I roomed with Charlie Root. He was a nice guy, but when he was out on that mound, don't take too big a toehold on him. You'll get one right behind your ear. He was a sidearm pitcher, threw hard, had a good curve ball, and was a competitor all the way.

"That day Ruth and Gehrig each had homered. Ruth got up again, and it was funny. He had two strikes on him. I was playing third base. I was right close to it. He's got two strikes on him. The guys are yelling at him from our dugout. He's looking right in our dugout, and he holds up two fingers. He said, 'That's only two strikes.' But the press box was way back on top of Wrigley Field, and to the people in the press, it looked like he pointed to center field. But he was looking right into our dugout and holding two fingers up. That *is* the true story. I've been asked that question five hundred times.

"Ruth would never do a thing like that, point. Charlie Root would have murdered him. Yeah. But I'll tell you, Ruth hit the heck out of the ball. The Yankees just had too much power for us. It was discouraging.

"All I remember about that Series was that they murdered us. We couldn't retaliate because they got so many runs.

"After the World Series, Burleigh Grimes, who was with us in 1932, said, 'Let me be the agent, and we'll get all kinds of money from different companies. We'll let them use our name on this and that.' The way he was talking, he was going to get us rich. You know what we wound up with? A hundred dollars apiece from Wheaties and a hundred dollars from Camel cigarettes. There were so darn many boxes of Wheaties up in the clubhouse, you could never believe it!"

BILLY HERMAN: "We had a lot of fire and spirit on the Cubs, but when we went out that first day and watched the Yankees take batting practice, our hearts just sank. They were knocking those balls out of sight. We were awestruck.

"That was the Series in which Ruth supposedly called his shot. I say 'supposedly.' He didn't really do it, you know. I hate to explode one of baseball's great legends, but I was there and saw what happened. Sure, he made a gesture, he pointed—but it wasn't to call his shot. Listen, he was a great hitter and a great character, but do you think he would have put himself on the spot like that? I can tell you what happened and why it happened.

"We were a young team and a fresh team. We had some guys on the bench that got on Ruth as soon as the Series started. And I mean they were rough. Once all that yelling starts back and forth it's hard to stop it, and of course, the longer it goes on, the nastier it gets. What were jokes in the first game became personal insults by the third game. By the middle of the third game things were really hot.

"It was the fifth inning when Ruth came up. He'd already hit a home run, in the first inning with two on, and the Chicago fans were letting him have it, and so was our bench. I was standing out on second base, and I could hear it pouring out of the bench. Charlie Root was pitching. He threw the first one over, and Ruth took it for a strike. The noise got louder. Then Root threw another one across, and Ruth took that, for strike two. The bench came even more alive with that. What Ruth did then was hold up his hand, telling them that was only two strikes, that he still had another one coming and that he wasn't out yet. When he held up his hand, that's where the pointing came in. But he was pointing out toward Charlie Root when he did that, not toward the center-field bleachers. And then, of course, he hit the next pitch out of the ball park. Then the legend started that he had called his shot, and Babe went along with it. Why not?

"But he didn't point. Don't kid yourself. I can tell you just what would have happened if Ruth had tried that—he would never have got a pitch to hit. Root would have had him with his feet up in the air. I told you, Charlie Root was a mean man out on that mound.

"But like I say, it's still a great story, and those who want to believe it will go on believing it, regardless of what anybody says."

CHARLIE GRIMM: "All this time a noisy battle of words was mounting from the rival dugouts. This brings us up to Ruth's famous visit to the plate with one out in the fifth inning. [Guy] Bush, leading the tirade from the bench, turned a blast on the Babe. One of the nicknames he didn't like was 'Big Monkey,' and I'm sure Guy included it. Even before Root got over his first of two pitches for strikes, Babe pointed straight away and turned toward our dugout—no doubt for Bush's benefit. Those who saw Ruth's pointing finger chose to believe, when he drove the ball over the center field bleachers, that he was calling his shot.

"I hesitate to spoil a good story, one that has been built up to such proportions down the years that millions of people have insisted they saw the gesture, but the Babe actually was pointing to the mound. As he pointed, I heard Ruth growl: 'You'll be out there tomorrow—so we'll see what you can do with me, you so-and-so tightwad.'

"Well, the next day, Ruth didn't hit any home runs off Bush. He was plunked by a pitched ball the only time he faced the Mississippi Mudcat, who didn't have the stuff that day, lasting only a third of an inning.

"Root never squawked as the legend grew that Ruth had called his shot for baseball's most celebrated home run. But he did balk when he was offered a chunk of money to re-create the scene in the Babe Ruth movie made later in Hollywood. If old Chinski [Charlie Root's nickname among the Cubs players] could have called back any one of the thousands of pitches he made for the Cubs, the one Ruth picked on would have been his choice. Let's face it, though, a great guy hit that homer, the greatest slugger of all time. And if you want to believe he really planned it that way, you just go right ahead."

JOE MCCARTHY: "That's the Series where they say he called his home run. That's a good story, isn't it. A lot of people still believe today that he really did that. Did he? No. You see, the Cubs were riding him from the bench every time he came to the plate, and finally he pointed over at them. Then he hit the next pitch out. After he hit the ball, somebody said, 'Did you see where he pointed?' Well, a lot of them did see his hand go up and they said, 'Maybe he did point that way.' That's how the story began. To tell the truth, I didn't see him point anywhere at all, but I might have turned my head for a moment.

"Babe went along with it. He was a great showman, you know. But later on he admitted that he never pointed to the bleachers. Gabby Hartnett said the same thing, and he was the catcher. Charlie Root, who was the pitcher, also said that. They said he pointed to the Cub dugout."

BILLY JURGES: "At first Babe said he didn't call his shot, but it was such a good story, later on he said he called his shot.

"He didn't point to the fence. He pointed to the dugout. He made a motion to the Cubs dugout. The Cubs ballplayers were riding Ruth, and he said, 'Well, that's only two strikes.' Gabby Hartnett, our catcher, heard him. Gabby said that Babe Ruth said, 'Well, that's only two strikes.'"

The way Hartnett remembered it, there was one strike, and Babe put up one finger as he pointed. In fact, he had put up one and on the next pitch put up two. But one finger or two, Hartnett's conclusion was the same: Babe was *not* pointing at the center-field fence.

GABBY HARTNETT: "Babe waved his hand toward our bench on the third-base side. One finger was up, and he said quietly—and I think only the umpire and I heard him—'It only takes one to hit it.' Root came in with a fast one, Babe swung, and it landed in the center-field seats. Babe didn't say a word when he passed me after the home run. If he'd pointed out at the bleachers, I'd be the first to say so."

*   *   *

Charlie Root gave his version of the matter in a speech to a Los Angeles high school assembly.

CHARLIE ROOT: "Sure, Babe gestured to me. We had been riding him, calling him 'Grandpop' and kidding him about not getting to be manager of the Yankees. We wanted to get him mad, and he was when he came to bat. As he stepped up, he challenged me to lay the ball in. After I had gotten the first strike over, Babe pointed to me and yelled, 'That's only one strike.'

"Maybe I had a smug grin on my face after he took the second strike. Babe stepped out of the box again, pointed his finger in my direction and yelled, 'You still need one more, kid.'

"I guess I should have wasted the next pitch, and I thought Ruth figured I would, too. I decided to try to cross him and came in with it. The ball was gone as soon as Ruth swung. It never occurred to me then that the people in the stands would think he had been pointing to the bleachers. But that's the way it was."

DICK BARTELL: "For years nothing made Root madder than hearing about how Ruth called his shot. But he just had to live with it."

Ed Froelich knew both Charlie Root and Babe Ruth. According to Froelich, he was told with certainty that the Called Shot never happened. Root, for one, told him so. Most convincingly, so did Ruth.

ED FROELICH: "Let me tell you about Charlie Root. He was one of the roughest, toughest competitors who ever lived. I mean tough. He believed that when he got two strikes on a hitter, that hitter was going down into the dirt. He was one hard-nosed, hard-assed pitcher. He asked no quarter and gave none.

"I remember a ball game in Chicago when he was hooked up in a pitcher's duel with (Giants pitcher) Adolpho Luque, who was also a hard-nosed, hard-assed pitcher. They got to knocking down some hitters, and the umpires, as you might have guessed by now, didn't step in in those days like they do now. Today it's bloody murder if a pitcher knocks down a hitter. In the old days everyone accepted it. It was part of baseball. And though they didn't have those big diving helmets that batters wear today, hitters didn't get hurt as much. They were alert. They expected to be knocked down, and they protected themselves at the plate.

"This particular day Root and Luque were pitching against each other, knocking batters down, and when it was Luque's turn to hit, Root hit him right in the squash. You hit a man in the head like that, and you don't know whether you've killed him or not, so Root ran up to the plate, bent over Luque along with everyone else, and asked him, 'Are you all right, Dolf?'

"Luque said, 'Get away from me, you rotten son of a bitch.'

"Root said, 'OK, if that's the way you feel about it.'

"When it came Root's turn to bat, Luque went after him, and Root just did get his elbow up in time to stop a pitch headed for his skull. The pitch nailed his elbow real good, but Root didn't say anything. He went down to first base, and he told George

Kelly, the Giants first baseman, 'George, when you get back to the dugout, you tell your guys to be plenty loose up there because I'm going right down the batting order, twice, each man.'

"Kelly was the batter the next inning, and he told the umpire, Cy Rigler, what Root had said. And Rigler didn't do a thing. Root went right down the batting order, knocked each guy down twice, and after he had knocked the ninth guy down for the final time, Rigler called time, walked out to Root, and said, 'Charlie, you said you were going to knock nine guys down, and that's the ninth guy. No more.'

"Root said OK. That was the end of it for the day.

"I never saw another ballplayer before or since who could do what I saw Root do. One day I was walking through the Cubs clubhouse getting some baseballs autographed, and I said, 'Charlie, would you sign these balls?' He growled, 'What for?' But he was kidding. Charlie was really a nice guy. I said, 'For Hack Wilson.' He said, 'OK.' He signed the last one, dropped the pen in the box, and took the ball, squeezed it real hard, and tossed it to me. He had raised the seams of the ball! I was flabbergasted.

"And after that, I'd watch him a little closer when he pitched, and I could see that every once in a while in an important situation when he needed a strikeout, he'd turn his back to home plate, squeeze that ball—give that ball a howsengrowser— meaning he was doctoring it up. With that seam raised, the ball would drop straight down. Root was wicked on right-handed hitters. He was a sidearm, sinker ball pitcher, except when he was throwing it at your head, which was often.

"You know that Charlie Root was the pitcher against whom Babe Ruth supposedly called his shot in the 1932 World Series.

"After the game Grantland Rice and all the rest of the New York newspapermen were around in the clubhouse, and Rice said, 'Babe, damn if it didn't look like you pointed when you hit the ball.'

"Ruth said, 'The hell it did.'

"That's all he said. And the newspapermen created a legend from that.

"The only thing Root ever said about that was that was a lot of bullshit. Which it was. I once had a conversation with the Babe about that Called Shot incident. If anyone knew whether or not he had called his shot against Root, the Babe did.

"It was 1938. I was the trainer for the Brooklyn Dodgers at the time. Dodgers owner Larry MacPhail had hired Ruth to be a Dodgers coach. It was in his contract to take batting practice every day. Having been away from baseball full-time for four years, the Babe had some aches and pains, and he would be in the training room every day.

"We got to talking one day. I said, 'Babe, a lot of people in Chicago still say that you pointed toward the center-field bleachers before you hit that home run out there.'

"He said, 'Doc, can you hear me?'

"I said, 'Yes.'

"A little louder, he said, 'Can you hear me?'

"'Yes.'

"'Can you hear me good?'

"I said, 'Yes.'

"He said, 'You tell those people for Baby'—he always called himself Baby— 'that Baby says they're full of crap right up to their eyeballs. I may be dumb, but

I'm not that dumb. I'm going to point to the center-field bleachers with a barracuda like Root out there? On the next pitch they'd be picking it out of my ear with a pair of tweezers.'

"He said one final word, 'No.'

"Root said he never pointed, and so did Hartnett, the catcher. What did happen? Ruth was at the plate, and the Cubs bench was calling him every obscene name they could think of. He had his bat on his shoulder, and Root threw a strike and the Babe took it with the bat on his shoulder. He got another blast from the Cubs bench. With his bat still on his shoulder, Ruth lifted the pointer finger of his left hand off the bat as if to say, 'OK, that's one.'

"Root pitched again, the Babe took it, and it was strike two, and he got another blast. Ruth looked over to the Cubs dugout, raised two fingers of his left hand off the bat, signaling, 'OK, that's two.'

"Root pitched again, and Ruth hit the top of the ticket office in Wrigley Field's center-field bleachers.

"Have you ever seen a photograph of Ruth pointing? At the World Series the place is swarming with photographers. You'd think one would have gotten the picture. No.

"Finally, as a rule, Ruth didn't hit the ball into center field. Almost never. Would he be pointing to a spot where he almost never hit the ball? It doesn't make sense. But see, it's a legend. People like to believe in fantasy, even newspaper reporters."

38

The Death of William Veeck

With the death of William Wrigley in January 1932, the ownership of the team passed on to his son, Philip, a shy, quiet, enigmatic man. Baseball didn't interest Philip nearly as much as playing polo and racing motorcycles. He also had mechanical pursuits. He loved to tinker, to take things apart and put them back together again. He especially loved to work on car engines. Philip was once asked what he would have been had he not been born to wealth. His reply: "I probably would have ended up a garage mechanic." He could fix a wristwatch and a radio. At his palatial home he didn't allow workmen to fix things. He did those chores himself.

As a boy he had been a tightwad. When he was a student at Phillips Andover Academy, his allowance was $30 a month. When his father learned he was banking a significant part of it, he ordered the boy, "Spend all of it or get nothing."

After graduating from Andover, where he listed his favorite sport as "dice throwing," Philip avoided going to Yale by convincing his father to let him travel to Australia to oversee construction of a chewing-gum plant. His father was impressed by the job he did. He came back to Chicago to study chemistry, and in 1925 his father appointed the thirty-one-year-old Phil the president of his chewing-gum empire. When he was asked how he got the job, Phil was brutally honest about it.

"I'm not sure I'm succeeding solely on my own merits," he said. "I have a feeling that 'pull' and the fact I'm my father's son had something to do with my election."

Phil Wrigley demonstrated great skill in leading the gum company. By midsummer of 1932, when GE had plummeted from $403 a share to 8½, RCA from 114¾ to 2½, and U.S. Steel from 261 to 21½, the earnings of the Wrigley Co. dropped only from its high of $12,296,158 in 1929 to a low of $7,095,667 in 1932. The dividend was never cut from its standard of $5 a share. The next year profits began to rise again.

While his father spent much of his time running the Cubs, Phil showed little interest in the team in particular and baseball in general. Nevertheless, when he died, William Wrigley bequeathed the Cubs to his son personally, the only direct bequest in his will. When he took over the Cubs, Philip Wrigley made it clear he would keep the team under his personal control.

In 1933 he told a reporter, "The club and the park stand as memorials to my father. I will never dispose of my holdings in the club as long as the chewing-gum business remains profitable enough to retain it."

Said Bill Veeck, William Veeck's son, years later, "And so Phil Wrigley assumed the burden out of his sense of loyalty and duty. If he has any particular feeling for baseball, any real liking for it, he has disguised it magnificently."

So long as William Veeck continued to run the Cubs, Philip Wrigley had little with which to concern himself. With Veeck in charge, the policies of William Wrigley continued, as did the team's winning ways.

William Wrigley had held certain philosophies that he felt contributed to a successful team. One of those was his insistence that his players be content. Rarely did William Wrigley and William Veeck haggle over salaries. William Wrigley wanted to be fair, even generous, and William Veeck did everything he could to make sure it was so. Woody English recalled that halcyon era.

WOODY ENGLISH: "William Veeck was a wonderful guy. He always reminded me of a big Indian. He was tall, straight, a lot taller than Bill Junior, and he always had a pleasant smile and a good warm handshake for you.

"In 1930 I had a great year. It was my best year. I scored 152 runs, hit 14 home runs, a lot of extra-base hits (67), not bad for a 150-pound guy who was the leadoff man. I hadn't signed my contract for '31. I was living in Chicago, and I got a call to come down to the Wrigley Building.

"I went down to his office, and the very first words he said to me were, 'Woody, you're one hell of a ballplayer.' Just that. I said, 'Well, thanks.' He said, 'Sit down there.' We talked about the weather, whatever, and he said, 'Now, you're going to sign your contract. What we're going to do, we're going to give you a blank contract, and you fill in what you think you're worth. Now don't ask for the Wrigley Building, because that doesn't belong to me. That belongs to Mr. Wrigley.'

"He called Miss Donohue in. 'Bring in a contract for Woody. No figures on it.' She brought it in. He said, 'Write down what you think you're worth, and I'll sign it.' That was something, wasn't it?

"I said, 'Well. . . .'

"He said, 'I told you not to ask for the Wrigley Building.'

"Anyway, I knew Hartnett was making $18,000. No one outside of Hack Wilson was making money. He was making $35,000. And that's what Hornsby got too. Anyway, Hartnett had been there about six or eight years longer than I had, and I figured I was young yet, so I said, 'How about $14,000?'

He looked at me and smiled as if to say, 'Dummy.' He said, 'You satisfied?' I said, 'That's right.' And I got another $750 a year for being captain.

"I bought a farm for my grandparents, I bought a house for my mother, and I helped my sister and her husband to own a farm. I always had nice cars, convertibles. I had a Packard convertible in 1935, and I had a Chrysler convertible, and now I have a Ford Pinto. So, you see, I'm not making that big money anymore."

Another of William Wrigley's philosophies was that the Cubs should feature big-name, big-production players on their team. In November 1932, William Veeck continued that policy when he traded four players for Babe Herman, a slugger with a lifetime .324 batting average. Herman, a real character, was known for his antics while a member of the Brooklyn Dodgers' Daffiness Boys. Once he lined a shot into the outfield, rounded second, and pulled into third, only to find himself standing on the base along with *two* other Brooklyn runners. In the outfield, players would hold their breath when a fly ball came his way. When Babe Herman became a Cub, he not only hit around .300, but the players were surprised to find he could catch the ball as well.

WOODY ENGLISH: "He was quite a character, a colorful guy. You'd have to be around him to hear him talk or see his actions. He'd go in the clubhouse, and he'd wear one of them skimmer straw hats, and he'd be shaving in the clubhouse with that straw hat on. It was comical looking.

"We got him for his hitting, but he didn't hit much with the Cubs [in 1933 he hit .289 and in 1934 .304, which wasn't great compared with the .393 he hit in 1930], but he made some spectacular plays in the outfield. He turned out to be a better fielder than a hitter for us."

In 1933 the Cubs continued to be strong contenders, finishing in third, six games behind the New York Giants, who were led by their star pitcher Carl Hubbell.

WOODY ENGLISH: "Carl Hubbell was the best pitcher I ever faced. A lot of the pitchers had a screwball, but his broke faster and sharper than anyone's. The other guys who threw it, you could pretty well see it coming all the way, but Hubbell's ball was right on top of you, almost on the edge of that plate, and boom, down it went, and that was his strikeout pitch. And he'd throw inside. He'd knock you out of there if you got too big a toehold. And he was fast, really fast—maybe not like Lefty Grove—but his screwball, that was his bread and butter."

One highlight for Woody English in 1933 was his appearance in the very first All-Star Game.

* * *

WOODY ENGLISH: "That first All-Star Game was one of the best things I remember. It was really thrilling because it was only supposed to be a one-game deal. Arch Ward was the *Tribune* sports editor, and the World's Fair was in Chicago that year, and he thought it up. Just supposed to be one year. They had 47,000 at the park, and it turned out to be such a hit, it's been going on ever since.

"I remember Babe Ruth hit a home run, and the American League won 4–2. Frankie Frisch hit a home run for the National League. I was a right-handed batter, but seventy-five percent of my hits went to right field. I went up to pinch-hit for Lon Warneke. Lefty Grove, who finished the game, threw me a high fastball, and I hit the ball good, but it was to right field, and the center fielder was right there.

"The game was held in Chicago, and they gave rings to every player. They were supposed to call the guys alphabetically. The first player up there to get his ring was Paul Waner. Somebody said, 'You're a *W*.'

"Paul said, 'I wanted to get my ring before it tarnishes!'"

With the depression at its worst, attendance in 1933 dropped dramatically at Wrigley Field, down 400,000 fans to only 595,000. In mid-September, tragedy struck the Cubs organization. After watching the Cubs battle the first-place Giants at Wrigley Field on a cold and rainy day, team president William Veeck contracted influenza. Within a month he was dead.

WOODY ENGLISH: "You know how Mr. Veeck died? He had a tooth extracted, and he sat out in the ballpark in the rain one day. It was chilly, and he got a cold, and it turned into some kind of leukemia. He lived outside of Chicago, and when he died, boy, that knocked everybody for a loop. That was sad. He and William Wrigley were two great men, such decent fellows. To us ballplayers they were like fathers, part of our family. They took good care of us, inquired about you and your family. They were wonderful."

BILL VEECK: "A few weeks after school started [in the fall of 1933], I was told that my father had been stricken with leukemia, an almost unknown disease in those days. I jumped into my car and rushed home.

"The doctors told me there was no hope. They also told me that the last thing a dying man can hold in his stomach is wine. I had done little enough for my father, I knew, and I was determined that he would go out in some comfort and some style.

"Prohibition had just ended. The bootleg supply was drying up; the legitimate wineries were not yet in full production. But there was one man in Chicago, I knew, who would know where the best champagne was to be had. Al Capone. I knew him slightly from the ball park and I knew some of his boys even better. Ralph Capone, Al's brother, was a great Cub fan. We had a ticket man, named Red Thompson, whom the mob guys always dealt with. Whenever I got a $100 bill in Red's bank in later years, I knew that Ralph Capone and his boys were at the game.

"I hurried to Al Capone's headquarters at the Hotel Metropole and told him what I wanted and why. 'Kid,' he said, 'I'll send a case of champagne right over.' The case was there when I got back. Every morning during these last few days of my father's life, a case of imported champagne was delivered to the door.

"The last nourishment that passed between my daddy's lips on this earth was Al Capone's champagne."

Before William Veeck died, he had been negotiating an important deal for the Cubs. After Veeck's death, Phil Wrigley appointed minority stockholder William Walker, a mogul in the fish business, to run the team. Wrigley made it clear then he still had no interest in taking charge.

Walker's first move was to complete the deal that William Veeck had been negotiating with the Philadelphia Phillies, the acquisition of one of the great hitters in the league, outfielder Chuck Klein.

In 1932 the Phils had featured a one-two combo that had even outslugged the combo of Ruth and Gehrig. The two hitters were the left-handed hitting Klein and first baseman Don Hurst. In 1932, Klein hit 38 homers and drove in 137 runs and won the National League's Most Valuable Player Award. That year Don Hurst hit 24 home runs and drove in 143 runs. The two Phils had amassed 737 total bases to 672 for the Yankees' legendary pair. If the fourth-place Phils had had any pitching at all, they would have been a championship team.

In 1933 the left-hand hitting Klein continued his great slugging, batting .368 with 28 homers and 120 runs batted in. The Cubs badly needed a right fielder who could hit with power. Klein seemed an exciting acquisition.

What enabled the Cubs to acquire Chuck Klein during the winter of 1933 was the precarious financial condition of Phils owner William Baker. William Veeck, with Phil Wrigley's approval, had offered the Phils $65,000 for Klein, substantial money in the heart of the depression. When William Walker completed Veeck's deal, it certainly appeared that Phil Wrigley would continue his father's philosophy of doing whatever was necessary to build a winning ball club.

The deal for Klein, a happy-go-lucky man, looked like a pennant winner, the same sort of purchase William Wrigley had made when he bought Rogers Hornsby from the Braves before the 1929 season. But once Klein arrived in Chicago, it became clear to everyone that he would have a far more difficult task hitting the ball 350 feet over the right-field wall of Wrigley Field than popping it up over the big Lifebuoy sign atop the 280-foot right-field fence in cozy Baker Bowl in Philadelphia. Klein's average his first year with the Cubs was .301, but his production dropped considerably. High fly balls to right and right center that would have been home runs in Philly became long outs in Wrigley. He hit only 20 home runs and drove in just 80 runs in but 115 games. His teammates were dissatisfied and disappointed.

CHARLIE GRIMM: "Klein had two things going for him. He was playing for a lowly club and he had a short right-field target in Baker Bowl. In Chicago he was coming to a contender and the fences would be more difficult to reach in Chicago.

"Klein was only ordinary for us. It developed he couldn't hit lefties. Obviously, too, he felt the pressure of being with a contender."

WOODY ENGLISH: "After a game one night at Wrigley Field, Billy Herman and I were walking along the runway up from underneath. You had to go up and out into the open to get up to the clubhouse, and as we were walking, we passed Chuck

Klein laughing, having a good time, and Herman said, 'Hey, Chuck, we lost today. What's so funny?' Klein said, 'I got my two hits today.' Billy Herman said, 'The Cubs lost, dummy.'"

The next year, in June 1934 the Cubs traded for the Phils' other slugger, Don Hurst. First baseman Charlie Grimm was nearing the end of his career. In the wings was young first-base prospect Dolph Camilli. Apparently, William Walker thought the slow-footed Hurst still had some productive years left and didn't think Camilli, a powerful batter, was ready to replace Grimm. He was wrong on both counts.

The Cubs sent $30,000 as well as Camilli to the Phils for Hurst, who flopped even worse than Klein. In 1934, Hurst played fifty-one games for the Cubs, hit .199 and ended his major league career. Hurst's fielding had been weak in Philadelphia. With Chicago his range at first shrank to that of a hydrant.

Camilli, meanwhile, had a spectacular twelve-year career, leading the league in homers in 1941 (with 34) and helping to bring Brooklyn a pennant that year. The Cubs players hated to see Camilli go. William Walker, the man Phil Wrigley put in charge of the team, was blamed for the disastrous deal, the first of several trans-actions by him and his successor that would cripple the Cubs by the end of the decade.

WOODY ENGLISH: "Dolph Camilli came in and played first for us beginning in 1934, and then they traded him away. He went to Philadelphia. William Walker had a fish market in Chicago. He was a big fish man. He was also one of the big stock-holders in the Cubs. I don't know what he was doing making trades. How could he trade Camilli for Don Hurst? I don't know. Everybody said he should have stayed in the fish business."

Despite the two deals that misfired, the Cubs continued to be contenders, finish-ing third in 1934. The team still had its great infield defense, with Charlie Grimm, Billy Herman, Billy Jurges, Woody English, and youngster Stan Hack all playing brilliantly. In the outfield the trio of Babe Herman, Kiki Cuyler, and Klein supplied the power.

If the Cubs could get one more pitcher, a pennant was in their sights. On Novem-ber 22, 1934, William Walker, who was being vilified for his trades, made one final move that would bring the Cubs a pennant the following year. With a young pros-pect named Augie Galan available for outfield duty, he traded Babe Herman, a too-old Guy Bush, and a young, lanky right-hander, Jim Weaver, to the Pittsburgh Pirates for southpaw Larry French and Hall of Fame infielder Freddie Lindstrom.

French had been a workhorse for the Pirates, winning 18 games in both 1932 and 1933. When he slipped to only 12 wins the following year, the Pirates made him available, and the Cubs grabbed him. The left-handed French would become one of the solid Cubs starters for the next half dozen years. He and Lindstrom, who could play both third base and the outfield, would help bring the Cubs a pennant in 1935.

At the end of the 1934 season Phil Wrigley fired William Walker because Wrig-ley didn't possess enough knowledge about baseball to know whether Walker was competent or not. All Wrigley knew was that he was getting pounded in the press by reporters who believed his man Walker, the fishmonger, had made bum deals that brought Babe Herman, Chuck Klein, and Don Hurst, three aging or over-the-hill stars, and sent away Dolph Camilli, the phenom who would pound Cubs' pitching unmercifully during his career.

Despite the strong criticism in the papers, William Walker hadn't done a bad job at all, considering the disaster that would follow his departure when at the end of the 1934 season Phil Wrigley decided he would take control of the team himself.

Wrigley told reporters, "If you own the club, you get the blame for what happens, whether you're president or not. So you might as well be president."

And with that Philip Wrigley, who had little knowledge of and even less love for the game of baseball, named himself president of the Chicago Cubs.

Had it not been for three miracles—a twenty-one-game winning streak, a seemingly impossible home run hit in darkness, and a season in which all the teams except the Cubs lost their best players to a world war—Philip Wrigley would have presided over a thirty-five-year stretch in which the Cubs were submerged in the bottom half of the National League standings. Because of those three pennant victories, the wait for another pennant has stretched only since 1945, a full fifty years.

Cubs fans would soon learn to love their team, serious flaws and all. They would have to because they would have no choice. The players would become part of their family, albeit a dysfunctional one.

Before that day came, though, those fans would be treated to a deserved pennant in 1935, the last hurrah of this great team in 1938, and a big surprise in 1945—and then, the abyss.

39

Philibuck

The Dolph Camilli for Don Hurst trade didn't devastate the Cubs because in late September 1934 management brought up to the big club an eighteen-year-old first baseman by the name of Phil Cavarretta. Cavarretta was not imposing—he stood around five foot eleven and weighed about 165 pounds—but he was a skilled batsman, and rarely was there a player of such determination and pluck. In the field he became a slick-fielding magician with the glove, and at bat he was a vicious line drive hitter who would also hit an occasional home run in a key situation. Cavarretta, whose lifetime batting average was .293, every day battled hard on the field. Philibuck, as his teammates called him, was the quintessential professional player, the digger who gave a hundred percent. During his twenty-year career in Chicago, Phil Cavarretta was the embodiment of the Chicago Cubs. The apex of his career came in 1945 when he hit .355, led the team to a pennant, and was named Most Valuable Player in the National League.

When he entered the big leagues in the fall of 1934, it was the depths of the depression. Cavarretta, who came from Chicago's North Side, had dropped out of high school to play pro ball because his father was out of work and the family didn't have enough money to eat. When the Cubs signed him in 1933, they sent him to A ball. They had no idea he would make the Cubs the following year at age eighteen and remain a member of the Chicago Cubs for the next twenty seasons.

Cavarretta recalled his earliest days as a Cub, a scared, inexperienced teenager playing in the big leagues.

PHIL CAVARRETTA: "When I was a youngster, going to grade school in Chicago on the North Side, I loved to play ball. Day after day I'd play and come home all dirty and sweaty, and at dinnertime my dad would look at me and in broken English, he would say, 'Phili, where you been? You dirty. Look at you.' I'd say, 'I got that at the school playing baseball.' He'd look at me with sharp eyes. He'd say, 'Base-a-ball. What is this base-a-ball?' I would explain to him what baseball is. I said, 'I have fun. I like it.' He said, 'You no play base-a-ball no more. You go to school, or I breaka you head.' My mom and dad weren't real big baseball fans. Both of them came from Palermo, Italy. They didn't understand baseball. I still kept playing, and he kept telling me to go to school. I *was* going to school, but he didn't want baseball to interfere with my education.

"I went to Lane Technical High School in Chicago. I played what we used to call hardball. Percy Moore, my coach, may his soul rest in peace, was a wonderful man and a great high school coach, but the thing we all enjoyed was that he was so good to us, like a second father to us. I made the team as a first baseman and pitcher. In those days if you could throw hard, you were a pitcher too. I played for three years, and we won championships upon championships. The last game I played in high school, I pitched a no-hit, no-run game. If you have a pretty good curve in high school, you win. I had a pretty good curve.

"Just before school was out, I went to my coach. I had to see him, because this was during the depression, and things were tough. Real tough.

"My dad was a janitor at a school. He was a hard worker, but being uneducated, he was unable to get a good job. In 1933 my dad was out of a job. I went to Percy Moore. I said, 'Coach, I'm going to have to leave school 'cause I'm going to have to go out and make a couple dollars so we can eat at home.' Things were that tough. He looked at me and said, 'Phil, are you sure about this?' I said, 'Coach, I just have to. I want to see if I can play professional baseball.'

"He said, 'I sure hate to see you leave, but let me see what I can do.' He knew Charlie Grimm, the Cubs manager, and he arranged a workout for me at Wrigley Field. I was seventeen years old.

"I wasn't very big in high school, about five foot ten, 150 pounds. I went out onto Wrigley Field. The Cubs were taking batting practice. Pat Malone, one of the best pitchers the Cubs ever had, a tough old guy, was on the mound. In those days the starting pitchers would pitch, rest two days, pitch batting practice, and then go in and pitch. Pat must have had a bad night. He was really growling out there. Charlie Grimm said, 'Get your bat, young man, and take about five or six swings. Let's take a look at you.'

"I went up there and started hitting line drives all over the place, hitting the ball pretty good. I think I hit one into the bleachers. The regulars were all around the batting cage, and they kept looking at me and said, 'My God, who is this skinny little guy hitting the ball so good?' I went up there three or four different times, always hitting the ball pretty good.

"So the Cubs signed me to a minor league contract. They didn't give me any money. They sent me to Peoria, Illinois. At that time it was the old Central League, now the Three-I League.

"I went home, packed my bag. Pants Rowland, a former big league manager and the Cubs' top scout, drove me to Peoria.

"When I was young, I was very, very quiet. On the way to Peoria, it was about noon, time for lunch. Pants looked at me and said, 'Would you like to have something to eat, young man?' I said, 'Yes, sir.'

"We stopped, and it was time to order lunch. I never was outside the North Side of Chicago. I didn't know what to order. Pants ordered a sandwich and a glass of buttermilk. I didn't know what buttermilk was. The waitress said, 'What would you like to have, young man?' I said, 'The same thing.' They brought the food. I ate my sandwich, and I took a sip of the buttermilk, and I said to myself, 'My God, this milk is sour.' I just left it there.

"After lunch, we went to Peoria. Pants checked me into a boardinghouse there, and I reported to the club the next day. We had a little old manager named Bob Murphy, a little bitty old guy, built real strong, tough as could be. He was another one who would growl at you.

"Murphy started me the first game. It was cold and windy out there. Very few people were in the stands. The first time at bat, I hit a home run. Then I hit a single, a double, and a triple. After the game was over, Murphy came over and said, 'Boy, you hit the ball pretty good, young man.' I said. 'I'm glad to hear you say that. Thank you, sir.'

"It was cold in Peoria, and they weren't drawing too many people, so the league folded.

"Pants Rowland came in and said, 'We're going to send you to Reading, Pennsylvania.' In the old New York–Penn League, Class A. I packed my bag, got on the train, and went to Reading. I got off the train, and nobody met me there. I was lost.

"I asked the cabdriver to take me out to the ballpark. He took me to the park. I went into the clubhouse, and I didn't see anybody but the clubhouse man. I told him who I was. He said he was expecting me. I said, 'Where is the ball club?' This was in the afternoon. I thought maybe we were playing at night. He said, 'They're on the road, Phil.' I said, 'My God, I don't have a room to stay in. I don't know what to do.'

"He said, 'Let me help you with that. Some of the players stay across the street at a boardinghouse. I'll see if there's a room available.'

"He took me across the street. I met this little old lady. She was so nice. She said, 'Yeah, we have one room upstairs.' It was a three-story house. She took me upstairs. This was in the middle of the afternoon. She opened the door to my room. The shades were up, but the room was almost absolutely dark. I took the room and waited for the club to get back.

"I got something to eat, and I came back to my room, and I was lonesome. I was scared to death. I said to myself, I'm gonna go home.

"As it happened, the club came in the following day. I went out to the ballpark, and Nemo Leibold was our manager. A beautiful man, may his soul rest in peace. I went up to him and said, 'I'm really lonesome. I have a room across the way. I'm not very pleased with it. I think I'm going to go home.'

"He called me into his office and he said, 'Look, young man, we've heard a lot of good things about you. Don't make a decision too fast. Give yourself a chance. Stay here for a week or so, see what happens. Get acquainted with some of the players. Maybe you'll enjoy it.'

"I said, 'OK, I'll give it a try.'

"Until this day, I was so happy he talked me into staying, because if I'd-a-gone home, I'd have never made twenty years in the big leagues. I'd have never been in three World Series, three All-Star Games. So I stayed and finished the season there and met a lot of good young players like Dim Dom Dallessandro, our right fielder. He later was a Cub. As one Italian to another we got acquainted pretty well. Dom took me out to his house, and we had spaghetti, and I really enjoyed it, and I went out and finished the season and hit .308, and the Cubs called me up in September 1934. As it happened, the Cubs needed a first baseman. Charlie Grimm was our manager. His playing days were just about over with. His back was bad. He had lumbago, sciatica.

"I was in the Reading clubhouse, packing my bag to go home at the end of the season, and I was homesick. I missed my mom and dad, brother and sister, and I was looking forward to going home, and while I was packing my bag, I received a telegram: 'Report to the Chicago Cubs in Boston.' Well, in a way I was happy, but then again, I was lonesome and looking forward to going home. I figured, What's a couple more weeks?

"I picked up the club in Boston at the Kenmore Hotel. Again, I was lost. I registered and went up to my room, had my dinner, went up to my room again, went to bed, and I woke up in the morning. I went down and had breakfast. It was time to go to the park, but being young and inexperienced, I didn't know where the ballpark was.

"I was sitting in the lobby looking for someone to take me out to the ballpark. The players were walking by. We had never met. They were going out to the park. I was sitting out front.

"The late Kiki Cuyler, who was our player-coach at the time, a beautiful man, a nice guy, he looked at me and said, 'Young man, can I help you?' I said, 'Yeah.' I told him who I was. He said, 'We had some good reports on you. How would you like to go out to the ballpark with me?' I said, 'Yes, sir.' I was always taught to say, 'Yes, sir.' That's the way I was brought up at home. On the way to the park Kiki Cuyler and I were talking. He said, 'You have a big opening here. If you have the ability to do anything, I'm sure our manager, Charlie Grimm, will give you a good shot at it. Because Charlie is kind of on his way out.' I said, 'I'm here, and I hope to do the best I can and make this ball club.'

"We went out to the ballpark, old Braves Field. In those days they were called the Boston Bees. I went with Kiki Cuyler to the clubhouse. He showed me where my locker was. I began to get undressed, ready to put my uniform on.

"In those days in Boston, the two clubhouses were right across from each other, and in the middle they had a stairway which led to the dugout. I'm sitting there, and all of a sudden I hear a voice that sounds like a big ole bear. The voice says, 'Where is Andy Lotshaw? I want to kill that son of a bitch Dutchman.' I look around, and who do I see, the big guy, Babe Ruth. To me, to this day, it was one of the biggest thrills I ever had in baseball. I looked around, and boy, Babe Ruth was talking. The Babe and the late Andy Lotshaw, our trainer, were very, very good friends, and they were always kidding, happy, and having a lot of fun.

"Babe was in his shorts, had a top piece on, with a big ole belly hanging out, but had a face that was a beautiful thing to look at. He was quite a guy.

"The next season Babe joined the Braves. Babe would put on exhibitions of hitting when the Braves were taking batting practice. When Babe came up, I would watch, really excited. Even at his age and the shape he was in, he would put on one of the greatest exhibitions of batting practice hitting I've ever seen in my life. He would hit them so *far* and so *high*. Babe had an uppercut swing, and it was just amazing to see this man. He must have been forty years old then. I remember so well, watching the Babe, who in those days made baseball. If it hadn't been for the Babe, salaries would have been terribly low.

"There was a photographer in the clubhouse from the *Boston Herald,* and he thought of the bright idea of taking a picture with an eighteen-year-old player coming up to the Cubs, and the Babe, who was on his way out. He came over and asked me, 'Do you mind if I take a picture of you and the Babe?' I said, 'I'd be happy to.' I still had my street clothes on and the Babe was in his street clothes, and in those days we had these great big old trunks with six compartments in there where we kept our equipment. So I sat on this trunk, and the Babe came over.

"'Hiya, kid. How are you?' I said, 'I'm feeling fine.' He said, 'Glad to see you. God, you look like just a little old high school kid to me.' I said, 'I'm only eighteen years old.' He said, '*What?*' His voice shook the room. 'Eighteen years old. You should be in high school.'

"This is the picture the photographer took."

Babe Ruth and Phil Cavarretta

40

Twenty-one in a Row

It didn't take very long for the Cubs to discover that the eighteen-year-old Cavarretta wasn't just an ordinary ballplayer. The next spring training they learned that this kid had intelligence and nerves of steel.

PHIL CAVARRETTA: "My first spring training, I traveled to Catalina Island. I checked into the St. Catherine Hotel, where the Cubs were training. I was just eighteen years old, didn't have any money in my pocket. We would get meal money, seven dollars and fifty cents a day.

"At night, six, seven of the guys would play poker. We bet a quarter and a half, three-raise maximum. This one night I got in the game. I had a couple bucks. Jack Doyle, who was our top scout, was in the game, and so was Gabby Hartnett, Augie Galan, and Billy Herman. I was sitting across from Mr. Doyle, and Gabby was between us. We got down to the last deal of the evening. It was twelve o'clock. We put in fifty cents, and I opened for a dollar. Mr. Doyle raised. It went around. Call. Call. Gabby raised. I raised. Three raises.

"'OK, how many cards you want, Phil?' I said, 'I'll stand pat. I don't want any cards.' They all looked at me. Jack used to call me Dago. He said, 'Hey, Dage, you don't want any cards?' 'No, sir.' I asked, 'How many cards you want?' 'Two.' They went down the line to Gabby. He said, 'Two.'

"Now it was my time to bet. I said, 'A dollar.' Mr. Doyle said, 'I know you have three of a kind, I think.' He raised me. It went around, and a couple of guys dropped out. It went to Gabby. He said, 'I raise you.' I said, 'I raise you both.' Now there's a pile of money in there. I was this little eighteen-year-old kid from Chicago, and all I saw was all this money. Gee.

"We had said that in the last game we could raise as many times as we wanted to. Mr. Doyle raised. Gabby raised. I raised them both. Mr. Doyle raised me. He had real sharp eyes, real BB eyes. He was staring at me. Then Gabby dropped out, even after all those raises. He figured I had a pat hand.

"Mr. Doyle raised me again. I asked him, 'How many cards did you take?' He said, 'None of your goddamn business.' I said, 'You have to tell me, Jack.' I was eighteen years old. He said, 'I took two cards.' He asked me, 'How many did you take?' I said, 'I'm pat. I raise you.' And Jack dropped out.

"First I raked in the pot, then I took my cards and messed them all up so they couldn't see what I had. Jack Doyle said, 'Son of a gun, you. What did you have?' I said, 'Well, it's in the middle there someplace.' He said, 'We gotta know.' I said, 'No, you don't. You could have called to find out.' And Gabby said, 'Philibuck, you gotta tell us.' I said, 'No I don't, Gabby.' Gabby said, 'Jack, what did you have?' Jack said, 'I had three kings.' Gabby said, 'Why the hell didn't you call him?' Doyle said, 'He was pat.'

"You know what I had? A pair of jacks. That's the truth. And someway or another, Jack Doyle found out I had a pair of jacks, and he was going to kill me. The next day he came up to me. He said, 'You had a pair of jacks? I could kill you, Dago.' I said, 'Well, I won.' He said, 'Young man, you're a young player. We got good reports on you. If you play baseball the way you play poker, you're going to be an all-star.' I said, 'Thank you, sir.'

"I happened to have a real good spring. I played almost every game, because Charlie (Grimm) wanted a good look at me. He was unable to play, and he was unsure about Don Hurst, who was at the end of his career, so I played in every ball game, hit the ball real good, fielded real good, and made a good impression on Charlie. Still, in the back of my head, because of my inexperience—I had only played in Class A—I felt the Cubs would leave me there with their Triple A club, the Los Angeles Angels. And I was willing to accept that, 'cause I knew I would get experience, and I wanted to play every day.

"In those days they would put up a list of the players cut and the ones who would stay on the club. After the last game we played in Los Angeles, I figured I would be left there. And so I was afraid to go up and look at the board. I finally went, and sure enough, my name was on the list of the team that was going north.

"I couldn't believe it! I said, 'My God, this is great.' And because I was in the major leagues, I got a raise. I was paid the major league minimum, $3,500 for the season. I got five hundred dollars the first and fifteenth of every month!

"I started the 1935 season with the Cubs, and I went on and played 146 games, hit .275, and to me, the 1935 club, in all the years I worked with the Cubs, that was the best team I ever played on. That was also the best infield I ever played with. We had one of the best infields in the league.

"Our '35 infield was young, and we were all hungry. Billy Jurges and Stan Hack, our shortstop and third baseman, came up in '33, and second baseman, Billy Herman, was only there a couple of years.

"Billy Herman and I roomed together for eight years. Billy helped me so much, giving me a rundown of pitchers, what to look for, and how to play hitters. Billy was one of the most intelligent infielders as far as positioning himself. In those days we'd have meetings how to play the hitters. The pitcher would say, 'I'll pitch him low and away,' and we had to know to move to the opposite field. Billy knew I was inexperienced, and he said to me, 'When we're out in the field, you watch me, and when I move, you come and move with me.' I would look at Billy, and if he would move toward second base, I'd move with him. That was great.

"He helped me so much learning how to play the game and how to position myself, what to look for when facing certain hitters. It made me a better ballplayer.

"Stan Hack at third was a happy-go-lucky man. He enjoyed life, enjoyed playing the game. Stan really was never given the credit he deserved. Stan was a great fielding third baseman. He could field bunts as good as anybody. He had a good arm, not a strong arm, but good enough for a third baseman, and very accurate. And he was a good hitter. He had 2,200 hits, a lifetime batting average of .301 for sixteen years. He was a good team player, never caused any trouble, and to me, with his stats and knowing Stan Hack, I can't understand why he isn't in the Hall of Fame.

"Billy Jurges was our shortstop. A great fielder. He thought he was a good hitter, but he really wasn't. When he was a player, Billy Jurges was a loner. When I first came up, he was a tough guy even though he was young. It seemed like he was always mad at something. And this was the way he played. He played hard. He played to win. And if you made a mistake, he would let you know about it. Instead of trying to explain it to you in a nice way, he would let you have both barrels. I was just a young kid. If I made an error, we'd go in the dugout and he would say, 'What in the world are you thinking about? You should be able to play better than that. You're in the big leagues. You don't do things like that in the big leagues.'

"One habit that I had—when I first came up, we didn't have a batting instructor, a fielding instructor, pitching instructors, we had to play with our ability itself, period. No one showed me or told me how to play first base. I had to do it on my own. And I had a habit on a low throw, I would field it with the glove down, which is the incorrect way of fielding a low throw. Nine out of ten times it was an error on me, and this is where Billy Jurges would really come after me. I mean, he would really chew me out. Finally, Charlie Grimm had enough of this arguing, and he called Billy Jurges and me into his office one afternoon.

"He said, 'Look, we have a good team here. We have to get along with each other. We're going to be together for five months. Let's try to get along.' He said to Jurges, 'Billy, this young man is trying to do everything possible to help us win a pennant, and I'm sure you are too. In making those errors, I'm going to take Phil out there this afternoon, and I'm going to show him how to field a low throw. But let's try to get along with each other.'

"Billy was still angry, to be honest with you. I made so many errors, a few times they gave Billy the error for a low throw. Charlie Grimm finally showed me how to field a low throw with an open glove.

"I'm sure you read about the incident at the Carliss Hotel in Chicago. A girl who had a thing for Billy shot him in his hotel room. He would never talk about it. I wouldn't tease him about it because, to be honest, he would be liable to pop me one.

"But Billy Herman would. They came up together and were very good friends, and they understood each other pretty well. Billy Herman would kid him about it.

Grimm, Herman, Jurges, and English

When this happened, this young lady shot Billy in the seat, so to speak. Billy would kid him about the two holes in his ass, and Jurges would get so upset he'd be ready to fight. Because Billy Jurges had a short fuse. He wasn't the easiest guy to be a friend of. He just would stay by himself, but later on, during the latter part of his career, he was traded to the New York Giants for Dick Bartell. When he was with the Giants, he became a pretty good guy. Instead of being enemies—he was on the Giants and I was on the Cubs—he'd come up and talk to me, and I thought, 'Geez, this is pretty good.' Later on he went with the Red Sox and managed there, and his personality absolutely changed, and to this day he's a great guy.

"That '35 team had one other young player who was important to the team, our center fielder, Augie Galan. Augie was the opposite of Billy Jurges or even myself, because once in a while my Eye-talian temper would get the best of me. Augie Galan was always happy. He was happy to play every game. In 1935 he played in 154 games and didn't hit into a double play, a record today.

"Augie Galan originally was a second baseman, but we had Billy Herman, so Charlie moved him out to center field, because we needed a center fielder, and Augie turned out to be one of the best fielding center fielders I've ever seen. He had a great arm, and he was a good little hitter. He was our leadoff man. Billy Herman was hitting second, and I'm not saying this just because they were my teammates, but as far as hit-and-run men are concerned, to me Augie Galan and Billy Herman were the best. Galan that year drew a lot of bases on balls and got over 200 hits. Billy Herman was a great hitter, could hit to all fields, and on the hit and run he had a knack of knowing who was covering, so they made some combination.

"Maybe the Cardinals had a better team. They had Dizzy and Paul Dean, Frankie Frisch, Pepper Martin, Joe Medwick, Leo Durocher. They won the pennant in '34, and then went to Detroit and had that big skirmish with Ducky Medwick, beat the Tigers in the Series. [Medwick had slid hard into Tigers third baseman Marv Owen, inciting the crowd to later throw things at him and force him to leave the game.] Their club, really, position for position, maybe they had a better ball club than we did, but as I said, we were young, and we were hungry. We wanted to win more than the Cardinals. They had won the year before, and they had the same club, and they figured, 'We're the Cardinals. We're going to beat you,' but it didn't wind up that way.

"We won the pennant because of our complete team, especially the regulars who played every day, and our pitching staff. They all did their job, and they did it right because the determination was there.

"The last trade Mr. Walker made, the one with the Pirates, was an outstanding trade, because Freddie Lindstrom came over. He played center field, and he also played third base for us, and we also got Larry French. He did an outstanding job, won 17 games.

"Let me tell you about our pitching staff. Start with Lon Warneke. To me, during the years I saw him pitch with the Cubs, and later on with the Cardinals, he was one of the best pitchers I've ever seen. With the Cubs, he'd win 18, 19, 20 games for you. The thing about Lon, when he started, you could bet he was going to complete the game for you. His best pitch was an overhand curve ball, an outstanding curve ball, and he threw his curve ball hard but he could also get a real big break on it. It would come up and look like a fastball and just as it got four or five feet to the hitter, you'd get a big down movement. He also had a good change and a good fastball. By good fastball, it's not the velocity so much as the movement of the ball. His fastball had good movement. It would rise, and he could make it sink. So to me, Lon Warneke was outstanding.

"In the clubhouse Lon was on the quiet side. They called him the Arkansas Humming Bird. He'd be by his locker, and he had a little ole ukelele, and he'd play that and hum and sing, which was fine. As long as he kept winning ball games, why complain?

"Bill Lee also was a quiet person, from Plaquemine, Louisiana, a good guy, a real nice guy. If you wanted to talk to him, you'd talk to him, otherwise he was quiet. He wasn't a loner like Jurges. He would associate with us, but he was quiet. They used to call him Handsome Bill. Bill was a good pitcher, but Lon was a little bit better 'cause Lon had a better variety of pitches than Bill. Bill had a good fastball, outstanding curve. His curve was his best pitch. He would throw you a curve ball three and two and throw it for a strike, and if you can do that with the good rotation, you're going to strike people out, and this was Bill Lee's strength. He would pitch you inside. His fastball wasn't that bad. He wasn't afraid of the hitters. He tried a change once in a while, but he was a fastball, curve ball pitcher with a good command of his pitches.

"Larry French, who we got from the Pirates before the '35 season, was the opposite of Bill and Lon. Larry was a good guy. He would talk to everybody. Again, I was just a young player, and he'd come up to me and kid me and invite me out to dinner. 'Let's go have a beer.' Larry was happy all the time. He was from California. He was a jokester. You'd sit in the lobby of the Commodore Hotel in New York—we did a lot of sitting—and what he would do, he and Lon Warneke, but mostly Larry French, he'd get a long string and he'd tie a five-dollar bill onto it. There were a lot of old people staying at this hotel. He would place the bill in the middle of the lobby, and he'd sit and wait. The people would reach for the five-dollar bill, and he'd pull on it a little bit. They'd try to pick it up, and he'd yank on it again. He would do crazy things like that to have fun.

"Again at the Commodore Hotel, Larry would get balloons, fill them full of water, and he would throw the balloons from the top floor all the way down. This thing would go off like a bomb. Scare the people. Finally the manager of the hotel had to come up, and he told them to stop it.

"And when we were sitting in the dugout, Larry was one of those guys who would give you the hotfoot. This was during the ball game. We'd always watch the pitcher to see what he was throwing, see what kind of stuff he had, so when we'd get up there, we'd have an idea of what he threw. You sat there, and Larry'd sneak up behind you, and always he had someone going along with him, and he'd put two matches in your shoe and light the match, and the next thing you know, boy, you had a hotfoot, and you'd scream and yell.

"After a while, we got upset because sometimes the match would go too long, and you'd get a blister from it. Charlie Grimm had to step in and stop the hotfoots.

"But Larry had such an outstanding personality. And he was a good pitcher, a better pitcher than a lot of people thought he was, because he didn't throw hard. He had a real good screwball, had a pretty good curve, but his best pitch was the screwball, which he threw to right-hand hitters.

"Larry had a lot of determination. He would never beat himself. You had to beat him. So many hitters went up and faced him and would say, 'Jesus, with that garbage you're throwing, how the hell can you get anybody out?' They'd say, 'I can hardly wait to go up and hit against you.' He'd come up and he'd get you out.

"Larry didn't get the credit he deserved because these hitters who would make these remarks would look at him—he didn't throw hard or have a Bill Lee curve ball. But he would get you out. He would win, so what more can you ask?

"I hadn't mentioned Charlie Root. *He* was a great pitcher. In 1935 he won 15 games for us. We used to call Charlie Root the Old Bear because he was built real strong. He was the type of pitcher you had to beat him. If you handled him pretty good, got too many hits off him, he would knock you down or hit you. Charlie Root wasn't given enough credit in 1935. It went to Bill Lee and Lon Warneke and French. But Charlie went out there and did his job, threw hard, had his curve, and he was a great help to our younger players on the pitching staff 'cause Charlie was in the league ten years by then, and he would help the younger pitchers, and during that twenty-one-game winning streak, he was a big help, not only as a pitcher, but as a coach to our younger pitchers."

For most of the 1935 season the Cubs held third place as the Cardinals battled the New York Giants for the pennant. And then the Cubs got hot. The half year of seasoning for the kids—Galan, Jurges, Hack, and Cavarretta—enabled everyone to jell. In September the team played an eighteen-game home stand and won every game. The team then went into St. Louis for a five-game showdown with the Cardinals. If the Cubs could beat Dizzy and Paul Dean, brothers who had won 49 games in 1934 and 47 in '35, the pennant would be theirs.

But beating the Cardinals would not be easy. The Gas House Gang was a powerhouse. Dizzy Dean was the best right-handed pitcher in the National League. Paul Dean, Diz's younger brother, was almost as good.

PHIL CAVARRETTA: "During that winning streak, one day I would get the hit to win a ball game, maybe the next day Chuck Klein would hit a home run, maybe the next day Lon Warneke would pitch a great game, and by the time we faced the Cardinals, it was, 'Hey, we can win this thing. We believe we can do it.'

"After winning eighteen in a row, we played the Cardinals. Lon Warneke was pitching for us against Paul Dean. Paul Dean gave us trouble throughout the whole season. He could beat the Cubs pretty good. Like his brother he threw a good, hard fastball. He had a better curve than Diz. And he had good control. This was in St. Louis. We had a five-game series. We needed two in a row for the pennant.

"It was 0–0 in the seventh inning. The year before I had hit a home run against Whitey Wistert, a rookie pitcher for Cincinnati. [It was one of only two career appearances by Wistert.] The score was 0–0, and I hit a home run, and we won the ball game 1–0.

"Exactly a year later, I hit a home run off Paul Dean to win a game 1–0. Paul threw me a fastball, and I hit it into the right-field seats in St. Louis, and we won 1–0. This gave us a tie for the pennant.

"The next day we went out and won our twentieth game in a row. Against Dizzy. Bill Lee pitched against Dean in that game. We got to Diz pretty quick. We handled

Diz pretty good. We hit him good, especially my old roommate, Billy Herman. Billy Herman hit Dizzy Dean, and Diz was tough. He was a Hall of Famer. But Billy Herman hit Diz unbelievable, 3 for 4, 4 for 4.

"Billy could call Diz's pitches. Like if his glove came over his head, it would be a curve ball, or if it went to the peak of his cap, it was a fastball. This is my thinking. I didn't know. But Billy knew, and until the day he passed away, he refused to tell me. He was my roommate. We played together for eight, nine years, and he would *never* tell anybody how he was getting his signs from Diz. Not even me.

"I said, 'Hey, we're teammates. We're trying to win a game.' He said, 'You never know. I may tell you, and maybe it will slip out, and you may tell someone from the Giants the delivery and what he's throwing, then he's going to tell someone else, and before I know it, I'm going to go 0 for 4 against Diz.' Which in a way makes sense. But Billy could have told his teammates. Cause we were fighting for the pennant, and in '34, '35, and '36 the Cardinals were really the team we had to worry about. But Billy would never tell us.

"Even after we both retired as players, I'd see Billy many a time. He lived in Palm Beach, and I used to visit him, and I'd bring it up. I'd say, 'Billy, we're all through as players. Tell your old roommate, would you please, how did you do it? What did Dizzy throw?' He would never tell me. He'd say, 'Here, have another drink.'

"After we beat Diz, we beat the Cards one more time to give us twenty-one in a row. When we lost the next day, the Cardinals had finally beaten us, but by then it didn't matter.

"So, in my first full year in the big leagues, at the age of nineteen, I got to play in the World Series."

41

Stan Hack Stands on Third

PHIL CAVARRETTA: "On the train to Detroit and in my hotel room the night before the Series in '35, I was nervous, scared to death. I was just nineteen, and I was in the World Series! This is what players dream of.

"The Tigers had an outstanding pitching staff. Schoolboy Rowe and Tommy Bridges were just great. Tommy Bridges had an outstanding curve ball. Like Bill Lee, he was strictly a curve ball pitcher, but he threw it a little harder, and he was a little faster than Bill. He had great control, and in the two games I faced him, I think I went 0 for 8 and struck out about five times.

"At bat the Tigers had three Hall of Famers, Hank Greenberg, Mickey Cochrane, and Charlie Gehringer. Hank Greenberg, a gentle man, a giant of a man, played first base. I watched Greenberg in batting practice, and he must have hit ten out of the park, and I thought, My God, what are we in for?

"Mickey Cochrane, their catcher, was a star, and at second Charlie Gehringer was another gentleman, a very, very quiet man who did his job, fielded his position, and to me was one of the best hitters I've ever seen.

"Those four people really impressed me, and to think I was in the World Series playing against them. At shortstop was Billy Rogell, feisty, tough. He was a mediocre hitter. He reminded me so much of our Billy Jurges. They were both feisty, average hitters. They thought they were good hitters, which is positive. They were the same type of guys.

"In the third game of the Series, Rogell almost started a fight with Jurges. Rogell slid into second base with spikes high. Billy covered, and he upset Billy pretty good. They started rolling around a little bit, the typical baseball fight. Right away they stopped it, but these are the things you remember.

"The Tigers beat us in six games, but it was a good Series. I remember real well the final game, in Detroit. Tommy Bridges started the game against Larry French, and we were tied 3–3 going into the ninth inning.

"Stan Hack led off the Cubs ninth with a triple. We figured if he could score, we'd win, and the seventh game would decide. The next two batters were Billy Jurges and the pitcher, Larry French.

"Now Charlie Grimm starts looking for a pinch hitter. But we don't have a pinch hitter because earlier in the game umpire George Moriority had cleared our bench, threw them all out of the game.

"Throughout the Series we had had trouble with Moriority, either on the bases or behind home plate. In the final game he was behind the plate, and we felt he was giving us bad calls on balls and strikes. As hitters, we felt when the pitch was a ball, he would call it a strike, and around the seventh inning the bench started getting to him. We were swearing at him pretty good. Moriority was tough, and he finally had enough of it, and he threw three or four of our bench jockeys out of the game. He told them, 'You're out of the game. Go up to the clubhouse.' Tuck Stainback was one of them. Woody English was another. These were the players we needed as pinch hitters in the ninth inning, and when Charlie needed them, the bench was in the clubhouse.

"Jurges batted. Bridges threw him three curve balls and he struck out. Then Larry French came up. We didn't have anybody to put in. He grounded out. When Augie Galan hit a long fly ball, it was one batter too late.

"In the Tigers ninth I was playing first base, holding on the runner, Mickey Cochrane. Charlie Gehringer hit a line drive almost right at me, but he hit it so hard I didn't have time to put up my glove. The natural instinct is to try to stop the ball, and not being very smart about it, I threw up my bare left hand, and I really thought I had broken it.

"I thought of throwing to second base to get the force, but my hand hurt so much I couldn't. I was afraid of throwing the ball into left field. I stepped on first base and Gehringer was out as Cochrane went to second base.

"The next batter, Goose Goslin, singled to right, kind of a blooper between Billy Herman and Chuck Klein. Back then we called it a Texas Leaguer.

"The ball dropped in. Chuck Klein got the ball, and I was the cutoff man for the throw home. While I was in my position waiting for the throw, I was peeking with my left eye to see where the runner was. I watched as Cochrane came around third, made his turn, and I could see he was going to score easily. He was halfway home before the ball even got to me, and as it got to me, he slid into home and scored the winning run. That was the game, and the Series.

"But the media didn't look at it that way. The media criticized me for cutting the ball off, not letting it go on through to home. But I saw the runner. He had already scored. Gabby Hartnett was the catcher. He was almost ready to walk away from home plate. They said, 'Cavarretta blundered the play.' I didn't say anything. In those days we accepted whatever they said. Not like today.

"We all felt bad because the players on the '35 club were close to each other. We were friends and buddies. The harmony on our club was very, very good. We would have our disagreements, skirmishes, off the field, but when it came to playing together on the field, as a unit we were out there to win ball games.

"I can still see Goslin's blooper falling in. Herman was a few feet away, and so was Klein, and so was Frank Demaree, our center fielder. We were so disappointed. We had played so well and had come so close to winning."

42

The Home Run in the Gloaming

PHIL CAVARRETTA: "In 1936 we had the same team, but Lon Warneke, who pitched outstanding in the '35 World Series, came up with a bad arm. It was just serious enough to take away some of the velocity from his fastball and take a little spin from his curve ball, and after winning 20 games for two years in a row, he was only able to win 16 games that season.

"In those days the brilliant medical people who are here today weren't with us. Today the medical people can work such miracles, especially with pitchers and their arms. Tommy John injured his rotator cuff, and if he had done that in our day, he would have been finished. In those days the medical people didn't know what to do. They would give you a cortisone shot—that will stay two or three days, and you go out and pitch. It was all they could do.

"The Giants had a great club, with Bill Terry, Mel Ott, and Carl Hubbell. We finished second to them two years in a row in 1936 and 1937. Their star was the great screwball pitcher Carl Hubbell. He didn't throw hard. You'd sit on the bench and look at his stuff and say, 'How in the world does he get me out?' You'd say, 'Give me my bat. I want to hit against him.' You go up there, and he gets you out. Carl Hubbell's screwball was the funniest pitch you'd ever want to see because there weren't too many pitchers who threw it. Our own Larry French was the other one. Being left-handed, he'd throw it, and as the ball was in flight, it would look like a fastball, not very fast, but you could see the rotation of the ball as it was coming to a left-handed batter like myself was the opposite of a fastball, going the opposite direction, and you'd watch it and watch it, and it would start on the outside part of the plate, and as it got to you, the ball would spin way inside on you. You would swing, and you'd either miss it or get jammed. You couldn't correct yourself to the pitch. Actually, left-hand hitters had better success against Carl Hubbell than right-handers. If a left-handed batter opened up, you could get a good piece of the ball, but the right-hand hitters, I don't know how they even made contact, because this ball would come up there and spin away from you on the outside part of the plate unbelievable, and as far as making contact, right-hand hitters had a tough time with him. Even Billy Herman had a tough time against Carl Hubbell. Billy was always looking for help. He'd talk to the batters around the league. Even with all the good information he received from other players, he still had a problem with Hubbell.

"In 1936 I hit .273, but I only drove in 56 runs, and in 1937, Charlie Grimm supposedly got sick, and Gabby Hartnett took over for him. I'll tell you really what happened there.

"What Charlie's problem was, I don't know. But he seemed to be losing his drive as far as the game was concerned. Because sometimes a person gets to a period in his life itself, going day in and day out to a job, and you get burnout. You say, 'I don't want anything to do with this anymore.' This is what I think happened to Charlie. Gabby Hartnett was our acting manager toward the end of the season. And Gabby made Rip Collins, who we had gotten from the Cardinals, the first baseman.

"I love Gabby, don't misunderstand me, he was a good guy. Being an intelligent Irishman, he would remember the .273 I hit in '36. So we got Rip Collins, and when you make a deal, you have to play the guy who comes to your club. Rip became our first baseman. I was sitting on the bench, playing the outfield once in a while. I played very little. I didn't say very much about it, didn't complain. I was a team player. If we win, fine. When I played, I did the best I could and tried to win a ball game. *But*, to anyone, especially to me, it's difficult to sit on the bench four or five days, go up and pinch-hit once or twice. Your timing is way off. Some players can do that. Dim Dom Dallessandro was one of them. Dominick didn't want to play every day. He loved to pinch-hit, and he could do it. I couldn't.

"In 1938, Charlie Grimm again started the season as manager. Rip Collins again began the season at first base. And I'm left out of left field again. But we were winning. I played a little outfield, played first once in a while, but again Charlie got so he couldn't manage, and this time he quit.

"Charlie wanted Billy Jurges to manage. And Charlie talked to Mr. Wrigley and the board of directors, he still wanted Jurges to come in and manage. And Billy turned it down. Billy told me that he felt he wasn't quite ready to manage. And so once again Gabby came in to be the manager.

"Gabby, may his soul rest in peace—I love Gabby as a person *and* a player—I fell in his doghouse for some reason or other. I didn't do anything to the man, but he put me there and just left me there. He figured I was not the guy to play regular. That was why I didn't play.

"And when Gabby took over the club in 1938, Gabby wanted to trade me to Cincinnati. I heard this through the grapevine. Gabe Paul was their general manager, and Bill McKechnie was the manager, and they liked the way I played. Gabby had meetings with Mr. Wrigley, and I don't know whether it was because I was born and raised in Chicago or whatever, but I was told Mr. Wrigley told Gabby, 'As long as

I am owner of this ball club, Phil Cavarretta stays on this team.' This is the story I heard. I *know* Gabby wanted to trade me to Cincinnati. This is a fact.

"And because Mr. Wrigley wouldn't let him trade me, I was given the opportunity to play on my second Cubs pennant winner.

"That was the year, too, that the Cubs acquired Dizzy Dean from the St. Louis Cardinals. Mr. Wrigley paid a fortune for Diz [a reported $185,000 and three players] even though we knew Diz's arm was shot.

"The players knew it when he was still pitching with the Cardinals in the fall of '37. 'Cause if you remember in the All-Star Game, Diz was pitching. [Cleveland outfielder Earl] Averill lined a bullet that hit Diz on the toe and fractured it. And the Cardinals manager Frankie Frisch—I had a lot of respect for Frankie Frisch, especially as a player, maybe not as a manager, but as a player—was a hard-nosed guy. They were fighting for the pennant with the Cubbies in '37. Diz fractured his toe, and I don't even think they put it in a cast. Frank said, 'No, he isn't going to miss one turn, because we're fighting for the pennant.' They taped it up and Diz went out and pitched. And this is how Diz hurt his arm. And we knew. When we faced him in the fall of '37, we couldn't believe it. 'Cause before he got hurt, this guy threw smoke at you. Never mind ninety miles an hour. This guy sometimes threw a hundred miles an hour, believe me.

"But after the All-Star Game, Diz was throwing up garbage. We didn't know *what* happened, and then we finally got the story that he pitched when he shouldn't have with the fractured toe, and Diz being such a great competitor, he said, 'Frank, give me the ball. I'll pitch for you.'

"His arm was shot in '37. We all knew it. But Mr. Wrigley decided to trade for Diz anyway. His advisers thought our doctors could help him with the sore arm problem. They also felt with his knowledge and his moxie, he could still win a few

Dizzy Dean

games for us. Then again, they looked at it another way: When ole Diz pitched for the Cubs, and the Cardinals came into Wrigley Field, the place would be full, and this was where they were going to get their money back. And they were right about that.

"Diz was a fighter, believe me. And what a lot of people didn't know, when ole Diz came over, Andy Lotshaw, our trainer, came up with some kind of salve, real hard stuff mixed up with something else, and he would rub this on Diz's arm before he would pitch. He would plaster it unbelievable and rub it and rub it into the back of his shoulder. By that time his arm was almost numb.

"One time I went into the trainer's room, and Andy was working on Diz. Diz was sitting there after this rubdown stuff was on his arm. I looked at Diz, and his arm was as red as a lobster. It was unbelievable. I said, 'Diz, what's the problem?' He used to call everybody Pardner. He said, 'My pardner Andy is taking care of me. He's kind of deadening my arm.' Like I said, his arm was as red as a lobster.

"And he'd go out and pitch. You talk about determination. 'I want to beat you any way I can.' This was Diz pitching.

"Diz couldn't throw hard. We said, 'He'll just dazzle you with his motion.' Once in a while he could zip one in there. But his control was so good, the command of his pitches outstanding, even though he couldn't throw hard. He actually came up with a little bit better curve ball, because with his fastball he hadn't needed a curve ball, but after his injury he would throw that curve at you, then sneak in a fastball and throw one slow and another one slower. But the key with Diz in the seven games he won for us in '38 was the command of his pitches and what we call intestinal fortitude.

"And whenever he pitched, the park was full.

"In 1938 the Pittsburgh Pirates were in first place almost throughout the whole season. The Pirates had a great club, with the Waner boys, Paul and Lloyd, and Gus Suhr at first. Pie Traynor, their manager, had been an outstanding third baseman, a Hall of Famer. Pie was a great hitter, a great fielder, very intelligent, like my roomie Herman. He'd move around just about on every pitch positioning himself. And nine out of ten times he would be right.

"Pittsburgh had good starting pitching, and Mace Brown was their ace relief pitcher.

"On September 27 the Pirates came into Wrigley Field for the series that would decide the pennant. They were leading us by a game and a half. Dizzy started the first game. His arm was hurting him badly, and he hadn't pitched in a week to ten days.

"The thing I remember best watching this man pitch, his presence on that mound encouraged us to go out there and play hard. Watching him pitch was an inspiration. You could see the man was suffering out there, and here we all were healthy, strong, and young. You'd say, 'My God, let's go out and win it for Diz.'

"That day Diz held the Pirates scoreless all the way until the ninth inning, when he gave up a couple of hits. Bill Lee came in and got the last man out, and we won 2–1. It was an incredible performance.

"The next day, Gabby hit one of the most famous home runs in the history of baseball. It was the home run in the gloaming, so to speak. It brought us the pennant.

"Wrigley Field didn't have lights, and it was getting dark. It was fall, the days were getting shorter, and it was an extra-long game. There had been a lot of hitting, a lot of bases on balls. It was one of those two-and-a-half-, three-hour games. I remember so well how tough it was to hit up there. The batter and the pitcher and almost all the infield were in the shade. But in the bleachers the sun was still out.

"Mr. Wrigley had built the center-field bleachers the year before, and if I may, that was one of the toughest backgrounds to try to hit against. The fans wore white shirts out there. You had a white ball and white shirts as a background, and because you were in the shade in the batter's box, it was almost impossible to see that ball until it was right on top of you.

"That day I played center field. I went 0 for 4 or 5. What I remember best, the umpires really wanted to call the ball game in the eighth inning because it was getting really tough to hit up there.

"But it was such an important game, two clubs battling for the pennant, home plate umpire Jocko Conlan said, 'OK, we'll go nine, and that's it.'

"The score was tied in the ninth. I was the first batter. I faced Mace Brown. I flied out to center field. And the next batter made out.

"It was tough to see out there. Really, to this day, I don't know how Gabby did it. It was twilight. Mace threw very hard, and he had a real good slider. In those years Mace Brown was one of the best relief pitchers in baseball. This guy was so good for an inning or two.

"Two men were out, and Gabby came up, and I figured, Well, we'll have to play a doubleheader tomorrow. I was sitting in the dugout. I had been the first hitter, and I could hardly see the ball, and they had a pitcher who was throwing BBs.

Gabby Hartnett

"The first pitch, Mace threw Gabby a slider, and Gabby swung and missed. I figured, Oh well, two more and that's the game. And the next pitch he threw a fastball, a waste pitch for a ball. Why he wasted it, I don't know. I could hardly see the ball.

"Mace's best pitch was a fastball. The ball was live and moved. He didn't have too much of a curve, so instead of a curve he would throw a slider. Al Todd was the catcher. He was the one who called for the pitch. The next pitch, for some reason or another, was a slider. If Mace had thrown a fastball, he would have struck him out, believe me. Gabby couldn't have seen it from the velocity. With the slider, it was a little slower. Todd called for a slider—and why he called for it I don't know—and Mace threw a slider.

"The ball was up, and Gabby was a good high-ball hitter, believe me. I don't know whether the pitch got away from Mace or not. Gabby hit the ball, a line drive. It didn't look like it was going to get into the bleachers. It looked like it was going to hit the bottom of the bleachers, two bases. We figured it would hit the brick wall out there and come back. But some way or another—I don't know whether it hit an air pocket or the good Lord said, 'Move up a little bit'—but the ball went into the first row of the bleachers, just made it, went right into the first row, home run!

"We were sitting there, thinking it was a two-base hit 'cause the ball hit, went in, and bounced back. The umpire at third ran out there, and he made the right call. It *did* go into the bleachers. There was a full house at Wrigley Field, and everybody was running out onto the field. From the dugout we still didn't know what the hell was coming off. Finally, it came to us. Gabby had hit a home run! We won the game! The fans were yelling, and then we knew it was a home run.

"Pat Peiper, may his soul rest in peace, he was our public address man, and over the loudspeaker he yelled, 'Home run! Home run!' I thought, Oh boy, a home run!

"We won the ball game and went into first place. Till this day I don't know how the ball got up there. Somebody must have boosted it.

"And to this day I feel that home run in the gloaming demoralized those Pittsburgh players so badly. We had two more games to play against them, and we swept the series. They came out and played, but they weren't the Pirates team we saw earlier. From that one home run.

"Al Todd came over to the Cubs later on [in 1940]. I wasn't going to ask him, 'Why did you call for a slider,' 'cause he was a big, strong guy.

"But I'm glad he did."

43

Diz's Last Stand

PHIL CAVARRETTA: "We played the New York Yankees in the '38 World Series. They wiped us out four in a row. They swept us. They were a great ball club. They had Joe DiMaggio, Lou Gehrig, Bill Dickey, Frank Crosetti, Joe Gordon.

"The closest we got to beating them was in the second game. This was in Wrigley Field. Diz was pitching, and he was really goosing them up there. But he was getting them out! His ball was hardly getting up there, but those heavy hitters were swinging and throwing up a lot of air.

"I was playing center field. After every pitch I could see the man flinching his arm. I could see, boy, he was hurting. He was pitching against DiMaggio and Dickey, and Gehrig, those heavy hitters, and he was getting those people out!

"It was 3–2 Cubs in the eighth with two outs and a runner on first and who comes up, Frank Crosetti, who couldn't hit a lick. But Crosetti hit a two-run home run into the left-field seats off Diz, who was just about wiped out by then.

Diz shouted at Crosetti, 'You'da never done that if I'da had my fastball.' Crosetti yelled back, 'I know, Diz.'

"I remember Joe DiMaggio trying to hit off Diz in that game. Joe was a great hitter, and here was Diz, throwing up all this slow stuff, and it was frustrating to Joe, and a couple times he flied out weakly to the outfield, and he'd kick the dirt. He wouldn't cuss, but he'd give it that kick, and to see him trying to hit against Diz, it was almost kind of funny. Then in the ninth inning Joe hit a two-run home run off Diz into the left-field stands.

"The thing I'm trying to get to: What courage this man had to pitch in the World Series under those conditions. It was one of the finest exhibitions of pitching I've ever seen, believe me, and I've seen a lot of good games.

"We went up to the clubhouse after the game. We just didn't get any runs, and it was sad, really, because we were getting our brains beat out. We felt bad because we knew our ball club was better than we showed. We knew we could have done better. I'm sure all the players felt that way. Diz pitched such a great game, and to see him out there with all that heart, and then get beat. . . . The clubhouse was pretty quiet.

"I went to Diz by his locker, wrapped my arms around him, and told him, 'Pitched a great game, Diz. Sorry we couldn't help you out.' Diz was very quiet, and he nodded. Usually you could say, 'We'll get 'em next time,' but this was the World Series. It was a little different.

"The final game I was playing right field, and Red Ruffing was pitching against us. I wasn't playing every day, I'd just fill in, but this day I was playing, and the Yankees were beating us again. I hit a shot down the right-field corner, got a two-base hit.

"I had always been a Lou Gehrig fan because when I was a kid, the top high school team from Chicago would play the top school team in New York, and when I was in grade school Lou Gehrig was on this team and he played in Wrigley Field, and he hit a home run. From that day on, I was a fan of Lou Gehrig.

"So I was on first base. Lou was holding me on. Lou was very quiet. Looking back, I could tell from his voice he was starting to get sick then, as young as he was. His voice was very weak. It wasn't a good strong voice.

"He said, 'Young man, you've only been in a couple games, but I've watched you play. From what I've seen of you, the way you hustle and the way you give it your best'—this I'll always remember—'don't change.'

"For Lou Gehrig to say this to a young player filling in . . . coming from this man, a Hall of Famer, a power hitter . . . the words attached to it when he said it . . . it was unbelievable. Just unbe-*liev*-able.

"The next year Lou had to retire, and not long after that he was dead [in June 1941]. I still feel sad when I think of him.

"Riding back to Chicago on the train we were all down. The Cubs had played hard, really. We had played to the best of our ability, but we had faced a team that was so strong, they would have beaten anybody four in a row.

"If you say, 'We didn't get any breaks,' everyone says, 'You're alibiing.' But in that Series we didn't get too many breaks. Maybe we could have won a couple games if we had gotten the breaks. And this is not an alibi.

"The players had their own compartments in their own Pullman car, and in those days you could play poker, not big stakes, a quarter and a half, three raises, and that was it, and so during the ride home we were playing poker, having some refreshments along with it. In the game were Augie Galan, Billy Herman, Diz, and I.

"Gabby Hartnett was our manager. He had his own compartment, and he was enjoying his own refreshments, let me put it that way. Gabby came into our compartment. I figured he would say a few words, try to build our spirits, but I was wrong. He was very upset. He came in there steaming.

"Gabby shouted, 'Look at yourselves. You call yourselves ballplayers?' We didn't know what to do. He said, 'You guys were terrible. To let those people beat you four in a row.' I was still a young player. I couldn't get up and say anything. And he was still the manager. You have to respect him. And in a way he was right, but still, you can't come out and use the language that he did. It upset us more because we were still upset from the defeat we had just received. And I'll never forget the last thing he said. Quote: 'A lot of you people here will not be on this ball club next year. I'm going to try to make some deals, get rid of some of you people. A lot of you are *not* going to be here next year.' And he walked away.

"We had all the respect in the world for Gabby as a person, as a player, and as a manager, but this bawling out was tough to take.

"And Gabby did make some deals. He got rid of Billy Jurges. Got rid of Frank Demaree. Got rid of [catcher] Ken O'Dea. How could he justify getting rid of a Billy Jurges?

"We all talked about it in spring training. Billy Jurges would go out, play hard, go through a brick wall for you. And a guy named Cavarretta would do the same thing for you. And Ken O'Dea, a second-string catcher, he was the same way.

"Why trade a Billy Jurges? We couldn't understand it, really."

44

The Crazy World of PK Wrigley

Philip Knight Wrigley had been highly successful at selling chewing gum since he took over the William Wrigley company in 1925. That year sales were $23 million. By 1971 sales had soared to $190 million, thanks largely to his stewardship. In the world of chewing gum, the innovative, brilliant PK Wrigley was Branch Rickey or

Ed Barrow. If his chewing-gum company had been a baseball team, it would have been the New York Yankees, if not his father's powerful Chicago Cubs.

A large part of PK Wrigley's success was in convincing people that chewing the sugarcoated chicle was not only fun but good for one's disposition. He disseminated that information widely by following his father's policy of spending millions of dollars, a full quarter of the company's revenues, on advertising, first in magazines and then on radio. No company in America spent more money on pushing its slogans and jingles.

"Enjoy delicious cool-tasting Wrigley's Spearmint gum right while you work . . . every day."

The national advertising was pervasive, and by the 1920s the Wrigley Company had captured 60 percent of the gum business.

When World War II broke out in 1941, PK Wrigley spent much effort campaigning to have chewing gum declared a war necessity. Ads stressed that gum "keeps your mouth moist—helps relieve monotony and nervous tension" during work.

In a letter Wrigley wrote a customer, "That chewing gum is not an unessential is proven by the fact that the demand for it increases by leaps and bounds under any conditions of stress. We have known of the benefits of gum for years. . . ."

In 1939, Wrigley commissioned a study by Professor H. L. Hollingworth of Columbia University, who wrote a monograph, *Psycho-Dynamics of Chewing*. This was proof, Wrigley said, that chewing gum lowers "muscular tension." For years, he conducted studies in the Wrigley Building to prove that gum chewing lowered nervous tension.

According to an article in *Fortune* magazine, "Researchers sit with metal tubes clamped to their salivary or parotid glands, located in the cheek next to the molars.

PK Wrigley

They solemnly record the drip of the saliva from the tubes into beakers. Then they chew gum and record again."

Concluded the study, "Almost invariably, they have discovered, the rate of drip goes up 100 to 200 per cent."

With a straight face, the unnamed author of the article commented, "How long the parotid glands can go on manufacturing saliva, if their owner drinks no water, is a question they haven't tried to answer."

Always, for PK Wrigley, gum's strongest selling point was its utility. He told the *Fortune* reporter that chewing gum could "relieve nervous tension, thirst, monotony." In the mouths of essential workers, he suggested, it might contribute to higher war production. To stress this point, Wrigley made a fifteen-minute video in which an actor playing Adolf Hitler contends that he has friends slowing down production in every factory in America. Cut to three women tempting the workers to slow down. Says the narrator, "Monotony . . . fatigue . . . false thirst . . . nervous tension. Yes—these are the agents of the Axis."

The president of a company then asks his foreman why one production line is doing better than the others. The answer: gum chewing.

Booms the president, "Make gum chewing available to every person who is employed in the plant." The curtain drops.

If you didn't buy that argument, PK Wrigley had others he promoted just as strongly. In plants where smoking was prohibited, he proclaimed that chewing gum would relieve the craving to smoke, "thus eliminating many trips to the rest room for cigarettes."

And for those who didn't buy that one, Wrigley argued that an employer should stock chewing gum because it induced among employees "a more harmonious attitude."

Wrigley concluded, "To help your workers feel better, and work better, just see that they get five sticks of chewing gum every day." (Dentists all over America gleefully rubbed their hands together at that advice.)

With Wrigley's millions spreading the word through advertising, during the war it became almost unpatriotic *not* to chew Wrigley's Spearmint gum. Demand for gum soared.

Not only was gum declared essential to the war effort, but PK Wrigley eventually got his gum included in the army K rations, the packets of ready-to-eat food sent overseas to the fighting men. He set up a rations-packing plant in his factory in Chicago and packed a large percentage of the K rations sent overseas.

Usually when faced with a problem related to the gum company, PK Wrigley found a solution. His marketing and advertising people informed him that "Wrigley" and "Spearmint" could not be translated into certain foreign languages. His decision: Package the gum with the Wrigley arrow—the trademark—without any name on it at all.

"Then just sit back and see what the people call it," he advised. In Hong Kong it became Rider of the Arrow gum, and in some Middle Eastern countries it became White Arrow gum.

One of Wrigley's pet projects was to make a gum that didn't stick to false teeth. When he couldn't do that, he sought to invent false teeth that wouldn't stick to his gum.

After the war, when it seemed gum production would have to be cut severely because of the lack of transportation of chicle gum base from Central America, Malaya, and Borneo, PK Wrigley found a substitute in Brazil.

As brilliant as he was selling chewing gum, it was a different story when it came to his baseball team. For one, he was not running it out of passion for the team or love of the sport. He ran it because he had promised his late father he would not sell it, in order to keep the team from being moved from Chicago. He also ran it because he was wedded to tradition. After all, the team played its home games at Wrigley Field, a ballpark built by his father, whom he adored.

And so, when PK Wrigley took over control of the Cubs after his father's death in January 1932, PK Wrigley made it clear that his first priority in running the Cubs was to make his father's ballpark a monument, and he set about refurbishing it and making it the most beautiful ballpark in America.

The reason he did this, he told Bill Veeck, the son of the Cubs' late general manager, was that "a team that isn't winning a pennant has to sell something in addition to its won-and-lost record to fill in those low points on the attendance chart."

Wrigley told another assistant, Charles Drake, the same thing. During a conversation, Drake mentioned to Wrigley that "the public had been conditioned to demand a winning team." According to Drake, Wrigley replied he wanted to shift the emphasis.

"The fun, the game, the sunshine, the relaxation. Our idea is to get the public to go to see a ball game, win or lose."

His father, William Wrigley, never would have conjured a strategy built around the anticipation of a losing team. But Phil Wrigley did just that, and his direction became prophecy. As much as any other factor, Phil Wrigley's idea of fun and sun as a substitute for a winning team shaped the relationship between the Cubs and their fans over the next fifty years. For his grand promotion, the beautifying of the ballpark, Phil Wrigley enlisted the aid of Bill Veeck, who had begun working for the Cubs in 1933 as an office boy for $18 a week.

BILL VEECK: "His solution was to sell 'Beautiful Wrigley Field'; that is, to make the park itself so great an attraction that it would be thought of as a place to take the whole family for a delightful day. It was not accident that the title of the [Cubs] magazine I edited for him was called *Fan and Family.*

"We sold 'Beautiful Wrigley Field.' We advertised 'Beautiful Wrigley Field.' The announcers were instructed to use the phrase 'Beautiful Wrigley Field' as often as possible.

"'Beautiful Wrigley Field' was a marvelous promotion based on a completely valid premise. The trouble was that I could never get its creator to take the next logical step; to give the customers what they really set out for the ball park hoping to find—entertainment and excitement."

The reason lay in the nature of Phil Wrigley. He was a man who was fascinated by *things*—cars, boats, horses, and horticulture were just some of his interests. People, they didn't interest him, and in a large group, they scared him.

BILL VEECK: "Phil Wrigley has one overriding flaw. He knows more about things and less about people than any man I have ever met. In the eight years I worked for him, he almost never had a visit from a personal friend. He has few personal friends. Business associates, yes; friends, I don't know."

He *was* a man without friends. Said Wrigley about himself, "If I were absolutely honest, I probably would say I have no really close friends." When he and his wife, Helen, married, he could think of only one person he wished to invite, Gus Suttergren, a childhood playmate who had become his chauffeur and later would be an assistant traveling secretary.

In Phoenix, Wrigley built a huge mansion on the top of a butte. The house had many rooms but no guest bedroom. "There is no need for anyone to stay overnight," he would say.

A baseball owner is a public figure, like it or not, and PK Wrigley didn't like it at all. He valued his privacy, and he rarely went to the ballpark. Like Howard Hughes, PK hated to be recognized and shunned having his picture taken. During the 1945 World Series he was conspicuously absent, and later he would brag that he was the first owner ever to go through an entire World Series without being photographed.

In his whole life he admitted to making two speeches. In the first, he said, "Thank you." In the second, he said, "Thank you very much."

Wrigley once told a reporter, "My ambition is to go hide in a cave somewhere with no telephone and a big rock over the door."

And so when Phil Wrigley took over the Cubs, he neglected the people side of the business while concentrating on what interested him the most, the inanimate, physical plant, Wrigley Field.

When it came to improving and beautifying Wrigley Field—honoring his dad by doing so—PK Wrigley held open a bottomless pocketbook. During the building of the center-field bleachers in 1937, Wrigley decided he wanted a "woodsy" motif. Bill Veeck suggested copying the ivy of Perry Field in Indianapolis and planting trees in the back of the bleachers. Veeck had meant planting the trees *outside* the park, but Wrigley decided he liked the idea and wanted the trees planted *inside* the stadium. Wrigley told Veeck he didn't want to have to wait ten years for them to grow.

Veeck had carpenters build tree boxes into the bleachers. To hold the weight, concrete footings and steel supports had to be built at a cost of $200,000. After that was done and the Chinese elms were planted, Veeck soon discovered that the wind blowing off Lake Michigan was so strong, it blew all the leaves off the newly planted trees. Wrigley, who didn't give up easily when he backed a project, had Veeck pull out all the trees and plant new ones. Again and again, Veeck would plant the leafy trees and the wind would blow off all the leaves.

Said Veeck, "We could have turned the Grand Canyon into a forest with all the trees we planted, since it took about ten sets of trees before Mr. Wrigley began to spot a trend."

Wrigley finally had to give up on having Chinese elm trees inside the park. The footings remain, however, and today knowledgeable bleacherites spread blankets down on those areas and relax, even on days when the park is full.

As for the ivy, Veeck had intended to plant it after the season and have it ready for the spring. During a long road trip, the last one of that year, Wrigley informed Veeck that he was inviting some people to the park for the final home stand in order to show off his newly planted ivy.

"Holy smokes," Veeck said. "I haven't even ordered it yet, let alone planted it. But I'll see what I can do."

He had a crew working all through the night planting bittersweet, which was hardy, looked like ivy, and wouldn't die.

Said Veeck, "When the morning sun broke over the grandstand roof, it shoné upon a bleacher wall entirely covered with bittersweet. We had planted the ivy in between and, in time, the ivy took over."

When PK Wrigley was done with his three-month renovation project, Wrigley Field indeed was the most beautiful ballpark in the country in which to spend an afternoon and watch a ball game. It was outdoorsy but intimate. Every seat was close to the field. The ivy gave a touch of class, as did the center-field scoreboard with its boating motif and fluttering yacht flags. Beautiful Wrigley Field. What fan wouldn't want to come to the Cubs ballpark, win or lose?

But very soon after coming to work for PK Wrigley after his own father's death in December 1933, Bill Veeck saw that Phil Wrigley's interest in the Cubs was out of familial duty more than anything else.

When William Wrigley bought the Cubs, he boasted of his intentions to make his team a winner. When Phil Wrigley took over the team from his father, he made it clear what he *wouldn't* do in order to make his team a winner: No money from the gum company would ever be spent on the team, he vowed.

PHIL WRIGLEY: "There are a great many stockholders in the Wrigley Gum Company who would be the first to complain if any of their money was used in baseball. So none of it ever has been used for that purpose, or ever will.

"We aim to have the Cubs pay their own way, as if they were my only interest. In this the Cubs are no different from any other major-league club whose owners have no outside interests."

What PK Wrigley *didn't say* was that he also had no intention of risking much of his own money on the team. He had plenty of money to do so even during the depression, and at the time of his death in 1977 he was making $50,000 *a week* in dividends from his stocks. But at no time during his stewardship did he ever spend the kind of money on baseball talent, either well or wisely, to make the team a contender, never mind a winner.

Baseball has had a dirty little secret ever since its inception: A percentage of team owners don't *care* whether the team wins. They are only interested in making money. Phil Wrigley cared only that the team didn't *lose* money.

PK Wrigley—unlike his father, who loved the game and his Cubs—for forty years was one of those owners who really didn't care whether the Cubs won or not. Much later, after being lambasted in the press year after year, Wrigley would huff and puff mightily about how hard he had tried and would boast about all the steps— all futile—he had taken to put a winning team on the field.

Had he cared, *really* cared, about winning, he could have spent his money to buy ballplayers. Had he cared to win without making large expenditures, he could have built a low-cost farm system, hired a team of talented scouts, and built his team over time. (By 1940, Branch Rickey of the Cardinals had a farm system that included thirty-two Cardinal-owned minor league teams, plus working agreements with eight other teams. The Cubs, in comparison, didn't own any minor league teams.)

Sure, Phil Wrigley hired a scouting director and paid a handful of scouts, and every once in a while the Cubs would find a player. But Phil Wrigley, who was a hermit by nature and shunned personal interaction, never hired the top people to get the job done. The reason: Phil Wrigley was a terrible judge of men in the business of baseball, in which outsiders like Wrigley can't succeed unless they pick their executives wisely.

PK Wrigley, moreover, was not the sort of man to give up control to others without retaining the right to say yea or nay. In his official biography, *PK Wrigley: A Memoir of a Modest Man*, by Paul Angle, Wrigley asserted he had approved every trade since 1932. He said, "When a question of a trade comes up, I talk to them about it. I listen to what they say, and if I can see they are unduly influenced by something that I don't think should be in the picture, I will say 'no, that trade is off.' That happens very seldom."

That might have worked well had he picked competent decision makers, but Philip Wrigley also was not the type of man to hire a strong-willed baseball brain to make his team a winner. He could not have worked with a Branch Rickey or a Larry MacPhail. They would have overwhelmed him because Wrigley would have had to do what *they* wanted rather than continue to make all the decisions himself. And all along, PK Wrigley made it clear that no one was going to make the decisions but him, no matter how arbitrary or wrong he might have been.

WOODY ENGLISH: "Phil Wrigley was a different man altogether from his father. His interests was in planes and boats and motors and things like that. He wasn't really into baseball like his dad. He was the type of person, if I said the sun was shining, he'd say it was cloudy.

"I remember one year he wanted to put in a sound system on Catalina Island so he could play Hawaiian music out over the bay there. One time after practice I was down by the water, and he said, 'Come on, Woody, get on the boat with me. We'll go out and see how that music sounds.' So I went out there, and it sounded pretty darn good to me. He said, 'How does that sound to you?' I said, 'Real good.'

"He said, 'It ain't worth a damn.'

"You know, when Charlie Grimm was the manager, I was his captain. Charlie would go up to the office and meet with him. Charlie told me, 'Whatever we used to say up in the meetings, he'd always say, 'No, that ain't right, let's do it this way.'

"Charlie said, 'And no matter what Mr. Wrigley says, after he goes up and leaves the room, everyone who's in that meeting will say, 'Can you imagine him saying that? He's absolutely wrong about everything.'"

If Phil Wrigley was going to make all the decisions and wasn't going to listen to advice—even from a man as knowledgeable about baseball as Charlie Grimm— then the best way for Wrigley to cut down on any interpersonal angst between him and his baseball head was to choose men who were quiet, even diffident, and then thwart them at every turn by not allowing them to make a decision.

The problem with hiring competent, knowledgeable people was that they tended to become frustrated after a few years and quit.

William Walker wasn't the type of person to stomach watching Wrigley wreck his team, and so he quit in anger. Wrigley then brought in Boots Weber to be the general manager. Weber had been hired by William Veeck to run the Los Angeles Angels, the Cubs Triple A team. He spoke in a whisper and was claustrophobic, which kept him from traveling with the team. Boots wasn't a great baseball mind, but he wasn't a hack, either. Unfortunately, Boots, like his assistant, Bill Veeck, constantly was thwarted by Philip Wrigley.

Phil Wrigley could have rebuilt the Cubs using several different methods. He could have bought players from other teams, the way his father did. In the beginning, when William Walker was pushing him, he purchased Babe Herman, Chuck Klein, and Dizzy Dean, though to less than rave reviews. Wrigley, who was excessively sensitive when it came to criticism, came to view this method of procuring players as both expensive and inefficient.

He could have built a farm system, the way the Cardinals and the New York Yankees did. But once Wrigley accepted the idea of buying farm teams, this strange man held the notion that it was important for each team to be monetarily successful. As a result, when his Triple A teams in Los Angeles and Milwaukee came up with a talented player, he insisted that player be offered to *all* teams, not just sold to the Cubs. Wrigley was thus using his farm system to provide *other* teams with the talent he was developing.

Pitcher Whitlow Wyatt, for example, showed promise with the Cubs' Milwaukee franchise. He did not become a Cub. Branch Rickey and the Dodgers offered to pay more than Wrigley and his advisers were willing to spend, so the Dodgers, not the Cubs, got Wyatt. Wyatt's league-leading 22 wins helped the Dodgers to the 1941 pennant.

Wrigley could have spent money hiring and training scouts to stock the team with young, talented players, but to do so required him to hire a talented farm director. He didn't do that.

And because he didn't know baseball and refused to take the advice of others, he made arbitrary decisions that often didn't seem to make any sense.

With Philip Wrigley cutting off all avenues of improvement, the team's destiny was assured. He wouldn't spend money, wouldn't build a farm system, wouldn't listen to his baseball people. The Cubs would continue to remain competitive only so long as the players inherited from William Wrigley and William Veeck stayed healthy and didn't age and retire or if they weren't traded away foolishly. Both circumstances occurred.

Also harmful were PK Wrigley's quirky ideas. What the Cubs desperately needed was an influx of new, young players, but rather than take the steps to ensure that, PK Wrigley determined that the key to winning was not the hiring of scouts to bring the team talent but the hiring of Coleman Griffith, the director of the Bureau of Institutional Research, to study the reflexes of his players in order to determine their skills.

PHIL WRIGLEY: "We figured if we could measure the physical characteristics and reflexes of an established ballplayer, we could test prospects and know what to look for. If you want to make the best knives in the world, you buy the finest steel. You can go out and spend $250,000 for a ballplayer, and he may not be able to cut butter. But if you know what makes a player who does come through in the major leagues, you have something. It's surprising how many ballplayers can play Triple A ball, but still not make it to the majors."

It was not unlike Wrigley's studies of workers to see if chewing gum could make them more productive. But Wrigley was dealing with ballplayers, not factory workers. The Cubs players saw Wrigley's scheme as harebrained, and they refused to cooperate. When the Chicago press found out about it, Wrigley became a laughingstock, and Coleman Griffith disappeared as fast as he had come.

The whole time Phil Wrigley owned the Cubs, his crazy schemes continued as substitutes for hiring scouting, building a farm system, and installing a talented manager.

His most outrageous innovation, which may have reflected his panic over not knowing what to do or may just have been a reflection of his oddball personality, was the squandering of $20,000 to hire a man whose job it was to travel with the team and put a hex on the opposing players. Wrigley, who became known for paying low salaries, hated to spend $10,000 for a player's yearly salary, but apparently he had been listening to professional wrestling on the radio or had gone to one of the matches and had seen one of the wrestlers' managers "hexing" the opposition. Wrigley, who was not knowledgeable about sports, must not have known the true nature of professional wrestling, for he went out and hired a man who duped him into thinking he could do the same thing to the Cubs' opposition. Bill Veeck, who had little regard for Wrigley's twisted thinking when it came to baseball, ruefully recalled the day Phil Wrigley approached him with his hex idea.

BILL VEECK: "One afternoon, I was called to Mr. Wrigley's office. It's a big office with a big desk in front of a big window. Seated in one of the easy chairs alongside the desk was a ferret-faced, wizened little guy in a checkered suit. He was puffing on a cigar in that self-pleased, self-important way that only a cigar can bring out.

"You could see that Mr. Wrigley was pleased with himself, too. 'He's going to help us,' he told me. 'He's going to give us a psychological advantage.'

"From the look of this little bum, I'm thinking that the only psychological advantage he could give us would be to sneak into the visitors' locker room before every game and steal the spikes off their shoes—an assignment for which he seemed eminently suited.

"Almost as if he had read my mind, he jumped out of the chair, fixed me with an awesome and terrible glare and began to circle around me, making cobralike passes at me like Bela Lugosi.

"While I was watching this dance, fascinated beyond belief, Mr. Wrigley was comparing his discovery to a wrestling manager who was supposed to be able to put a whammy on his boy's opponents, a wonderful publicity gag that was getting a big play in the Chicago papers.

"Holy smokes, I thought, suddenly getting it. Old Phil has come up with a real good one. Who'd have thought the old boy had it in him? I had finally got to him, I figured. Things were going to get interesting around Wrigley Field.

"Two days later, during a meeting in Wrigley's office, I began to talk up our whammy man, because I thought it was pretty funny. 'What are we holding back for?' I said. 'Let me give it to the papers today.'

"A chill came over the room. 'There's nothing funny about this,' Mr. Wrigley said evenly. 'This man may help us. And don't go talking to your newspaper friends about it. Or anybody else, either.'

"What can you say to a multimillionaire? I could think of a lot of things. Like, 'When I was a boy, my daddy told me that if a little man ever came up to me in a checkered suit, took the cigar out of his mouth and told me he was going to win a pennant for me by putting a whammy on my opponents, I should, despite my sweet and trusting nature, take the elementary precaution of checking him out with the Better Business Bureau for past performance.'

"He had contracted to pay the guy—may Ford Frick be elected to another term as Commissioner if this is not the truth—a flat $5,000 fee plus an additional $25,000 if we won the pennant.

"For the rest of the year we carried our Evil Eye around the league with us. At home, he sat directly behind the plate, gesturing furiously at opposing pitchers, none of whom seemed disposed to enter into the spirit of the thing at all. (He was, I must admit, able to cast his strange spell over the customers sitting nearby, most of whom could be seen edging cagily away from him—which proves that Beautiful Wrigley Field did attract a most discriminating clientele.)

"Our man operated under a severe handicap for such a chancy profession. He could not stand cold weather. (Which led me to believe he was a fraud—not an Evil Eye at all but a voodoo chief who had served his apprenticeship in Equatorial Africa.) On cold days, he would go up to the office, stand over the Western Union ticker and put the whammy on the tape as the play-by-play came in.

"Let me make it clear that I don't want this to be taken as a blanket indictment of all Evil Eyes. Most Evil Eyes, I'm sure, are honest, tax-paying, respectable citizens. It's only that rotten 3 percent who don't give you an honest day's work for an honest day's pay who give the whole profession a bad name."

Perhaps the hexer should have fixed his glare at the Cubs front office. The deal for Dizzy Dean was the start of the slide. Though Phil Wrigley had been told in no uncertain terms that the pitcher's arm was dead, he still wanted Dean because of his box office appeal. Boots Weber, who considered the won-lost record before the PR value, didn't want Dean, who had succeeded Babe Ruth as the game's most popular player, because his arm was so bad he couldn't throw hard anymore. Wrigley heard Weber's arguments and overruled him.

Everyone remembers Dizzy Dean went 7–4 for the Cubs in 1938. They forget that one of the men traded for him, Curt Davis, won 22 games for the Cardinals in 1939 and then went on to help the Dodgers to a pennant in 1941. And after the '38 season, Dean was ostensibly through.

In June 1939, Dean got in Gabby Hartnett's doghouse when he showed up in the clubhouse one day and told reporters a lion had attacked him in a taxicab. Then he changed his story, concocting a tale about cutting his arm on a glass table in a hotel room.

*   *   *

DICK BARTELL: "One night in New York Dizzy and his wife Pat went to an Italian restaurant with Hartnett and Larry French. On the way back in a cab, Diz said, 'Let's go down to Greenwich Village.' The others wanted to go back to the hotel, so back they went.

"In the morning French ran into the trainer, Andy Lotshaw.

"'Phew, what a night,' Lotshaw moaned.

"'What's the matter?'

"'Dean cut his arm. His brother is in town, and he claims he reached across for the telephone to call him and cut his arm on the glass top table. Needed stitches.'

"Some writers tried for hours to see how they could cut themselves on one of those tables and couldn't do it.

"Dean had a different explanation for everybody who asked him. What had happened was, Pat had cut him with a nail file."

Hartnett lost patience with his ailing pitcher and sent him home. In April 1940, Dean was sent to the bullpen, and after a failed try in the Texas League, he retired (although he did come back for one final appearance in 1947 with the St. Louis Browns).

In three seasons, Dean won 16 games for the Cubs. He won but 6 games in '39 and 3 more in 1940 before going to the minors. By 1941, he was back in the limelight, as an announcer for Falstaff Beer and the St. Louis Cardinals.

By the end of the 1930s, manager Gabby Hartnett broke up the 1935 winning infield combo of Herman, Jurges, Hack, and Grimm. Phil Cavarretta seemed to have replaced Grimm nicely, but Gabby didn't want an inexperienced player there. He preferred Rip Collins.

Hartnett, whose popularity as manager was coming to an end, had hurt himself badly among the players after his threat on the train after the final game of the World Series to trade everybody after the '38 season.

PHIL CAVARRETTA: "Some players you can be tough with and let them have it, scream at them, but a lot of them, as the years go by, you can't do that anymore. Going into '39, we didn't absolutely say, 'The heck with this.' We still gave it our best, but deep inside the best wasn't coming out. He was our manager, and we still carried respect for the man because he was our manager, but after the train thing, he lost a lot. Billy Herman and Gabby had been buddies, and they lost something."

Upon his return to Chicago, Hartnett had instigated the departure of the Cubs' great shortstop, Billy Jurges, which further hurt the Cubs morale. Perhaps Hartnett was hearing footsteps and got rid of Jurges because Billy had been the first choice as manager in '38, or perhaps Hartnett felt the shortstop had lost a step. Regardless, the loss of Jurges further damaged the Cubs.

Dick Bartell, who was acquired for Jurges, recalls the situation when he reported to the Cubs for the 1939 season. Even then, the acerbic Bartell could see that the Cubs organization was in disarray.

DICK BARTELL: "Throughout the 1938 season Hartnett's future was rumored to be in doubt. But the dramatic victory in the pennant race made it impossible for Wrigley to fire him in '39. He had one more year.

"He also had a lot of front office interference to put up with. It didn't come so much from the Wrigleys as it did from the general managers and other executives who came over from the chewing gum business. Managing by committee and rotating skippers came later.

"Pat Malone said the players had tried to count up the number of executives with the club.

"'We started with the clubhouse attendant, who has an assistant. There was somebody to survey the fans to see when they bought the most popcorn, things like that. We got the list up to 21.'"

The outspoken Bartell discovered Gabby Hartnett didn't have what it takes as a manager.

DICK BARTELL: "I came to Chicago respecting [Hartnett] as a player. But I lost respect for him as a manager. To put it plainly, he couldn't manage my Aunt Kate. He was very difficult to get along with. As Gabby as he was behind the plate, he was just as noisy in the dugout, pacing up and down, always chattering. But it wasn't positive noise. He seemed to have a smile on his face, but there was a lot behind the smile that wasn't very happy. He was highstrung and would get into arguments with players.

"I'm sure he was disappointed with me, expecting more out of me than I could deliver. I was giving it my best. Getting on my back all the time wasn't the most effective way to improve my performance. He'd chew out a player for not hustling right in front of all of us on the bench. Players don't like that. It brews resentment.

"One day at the Polo Grounds he got on me about something and one word led to another and it got a little heated and he said some derogatory things to me and I was ready to challenge him. But he was 6-2 and I was 5-7, so I grabbed a bat and was going to let him have it until a few players grabbed me and stopped it.

"Gabby had an ego that wouldn't quit. It got in the way of his managing. That's another reason so many star players are poor managers. He made life miserable for Gus Mancuso, because Gus didn't handle the catching job the way Gabby did.

"Gabby lasted through the 1940 season."

Under Hartnett the Cubs finished fourth in 1939 and sank to fifth, with a record under .500, in 1940. It was a turning point in Chicago Cubs history. Phil Wrigley was faced with his most important decision. Boots Weber, like Bill Veeck and Dick Bartell, realized that Phil Wrigley and his tightfisted gum people were running the Cubs, and so he resigned as general manager in 1940. Wrigley needed to hire someone to replace him. PK looked to his father for guidance, but so characteristic of Phil Wrigley, he misinterpreted what his father had tried to tell him.

When William Wrigley had needed a general manager, he had picked the bright, intelligent William Veeck, a former sports reporter for the *Chicago Tribune*. Veeck had done his job quite well.

Phil Wrigley, who for several years had worked side by side with William's son, Bill, could have chosen him for the post. But Bill Veeck was a confident, strong-willed man who history shows knew what it took to succeed in baseball. Veeck was just the sort of man Phil Wrigley shunned.

It wasn't for more than thirty years, until 1966—after interminable years of failure and bitter blasts of condemnation from the Chicago media—that PK Wrigley did hire a strong-willed, certified baseball expert to turn around his team: Leo Durocher, who came oh so close to winning a pennant.

To PK Wrigley, Bill Veeck was too much a maverick for his taste. Veeck, who once fell out of an upper-story dorm window while drunk at Kenyon College, liked to raise hell. He also liked the spotlight, something the reclusive Wrigley studiously avoided.

Young Veeck recognized the type of man Wrigley was, uncomfortable with the outgoing baseball personnel, comfortable with the more stodgy gum executives.

BILL VEECK: "Because [PK Wrigley] is such a shy man, the associates he feels more comfortable with are not the ball-club employees—who are a gregarious, outspoken lot—but the gum company people. And so while he kept all my father's employees, he also surrounded himself with a kitchen cabinet of gum executives who were always undercutting Boots and me.

"The one point on which we clashed, perennially, was promotion. I wanted it. He didn't. He was the boss. He won every argument. Mr. Wrigley, as a shy man, isn't interested in the press. It's more than that, though; he's a little afraid of writers. He sometimes leaves the impression he is afraid that if he opens himself up to them they'll compare him unfavorably to his father."

Bill Veeck wanted Wrigley to build lights for Wrigley Field so the team could play night baseball. PK adamantly refused to allow it.

BILL VEECK: "There was one thing I was unable to persuade Mr. Wrigley to do, even for the park. In 1934, the year before Larry MacPhail installed the first lights in a major-league stadium, I tried to get Mr. Wrigley to put lights at Wrigley Field. 'Just a fad,' he said. 'A passing fad.'

"Every year, I'd bring it up again. Every year he would come up with a new reason for not doing it.

"'Those light towers look terrible sticking up there,' he'd say. 'They'll spoil all this beauty we've worked so hard to create.'

"Old men, playing dominoes across the hearth, like to say that Phil Wrigley is the last of the true baseball men because he is the only owner who still holds, in the simple faith of his ancestors, that baseball was meant to be played under God's own sunlight.

"I know better. Having blown the chance to be first with lights, Mr. Wrigley just wasn't going to do it at all."

On November 12, 1940, a press conference was called to announce the firing of Gabby Hartnett and the resignation of Charles Webster as treasurer. At the meeting Hartnett said to Wrigley, "Well, thanks, anyway, Mr. Wrigley; not thanks for firing me, but for coming down here with me to announce it."

Without Hartnett, the team became less powerful at bat and a little drabber at the box office.

A few days later Phil Wrigley announced the appointment of his new general manager.

It was not Bill Veeck, the man he should have named. Bill Veeck was named treasurer to replace Webster.

Not hiring Veeck to run the Cubs was the single worst personnel move in the entire history of Phil Wrigley's reign as owner of the team. There were other egregious gaffes, to be sure, but this one had the greatest impact on the future of his team.

Rather than choose Veeck, Phil Wrigley followed his father's example by hiring a sports reporter. The man's name was Jim Gallagher. He was thirty-six years old and had gone to Notre Dame, worked for the *Chicago Herald-American*, and like William Veeck, had been sharply critical of the Cubs in the paper. In 1938, Phil Wrigley had hired him to take charge of press arrangements for the World Series. Wrigley was impressed with the job he did.

Unlike Bill Veeck, Jim Gallagher wasn't outgoing, lacked patience, and had no talent for judging horseflesh. Truth to tell, when Gallagher took the job he didn't know much more about professional baseball than the average fan at home. Which may have been just the way Philip Wrigley liked it. Over the next decade Gallagher would consistently be fleeced in trades by rival general managers.

Veeck, whose ambition was to own a team, well knew that Phil Wrigley had no intention of making him the Cubs' chief executive, and so on June 23, 1941, he quit the Cubs, borrowed $25,000 from a banker friend of the son of Cubs scout Pants Rowland, and bought the bankrupt Milwaukee Brewers team in the American Association. Veeck was twenty-eight years old and dead broke. Before long the imaginative and innovative baseball entrepreneur would sell the Brewers for a substantial profit, buy the Cleveland Indians and lead them to a pennant in 1948, and then buy the St. Louis Browns and become the most famous promoter in the game after signing a midget, Eddie Gaedel, and sending him to bat in a 1951 game against the Detroit Tigers. Bill Veeck brought excitement and enthusiasm wherever he went. Jim Gallagher brought frustration and anger to his team's fans.

Gallagher differed from his precedessor, Boots Weber, in that he was a man who enjoyed making decisions. Unfortunately, most of them turned out harmful to the team. Gallagher's first decision was to do what every new general manager does: Fire the incumbent manager. He pushed Phil Wrigley to replace the longtime all-star and fan favorite Gabby Hartnett with another catcher, a colorless, put-'em-out-there-and-let-'em-play manager named Jimmie Wilson.

Hartnett, a lifelong Cub, to the fans had been part of the family. Wilson was a total stranger, a cipher. He had managed the Phillies for five bleak seasons (1934–38), during which time the team finished no better than seventh, but late in the 1940 season and in the World Series he left his coaching role to fill in heroically at catcher for the Cincinnati Reds when Ernie Lombardi was injured. Wrigley had been content to keep Hartnett, but Gallagher thought the fans would warm up to this Series hero and felt he'd be a good choice to rejuvenate the Cubs. The fans soon came to dislike Wilson as much as they disliked Gallagher. Before long the fans would be referring to the combination as "the James Boys." The phrase would not be used fondly.

Gallagher's next major move was to give away the Cubs' all-star second baseman, Billy Herman. The Cubs had a minor league second baseman named Lou Stringer, and Gallagher expected him to become a star. He didn't. (In a six-year career with the Cubs and the Red Sox, he batted .242, striking out ten times for every home run he hit.)

If a general manager trades a star like Herman, he had better get another star back, or at least three rookies with strong potential. Gallagher got virtually nothing in return for Herman.

Branch Rickey, whose Dodgers desperately needed a second baseman to team with shortstop Pee Wee Reese, offered Gallagher the choice of either the youngster Pete Reiser or another youngster, second baseman Charlie Gilbert. If Gallagher had taken Reiser, who hit a league-leading .343 in 1941 and led the league in stolen bases in 1942 and 1946 (Reiser was in the military from 1943 to 1945), Cubs fans might not have been so hostile to the trade. But it was part of Branch Rickey's genius to give the other general manager a choice of two players and then steer him to pick the lesser of the two. As Rickey had anticipated, Gallagher picked the wrong guy. Reiser went on become an all-star with the Dodgers. Gilbert hit .279 in 39 games with the Cubs in 1941, then hit .184 in '42 and .150 in '43. Herman, who was in his prime at the time of the trade, became an important cog in the Dodgers' 1941 pennant.

PHIL CAVARRETTA: "When we traded Billy, I was sick, believe me. Billy Herman was still an all-star. He went over to Brooklyn and won pennants. As we all know, Branch Rickey, who had moved from St. Louis to Brooklyn, was one of the shrewdest and smartest dealers that baseball has ever seen. That's because he always had an outstanding scouting system. Rickey built up his minor league system. We were always concentrating on the big club, which is a mistake, believe me. You have to have kids coming in. Our scouting system wasn't that good, and it showed in our minor league system, and then on the Cubs themselves."

Gallagher did one more thing to sink the Cubs. He codified Phil Wrigley's insistence on not spending much money on ballplayers' salaries. He and Wrigley worked out a draconian budget, a salary cap in a way, one that changed the Cubs from being one of the better-paying teams in the league to one of the worst.

During his reign Gallagher kept to that budget with a slavish adherence. At first some unknowing top prospects continued to sign with the Cubs, thinking the team was still playing as it had under William Wrigley. It took a few years until word got around that the Cubs paid as poorly as other second-division organizations like the Phils and Reds.

The fault would lie primarily with Phil Wrigley, but because most fans are too in awe of men with money and because they feel an indebtedness for allowing the team to play in their city at all, rarely would Wrigley feel the heat for the bad baseball that soon would come. Instead, the fans and the press focused their wrath on Jim Gallagher, the Cubs general manager from the winter of 1940 through his firing in June 1949. Gallagher would be castigated for allowing the curtain to drop with a thud on the glorious reign of the Chicago Cubs.

Charlie Grimm, who would quit as manager during the 1949 season under the weight of having to manage too many bad ball clubs, said of Jim Gallagher: "He was the most honest man I ever knew. I admit I was impatient at times with the slow flow of talent to the Cubs and with the ability of these replacements. But that wasn't basically Jim's fault."

Even Grimm was too in awe of the Gum Magnate to directly point the finger at him.

One great year during a long world war would magically give the illusion that the Cubs weren't a second-division ball club, but as quick as it took for the boys abroad to come home and make whole the Cardinals, the Dodgers, the Braves, and the Giants, the fall of the Chicago Cubs would be as certain as the fall of the Axis powers, as the Cubs would finish in the second division twenty-four years out of the next twenty-seven.

When Branch Rickey was asked about the plight of the Cubs, the Mahatma pontificated, "This team has to approach cooperative perfection to remain in the shadow of last place. There is artistry in ineptitude, too, you know."

Phil Wrigley would artistically create a baseball anomaly: a cult of successful losers. At first the fans would complain bitterly, but after a number of years of losing under an owner who made clear he would not sell, they would accept their plight and love the team as they would a doddering aunt or a child with crossed eyes. It may have been flawed, but it was theirs to love.

When the fall came, as Phil Wrigley had ordained it, the chewing gum kingpin would have one crucial hedge against what otherwise would have been economic disaster for his team: the advertising-induced aura of Beautiful Wrigley Field. Win or lose—and usually it would be lose—Cubs fans would be told over and over that going to the ballpark on Chicago's North Side would be a wonderful way to spend a glorious afternoon in the sunshine.

The ads, moreover, would not be wrong.

45

Wartime Ball

Don Johnson, who joined the Cubs in the final weeks of the 1943 season, was the typical World War II ballplayer. Johnson, who was born in 1911, was the son of Ernie Johnson, who played in the Federal League, replaced shortstop Swede Risberg on the White Sox when the eight Black Sox players were banned, then played with Babe Ruth on the Yankees. Don Johnson had grown up in Southern California, then headed for college, where he played at Santa Ana Junior College and then Oregon State, and for the next ten years, starting in 1932, made a minor league pilgrimage beginning with the Seattle Indians, then going to the Reading Red Sox, back west to Sacramento, to the San Francisco Missions, to the Hollywood Stars, then three years with Tulsa, then a year in Milwaukee with Bill Veeck and Charlie Grimm, where he got to watch Veeck's farsightedness as a promoter, to marvel at his combative nature. Johnson also played for manager Charlie Grimm, a banjo-playing fun-loving imp who could be tough when he had to be.

When Johnson finally made it to the majors with the Cubs in September 1943, baseball life would seem mundane compared to his days with Milwaukee.

Then in 1944, Grimm would return to Chicago as manager and breathe new life into Johnson's career and that of the wartime Cubs.

In the spring of '44 the Cubs' candidates for second base were Johnson and Eddie Stanky, who off the field was religious and on the field was Beelzebub on spikes. The dirty play of Stanky, a confrontational player like Ty Cobb and his future manager, Leo Durocher, was deemed too offensive by the Cubs. A month into the 1944 season Stanky was traded to the Dodgers for journeyman pitcher Bob Chipman. Stanky went on to a tumultuous eleven-year career during which he battled for and led three National League teams, Brooklyn, Boston, and New York, to pennants.

In 1944, Johnson hit .278 and made the All-Star team. The next year he hit .302 and helped lead the Cubs to a pennant.

In 1946, Johnson suffered a broken hand, and his batting average dropped significantly, to .242. By 1948 he was out of the game.

DON JOHNSON: "The most impressive thing any hitter ever told me was what I heard Ted Williams say when he was playing for San Diego in the Pacific Coast League. I was with the San Francisco Missions then, and we were fogged out one day in San Diego. Players from both teams got together in our dugout. We had a catcher by the name of Chick Outen, a good hitter, and Ted was there. It was his second year in the league. Chick said to Williams, 'Hey, kid, how come you hit so good?'

"Williams looked him right in the eye and didn't hesitate at all. He said, 'You know, that ball seems to hang there until I'm ready to hit it.'

"I thought to myself, Gee, I never had that experience.

"After three years with the Missions, I was sold to Hollywood. I wasn't there long when they sent me to Tulsa, a farm club for the Cubs. I was down there three years. I was with Lennie Merullo, and Dizzy Dean for a while when he came up with a sore arm.

"Lennie was a real jokester, a really great guy, my best friend in baseball, a sharp guy. I remember on a train one time going from Tulsa to Houston, we had some young ballplayers, a young kid named Zelosko, a shortstop, and other guys. Lennie is eight or ten years younger than me, but he was older than these kids. We got to talking about the war, and Lennie said, 'I was over there.' I knew he wasn't in the war. One of the kids asked him, 'What did you do?' He said, 'I was a submarine captain.' And he went on to explain all the stuff about a submarine. I said to Lennie, 'Where did you pick up all that crap?' He laughed.

"Of course, Diz impressed me. He was a great ballplayer, and he wanted to win real badly. With his sore arm he could hardly throw, but he could still pitch fairly good. I can remember about the sixth or seventh inning of a ball game, he was having a rough time. There were men on first and second, and the batter hit a ball off him, and it looked like the runner at second was going to score, so Dizzy stood ten or fifteen feet from home plate right on the line, where the runner couldn't get by him unless he ran out of the baseline.

"The umpire called the runner safe because he said Diz was blocking the plate. Dean said to him, 'Listen, they don't come out here to see you. They come out here to see Dizzy Dean, and I was standing close to the fans!'

"We traveled by train then, and we'd come to a stop, and he'd get off the train, and you wouldn't see him, and pretty soon he'd come back loaded with groceries, sandwiches and everything, pies, cookies, and we would all eat it up on the trip.

"Another thing that impressed me about him was in the Rice Hotel in Houston, he had two or three phones in his room hooked up, because he loved to bet on the horse races. I guess he was pretty good at it, because he had to pay for it himself, because he couldn't sign any checks without his wife Pat's signature.

"While he talked on these phones going all the time up there, us kids would sit around—I wasn't so much a kid as the other guys—but I was a kid in comparison to him, and watched him make bets. I remember him talking several hundred dollars, and that seemed like a lot at the time. Later he'd go down to the bookies and pick up the money.

"He did this on the road. At home in Tulsa, why, the wife would be with him, and she'd dish out the money.

"He was a great guy, though. He was eager to win all the time. He told us that in 1934 he and his brother Paul pitched practically the whole season, every other day, and said that he weighed 164 pounds at the end of the season.

"After spending '40, '41, and '42 at Tulsa, I was sent to Milwaukee in 1943 to play for Bill Veeck and Charlie Grimm.

"We drew like mad in Milwaukee. Bill was German, and he was up in Milwaukee with all those other Germans, and they thought he was God. Bill was way ahead of his time. *Way* ahead.

"Bill always had special promotions and giveaways for the fans. This was during the war. We played ball games at nine and ten o'clock in the morning so the factory workers on the night shift could see ball games. And even at that hour we loaded the park. He served them Wheaties and cream. They had those cardboard containers with plastic around them, and they could pour the cream in there, and everyone had a plastic spoon, and everyone ate Wheaties and cream.

"One time he had a special night for the fans, and out of nowhere from way in the outfield there was a great big gate, and the gate opened, and here came this great big package, and they put it right on the mound. Veeck had brought in a left-handed pitcher from the Mexican League or someplace. We never heard of him. A pretty good pitcher. I guess he had been warming up under the stands.

"There was a drum roll, and he popped up out of the box. They took the box away, and he pitched the ball game.

"Veeck was not the type of person who liked to lose. I remember one time we had a decision go against us that Veeck thought was unfair. I got dressed after the ball game and was walking out. I had to pass the umpires' dressing room, and [Veeck] was standing right outside the door. I said, 'What's cooking, Bill?' He said, 'I have to talk to those . . .' He was really mad. I said, 'Why don't you let them go. You just hurt your ball club that way. They'll suspend you.' But he wouldn't pay any attention to anybody. He was going to talk to those umpires no matter what.

"He was a great guy to play for, Veeck was. He was a fantastic guy. He'd be down in our clubhouse before the game talking to the players, not a pep talk, just friendly. And he'd get out and pitch batting practice for an hour on that fake leg of his. He was in the service, and they had to amputate that leg. They cut it off a little at a time. He had that left prosthesis on there, but he could pitch good batting practice.

"He did everything he could for the ballplayers, even in those times. And of course, he had Charlie Grimm as his manager there. Oh, Jesus, Charlie was really funny. In Indianapolis one ball game, it started to rain about the seventh inning. It just rained, rained, rained. All through the seventh and part of the eighth. And the umpire wouldn't stop the game.

"Grimm found a great big beach umbrella someplace. Where in the hell he ever got it, I don't know. He walked out to protest to the umpire, and subconsciously the umpire got under the umbrella with him! When he realized what he had done, he kicked Grimm out of the ball game with his umbrella.

"Where he came up with these things, I don't know. Another time we were playing, and it was so darn dark you could hardly see. The clouds were coming in. Grimm had one of these lanterns the railroad people carry. He walked out there and held it up over the umpire's head and got kicked out again!

"As a player Charlie was a good hitter and a hell of a good first baseman. I don't know why he isn't in the Hall of Fame. As a manager the players had respect for Charlie because even though he was funny in the clubhouse, he really had control of a ball club. I remember a young knuckleballer. He was one hell of a good pitcher. He was having a rough time, and he got knocked out of the game about the fifth or sixth inning, went up to the clubhouse, packed his stuff in his duffel bag, and just as we were coming up the stairs, he was finishing packing. Grimm sat down by his locker and watched him. The kid started out the door, and Charlie said to him, 'Listen, lad, if you go out that door, you're going straight to Nashville, and you're not coming back.'

"And you never saw a guy unpack his stuff so quick in his life. Charlie was a good psychologist. He wasn't boisterous, never bawled the guys out.

"Some managers would have called him an SOB and a quitter, but Grimm let you know darn well he didn't like what was going on without belittling you.

"Charlie hired Jimmie Foxx. Foxx was our hitting coach. He was great. Even though he wasn't playing he watched the ball game, every second of it.

"One time I made a play. As I came into the bench, all I saw was this finger of Jimmie Foxx pointing over to me. 'Come over here, kid.' I went over there, and all he said to me was, 'What was your thinking before you made that play?' And I told him exactly what I was trying to do.

"The bases were loaded, and the infield was in. I was playing second base, and a ground ball was hit to me off to my right. I had to take two steps to get it, and I looked at the runner coming home and I thought, Hell, I can't get him. So I threw to first base.

"I told Jimmie what I was thinking before he hit it. 'This ball has got to be hit right at me, 'cause that guy at third is fast.'

"He said, 'OK. That's all right.' It's all he said. I appreciated Jimmie. He was like a lot of old-timers helping out the guys who haven't had the experience.

"At Milwaukee our clubhouse was loose as a goose. We won our division, and then we played Columbus, and they beat us in the playoffs. After Columbus beat us, I packed my stuff and was ready to go back to Laguna Beach, and Charlie came up to me and said, 'Do you want to go up and finish the season with Chicago?' I said, 'Hell yes.' He said, 'That's where you're going.'

"I was happy to go to the major leagues, hell yes, even though it really wasn't the major leagues anymore. So many of the good ballplayers had gone into the service, the competition was about the same as it was in Triple A. There were a couple hundred major league ballplayers taken into the service, and in the minor leagues a little over three thousand went. That's 'cause there were a lot of minor leagues then, a heck of a lot of them.

"But we had darn good attendance, and President Roosevelt thought it would be a good pick-me-up sending the baseball results over to the soldiers, and I was tickled to death to be in Chicago. The only reason I didn't get drafted was we had three children at the time, and I guess the government didn't want to have to support my family if I got bumped off.

"When I joined the Cubs ball club in September of '43, Jim Gallagher, the general manager, took me down for a luncheon at the Wrigley Building and introduced me to Mr. Wrigley. Gallagher said to him, 'Mr. Wrigley, this is your new second baseman.' And he kind of looked at me and said hi and then he walked off. I didn't understand that. That was the only time I met Mr. Wrigley.

"Gallagher was a newspaperman who didn't know anything about baseball. He had been associated with the game but never had been in it in a capacity where he had to make decisions. He was a stubborn little guy, honest, but he had no business trading with Branch Rickey.

"I only got to play a few games when I got to the Cubs in '43. Everything was new to me. I felt like I really had to produce in a hurry, and I didn't do too well at the end of '43. Jimmie Wilson was a different type from Grimm altogether. He didn't say much. I don't remember him ever having a meeting. As far as I know, I forget even who his coaches were.

"We held spring training in '44 in French Lick, Indiana. It wasn't much of a spring training. It rained most of the time we were there, and the place was flooded. I only remember playing a couple of ball games in French Lick. There was a lot of card playing. Guys would go for a walk if they could.

"Mainly what we did was have mud baths there in French Lick. We'd get in one of these slabs, and they filled them with mud, and you got in, and they shoveled more mud on us, and you stayed in there for a while. It was really great for the fat guys but with my build [six feet, 170 pounds] I only could stay in there ten or fifteen minutes. I didn't need to sweat the meat off.

"Then they'd have you stand up, and this guy with a hose would about knock you over knocking the mud off you, and then you'd take a shower and maybe you took a walk. It really wasn't much of a spring training. But we felt it was better to be in French Lick than in Europe.

"When I came up in '44, at second base they didn't have too many choices: Me and Eddie Stanky. He was younger than me [by five years]. Most everybody was younger than me. When the '44 season began Wilson was the manager, and I wasn't playing. I was decoration. When we started 1–9, Wilson quit, and Grimm came in [after Roy Johnson was interim manager for one game, a loss]. I thought it was great, 'cause I had played for him for a whole year, knew his habits. And when he came, the whole club loosened up.

"Stanky and I were together for about a month. After Grimm came, the Cubs traded him to Brooklyn for a left-handed pitcher, Bob Chipman. Eddie was kind of a quiet guy off the ball field, but on the ball field, he was a battler.

"One time after he went over to Brooklyn, Stanky slid into me at second base, and I tagged him out and he tried to grab the ball out of my hand. I would never tag him with the ball in my glove, because he was inclined to kick the back of your hand or try to knock the ball out of your glove. You can hold the ball tight in your hand and have the thing covered pretty darn good. In the glove, it might pop out. Which would mean you didn't have control over it. He had his own way of playing. He was geared that way, and there was nothing in the world to stop him.

"Leo Durocher liked that type, and that's why he picked him up. I never did question anything the owners did, because there was no use in doing that. I welcomed the opportunity to be able to play.

"We had a team of really good guys. Stan Hack was on third. Stan always seemed like he was ready to smile. Cavarretta, who hated to lose, was on first, and myself on second and Lennie Merullo at short and in the outfield we had Andy Pafko, Bill Nicholson, and Peanuts Lowrey [who missed the '44 season because of military service].

"Nick [Bill Nicholson] and I went to Pittsburgh together to the '44 All-Star Game. He hit a triple. I didn't get to play. [Cardinals manager] Billy Southworth came up after the game, and he said, 'Everything was going so good, I didn't put anybody else in.'

"I said, 'That's the way it goes.'

"Nick was one of the neatest guys you ever wanted to meet. He was a powerful guy, built like a fullback, a quiet guy. He could hit a ball a long ways. If he'd swing and miss on a ball, all the audience would go, 'Swish.' That was his nickname, Swish. Half the time they wouldn't say his name. They announced him as Swish.

"He was a real good outfielder. I don't think I ever saw him throw to a wrong base. He could go get a ball. He'd fool you. He covered more territory than you thought. He and Pafko and Lowrey out there did a great job.

Bill Nicholson

"Peanuts was a funny, little guy. I'd be standing in the lobby of the hotel and he'd start a conversation with me like he was a big vegetable dealer. He'd come up to me and say, 'You know, we have a load of carrots coming in. We'd better get together and pick out a price.' He'd do it in the hotel lobby, where a number of people would be standing around, listening. I'd go along with him. Sometimes we'd have a little argument about the price of vegetables.

"At catcher we had a guy by the name of Dewey Williams. He was a farmer boy, and he walked just like one. He was a good hustler back there, a heck of a good guy.

"And by the time 1945 came around, it wound up that we had some pretty darn good pitching. For an infielder, it's so much easier playing behind a real good pitcher.

"Paul Derringer didn't fear anybody. He was mean on the mound. He was out to win. He showed it all the time. If things weren't going right, he'd pop off, not directly to guys, but about situations. 'This should have been done this way.' He'd cover a situation that came up. He wouldn't mention names. You'd know that if you didn't do something, even if it was a physical error, he'd make you feel you wished you could have done better. But that isn't bad on a ball club.

"Claude Passeau was a southern boy, and he had a lot more composure than Derringer did but Claude also could be pretty mean out there on the mound. I know one time we were playing St. Louis in St. Louis, and [shortstop] Marty Marion beat us the first two ball games with some good plays in the field. Before the third game Passeau walked up to the batting cage while Marion was practicing batting, and he yelled at him, 'You're not gonna beat us today, you big, long drink of water.'

"The first time Marion came up, Passeau hit him in the ankle with a pitch. That hurts. You have no muscle there to protect you. Passeau ran up to him and said, 'How are you, Marty?' Marty said, 'You SOB, you.'

"We won that ball game.

"And Hank Wyse could be a tough character as well. I remember when we were playing in Tulsa together. We were on a train traveling with the Houston ball club. "They must have been on their way north, because it was only a few days before we played them. Sitting there playing cards was a guy by the name of Bill Norman, they used to call him St. Louis Bill or something [Norman was born in St. Louis], a big outfielder. And Hank Wyse had a walk on him just like Jack Benny. Hank walked through their car on the train, and Norman made some kind of remark, 'Who in the hell is that guy with that funny kind of a walk?'

"Hank didn't say anything, but the first two times up, Hank really lowered the boom on him. Norman dusted himself off the first time, and he said to our catcher, 'What in the hell is coming off?' The catcher said, 'I don't know.' The next pitch was the same thing. He *really* lowered the boom. Hank just wanted him to know that that walk didn't mean there was anything insignificant about him.

"Guys like Derringer, Passeau, and Wyse, they understood that everybody behind them was part of the team but that they were the main part out there.

"In June [1945] we got Hank Borowy from the Yankees. Without Borowy we could not have beaten the Cardinals. I think everybody felt that way. He came in and won 11 ball games for us. I have no idea why the Yankees sold us Borowy. They didn't need the money. It did seem kind of strange to all of us.

"He had a good live fastball. It was *really* live. Sometimes the ball would break away from the hitter and other times toward him. Some guys are faster than the devil, but the ball doesn't do too much. This sucker had a beautiful, easy motion, very deceptive. He looked like he wasn't going to throw hard at all, and that thing, 'Ping,' boy, I'm telling you, he really let it go. It was really fun playing behind him, because they hit a lot of fly balls off him.

"The Cardinals had won the pennant in '42, '43, and '44, and even though they had lost Musial and [Enos] Slaughter and some of their top pitchers to the war, in '45 they still had Marty Marion at shortstop and Emil Verban at second base. The Cardinals always had players because they had so many farm teams to choose from. And in '45 they again had a pretty good pitching staff: Red Barrett, Ken Burkhart, and Harry Brecheen.

"That reminds me. Brecheen was always tough for me to hit. He threw a lot of different speeds. But this one game in Chicago he let a high fastball get away from him. He wasn't that fast, but he was fast enough. And I hit a home run off him. The wind was blowing out, and anyone could have hit a home run that day. When the wind blows out in Chicago, it's great. And he followed me all around the bases.

"He shouted, 'You'll never hit another one off me.'

"I told him, 'I'll take it, Harry. That makes up a little bit for all the other times.'

"I remember about two weeks or ten days before the end of the season we were still in first place with the Cardinals right behind us, and we had won a ball game in Chicago. I was walking up the ramp from the dugout into the clubhouse along with Ed Sauer, a reserve outfielder, a big guy. He said to me, 'Hey, DJ, do you think we're going to win this?' I said, 'Hell yes, no doubt about it.' And I kind of surprised myself.

"I had a good feeling we were not going to lose. 'Cause when you're losing, you feel you're going to lose. But I had that feeling we were going to win.

"Later I got to thinking: Gee, we *are* going to win. There's no doubt about it, is there?"

46

The Workhorse

Even though the Cubs farm system and scouting staff was by far inferior to those of other major league teams, sometimes the Cubs attracted a solid prospect just because it was a team without great depth and a young player figured playing for the Cubs would be a quick way to reach the majors. Hank Wyse, who won 16 games with the Cubs in 1944, 22 in '45 (second in the league to Red Barrett's 23), and 14 in '46, had wanted to sign with the Yankees, the Cardinals, or the Cincinnati Reds but was talked out of doing so by his semipro manager, a former major leaguer who felt that the pitching-poor Cubs needed him most.

The fearless Wyse, an oil-field worker in the off-season, was as tough as they came. With Paul Derringer, Claude Passeau, and Hank Borowy, who came from the Yankees midway through the '45 season, Wyse would be an important wartime performer for the Cubs.

HANK WYSE: "I grew up in Lunsford, Arkansas. We played a lot of baseball since I was a little bitty kid. I played ball in school, and because there were no jobs during the depression, I went to Kansas City, where I played semipro ball and worked for a lumber company, and Singer sewing machine, and Goldman's Jewelers, which won the Ban Johnson League a couple years in a row.

"Roy Sanders was managing Goldman Jewelers. Roy had pitched for the Pittsburgh Pirates [and the Reds]. Roy and I built a mound and a rubber out back the apartment where I lived. And he built a canvas on the back with two stakes on it for a right-handed hitter and a left-handed hitter and put a home plate on it, and he told me when I could throw seven curve balls out of ten, I'd be ready. And I throwed at that for almost a year. I had two younger sisters who would bring the balls back.

"When I was about twenty-one, livin' in Kansas City, one of the pitchers I faced was Satchel Paige. His third baseman with the Monarchs, [Jack] Saltzgaver, got together a bunch of kids from the minors and took two of us from the Goldman Jewelers team to play against Satch and his bunch. Satch was better than anybody I ever saw in my life. He throwed harder than anybody I've ever seen.

"I went up to hit the first time, kind of loose, the bat on my shoulder, and he threw the ball for a strike, and I stepped back. He said, 'Stand up there, white boy, I ain't gonna hit you.' I said, 'I know damn well you ain't gonna hit me.' He threw three pitches, that was all, all strikes.

"Saltzgaver had brought two or three balls that weighed only six ounces, instead of seven ounces, and he had me throw them, and I was throwing that little ball right by them guys. They couldn't believe it. Satchel threw with the regular major league ball, seven ounces, and he was throwing the regular ball by us, and we didn't believe it.

"I remember I struck this one colored guy out three times in a row. I'd start about waist high, and then a little higher, and a little higher, and he'd shake his head. The last time he came up I threw one right down the middle real hard, and he said, 'White boy, throw that fastball one more time.' He just couldn't believe it.

"Well, that catcher [Josh Gibson] came up in the eighth or ninth inning, and they changed balls with me, and I threw the seven ounce one, and it felt like a softball then. He hit it so far I think a blackbird built a nest in it before it came down.

"Roy sent out five letters to the major leagues about me and got all five letters back. He called and we met, and he said, 'Where do you want to go?' I said, 'I want to go with the Yankees.' Bill Essick was the scout in Kansas City, and he had been trying to sign me. He offered me $75 a month and $75 a month for my mother and two sisters if I would sign with him, but I wouldn't sign then. I told Roy I wanted to go to the Yankees, and he said, 'No way.' I said, 'Why?' He said, 'They have three 20-game winners now and two more in Kansas City. It'll be ten years before you get up there.' I told him, 'Well, how about St. Louis?' He said, 'No way. You can't go there, either.' They had Mort Cooper and two others. I said, 'Cincinnati?' He said, 'You can't. They have Paul Derringer and Bucky Walters and Vander

Meer.' I said, 'Where do you want me to go?' He said, 'The only place to go is Chicago.' I said, 'How come?' He said, 'They need pitchers today bad. Start playing pro ball now, and if you can't pitch in the big leagues in two years, retire and come home.' He said, 'They need you now.' So I took it. They paid me $300 a month.

"I started at Tulsa in '40 but soon they sent me to Moline, Illinois. We lost four, five in a row, and I was discouraged because I wasn't pitching. I wanted to go home. After this one game we lost I was setting in the clubhouse by myself. The manager, Mike Gonzalez, undressed, went in and took a shower. So I undressed and went in there. He had soap all in his eyes, washing his hands. He said, 'Gol dern, I don't know who to pitch tomorrow.'

"I said, 'If you don't pitch me, I'm going home.' He rubbed his face and said, 'Who said that?' I said, 'I did. And I mean it too. I left a job to come here and pitch. I didn't come here to sit on the bench. We're losing anyway.'

"He said, 'You want to pitch that bad.'

"I said, 'That's why I signed a contract.'

"He said, 'All right.'

"Sure enough, he pitched me, and I won. After I won that first game, Mike came out every day early with me with a catcher. He'd say, 'I don't want you to throw the ball over the plate. I want low and inside, low and outside, high inside, high outside. Whatever pitch you throw, I want you to know where it's going.' He worked with me a week or two.

"I won two or three in a row, lost a couple, won a couple more, and Tulsa sent a telegram. My wife and I were watching a Western show, a double feature for a quarter, and he had us paged, and we come out, and he said, 'Go get your clothes and get out of here. Catch a bus. It's about an hour before it leaves. You're going to Tulsa.' He showed me the telegram. He said, 'They told me to send my best pitcher.'

"I said, 'OK.'

"He said, 'Well, hurry up.' Then he said, 'Hey, they told me to send my best pitcher. You're not my best pitcher, but you got the best chance of going to the big leagues. You keep doing what we've been doing here.'

"So I came back to Tulsa, where I won three or four games.

"I worked that winter in the oil fields. It was dangerous. I had a little trouble. You rack all the pipes and hold the rope to run the pipe in. They usually chain you to do it. I wouldn't use chains. I said, 'I ain't gonna lose my hand.' So I used a rope instead. When it got wet, it was hard to hold.

"One day the driller kept jerking that, running that cathead wide open. I said, 'If you don't quit jerking me around up here, I'm going to turn loose this rope and wrap you around that thing.'

"He said, 'You do and I'll whip your ass.' And nearly everybody who was working for him was kinfolks, nephew, brother-in-law or something. We come out . . . we were wrapping six-inch pipe then. We come out of the hole, went back in, and after we screwed in the last piece of pipe, I turned that rope loose, about ten foot flopping around over him. If he hadn't jumped off about ten or fifteen foot, it would have killed him.

"He come back up. He said, 'You know what I told you.' I just walked out and picked up a twenty-four-inch pipe wrench. I said, 'Well, this is one guy you ain't gonna whip.' He said, 'How come?' I said, 'If you can whip this wrench, you got it.' I said, 'If you want a ride home, you better shut this thing down, because I'm leaving.' It was about an hour before we were scheduled to quit for the day. He said, 'You can't.' I said, 'Yes I can.' There were about fourteen inches of snow on the ground with about zero weather. And I was driving. I went and got me a rope and cut it up in pieces and made a chain to put on the back wheels. He caught me cutting up a brand-new rope and told me I had to pay for it. I said, 'I'll send you the money. I'm going to spring training in two weeks.' He shut her down, and we got along all right after that.

"I went to spring training on Catalina Island in 1942. I'd have been more impressed, but, see, the war was going on. We were afraid to do too much. We were playing golf one time, and I looked up and one of the navy's training planes came off the water and was heading right for where we were, and we dove in the bushes. It hit the top of the tallest trees around there, hit the electric line that fed the hotel. There was this noise, and then you looked around and saw all that fire coming from the wires. The pilot turned it around and just barely got into the ocean.

"About that time there was a Japanese plane they shot down over Long Beach. They say they didn't do it, but they did. I saw a guy who picked up some of the pieces of it. It was a Japanese plane. They didn't want anybody to know it.

"Another time we were about two hundred yards from the back side of that island, and a Jap boat came up and took fuel while we were there, and that about scared us to death.

"I started the '42 season with the Cubs. I was supposed to stay there. It was April, around the first, and we were supposed to play an exhibition game in Tulsa. I got up the next morning, looked in the paper, and saw, 'Hank Wyse Is Left in Tulsa.' I liked to have a fit. I had been 20–4 with Tulsa in '41.

"I went home to drill wells. They sent me another contract, but I tore it up into pieces, put it in an envelope and sent it back. So the business manager in Tulsa, Don Stuart, he called me and told me to sign, and I told him, 'No way.' But I finally did. I got a little more money, $750 a month.

"I went 22–10 for Tulsa in '42 and went up to the Cubs. That year I pitched my first four major league games. Jimmie Wilson was a pretty strict manager. I didn't know much about managing in the big leagues. He had an awful close curfew. He didn't seem to talk to the players very much, only the older players. He didn't talk to rookies or nothing. Roy Johnson, who was a coach with the Cubs, had been my manager with Tulsa. We called him Hardrock. He was an old veteran who had pitched in the big leagues. He was my buddy. He called me Buddy Boy all the time, so at least I had someone to talk to all the time.

"Let me tell you something funny. When they called me up in '42, they was playing in Cincinnati. They were playing a doubleheader, and I sat on the bench through all the first game. When the game was over, Wilson said, 'Go inside and get a sandwich and a cold drink.' I said, 'No. I'd rather just sit out here and enjoy it.' There was a big crowd at Crosley Field that day. It was the first big league ballpark I had ever played in. Me and the batboy sat there and talked all during that break, and when he came back down, Wilson told me the ball was still in the box. He threw it in my lap. 'Warm up. You're the pitcher.' I took my time and looked at the package and found the ball. He said, 'Well, warm up. You're the pitcher.' I didn't know I had to jump up there. So I got up and said, 'I need a catcher.' He said, 'Your catcher is already down there.' I didn't know that he came from another way and was sitting there waiting on me.

"I went out there and started warming up. Wilson come up behind me, and he said, 'Are you all right?' I said, 'Yeah.' He said, 'You don't look it. You're white as a sheet. If you don't want to pitch . . . why, I guess I should warm somebody else up anyway.' I turned around and said, 'Why the hell don't you do that? You told me to pitch, and I will. But if you keep on, I ain't going to.' So he just walked off.

"I didn't understand why he was doing it. I didn't know why he came out there. When I walked out on the mound, it didn't help anything that Johnny Vander Meer was warming up on the side, and his pitches sounded like a shotgun going off. I couldn't think of anything but them two no-hitters in a row he had pitched.

"So I went out there. Lonny Frey was the first Reds hitter. He hit a triple off the first pitch. I turned around and picked up the resin bag and thought, Hell, maybe it is too difficult up here. Maybe it is the big leagues!

"But I got 'em out without 'em scoring. I shut them out until the seventh inning, and I won 7–3. That was my first win.

"I don't know why I didn't start until '43 with the Cubs. I was 20–4 in '41 at Tulsa and then 22–10 in '42. I thought I ought to be starting up there. I guess they didn't think a rookie could pitch till he knows his league, but I don't believe that. If he knows how to pitch, he can pitch anywhere.

"Jim Gallagher, a newspaperman, was their general manager. And back then you couldn't get no money, 'cause in '44 they froze the salaries so you couldn't get no raises.

"In April of 1944, Wilson was fired, and Charlie Grimm took his place. It made a difference. Charlie was a fun guy, always called everyone by a nickname. I was Hankus Pankus. He was always making fun of the umpires, had everybody laughing, but he didn't actually talk to us young guys. He didn't talk to us at all. In fact, nobody talked to us hardly at all. The only guy who did was Red Smith, the bullpen coach. He was kind of Grimm's stool pigeon. He talked to everybody out in the bullpen. Everything that was said Grimm knew about it. Red, who used to be a football player, talked to everybody down there, and because of Red, Grimm knew everything that was going on.

"One of my teammates was Claude Passeau, a mean, rough pitcher. He'd knock you down. This is kind of interesting: In '45 him and I pitched all the doubleheaders. I'd start the first game, and he'd go the second game. Most of the time I'd win and he'd lose. He'd get beat 2–1, 3–2, or 1–0. I'd win 6–0, 6–2. He said by the time they got around to his game, we were all wore out.

"And he went to the manager, and I think he went to the front office, he wanted to pitch the first game instead of the second game. Of course, I didn't know anything about this. He then told Roy Johnson about it, and Roy come in and said to me, 'What do you think about it?' I said, 'Well, that ain't fair.' He said, 'No, really it's not.' He said, 'We're trying to win a pennant. I don't think it will make a difference in your pitching, would it?' I said, 'It won't make any difference with *my* pitching, and I don't think it will make any difference in his pitching, either.' He said, 'Well, he seems to think so, and if it does, he might just win us the pennant.' I said, 'I'll do it under one condition.' He said, 'What's that?' I said, 'If you don't come back and tell me he wants to pitch the second game instead of the first one.'

He said, 'I'll guarantee you he won't do that.' So I just kept winning. And the reason he was getting beat, he was arguing with the umpires all the time. If somebody booted one, he throwed a fit. The guys weren't ready. They were on their heels.

"When I was pitching, as soon as I got the ball, I fired the ball in, and they made plays for me they didn't make for him. And he was mad all the time. He couldn't understand that. He'd stomp around on the mound, and he'd throw spitters, and they'd accuse him of that. The ump would ask him to throw the ball in, and instead of throwing it back in, he'd roll it back in just to aggravate 'im. I actually believe the umpires gave me some strikes that they didn't give him. Claude was a good pitcher. He had the best slider that I had ever seen. Weren't very many throwing them then. They didn't know what it was.

"Paul Derringer was a nice guy, a good pitcher. Of course, he didn't have the stuff he had when he was with Cincinnati, but he knew how to pitch. He won 13, 14 games. [In 1945 he was 16–11.] I roomed with him on one road trip. He took me to some of the nicest places I ever seen before. He went first class. I thought that was pretty nice. Took me to restaurants I never heard of.

"Clyde McCullough, our catcher, was in the navy. We had Paul Gillespie, Dewey Williams, Mickey Livingston, and Bob Scheffing. Dewey was the best of that bunch. He caught the best game. Dewey didn't get upset much.

"The guy who really helped us in '45 was Don Johnson. He's a great guy, one of the best. He wasn't supposed to be a great fielder, but he was great on double plays and hitting and running. He hit over .300 for us [.302]. He never argued with no one, never cussed no one, never got in trouble, and once in a while he'd pat somebody on the back and say, 'We're going to win this game,' and we'd win it.

"I remember late in the season, Brooklyn came in, it was close to the end of the season, we had about a two-and-a-half-game lead, and as we sat in the dugout the Dodgers walked around talking to us, asking how the wife and kids were, and Don come around and said, 'Don't be listening to them guys. They're just trying to talk you out of the game. Let's just kick the devil out of them.' And we did it two out of three.

"St. Louis came in, and they began doing the same thing, asking the guys how their wives and kids were, 'You come down and we'll go hunting or fishing,' and Don said the same thing. 'Let's go get them. They're doing the same thing. Let's don't let down. Let's beat them too. We can win this pennant. All we got to do is beat them.' We beat them two out of three.

"Stan Musial was their hitting star, a tough out for everybody, but I got him out good that year. I used to take a big windup and just pump once and throw the ball. One time we were playing Boston, and I beat Nate Andrews in a ball game—he was a good pitcher—and after the game he called me and wanted to know where to get in touch with Nick [Bill Nicholson] or Stan Hack, and I told him I didn't know, I hadn't seen 'em, and he wanted to know if I would come and help him. I said, 'What's the trouble?' He was drunk. He had to get a doctor. So I called a cab and went to his apartment. I got there, and he was laying in the bed, and he said, 'The doctor's name is out on the dresser. Call him.' So I called him, and he came over. And I asked him how he was, and he said he had drunk quite a bit after the ball game. He said, 'I have to go to the park tomorrow.' The doctor pulled a needle out of his bag, went into the bathroom, and washed it off. I don't know if he had water in it when he shot him or not, but he didn't give him nothing. He came back in there and said, 'This will fix you up.' Nate said, 'Good. All I need is to go to sleep.' He stuck him in the hip, and he turned over and said, 'Aah,' and just passed out. And I don't think he gave him anything. Might have been water.

"The next day Nate came over and said, 'How do you get Musial out?' I said, 'Don't nobody get him out. What are you talking about?' He said, 'Yes, you can.' He told me, 'When he gets the bat cocked and the leg cocked back, don't pump once, like you usually do, pump twice. When you see a wrinkle in that right leg, when that knee relaxes, throw then. If it don't do it on the second pump, pump again. If you don't see it then, pump again.' And I did, and I got Musial out so it was pitiful. I'd see that leg give a little bit when he relaxed, and I'd throw, and he'd pop up, hit into double plays, strike out.

"[Musial] would take high school kids out to the ballpark, they'd chase balls for him while he was hitting, looked at all the pictures every time I'd pitch, to see what I was doing.

"One day I was pitching a game and he hit a line drive right between my legs about a hundred miles an hour. He got on first base and laughed. He said, 'You're not going to do it anymore. I know what you're doing.'

"And I didn't get him out quite as good after that.

"I always was a pretty good study of baseball. During batting practice when the other guys were up, other pitchers were eating a sandwich or playing cards. I was setting in the dugout and watching the visiting club hit. I picked up a lot of things. I studied the game, and old Hardrock would help me. I'd tell him about it, and he'd say, 'It might work. Try it.'

"During the All-Star Game [Brooklyn outfielder] Dixie Walker was hitting. He was leading the league then, and nobody on our club was getting him out, and I threw practice instead of playing in the game, and I threw him down the middle— during batting practice that's what you're supposed to do—and he could hardly hit one out of the infield. I thought, That's funny, as good a hitter as he is. We used to pitch him outside, and he'd hit to left field. We'd pitch him inside, and he'd hit to right field. Pitch him down the middle, and he'd hit through the box. You could hardly get him out. After that, I pitched him down the middle, and I got him out so it was pitiful. I don't know what it was, him looking to where I used to pitch him, I guess, but it wasn't there.

"I enjoyed pitching against Cincinnati. They had [Frank] McCormick on first, Lonny Frey on second, Eddie Miller at short. I used to go down and watch them take batting practice from the dugout. One time Miller came over—I knew Miller when Eddie Joost played at Kansas City. I used to throw batting practice for him. I was setting down in the dugout, and he just got through hitting, he ran around the bases and come by and said, 'Goddamn, are you pitching again? Just throw your damn glove out, and you got us beat again.'

"I think I beat them six or seven times that year. I beat them an awful lot.

"Of course, that year I got a little tired, pitching all them games with two days' rest. Before they got Hank Borowy from the Yankees [in 1945] they sat down with me, all the coaches, Hardrock, the manager, wanted to know if I could pitch on three days' rest and sometimes two days' rest. They said, 'We're going to get Borowy, but we're having a little trouble, but we're going to get him. If you can pitch a few times with two days' rest, maybe we can win this.' I asked them, 'What if I hurt my arm?' He said, 'Mr. Wrigley will take care of you the rest of your life.' I said, 'All right, I'll try it.'

"On three days' rest I'd win 3–2, 4–2. On two days' rest—I did that two or three times—when I'd warm up, my arm felt dead and tired. I thought, Jesus, I ought to tell him I can't pitch today. Then, Oh well, it ain't hurting, it's just dead, so I'd go out there and shut you out. I could throw it to within a half inch of where I wanted to. I just kept doing that until they got Borowy, and I went back to three days' rest.

"I was in good shape. I throwed in-between times too. I threw batting practice or in relief. I wanted to keep it loose so it wouldn't stiffen up.

"In the middle of the season we finally got Borowy from the Yankees. The Yankees asked waivers for him. They wanted to help the Cubs. The Cubs had been helping them, and the Cubs thought they could win with him, and the Yankees was going to give him a shot at it. They put him on waivers I don't know how many times, and everybody in the American League claimed him, so they waited until about five minutes to twelve one night and put him on the list, and nobody claimed him, and that's how they got him out of there.

"In 1945 we beat out the Cardinals because Claude Passeau and Hank Borowy pitched agin' 'em and beat 'em. I only pitched once or twice agin' 'em. I shut them out once. But Passeau and Borowy done a pretty good job agin' 'em.

"When Borowy came, he was terrific. He had awful soft hands, and he always got a blister on his hands, and he wouldn't put nuthin' on them to toughen them up. I don't think he had ever worked a day in his life. He had tender hands, and he'd get blisters on the second finger of his right hand, and he couldn't pitch hardly. 'Cause Andy Lotshaw helped him a lot getting him ready. He didn't finish all of them games. He had some relief help in the ninth. But he had a good fastball. That was his best pitch. Later in the season the guys would get tired, and he got stronger. They hadn't seen that kind of stuff. He was 11–2 with us. He won the pennant clincher against Pittsburgh. I had won the day before in Cincinnati.

"I thought Chicago was a real good baseball town. In '45 we had a pretty good crowd all the time. I had quite a few friends, got along real good with the fans, and I kinda enjoyed it. I really enjoyed it that year."

47

Jolly Cholly

In November 1940 the Cubs fired Gabby Hartnett as manager and replaced him with Jimmie Wilson, the former Reds catcher. The general manager, Jim Gallagher, hired Charlie Grimm to be one of his coaches. Gallagher had warned Wilson that if things didn't go well, Grimm would be right there to take over, but Wilson wasn't concerned because the following June, Grimm went to manage the Cubs' top minor league farm club, the Milwaukee Brewers, owned and run by Bill Veeck.

But in 1944, after the Cubs under Wilson started the season 1–9, Phil Wrigley decided he had made a mistake letting Charlie Grimm go. Once again, Jolly Cholly became manager of the Chicago Cubs. Cubs shortstop Lennie Merullo, who flourished under Grimm's jovial reign, recalled the camaraderie under the man who over the years led the Cubs to three different pennants, including his last in 1945.

LEN MERULLO: "The day Charlie Grimm rejoined the club in '44, we were picked up at the train station in St. Louis in two small school buses. We were saying, 'What the hell is going on?'

"We drove right by the Chase Hotel, and then you should have heard the writers and the ballplayers. . . . 'Where the hell are they taking us now, out to the zoo?' 'Cause Charlie Grimm had a pal who was the manager of the St. Louis zoo.

"Turned out they took us forty miles out to Charlie's home. He had a picnic, all the beer you could drink, all the drinks you wanted, a big, big barbecue, and we had so much fun. The whole idea was for him to get to know the ballplayers, which was a great idea. He took a fellow like myself aside, 'Hey, come on now, you're not playing up to snuff. What's on your mind?' 'I don't like hitting eighth. I should be up in the second spot.' And sure enough, I was up in the second spot. And then he put me back in eighth, because I didn't earn my spot. But at least he got to know what was on your mind. And he did it with all the ballplayers. Even if he didn't ask, you had a chance to talk with him, away from the ballpark. It was great. He had a beautiful, beautiful place. Charlie and Bob Lewis, the traveling secretary, and one of our coaches, Red Smith, they were always putting on little acts, like Hermann Göring and Goebbels and Hitler. They were famous for that. And they were great. Charlie was German himself.

"Under Charlie we all enjoyed each other, had a lot of fun with each other. When you played for Charlie Grimm, that's the type of ball club he had. He coached at third base, and he did his best to keep you loose. Some players if you get in a rut, you beat yourself to death. You try all the harder, and you stop getting any base hits, and for me, it would affect my fielding. I was that type of ballplayer. I needed a guy like Charlie to snap me out of it.

"And I was not a fellow who went out or had drinks. I'd have a lot of fun and get along great with the ballplayers, had a lot of fun with them, make believe I was pinning Bill Nicholson down on the floor—he'd let me do it, and then he'd just flip me over like I was nothing. But there was always something like that going on in the clubhouse. We got along great with one another. I was the champion Wheaties eater. Bill Nicholson led the league in home runs in '43 and '44, and every time Nick hit a home run, in those days he got a case of Wheaties. They'd slide them down the backstop. And after you hit your home run, the batboy would catch the Wheaties off the screen and hand it to the home run hitter. That box always went into my locker. I didn't have to hit home runs to eat!

"Our catcher, Clyde McCullough, was not an educated guy, and we used to kid him all the time. Clyde was a great defensive catcher. Nobody had a better arm or was a better mechanical catcher than Clyde. He was tough, strong as a bull.

"We'd have the preseries meeting out there on the floor of the clubhouse. The catcher and the pitcher would get in the middle, and we'd go over the whole ball club we were playing. If we were playing a team like Brooklyn, we knew Charlie

Dressen was a sign stealer, so we'd have to switch signs about the second or third inning, and geez, it was always very, very confusing to Clyde.

"We used to work with him, the second baseman, and third baseman. If we went to a scoreboard sign, we'd let him know with a signal from either Don Johnson or me just where we were going to go. But Clyde had trouble with the signs, so we'd kid him. We would overexaggerate. We used to swear he had to put his head down and see how many fingers he was putting down!

"But he could throw with anybody. He had that catcher's body, a long torso and short legs, and a great arm, and he liked to show it off. And in infield practice Don Johnson or Stan Hack, when he made those throws to the bases, you could hear the crowd 'OOOOooooh,' and when they'd catch the ball, they'd snake their gloved hand, as if to say, 'That ball stung,' putting on an act.

"Well, one day Don Johnson covered on the throw to second base while Clyde was showing off his arm. Don looked like he did it accidentally, but he did it on purpose, he dropped his glove and caught the ball barehanded, and that goddamned McCullough was so mad he chased him out to center field!

"Peanuts Lowrey, who played center field, we called Goober, because he had buckteeth as a kid. He had those teeth taken out and replaced with false teeth, uppers. He was one of those guys who had that look on his face, a good-looking guy. He had beautiful eyes, with long, long eyelashes. He lived in Culver City, working part-time in the movies. He once was in the movies with Spanky and Our Gang.

"Peanuts was a good player. He was the only player I knew who would come in without a signed contract, always carried it, even though the rule was you couldn't report unless you were signed. He was an infielder-outfielder, never had a job starting out, but he would always wind up a regular within ten days. That's the way he was. He always would have a good year, and they used him where he could help the team best. Sometimes he played third, sometimes a little short, mostly left field. He could play center field as good as anybody, but he didn't have the arm.

"Years later, I was scouting for the Cubs. Jim Gallagher was working out of the commissioner's office. I asked him one time, I said, 'Jim, it always bothered me that that goddamned Peanuts Lowrey, in negotiating with you every spring, he would bet me a suit of clothes every spring that he would hit more home runs than me.' Peanuts was another Leo Durocher. He could con you, he was sharp, he would play pool. If he had to cheat to beat you, he would do it. That was Peanuts Lowrey.

"I said, 'I'm just curious about Peanuts Lowrey. He was my friend and Phil Cavarretta's friend. He would come into camp, and I know he lived in California, but you would always give him permission, "OK, I'll see you in camp." He would pat his inside sport-coat pocket, as if to say, "The contract is there, kid, and I'm going to talk to them."'

"Jim said, 'Let me tell you about that little son of a bitch. You know, he made more money on that ball club than Stan Hack, Bill Nicholson, and Claude Passeau.'

"I believe it. They didn't believe in incentive clauses in those days, but he would make agreements with Gallagher because he knew how they used him, and he'd have good years. I don't know just what kind of side agreements he'd make, probably the number of games played, or if he hit for a certain average, or if he played more than two positions, things like that, but he would work out something with him.

"Gallagher said, 'The easiest guy to sign every year was Stan Hack.' Stan was such an easygoing guy.

"Smiling Stan. Everybody loved Stan Hack. Stan was a very, very popular player. Stan was an outstanding stick. He hit from foul line to foul line, a line drive type of hitter. He was like Wade Boggs. He was a lifetime .301 hitter. He didn't have a great arm, but he had such a nice soft throw. It was never off the mark, and he'd always come up with the ball. He looked a little unorthodox, those knees would go together. Don Johnson and I would have a lot of fun imitating him.

"But that Peanuts, he probably made twice as much money as Stan. Send him a contract, and Stan'd sign it and send it right back. Now, there is a guy who never got the money he deserved. Nick was making around $18,000, which was a pretty good salary. I'm sure Bill Nicholson got what he deserved, because he was a good, smart country boy. And Passeau was the same way.

"When Gallagher told me Peanuts was making more than them, I believed him, knowing Peanuts.

"My own son was around the ballpark. He didn't idolize me. He idolized Peanuts. He followed Peanuts around, and Peanuts made so much of him, 'cause he had lost his own boy, I suppose.

"'Who's your favorite ballplayer?' I'd ask my boy.

"'Peanuts Lowrey.'

"He was a great clutch player.

"Bill Nicholson had a great sense of humor, even though he was very quiet. He had a dry humor. Everybody loved him. He had those shiny white teeth and always had a smile on his face. He was about six feet tall, no more, and strong as a bull. He was a farmer. Bill and Stan Hack were roommates, and they were complete opposites.

"Stan's idea of having a great time after a ball game was to sit down and have a couple of bottles of beer and talk about the game. Charlie Grimm always had a couple of cases of beer for the players after the game instead of having the fellows stop off at a saloon or the hotel lounge and get in trouble—many of the fellows did get in trouble that way—Charlie started that idea, which I thought was a great idea; even if you didn't have a bottle of beer, you got in the custom of sitting with your teammates and talking about the ball game.

"Nick was in the clique I was a part of. We loved to play poker. We played for hours until it was time to go to bed. And Stan would just stand around and look at us. He'd never play.

"The card players were Phil Cavarretta, myself, Peanuts Lowrey, Bill Nicholson, and Clyde McCullough, when we could keep a hold on him. Clyde was always on the prowl. He loved to play poker with us, but he was too active. He had to be going here, going there, doing this and doing that. And he was not a drinker. Hank Wyse played, and once in a while our catcher Mickey Livingston, a great guy. That was the clique. There were always five or six in the game. We had a dollar ante, couldn't go over. The year that Eddie Stanky was with us [1943], we didn't want any part of him in the game because he was always trying to up the ante. Christ, he and Peanuts Lowrey really got into it one time. Ow.

"This time we were playing dice, and what we would do, we'd take one of the rugs and put it up over the radiator, and this happened at the Biltmore Hotel in Los

Angeles during spring training. We put it up over the radiator so it would be quiet, 'cause we threw the dice against the radiator, and with the rug you wouldn't make any noise. So Stanky came in. And we always had the limit. He waited for his turn, and then he threw out a twenty-dollar bill. We just looked at him. 'Hey, Eddie, a dollar. A dollar is the limit.' He insisted. 'Cover it.' So everybody took a dollar or two, and he lost it. But the second time around he threw out a twenty-dollar bill again, and again we all jumped on him. We thought, Let's teach him a lesson. He's going to lose it again. Well, he rolled it up to a couple hundred dollars. Yeah, just like that. And then he dropped the dice on the floor and started to pull the money in. Peanuts said, 'What are you doing?' Stanky said, 'That's it for me. I got what I wanted.' And he started out the door. Before you knew it, they were wrestling, really going at it! But that was Eddie Stanky.

"Eddie was a wonderful guy—off the field a tough kid from Philadelphia, a little guy [five-eight, 170], loved to dress impeccably. He fell in love with the daughter of Milt Stock, when Milt was managing in Macon, Georgia. She was a tall, beautiful southern belle. If you saw the two of them together, you'd say, 'How did they ever get together?'

"Eddie was a clean-cut, snappy-talking guy. They didn't look like a match, but Milt was the same way. He was a little bowlegged guy who married a beautiful woman, the mother of this girl, when he was playing in that Southern League.

"I always kidded Eddie, 'If it wasn't for me, you never would have become the ballplayer that you did.' If you remember right, a little research will tell you that in 1942 he was the MVP on the Milwaukee ball club, led that league. He was a shortstop. I'm a shortstop, supposedly with a bright future. I was a lean kid, I could run, and I could throw. And kind of a colorful type of ballplayer, and I was brought up in the Cubs system. And he had played a lot of minor league baseball, never went to school. He had a great year there, and now what are they going to do with him? When they brought him up, they made him a second baseman, and we paired up. And we got along great.

"He didn't have many friends on the ball club. He was one of those guys who was a little arrogant, a little smart talking. That was his way. But that wasn't the real Eddie Stanky. That was his way so he could be noticed. He didn't have a great arm, wasn't a great runner, didn't look like a great hitter, but he was a hell of a ballplayer.

"He used to do little things, the little things I didn't feel I had to do. He was one of these guys who would step on the first baseman if he was reaching across the bag. Little things like that, hoping he would drop the ball. Or tag the runner hard coming into second base, try to slap him in the face with the ball. Little things like that.

"I can remember we were playing against Boston. They had a big tall guy from the South by the name of Connie Ryan, a second baseman. They had a little altercation, and I don't think Ryan ever forgot it. Stanky slid into him pretty hard one day, and boy, that started it. The next time he took a high throw, with Stanky stealing—Stanky couldn't run that well but he was a good base stealer—I remember Ryan taking that high throw and coming down right in his neck with his spikes. I know that was done purposely. I don't think he meant to get him on the neck, but he meant to come down on top of him. And he really cut him pretty good.

"That was the kind of player Stanky was. Nobody really liked him when you played against him. When you played with him, he was a winner. And he would stir you on, get you going, but then he was traded for a left-handed pitcher, a good friend of mine who died a young man [at the age of fifty-five], from the Brooklyn Dodgers, Bob Chipman. We called him Chipmonk.

"Why did they trade him? Simple. We had Stan Hack, the best leadoff man in major league baseball. Great on-base percentage, good hitter, and just a natural leadoff man. That's Eddie Stanky's best spot. His most valuable spot. When he played with us, I hit second a lot more than anybody else on that ball club. And where was Eddie Stanky hitting? Eighth. He never would show his true value. He was a base on balls guy. He made you throw strikes, and foul off pitches, hoping to get a base on balls. Or he'd hit doubles down the left-field line or the right-field line, with that thirty-ounce bat he used. That was his value, and Leo Durocher knew it. The Brooklyn organization knew it. They said, 'Let's go after Stanky. He doesn't cover that much ground, but he's a good infielder and knows how to play the hitters, turns a double play pretty good.' The first thing Durocher did, he put him right into the leadoff spot, with Reese hitting second. That was it. Leo made him a ballplayer.

"Leo Durocher was *the* most hated man in baseball. That's when you played *against* him. If you played for him, fine. But when you played against him, you didn't like him. You didn't like his coaches, either, except for Red Corriden, a little freckle-faced guy, red-headed, an ex-Cub, who was great. Nobody liked Charlie Dressen, his third-base coach. We didn't like him at all. We would always get on him, because he had the reputation as a sign stealer. But Durocher was a good baseball man. What the hell, we all knew that. He was a hunch player, a hunch manager. He knew who to get on and who not to get on. He never got on Cavarretta. Never got him mad. Let him sleep. But he'd get on fellows like me, who would want to get back at him, and you'd tighten up.

"He would get personal. Sure. Yeah. Even his own players didn't like it. But they knew what he was doing. And he got results. He got on Paul Erickson one day, and got on Hiram Bithorn one day, and they wound out throwing at him in the dugout! Throwing the ball *at him*! That's how mad he could get you.

"The Cubs and the Dodgers were great rivals. Hated each other. The Brooklyn fans were really outstanding, at the old Ebbets Field. They were almost on the foul line, and the fans—if you made a good play, they let you know it, and if you didn't, they let you know that too. Oh, they could get on you. And they were right on top of you. Even closer than in Fenway Park. But you liked to play there because there was always so much excitement. There were cops on the bench. Every ballpark had cops on the bench.

"They still talk about the terrific fight I got into with Dixie Walker. It was the only time they ever made a circle and let two guys fight it out before a ball game.

"The only two things they remember about me, it wasn't my hitting or fielding, it was the fight I had with Dixie Walker, and my four errors on the day my oldest son was born.

"Lew Riggs was playing third base. Riggs and Cookie Lavagetto used to alternate at third base. I was on first base, and Peanuts Lowrey was hitting. We put on the hit-and-run play, and I was on the move, a bang-bang play at third base, and I got to second base the same time as Stanky, and I slid into him hard. I took him out. The next thing I know, we're rolling on the ground. He's hitting me in the face with the ball. And somebody else was punching me. We both got kicked out of the game.

"I heard Charlie Grimm say, 'That goddamn Reese. That little son of a bitch Reese.' He had been the one who had jumped in there. And all night long my roomie, Cavarretta, had me so wired up. We were staying at the Commodore Hotel. Of course, I had some pretty good welts all over my face. Phil just kept talking out loud to me. I couldn't wait to get to the ball game the next day.

"Pee Wee was a good ballplayer and a good fella, but geez, I was so angry at him for jumping in on it, I couldn't wait to get out to the ball game and have it out with him.

"I foolishly waited until he got into the batting cage. We were warming up pre-game. In those days you had cops on both benches to keep the crowd off the dugout. We had one cop we all knew. He had been there for years, a very popular guy, a great big Italian fella. So I went in and stepped right in front of Pee Wee. I showed him the welts on my face. I said, 'Pee Wee, I understand you jumped in and let me have it.' He explained it.

"He said, 'Geez, I started to pull you off Stanky, and somebody started belting me.' Which was the way it was, I'm sure. So I turned around and said, 'Look, Pee Wee,' and I was no bigger than he was, even though they called him Pee Wee, 'Well, Pee Wee, I think I can handle you. So if we ever get into it again, you stay the hell out of it.' And I started to walk away. Meanwhile, all my ballplayers are watching what the hell is going on. They can't imagine me going in there and talking to Pee Wee.

"Anyway, about fifteen or twenty yards away from me, Pee Wee started yelling at me—and I don't blame him. He said something to me, so I started to walk back to him, and now we're going nose to nose, just yelling at one another, and then I got hit right behind the ear, and the punch came from Dixie Walker. He was *the* hero back in those days, a hell of a ballplayer, but among the ballplayers he was not too popular. So when that happened, my ballplayers all jumped in there, and of course, Dixie took off, and I took off after him, tackled him near the dugout, and then the cops had us both.

"Charlie Grimm then said to the cops, 'Get your hands off of them. I'm responsible for my ballplayers.' Geez, the next thing I know the big cop on our bench threw me out there. He said, 'Well, go get him.' And they made a circle and let us go at it. We both got fined $1,500 and were suspended for ten days. That was a lot of money back in those days. It was paid by the Cubs.

"But they tell me during our fight, everybody went after Durocher, the hell with the other guys, and they practically undressed him.

"In 1945 we finished ahead of the Dodgers, and ahead of the Cardinals, too, which was the only time between 1942 and 1946 anyone beat out the Cardinals.

"The Cubs and Cards, that was a better rivalry than Brooklyn. Oh sure. You had a lot of Illinois fans who was Cubs fans, and in the lower part of Illinois, they were Cardinals fans. And it was only a three-hundred-mile hop.

"Their star was, of course, Stan Musial. Stan Musial? You couldn't play him. You say to yourself, 'Let's see, he's a left-handed hitter. I'll play him toward second base.' Or, 'I'll play him deep.' Or, 'I'll play him to the right side.' Didn't matter. Nothing worked. He had that unorthodox style of hitting, had his fanny facing the pitcher, the left toe in. If that ball was outside, he'd hit it to left field. If the ball was inside, he'd hit it to right. If the ball was over the plate, he's liable to hit it out of the ballpark. And then at times he'd come around and give that inside-out swing and hit it between third and short. He always got a good piece of the ball. And you couldn't play him deep because he could run like a son of a buck. Really, Musial was fast. Look up the number of ground ball base hits that he got and you'll realize. He had plenty of them.

"In 1945 we had a good ball club. The other teams weren't at full strength as yet because a lot of the players hadn't come out of the service. It was taking a little time for some of those outstanding ballplayers to get back. But it was a good ball club. Even so, we couldn't have won the pennant if Jim Gallagher hadn't gotten Hank Borowy from the Yankees. I don't know what the deal was, what the Yankees had promised Gallagher. All I know is the Yankees were able to help the Cubs out at that time. I don't think anyone realized how serious the Yankees were when they put him on waivers.

"Hank was a very quiet, laid-back fellow, not an overly big guy [six feet, 175], but he had long arms and big hands and a beautiful nice, smooth, easy motion. I had faced him a couple summers and then in college. And he won the pennant for us.

"Hank went out there, never missed a turn, and you'd be damn sure he was going to pitch a hell of a ball game. Boy, he rode that ball in there. He was on a roll. I mean, he picked up that whole ball club. He absolutely picked up that ball club. Fellows like Philibuck [Cavarretta], Stan [Hack], and Nicholson just rolled right along with him, having real good years. I hit about .240, but I played every game, and boy, it was fun. And beating the Cardinals was more fun.

"We clinched the pennant in Pittsburgh. I remember the party afterward more than the game. William Benswanger was the owner of the Pittsburgh Pirates, little Mr. Benswanger, and Paul Derringer, who was six foot four, a big son of a buck, nice guy but not too popular. He had a little crude way about him. His sense of humor was never what it was hoped it would be for a big star like he was. I remember he got into a very vocal thing with Mr. Benswanger, who came over to congratulate everybody, including Charlie Grimm. In a kidding way, trying to be humorous, Paul got a little rough with Mr. Benswanger, even got a little physical with him, which kind of spoiled the party.

"Paul said, 'Wow, we booted you guys.' And he gave him a kick in the fanny. That was very uncalled for.

"Of course, I tell the story, I don't know how true it is, but it is certainly partly true: Derringer was traded from Cincinnati to the Cubs in 1943. I had hit a home run with the bases loaded off him not long before that. I think I hit 6 home runs in the seven years I played. One was that grand slammer off Paul Derringer.

"I can remember it just got into the left-center-field stands, and his arms were up in the air. I don't blame him. It was a curve ball. That's what he was, a big curve ball pitcher. He'd lift that leg way up there and let you have it, curve ball after curve ball. He could hum it too. But his curve ball was his best pitch.

"Of course, I tell everybody, they must have figured his career was over with when I hit that home run because it was not long after that they traded him to the Cubs."

48

Roomies

Two members of the Cubs' fine infield defense on the 1945 pennant winner were first baseman Phil Cavarretta, who that year led the league in hitting with a .355 average and won the Most Valuable Player Award, and Lennie Merullo, the pepper-pot shortstop from Boston who had to leave Villanova University early when it was discovered that Phil Wrigley had paid him $1,500 for a commitment to sign with the Cubs while he was still in college.

Merullo played an excellent defense at shortstop; he spent much of his time on the bench as Phil Cavarretta's unofficial batting coach. The two roommates, both Italian, were nicknamed the Grand Opera Twins. For almost a decade they roomed together, two feisty ballplayers who had a deep mutual affection but who not only battled the opposition but at times liked to get on each other as well.

PHIL CAVARRETTA: "Lennie Merullo was my roommate for nine years. Boy, he used to worry so much about his hitting! He wasn't a very good hitter but a super competitor, a good infielder, kind of a miniature Bill Jurges, the same type of player. Billy couldn't hit, either.

"All the time I had to listen to him explain how he attempted to hit [Reds righthander] Ewell Blackwell. Oh God. Ewell was great. Even left-handed hitters had trouble with Ewell Blackwell. 'Cause he was so fast, and his ball would sink about a foot and a half. And he had a riser. He came from the side. I told Lennie, 'If I was a right-handed hitter, I wouldn't even go up and hit against him.' He said, 'Roomie, tell that to Charlie, will you. Tell him to take me out when he pitches.'

"He would try to hit Blackwell, and every time he went up there, he would get jammed and break three or four bats.

"We'd room together, have dinner, have a couple beers, come in. We'd go to the movies. I loved movies. In New York we'd go to the Palace Theater and come back to the hotel, go upstairs, get ready to go to bed, and I'd be laying down, trying to fall asleep, and all of a sudden Lennie would start: 'Jesus criminy, why the fuck can't I hit. That guy today, I should have killed him.' I said, 'Lennie, go to sleep. We have a doubleheader tomorrow.' He said, 'I *know* I can hit.' I said, 'Lennie, you could live to be eighty-nine and you'll never learn how to hit. Face it. You can't hit.'

"And boy, would he get mad! He'd put his clothes on, and he'd leave.

"I'd say, 'Good-bye.'

*   *   *

L ENNIE M ERULLO: "I roomed with Phil Cavarretta for nine years, seven in the big leagues and two in spring training. You ask him and he'll tell you I was the best roomie he ever had.

"Phil's a great guy, a tremendous person, a good family man, but he's a little different, hard to get to know, hard to get close to. We were thrown together soon after he reported to the Cubs when I was working out with the Cubs in old Braves Field. They took kids like me and put us over by the shower. Our trainer, Andy Lotshaw, would throw a uniform at you and say, 'OK, kid, get dressed in the dugout, and the coaches will take care of you.'

"I got in there early. You're wide-eyed, taking everything in. I put on the baggy old flannel road uniform and was ready to go out there, and the Cubs came filing in, having a lot of fun with each other. Larry French and Pat Malone, the whole gang, Gabby Hartnett especially, screaming, yelling, typical, and if you are just a kid, you're drinking all this in. This is exciting! And then I see Joe Marty, with his great ability. He was going to be another Joe DiMaggio, which he never did. Frank Demaree was there. Charlie Grimm. Boy, talk about excitement. Augie Galan, a young, good-looking guy.

"Augie asked me, 'What's your name, kid?' He wasn't much older than I was. He said, 'Grab your stuff and come on over.' Augie said, 'Put your stuff in his locker. You two guys should get along great. Merullo, Cavarretta. Hey!' He was doing this just to agitate Cavarretta. Cavarretta hadn't come in yet.

"I said, 'Do you think it will be all right?' I was excited to do that. I had been reading all about this young ballplayer. So I put my stuff in there, and in comes Phil Cavarretta, and the next thing, we're looking nose to nose at one another, and Augie Galan says, 'Which one is the high-class Italian? You or him?' And we both said, 'I am.' And kiddingly I said, 'Nah, you're a Sicilian.' And he looked at me with fire in his eyes. I thought he was going to knock me down on the floor. He said, 'What do you mean I'm a Sicilian? My people are from Palermo.' He didn't realize Palermo was in Sicily.

"I went back to school, and he was playing in the big leagues, and when I went to spring training in '39 he asked me to room with him. And we roomed together every year.

"He was not the easiest guy to room with because he is high-strung, a great athlete, and the madder he got, the better ballplayer he was. He didn't have that nice personality that people expected. He was a local boy, and he had to really mature, had to learn he had to spend some time with the fans, stand there, sign autographs, instead of brushing his way through.

"He was a good roomie, but he was our star, our captain. I kept him on an even keel. They used to call us the Grand Opera Twins. Two Italian boys. He was the star, and I was his roommate. I was the streaky ballplayer. I had good streaks, and then I'd have a bad streak. But he was very consistent, and we had to keep him happy, because gol dang, he was our ballplayer.

"We'd have fun with him in infield practice. Me, Don Johnson, and Stan Hack. To me the biggest difference in baseball today and years ago was that everybody talked it up. Talk, talk, talk. Today it's a quiet game. You don't hear a peep out of the catcher, a peep out of anybody. Then, if you didn't talk it up in the infield, your second baseman or third baseman would say, 'Hey, shake it up. Let's go.'

"When we had infield practice, we used to do the same thing, have fun with each other. Phil had a way, he sounded like a god-dang dog. 'Errrrrrrrrrerrrrr.' Soon as he opened his mouth, we all started barking. 'Owwwoooooowooooooo.' And he'd get so goddamn mad. 'All right, you sons of a bitch.' That was fun.

"When Phil was breaking in he used to be a stand-up hitter, got close to the plate. He could hit, but he'd pull everything foul. You could see he had that real quick bat. He was a tough out. Then as his career went along he made a change. He got off the plate with a closed stance, was stooped over, his right arm straight out, and he'd aim right at the shortstop. He was in a crouch, stayed down.

"Before Phil stepped into the batter's box, he'd spit, and he'd try to hit that spit, and if he didn't, he wouldn't get into that batter's box. That was a habit of his.

"But it was my job—most of the time I hit eighth, which is the worst place in the lineup 'cause the pitcher hit after you, so you never got a good ball to hit. You'd get overanxious. I could run like a son of a gun, and if I was in the groove and felt like that, I would be hitting second after Stan Hack. Most times I hit eighth. So Phil was always hitting either number three or number six after Bill Nicholson. Anyway, he had a bad habit of coming out of his crouch a little too soon, and if you live with a guy and play with a guy every day, you get to know each other's habits. And when he didn't hit the ball good, if he was unhappy with that at bat, I'd say, 'Phil, looks like you're coming up a little bit.' He'd say, 'Let me know, for Christ sake.' Like I was at fault.

"So that was my job. I'd have to watch him, and I'd have to yell out if I noticed that. If he was fouling off pitches, I'd yell out, 'Fill-a-buck.' That was our word code. He knew exactly what I meant. And he'd stay down.

"Everybody on the ball club knew what we were doing. Sometimes Phil would pop one up or wouldn't hit the ball or hit a weak ground ball back to the mound. 'Here it comes, Lennie. You're gonna get it.' Sure enough, he'd come over. 'You son of a bitch, roomie, you're not looking.'

"He led the league in hitting in '45. A tremendous person.

"And I always like to tell the story, toward the end of my career when I had a sciatica condition and I went to a utility role, we had a kid, Roy Smalley, who was on the horizon and it looked like he was going to be outstanding, a big guy, six three, great arm, good power, not that good a runner but good hands. He looked like he was going to become the next greatest shortstop, so I could see the picture on the wall, and toward July in '48 I was expecting any time to be called down the office and released.

"I finally got the call. Joe, the clubhouse man, said, 'Mr. Gallagher wants you down the office.'

"I said, 'This is it.'

"I went down there, and he said, 'Sit down, Lennie.' I sat down facing him across that big desk. Gallagher was a big fella, bushy eyebrows, little mustache, adopted son, a good Roman Catholic, went to Notre Dame. Everyone kidded him about that. They talked behind his back. He wasn't the most popular guy, but a good person.

"We sat there for what seemed like twenty minutes without saying a word. And finally he came out with, 'Lennie, who can I get to room with Phil Cavarretta?'

"That's a true story."

49

The War Pennant

The St. Louis Cardinals had won pennants in 1942, '43, and '44. In 1945 the Cardinals were weakened by the loss of stars Max Lanier, catcher Walker Cooper, and outfielder Stan Musial. The four stars had played in 1944 but had been drafted for the final year of the war.

The Cubs, at the same strength as in '44, found themselves on the trail of the champions. The Cubs had players who were close-knit and liked to have fun. Dewey Williams, one of the Cubs catchers, was another of those players whose bubbly personality and catching skills contributed to the Cubs' success that year.

DEWEY WILLIAMS: "Oh, we had a good ball club in '45. We won eighteen out of nineteen doubleheaders. We beat Cincinnati twenty-one out of twenty-two games. And we'd have won the twenty-second if Hy Vandenberg had covered first. I was jumping up and down, hollering at him to get over there, and we lost the game 2–1.

"I can remember we always had two big tin tubs, and it was always full of beer when we got through with the game. We took them on the road, along with our equipment, and that would sit in the clubhouse before the end of the game, and they had beer, and soda pop for the other guys who didn't drink.

"Andy Lotshaw was our trainer. He called me Huey because he couldn't say Dewey. He always had a Coca-Cola bottle with him, and when the pitchers went to him for a rub-down, he'd be bullshitting with them, and all he was putting on their arm was Coca-Cola. He'd say, 'Huey, they don't know what they're doing anyway, so what the hell.' Claude Passeau was one of those. He wanted and got special treatment from Andy.

"Passeau was a character. You'd get to New York, and you'd go down in Grand Central to catch the subway to Ebbets Field, and you'd stand there bullshitting with him, and you'd get on the subway, and then when the doors got ready to shut, he'd get off. He'd step off just as the train was pulling out, and you'd be on the wrong train. Hell, some of the ballplayers wound up in Coney Island. One time Heinz Becker and Dom Dallesandro didn't get to the ballpark until the third inning!

"Paul Derringer won a lot of games [16] for us that year. I can remember in a game in Brooklyn I never gave Paul but one sign all day long. That was because Leo Durocher was coaching first. Brooklyn would steal your signs. Every time one of the Dodgers would hit a line drive, Eddie Stanky and a few of the other players would jump up and down, like they were calling our pitches.

"We won 3–2, and after the game we went into the clubhouse. Derringer was about to fight our players on the bench because they kept saying the Dodgers were calling our pitches.

"I asked Derringer, 'Are you going to tell them, or will I?' He said, 'I will.' Derringer told them, 'Dewey didn't call but one pitch all day long. How in the hell were they stealing our signs?'

"Don Johnson, Len Merullo, and Passeau and quite a few of the others would put things over on the sportswriters. Hell, Johnson was good at it, and so was Merullo. They'd have Joe DiMaggio traded to Cincinnati, Ted Williams going somewhere. They'd make stuff up and tell it to the sportswriters. And that's the reason the sportswriters never came around us.

"We had so much fun. I can remember after a Sunday game against St. Louis, we were on our way home. Andy Pafko was sitting next to me and Don Johnson was sitting across the aisle. I began talking to Johnson, but I was just moving my lips, and he was doing the same thing. Pafko was going, 'Huh? Huh?' Andy thought he was going deaf!"

The 1945 Cubs were loosey-goosey, a reflection of their manager, Charlie Grimm, and they clung to first place despite the mysterious loss of power from Bill Nicholson, the two-time league home run champion who was mired in a disastrous batting slump. Grimm even had to bench his star slugger, who finished the season batting only .243, with a mere 13 homers.

Just two years earlier, during a season in which Nicholson struck 29 homers and drove in 128 runs, in a game against Boston, Braves manager Casey Stengel had walked over to Cubs manager Jimmie Wilson. He pointed to Nick in right field and said, "Take that guy out of there."

Wilson, confused, asked Stengel what he was talking about. "Take him out and I'll let you play two men in his place," said Stengel, "and I'll agree to use only eight men against your ten. Just take him out."

It would not be until 1950 when Nicholson would be diagnosed as having diabetes, back then a mysterious illness that can affect one's eyesight. It was the diabetes, it turned out, that had sapped Nick's power.

Even without the hitting of Nicholson, on July 8, 1945, the Cubs climbed into the lead. But Cubs general manager Jim Gallagher suspected his pitching wasn't strong enough to fend off the Cards, and he began his search for a fourth starter to go along with Claude Passeau, Hank Wyse, and thirty-eight-year-old Paul Derringer, who was at the end of an illustrious career.

Gallagher hadn't been looking to buy a star. Teams didn't ordinarily make their best players available in the middle of the season. He was hoping to pick up a veteran who perhaps was in a slump, with the hope that manager Charlie Grimm might be a positive influence and turn him around.

Among the team executives Gallagher called was Larry MacPhail, an owner and general manager of the New York Yankees. Gallagher was angling for Ernie Bonham, who had been slumping.

During a conversation with MacPhail, the unpredictable Yankees boss asked Gallagher, "How would you like Borowy?"

Hank Borowy at the time was considered the best pitcher in the American League. He had ten wins and an excellent earned run average.

Gallagher didn't really believe the Yankees executive would make Borowy available and told MacPhail so. MacPhail told Gallagher to make an offer.

When Gallagher relayed the offer to Phil Wrigley and Charlie Grimm, all agreed that the acquisition of Borowy would bring the Cubs the pennant. Gallagher still wondered whether perhaps MacPhail was pulling something. (MacPhail well may have been pulling something. Even though the war was over, Borowy was draft eligible. He was scheduled to appear before his draft board momentarily. So there was still a chance Borowy would be drafted.)

When Gallagher came home around midnight, his wife told him MacPhail had called six times. Gallagher then knew MacPhail was serious.

At three in the morning Gallagher called him back.

Asked MacPhail, "How about it, Gallagher, do you want Borowy or not?"

"Of course we want him," said Gallagher, "but you know the other American League clubs won't give you waivers on him."

"Oh yes they will," said MacPhail. "As a matter of fact, they have. Borowy's free to go to the National League right now."

By the next morning Gallagher had an offer. On July 27, Phil Wrigley made his last coup, paying $97,000 for a pitcher whose lifetime record had been 46–25 during the last three years.

When the deal was announced those who knew MacPhail wondered whether Borowy would show up with a sore arm or be damaged goods in some way.

At the time of the deal, Larry MacPhail intoned, "Borowy appears to have outlived his usefulness with the Yankees. Since April he has pitched only four complete games and appears to have outlived his usefulness to us."

Cubs manager Charlie Grimm couldn't figure out why MacPhail let his star pitcher get away. Grimm told the press, "A few years before, when Larry was with the Brooklyn Dodgers, he had made a slick deal with the Cubs for Billy Herman. I've often thought he showed his appreciation by clearing the way for us to land Borowy."

Hank Borowy

Cubs first baseman Phil Cavarretta had his own theory, one about Borowy's blisters. But whatever the reason why MacPhail let Borowy go, Cavarretta was happy the Cubs had acquired the great pitcher.

PHIL CAVARRETTA: "What I heard, the reason they got rid of him was that Hank Borowy had a history of blisters on his pitching hand, and he had to skip two or three turns sometimes. The Yankees were always battling for a pennant, and he was one of their aces. You can't have an ace miss two or three turns. He kept getting blisters, and so they sold him to the Cubs, and the same thing happened here. It was the most ugly thing you'd ever want to see. In Hank's middle finger it would break the skin, and actually you could see the inside of the finger, the veins and all, and a funny part about that, the fans knew about it and sent in different remedies like pickle brine. One guy sent urine. And poor Hank. He is a very, very quiet guy. He wouldn't say boo to anybody, but he was a good pitcher.

"If we don't get Borowy in '45, we don't win the pennant, and I'll tell you why. 'Cause Hank Borowy beat the Cardinals himself four times. We only won the pennant by a couple games [three]. But he could beat the Cardinals. Four times is four full games.

"Hank had a good live fastball. That ball would jump. He could pitch high-ball hitters high and get them out because his high fastball would rise. It was like a breaking ball. He had a good curve, good command of his pitches, very intelligent, and he'd give you a hundred percent at all times.

"We used to kid him all the time, especially Lennie Merullo, our shortstop. Lennie was always teasing guys. Hank would be quiet, sitting there, and Merullo would say, 'Holy mackerel, Hank, for crying out loud, move a little bit. You all right? We think you're dead, man. Say something.' Lennie used to call him the Fordham Flash because he went to Fordham. Hank'd sit there and look at Lennie and say, 'Hey, Dage, be quiet.'"

Borowy reported to the gleeful Cubs and won his first two games. In one of the last big breaks the Cubs would ever get, Borowy's draft board gave him another deferment. By the end of the year his record with the Cubs was 11–2, as he helped pitch the Cubs to the pennant.

With Borowy rounding out a solid pitching staff, the Cubs continued to hold off the still-strong Cardinals. As a team the Cubs led the league in hitting, pitching, and fielding. Phil Cavarretta hit .355, best in the league. Stan Hack hit .323. Don Johnson hit .302. Young, talented outfielder Andy Pafko, who before long would be given away to Brooklyn, hit .298, struck 12 home runs and drove in 110.

With the Cubs still ahead of the Cardinals by a game and a half with six remaining, they met for two games at Wrigley Field. Hank Borowy won the first game 6–5, for the pitcher's twentieth victory of this split season, ten wins for the Yankees and ten for the Cubs. The Cards won the second game, but the Cubs ended any chances the Cards might have had by winning a doubleheader against Cincinnati and one against the Pirates.

On September 29, the Cubs defeated the Pittsburgh Pirates to win the 1945 pennant. The Cubs finished the 1945 season with 98 victories, three games ahead of the frustrated Cardinals.

At the team victory party, manager Charlie Grimm took a pair of long scissors, cut off the end of each player's tie, and had a quilt made.

The World Series was played against the Detroit Tigers, the team the Cubs had defeated twice, in 1907 and 1908. The Tigers had defeated them in the 1935 Series. Stan Hack and Phil Cavarretta had played in that Series. Ten years later they were looking for revenge.

The Series opened in Detroit for the first three games. In what was supposed to be a fun gesture toward the Cubs players, the Tigers booked them into staterooms on a cruise ship that was parked at the waterfront. When the players arrived on the ship, their reaction turned to anger.

LEN MERULLO: "The first thing they wanted to do was put us aboard a boat. They had a boat in the harbor, a big cruise ship, and of course the wives went out and bought special clothes, and they had us rooming on this boat. The women rebelled. Oh yeah, the wives rebelled. The wives of the writers rebelled. Then the ballplayers said, 'We're not staying here.' So we wound up at the Book Cadillac."

HANK WYSE: "Phil Cavarretta and his wife, my wife and I, Peanuts Lowrey and his wife, we didn't stay on that boat. It was as big as a small bathroom, couldn't even get our bags in there. I put mine up, and my wife didn't like it—Good Christ, I thought it would be fun. Cavarretta called me and said, 'Let's get out of here.' I said, 'What do you mean?' He said, 'Come on. Let's go. We're going back to the hotel. We ain't gonna stay in this tub.' We went back to the hotel, and they said they didn't have any rooms, and Phil said, 'Call the traveling secretary.' He got ahold of Bob Lewis. He told him, 'If we don't get a room in this hotel, we ain't gonna play tomorrow.' In about five minutes we all had rooms."

Hank Borowy faced the Tigers' Hal Newhouser in the first game. Borowy, who knew the Tigers from his American League days, made short work of their hitters, shutting them out 9–0 on six hits. Hank Wyse pitched Game 2.

HANK WYSE: "I remember when we got to warming up, they wanted to take pictures of Virgil Trucks and me shaking hands. I shook hands and wished him good luck and walked off and he beat me, and I told myself, 'Damn, you all will never get me to do that again.'

"I had pitched a game in the minor league against Trucks. That day I pitched a one-hitter, and he pitched a no-hitter agin' me. He was with Beaumont. He didn't give us as much trouble in his second start against the Cubs. But that day he had a good slider, and he was throwing pretty hard.

"I was ahead 1–0 in the fifth. I thought I was getting them out pretty good. Then one of them, Jimmy Outlaw, got a base hit, and I don't remember how the next one got on. Then Hank Greenberg came up. I had made him look bad the first two times. I was throwing three-quarters, fastballs away from him, throwing him curve balls in, and he really looked bad.

"I had two strikes on him, and I thought I'd show him my good curve and come straight overhand, and I hung it a little bit inside about waist high, and he hit it about a mile high, but it just barely got into the seats. It went out about a seat or two.

"I heard later that Jim Tobin, who used to be with the Boston Braves, was calling pitches from the catcher. He was in the scoreboard calling pitches. I don't know that for sure but I wouldn't doubt it."

In Game 3, Claude Passeau pitched a one-hitter, allowing only a single to Rudy York in a 3–0 victory, but Detroit left-hander Dizzy Trout came back to win the next game 4–1. Hank Borowy finally showed he was human in Game 5, as the Tigers knocked him out in the sixth in an 8–4 loss.

Game 6 demonstrated the Cubs' tenacity. Claude Passeau had held the Tigers to but one run when in the sixth inning a little drive caught him in the pitching hand, tore off a nail, and forced him from the game in the seventh inning. What made the incident so crucial was what happened after that: Cubs manager Charlie Grimm brought Hank Borowy into the game in the ninth inning with the score tied at 7. Borowy had been scheduled to pitch the seventh game. One inning would not have tired him. But because the game lasted twelve innings, Borowy had to pitch four innings before the Cubs finally won it. Had Passeau not been injured, the Cubs would not have had to use Borowy in Game 6. The outcome hung on that one fingernail.

CHARLIE GRIMM: "I'll always think we would have brought the Wrigleys their first world championship had not Passeau suffered a torn nail on the middle finger of his pitching hand in the sixth inning of the sixth game."

Game 7 was the decider. Manager Charlie Grimm was faced with a dilemma. Who should he start? Hank Wyse was used up, and so was Paul Derringer. Passeau was injured and couldn't pitch.

DEWEY WILLIAMS: "In the sixth game of the World Series I went in to catch in the ninth inning, and Borowy was pitching. In the twelfth inning I can remember Joe Hoover was on first base for Detroit, and Steve Owens, I could see he gave him the sign to steal. Eddie Mayo was hitting and we got two strikes on him, and if we got Mayo out, a left-handed hitter wouldn't be leading off the thirteenth inning. So we got two strikes on him, and I walked out to Borowy and told him, 'This is one guy I want you to strike out to keep him from leading off the next inning.' I wanted Borowy to get something on it. He threw a high curve ball that didn't get down far enough, and then Hoover took off for second base. I threw him out even though Merullo came over and Hoover cut Merullo on both arms.

"We won the game. Right after the game we went into the clubhouse, and Borowy was over there with Grimm. We had one day off the next day, and Borowy told Grimm, 'Let me pitch the seventh game.' With one day rest. He had just pitched four innings. Boy, did he ever wheel that ball, just like pitching two games. And I told Merullo and Cavarretta, 'If he pitches, there goes our money.' And I tried to get Milt Stock to go through Grimm and not let Borowy pitch the game, but I couldn't shake him.

"So, the day the game started, I warmed Borowy up. I always warmed the pitcher up so I'd know, whether I was catching or not. And he just didn't have it.

"I went down to the bullpen and got Hy Vandenberg up. Vandenberg would have beat them. That's the guy I wanted to pitch. I got him up and started warming him up. Out on the field against Borowy the first three hitters got on. Grimm went three hitters with him.

"When I got Vandenberg warmed up, damn Grimm sent Derringer down there to warm up. He put Paul in, and Paul got the shit kicked out of him. That cost us the damn game. Paul, he was a hell of a pitcher the first of the year, and then after he'd pitch, he'd take off. He wasn't with the ball club a lot of the time. He'd take off to St. Louis. He got fat again.

"Grimm didn't like Vandenberg because he had had a little trouble with him during the season. Hy was having a little fun in New York. Derringer could lead Vandenberg around by the nose, and then Grimm got mad at Vandy. Hy got in a fight with the house dick at the Commodore Hotel. Vandenberg knocked the house dick on his butt."

LEN MERULLO: "The Cubs should have won that Series, no doubt about it, against Newhouser and all. I still think the Cubs had the better ball club. Geez, we started off great, but we just didn't do it.

"Borowy never should have pitched in that last game. Never should have. He *never* should have. I was on the table in the trainer's room getting stitched after I was spiked in the sixth game. The game was over. This is a moment I will never, ever forget. Everybody comes up, we won that exciting ball game. The ball bounced over Hank Greenberg for a double by Stan Hack. We won, so we're going into the seventh game.

"We had a day off the next day. I'm in there getting stitched and all the writers and players come in, and the last one in there was Borowy. He had come in to relieve, pitched a bunch of innings. And I'm there, right there. And Grimmy, loud enough for everybody to hear, said to Hy Vandenberg, 'You're my pitcher for the seventh game.' Hy was a pretty good pitcher, a veteran pitcher. He was no Borowy, but a good pitcher. And then Borowy came in. And just like it happened yesterday, Borowy said, 'Skip, I'll go right to bed tonight, we have a day off tomorrow, and I'll be ready for that seventh game.' And Grimmy said, 'You're my man.' Just like that. That's just the way it happened. And the guy was all pitched out. They got five runs the first inning.

"If you ask me, how could Charlie have allowed that? The answer is: He went with his best. That was the reason. And I probably would have done the same thing. But it didn't work out. He should have stuck with Vandenberg, who was rested."

BILL NICHOLSON: "I knew Hank shouldn't have pitched. I knew when I was sitting there, 'cause he was a man who had to have his rest, and seven innings was top-notch for him, and when he didn't get his rest, I knew we were in for a rough day. I didn't say anything to Grimm, but he couldn't get anybody out. He didn't have his proper rest. And he was a seven-inning pitcher too.

"We had a chance to win the Series that year, but when they got five runs in the first inning of the seventh game, we didn't have a chance. And it was tough being a left-handed hitter. Hal Newhouser was a good pitcher. Yeah. We should have stayed in bed. I got a hit off him, but we couldn't improve on things after the first inning."

HANK WYSE: "It was Grimm's fault. He didn't pitch the pitchers right. I don't know why he couldn't have pitched Paul Erickson or why he couldn't pitch Vandenberg in that seventh game. They were furious, and so was I.

"I didn't talk to Charlie about it. It wouldn't have done any good. We talked among ourselves. Oh yeah. Erickson even went up to the office and asked to pitch.

"We knew for him to be effective Borowy had to have four days' rest. He always had a blister on his hand. He had won in relief the game before. None of us thought he ought to pitch. Borowy went out there, and they scored five runs the first inning.

"The only thing I could figure out, he pitched Borowy because Borowy had pitched in the American League before and he knew how to pitch them. That's the only thing I could think of. I also knew he had to have four days' rest, and he hadn't had none at all."

DON JOHNSON: "Asking Borowy to pitch the seventh game was asking an awful lot from him. 'Cause he had been pitching a lot. Then he wanted to pitch that last game. You have to admire a guy for wanting to do it."

PHIL CAVARRETTA: "The World Series was over in the first inning. And of all the people to get the big hit, Paul Richards, the Tigers catcher, hit a double to left field, and in all the years he played, he never pulled a ball in his life. That shows you that Borowy didn't have a thing. Because we were all playing him to right field when Richards pulled him.

"They got five runs. We kept pecking away. Newhouser was tired, and we scored runs off him. I got a couple hits off him [three singles]. He was out of gas. They brought in Trout, and he did the job. Dizzy was the best pitcher in that whole Series. A lot of people don't realize it. They had Newhouser, [Art] Houtteman, and Stubby Overmire, but Diz to me was the best pitcher in the whole Series."

DEWEY WILLIAMS: "After the game we were shaking it up. We had music going. Borowy was the only one who had a few tears in his eyes. We were giving it hell, having a lot of fun. I mean, it was like we won the damn game. Nobody was worried about it. Borowy was sitting in the dugout crying."

DON JOHNSON: "After the game is over and you've lost? I don't think there was any animosity toward anybody. We just wished Hank had had more rest.

"You win, you win. You lose, you lose."

PHIL CAVARRETTA: "And that was the last time the Cubs were in the World Series. It's sad, really. It looked for a while like the Cubs were going to do it in 1984, when Jim Frey was the manager, but San Diego beat them, and then even with the great infield of Grace, Sandberg, and Dunston they didn't make it. What the answer is, I don't know."

50

The Depths

CHARLIE GRIMM: "In 1945, we had been fortunate that many of our regulars were not acceptable for military service. But, now in 1946, this edge was lost. The weight of years on our club was just enough to put the flag far out of reach."

HANK WYSE: "The main thing that happened, in '46, Cavarretta didn't have the same kind of year he had in '45, and Nick was having it worse, and we didn't have the pitching that we got the year before. Of course, St. Louis got their good players back. Musial started helping them a lot. But our club wasn't that bad."

In 1946 the Cubs finished third, behind St. Louis and Brooklyn. But in 1947, with the strong Cubs pitching staff reduced to a shadow of itself, the team finished sixth, twenty-five full games behind the Dodgers.

Paul Derringer was gone. He had retired immediately after the '45 season, in which he won 16 games. His arm had been used up. Wyse, Borowy, and Passeau had won 14, 12, and 9 games, respectively, in '46, but in 1947 Borowy won 8 games, Wyse 6, and Passeau just 2.

Wyse injured himself during spring training of 1947. Soon afterward, the Cubs got rid of him.

HANK WYSE: "I went out and threw batting practice in spring training, 1947. There had been bad weather, and a lot of guys hadn't been getting to hit good stuff. They came down early morning, I had already eaten breakfast, and I said to Hardrock Johnson, 'Where are you going?' He said, 'We're going out to take extra batting practice.' There were six or seven of them. The main guys. I said, 'Can I go with you?' He said, 'Yeah.' He threw batting practice. Of course, he couldn't throw hard. I said, 'Can I throw?' He said, 'You want to throw?' I said, 'Yeah.' And I was throwing curve balls and change-ups and fastballs that they hadn't seen, and he came out and said, 'That'll be enough. You've been throwing for thirty minutes.' Well, I didn't realize that.

"When the ball game started, the pitcher got in trouble, and Charlie Grimm told me to go and warm up, and I said I couldn't. He said, 'Why?' I said, 'My arm is all dead.' He said, 'How come?' I said, 'I threw batting practice this morning.' He said, 'Who in the hell told you to throw batting practice?' Well, I didn't tell him that Roy did. I just told him I thought the guys needed it.

"He sent me to the doctor for X rays, put it in a sling, and he sent me to Kansas City. I never talked to anybody after that, only somebody in the office. They done to me about like the Yankees did to Borowy. They put me on the waiver list. [Boston manager Billy] Southworth told me, 'You never would have gotten out if I had seen it. They did it so late I never did see it.' And Teddy Lyons from the White Sox told me the same thing. He said, 'I don't know how the hell they done it. I guarantee you, if I had seen it, we wouldn't have let you go by.'

"But they snuck me out of the league, and I got a telegram that I was being sent to Shreveport.

"After they took X rays and put it in a cast, they wouldn't tell me what was wrong with my arm. I didn't find it out until I got to the American League that I had seven chips in my elbow.

"When I was pitching with two days' rest in '45, Charlie Grimm told me, 'If you hurt your arm, Mr. Wrigley said you'd have a job for the rest of your life.' Well, when I hurt my arm, I was gone in about three minutes. He never even talked to me.

"I talked to Hardrock one time at a banquet dinner in Tulsa. I said, 'What about that deal you made with me in the dugout? You told me if I hurt my arm that Wrigley would take care of me the rest of my life.' He said, 'Why don't you call Mr. Wrigley?' I said, 'Are you kidding? Who in the hell would say that you guys said that? Would nobody say you did.'

"He didn't say nothing."

To replace these pitchers, the Cubs had a group of young, mostly mediocre prospects that included outfielder Clarence Maddern, Cliff Chambers, Bob Rush, catcher Rube Walker, Hal Jeffcoat and Russell Charles Meyer, known by his teammates as Monk, later as the Mad Monk. As a youth, Meyer had a vicious temper and didn't take to coaching. He could also pitch, but like many of the Cubs' better pitching prospects, he was traded away to shine for other teams. After winning 10 games in '48, including three shutouts, Jim Gallagher without explanation sold Meyer to the Philadelphia Phillies. Phil Wrigley pocketed the money, the Cubs continued to languish, and Meyer helped the Whiz Kids win the 1950 National League pennant. After a stint with the Phils, he went on to pitch for the Brooklyn Dodgers, appearing in the 1953 and 1955 World Series.

PHIL CAVARRETTA: "Meyer had a tough time holding anybody on, even when he was with the Cubs. That was one of the faults our scouts saw in him. He didn't pitch that much with the Cubs, 'cause number one, he had a bad move to first, and number two, he wouldn't take instruction. Monk Meyer had a real bad temper.

"In Chicago, when he was with the Cubs, he was a wild guy. Him and Bill Nicholson and Dominic Dallessandro stayed at the Sheridan Plaza Hotel, and the three of them used to go out.

"Monk was hardly pitching. He would mop up. And it looked like he was always mad at somebody. 'I want to get out of here.' 'I want to kill somebody.'

"Bill Nicholson told us the story. This one night he and Monk and Dallessandro went to the Sheraton Plaza to have dinner and a few beers. There Monk met a young lady he knew. She was in a wheelchair. Monk had kind of gone for her, took her to bed a few times. This one night she was by the bar in a booth.

"Monk saw her sitting there by herself and he went over and sat down with her. They had few beers, and she was very upset. Monk used to go with a lot of girls, and she was upset about that. So one thing led to another, and you could hear them arguing all over the room. All of a sudden they were nose to nose. She got so upset she bit Monk right in the nose. Bill said the tip of his nose was hanging off. She bit the shit out of him. Nicholson said, 'Poor Monk was bleeding like a horse.' They took him to the hospital. He had to have stitches.

"The next day when Monk got to the clubhouse, he tried to sneak past Charlie Grimm's door by walking in between Nicholson and Dallessandro. His nose was all wrapped up and swollen, and he had two black eyes. He was a *mess*.

"We traded him to Philadelphia, and then he went over to Brooklyn, and they used him, and he had one of the best screwballs I'd ever seen. Real good. He threw it hard.

"I really don't know why the Cubs didn't use him."

By 1948 the Cubs team was hopeless, perhaps the worst in the history of the illustrious franchise. The team in 1948 finished last, twenty-seven-and-a-half games behind the Boston Braves of "Spahn and Sain and pray for rain" fame. The Cubs were sixth in runs scored, fifth in earned run average and second worst in the league in fielding. One million, two hundred and fifty thousand fans still came out to Beautiful Wrigley Field to watch them as the Cubs proved that Phil Wrigley's calculated approach could work: You didn't have to win to be a financial success.

Most of the players from the 1945 team were gone. Before the '48 season Lennie Merullo, the heart of the Cubs' infield, had to quit when his sciatica made it impossible to continue. The Cubs' wartime crop of young hopefuls, all from the Los Angeles farm team—Billy Schuster, Dom Dallessandro, Don Johnson, and Ed Sauer—had turned out to be average, as did the rest of the team's prospects.

The '48 infield consisted of first baseman Eddie Waitkus, who later would become famous when as a Philly he was shot by a deranged groupie; second baseman Hank Schenz; a lanky young shortstop named Roy Smalley; and third baseman Andy Pafko, who by trade was an outfielder. In the outfield was Hal Jeffcoat, who after a half dozen desultory years trying to make it as a hitter would go back to the minors and return a pitcher with Cincinnati; a diabetes-ravaged Bill Nicholson; and Peanuts Lowrey. Bob Scheffing, who one day would manage the Cubs, was the catcher.

Left-hander Johnny Schmitz won 18 games, Meyer won 10, and no other starter on the staff won more than five games. Jess Dobernic, who had last pitched in the majors in 1939, won 7 games in relief, then after a little mop-up work in '49, returned to the minors forever.

Only Pafko, Nicholson, and Cavarretta supplied much offense. Pafko would be handed to the Dodgers in mid-1951 in a terrible trade. Nicholson's diabetes would reduce his output until he would be traded to the Phillies in early October 1948, leaving Cavarretta as the sole survivor of the 1945 pennant winners by 1952.

Playing on such a bad ball club was a terrible strain for Cavarretta, who hated to lose even one game. In 1948 he had to endure losing 90.

PHIL CAVARRETTA: "I was the type of guy, when I played, I gave a hundred percent at all times. I didn't like to lose. But I found myself on a club that didn't win too many games. There were players on the team who I knew shouldn't have been in the big leagues. That goes back to your organization.

"After playing in three World Series, then to play on a club that's bad, you wake up sometimes in the morning and say, 'Geez, I hate to go out to the ballpark.' Really. I wouldn't tell this to people, because I wasn't that type of guy. To go out there day in and day out and you do everything in your power to try to win a game, get a base hit, get on base, make a good play on first, and the results are always bad, you say to yourself, Gee, is it worth it? And you start thinking, 'I can still play. Should I ask to be traded?' I'd think it over and say, no. I'm just not made that way. I wouldn't go to the general manager or manager and say, 'I want to be traded.' I couldn't do that.

"But it was tough day in and day out to see games you think you have won, and then all of a sudden, you lose. And it hurt me when I lost. When I was a kid and I lost in marbles I got upset about it. In those days they had these big baseball cards, and we'd throw them up against the walls, play leaners. If I lost playing leaners, I'd get upset.

"Losing would bother me physically, 'cause I wouldn't feel too good after losing game after game. And it didn't make any difference whether I was 0 for 4 or 2 for 4. I played a long time, but to me, another thing you do to be a success, it isn't whether you go 2 for 4. It's 'Did we win or lose?' A lot of guys will say, 'That's a pile of garbage what you say.' But that's the way I felt."

In 1948 the press and the fans called for the heads of general manager Jim Gallagher and manager Charlie Grimm. One of the more humorous commentaries was written by Warren Brown in the *Chicago Herald-American*.

Evoking the comedy team of Gallagher and Shean, Brown slammed the Cubs braintrust by parodying them daily. Here's one example:

Mr. Gallagher and Mr. Grimm

Oh, Mr. Gallagher, Oh, Mr. Gallagher,
The schedule gives another day of rest
Which is something we don't need
To establish our clear need
For outresting all contenders, East or West.

Oh, Mr. Grimm, Oh, Mr. Grimm,
Our stout-hearted athletes are in losing trim;
To make it very terse
Their speed's always in reverse.
Battery weakness, Mr. Gallagher?
Clutch trouble, Mr. Grimm?

Oh, Mr. Gallagher, Oh, Mr. Gallagher
In another day we'll have to leave once more
To play Pirates, then the Cards
In their very own back yards
I hope it ain't what it was like before.

Oh, Mr. Grimm, Oh, Mr. Grimm,
These contenders may well tear us limb from limb
We may emulate the dive
Of the Cubs of '25
We ain't that bad, Mr. Gallagher,
That's what you think, Mr. Grimm.

In June 1949, Grimm, himself a hard loser, could no longer take the pressure and the abuse. The Cubs fixture stepped down again, this time in favor of a manager from the school of John McGraw: Frankie Frisch. Grimm, who was like a son to Phil Wrigley, selected Frisch and personally asked him if he would take the job. When Frisch asked his wife and his friends whether he should take it, they all told him that managing a team without decent ballplayers would be a daunting task. But Frisch loved to manage, so he took the job anyway.

FRANKIE FRISCH: "Early in June 1949, while I was enjoying a most pleasant job as coach of the New York Giants, I was on the bench with Leo Durocher, the club manager, watching the Giants in their infield practice. I was very much contented with my job.

"There was a telephone in the dugout at the Polo Grounds and it rang as Leo and I discussed the practice and the ball club. It was a call for Leo from the Giants' office, above the center field bleachers. Leo left me to take the call and when he returned he nudged me and took me aside. He didn't waste any preliminary words.

"'How would you like to go back to managing?' he asked in a whisper.

"'What club?' was my quick answer.

"'The Cubs,' he said, and I said, 'Oh, my God.'

"'I guess I will,' I then told Durocher, 'but I want a few days to think it over.'

"I went home that evening and told Mrs. Frisch about it. She didn't mince any words or hesitate about her reaction to the offer.

"'No,' she exclaimed, 'absolutely not.'

"I discussed the proposition with several good friends, in and out of baseball. Their advice was amazingly unanimous.

"'Don't do it, Frank,' they all said. 'Positively you ought to reject the offer with polite thanks. But don't consider it for a minute more.'

"I guess I always was a stubborn Dutchman. Regardless of what Ada and my friends said, I kept saying 'Yes.'

"So I called Charlie Grimm, then the Cub manager, at the Commodore Hotel and arranged for a meeting. Phil Wrigley, president of the Chicago club, also was in New York at the time and the call to me was the result of a decision Wrigley and Grimm had reached in a conference over the plight of the ball club. I didn't see Wrigley, but I saw Charlie and the deal was quickly arranged. He asked me if I'd like to take over the job as manager of the Cubs, and I said, 'Can I get a two- or three-year contract and at how much salary?'

"And that was it. I signed for the balance of the 1949 season and for two more years and took over the job on June 10.

"It was a rather unusual procedure in some ways. I probably was the only man ever signed by a major league manager to take over that man's job as field director of a ball club. The club was in a bad way, was last all year, I believe, and had finished last the previous season. Wrigley apparently was very fond of Charlie and so instead of firing him and hiring a manager himself, he put the job of getting a successor into Charlie's hands.

"Why did I take that job, when my wife and all my friends advised against it? Let me say first it wasn't because 'it was a challenge.' I despise that statement and that word. Somebody gets a job with a lousy ball club and people ask him why he took the job, giving up one in which he was much happier, and he says, 'I took it because it was a challenge.'

"Baloney and bosh! I don't care who the manager is, he's not going to take an eighth-place ball club and put it into the first division. The ballplayers make a ball club and they make a manager.

"I took the Chicago job because I loved to be a manager. It's a great job. If baseball's in your blood, as it is in mine, if baseball is your whole life as it is mine, you want to play as long as you can, you dream of being a manager, and you'll take any managing job that's open. That's why I took the job of managing the Cubs, despite the fact that they were in last place, with no immediate hope of getting out of the cellar.

"Few men have ever turned down a managerial job. I was glad to get the opportunity. I'd take the job again, regardless of the ball club's low status. But I would not make the mistake I made in Chicago. It was a big mistake, as I look back now.

"My big mistake was in not seeing to it that I got close to P. K. Wrigley, owner of the ball club. The first thing I should have done was to ask Mr. Wrigley to call a meeting of the baseball people in his organization, his scouts, his general manager, his coaches, and his manager. The Cubs and the whole operation of the ball club obviously needed a thorough overhauling."

Frankie Frisch was not the answer. He had a team of young, not-very-talented players, and he was the sort of manager who screamed and ranted and raved when things weren't going his way. In the three years Frankie Frisch was manager, the Cubs finished last in '49, seventh in '50, and were last again in 1951 at the time of his departure.

In mid-1951, Phil Wrigley fired Jim Gallagher after ten years as general manager. To replace him, Wrigley decided to pick someone from the very successful Brooklyn Dodgers organization, hoping some of Dem Bums' magic would rub off on the Cubs. The man Wrigley selected was Wid Matthews, who for eighteen years had been Branch Rickey's assistant with the Dodgers. Matthews, it turned out, hadn't learned much from the master, and he would be more of a dupe for Rickey than even Gallagher had been.

On July 21, 1951, Phil Wrigley and his new man, Wid Matthews, fired Frankie Frisch.

Phil Cavarretta remembered the Fordham Flash.

PHIL CAVARRETTA: "Frankie Frisch. Oh boy! Frankie was from the McGraw era. I knew he was a great ballplayer because I had played against him many times when he played for the Cardinals. As for his managerial skills, he was tough to play for. We were a young club, and you'd have a meeting before every series, go over the hitters, and some of the meetings we had, and some of the language he used—I used to watch the young players, Bill Serena, Roy Smalley, Bob Ramazzotti, Ransom Jackson, man, they were all quivering at the language he would use.

"He'd say, 'Ballplayers, you guys call yourselves ballplayers? Look at you. Serena, over there in the corner. Get your head up.' Jesus, these kids were scared. That was from the old school. McGraw was some kind of guy, and Frank, I'm telling you . . . he had done a great job managing the Cardinals, but he had a great ball club. He didn't have a bunch of young kids.

"It was late in '51. We were in Brooklyn, playing the Dodgers, a good club. And I mean, our club was *bad*. I was a part-time player. Wid Matthews was our general manager, and he went to Philadelphia for something. He had come back, but Frankie Frisch didn't know it.

"We were playing in Ebbets Field and Matthews came into the dugout about the third inning, and he sat in the corner where Frankie couldn't see him.

"Every time we would go into Brooklyn or play the Giants in the Polo Grounds, he'd say, 'Come on, guys. Get up and do something. Get this game over in a hurry.' I guess Frankie knew we were going to lose. We wondered, Why does he keep telling us this? Well, turned out he lived in New Rochelle. He loved to garden, dig around in the ground and raise petunias. He wanted to go home early. He would tell us, 'Come on. I gotta get home and raise my petunias. Let's get this game over with.'

"Well, this particular day, Wid Matthews was in the dugout, and he was hearing all this. And what really got Frank fired, he always had a book, a regular novel, in his hand, why, I don't know. On this day during the game he was reading a book in the dugout. We were running in and out, and he was turning the pages, reading. I thought, This guy is cracking up. Frank says, 'Come on, let's get this thing over.' And he's turning the pages of the book, and Wid Matthews saw this.

"I remember Bill Serena was the hitter, and like I say, we were getting creamed. Bill struck out. He was my roommate, a funny guy. When he struck out, Frank used a real cuss word.

"Frank said, 'God almighty. What lousy ballplayers!' And out flew the book. He threw it out toward the third-base coach.

"When he threw that book out, Mr. Matthews got up and left. Frank was fired that day. When he flipped that book out, that's when Frank got fired."

When Frankie Frisch was fired, the manager chosen to replace him was Phil Cavarretta, who had never before managed a team, either in the majors or the minors. One of Cavarretta's first moves was to get Wid Matthews to block off the center-field bleachers from the fans. For years players had complained that when they were batting late in the afternoon at Wrigley Field it was impossible to see pitches come out of the white shirts. Cavarretta cared enough about his players to get the Cubs to block off the section.

"If you don't," Cavarretta warned, "someone is going to get killed."

PHIL CAVARRETTA: "One day we were playing the Phillies with the Whiz Kids, a doubleheader at Wrigley Field. We had a packed house. Most of the fans were wearing white shirts. Robin Roberts was pitching. I had played the first game at first base, and when I got to bat it was tough to see then with the white background and the white ball. I hit a triple and drove in two runs, and I beat Robbie by myself.

"The second game started. Curt Simmons was pitching. I wasn't playing. About the seventh inning we started a rally, and I was the third hitter to come up, and now the batter's box was in the shade, the pitcher was in the shade, but the bleachers were in the sun.

"I was a low-ball hitter, and Curt Simmons was a high-fastball pitcher. He could throw hard. He threw me a fastball, and I tried to pick it up where he released the ball. He released it, and I didn't see it.

"I'm looking for the ball, and the next thing I know, the ball is right in front of my face. Your natural instinct, like if you're fighting, you throw a punch to protect yourself. I threw up my right arm, and he fractured my wrist. I was out quite a while.

"I would have been killed if I hadn't put up my arm. Because Simmons could throw. If I hadn't thrown up my arm, he would have hit me right between the eyes. I would have been dead.

"After I became manager, in 1952 I went up to my general manager, Wid Matthews, may his soul rest in peace. I said, 'Wid, we have to do something about this background. Somebody is going to get killed.' In those days we didn't have helmets. We had the inserts under our caps. I said, 'It's real bad, especially the second game of a doubleheader. You have all those white shirts out there.'

"He said, 'What do you suggest we do?'

"I said, 'Rope off a certain section,' which it is now, about twelve hundred seats. In those days admission was a dollar and a half to get into the bleachers. Now he starts to think about money. A dollar and a half a seat times twelve hundred. We played seventy-seven games at home.

"Wid said, 'I don't know how I can do that.'

"I said, 'We can make up for that by my hitters hitting better, 'cause they can see the ball better. We'll win. You win, and we'll put people in the park.' He said, 'Gee, that sounds pretty good. Let me think about it.'

"About three days later he called me up to his office. He said, 'We're going to do it.'

"I said, 'Hallelujah.'

"I would only wish today's players would know about this. If they had had to hit against that background with the white shirts, they couldn't have hit 45 home runs a year. Bill Nicholson and Hank Sauer were our home run hitters, and if they hit 35 against that background, that was a bundle. Those players, if they had played without the white shirts out there, they'd have hit 50 home runs.

"To this day, no one in Chicago, or Wrigley Field, or any place in baseball knows the man who said, 'Let's rope that off.' Who did it? Phil Cavarretta."

In his first year as manager, Cavarretta, who possessed a sharp baseball mind, was effective despite his lack of experience and hot temper. Led by Hank Sauer, who led the league with 37 homers and 121 RBIs to win the National League Most Valuable Player Award, in '52 the Cubs rose to .500 and fifth place. Then in '53 the team dropped back to seventh despite the acquisition of Ralph Kiner, who was nearing the end of his illustrious career.

In the spring of '54, Cavarretta could see that there was little talent to manage and no hope for improvement. Out of frustration and pride he asked for a meeting with Phil Wrigley to let Wrigley know that in order to be competitive the Cubs would need some better talent. Would the front office please do something?

Cavarretta got his answer. The Cubs fired him. Cavarretta contends he was the first manager ever to be fired *before* the season had even begun.

PHIL CAVARRETTA: "The club I had in '52 was not too bad a ball club. We had Hank Sauer, Ransom Jackson, Bill Serena, Roy Smalley, who was having a pretty good year. A lot of fans didn't like him, but Roy was a pretty good player.

"Our strength was hitting, offense. We hit the ball, and in '52 we played .500 ball. Hank Sauer was my most valuable player in 1952. He did a great job. A super job. Frank Baumholtz was my little center fielder. He was a great little basketball player, a professional with Cleveland. Stood about five eleven. As old as I was, I could have run as fast as Frankie. Don't tell him that. But I didn't have anyone else. I had Hal Jeffcoat. He was a terrible hitter, who later went on to be a pretty good pitcher. He couldn't hit, but he could run, and he had a great arm. But I wanted people who could hit. So I put Frankie out there.

"On his left was Hank Sauer, the right fielder. They were roommates, two great people. On his right was Ralph Kiner. Sauer and Kiner were two guys who couldn't run as fast as an elephant could. And just about every day Frankie was playing out in center field. The ball would be hit out to right center. All you heard from Sauer was, 'Come on, Frankie. Go catch that ball.' Even if Hank was closer to the ball than poor Frankie Baumholtz. And the same thing in left field. The ball would be hit out to left center, Kiner's ball, and Kiner would say, 'Come on, Frankie.'

"When the season started Frankie must have weighed 180 pounds. When the season was over he weighed 165, believe me.

"I could see problems developing in '53. Toward the end of the season you recall your best young players, you bring them in and you play them. You have to play them, because this is the way you evaluate people. You look at them and see what they can do. You don't have to be an Einstein to be able to say, 'This kid has good ability. He has a chance to be a big leaguer.' But with the kids I brought up I wasn't seeing that. In '53 I could see it was going down. And our club, it hadn't been a bad club. Our front line was pretty good, but our bench was pretty weak. You would say, 'Why don't you try to make a deal?' The players we had, number one, we couldn't afford to trade them 'cause I didn't have people to replace them, and actually the value we had on the players who were playing every day, and I hope they don't misunderstand me, the value wasn't that high to get a good player in return. So you really are in bad shape now.

"I could see it in '53. We brought up the best young players from the minor league system in spring training 1954. I was still player-manager. I worked hard to get myself in shape. Dee Fondy was my first baseman, who later on became a good ballplayer. So I went through the procedure of spring training, worked hard to get yourself in shape, legs and what have you, worked on fundamentals and cutoffs. So now we start playing exhibition games, and Roy Johnson was one of my coaches, Spud Davis one, and Charlie Root was my pitching coach. In spring training you watched and evaluated the players to see what you can do.

"The only one I could see who had great potential was Ernie Banks. He was a shortstop, and Gene Baker was also a shortstop. He had a great year at Los Angeles, a good player. He was a shortstop. To me, as far as his range, it wasn't that good, but I saw that Gene was a pretty good little hitter. I moved him over to second because I wanted him to play. I saw ability there. But I could see Ernie Banks, with the quick wrist action. I said, 'This guy has to play.' I knew he had very little experience. I didn't think we were going to win many games, so I figured we'd better play this kid, because this kid is going to be great. You don't have to be an Einstein to see it. And his fielding was good. He was a good fielder.

"We were playing and playing, and not winning.

"I've always been the type of man, I was brought up this way at home, number one, to be honest, and number two, to have pride in what you do. That's my mom and dad. Especially to be honest.

"The problem was that the front office, the minor league system—they are not going to like me for this, because that's the reason I was fired—they let their minor league system get away from them. They didn't sign good young ballplayers. They felt the ones they had were going to be big league ballplayers. But our scouting system wasn't doing the job correctly, not evaluating correctly. They couldn't have been, because our minor league system was really pretty bad.

"I have a lot of pride. I hate to lose. And I couldn't stand it any longer. The losing was getting to me. I was suffering.

"One night I was talking to the late Bob Lewis, our traveling secretary, a good guy. He was good to me. A lot of the players didn't like Bob because he growled once in a while. He was the ticket man. If you came for a pass, you had to go through his office, and once in a while, he's growl at them. Bob could see I was suffering. He said, 'Phil, come on. I'll take you out for dinner. We'll go to a Mexican restaurant.' We were in Mesa, Arizona. He said, 'We'll bring [equipment manager] Yosh Kawano with us.' We go and have dinner. Bob could see I was really down. He said, 'Phil, this is just a suggestion.' I said, 'What? I'll listen to anything. Tell me.' He said, 'Mr. Wrigley is very fond of you, whether you know it or not.' I said, 'I know that.'

"He said, 'Why don't you have a meeting with Mr. Wrigley tomorrow. He's going to come out to the game.' The next day we were going to go to Phoenix to play the Giants.

"Bob said, 'He'll listen to you, Phil. Tell him what's on your mind. Go over the whole ball club. Tell him who you think will help the club and the guys who won't.'

"I said, 'Geez, I don't know. That's kinda tough.' He said, 'Phil, Mr. Wrigley'll understand, believe me.' I said, 'I'll think it over.' I called my wife, Lorraine, up. We were living in Dallas at the time. I told her the same story. She said, 'I don't know, Phil. You do what you think is right. But be honest with Mr. Wrigley.'

"I called up Mr. Wrigley and made an appointment with him. He came out to Phoenix. We were playing the Giants. Mr. Wrigley came to the game. We met around eleven-thirty, while the Giants were taking batting practice. We went out in right field and sat in the bleachers.

"He said, 'What's on your mind, Phil?' I said, 'I'd like to go over the ball club, Mr. Wrigley. I feel the manager ought to do this every spring training.' So I start going through our ball club. I started at first base. Dee Fondy was our first baseman. I said, 'I'm satisfied there. I may play once in a while, pinch-hit. We're in pretty good shape there.' I went to Gene Baker. I said, 'He may be able to do the job. At shortstop, Ernie Banks, he's my star of the future.' It's just what I told him. Third base—Bill Serena. He had pretty good power, but he couldn't run, an average fielder. He had such a great arm, I almost tried to convert him to pitcher, but he didn't like the idea so we left him at third. Ransom Jackson—a great athlete, a great football player too. University of Texas, good guy. Jackson had good ability, but he was a real quiet guy. He wouldn't get too excited. Nothing would get him excited. Never get gung ho. And he didn't like to play every day. He was one of these guys, like Dom Dallessandro, who pinch-hit once in a while, preferred to play two, three times a week. I wasn't looking for that. I was trying to build a ball club.

"I said, 'Jackson, he'll fill in once in a while. I'm satisfied with him.' So then I started to go down the rest of the ball club, and some of the things I said, especially about my outfield and pitching staff and my catching . . . I guess I shouldn't have said. I wasn't very kind, but I was being honest. Clyde McCullough, may his soul rest in peace, was my number one catcher, but he was on his way out. It was in hopes we could make a deal here and there so we could improve ourselves.

"But the thing there, it was a mistake on my part. See, Wid Matthews, our general manager, was in Florida at the time, and in a way, I shouldn't have done this.

"Wid Matthews didn't like what I had to say, and I don't blame him. I should have waited until Mr. Matthews came back so the three of us could have sat in a room and gone over the club.

"I admit I pulled the trigger a little too quick on what I had to say, but again, I was telling the truth. I wanted Mr. Wrigley to understand that. And I wanted Wid Matthews to understand that. We should have done that all together.

"It wasn't very long when Wid Matthews came back, and I mean, our club was playing bad. Because—I'm just going to have to say it—the ability just wasn't there.

"My wife and I were living in Dallas at the time, and we were coming into town to play the Giants in a three-game series. Things were picking up a little bit. Wid had made a terrible trade with the Dodgers. He gave them Andy Pafko, our best power hitter, and in return I had [infielder] Eddie Miksis, [outfielder] Gene Hermanski, [pitcher] Joe Hatten, who had a sore arm. He came to me, and I'm supposed to live with him. And [catcher] Bruce Edwards, who I loved as a person but who couldn't throw. He had a bad arm. Those four guys came to me.

"It wasn't one of our better deals. But still the players were presented to me by Mr. Matthews.

"We're playing the Giants in Dallas. Like all managers playing in your hometown in spring training, you're going to have the press out and some of the players. I'm going to have a big party at my house. I bought a full fridge of steaks, a lot of beer, to have a good time.

"The first game we played, we lost, and after the game I told Bob Lewis about this big party at the house, but he didn't seem like he was too happy. Bob was a guy at times who was grumpy, but at times he was happy. He said, 'OK,' and we went out to the ballpark. We played, and we lost again.

"After the game was over, Bob came up to me and he said, 'Wid Matthews wants to see you at the hotel.' I figured he was going to go over the ball club, encourage me a little bit. We were staying at the Jefferson Hotel in Dallas. My three daughters were with me. They came to the game. I told them to wait in the lobby for Daddy.

"I went upstairs to Wid Matthews's room, and I said, 'Hi, Wid. Everything all right?' And there was no response. I could see he was upset about something. I figured it was the ball game. We had lost.

"He got to the point real quick. He said, 'Phil,' and these were the words, 'we feel that it's necessary to make a change in managers.' I was quiet for a while, and I said, 'Change of managers in spring training?' He said, 'We're going to make a change in managers. We're going to bring in Stan Hack to take over the club. We want you to go to Los Angeles.'

"Well, I'm fired. And now I'm getting a little excited. I started using language I shouldn't have used. I said, 'You gotta be kidding me. The season hasn't even gotten started. You don't fire people in spring training. You send kids to the minors. But a manager? At least give me a chance to open the season.'

"He had no answer. I said, 'Give me a reason.' I wanted to know why the hell he fired me. He said, 'I have no reason.' I said, 'That's a hell of a good answer to give a man, to fire him in spring training, to explain to him why you're firing him. And you say you don't have a reason.'

"He forgot that I did a great job in '52. In '53 we didn't play too good, but we needed help. And I didn't get it.

"He said, 'We want you to go out to Los Angeles and manage out there.' I had an ironclad contract. He had to pay me. And I was so mad, so upset, planning on this big party, my kids were downstairs, and I almost was in tears. That really was one of the saddest moments in my life. To this day I still can't get over it. I don't know if I should be bitter, 'cause there were so many things I didn't understand. The man should have explained different things.

"He said, 'I want you to go to Los Angeles.' And I was so upset, so mad, I used strong language. I said, 'Shove it. I'm not going to take it.' I said, 'I'm not going to go, Wid.'

"They had to pay me anyway. And I felt I could still play a little bit.

"After it was all over, and after finally coming to my senses, I should have accepted the Los Angeles job for experience. To be honest with you, when Wid Matthews called me in '51 and said, 'We'd like you to take over the club for the balance of the year,' I should have said no. 'Cause I could still play. But the reason I should have said no was that I had no experience whatsoever managing. When someone presents that package to you right away—you always dream of managing the club—you say yes. But after I thought of it, I should have said, 'No. Send me someplace for two, three years to manage, 'cause I have to learn how to manage.'

"When you become the manager, the game absolutely changes. The strategy changes. The handling of men changes. This is why I should have gone to the minors to manage.

"But when he offered me the job of managing in Los Angeles, I'm convinced he just wanted to get me out, believe me.

"But it was the first time a major league manager was fired in spring training, and I'll tell you another little thing. Years later, [in 1976] I was at home, and [A's manager] Alvin Dark called me up. Alvin was a good guy. He said, 'Phil, I'm a member of your club.' I said, 'What do you mean?'

"Alvin said, 'Mr. Finley just fired me too, in spring training.'

"I said, 'Congratulations!'"

The firing of Phil Cavarretta marked the end of an era. He had spent twenty years in a Cubs uniform, beginning back in 1934. He had played on three pennant winners, participating in almost 2,000 ball games as a Cub.

For Cubs fans of a certain generation, Cavarretta was Mr. Cub. With his bitter departure in the spring of 1954, Cubs fans were left to root for their individual heroes and hope one day things would get better.

51

The Minor Leagues

Jim Brosnan, who is best known for two outstanding diaries he wrote while with the St. Louis Cardinals *(The Long Season)* and the Cincinnati Reds *(The Pennant Race)*, began his career with the Chicago Cubs. He was signed in 1946 for $2,500 and for ten long, sometimes painful years toiled in the Cubs' wreck of a minor league system, fighting with managers and getting in trouble.

Brosnan was, and is, a very thoughtful, sensitive man who was seen as a maverick and a loner by many of his teammates and managers. Brosnan loved the game dearly, but he didn't always love the men who were in it. During the Jim Gallagher era of benign negligence, Brosnan spent almost a decade pitching in the minors before Cubs pitching coach Howie Pollet taught him the pitch that enabled him to get major league hitters out. But only after he got drunk and nearly got thrown off an airplane while with the Los Angeles Angels in the Pacific Coast League did Cubs management realize that Brosnan had what it took to become a Chicago Cub. To play in the Cubs minor league system for ten years, you had to be a little crazy.

JIM BROSNAN: "I pitched three shutouts in a row in American Legion tournaments in 1946, and a week after my seventeenth birthday Tony Lucadello, the Cubs scout at the time, showed up and said, 'I'm prepared to give you $2,500 as a signing bonus if you will sign with the Cubs.'

"Well, in my entire life I had never seen even five hundred dollars at one time. After I signed, I reported to St. Augustine, Florida, along with two hundred returning servicemen who were guaranteed a shot at a job. I wore number 172, which was pinned on my back. I didn't think that boded well for my future, but after the first ten days a lot of them quit. Whatever they had was gone, and they decided to get on with their life and not play a boy's game for very little money anymore.

"I was sent to Elizabethton, Tennessee, Class O, and I played my whole first year for five hundred dollars. That was my salary for the *entire* year. And since we only got $2.50 a day to eat on on the road—I spent about $3 a day on food—you could eat on that in 1947, not very well, but you could—so I was losing money on food. But I did win 17 games, and I was boosted all the way to Class B ball. And instead of $125 a month, they offered me $150 a month. For the 17 wins, I got a $25-a-month raise.

"I started out that second season at Springfield, when it was in the New England League. It was Bob Peterson's first year as manager. He had never managed anybody before—he had never managed anybody like *me* before.

"When I lost a game, it was suicide time. I went into a deep depression. Bob couldn't figure out a way to handle that. I don't think I ran into a manager who could.

"I spent five years in the minors before the Cubs finally sent me to George Mohr's Institute for Psychoanalysis, *the* place to be in Chicago at that time. I was diagnosed as being bipolar—today they call it manic-depressive. I was subject to mood swings, and being in the business, the sport, I was in, I could go from manic elation when I won, whether a good win or not, to deep depressions. After a loss, the depressions would always be severe. The downs were worse than the ups.

"Bob finally got rid of me. He sent me laterally to Fayetteville, North Carolina, which was still B ball. The Cubs kept me because the 17 wins was enough to show I had talent, and they figured the problem I had was psychological.

"Frank 'Skeeter' Scalzi was the manager. Old Skeeter and his wife, Jenna, were like parents, better than my parents ever were to me, so I enjoyed it at Fayetteville.

"I didn't have a good record, but I did pitch a no-hitter. After the game, by passing the hat I collected $175 dollars, which was more than my monthly salary. It was a big crowd, just before a playoff game, and we were fighting for a position. We had real good baseball fans, and a lot of soldiers from Fort Bragg would come out to the park.

"From Fayetteville, I went to Macon to play for the Peaches. Macon was an independent team with which the Cubs had a working agreement. Our manager was Don Osborn, the Wizard, of Oz, obviously, who had been a minor league pitcher for seventeen years on the West Coast. Oz was an excellent manager and very good for me.

"We had a very good team, won the pennant by ten, twelve games. I pitched .500 ball, though I should have been better than that.

"The next year, 1950, Oz went to Nashville, and I got shipped to Springfield. He then asked that I come down to Nashville and join him. He thought I was one of his projects, though I was becoming less and less a prospect.

"The reason: I still hadn't learned how to pitch. No one had taught me. In the Cubs organization back then there was no way for young players to develop unless they got lucky, picking something up from a teammate or even an opposing player.

"PK Wrigley was a very successful businessman, but he did not pick good people to run the Cubs organization the way he picked people to run his gum business for him. I was told that PK got talked into running the club, that his father made him promise to do it. It was a promise he had made to his father before he died that he would keep the Cubs in Chicago, not sell the club to outsiders who might take the club somewhere or run it here poorly—well, *he* did not run it well, no doubt about it.

"His general manager, Jim Gallagher, didn't know any more about baseball than the average sportswriter. The *Chicago Tribune*'s Jerome Holtzman, who is a Hall of Fame sportswriter, admitted to me many times, 'I really don't understand the game of baseball,' the tactics, the techniques. And Holtzman said, 'Many of the guys I work with don't understand it any better than I do.' Gallagher was not a good choice for general manager.

"It's always been a problem with the Cubs that the personnel director, whatever his title, has not been astute in judging talent. And of course they compound it by not having teachers of fundamentals in the minor leagues to improve whatever talent they get. I can't remember the last year that they had more winning teams in the minor leagues than losers.

"PK never thought things through in baseball the way he did in business. Remember the College of Coaches? Essentially he had a good idea, to pool the resources of a group of managers, but what he should have had was coaches down in the *minor* leagues teaching. He had the idea, but he didn't quite get it right.

"And even if PK had a good idea, he didn't hire the right people to carry it out. I can remember after Gallagher left and Wid Matthews came in, Matthews wanted to start a program to teach fundamentals throughout the Chicago Cubs organization. The idea was good. Other clubs had been doing it for years. Sure, every club should have a way of teaching fundamentals. But then PK put Rogers Hornsby in charge. Hornsby was absolutely the *worst* person in the world to teach. He was not a teacher. He was a bad manager because he expected people to do things they couldn't do. Certainly he was a good player. But to put him in charge of the program?

"Anyway, while Gallagher was in charge there was almost *no* teaching in the minor leagues. The Cubs had a roaming minor league pitching coach, Ray Hayworth, who had been a catcher. I didn't see him the whole time I was at Fayetteville. Ray came around at Nashville once. He knew Osborne. The Cubs had two real good pitching prospects on that club, Umberto Flammini and me, and they had two other guys, Jim Atchley, my roommate, who won 16 games, and Bob Spicer, who was about five eight, little bitty guy, but he was a bulldog with pretty good stuff.

"Osborne taught us how to throw the spitter. It amounted to a tar ball, a real good sinker. He taught us all how to pack our glove with tar. You could hold the glove upside down with the ball in it, and the ball would stay there. You got that stuff on the ball, and if you knew how, you could make the ball sink, either good, better, or very good, like a spitter. He could still do it, and he was forty-four years old.'

"From Nashville in 1950, I went to Des Moines, where the legendary Charlie Root was the manager. I don't remember much about Root except that he was a disciplinarian who didn't know how to do it. He knew a lot of guys were fooling around, and yet he couldn't stop it, but then again, he had played with legendary Cubs Pat Malone and Hack Wilson, though he hadn't hung out with them.

"Charlie and I didn't get along right from the get-go. It was just awful, a bad relationship. Yet I pitched very well for him. Two things happened. I was to blame for one. He was to blame for the second.

"The Cubs took up two of our prospects, third baseman Leon Brinkopf, and a shortstop, whose name I forget. The Cubs were trying to show the people that they had some prospects. The shortstop, who was related to our general manager, John Holland, never did play for the Cubs. He wasn't a big-league prospect in any way at all. Brinkopf, who was hitting the ball well, drove in a lot of runs, played a pretty good game. He played shortstop for the Cubs the following year [1952].

"So I said, 'It's a bad deal for us because they're taking two good players away from us, and we're not getting anything in return,' and Root thought that was a terrible attitude to take because here were two guys getting a shot at the big leagues.

"Charlie said, 'They really deserve it, and we should back them. You're taking a very selfish attitude.' Well, I was. Damn right I was. I win because the players behind me play well. So I was wrong there. But he looked at me askance.

"Then there was the twelve-inning game I pitched in Des Moines. I was winning 1–0 in the ninth inning, and there was an error and a bloop hit, and we were tied up, and in the twelfth inning a guy hit a ball. It wasn't a real high fence. The right fielder jumped up, the ball hit his glove, and went over the fence. I lost the game 2–1.

"Before the game I had been reading the latest issue of *Time* magazine. After it, I came into the clubhouse, sat down in front of my locker, picked up the magazine, and started reading it again. Root became enraged.

"'How could you read that trash?' He actually called *Time* magazine trash. He probably never read *Time* magazine in his life. Root said, 'How could you just sit there and read it after what just happened?' Because I had pitched very well and should have won the ball game. Root felt I should not have been sitting there reading a magazine, that I should have been pissed off, smashing the locker, doing something, crying, ordering a beer.

"And he wrote up a report on the game saying I had the wrong attitude and I would never be a big-league ballplayer, even though I had pitched twelve innings and kept his club in the game!

"And because of that report, the Cubs sent me down, even though they didn't know where to send me. Root didn't want me anymore.

"'Get him out of here.'

"The Cubs sent me to Decatur, Illinois, the dumping ground. This was where all the misfits and oddballs of the Cubs organization went, managed by Maury Arnovich, who couldn't tell he was handling misfits and oddballs because we were all like him.

"I don't remember much about Maury because nobody paid a damn bit of attention to him. He may have had signs, but nobody knew what they were. 'Cause he once gave me the sign to bunt, and I didn't do it. In fact, I hit a double. It seemed to me there wasn't any point of me bunting. So he fined me five dollars, which was a lot of money. I said, 'I won't pay it. You'll have to take it out of my check.' And of course he forgot to do that.

"Nobody on that club made it to the big leagues.

"The last weekend of the season we were playing in Cedar Rapids. There was a Shriners convention in the hotel, and our catcher Bob Bortz and I and Birdie Thurlby, an outfielder, decided we wouldn't go to sleep all weekend. Thurlby was the leading hitter on the club. He couldn't run, couldn't throw, but he was funny. He was the one who decided we would stay up. No sleep was going to be our goal. We were going to pull two all-nighters. And with the convention there and the women who were hanging around, we had no trouble whatsoever.

"During the day we would doze, wake up, and somebody would tell a story about something that happened to them during the time. And then we'd doze off again. Then we'd play the ball game, Friday night and Saturday night. We met at breakfast after staying up all night.

"On Sunday morning Arnovich said to me, 'You're pitching.' I could hardly see. I was swaying. Bortz was laughing. Thurlby, the outfielder, may have told Arnovich on us. That's the kind of thing he would do. Because he didn't play. Suddenly he had a bad leg, so he couldn't play the last game.

"So Bortz was catching, and I was pitching, and I literally couldn't see the signs. Bortz said, 'It doesn't make a fucking bit of difference. You can't throw hard enough to hurt anyone.' And I could not. As hard as I was trying, I was throwing humpbacked liners, looked like easily hit eephus balls.

"Well, we were losing 7–0 and I had two outs in the first inning. Then Arnovich came out and said, 'You're pitching the *whole* ball game.'

"Naturally I didn't. I couldn't. But to that point my ERA that year wasn't so bad. It looks terrible now, but except for that two-thirds of an inning in that last game of the season, I had pitched fairly well for not a very good ball club.

"Another thing I remember. I was pitching against Waterloo, and we were losing 2–0. The pitcher for Waterloo was pitching a no-hitter. He was a young kid who hadn't pitched professionally as well as he had in high school. And he had this no-hitter.

"Our batter, Bob Anderlick was his name, was a real pain in the ass. With two outs in the ninth inning and Waterloo ahead 2–0 and this kid throwing a no-hitter, he made a perfect bunt. The poor kid picked up the ball and started to cry. And I was crying with him. What a silly fucking thing to do! A no-hitter. Two outs. Our club wasn't scoring any runs. We weren't going to tie the score.

"I should have been pissed off because I was the one who lost the game. But I was pissed off at Anderlick and told him so. Well, that didn't set well with other players on the team. Not only was I not pissed off because I got beat, but I'm mad at the guy who busted up the no-hitter.

"Bortz thought it was funny, but he couldn't think it was funny around anybody else. When we got back to the room, he said, 'That will go on your report,' because he knew about the Root incidents. He said, 'That's a good way to end the season, you big son of a bitch. You stupid asshole.'

"I was supposed to go into the army at the end of the season, but the army wouldn't call me. I had been waiting four months. I should have gone in in October, and here it was March. I wasn't wanted around the house. So I went to spring training with the Springfield team in the International League, and I was there when the draft call finally came.

"I left Cincinnati by train and went to Fort Meade, Maryland. We sat down for the opening address, and the special service officer came in and said, 'Anybody here play professional sports?' I raised both hands.

"We were all shipped in to a medical replacement training batallion. Which meant we had half the day off. I spent half a day learning to become a corpsman, how to do bandages. I could carry a stretcher, but that was all I could have done if I went over to Korea. We did that in the morning, and I had the afternoon off for practice or a game. We played eighty games a year.

"So I had it made that first year. Especially because I could throw harder than anybody else. I didn't have to pitch. All I had to do was throw. I lost one game to Johnny Antonelli. He struck out 18. He pitched for the premier freeloading team at Fort Myer in Washington, D.C. They marched to the cemetery at Arlington, were aides to various officers. They had the best team, had five major leaguers on that club. And I lost to Bob Turley in an amateur baseball tournament in Wichita. He struck out 16 in seven innings.

"Most of the time I won. We had a good ball club. What I got out of that experience was confidence that I really did have an exceptional arm. I won 37 games in two years.

"After I got out of the service, I immediately went to a ball club where I was 4–17. It was Springfield, Triple A, a Chicago farm team in the International League.

This is when I learned for the first time that the Cubs weren't a very good organization.

"Bruce Edwards, who was my manager, would talk about how piss poor it was. He had come from the Dodgers organization where (a) you really had to be a standout to get to Triple A and (b) everybody knew all the little things you had to know about professional baseball by the time they had spent five years as a professional. He said it was a shock to him that players in the Cubs organization had gotten to Triple A baseball and didn't know their fundamentals.

"It wasn't until 1951 that Wid Matthews, who brought Edwards over from the Dodgers, started to have teachers in the minor leagues. Before Wid, managers got hired because PK Wrigley remembered them. He'd say, 'He'll probably make a good manager. He deserves a job. If he can't find anything else, we'll let him manage one of our minor league ball clubs.' And there were a couple of managers like that.

"The Cubs had no coaching, no program, no fundamental method of teaching the young prospects. I don't know why they signed some of the people they did sign.

"This Springfield team was a bad ball club, a last-place ball club. A *bad* ball club. Bruce Edwards left the team to go back to play in the majors when one of the other clubs' catchers got hurt. Bruce said it was the best thing that happened to him because managing us was driving him crazy. He had all these prospects.

"Gene Hooks, who became a very famous baseball coach at Wake Forest, played for us. Sparky Adams played center field. We had a third baseman playing left field, and Ron Northey played right field. The left fielder couldn't run. And Northey, who was through by that time, couldn't run. And Sparky, who weighed 161 pounds when the season started, had to run so much that when the season ended he weighed 150 pounds and his feet were gone.

"It was Northey who gave me the nickname Reverend.

"'Why?' I asked him.

"'Because you look like a reverend.' It was because I wore glasses, I suppose.

"I was mighty happy when Frank Robinson later decided he'd call me Professor. It sounded much better, and it looks better in the Big Book [*The Baseball Encyclopedia*] than Reverend.

"We had Randy Jackson at third. Randy didn't know anything. He had come out of Texas. He had been a football player. He played baseball, but I don't think he loved the game at all.

"When he got over to Brooklyn, he loved playing for the Dodgers because he suddenly realized the difference between a truly professional major league team and what he had come from. Bruce could have told Randy that if he had asked right from the start.

"At Springfield I couldn't figure out what to do to win games. I decided to become a sinker ball pitcher. I remembered some of Don Osborne's tricks, how to pack the resin in my glove. But I never did really get it down. I went out there every fourth day. That's how I was able to lose 17 games. You have to pitch regularly to lose that often.

"I knew if I didn't pitch a shutout, or hold them to two runs or less, I wasn't going to win. Seven times the scores were 3–2, 2–1, 2–0. It finally got to me. At the end of the year, I decided to quit.

"The army offered a service. I took a battery of tests, and they told you what sort of career you ought to get yourself into. I went to Worcester, Massachusetts, took a day off, and took the test, and they said, 'You should be either an accountant or a writer.'

"Knowing that writers starve to death, knowing no writer who did not look like he was starving to death, I decided to become an accountant, and they got me into Benjamin Franklin University, a specialized accounting school in Washington, D.C.

"I entered the program right after the '53 season ended. I was through. That was it. I was married. I had lived in Laurel, Maryland, when I was at Fort Meade, liked the area. My wife was working while I was going to school. We were getting by.

"In February 1954 I got a letter saying, 'You are invited to spring training with the Cubs. We will send you a major league contract.' Which they did. Five thousand bucks. But only if I stayed in the big league would I get the $5,000, otherwise I would get $750 a month. This was customary. Still is.

"I went to spring training. Here was a shot at five thousand bucks. I still had not seen more than $2,500 at one time. I figured, Why not give it a shot?

"I made the club despite the fact that I arrived weighing 235 pounds, which was a good 25 pounds overweight. 'Cause I wasn't going to play anymore, so I didn't work out. I love to eat, and it looked like it.

"I would run with the pitchers, and by the end of the workout I was puking on the sideline. I would run around next to the fence, and I'd empty myself over the right-field line. I had shin splints. Everything that could go wrong seemed to go wrong, but my arm was fine. I was throwing the ball hard, and the Cubs had nobody else. Bob Rush got hurt, so they were going to be short on pitching, and then I pitched a good game in Dallas, the day that Phil Cavarretta was fired. This was when Cavarretta said, 'This club is a fifth-place club at best.' And PK Wrigley said, 'That's damaging to morale. You're fired!'

"Stan Hack took over. He was one of the sweetest men on the face of the earth. He was embarrassed by the players he had to deal with but determined to carry it through for Mr. W.

"Stan said, 'If Mr. W says I manage, I'll manage.' Bob Scheffing was one of his coaches. Scheffing was a good man, but not the sweetest man in the world. He couldn't be because, as I said, Stan Hack was the sweetest man in the world. So Scheffing was in charge of discipline, and he had been an officer in the service. He knew how to discipline people. He also could tell a prospect from a suspect, and the way I hear it, and since it came from Mary Scheffing, his wife, I have to assume it is true. He said, 'Every time Brosnan sticks his head out of the bullpen, somebody hits a line drive.'

"And he was probably right. In '54 I had an ERA of 9.45.

"Howie Pollet won 20 games that year, and Howie decided he could help me. He was not only helpful as a counselor, but he taught me how to throw a slider. He told me, 'Don't tell anybody else I'm teaching you this,' because his reputation was a big overhand curve ball, which was the way Howie Pollet pitched, and which he taught all the other pitchers, because he thought that was the best pitch. But he decided I couldn't throw that pitch, and he was right. I couldn't. So he taught me the slider, and all of a sudden I could be a finesse pitcher, not a power pitcher. I really didn't throw hard enough or have enough movement on my fastball to really be a power pitcher.

"I had had two pitches, a fastball and a change. I could throw a pretty good change. Now I had a third pitch, the whole shebang, but I had no place to use it because every time I stuck my head outside the dugout, bang, a line drive. Right?

"So they sent me to Des Moines. I pitched very well there. And hell, I had turned into a cheerleader. There were no coaches on the minor league clubs. Players coached. Pitchers who weren't pitching, they coached first base and third base. 'Hey, hey, I'm out there, let's go.' Younger players listened to me, and now the Cubs liked my attitude. My attitude had changed. They loved it.

"During the season one of the Cubs pitchers, Bubba Church, got hit in the jaw by Ted Kluszewski's line drive, and he was through for the year. Who did they bring up? Moi. To the great disgust of Walker Cooper, who simply could not understand it. I had already proved to him I couldn't pitch in the big leagues. 'What the fuck do we have here? We got nothing! We lose Bubba Church, and we get this guy?'

"Well, I didn't pitch too badly. I didn't change his mind, but I convinced somebody in the organization that with this stuff I was using I had to go out and work. I had to pitch somewhere. They sent me to Beaumont, Texas, and I pitched very well, finished 8–1.

"On the last day of the season I pitched a game against Doyle Lade, the first game of a doubleheader against Shreveport, a team that had clinched first place the night before. They were all drunk. Doyle Lade was drunk too. I loved the idea of pitching against them. It took me fifty-five minutes. I won 2–1.

"My wife was pregnant. I wanted to go back to Chicago, and so I asked my manager, Mickey Livingston, 'Now can I leave?' I hadn't seen my wife for two and a half months. And he wouldn't let me go. I had to sit there and watch the second game. Max Lanier pitched the second game and won it in an hour and forty minutes. We had played two full games in less than three hours. So I had plenty of time to catch the train. I made it to the station, and I got away.

"I can't figure out why Mickey would be so pissed off. Sure I do. I didn't want to pitch that day. I wanted to go home. I was 7–1. I had done my job. It didn't make any difference whether we won or lost. So when I went out there it didn't look like I was pitching. I looked like I wanted to get knocked out.

"I walked the first two batters. Mickey came out and chewed my ass. But after they got one run, that was it. They didn't get anything else. So why shouldn't he let me go? Well, he didn't. He was showing his need to discipline me.

"I didn't care whether I ever saw Beaumont or Mickey Livingston again. It was the hottest place I'd ever been in my life, no beer on Sunday. You couldn't buy a drink, unless you went to one of the brothels. Ben Taylor was our first baseman. He played with Detroit, a big guy from the Pennsylvania coal mines. He and Red Hollis dragged me to the whorehouse one Sunday afternoon, 'cause it was our custom to have a couple brews after the game, usually at night. Sunday afternoon was the only afternoon we played, and Benny was proving how cosmopolitan he was. He knew where you could get a drink on Sunday. That's all we did. The girls, who weren't too attractive, they were not tasty looking, they talked baseball. They were baseball fans.

"Beaumont was a bad place. It had a nice ballpark, but the mosquitoes were gigantic. Alan Russell, who ran the team, told me, 'I'm losing money on the bug spray.'

"The Cubs then sent me to Los Angeles, where I pitched for Bill Sweeney, the legend on the coast. He had managed many clubs up and down the coast. He had been an alcoholic for twenty years, and it was beginning to show. One day we were taking batting practice, and I was going to pitch that game. I came back from the batting cage and Sweeney was sitting on the bench, and he said to me, 'Steve . . .' I said, 'Yeah, Bill.' [First baseman] Steve Bilko had been standing ten feet away. Sweeney had probably seen Bilko out of the corner of his eye. He knew he wanted to say something to him, but he was looking right at me, me with glasses, and I was in very good shape, fifty pounds lighter than Bilko, and he's telling me something he wanted Bilko to know. I started to laugh, and Bilko was just disgusted that he had to play for this drunk. Bilko could put away a case of beer after a ball game and you couldn't tell he had had a drink.

"Sweeney didn't last long. The organization finally did something right. Bob Scheffing said, 'I want to manage, but at a high level,' and they said, 'All right,' and they sent him to manage the team, and we finished third that year, and he won the championship the next year. He had Gene Mauch playing second base. Bilko hit 55 home runs the following year.

"After Scheffing got there, the team did start to play very well. I was 8–7. We were playing at Oakland, and it was almost a repeat of the Charlie Root game. I'm winning 2–1 in the ninth inning, and there's a man on first and George Metkovich was hitting. I know Metkovich, know how I'm going to pitch him, and I know how he's going to hit the ball if he hits it. I turn around to face the outfield. Gale Wade is playing center field, and I motion for him to move to over, to get to left field, because I'm going to pitch him away, and he's going to hit a fly ball to center field. Gale Wade doesn't move. I signal, 'Move over.' I had no authority to tell him what to do. It would have to come from the manager, according to Gale Wade. Or from Gene Mauch, who was the second manager on our team. From somebody else, not me. So he didn't move. In fact, he moved the other way. He was a hardheaded little son of a bitch from West Virginia, and he just made up his mind he wasn't going to pay attention to anybody else. He thought he was the greatest center fielder in the world. And he *was* pretty good.

"I threw Metkovich a high fastball. He hit a high fly ball to left-center field, right in the gap, but if Wade had moved over where I told him, he would have caught it right there.

"Tie score, 2–2. Eleventh inning. I don't recall who hit the ball, a fly ball to right field, a kid leans from the stands with a first baseman's mitt, catches the ball, takes it right out of our outfielder Bob Coates's glove. Coates wasn't very big. He could have reached up, but he was waiting for it. And the guy reached out and grabbed it. In the Oakland ballpark the lights weren't very good anyway. This was enough for whoever was umpiring first base. He said he didn't see it, and I lost the game 3–2.

"This time I was a little depressed. We had an hour to wait to go to the airport, so I went into the nearest bar, and [former Dodgers third baseman] Spider Jorgensen and [outfielder] Wally Westlake were there. They were Oakland players. 'Nice game. Tough luck. Have a drink.' OK. I had three Gibsons in twenty minutes.

"I had pitched eleven innings in the heat of the summer, and I hadn't had anything to eat. I got on the bus, and right away I was a little manic, high, not just from the alcohol, but it was part of my psychological history. Gene Mauch saw it right away. 'Tough game. We'll have a drink at the airport.' And he got [infielder] Bud Hardin and [outfielder] Hal Rice, who were the real heavy drinkers on the club, to line up five Gibsons. We have a half hour to get on the airplane. I knocked four of them back, so now I've had seven Gibsons on an empty stomach in less than an hour and a half.

"On the plane I couldn't sit down. I wouldn't stay down. I was wandering up and down the aisles, on this commercial flight, annoying everybody. The copilot came back and said, 'We're going to have to put you off at San Francisco.' Scheffing talked him out of it. It wasn't until we were down over Bakersfield that they could get me in my seat and keep me down.

"My wife had driven out to the airport with Mary Scheffing. We lived in the same neighborhood in Hollywood. Everybody was off the plane except me, Hardin, and Rice, and we came down the ramp singing. I couldn't walk. My legs were gone. They were carrying me. My wife said it was the most embarrassing moment of her life. She got back in the car and waited for me. Bob Scheffing said to his wife, 'We'll take a cab.'

"I got in the car, and I said, 'Where's the baby?' My firstborn was born March 18 in spring training. The baby was sleeping in the backseat. I wanted to get in the back. My wife, who was driving the car, said, 'Sit right there. Don't move. I don't want you near my baby.'

"I don't remember much about the night, but the next day was pretty bad. A lot of bile. Nothing in me. I was throwing up little bits of little onions. I have never been able to eat one since. It makes me sick to look at a jar of those Gibson onions, even today.

"I got to the ballpark and Scheffing said, 'Why are you here?' I said, 'I'm going to get in the whirlpool and stay there for a couple of hours.' He said, 'Come back tomorrow. You're no good to us. Tough game.'

"Scheffing wrote a report about the game. The first line: 'Brosnan finally joined the club.' Then he went on to describe the game and what happened afterward.

"I had gone from an almost sociopathic loner, always by myself, to suddenly becoming one of the guys, especially one of the guys who drank, the social guys. And then all of a sudden I was everybody's friend.

"I went 9–2 the rest of the year, and at the end of the year, we had a little party, and Bubba Church, who was now pitching for our team, said to me, 'You're the guy who's going to make the Cubs next year.'

"And I was that guy."

52

Boyhood Memories

LIFETIME CUBS FAN JIM SHAPIRO: "I was born in 1938. One of my earliest memories is the 1945 World Series. I was seven years old. My father went. I remember begging him to go. Of course, it was impossible.

"I did get a pennant from the Series, which I kept on my wall for years and years. It had all the names of the players on it. I remember when I was going to college I still had that pennant, and in one of the moves in a gesture of 'Who needs this?' it got tossed away, and I've been wringing my hands ever since.

"I grew up on the North Side of Chicago. I was born near the corner of Foster and Sheridan Streets. You could ride your bike from there to Wrigley Field. It would be a pretty good walk, but you *could* ride your bike. When I was quite young, we moved to East Rogers Park, very much in the heart of the North Side of the city.

"The fact of the matter is, growing up where I did, I didn't know White Sox fans. It was like the White Sox simply didn't exist. There wasn't a lot of conversation about them. They were over—there. It was a long elevated and streetcar ride to get over to Comiskey Park.

"I had a first cousin, Ed Stone, who grew up in Marquette Park, which is on the South Side of Chicago. He was about my age, a rabid baseball fan and rabid White Sox fan. Forty-five years later, we still endlessly argue Cubs-Sox. But it was not so much a scientific analysis of which team was better, position by position, statistics by statistics, but rather, 'Cubs stink and White Sox are great,' or 'White Sox stink and Cubs are great.' You just were extraordinarily loyal and dedicated to your team.

"In my lifetime I've been to Wrigley Field between a hundred and fifty and two hundred times. I remember going to White Sox Park three times. Once I went to a night game there with a couple of buddies to see what that was like.

"I was scared. It was on the South Side. I didn't know a lot of people. You sensed it was not your area, not your neighborhood. Comiskey Park was, then and now, in a little bit of a rough neighborhood. If I was going to spend the time, I was going to spend the time with the Cubs at Wrigley Field, which was and is a neighborhood baseball park. It's a *park*, not a stadium. You feel at home.

"At Wrigley Field I always felt safe. You could take the A train and you got off at Addison and you walked not even one block. There was no transfer, no long walks, you couldn't get lost. You felt *very* safe.

"Wrigley Field had a lot of tradition about it, in that if you followed the Cubs, the Cubs and Wrigley Field were, and still are, inseparable. I cannot imagine the Chicago Cubs playing anywhere but Wrigley Field. So if you followed the baseball team, the ballpark was an integral part of the team, as important, maybe even more so, than following any particular player. It was part of the heritage and fabric of the baseball team itself.

"Wrigley Field was such a pretty place. If you sat in the bleachers, it was great. You got some sun. You could see the game very clearly. You always felt you were close to the game, even if you were in a far seat. If you didn't sit in the bleachers, you could overlook the skyline. It was lovely. And it was intimate. You were never far away from the action.

"I've been in many major league ballparks, and in other stadiums even when you have relatively good seats, you can feel far away. I once went to the SkyDome in Toronto, a magnificent stadium, very beautiful with a retractable roof, and I had good seats, and I remember sitting there thinking, 'I'm really far from the playing field. I'm *very* far.' I remember many, many times looking up at the Diamond Vision screen to see really what happened. I cannot imagine in my life having to look up at any screen to see what was going on at Wrigley Field, even if you were in the bleachers.

"The one smell I can remember were the peanuts. When you went to the game you just had to have a bag of peanuts. And of course, the hot dogs. Wrigley Field had a famous hot dog vendor, Gravel Gertie. The reason he was called that was that he had a very hoarse voice from yelling out over thirty years, 'Red hots and hot dogs.'

"Gravel Gertie was a great kibitzer. He would insult you. 'What's the matter, you too cheap to buy your son a hot dog? Buy him a darn hot dog.' And people would laugh. 'You're only going to buy one? You're going to starve on one. Buy two.' He had a great gift of gab about him.

"One of the great thrills was not only to go to the ballpark, not only to eat a hot dog, but to eat a hot dog sold by Gravel Gertie. He had a station just in back of the visitors dugout on the first-base line. I didn't always like to sit behind the Cubs dugout along third base, because I liked the sun, and it was sunnier behind first. If you sat on the first-base side, you got a little bit of an afternoon of sun. Of course, if you sat in the bleachers, you got all-day sun.

"When you went earlier in the year, April and May, it could be cool, frankly cold. So if you had a chance to get a couple extra hours of sun, that was helpful.

"Gravel Gertie's voice eventually literally gave out. But he was so well known that he actually could sell hot dogs and outsell anyone else by just walking around the ballpark and banging a bottle cap against his tray. He could bang the tray, and you knew that was Gravel Gertie selling his dogs, and you bought a dog from him. It was a loyalty to him, part of the fabric of the park, and it made it all that much better.

"So Gravel Gertie was a Wrigley Field tradition, and so was Pat Peiper. Ever since I began going to the ballpark when I was a boy, Peiper was the PA announcer. He would sit on the field. He was *never* up in the stands. He would get the lineup from the managers, who would go from the dugout right over to him, and then he would give his famous, 'Attention, attention please, have your pencils and score-cards ready and we'll give you the lineup for today's game.'

"My wife's father, Manny Schwartz, for many years was the stand-in announcer at Wrigley Field should Pat Peiper retire. For thirty-five years Pat was about to step down, but he never did, or at least not till he was eighty, and by that time Manny had moved down to Florida.

"Pat Peiper originally was hired by Charlie Weeghman, who built Wrigley Field. Weeghman earned his money for development by owning restaurants, and before he owned restaurants he worked in restaurants as a waiter. It was a Horatio Alger story, from waiter to restaurateur to developer to builder of a legendary ballpark.

"Weeghman, as would be expected, was partial to waiters. When Peiper was a young waiter working in a restaurant in Chicago called the Ivanhoe, he came to him for a job at Wrigley Field. Weeghman said he had an announcing job. He gave Pat a megaphone, and he would bark it out. That was his day job, and at night he waited tables at the Ivanhoe. Through much of his life until he was well into his sixties, he would still go to the Ivanhoe. Peiper was a walking legend.

"By the time I was a boy, Peiper was making his announcements over the PA system. After I would arrive, I would wait to hear Pat Peiper's voice. He was part of the fabric of tradition, hearing him announce for more than twenty-five years of my going to the ballpark.

"There was, and still is, a sameness, in a beautiful sense, a stability about the park. The area around Wrigley Field didn't dramatically change. It didn't deteriorate. It didn't get fabulous. It stayed very steady for all the years I remember it. Everybody talks about the vines. You go there and see the vines. Well, Pat Peiper was part of that stability for my whole youth, even into my young adulthood. It was the same announcer with the same voice making the announcement in the very same way.

"The Cubs did not have very good teams when I was growing up. After the '45 World Series, the team went downhill quickly. For twenty years the players were nothing to write home about.

"As a youngster the player I had a long love-hate relationship with was number 39, Roy Smalley. He was our shortstop. He was a great fielder. He could pull some electric plays.

"It was his fielding more than his batting that appealed to me. I was an infielder. I played second base when I played grade school on a local team, but it was Smalley I liked, not Eddie Miksis or Wayne Terwilliger. I was never enamored of those guys. I'm not sure why.

"Smalley was a crowd favorite in terms of his fielding, and I either loved him or hated him, depending on his fielding for the day. [In 1950, Roy Smalley led the league with 332 putouts, 541 assists, and 115 double plays.]

"But Smalley could also make some incredibly bonehead plays, particularly throwing to first base. [Smalley in '50 also led the league with 51 errors and at bat with 114 strikeouts.] Smalley had the habit of tossing it right into the stands.

"I remember very clearly the talk in the neighborhood was that the Cubs had a great double play combination, Miksis to Smalley to Grandstand.

"The first Cubs radio announcer that I remember was Bert Wilson. There was a period of time, a stretch of about ten years [from 1944 through 1955], and those were formative years for me in grade school and early high school, that the voice of the Cubs to me was Bert Wilson.

"It was Bert Wilson who originated, I'm sure at the prompting of Phil Wrigley, the discussion of 'Here we are at Beautiful Wrigley Field.' It would be as if you couldn't just say 'Wrigley,' and you couldn't just say 'Field.' The name of the ballpark was three words, it was 'Beautiful Wrigley Field,' and probably woe to Bert if he didn't use that expression.

"There was another expression that Bert used that I still remember to this day, which he said usually at least once and probably three or four times during any given game, particularly at the early part. He would say, 'It's such a beautiful, cloudless day, and frankly it's such a beautiful day, I don't care who wins as long as it's the Cubs.' That was his expression. 'I don't care who wins as long as it's the Cubs.' It was his way of saying, It's beautiful, but boy we would sure like a win. That was my early remembrance as the voice of the Cubs.

"In the early 1950s we discovered television. Jack Brickhouse was the pioneer when the Cubs started with WGN-TV at that time. He was the voice behind the camera. Brickhouse was the master of knowing you didn't have to be talking all the time. He saw you could let the visual image carry the day.

"When I couldn't get to the game, or when I'd come home from school, I'd catch the last half of the game on TV.

"Of course, watching the games on television was a whole new phenomenon, to be able to see it right there, no matter how tiny the screen was. It was fabulous, but in no way did it take the place of going to the games.

"Phil Wrigley was a pioneer in the broadcasting of the games on TV. I'm sure there was a huge argument at the time, 'My God, if you showed the games, people could watch for free, and they would never come to the park. Why would they?'

"Literally, it was just the opposite. Watching the games on TV made you hunger more to go out to the ballpark. You were interested, you saw the game, you saw the action, and you said, 'By gosh, I gotta be out there.'

"Because you knew there was no substitute for being there and smelling the peanuts and hearing Gravel Gertie, and being part of the crowd and taking it all in. For me to watch the Cubs games on television, it just added gas to the fire."

LIFETIME CUBS FAN PAUL BUCHBINDER: "I was born in '49, and in the mid-fifties the notion of the World Series in Chicago was an impossible notion, so the best thing you could hope for was that your team would be better than the White Sox. Growing up as a kid, all my friends divided up by Cubs fans versus White Sox fans, with the exception that there always was one kid who would be a Yankees fan.

"In the beginning I was a White Sox fan, but I quickly became a Cubs fan, and I *am* a Cubs fan. I started as a Sox fan because it was as though I was being torn to choose sides between my parents. My father was Jewish and he was from the North Side and a Cubs fan, and he would promote the Cubs. My mother was Catholic and grew up in back of the stockyards, and she was a Sox fan. But even though my mother was a Sox fan, we used to go out to Wrigley Field because the Cubs held a promotion called Ladies Day, which were typically on Tuesdays or Fridays, and they were also during the day, which during the summer, if you've got kids, is a great place to go.

"I can remember the way the Cubs used to promote Ladies Day. The thing was, the Cubs rarely even promoted baseball. Jack Brickhouse would read the ads, and he'd say, 'Hey Mom, Fridays are Ladies Days at Wrigley Field. Grab the kids. Pack a lunch or better yet . . .' I can still hear the way he used to say it. ' . . . or better yet, buy a ballpark frank at the hot dog stand. We have everything you need. And while you're at it, see a major league baseball game, as the Cubs host the . . .' The game itself was incidental to the family event.

"And I can remember on the Cubs scorecard the images of a little Cubbie bear holding a hot dog. It meant that all my needs would be met. To me ballpark franks taste the same as they did when I was a kid. That's a bit of nostalgia that has never disappointed. And even though today I'm a vegetarian, I'll eat a ballpark frank. It's my one exception.

"Going to Wrigley Field was a thing my mom and I could do together, and it was a safe place to go. We could get on the bus and then get on the El, and you'd see this ballpark, this enormous monument. And when you entered the ballpark, even if you were sitting in the grandstands, you had to go through these tunnels, which are like the one at the end of the movie *The Pride of the Yankees*, when Lou Gehrig/Gary Cooper walked through the tunnel. It's the same feeling walking through the tunnel at Wrigley Field. And then you come to the opening, and a whole new world just sort of opens up in front of you. You're in a dark room, and all of a sudden you have this panavision screen, and it was green—the field was *really* green—and it was moving, and it was just so engrossing.

"Even as an adult, I always felt inside a ballpark was like a cocoon. You have the ability to forget about everything else except what you hear and see inside. The only sound outside is an occasional rumbling of the El.

"I can remember when I was growing up, the hot ticket if you were young was the city series game against the White Sox, because that was the game that would settle the arguments before the season. My brother, who was two years older, was a White Sox fan, and he and I would have arguments centering on the players. We would compare them, like comparing Minnie Minoso versus Hank Sauer, Frankie Baumholtz versus Jim Rivera.

"Frankie Baumholtz almost won the batting championship. In 1952 I can remember Baumholtz and Stan Musial were going for the batting title, and it was September, and Musial was ahead of Baumholtz, and Cards manager Eddie Stanky brought in Musial to pitch against Baumholtz. Here were two guys going for the batting title, and to me this is what baseball should be about when it comes down to something like the batting title, to have that confrontation between the two people who are actually battling for the title. That's the same as when you're kids. 'Think you're so good. Think you're a better hitter than me? Hit this.'

"If only Baumholtz had come in to pitch to Musial, except that Musial probably would have clobbered him. It was a great, great moment. Baumholtz, of course, didn't win the batting championship. [Musial finished at .336, Baumholtz at .321.]

"Each year during my childhood, the Cubs would finish eighth or maybe seventh, but every spring I became convinced the Cubs would win the pennant. I always bought into the spring training assessment of Jack Brickhouse and Jack Quinlan.

"They were so enthusiastic and such great guys to listen to that when they told us the Cubs had really changed this spring with this acquisition or that acquisition, rather than realize it meant it would bring them up to the top of the second division, we *really* thought, 'They're going all the way.' And it's that renewal thing of spring.

"Remember Frank Ernaga? In '57, Frank Ernaga was one of those bonus babies. Brickhouse had us convinced that he was a great prospect. In his first at bat he hit a solo home run. His next at bat, a triple. A couple of days later he ran into the vines chasing a fly ball, got hurt, and was finished. [After going 1 for 8 as a pinch hitter in 1958, Ernaga hung up his spikes.]

"As I look at it now as an adult, it was a matter of hope. The Cubs represent hope. As bad as they might have been, it didn't seem dismal. I was always able to maintain that childhood experience of being able to feel faith going to a game.

"And the Cubs always seemed to be in it to the end. The Cubs always seemed to raise a bit of hope into the ninth inning. And most of the time you got your money's worth to go to a Cubs game, because you got a *full* nine innings. Most of the time the Cubs would come to bat in the bottom of the ninth!

"My favorite ballplayer was Paul Minner. One thing I remember, there was a newspaper in Chicago called the *New World*, which was put out by the Catholic Church. The *New World* would have a poll; pick your favorite Cub and White Sox player, and this goes into why Paul Minner may have been my favorite: because my brother Ned knew that everybody would go for Ernie Banks, and either Nellie Fox or Luis Aparicio or Minnie Minoso, so he wanted to bring attention to another player, and he tried to do it by stuffing the ballot box. He went down to the office of the newspaper, and they had Xerox copies of the ballot, and he started a whole campaign to write in two unknown players: Jim Brewer for the Cubs, and Jim Lemon for the Sox. And this leads me to Paul Minner. Everybody *was* going for Minnie Minoso, Hank Sauer, and Ernie Banks—and this was something that continues in my life now—like my brother, I felt I had to find somebody distinctive with whom

I could somehow identify, whether it was the way they played or the way they looked. And so I picked Paul Minner.

"One element about him was his name. I'm Paul. He's Paul. It was something my father was able to engage me with by saying, 'Here is somebody with your name out there playing the game.' Another thing that hooked me on to him was that he came to the Cubs the year I was born. My father said, 'This guy has been here as long as you've been here.'

"My dad would usually get my brother and me Cubs tickets for my birthday, which was in May, and one of my early memories is a game that Paul Minner pitched. We sat in the box seats, so we could see his face.

"His face was interesting. It reminded me of that famous Norman Rockwell painting in the dugout, the way his uniform fit. He didn't look like an athlete. He looked like a real guy, and his face was sort of drawn and his cap was pulled over his head. He was pretty big and lanky. My father knew a little bit about him, and he said, 'This is the Cubs' best pitcher.' He *was* the Cubs' best pitcher in '53. Which means he won 12 games and lost 15. It was all relative, of course, but this was our best. And I latched on to him. You wouldn't read about him much in the paper, but he was number one in the stats. This was the player I always looked for in the box score to see how he did. I would watch the Cubs game to see if he would win or lose. He usually lasted four or five innings.

"I never met him, but I have always felt warmth toward him. On my fortieth birthday, a friend of mine, Bill Young, somehow found Minner, and at my surprise party, he had him call me. I was stunned. I couldn't believe it. And he was incredulous that somebody could have picked him as a favorite player.

"It was my birthday party, and it was a surprise party, so from the first surprise I had a shock, and then the phone rang, and it was Paul Minner, and everybody was standing around me, looking at me on the phone, and I was surprised, of course, and speechless. He just seemed like a real gentle person, a nice guy. And he told me about himself, his family.

"If becoming forty is not a great experience, talking to Paul Minner on my fortieth birthday will be the wonderful memory I carry away."

LIFETIME CUBS FAN BRUCE LADD: "I was born in 1936 and grew up in Chicago. Why else did I get this nonfatal disease? My favorite player was Andy Pafko. How can you explain taste? He was at that time the star of the team. Nicholson was fading. Passeau was fading. Borowy had come over from the Yankees, and he was fading. Andy was the star.

"In '48, he had his best year. He hit .312. That was the year he moved to third base. At that time Pafko was my hero. Still is, for that matter. Number 48.

"If you recall, Pafko was considered an absolute coup for the Dodgers when they got him in '51. That was exactly what they needed. The guy went on to play in four World Series, three with the Dodgers and the Braves, so hell, he was a great ballplayer.

"It was a four-for-four trade with the Dodgers. The Cubs really took gas on that one. Oh, they gave away some decent ballplayers for *nothing*. Absolutely nothing. The one-for-one on Andy was Gene Hermanski. Wid Matthews made the trade. He had worked for Branch Rickey, and he probably owed him something from a crap game and paid him back that way.

Emil Verban

"And when I heard about that trade, I went down and declared—and my mother remembers it to this moment—'I am never, ever going to pull or root for the Cubs ever again in my life, period, finis, over and out, end of it.'

"Of course, it didn't last. Two days later I came back.

"Today I am the historian of the Emil Verban Memorial Society, a group of seven hundred Cubs fans, living mostly in the Washington, D.C., area. Ron Reagan is a member, Hillary Clinton. She was our featured guest at our luncheon in April. She was born and raised in Park Ridge, Illinois, and is very knowledgeable and still an excited Cubs fan.

"She hosted us over at the White House for a nice hour and a half breakfast, took us in to see Bill. Right into the Oval Office. We whizzed right in there. He didn't know we were coming. And then she came over and spent an hour and a half with us for lunch.

"We have guys like George Will, and Tom Bosley of *Happy Days*, and Bryant Gumbel, and a bunch of congressmen and senators, luminaries around the political part of town. But basically just people who were in Chicago at one time or another, who find themselves out here.

"Every two years we have a lunch whether we need to or not. There are no activities other than the historian periodically issues a memorandum to the membership. We don't have any dues, we don't have any officers, we don't have any obligations of membership whatsoever, and that's why everyone likes it.

"It started in 1975 when some guy sent me the most wonderful *Esquire* review of Leo Durocher's new book, *Nice Guys Finish Last*. The guy who did the book review talked about the book, and he said, 'I had a chance to talk to Durocher,' and he said he asked him, 'Mr. Durocher, how do you do it with the women? You're older, and you're balding. How do you do it?' He said, 'Son, I'll tell you how. You make a date with one for eight o'clock. That's sharp, eight o'clock. Now, at eight-oh-five, you put your hand on her snatch. One of two things is going to happen. Either she is going to push your hand off, or she isn't. Remember, if she pushes your hand off, it's still only eight-oh-five!'

"Having this in my hand, I thought, Oh gee, here I am in Washington. I'm going to send this to all these guys I hang around with at receptions and work with in the White House. They are going to get a kick out of it. I grabbed a list of about five or six guys, and I was going to put a cover note on this.

"First I wrote, 'To um, to the Cubs fans . . . to the Cub fan club, uh, to the Roy Smalley Fan . . .' All of a sudden, Emil Verban, an obscure player, to say the least, leapt into my mind, and Emil's name went right on there. 'Emil Verban Society . . . no, wait a minute, we need a touch there, Emil Verban *Memorial* Society.'

"I didn't know if Emil was alive or dead. I named myself the historian of the society, and I put, 'Memo number one.' Never intending that there would be a memo number two. And the short of it is, these guys wrote, called, and said, 'Jesus, this is funny, really terrific. When's memo number two?'

"About three weeks later, the Cubs got beat 23–3 by Pittsburgh, so I tore that out of the *Washington Post*, and I sent that with a trivia question, and the next thing I knew they were calling me nominating members. Well, the thing began to grow until we have seven hundred members. I'd say more than three-quarters are residents in the D.C. metropolitan area. All Cubs fans.

"Emil died in '89 unfortunately. Today, he'd be making 1.2 million. He hit a career .272, .280 with the Cubs in '48, '49, and '50. He was the pick of the litter with Marty Marion of the double play combinations in the mid-forties. At our lunch in April, which Hillary Clinton and Ernie Banks and a lot of the old players attended, along with 350 guests, we put on highlights showing Emil performing in the '44 World Series for the Cardinals. He did well in that Series. He hit in the winning run in the sixth game. The guy was way better than your average ballplayer, and yet people think we picked him because of his mediocrity.

"We might have picked him because of his obscurity, but *not* because of his mediocrity, by any means."

53

Mr. Cub

The first Cubs superhero to appear on the scene since the days of Hack Wilson, Kiki Cuyler, and Riggs Stephenson was thin, lanky, and black. This man, who wore uniform number 14, turned out to be perhaps the most popular player in the history of the team. He was loved the way Mike Kelly and Cap Anson had been loved at the turn of the century. (What would the racist Anson have thought of that?)

The man, whose name was Ernie Banks, was idolized by the Chicago faithful. He arrived at Wrigley Field in the fall of '53, just six seasons after the racial revolution brought about by the coming of Jackie Robinson in 1947. The difference between the way the Cubs players and fans accepted Banks and the way Robinson had been treated spoke volumes about the way the country had changed in just those few years.

When Jackie Robinson played his first game for the Brooklyn Dodgers in April 1947, white society in America was forced to rethink its segregationist policies and adapt. The Cubs players, like everyone else then in the game, didn't want a Negro playing in the National League. Jim Crow had been a way of life in America since the end of the Civil War, and most everyone North *and* South was steeped in an acceptance of segregation and intolerance.

Hank Wyse, an Oklahoman who was a pitcher for the Cubs in 1947, recalled when Robinson first came into baseball.

HANK WYSE: "We had a meeting. Well, every club had a meeting, and like every other club, we weren't going to play if Robinson played. Cavarretta was the captain. He called the meeting. The manager and the coaches wasn't in it, just the players. And he told us that every club was voting agin' it, so we voted agin' it too, not to play if Robinson played. I didn't care. It didn't make me no difference to me. But I just voted along with the rest of them.

"Cavarretta was the only one who talked. We voted. I voted against. I know some of them didn't. But the majority voted against.

"We went back out on the field, and I don't know who brought the telegram back, but the commissioner [Happy Chandler] sent a telegram saying that if we didn't play, every player would be barred for life. So we had to play.

"I remember the first game against him. I don't remember who started, but every time he come up, we knocked him down four times. The pitcher would stay in there until it was his turn to come up, and they'd knock Robinson down four more times. When it come time for the pitcher to come up, we'd take him out and let somebody else in. 'Cause you knew darn well that the Dodgers were going to knock him down. So we changed pitchers during the ball game. Paul Erickson was the last pitcher, and the last time he came up, Erickson throwed it at his head, and he went down. He got back up, and he stuck one in his ribs. All four times he got up, they knocked him down. All four pitches.

"He didn't say nothing. He just got up and trotted down to first.

"He wasn't the best shortstop or first baseman when he came up. Branch Rickey had schooled him a little bit, 'cause he had a college education, but they kept it a secret that he had raped a white girl in college. [This was one of the scurrilous rumors spread about Robinson. There is no evidence whatsoever that Jackie had raped anyone.] They told him not to say nothing about what they done or anything, just hit, run and throw. And that's what he done for a while.

"He was a pretty good hitter, but he didn't run as fast as some other guys. He stole quite a few bases. He looked like he was running about a hundred miles an hour because he was twisting and taking short steps, and guys overestimated him."

LEN MERULLO: "Of course, we had a lot of southern ballplayers on the club at that time. A lot of them, and they would make remarks. Hey, we had McCullough,

Claude Passeau, Bill Lee, Dewey Williams, Hank Wyse, we had a bunch of them on that ball club, and they would all make remarks. I was there when he broke in, and you had to be there to appreciate what Jackie Robinson went through.

"He was a quick guy, but I wouldn't say he was the fastest guy, and he was a good-sized boy, a big strong boy, but I'll tell you, if he was white, this is my impression, if he was white and the way he played the first month say or even more at first base, he would have been back in the minor leagues. He didn't play with any confidence at all. He didn't do anything with the bat. He was hitting about .150—I may be exaggerating, but that's the way it looked to me, and he was having trouble at first base, but they kept him out there. Nobody talked to him from the opposing teams. Even some of his own players didn't.

"But as time went on, I don't care who you were, you *had* to respect what that young man was going through. He was about twenty-eight years old. He wasn't a kid, but he was going through some ordeal, and you had to respect that.

"I can remember getting on first base, and I whacked him on the fanny, where no one could notice it, and I said to him, 'Keep going, Jack.' And I'm sure others did the same thing. I'm sure they did, because you had to see what the poor guy was going through. I think that helped him more than anything else, because you could just see the confidence coming up into him, and then when they put him on second base, he was on the way home. He had that small glove that he used, didn't look like the typical quick middle man, but he could use that bat. He was so quick starting, but he was still the black type of ballplayer, that jigging off first base, and I can remember I had an incident with him. Bill Lee was pitching, and Bill was a big, slow, deliberate curve ball pitcher. Jackie was on first base. No outs. And when you're playing the infield and see the pitcher, very deliberate, slow, throw to first base, wind up again, to first base, you're up and down. Next thing you say to yourself, 'You nigger son of a bitch.' You're getting a little aggravated. Well, the throw goes to home, he steals second base. They walked the next guy. Now there were men on first and second. Bob Scheffing was the catcher. He didn't have a great arm, but he was a good receiver, had a quick arm. We put on the curve ball pitchout. You could do it with a good sweeping curve ball. The bunt is in order. He's going to bunt. You know he's going to bunt. We put on the play.

"When we put on the curve ball pitchout play, we don't do it on the first pitch, we do it on the second pitch. I don't remember the hitter. The first ball was outside. The play was on and I was supposed to give Jackie plenty of room, let him hear you behind him. But not run him back toward the bag. Let him get off there. And it worked out perfectly.

"Now this was in Chicago. The ballpark was loaded. I gave him room, the bat went out, and when you saw the ball going way outside, he pulled the bat back, and that runner was hung up, and we had him off by plenty, so much that instead of staying back on the bag, I moved up, and as he came in, his leg came over and hit me right on the shoulder. Well, I gave him a double tag. The second tag was around the head. Well, he got up, and you could have heard a pin drop. There were 42,000 people at the ballpark. And he had every right in the world to be angry. He was embarrassed. We had him out. And I had given him a hard tag, a double tag. He got up, and face-to-face, he didn't say a word, but he just froze there for what seemed like a long time. Then he turned around and ran right toward the dugout.

"Well, one of the magazines, *Collier's* or *Saturday Evening Post*, came out with a big article that I was one of the players who was against blacks and all that, because of that one incident. But that was Jackie Robinson."

PHIL CAVARRETTA: "When Jackie first came up he had a tough time. They jammed him so easy. He broke more bats. I feel there was so much pressure on this man that he wasn't playing to his true ability. They'd jam him inside, and it was sickening to watch him try to hit. Throw curves that he'd miss by a foot. We'd say, 'This guy is on a big-league roster? How can they sign this player? He should be in Montreal.' 'Cause he did look terrible. Fielding he looked awful. His range wasn't ten feet. But I can imagine him being so uptight coming in, being the first black player, with so much pressure on him. I think anybody would feel that same way, but later in the season he was outstanding.

"I don't know if they moved him away from the plate or whatever it was but later on, like any rookie, once you get your foot in the door and you feel you have the ability, you perform a lot better, and I'm sure that's what happened to Jackie. They said his wife had a lot to do with this. He would go home at night, and she would talk to him. 'Do the best you can. If you make it, fine. If you don't, we'll go back to Montreal.' In other words, she encouraged him, and he needed it bad.

"Later on when Jackie loosened up a little bit, Jackie was tough. If you had to pick a fight, you wouldn't pick one with Jackie. He would let you know about it if he was mad, not as far as words, but with his play. And he wasn't dirty. He was a hard player. But what he went through the first part of the season, to watch this young man hit big-league pitching, to field a ground ball, and actually he had outstanding speed, and he wasn't even showing his speed. But once he got his foot in the door and started to get a couple hits and encouragement from his coaches or whoever, to me even to this day what I've seen on TV, he was the most exciting player I've ever seen.

"When he got on first base, this was when he knew he could play. I'd be holding him on, and he'd start dancing around, and you could feel something was going to develop. He was going to steal a base or do something.

"And he'd get on third base, and he'd steal home, which was very rare. You hardly saw anyone steal home. We were his favorite club for stealing home. About three or four times. We knew he was going to do it, but whoever was pitching or calling the game started to call for a pitchout, and then he'd say, 'Ah, he's not going to steal home,' and he did it three or four times.

"He was exciting. Unbelievable. Dancing around. He upset the pitcher. You get that whole infield wondering what's going to happen."

Jackie Robinson helped lead the Dodgers to the 1947 National League pennant in his first year, and it didn't take other team owners long to realize that black ballplayers would help make mediocre teams into good ones—and good ones into pennant winners.

In 1942, five years before Robinson broke the color barrier, Bill Veeck had been in the process of buying the Philadelphia Phillies. During the negotiations he let slip to National League president Warren Giles that after he bought the perennially woeful Phils, he intended to stock it with an all-star team of Negro League players including Satchel Paige, Josh Gibson, Cool Papa Bell, and Buck Leonard. Veeck well knew that not even the St. Louis Cardinals would have been able to compete with that powerhouse. But Veeck made the mistake of telling Giles prior to the sale, and as soon as word got out to Commissioner Landis, who was a virulent racist, the National League bought the Phils and sold it to another buyer for less than what Veeck was intending to pay.

By 1948, Veeck owned the Cleveland Indians, and he signed the second Negro player after Robinson, outfielder Larry Doby, the first black player in the American League. Doby and former Kansas City Monarchs star Satchel Paige helped lead the Indians to the 1948 pennant. Veeck also signed Luke Easter, who played on the Indians pennant winner of 1954.

After Branch Rickey signed Robinson, the Dodgers general manager added Roy Campanella, Don Newcombe, Joe Black, Junior Gilliam, and Sandy Amoros, and these men along with Robinson helped the Dodgers to pennants in 1949, 1952, 1953, 1955, and 1956.

At the Polo Grounds, Horace Stoneham signed for his Giants a youngster from Birmingham, Alabama, in the Negro Leagues named Willie Mays, along with a third baseman named Hank Thompson and an outfielder named Monte Irvin. The Giants won pennants in 1951 and 1954.

Phil Wrigley, like every other major league owner (except Rickey), had voted against Jackie Robinson coming into the league. The notion of integrating baseball went so against the grain of the times that it was revolutionary in scope. Men like Wrigley were not revolutionaries by nature.

Robinson's entry into the game would change not only baseball but the country itself. The prejudice was, and still remains for too many, that people of color are inferior in every way. But when Jackie Robinson began playing major league baseball, he proved to his people, and to a lot of whites as well, that blacks could not only perform capably, ending one myth, but they could play superbly.

In the next decade barriers of racial segregation would begin to fall as public transportation, schools, and places of public congregation such as restaurants and hotels would slowly become integrated.

During the 1950s most Chicago restaurants wouldn't seat blacks, and most hotels wouldn't accommodate them. The Loop was considered off limits to blacks. According to one of the keenest observers of Chicago, Mike Royko, the city government followed a policy of containing the movement of blacks, limiting them to certain neighborhoods, using the walls of the new highways to help form the parameters of ghettos. White neighborhoods wouldn't even build housing for the elderly for fear that white wards might attract elderly blacks.

As a result, Chicago's slums were among the nation's worst. At the same time, the fear of blacks by the whites in Chicago was great. According to Royko, South Side whites hated blacks more than North Side whites did because the blacks were closer.

Said Royko, "Most Chicago whites hated blacks. The only genuine difference between a southern white and a Chicago white was in their accent."

Edwin Berry, the executive director of the Chicago Urban League, called Chicago the most residentially segregated city in the United States. It was a place, he said, where "a Negro dare not step outside the environs of his race."

Into this milieu came a black man who today is called Mr. Cub. The impact this quiet man made on a populace so firmly entrenched against blacks in general was amazing. It is Ernie Banks's greatest legacy, more important than all the home runs he hit.

After Robinson signed and played for the Dodgers, Phil Wrigley had some apprehension about signing a black player, in large part because he feared an adverse reaction from the Cubs' almost totally white North Side constituency. But though Phil Wrigley may have dragged his feet in bringing black players to the Cubs, in practice he did not act or talk like a racist.

While he was developing Catalina Island, one of the men responsible for the development made a frantic call to Wrigley.

"A Negro," he said, "a *Negro* wants to settle on Catalina? What should we do?"

Wrigley did not hesitate. "See if you can find a history book," he said coldly, "and read the Constitution of the United States."

On March 8, 1950, the Chicago Cubs signed their first black player. He was a twenty-five-year-old shortstop from the Kansas City Monarchs by the name of Gene Baker, a flashy operative from Davenport, Iowa. Baker had a strong arm, covered a lot of ground, and was durable. Scouts rated him a major league prospect. But Cubs general manager Wid Matthews, who did not have the pioneer spirit of his former boss, Branch Rickey, did not rush to bring Baker to Chicago. Baker toiled parts of four seasons playing shortstop in 420 consecutive games for the Los Angeles Angels in the Pacific Coast League while the Cubs played the boo-birds' favorite, error-prone Roy Smalley.

Under a lot of pressure to bring up a Negro player, the Cubs finally brought Baker up for a look-see in September 1953.

Jim Brosnan was a pitcher on the Cubs when Baker came up in '54.

JIM BROSNAN: "Gene Baker was bright, knew the game well, the fundamentals. He had good range, but not great range. He had a second baseman's arm and he could bunt, hit and run, and do the little things a number two or a number seven or eight hitter could do. And he was very consistent at what he did.

"No one ever expected him to be a star, but he *was* a professional. He gave that impression right from the start."

A few days before Baker came up to the Cubs, general manager Wid Matthews informed Wrigley he had hired another "Negro player" from the Kansas City Monarchs.

"Who?" Wrigley asked.

"Fellow named Ernie Banks," Matthews replied.

"Gee whiz," Wrigley answered, "we are bringing up one Negro player. Why go out and get another one?"

"Well," Matthews replied, "we had to have a roommate for the one we've got."

LEN MERULLO: "They knew we were going to bring Baker to the Cubs, and they knew he'd need a roommate. One reason they signed Banks was so Baker would have a roommate. That's true. You had to have a couple on the ball club. You couldn't isolate a guy.

"The Cubs scouts, Vedie Himsl and Ray Blades, were covering the Kansas City Monarchs as they came into White Sox park. They were told, 'Give us a rundown on who you like on that ball club.' And they wound up signing three of them. One was Ernie Banks. And I was in the office when they signed Ernie, and they played him the next day. He went right from the Kansas City Monarchs to Wrigley Field."

Without Baker, the Cubs might not have signed Banks. Without Banks, who knows how low attendance to Cubs games might have sunk in the 1950s and early 1960s.

Banks, who had taken over Baker's shortstop job on the Kansas City Monarchs, was five and a half years younger than the twenty-seven-year-old Baker. The Cubs, who had finally tired of Roy Smalley at shortstop, had to move one of them from shortstop to second base. They moved Baker because they felt that Gene had more experience and could make the change more easily than Banks.

Baker not only adjusted to a position he had never played before, but he taught Ernie Banks everything he knew about playing shortstop until Banks more than held his own. It took a little while before his teammates noticed something special about the rookie's hitting style: The skinny kid had raw power.

JIM BROSNAN: "What I remember about Ernie when he first came up was that he sometimes got down on himself if he made an error or struck out. Banks had pretty good range, but he wasn't very aggressive. He had nice hands, but his arm wasn't very strong. His swing was so smooth, almost effortless, that you didn't notice the last movement of his wrists just before he hit the ball, how quick it was. Ernie's swing was both a long swing *and* a very compact swing, all in the same swing. 'Cause it was a looping swing, and then bang. The ball would fly off his bat."

Jim Brosnan returned to the minors in 1955. When he returned to the Cubs in '56, he couldn't believe the difference in both Baker and Banks. Baker had become a mainstay. Banks had become one of the dominant home run hitters in baseball.

JIM BROSNAN: "All of a sudden, in '56 they were the key guys on the ball club. Hell, Baker to me was just as good for our club as Gene Mauch had been for the Los Angeles Angels the year before. Pitchers would pay more attention to what Mauch would say than the catcher or our manager. Baker was the same way. Gene always sounded like he knew what he was talking about. He knew the game well. Gene Baker had become a leader. He didn't get any press, and I don't think he got a lot of support from the other guys on the club, though I can't think of anyone who minded that Baker and Banks were on the team. They weren't accepted socially, but since they were both rather quiet men who didn't need to be gregarious, all they needed were each other. The year I was in L.A., Banks became a hitting star, and the Cubs fans loved him. A Cubs fan will embrace any kind of human being if that human being can hit the ball, catch the ball, throw the ball, score runs, and help win ball games, so it may have been easier for Ernie here in Chicago as a Cub rather than if he had been a White Sock.

"In his prime Ernie Banks was one of the most dangerous batters in the game."

* * *

Born on January 31, 1931, Ernie Banks was the second of twelve children. His father, Eddie, had been a semipro ballplayer around Dallas. As a child, Ernie worked with his father in the fields picking cotton, doing backbreaking work from six in the morning until sundown for a couple of dollars a day.

When he was high school age Banks starred as a softball player, barnstorming with an all-black team called the Amarillo Colts. At age nineteen, he played with the Kansas City Monarchs of the Negro Leagues for $300 a month, which at the time seemed to his family a fortune. Among his teammates were black stars Satchel Paige, Josh Gibson, and Elston Howard. After the season he barnstormed with the Jackie Robinson All Stars, a collection of black greats, as he at short and Robinson at second formed an exciting double play combination.

Banks spent two years in the U.S. Army with a black unit. After basic training he was asked by Abe Saperstein, the owner of the Harlem Globetrotters, to play in a Globetrotters basketball game. According to Banks, at the meeting Saperstein, who was white, asked him to sit down next to him.

Said Banks, "I'd never sat down next to a white man, and I wasn't sure what to do."

Banks was shipped to Germany, where he was assigned the job of playing baseball. Bill Veeck was the first major league owner to approach Banks. He wrote him a letter telling him to try out with the Indians when he returned from overseas. The Brooklyn Dodgers also contacted him.

But when Banks returned home to Dallas in March 1953, he ignored the invitations and made a beeline to his old team, the Kansas City Monarchs, where he hit .386, with 20 home runs.

On September 7, 1953, the Cubs' Wid Matthews met with Monarchs owner Tom Baird, manager Buck O'Neil, and Banks. Banks was offered a major league contract to play for the Cubs for $800 a month. The Cubs paid the Monarchs $20,000 for the rights to sign Banks and a young pitcher, Bill Dickey, who never made it in the majors.

When the twenty-two-year-old Banks first reported to the Cubs, he didn't have a glove of his own. Cubs infielder Eddie Miksis lent him one. Ray Blades, a Cubs coach, offered his help by giving him a book called *How to Play Baseball*. That was how deeply racism was ingrained into the soul of America.

Ernie Banks didn't need an instruction manual, of course. All he needed was an opportunity and an equal chance. Banks played for the Cubs from 1953 through 1971, nineteen years (and twelve different managers), during which he played in 2,528 games, breaking Cap Anson's long-standing record (an irony considering that it had been Anson who had set the policy of keeping blacks out of baseball in the 1880s), smote 512 home runs, including 12 grand slams, drove in 1,636 runs, was named Most Valuable Player in the National League in 1958 and 1959, and in 1977 was elected into the Hall of Fame.

Ernie Banks shone like a beacon during so many years of Cubs ineptitude that White Sox manager Jimmy Dykes once was prompted to say, "Without Ernie Banks, the Cubs would finish in Albuquerque."

With a glove Banks was decent, but what the fans came out to see was Ernie Banks swinging the bat. In his hands, it was a powerful weapon. He snapped the bat at the ball, like cracking a whip. The ball would leap off the bat and be propelled as

Ernie Banks

if shot into the left-field bleachers. About his wrists and forearms, Cubs manager Bob Scheffing once said, "You grip them and they feel like steel."

In his time Ernie Banks had not merely played the game of baseball, he had revolutionized it. He was the first great slugger of the Era of the Lively Bat, which he had introduced by going to a lighter, snappier bat.

As a result, he became the hardest-hitting shortstop in the history of the major leagues. Consider the history of the game. What other shortstop could hit like Banks? There was Honus Wagner, who hit .329 lifetime, but Honus hit only 101 homers. Cal Ripken Jr. has been a great hitter, but it's unlikely Ripken will hit 400 homers. There isn't another shortstop anywhere near him.

To Cubs fans, Ernie Banks stood out on the field in a Cubs uniform like a diamond standing among chunks of coal. For almost twenty years, as the supporting cast shuffled in and out around him, Ernie Banks was their star. Chances were the Cubs wouldn't win, but it was likely that Banks would do something wonderful at the plate during the ball game. He was a shortstop who hit long home runs. What fans of other teams could say that?

But as great as Banks was, he never forgot where he had come from and how nice the members of the Cubs community, the executives and players, had been to him.

Recalled Banks, "The sudden association with so many white people often left me speechless and wondering why they were so kind."

Always, he would be gracious and grateful. As a result, Ernie Banks didn't antagonize or frighten the white fans. They noticed he wasn't a militant, that he went along, didn't make waves. All of Cubdom embraced him. Here was the one black man they would be happy to have move into their neighborhoods.

Banks over the years was attacked by blacks and whites who wanted to see him be more aggressive in the field of civil rights. But Ernie Banks was a man who opted to go along and get along. It was a philosophy he could live with.

ERNIE BANKS: "Some people feel that because you are black you will never be treated fairly, and that you should voice your opinions, be militant about them. I don't feel this way. You can't convince a fool against his will. He is still going to hold to his opinions, so why should I tell him, 'Look, you are prejudiced. You don't like me because I'm black.' If a man doesn't like me because I'm black, that's fine. I'll just go elsewhere, but I'm not going to let him change my life. I don't think it's up to black athletes to get involved in political or racial issues. Our main objective should be to play whichever sports we are involved in and play well. We can't use prejudice as an excuse or as a crutch. In athletics, I feel, you are judged on what you can do. If you can play, you will play. If you can't play, you won't play.

"An athlete, like everybody else, has to live with himself. He is called upon to do many things others aren't. He talks to newspapermen. He is interviewed on radio and television. It is not his duty to comment on things outside of his game or to bum-rap somebody else in airing his personal feelings. It is important to be yourself, be a man, accept things as a man."

And Ernie Banks was good to his word. No matter how bad the Cubs might have been, he had only positive and uplifting things to say. The younger Cubs players worshiped him, even if his eternal optimism seemed a little strange.

GLENN BECKERT, CUBS SECOND BASEMAN, 1965–73: "I saw Ernie Banks when I was a knotholer in Pittsburgh. It was an American dream that one day I would wake up and be playing next to him.

"Ernie was the eternal optimist. Everything is fine, a 'great day.' You'd go back to Chicago from the nice weather in Arizona. A lot of times we'd open against St. Louis, and when you did that, Bob Gibson was going to be their pitcher. Gray, overcast, thirty-two degrees in Wrigley, big crowd, start snowing about the sixth inning, and Ernie says, 'Isn't this a great day. We'll keep nice and cool so we don't get overheated!' I mean, he'd actually say horseshit like that!

"He was not college educated, but he was so educated about different towns, different historical places. This one time we had to fly to Tacoma, our Triple A team at the time. We had finished a night game in San Francisco, and the plane was delayed. We didn't get into Tacoma until three in the morning. And we were giving up one of our off days. The players hated it.

"Guys were trying to get some sleep on the way to the hotel, and Ernie said, 'You guys, tomorrow morning at eight, Tacoma, Washington, has the biggest totem pole in the world, and for all you young guys who have never seen it, I'm taking a tour out there tomorrow morning.' Can you imagine? Who wants to see a damn totem pole at eight in the morning after two hours' sleep?

"And he had little sayings. He'd keep you loose, like in Philadelphia he'd say, 'This is where that Benjamin Franklin cracked that bell.' Crazy stuff, but he was always nice to the people. He had a way . . . he'd never say no to a writer. They'd come up to interview him, but he had this little game he'd play. He'd call over Don

Kessinger and myself. 'Hey, Kess, Beck, come here.' We were young kids. He'd say to the reporters, 'Hey, I want you to meet Don Kessinger, Glenn Beckert. They are going to be the greatest ballplayers.' And he'd walk away, and you ended up talking to the writer who didn't want to talk to you in the first place. So that's how he'd get out of it. Half the time the writer would listen to Ernie and say, 'What did he say?' And we'd be standing there like two young kids. Me and Kess and the writer would all be looking at each other, 'How are you?'

"If he did it once, he did it a hundred times."

At times Ernie's sunny disposition grated on his teammates. Here was a star who played in more losing games than anyone in the history of the game, and it never seemed to bother him. He never played in the World Series, and he didn't seem to mind. Jim Brosnan, for one, wondered what sort of person was behind the Ernie Banks mask.

JIM BROSNAN: "Ernie was the ultimate politician. He was like that right from the start. It was almost impossible to get to know Ernie Banks. He would say exactly what he was supposed to say. 'It's a beautiful day. Let's play two.' 'The friendly confines of Wrigley Field.' I don't know if he invented that or not. He wouldn't say much, but what he did say was all clichés. And they weren't even funny. If he had spoken black and had been a little funky in what he said, it would have been entertaining, and we would have talked more to him. I don't recall having more than a couple minutes of conversation with him. 'Did you have breakfast?'

"You never knew what Ernie was feeling. I was at a dinner party with him once. We were the only ballplayers there. Matter of fact, no one there cared much about ballplayers at all. I was there because I had written a book, and Banks was there because the host thought he ought to invite someone I could talk with! Anyway, someone asked Ernie the question, 'Did it bother you that you played so well, played so long, are in the Hall of Fame, and never got into the World Series?' And he gave one of his bullshit answers, 'I would have loved to have done that, but I enjoyed every minute of my career with the Cubs, and if I could have played two games every day, it would have doubled my happiness.'

"By this time I had heard bullshit about him and from him, but had read no stories about what he really was like, 'cause I couldn't believe he could be that way with everybody.

"[Journalist] Jerry Holtzman once told me he and Ernie once were together in a bar late at night after a game. Holtzman said to him, 'Ernie, cut the bullshit and tell me what you really think.' And Holtzman says he thinks he did, but he's not sure. That's the way Jerry put it.

"But there is another side to Ernie Banks, and I would like to know it. He had had a tough time with the wife, who didn't respect him as Mr. Cub. After baseball, he didn't work very hard. He went to work for the Cubs after he was through, and he wouldn't show up where he was supposed to be, didn't do much when he did, but he loved to play golf. He went from playing baseball to playing golf. But when you talked to him you couldn't get to the real him. As I got a little older, I wondered why he couldn't be more like [pitcher] Brooks Lawrence or Frank Robinson. They spoke up, had something to say, and it was worth listening to. I never heard him take an opposite viewpoint, resenting the discrimination, wishing something else was done—not that he would do much.

"But you couldn't get to him, especially if you were press, 'cause he's got a reputation and doesn't want to foul it in any way."

The fans, unlike any skeptical teammates, loved that Banks always had a kind word for the inept Cubs organization and a corny phrase or slogan for the media and fans. "Let's play two" became his watchword. Even if his teammates could never figure out whether Ernie was sincere, the fans didn't care. He liked to repeat, "In the bee-yoo-ti-ful confines of Wrigley Field." The fans loved it. Every spring Banks predicted the Cubs would win the pennant. One year his slogan was "The Cubs will come alive in sixty-five." (They finished eighth.) Then it was "The Cubs will be heavenly in sixty-seven-ly." (That year they only finished fourteen games out.) Every year the fans believed him.

The other aspect that the fans loved about Ernie Banks was that though he may have played in more losing games than any other player in the history of the game, he seemed unaffected by the losses and at the same time appeared utterly convinced that tomorrow the team would win.

By the time Ernie Banks took the field as a regular in 1954 the fans had come to recognize that losing was something that seemed to go with being a Cub. But with Ernie Banks out on the field playing for them, there was *always* hope for the future. And it is Ernie Banks's hope that has symbolized the Chicago Cubs.

Like Banks, Cubs fans don't get angry. Banks seemed almost sweet. Cubs fans take the same approach toward their team. Banks never complained. Cubs fans never complain.

Ernie Banks was a regular guy who went along in the face of adversity, just like the fans. He became their Moses, leading them to the Promised Land, and like Moses, never quite got there. But like Moses, Ernie was the moral and spiritual leader of his people. He always did and said the right thing. During games Ernie Banks even chewed Wrigley Spearmint gum.

Oh, how the fans loved him.

PAUL BUCHBINDER: "He was so fluid, so smooth, so long. It looked like he could range with his arms at a stretch all the way from third to second. And he did it with such ease. My best friend growing up, Bill Behnke, had an older brother Ray, who was very tall. His nickname was Ernie, because he had those long arms and long legs.

"Ernie Banks was symbolic of the Cubs fans in that you knew when he went out there the next day, he was optimistic. He represented a type of hope as well. And he was such a gentleman.

"I actually played against Ernie Banks in a summer softball league. When he was still a coach with the Cubs, he was working for the Ravenswood Bank as a roving ambassador. So he played on the Ravenswood Bank softball team in Wells Park. He played third base, and I hit the ball to him, and when he fielded it and made the throw, I was only five steps from the plate because I was watching him. Everybody on my team tried to hit it down to Ernie Banks, not to whack it past him, but to be able to say, 'Yeah, Ernie Banks threw me out!'

* * *

JIM SHAPIRO: "When Ernie Banks joined the Cubs, I never gave it much thought that he was black. The Cubs were one of the last teams to get black ballplayers, so by the time you had black ballplayers joining the Cubs, it was so standard in major league baseball that it wasn't any big thing to even talk about.

"The thing Cubs fans still remember about Banks was the fact that there were many, many years when there wasn't a lot for Cubs fans to talk about. You talked about the vines, the tradition, the die-hard fans, and that was about it. They had a long drought of losing seasons, with an appropriate level of negativism and hand-wringing both in the newspapers and from the fans. But Ernie Banks brought an unquenchable spirit to the team and to the fans. His famous 'Let's play two' was another way of saying, 'Hey, there is more to this than winning.' Banks was giving us a reason to go on, saying, 'What's important is being out there, having fun, enjoying what you're doing. It's not getting yourself down 'cause you didn't win.' And of course, the longer that went on, and the fact that his spirit never seemed to flag at all, he became an even greater phenomenon.

"What I remember most about Ernie was that he smiled a lot. He was a happy-faced kind of guy, when there were a lot of Cubs players and Cubs fans and Cubs managers and Cubs reporters and Cubs commentators with long faces. He was hustling when not everyone was hustling. He wasn't given a nickname like Charlie Hustle like they did for Mr. Cincinnati [Pete Rose], but anyone going to the park could see he was running out every grounder, hustling on every play. You had a much better appreciation for it when you were at the park, not watching it on television, because you could really see the effort he put forth. So he didn't have to say that much to endear himself to the fans.

"Since the Cubs had so many lean years, you had a special appreciation for *anyone* who gave you not just hope but a little spirit and a little joy, when at times no joy was there.

"There are a lot of people who have special reverence for Ernie Banks and his spirit and his optimism who have no idea what his batting averages were, or how well he played, or exactly when he played, or even what position he played. They just remember, 'Ernie Banks was the guy who kept the team together.'

"And there's a lot to be said for that."

54

The Professor

The mid-'50s, even with Ernie Banks playing shortstop and hitting long home runs, was a period of mediocrity for the Cubs. Under manager Stan Hack, who wasn't smiling as much as he once had been, the Cubs finished sixth in 1955, then fell into the cellar in 1956, as the pitching staff of young prospects, including Moe Drabowsky, Dick Drott, Glen Hobbie, Bob Anderson, Johnny Briggs, and Jim Brosnan, faltered or were taken into the armed service.

By '56, Brosnan, no longer young, was part of a team that won 60 games and lost 94. Phil Wrigley, who never did understand why, rued that the team seemed to be going backward and after the '56 season fired Wid Matthews and Stan Hack. He hired as the new general manager John Holland, who had been a general manager in the farm system. From Los Angeles, Wrigley selected Bob Scheffing, a competent manager.

The Cubs won 62 games under the new regime in '57, tying for last. In the spring of '58, the Cubs' three top pitchers were either hurt or in the service. The bespectacled Jim Brosnan, who would not find fame or success until after he left the Cubs, was named as the opening day pitcher. That spring he was the best the Cubs had to offer. All year Brosnan had to face powerful teams like the Brooklyn Dodgers, the Milwaukee Braves, and the New York Giants, with little to support him but prayer and Ernie Banks.

JIM BROSNAN: "My first full year as a Cub was 1956. The team to beat that year was the Brooklyn Dodgers. They finished thirty-something games ahead of us [thirty-three]. They were a right-handed hitting club, and I was one of the right-handed starting pitchers.

"I remember Duke Snider hitting a home run off me in the eighth inning of a ball game to beat me 3–2. And I thought I had them beat. In another game Campy [Roy Campanella] hit a slider off me, a bad pitch, into the upper deck in left-center field. Gil Hodges hit one too. I always remember the home runs.

"I remember knocking Jackie Robinson down three times. He never said a word, and the third one was right in front of his nose. He stood right on the plate, so you had to back him off. If you could back him off even six inches, you had a shot at getting a strike on the inside corner, otherwise you had no shot at all. He just stared at me—his head-of-the-gang stare. But he stared at everybody. He never said a word. And I got him out.

"I kept pitching him inside, threw change-ups away, pitching inside, and then I'd get the ball on his hands and he couldn't quite get the bat out in front of it. Sometimes my ball tailed in, and if it did, he had to be ready to bail, so he would be a little late with the bat.

"The Dodgers were the best-hitting club. They were all veterans, and as such the umpires gave them all the breaks. As a young pitcher, the umpires would never give me a pitch off the plate, a perfect-pitch slider, low and away. If you're pitching to Campanella, it was called a ball. And that's where you had to pitch him. Hodges, if you could get a slider on the corner, he couldn't touch it. He just could not hit it. I often wondered how this guy hit 30 home runs a year, if you could pitch him so easily. And then I began to understand that if he didn't swing at that ball, the umpire called it a ball. A young pitcher didn't get that for a strike. I saw that if you were established, like Robin Roberts or Warren Spahn, you could pitch six inches off the plate, and they would be strikes. Spahn didn't throw a ball over the middle fourteen inches of the plate the last couple years he played, unless it was 3–0 and the batter was taking. I learned that it takes years for a pitcher to develop a rapport with the umpires. The umpires have to know you can do certain things, realize that you're trying to do them, and then they start giving you pitches.

"In '56 the Dodgers were not only powerful but smart. The Milwaukee Braves were another right-handed hitting team, but one thing the Dodgers did that the Braves didn't do was play very smart baseball. The Dodgers were grounded in fundamentals. The Braves weren't. Shortstop Jimmy Logan would make all sorts of mistakes. [Third baseman] Ed Matthews, too, early on in his career. And they didn't have much speed. The Dodgers had that, even though they didn't steal many bases. The Braves had hardly any at all. Billy Bruton was the only one who could run. [Bruton led the '56 Braves with a mere 8 steals.] Hank Aaron could run, but he didn't do it. When the Dodgers started to get old, the Braves won the pennant in '57 and '58.

"Willie Mays of the Giants was another right-handed batter I had to face. I struck him out three times in one game in Wrigley Field. Somebody made a big issue out of it, as though it hadn't been done before. But Willie was just having a terrible day, and I had a good high fastball and struck him out three times, twice on 3–2 pitches, 'cause he wanted to hit the ball and he swung at bad pitches. He got even with me, hit a slider at the Polo Grounds to left center. I would have sworn it went over the roof. Oh God, if it hadn't been for [Pittsburgh first baseman] Dick Stuart it was the longest ball ever hit off me.

"Stuart hit a hanging curve ball off me in Pittsburgh that—this sounds apocryphal, but a guy came up to me the next day at the ballpark outside with the ball and said, 'Would you sign this? This is the ball Stuart hit off you last night.' He had found it in Schenley Park. He was sitting there listening to the game, a good five to six hundred feet away, and it came rolling toward him.

"Later I was eating dinner when an American Airlines pilot came over to talk to me. He said, 'I saw the ball that Stuart hit. It went right past the nose of the plane as we were coming in for a landing.'

"In 1958 I was designated by Bob Scheffing as the Cubs starting day pitcher. Bob Rush was hurt, Moe Drabowsky and Dick Drott were serving their army hitches, and I was the fourth pitcher of the staff. So by default I opened.

"I had had a very good spring training, and Mr. W was there at the ballpark. Art Meyerhoff, who was hired by Mr. Wrigley to do the advertising for Doublemint gum, Catalina Island, and the Biltmore Hotel, invited me over for dinner. I had worked for Art in the off-season while I was in the minors. Art was in charge of advertising for just that one gum, Doublemint. He didn't have Juicyfruit and the other gums. He worked on the Doublemint Twins.

"Art said, 'We'll ride with Gus.' I didn't know who Gus was. Gus was PK Wrigley's chauffeur. We got in the car, and PK was in the back. Meyerhoff got in the front seat, and I sat in the back with Mr. Wrigley, and he said, 'Congratulations.'

"'For what?'

"'That you're starting, that you're our opening day pitcher. I think you deserve congratulations.' Then he said, 'What do you think of my new idea about paying starting pitchers $15,000 a year?' His idea was that as long as you started for the Cubs, he would pay you $15,000 a year. If you didn't remain as a starter, then you would get paid for whatever you signed for. I had signed for $10,500. Which was what I deserved after three barely competent years.

"I said, 'I think it's an excellent idea, sir. I really do. Thank you, sir.' It was an incentive, a one-time offer, just that year.

"We took the limo back to Mr. Wrigley's mansion. He had a true mansion up on a butte overlooking the grounds of the Arizona Biltmore, and he pointed out various Frederic Remingtons he had, introduced me to his wife, who was standing at the top of the stairs.

"'This is our starting pitcher for opening day.'

"'Yes, dear.'

"She gave less of a shit about baseball than he did.

"We never had a deep pitching staff because the Cubs always had a budget and never spent enough on pitchers. Once Mr. Wrigley began paying $60,000 for their starting pitchers, that didn't leave much in the pitching budget for the other guys, who had to be under ten grand or less.

"They had budgets. Marvin Miller said that when he came into the game he found out that seventeen percent of the gross proceeds they took in went to the ball club to pay the ballplayers.

"Talk about a bad businessman. Shit, Phil Wrigley *gave* away the radio, *gave* away the television rights. He should have been charging for those things. It could have been a source of income. And he spent a lot of money on marketing ideas that had nothing to do with winning ball games.

"His slogan was Come Out and Have a Picnic, and the other teams usually did.

"The Cubs pitching staff at that time was divided into two separate groups of players, the bullpen and everybody else. Except for the year the starters got fifteen grand, all the starting pitchers wanted to be in the bullpen, because that's where all the fun was.

"In the bullpen we kicked around the Cubs' plight. We had a cynical bunch, but not to the point where we would feel sorry for ourselves. We *were* in the big leagues. If you're there a couple years, you think of yourself as being among the four hundred best players in that business, and so that's a mark of pride even if you're not winning. 'Cause no matter what we looked like, I don't recall anybody not feeling he was doing his best.

"There are two things, winning as a team, and the individual pride. Your own statistics are important because you might be traded to another club. You had to perform as an individual, and you had to be part of the team, knowing your performance adds to the team's. You say to yourself, 'I'm going to prove I'm good enough to play with any ball club.' Or, 'If I do well against this club, I'm going to feel better about my performance. Feel better about *myself.*' I never even thought about other clubs.

"A lot of malcontents ended up playing for the Cubs, or it seemed that way because they bitched a lot. That club had more than its share of gripers. They griped about meal money, travel, griped about what time the game started, everything. Some people just griped. It was part of their personality.

"Don Hoak, my God, the redass of all time. Great heart. He'd stick his nose in front of any ball hit to him. He broke it seven times. Walt Moryn still gripes about everything. He gripes about leaving the Dodgers and coming to the Cubs, where he was a star. He couldn't make the Dodgers, but he gripes because he could have been on a World Series team. Dee Fondy, oh my God. He had a hard-on for the world.

He's mellowed since he became a scout, and he's a good scout. When you're a scout you don't have to get along with anybody except the other scouts. You don't have to talk to the players.

"I always thought a manager should know what that does to a club, even if the griping doesn't appear to be insidious. And if he knows that, he should trade the gripers for somebody else of equal talent, but with a better attitude toward life.

"In the winter after the '57 season my wife and I moved into our house outside Chicago. I had gone to John Holland, the general manager who replaced Wid Matthews, and I said, 'John, am I going to be around? We have to buy a house.' He said, 'Jim, of course you are. You're going to be one of our starting pitchers next year.' And I was. Until I was traded in May.

"But thanks to Mr. Wrigley, I went into St. Louis with that $15,000 contract. I had been a starting pitcher, so I was making $15,000. And the Cardinals had to honor it. The GM at St. Louis asked me, 'Who do you know?'

"Because the Cardinals pitchers, who had far better records than mine, were making much less money."

55

The Kid from Garlic Gulch

In the mid-'50s the Cubs scouting and farm systems were inferior to those of other big-league teams. During the 1950s, the handful of Cubs scouts found few gems. Those who had potential often were ruined by their minor league experience. The Cubs didn't like to pay big bonuses like some other teams, and few of the prospects they did pay money to ever made it.

One of the problems was that although Phil Wrigley authorized his farm director and general manager to make decisions, they also knew that Wrigley liked to be consulted. Before the draft of players, which began in 1965, the first team to sign a player was the winner. Too often, after the scout checked with the farm director and the farm director checked with Mr. Wrigley, the prospect would already be signed elsewhere.

Lennie Merullo scouted for the Cubs for many years under Phil Wrigley. Merullo recalled his frustrations.

LEN MERULLO: "To me, even John Holland should have said, 'OK, we don't have to go to Mr. Wrigley. Go out and sign that guy.' Sometimes it was just a matter of another $5,000. We lost some *real* good ballplayers because of the hesitancy.

"I can remember the big pitcher with the [Milwaukee and Atlanta] Braves, Tony Cloninger. He was one. Rube Wilson, our scout in that area, was very very close to Tony. And for a matter of $5,000, there was a big hesitation. 'We got to get ahold of Mr. Wrigley. He's up in Geneva. We can't get ahold of him.' By the time they asked for permission for the measly $5,000, we lost him."

*   *   *

A brilliant scout who can judge talent is the lifeblood of an organization. The Cubs' head scout was Hardrock Johnson, a grumpy, tactless man who ended up signing one of the finest third basemen in the history of the game even though first he denigrated the boy's talent and then offered him a pittance compared with what the competition was offering.

The prospect, Ron Santo, was born to be a Cub. He was an emotional, sensitive youngster who didn't care about winning and losing or about money nearly as much as he did about loyalty and doing what was right.

In 1958, Santo was a high school senior in Seattle, Washington. He was a third baseman who had sacrificed himself for the good of the team when he volunteered to play catcher his senior year. All sixteen major league teams knew Santo was a strong prospect for stardom.

The Cubs had two things going for them with Santo. A Cubs bird dog had followed and befriended the youngster since he was a freshman in high school. The other plus was that because the Cubs were so bad, Ron figured he had a good chance to reach the majors quickly.

The other major league teams offered him signing bonuses of between $50,000 and $80,000. When the Cubs' Hardrock Johnson came to see him, he told Santo and his father that he didn't think he'd make the majors as a third baseman, and then announced he would offer him only $20,000. Then abruptly, he left.

Santo, who would have a fifteen-year Hall of Fame career, was a sensitive kid who felt a deep loyalty to the Cubs' bird dog who had remained with him his entire high school career, encouraging him, befriending him. And so this kid, who suffered from diabetes and all his life rooted for underdogs, ignored Johnson's insults and slights, spurned the extra sixty grand, and did what his heart told him: sign with the underdog Cubs.

Santo was the kind of minor leaguer who *demanded* he be noticed and, when given the chance, would perform.

He was the sort of player the Cubs fans hadn't seen in a long time: a supertalented kid with arrogance, someone who believed in himself and in his team. And when the Cubs won, after the last out Ron Santo would rejoice, sometimes jumping up and kicking his heels together in a victory dance. After joining the Cubs, Ron Santo's play, as much as any player's, defined a ten-year period when the Cubs fought and scrapped and played exciting, aggressive baseball.

RON SANTO: "I knew I was exceptional because I made the high school team as a freshman, where you weren't allowed to make the team as a freshman. I played third base, and I played it all the way through my career except my senior year in high school. Our catcher got hurt, so I went behind the plate because I had a good arm.

"My sophomore year Dave Koscher began scouting me. He was a bird dog scout with the Chicago Cubs. One day my sophomore year he walked up to me. I didn't know who he was. He was a spastic. He walked funny. He talked funny, but I could understand him. I didn't know he was a scout.

"Dave followed me all three years. We became very close friends. I later learned that he was friends with Rogers Hornsby, the great Hall of Famer. Dave later told me, 'I was in a wheelchair when I met Rogers. And he convinced me I could get out of the chair.' That's the kind of inspiration Rogers Hornsby was to Dave Koscher.

"My sophomore year Dave told me, 'Someday you will be hitting the ball out of Sicks Stadium, and you'll play in the major leagues as a third baseman.' Dave said that to me. He knew talent. He knew the game of baseball. He was a great inspiration for me.

"My senior year in high school I won the Hearst All-Star Award. Sixty high school players in the state played in a doubleheader. You played three innings, and they picked the best two players that day. They did this in each state. Then in New York they played the New York All-Stars against the United States All-Stars. You had to be pretty good to get on. I played in this game in New York.

"It took fourteen hours to fly to New York one way, because of the milk runs. At that time they were D-6s, propeller jobs, and it was up and down, up and down. That was something because I had never been out of Seattle in my life. That was an experience I got at the age of eighteen, which was unbelievable.

"If you played in the Hearst All-Star game, you came down there with all these all-stars. You worked out, and I happened to start the game as a catcher. Joe Torre was the third baseman on the New York All-Stars. He was from Brooklyn. Joe ended up in the major leagues as a catcher.

"The New York All-Stars beat the United States All-Stars 9–0. They had a pitcher about six foot six, could throw ninety-plus. We got only two hits, and I had them both. I did try to throw two runners out, and I threw the ball into center field, and then there was a ball hit to center field, and I forget who was coming in, but I had him out by five feet, I had blocked the plate, but I dropped the ball. So defensively I didn't do a good job, but they knew that I had a good arm. But my heart was not in catching. My heart was at third base. But I didn't care where, as long as I could get to pro ball.

"A lot of scouts were there. Everybody was interested in me. The New York Yankees scout wanted me to stay in New York and work out with the Yankees. I can't remember the names of the scouts, there were so many of them. I didn't want to stay. I wanted to go back home. I had been gone a week and wanted to get back home. The Yankees told me they were going to send a scout to Seattle to sit down with my dad and me.

"I had a stepfather. My real dad had left us when I was five years old, never saw him until I was nineteen, when he showed up after I was in pro ball. I had a lot of confidence in my stepdad. I loved him very much. He was a wonderful person, came into my life when I was twelve years old. He watched me play.

"Anyway, I got back home, and I started to get phone calls from different teams, so we set up meetings with all sixteen major league clubs.

"I lived in a place called Garlic Gulch—monetarily we didn't have a lot, but lovewise it was wonderful. The first scout who walked in was a Cleveland Indians scout.

"My dad and I sat down with the Cleveland scout, and this was the killer. Very quick the scout said, 'We're very interested in your son. This is our deal. We'll give him $50,000 to sign.'

"My dad and my mother together might have been making $4,000 a year. When he said, '$50,000,' my dad and I looked at each other, and it was like I couldn't swallow.

"And my dad right away said, 'And where will he be playing?' Very calmly. Because I wasn't thinking where I was playing. And my dad had also said we were going to talk to all the scouts. I hadn't made up my mind about a team, or who was my favorite team. I was more of a National League fan, because I used to watch the game of the week on Saturdays and Sundays. Saturday was the National League, Sunday was the American League. I missed a lot of Sundays. I never missed a Saturday. I was a National League fan.

"I rooted for the Brooklyn Dodgers in the National League, the Yankees in the American. There was no one ballplayer I liked. It was the Dodgers and the Yankees, and of course, Mickey Mantle and the others. Those were the teams. But it wasn't like I was crazy about them.

"Anyway, the Cleveland scout said, 'Go to Double A ball, we'll give you $500 a month. We know you're seeing other scouts. You let us know.' It was done very well, very nicely.

"'We'd really like to have you.'

"The next hour, another scout came in, then another. Every team made an offer. The Cincinnati Reds made the highest offer. I had worked at Sicks Stadium in Seattle since I was a freshman in high school. The Seattle Rainiers was the Reds' Triple A farm team. I had worked in the press box, and I became a batboy, then I worked as an usher, and then my senior year I worked as a clubhouse boy. I shined Vada Pinson's shoes before he went to the big leagues.

"My senior year, Cincinnati came in to play an exhibition game against Seattle, and that year Vada was with Seattle. Freddie Hutchinson was the manager. He was the most wonderful man for a young kid. I highly respected him because he was a guy who was tough, but tough in a different way. You knew when Fred said something he meant it, and you had respect for what he said. He wasn't an angry person. He was very calm, but you could see in his face when he was upset about something. He got nothing but respect. And he could handle himself. I never saw him fight, but you knew he would. That was the respect his players had for him. He was a tough, tough person. And a real good manager.

"I used to listen, and I saw how much they thought of this man, a wonderful man.

"The Rainiers general manager, Dewey Soriano, told me the Reds were coming to play an exhibition game, that Fred would like to have me take batting practice. Freddie saw me when I was young, saw I could swing the bat. I couldn't hit it out of the park, but my freshman year I was only five two and it was one hop to the wall.

"And then I grew. The next year I was five eight and by my senior year I was six feet.

"So we were at the ballpark, and the Cincinnati Reds had those vests, and I had put one on, walked out to the field, had my thirty-one-ounce bat, thirty-four inches. I was 165 pounds. And I thought they were going to have a batting practice pitcher. Well, they had Don Newcombe throwing batting practice. OK?

"I looked and uh, Don Newcombe? He threw ninety-plus, his ball ran in. I'm thinking, He's not going to be letting me hit.

"I really wanted to impress them, and my timing was sharp. I always felt I had a quick bat. It didn't matter how hard somebody threw. I had this gift. I knew that . . . but this was a major league pitcher.

"Ed Bailey was the catcher on the Reds club at that time, and I got into the cage, and the first pitch Newcombe threw was a fastball inside. The ball ran in, and I busted my bat. First pitch! It was the only bat I had. Now Ed Bailey throws a bat to me. He said, 'Here kid, try this one.' This bat had to be thirty-eight ounces, with a thick handle. I was embarrassed to say, 'I really can't use this,' so I just grabbed the bat. What could I do? It was thirty-eight ounces against Newcombe. I'll be honest with you. I looked like a piece of shit.

"That was pretty much it. I didn't hit the ball well. I didn't show anything, but it's funny—at that time of course I didn't know this, but Freddie Hutchinson had a lot to do with why Cincinnati was so interested in me, along with Dewey Soriano, who was the general manager, who had watched me play ball in high school. They knew I was touted, but I really thought I had ruined my chances with Cincinnati.

"To get back to where Cincinnati comes in, Dewey came over to our house with the scout. They were about the fourth club. Everyone else was fifty to sixty thousand dollars. No one was below fifty, as a signing bonus. But everyone was $500 a month. Everyone.

"So Dewey and the Reds scout came walking in my home. I said, 'Dad, I don't think they're that interested.' Dewey said, 'Your son has been a great employee at the ballpark, a wonderful kid.' And then the scout stepped in and said, 'Ron, we're very impressed. We know you can play third base.' That was important to me. 'But we also know you can catch, and there are more catchers needed in the big leagues than third basemen. So here's what we're offering. Here's $80,000 to sign, and a Double A contract. We would like you to start off in Seattle with the Triple A ball club, but we will give you a Double A contract. We don't want to rush you, but we feel, being the hometown boy, that you can probably play there. I said, 'I'd rather *not* play in my hometown. I'd rather go to Double A.' Playing at home, that's a lot of pressure. They left.

"I had heard from everybody, but not from the Cubs. I hadn't heard from Dave Koscher. He did not call me in two days. And I was surprised.

"I said, 'Dad, I don't understand this. Why aren't the Cubs calling?' Because I loved Dave. He had had so much confidence in me.

"The next morning I got a call from Dave Koscher. He had this voice, almost like he's crying all the time, and he says, 'Ronnie, I know all the scouts, all your deals. The reason I haven't stopped over, first of all, I spoke to Hardrock Johnson, the head scout, and they've already told me all they're going to offer you is $20,000, a Double A contract at $500 a month.'

"I said, 'Dave, tell him to come in anyway.'

"Dave wasn't in town. So he flew in. He and Hardrock Johnson came to the house.

"My dad knew I had a lot of love and respect for Dave Koscher. And I had feelings for the Cubs. I used to watch the Cubs on national TV, and for some reason Ernie Banks was somebody I just idolized. I thought he was an outstanding hitter and seemed like a fine person. And I always felt sorry for the Cubs. Because they weren't a winner. I was always for that underdog, especially the Cubs. For some unknown reason, I might have seen them in my life maybe seven or eight times, but I always had feelings for them, always wanted them to win.

"Hardrock walked in, did not even sit down. He said, 'Lookit, I've come all this way. Dave told you, we're going to offer you $20,000. You're going to sign as a catcher, 'cause I don't think you can play third base in the big leagues.' He had never seen me play. Right there, that bothered me, because Dave told me I'd be a third baseman. But Dave was a bird dog. And in front of Dave, Hardrock said, 'Here's the deal. Take it or leave it.' I would have told him to get out of there. But my dad handled himself really well. Even though he's Italian, my dad didn't have a temper. He said, 'Thank you very much, Mr. Johnson. That will be it.'

"But he was upset, and so was I. 'Cause Hardrock Johnson had no respect. He had driven Dave, 'cause Dave didn't drive. I said, 'Dave, why don't you stay. I'll drive you home.' So Hardrock took off.

"Dave couldn't apologize enough. 'Oh, Ron, how could he do this? How could he say these things to you?' I said, 'Dave, if I sign with the Cubs, it will be because of you. I'm going to sit with my dad tonight. We're going to go over everything, and I will call you the first thing in the morning and let you know. You're not out of the picture. I want you to know that.'

"I said to him, 'You've always believed in me, Dave. First of all, money's not important to me. Making it into the big leagues is the most important thing in my life.'

"I sat down with Dad that evening and talked about everybody, talked about money. My dad said, 'I can't believe the money that's there.' It was like I was set for life in 1958. Geez. To my dad, boy, you can imagine. He said, 'But I want you to know something. I believe very strongly that you can play in the big leagues. I believe you can get there. I know this. But it's a matter of saying, Where would you get lost? How many years would you spend in the minor leagues? There are twenty minor league teams with every team. You want to play third base. Why don't you look at it this way. Do you want to take the money, give it four years, put the money in the bank? If you take Cincinnati and don't make it, you have money in the bank. It'll give you a start.'

"Then he asked, 'Does the money matter?'

"I said, 'No, Dad, it doesn't.' He said, 'Then it's up to you. I'll tell you one thing. Dave Koscher has as much confidence in you as I do. Think about that. Sleep on it.'

"I did, woke up, no doubt in my mind, I'm going with the Cubs. I called Dave, and he was so excited. I signed as a catcher with the Cubs.

"I spent one year and two months in the minor leagues, and then I was in the big leagues.

"I went to a three-week camp with all the Cubs' top prospects in Mesa, Arizona. This was February. Rogers Hornsby was the batting instructor and one of the coaches there. He was *the* key man for hitting.

"I remember coming to Mesa, living in a barracks with thirty top prospects. There were five catchers competing with me, including Moe Thacker and Sammy Taylor, who were top receivers but not great hitters. And they had higher bonus babies than me, Dick Bertell, a couple other guys who were high bonus babies. I was not considered a high bonus baby.

"Elvin Tappe was the manager for those three weeks. We had intersquad games. Rogers Hornsby had walked up to me the second day and said to me, 'Ron, I wouldn't change anything with you.' My feet used to be even with the plate. I was a little bit up. He suggested to me no mechanics change but to move back away a little bit to get a better perspective of the curve ball. And I did that, and I felt comfortable. And I was a pull hitter. Not that I was a home run hitter. I didn't know if I was. I just hit line drives, and a few became home runs—they didn't have fences. You had to run around the bases.

"A week went by, and I was not playing because Tappe was using these bonus baby catchers. All I was doing was catching batting practice, picking up the equipment after, not getting an opportunity. Rogers liked my swing, but he wasn't managing. He was a hitting instructor. I walked up to Elvin Tappe, and I said to him, 'Mr. Tappe, am I going to get an opportunity to play?' He said, 'Who do you think you are?' He never cussed. He was very clean living. He said, 'I'll tell you when you play.' I didn't like the way he did that.

"Even though I was young, eighteen, I said, 'Hey, I don't think I'm anybody, but I've been here a week and I haven't played. How do you know how good I am until you play me?' He said, 'You'll sit there until I tell you. You'll pick that equipment up until I tell you.' And I just walked away.

"That day, which was a Saturday, a catcher got hurt, got a ball underneath the cup, and he was out. I was sitting there and Tappe said, 'Get the equipment on. You're in there.' My first time at the plate. Gone. I hit a line drive over the left-field wall. The first time. Know what I mean? I can't tell you what I felt like. I didn't expect that. I came up the next time, and I hit a line drive down the left-field line, a double.

"The next day I was starting, and from then I played every day. I hit four home runs that week. After the three weeks were up, Rogers Hornsby took twenty guys, ran us over to a bleacher bench, and I was sitting in the second row with Billy Williams. Billy and I became friends. It was funny how we hit it off. I saw the talent with his bat. This guy was exceptional. And a wonderful person. I think we had maybe three blacks on the ball club. Weren't many. All wonderful guys, and all had talent.

"So Rogers went down the first row. Rogers Hornsby was a person who didn't hold back with anything. There were maybe seven guys in the first row. He looked at the first guy and he said, 'You might as well go home. You won't get by A ball.' He went to the next guy, 'Forget A ball. You won't even get to C ball.' And he went right down the line.

"Can you imagine me sitting there with Billy, and he's saying this to the prospects? Rogers Hornsby was saying this. If Rogers Hornsby had said to me, 'You might as well go home,' do you know where my confidence would have been? I would have felt like I had *no* chance.

"To the first guy in our row he said the same thing. He allowed that a couple guys might make Triple A, but not one to the majors. Rogers said to Billy, 'You will play in the big leagues. And you could play now.'

"Rogers said, 'You,' meaning me, 'can hit in the big leagues right now.' And then he went through the rest of the guys, and it was back to the same old thing. It was everybody but Billy and me.

"I was thinking, These are prospects, young kids. What does he know?

"We were the only two that made it to the big leagues."

56

The College of Coaches

Don Elston was signed by Cubs scout Tony Lucadello in '48. He toiled in the minors through '54 and in the winter of '54–55 was traded to the Brooklyn Dodgers as a throw-in, along with Handsome Ransom Jackson, the player the Dodgers really wanted. Elston, who couldn't crack the deep Brooklyn pitching staff, came back to the Cubs in May '57 in a trade for Vito Valentinetti, Jackie Collum and Solly Drake.

Beginning in 1958, when manager Bob Scheffing made him a reliever, Elston anchored the Cubs pitching staff, leading the league's pitchers in '58 and '59 in most games played. In '59 the sinker ball specialist accounted for 10 wins and 13 saves on a team that rose to a fifth-place tie in large part on the strength of a superior bullpen.

At the end of the '59 season Bob Scheffing was fired as manager, and in '60 PK Wrigley once again brought back Charlie Grimm, who had left the team in '49. Grimm had managed the Braves in '52, their last year in Boston, and then piloted them during their first four seasons in Milwaukee.

This was to be Jolly Cholly's nineteenth season as manager, and his last, for this time he was too old (sixty-one) and his indigestion no longer could handle the rigors of the job. After starting the season 6–11, he switched places with the Cubs' television broadcaster Lou Boudreau, who finished out the season. This would be the former Cleveland Indians star's sixteenth year as manager, and his last. The broadcaster/manager switch, which was orchestrated by Phil Wrigley, was chortled at around the league. The Cubs under Wrigley were known to do some strange things. This seemed among the strangest. Jack Brickhouse, the Cubs announcer, was privy to the details of the manager swap.

JACK BRICKHOUSE: "Phil Wrigley called me in, this was in May, and he said, 'Jack, I want to make a trade, and I want you to take care of it.' I said, 'Oh, who's involved?' And Mr. Wrigley looked at me and said, 'I want to trade Boudreau for Grimm.'

"'Boudreau for Grimm?' Brickhouse repeated.

"'Yes,' Wrigley answered, 'Charlie's worrying himself sick over the team. He's out walking the streets when he should be resting. And between that and his coaching first base, if the Cubs don't kill him first, his sore feet will.'

"A manager for a broadcaster. Only with the Cubs."

Lou Boudreau, who was a fine manager, finished the season and never returned. Lou had wanted some security and asked that his contract be extended. Wrigley, who seemed often to be paying men *not* to manage, refused the request, then offered Boudreau an opportunity to be part of a bold experiment.

PK Wrigley, who didn't understand the game much better in 1961 than he did when he took over in 1933, decided to implement a radical change in the leadership structure of the team. He had had it with always having to fire and then hire managers. How to avoid that? Get rid of the post of manager. His scheme was one of the more poorly conceived ideas in the history of the game of baseball: the College of Coaches.

The man who started Phil Wrigley thinking—always a dangerous risk—was Elvin Tappe, the Cubs' longtime coach, whom Wrigley called in for a meeting at the end of the 1961 season. Wrigley wanted to know why the team didn't perform better. Tappe told him, "You're making too many changes. Every time you make a managerial change, you make a pitching coach change and all coaching staff changes. We've gotta systemize the thing. You've got too much talent to be changing all the time. That's like going into the school and changing the teacher halfway through the school year."

Wrigley asked what Tappe would recommend. Tappe suggested hiring a corps of coaches and keeping them as coaches, no matter who was the manager. Tappe also suggested that he write a book explaining the Cubs system so that the same methods could be used at every level of the organization. As Tappe outlined it, half of the coaches hired by the Cubs would manage in the majors, and the others would teach the Cubs system at each level of the minors.

If Wrigley had listened to Tappe, the Cubs might have had some continuity. But Phil Wrigley wasn't satisfied with Tappe's system. He wanted a system of his own he could implement.

Wrigley asked Tappe, "Could one of the rotating coaches be manager?"

Though he was against the idea, Tappe, the loyal soldier, said, "Well, yeah."

So rather than keep a central corps of coaches no matter who was the manager, as Tappe had suggested, Wrigley made the decisions that (a) the Cubs would be better off not having a manager at all; (b) there would be a pool of coaches from which to pick a head coach; and (c) every few weeks he would switch them around. The players, Wrigley decided, could thus benefit from the accumulated knowledge of the group. In other words, if one coach could help a team, imagine what eight coaches could do!

When Wrigley asked Lou Boudreau if he wanted to be one of the team of coaches, the skeptical and savvy Boudreau turned Wrigley down flat and asked to be allowed to return to the broadcasting booth.

Said another mocking critic of Phil Wrigley's new scheme, "The Cubs have been playing without players for years. Now, they're going to try it without a manager."

Unfortunately, it became a case of too many cooks trying to stir the broth, with each of them adding his own spices, as the coaches sought to outdo the competition and vie for Mr. Wrigley's favor. With each midseason coaching change, the roster would also change. The turmoil became so great that by the end of two years of the grand experiment, the team was mired—seemingly forever—in the muck of eighth place.

One trivia question: Who were the original eight coaches in the College of Coaches? They were Charlie Grimm, Harry Craft, Rip Collins, Bobby Adams, Vedie Himsl, El Tappe, Verlon Walker, and in the minors, Goldie Holt.

Wrigley added to this group of coaches Lou Klein, Freddie Martin, and Charlie Metro, who came from the Detroit Tigers. In 1963, Wrigley hired a new head coach, Bob Kennedy. That same year Wrigley hired Colonel Bob Whitlow as the team athletic director.

Don Elston recalled his years with the Cubs, including the fallout from PK Wrigley's oft-discussed five-year sociological experiment in team dynamics. The funny thing was, the players may have hated PK's ideas, but they still retained a fondness for him. Elston recalled his days of turmoil with the Cubs.

DON ELSTON: "I got shafted in spring training of '54. That was the year the Cubs fired Phil Cavarretta in spring training and they brought Stan Hack in. The first day Stan joined the club I was supposed to be the starting pitcher in Shreveport. Stan came to me. I had never met him. He said, 'Don, I want to start Dave Cole. I want to see what he looks like. We'll start you tomorrow or the next day.'

"Five weeks later, I hadn't pitched an inning. I never pitched again, and they sent me back to Class A ball. Dave Cole didn't stay either.

"The Cubs traded me to the Brooklyn Dodgers in December of 1955. I looked at the Dodger ball club when I got there. I knew there was no way I was going to make that ball club.

"I was a year and a month in the Dodgers organization. I pitched one inning for Brooklyn the whole time I was there. I had a fairly good spring. I got to pitch by accident. One time we were in Miami, playing the Boston Red Sox, and I hadn't thrown for several days, so I got up in the bullpen, and I don't remember who was pitching, but he hurt his arm, and Walter Alston looked down and saw me throwing and he said, 'Bring him in.' So I pitched two innings against Boston. Those was the two times in my career I faced Ted Williams.

"It was scary. I threw him a knuckeball I didn't even throw. Campanella was catching. I got Williams out both times. He popped up foul once and he almost killed Gil Hodges at first base with a line drive.

"That Dodgers ball club had a tremendous pitching staff. That was also the year [1955] they had signed Sandy Koufax, and they had to keep him on the club roster. They had the greatest starting pitchers in the world, and they had Clem Labine and Ed Roebuck and a couple others in the bullpen who are tops in the field, so there was no way a kid who had never pitched in the big leagues was going to make it.

"When I was in spring training with the Dodgers, I saw that the Dodgers worked harder than the Cubs did. Their fundamentals were worked on a lot more than the Cubs'—of course, they had a lot more coaches in spring training. Dodgertown at Vero Beach was a factory, and you had people from the minor leagues coming in to help. You always had somebody tutoring you, teaching you, where the Cubs didn't have the personnel, and what coaches they had were not of the quality the Dodgers had. Dodgertown was an experience. It was quite different from anything I had ever seen with the Cubs.

"But when the Cubs got me back from the Dodgers in May of 1957, I was very happy because I had been sitting on the bench at Brooklyn. I knew I wasn't going to pitch, and I didn't have any options left.

"My wife and I consider '57 my first year in the major leagues. I was twenty-eight years old when I came to the major leagues to stay. I had been around for a while. Not many people stayed around that long and hung in there.

"The reason the Cubs got me back from Brooklyn was Bob Scheffing. I had pitched well for him in Los Angeles, starting and relieving, and when he took over as manager of the Cubs, he brought me back. The first day here I was a starting pitcher in the major leagues.

"The Cubs needed pitching, and the Dodgers didn't. I pitched well for Scheffing that year. I started 14 ball games, and on the last day of the season Bob called me into the office and he said, 'Don, next spring we're going to put you in the bullpen and leave you there.' That's how my career started in relief.

"I liked to pitch against the Dodgers, even when they moved to the Coliseum in '58. I liked the ballparks where that backstop was real close to home plate. It made you feel like you could throw harder. What I did was throw hard. I didn't have anything else. I felt like I had a psychological advantage by having that backstop close. I loved to pitch at Ebbets Field, the Polo Grounds, Crosley Field in Cincinnati, and in Philadelphia. St. Louis I hated. With me and the sinker, they hit it on the ground anyway. My outs were usually ground balls.

"I didn't have much trouble with right-handed hitters. I had pretty good luck with Hank Aaron. I had good luck with Willie Mays. He was such a guess hitter. He got his hits, but I had real good luck with him. I didn't mind even when he did get on, because I didn't let him run. I had a good move to first base, so Willie didn't steal many bases. Nobody stole many bases off me. At that time you could cheat a little bit, whereas today what I did would be a balk. I used to bend the front knee a little bit. Don Drysdale taught it to me when I was with the Dodgers, and I brought it into the Cubs organization. I taught everybody over here. So I didn't mind anybody on base, which helped, being a relief pitcher.

"I didn't like any left-handers at all. I didn't like to face *any* left-hander. I don't care if he was hitting .110, like Warren Spahn. In nine years I don't think I ever got Stan Musial out. I hated that man. I could not get him out. I threw everything, tried everything. One night I had him 2–2 in St. Louis. I threw a pitch that just covered the outside corner of the plate, and Jocko Conlan called it ball three. Next pitch, Stan slapped one for a base hit.

"The next night I came out of the dugout, and Stan was standing in the cage, and I walked up and grabbed him by the rear end of his pants and I pulled. I said, 'Damn it, I finally had you.' He turned around and said, 'I know it.' That's all he said. If it was Musial or Williams or one of those big hitters, it was a ball. That's all there was to it. That was the only time I know I would have had Stan Musial out.

"In '58 we had a good-hitting ball club, five guys who hit 20 or more home runs. Ernie Banks was the Most Valuable Player. Bobby Thomson, Walt Moryn, Dale Long, and Lee Walls all had great years in '58. They hit a ton, and we finished [tied for] fifth. Then in '59 only one of them played full-time, and that was Banks, who hit 45 home runs, drove in 143 runs, and was the league's Most Valuable Player—again. But none of the others got to play like they did in '58. Thomson and Walls only played in 120 games. Long and Moryn played in less. We talked about it all the time. They changed the ball club around. George Altman came in, Irv Noren played a little. That year we were tied for fifth.

"I really liked Bob Scheffing. Bob was very steady, good with his people. His philosophy fit perfectly with the Cubs. At the time we were having a good time, we weren't winning anything, and nobody seemed to really give a damn. I thought Bob was the best to play for. After being either last or seventh, he led us to fifth.

"Bob was a really hard loser. I can remember in '59, I was pitching against Cincinnati. John Powers, a pinch hitter, came up. That game my hometown folks threw me a night. Powers hit a home run off me. He had reached out and pulled it. He didn't leave anything in the rack. He creamed it. Scheffing and I went to the clubhouse nose to nose.

"'Why the fuck do you throw him a fastball? I told you to throw him nothing but breaking balls.'

"'Bob, I threw it a foot outside and a foot low.'

"We just walked off the field.

"He wanted to win. I respected him.

"In '59, PK fired Scheffing. We all thought he fired Scheffing due to something Bob's wife, Mary, said to PK, about how poor the talent was on the ball club. Mary popped off about something during spring training at one of our functions, and PK didn't like that. We didn't know for sure, but we thought that very likely was why they got rid of Scheffing.

"The next year, which was 1960, Charlie Grimm started off the season as manager. I don't remember enough about his managing to say much. They didn't fire him. He traded places with Lou Boudreau, who finished out the season. At the time we were dumbfounded when PK switched Charlie and Lou. 'My God, something like this has never happened before.' The newspapers had a field day. It gave them copy for a month.

"There was a lot of conversation about it among the players. In fact, we were in favor of it. The players didn't have a lot of confidence in Charlie. Everybody loved Charlie. Charlie was a party animal, a great guy. He and Marianne were a great couple, but we thought that Boudreau could do something for us, and it turned out that it didn't happen.

"I was very happy about the switch. Everybody got along with the Good Kid. Lou was great to work for. He had the best philosophy of any manager I ever played for. He let everybody go and do what they wanted. He didn't overmanage like some did. He was extremely intelligent handling the people. If you got in a big slump with Lou, he might say, 'Hey, I don't want to see you in the hotel tonight. Don't come home. Do something different. Change something.' He was innovative in trying to think of ways to relax the ballplayer, and I liked that about him.

"But that ball club in '60 was a lousy ball club. Ed Bouchee had just come over from Philadelphia, where he had been having emotional problems, and he still had them here. In fact, he was in therapy. George Altman wasn't steady enough. He was streaky, a pretty good outfielder, a journeyman, not an everyday full-time ballplayer.

"We had a rookie, Ron Santo, playing third base. He didn't start off like a house afire. It wasn't until the next year that Billy Williams joined the team [full-time]. There was a guy, the first time you saw him, you said, 'Here's a star.' Billy had so much power. When he hit the ball, it was like a rifle shot.

"We always lacked a steady catcher who could hit a little bit. Moe Thacker couldn't hit anything. Dick Bertell ended up being the best catcher of the whole group. We had Elvin Tappe. He was a great guy, but he couldn't hit his hat size. Cal Neeman and Jim Fanning were pretty good receivers. Sammy Taylor could hit a little bit. He's the only one who hit left-handed. We had good receivers, but nobody who could hit .250.

"We had some good arms on the pitching staff. One year [1963] Dick Ellsworth won 22 games. The next year he lost 18. Nobody could understand that. One year [1964] Larry Jackson won 24 games. The next year he lost 21. Nobody could figure out what happened. And we had Bob Anderson, Don Cardwell, and Glen Hobbie.

"Glen was my roommate. He got everything out of what he had. Glen didn't have the talent some of the others had, but he made up for it with his work habits. On the mound he worked very hard. He had a good heavy fastball, good stuff. He was the guy if you needed the ball game won, you put him out there, 'cause you knew you were going to get everything he had.

"We had Taylor Phillips, who we called T-Bone. He had good stuff, a good live arm, good natural ability. He didn't train well. He had a good time. He was not there long [1958–59]. Everybody liked him, a nice guy, but he never had any particular success.

"We had good arms, but we had nobody to work with us, no one to teach us. We had PK Wrigley cronies as pitching coaches. Charlie Root, when I first came up. Freddie Fitzsimmons. I played part of one year for Dutch Leonard. We had Freddie Martin, who taught everyone the split finger. He was there a year or maybe two.

"I never felt that I was learning anything from any of the coaches. I felt most of my learning was done from the mound after I got to the major leagues. I didn't see much teaching going on.

"Spring training you did what was typical spring training workouts, but no one was particularly working with pitchers individually. The person who helped me the most was our general manager, John Holland. John would call me in once in a while and say, 'You're doing this, or that.' 'Cause John had seen me in A ball and Triple A ball.

"I remember one night walking up one of the hills in San Francisco with John, and he was telling me, 'You have to go back to keeping the ball on the outside part of the plate.' Nobody else had said anything to me. So I felt our pitching coaches weren't helping the ball club enough. Whether that's the reason we didn't have good pitchers, or the reason they didn't have good records, I don't know.

"I would have liked to have played longer for Boudreau. If they had offered him a contract sooner in the year for the next year, it would have made a big difference. He wanted a contract for the next year. I remember Lou, Harry Craft, and I were sitting in a bar in Philadelphia talking. We were having a beer, and we were talking about the situation. Lou wanted a contract for next year, and PK did not believe in two-year contracts. PK would not give anybody a contract for more than one year. I don't think he ever did as long as he had the club. He didn't believe in it. It's the same way that he didn't believe in someone coming to his house and staying overnight. He had a mansion at the Biltmore Hotel in Scottsdale where he used to throw a big party for all of us every year. At the Biltmore Stables. I remember the first year, my wife said, 'The stables?'

"We got over there, and the stables were carpeted. His home was on a mountain and it was huge, and it had one bedroom. He didn't believe in people coming to his house and staying overnight.

"Anyway, PK didn't believe in two-year contracts, and so at the end of the year Boudreau didn't come back. And the next thing PK decided—do we have to talk about this?—was his College of Coaches.

"I have answered more questions about this College of Coaches crap than anything else I have talked about with people who say, 'Oh, you played with the College of Coaches, didn't you?' I say, 'Yes, I did.' This happens, I would say, once a week.

"'What was it like?' That's *the* question I get the most.

"I don't think you will talk to one ballplayer who played under that system that's going to say anything different than it *was* very hurtful, and it was a very bad situation. In 1961, it all went to hell, no question about it.

"We came to spring training, and we had a lot of coaches on the staff, Vedie Himsl, Elvin Tappe, Lou Klein, Charlie Metro. Who am I leaving out? If you look at that list, there is not one decent major league manager in the group. Not one. And yet, you've got them taking turns every five or six weeks.

"Our concern as players was that not one of them helped one of the others. My impression was that whoever was the manager—or the head coach—was pretty much on his own. All they did was wait until it was their turn.

"I had played with, for, and knew all of these coaches except Charlie Metro. I had played with Tappe, played when Vedie was in the front office, played when Lou Klein was a coach, and I played with Harry Craft, who had been coach with Boudreau and Charlie Grimm the year before.

"When I said there was not one of them qualified, I had forgotten about Harry. He would have been the best qualified, because he did manage a little bit in the major leagues [with Kansas City, 1956–59]. But it was very confusing. You didn't know what your status was on the day they changed from one to another. That day you found out.

"Continuity definitely was not there. The everyday players were in a different situation than the pitchers. They had to use us. But the guy who played third base didn't know on the day they changed from one manager to another if he was on the next guy's good side. 'I just got through playing for Vedie. Am I going to play for Lou Klein?' And it changed. Some of them did not play for Lou Klein. He would play someone on the club who he liked better.

"It seemed to us they were trying to make an impression on someone as if to say, 'I know more than the guy who managed in front of me. I'm the guy who should have the job all the time.'

"Rather than go through the whole year with four guys and each would do six weeks—that was the system the way PK set it up, and it never made any sense—we were under the impression that the Cubs were really looking for someone who would do a good job and they would stay with him. We thought that. I know I did. It never worked. And I have absolutely no idea what the criteria was for changing. 'Will he have it three weeks, four weeks, five weeks? And who's going to make the decision that we're changing?' I have absolutely no idea who made the decision.

"The first year Vedie managed for a couple months, then Harry Craft for two weeks, then Tappe for the rest of the year, except the last ten days when Klein had it.

"I remember Tappe had it the longest, and I had played with Elvin four or five years. I had 58 appearances that year [1961], which was quite a few. In '58 I led the league in appearances, and in '59 Bill Henry and I co-led the league. That tells you a hell of a lot about our pitching staff. That's when Jack Brickhouse gave me my name, Everyday Don. In fact, he still calls me that. Or the Old Number 36.

"The second year Tappe had it a month, then Klein a couple months, and then Charlie Metro had the team the rest of the season.

"Metro was my least favorite of the group. He and I had a lot of sparks. We had some personal sparks. I didn't like Charlie for the reason that he was the last one that took over, and while the first two were running the club, he was in the outfield with his son hitting him fly balls and fungoes and ground balls. He did nothing whatever to help the other two. And as soon as he took over, the other two had no job. They were there, but they had nothing to do. That was such a biased threesome toward themselves that it affected our ball club a lot.

"Charlie was a very, very abrasive person. I remember one incident. This was '62. At that time I had six years in the major leagues, and in all that time after the ball game, no matter where you were, after infield practice the guys would go into the clubhouse, shave, and go back out.

"We were in the Polo Grounds. It was before the ball game. We worked out, infield was over, we were waiting to go back onto the field for the ball game. Quite a few of us were lined up shaving. I was one of them.

"And he came in, boy, raising holy hell. He said, 'Everybody's getting ready to go out and party tonight, and we've got a ball game to play. No more shaving in the clubhouse from now on.' Nobody could shave in the clubhouse before *or* after the ball game. Couldn't shave before the ball game, couldn't shave afterward? Why? We didn't know. But this was one of his rules. And *that* was a morale knocker-downer that lasted a long time. Just that one incident. Really hurt the morale on the ball club.

"I would like to think it didn't affect my performance on the mound. On the mound it was always, 'Give me the ball. I want it.' It hurts when you go out to dinner afterward, having a beer, and this is the main topic of conversation. Now, that has to prey on your mind. Has to.

"I'm picking on Charlie. He was there the longest. His comment to us was, 'I've never managed losers before.' That helps a guy a lot too to have somebody say you're a loser. "We knew we were losing. We didn't need to have him tell us. If he'd have stayed in his job as chief scout, he'd have done a hell of a job, but he had no business managing a ball club. He had no idea what to do with people. It was a little hairy.

"I recall that our player representative, Don Cardwell, went to Mr. Holland and complained about Metro. This was not Don's decision alone, it was a consensus of several players. 'Get rid of him. We want him out of here.' It didn't happen.

"That was the year the Mets had the worst team in history, with [40] wins. The other expansion team, the Houston Colt 45s, won 64. We won 59.

"And this was not a bad team. They had moved Ernie Banks to first, Kenny Hubbs was at second, Andre Rodgers was at short, Ron Santo at third. We had an outfield of George Altman, Lou Brock, and Billy Williams. Dick Bertell caught. This was not a bad team. [Bob] Buhl, Ellsworth, Cardwell, [Cal] Koonce, Hobbie, me. That was *not* a bad team.

"Bob Kennedy, who was one of the College of Coaches, took over in '63. That's when they stopped it. When we started '63, we were relieved this thing was over. But at the same time we had another problem, something else we didn't like, which was another of PK's ideas, and that was the Colonel.

"PK brought in the Colonel, Bob Whitlow, an army man. His job was to train us during spring training. We didn't like what he was doing at all. He came out in the morning with calisthenics, jumping jacks, and all this jazz. Even with the Dodgers we didn't do that. But he was the Colonel. 'This is what we did in the army. This is what we're going to do here.' And we resented that. There was *a lot* of resentment about the Colonel. He was a nice man, but we didn't like that concept. He was the athletic director. In college maybe. Not in the major leagues.

"We were under the impression it was PK's idea. And I'm sure it was, along with the College of Coaches. The Colonel might have been a better idea than the College of Coaches, if you come right down to it, and if we had accepted it. But after the College of Coaches, maybe we were less likely to accept any new idea.

"We didn't rebel. Everybody did the calisthenics. The Colonel led it himself in uniform. He wanted us in shape, but in baseball you keep yourself in shape every day playing.

"Personally, I hated running. So I didn't a lot of times. I would go in behind the pitcher and shag the balls, and I would run around there keeping in shape, 'cause I might pitch five or six days in a row.

"I remember when I was with the Dodgers, Don Newcombe had no regimen. The Dodgers ran your butt off, but Newcombe never ran with the pitchers. He would go out, and he would trot around the periphery of the ballpark, and he'd never stop. He might trot for an hour and a half, and that was his way of keeping himself in shape.

Lou Brock

"And I liked PK. I talked with him a few times. He wasn't a visible owner. You didn't see him. He might come to Wrigley Field every two or three years, and yet he was a unique owner. John Holland and I were pretty close, and John told me he had to call Mr. Wrigley after every ball game no matter whether it was day or night, no matter what time it was or where he was, he had to call Mr. Wrigley after the ball game. PK insisted on that.

"The players' concept of PK was that he was a good owner. He thought about the ballplayers a little bit. I can remember, it had to be 1959. I had a $9,000 contract, and John Holland called me in and said that Mr. Wrigley had come up with the notion that anybody who was a starting pitcher in the major leagues should be making a minimum of $15,000. He said, 'You're not a starting pitcher, but he thinks you should be considered in that,' and from then on I made $15,000. 'Cause I was working more than they were. There were about five of us who got paid at the rate of $15,000, so we liked him. At the time that's what we were there for. We enjoyed it and had a good time, but you still had to eat.

"My last year with the Cubs was '64. I was thirty-five. I didn't get to pitch as much as I thought I should have in '63. I did go to Bob Kennedy about that and said, 'I got to throw more. I'm not effective unless I throw more.' Of course, in '63 they had acquired Lindy McDaniel, and he was extremely effective. So he took over what my role had been, which was understandable, but I said, 'Hell, let me be the setup man. Let me pitch in the middle of the ball game. I don't care. I want to throw.' And I didn't get to do it. Kennedy wouldn't even let me pitch batting practice.

"So '64 was more of the same, and I probably made a nuisance of myself, because I did complain that year quite a bit. 'I can't help you if you don't let me throw.'

"At the trading deadline that year, in mid-June of 1964, we made what arguably could have been the worst trade in the history of the Cubs. We traded Lou Brock to the St. Louis Cardinals for pitcher Ernie Broglio. Ernie had won 18 in '63. Lou was a young kid. It had to be John Holland's doing. Or PK's. I don't know if John's the one who just made the trade or who was responsible for it.

"I can remember sitting and talking with [veteran infielder] Don Zimmer and Larry Jackson. Everybody wanted to know what the hell happened. Why? Nobody could figure it out, because we all knew that Lou was going to be a star. Nobody could figure out who did the trade, or why the trade was made. We just could not understand what had happened, and why. We didn't understand it.

"Whenever we played St. Louis and saw what Brock was doing to us, we thought about it. Lou was a left-hander, another one I didn't like to pitch to.

"Too often in trades the Cubs got these pitchers who were through. Broglio was another one. Ernie had had phenomenal years with St. Louis, but when he came over here, Ernie did nothing."

With the Cubs, Lou Brock had shown flashes of superhuman skills. In '62 as a Cubs rookie he had homered over the center-field bleachers in the Polo Grounds, a distance of 485 feet. Only Joe Adcock of the Milwaukee Braves had ever hit a ball there before him. In '63, Brock stole 24 bases on a team not known for its baserunning. After the trade in June '64, Brock, then only twenty-four, helped lead the Cardinals to the pennant. In 1974 he broke Billy Hamilton's stolen base record [set in 1889, repeated in 1891] by seven with 118. He ended his career with 938 stolen bases, now second only to Rickey Henderson.

The trade was a terrible blow to the Cubs.

RON SANTO: "The system [College of Coaches] hurt Lou. I saw Lou's talent. He came to Wrigley Field, and in those days you could take batting practice, work out without signing. You knew this guy would be great. But they wanted him to do this, do that, play left field that way, not this way. Evidently, they didn't see what I and a lot of other players saw. I think if John Holland had to do it over again . . .

"The point I make is, for some unknown reason they thought Lou wasn't going to make it. Lou was young. When you get confused . . . if they had just let him play the game. Sometimes you have to leave people alone. And they didn't do that, and John felt that if we had one more pitcher—and of course Ernie Broglio won a lot of games the year before—but I knew that was a bad move."

WRITER LONNIE WHEELER: "The great unknown of the Banks-Williams-Santo-Jenkins-Beckert-Kessinger-Hundley Cubs was what would have been if Chicago had not traded Lou Brock to the Cardinals for Ernie Broglio in 1964. It wasn't bad luck, though, that sent Brock away. The Lou Brock who wore St. Louis colors and became the greatest base stealer in the history of the game would not have been the same man in Chicago's striped suit. The Cubs were not capable of producing a player like the one who kick-started the Cardinals when they took three pennants and two World Series in the sixties."

LOU BROCK: "To this day, the Cubs do not view baseball as a battle of foot soldiers. With the Cubs, a single was just a setup shot for the home run. We didn't run the bases, didn't steal. Nobody taught base stealing coming up in the Cubs organization. The Cubs might have wanted me to switch to that style, but by the time I learned to be a slap hitter, I was in St. Louis. My last hit in Chicago was a two-run homer to win a game against the Pirates. I was convinced I was a home-run hitter. I got to St. Louis, and the manager, Johnny Keane, said, 'We think you have the ability to steal bases.' I said, 'The what?' He said, 'We want you to steal bases.' I said, 'You've got to be kidding.'

"The Cubs, all they ever needed was a good leadoff man. If I'd been here, the Cubs would have won the pennant in '68 and '69."

57

The Cornerstone

If the way the Cubs ran things created consternation for the veteran players, imagine how disruptive it must have been for the kids. Ron Santo, who began his career in 1960, was a rarity, a young star playing on the Cubs. Phil Cavarretta, who began at age eighteen a quarter of a century earlier, had been the last young star before him.

During his fifteen-year career Ron Santo hit 342 home runs. The only career-long third basemen to hit more were Graig Nettles with 390, Eddie Mathews with 512, and Mike Schmidt with 548.

Santo saw firsthand that the Cubs organization of the early 1960s had certain philosophies: It preferred veterans to kids, even if the veteran couldn't play as well; it would trade top prospects for veterans, even if the veterans were at the end of their careers; and it wanted those veterans not to criticize the front office.

Santo recalled how the Cubs traded pitching prospect Ron Perranoski, who later pitched in three World Series with the Dodgers, for over-the-hill utility infielder Don Zimmer. When they couldn't bring themselves to start him at third, the Cubs soon got rid of Zimmer, not for any lack of skill, but because Zim publicly said he felt the College of Coaches, with its lack of stability, was injurious to the Cubs' young players.

Rather than change the system, the Cubs got rid of the messenger, the baseball-savvy Zimmer.

RON SANTO: "I was at spring training in 1958, my first year, eighteen years old. The Cubs had some young pitchers on their staff like Moe Drabowsky, Dick Ellsworth, Bob Anderson, Glen Hobbie, Dick Drott. You talk about guys who for some unknown reason other than Moe didn't make it. Ask Willie Mays about Dick Drott. He used to bend Willie's knees with his curve ball. These guys were big, threw ninety.

"I went through the first cut and the second cut. I went to Double A ball in San Antonio, Texas, with Grady Hatton. We won the division. We had Billy Williams, J. C. Hartman. My roommate was Ron Perranoski.

"At San Antonio, I hit .327, led the league in doubles, hit 11 home runs. I didn't consider myself a home run hitter, but I hit the ball on a line. I drove in 90-some runs. Billy had a great year too.

"I got married at the end of that year, and I got a letter from the Cubs inviting me to spring training as a nonroster player. Alvin Dark had retired, and they needed a third baseman. The other candidates were older guys like Harry Bright, Frank Thomas, and Sammy Drake.

"In spring training I was pretty well isolated. To give you an idea, at breakfast nobody would sit with me. Nobody. The only guy who would talk to me was Ernie Banks. 'Cause I was taking somebody's job. And you had to prove yourself to those guys, and to the players from the other teams who would razz you. In those days they yelled, 'Rook.' Opposing catchers would talk to you. Smoky Burgess would always talk to you, Ed Bailey. He'd say, 'Fastball inside.' It would look inside. The ump would call it a strike. Ed would say, 'That was a strike, rookie.' That kind of shit. There was a lot of razzing then.

"But you know what, you're oblivious to that too. It's funny. I remember it, but all I cared about was making contact, doing my job. All I was trying to do was do everything right and work hard.

"At spring training I got a chance to play. I got hot, started playing a lot of exhibition games. Charlie Grimm started the season as manager. I highly respected him. He was a funny man, let you play the game. A good guy to be around.

"Two weeks left. I've been hot, playing every game. Harry would get in there, Frank would get in there, but it looked like I would get the job. Nobody said anything to me. I was a nonroster player, but I felt strongly I was going to play third. I was thinking in my mind that I would not go back to the minor leagues.

"We have remaining a weekend and a following weekend, so there's only one week left. The Dodgers were coming into town the weekend before we were going to break camp. You have to remember the Cubs' ball club was a second-division ball club. It's not like they were going to win that year.

"Before the Dodgers series, Charlie Grimm called me into the office and he said, 'Ron, you have two good days here, Saturday and Sunday against the Dodgers, and you will break camp with the Cubs. You'll be our third baseman.'

"Now, you would assume that's pressure. But it wasn't. I can only say when you're young, you say, 'Oh shit, man, great.' And I was hot. I was having a good spring.

"We faced Stan Williams and Don Drysdale. My first time up against Williams, I hit a home run off of him. I got another base hit, went 2 for 4, made some plays. I was more intimidated by Drysdale, because I used to watch Drysdale on TV.

"I remember one day the Dodgers were facing the Milwaukee Braves, and Drysdale was facing Hank Aaron, and I'm watching it, my mother's there, and I said to my mother, 'God must have given Henry Aaron this natural gift, and Don Drysdale. They both have a gift, Mom. Can you imagine my playing with them?' I could never imagine myself facing Don Drysdale, who pitched inside, threw ninety-plus, was mean. And what a competitor!

"So I was intimidated. But I hung in there. And you have to remember one thing. These are established pitchers. In spring training they don't have the best breaking ball, the best fastball. I didn't know it back then. But against Drysdale I went 2 for 4.

"The game's over, he calls me in, and Charlie says, 'You're breaking camp.' I was in the minor league facility. He told me to move into the Maricopa Inn. I moved in, got my room, moved my stuff in, called my wife, and I told her, 'I'm going to the big leagues.'

"I hadn't seen general manager John Holland, hadn't signed a major league contract, but I was going. 'Cause Charlie told me.

"That evening I got a phone call at seven o'clock. 'Ron, this is John Holland.' I said, 'Hi, John.' He said, 'Would you meet me in Charlie Grimm's room.' 'Sure, I'll be right down.' I was walking over thinking I was getting a major league contract.

"I walked in the door, and I don't know if you've ever done this, but you know when you walk in a door something is wrong? I was nineteen. Charlie opened the door, and I walked in. Charlie sat down. John was already sitting, and I'm standing.

"I looked at Charlie Grimm and at John. John said, 'Sit down, son.' I said, 'I don't want to sit down. Something's wrong.' He said, 'Would you please sit down.' I said, 'No, I don't want to. Something's wrong.'

"Holland said, 'OK, son, here's what happened. We just made a trade, Ron Perranoski, Johnny Goryl, and Lee Handley for Don Zimmer.' I knew Don with the Dodgers, a kind of utility player, second base, third base. He said, 'Both Charlie and I have talked about this, and we feel you're maybe a little bit too young, and we need a veteran guy at third base.'

"I'm upset. I'm choked. I'm emotional. I feel like I'm going to cry, but I try to hold back.

"I turned to Charlie and I said, 'You promised me. You told me that when we break camp, I'm your third baseman.' I said to John, 'I *know* I can play. I'm not too young. I've proven it this spring.' And I said, 'I am *not* going to the minor leagues. I'm going home.'

"He said, 'Wait a minute.'

"I said, 'No,' because I was going to start crying. So I walked out the door, went down to my room, and bawled like a baby.

"I waited until I could speak and relax a little bit—and I called my wife. I told her, 'I'm coming home. I'm quitting baseball. He lied to me.'

"My wife said, 'No, no, you shouldn't do that.'

"I said, 'I can't help it. I earned this job. I deserved this. I know I can play there. And I'm going home.'

"She said, 'Well, you have to do what you feel, Ron.' So I hung up the phone. There was a knock on the door. It was John Holland. He came in my room.

"'Son, I know you're upset. We *know* you can play in the big leagues. We know you're going to be there. We just made a move here we had to make, so we've got to send you to Triple A ball, but you'll be back. We're going to give you a major league contract.' He had it with him. It was for $7,000.

"I said, 'John, I don't care about the money. Pay me $500. I want to play in the big leagues.'

"He said, 'No, we want to give you major league money to play in Triple A ball. We know you're coming up to the big leagues.'

"I said, 'Then I'm going home.'

"He said, 'Now settle down, son.'

Ron Santo

"John Holland was a guy like a father image. I knew I was emotional, and I guess what he said to me made a lot of sense. I knew he meant it when he said, 'You'll be back in a hurry.' I decided I'd sign, and I went to Triple A ball.

"I did that, but my heart wasn't in it. I got off to a terrible start. My manager was Enos Slaughter, a wonderful man. I loved Enos Slaughter. He loved to fight, and I was in that kind of mood. He used to start things and tell us to go after them. Enos was very aggressive. He loved speed, 'cause he had that speed. He loved guys who went the other way. He loved aggressive guys, guys who wouldn't take any shit, and I was in one of those moods all the time. I was always getting hot. I wouldn't back down from a fight, and if someone was in trouble, I'd be right in it, and he'd be right in it. He just loved it.

"We started the end of April, got off to a terrible start. I was picking up the paper every day seeing what the Cubs were doing. They weren't doing too well. You know how you say, 'Geez, maybe they'll call me. Nah. I doubt it. I'll probably be here all year.'

"And then Enos came up to me and said, 'I understand John's coming out.' This was the second week in June. I was hitting around .260. Not many home runs. I heard he was coming. I didn't know when, so I thought I'd better start picking up the tempo, and I did. I got hot. John came in, watched the team for a week, and then I got a call at seven-thirty in the morning, June 25, 1960, to head to Pittsburgh that night, and I started the next day.

"Earlier in the year Charlie Grimm had gone from his managing job to the broadcast booth, and Lou Boudreau went from broadcasting to the manager. In spring training Lou had told me, 'You deserve to be in the big leagues. You should have broke camp.'

"When I arrived, Lou started me, hit me sixth. Lou had a lot of confidence in me, knew I could play.

"I remember the first day I came to the big leagues, June 26, I put on that uniform and I walked out there, and I was sitting on the bench and Ernie Banks was sitting next to me, and he said to me in his joyful way, 'Are you nervous?' I said, 'Oh boy, am I nervous.' He said, 'Lookit, kid. Think of Bob Friend and Vernon Law as minor league pitchers when you go to the plate.' It was a great thought, but yet I knew it was Bob Friend and Vernon Law! But that was the kind of person Ernie was. I've only seen Ernie get mad once in my thirteen years with him.

"This was early in my career. Jack Sanford hit him for the twelfth time. For the TWELFTH time. In those days you could do that. Because Ernie used to nail Sanford.

"That first year Ernie Banks was tremendous to me. He was the only one. You couldn't sit and have a real serious conversation with Ernie Banks. Not about something that was bothering you, but he could be a real inspiration to a young kid.

"We played a doubleheader against the Pirates, and I went 4 for 7, drove in five runs, beat Bob Friend and Vernon Law. As a team, they won the World Series that year. We broke a nine-game losing streak. And that's how I broke into the big leagues.

"Lou Boudreau was a fine manager. Lou fined me $50, which was a lot of money, because I didn't slide. He was third-base coach and manager. I was coming into third, and he was laying on his stomach, and I stood up and got thrown out. He called a meeting the next morning, and in front of everybody he said, 'Young fella, you're fined $50 for not sliding.' From then on, to me, I was going to slide.

"And at the end of that year, Boudreau wanted a two-year deal. He liked the ball club. He felt we had a young pitching staff. But Mr. Wrigley did not believe in two-year contracts, so Lou went back to the broadcast booth, and that's when Elvin Tappe came up with the suggestion of the coaching system, the rotating coaches and Colonel Whitlow, the athletic director of the Cubs. He was in the military, and he would run spring training, and they ran it like a military camp. The only thing we didn't have was army uniforms. You couldn't believe. We never did things like this, different . . . always did sprints, but jumping jacks, this, that, you had to be in a straight line, you had to be in formation. It was something. An army colonel was running spring training.

"Being that young, I was only concerned about staying in the big leagues. You don't think about anything else. You don't look at your ball club even. You don't realize you're not winning. You're in that stage, and then after you establish yourself, *then* the team concept comes up, and you think, Geez, we don't have enough talent. This is bad. . . .

"My second year I hit behind Banks, and he hit 29 home runs, and I spent about 29 times in the dirt, and I used to say to him, 'You're hitting the home runs. Why am I spending the time in the dirt?' He just laughed. That's the way it was then. You accepted it. You didn't think twice about it. This was all respect.

"By my third year I made the all-star team. I started to get respect. As soon as I made the team, I knew I was a player, but you don't sit back. You keep going.

"And the other factor, I felt I had a gift. Although as a diabetic, I had to go through a lot, it was easy to play the game, and I loved working to be better. I had great work habits.

"To face a pitcher, no matter who he was, and to hit, it wasn't difficult. You have your bad days, but you knew you were going to bounce back. You knew you were good, and then as you got better, then it becomes a one-on-one situation. Who's hot, who's cold. Who's confident, who's not.

"And then when you walk to the plate you look at the pitcher, and if he doesn't seem confident, then you know he's yours.

"My second year, 1961, the Cubs began their experiment, the College of Coaches. It was a ridiculous system, because there was no stability. Don Zimmer, for one, thought it was ridiculous.

"I'll never forget during the season Don went on the radio with Lou Boudreau, who had returned to the announcing booth. It was the pregame show. I was in the clubhouse before the game, and the players could hear the interviews. Zim said, 'This coaching system is killing one of their best prospects, Ron Santo.' Meaning, after two weeks, you have a new guy in there, and he's telling you what to do, where to play, and the next guy is telling you something else, and Zim felt this kind of system could ruin a lot of young players.

"I had gotten close to Zim very early. I didn't drink through high school because I was so set. No beer, or just a sip or two.

"Popeye [Zimmer] was great to me. He respected me as a young, talented player, and so my first year we were in Milwaukee playing the Braves, and after the ball game him and [reserve first baseman] Dick Gernert invited me out to Fazio's, a bar there, and I thought, Geez, that's great. Zim invited me out. I'm going with the big boys. I was sitting between Dick Gernert and Zimmer, and he said, 'What do you drink, son?' I said, 'Well, I don't drink.' He said, 'Have you ever drank?' I said, 'No, I've had a sip of beer, but I'm not a drinker.' He said, 'You're gonna be a drinker.' I said, 'Tell me, what do you mean I'm going to be a drinker?' He said, 'Let me give you a drink.' I said, 'OK.' He said, 'Give this man a gin and tonic.' It tastes sweet . . . you don't taste the booze.

"I had about four or five gin and tonics, and we're talking baseball, and I was really into it. I got up to leave, and I went right to my knees. It was unbelievable. I don't know if they were giving me doubles, but I went to my knees.

"Popeye was very aggressive. I loved the way he was. He knew the game. He was a guy who sat on that bench and evaluated, not like me. All I was concerned with was how I was doing. A lot of players won't admit this, but when you're in the big leagues, and you're a big-league ballplayer, you're not worrying what the manager is doing. You're only worried about what you're doing. Now, sure, players say, 'Why is he doing this?' But you can't be paying attention to that. You have to be paying attention to what you're doing, not what he's doing. But there are players who become good managers, mainly catchers, because they see the whole perspective of the game, plus when they are sitting, they're thinking. That's why they make good managers. That's also why a lot of good players don't make good managers, meaning they never really paid a lot of attention to the strategy of the game. Popeye always did. He used to love to talk baseball, and he was so interesting about the game. He talked not so much to me—he knew I was a pull hitter. He knew I wasn't a guy they were going to hit and run with, but he would talk about the strategy of the game, about the game itself. I learned a lot just by listening to him about what the game is all about and what you have to be aware of, what goes on, and that was Popeye.

"But when he put down the coaching staff that way, they traded him a week later. Popeye was gone."

58

Kenny Hubbs

In addition to Ron Santo, the Cubs in the early 1960s also had another potential Hall of Fame infielder in Kenny Hubbs, who had signed in 1959. After two years in the minor leagues, Hubbs became the Cubs' regular second baseman in 1962.

As a Little Leaguer, Hubbs had led his Colton, California, team to the finals of the Little League World Series. In one game he hit four home runs. He set a Little League record with 17 straight hits. After the series Kenny and his dad visited Wrigley Field, where he watched Ernie Banks hit two runs.

In high school Hubbs starred in baseball, basketball, football, and track. He was president of his class.

His senior year Hubbs became ill. His wisdom teeth had become infected. Scout Gene Handley helped treat him with ice packs, then signed him to a Cubs contract.

With the Cubs in 1962, Kenny Hubbs was a twenty-year-old sensation on an old ninth-place team. He was in the starting lineup on opening day. On June 12, he made an error. He didn't make another one until 78 games later. First he broke the 56-game National League second-base record set by Red Schoendienst, and then he broke the 73-game major league record set by Bobby Doerr. Doerr also held the record of 414 consecutive chances without an error. Hubbs broke that too, handling 418 chances in a row before throwing away a routine grounder on September 5.

At the bat, he hit only .260, but he drove in enough runs to make him one of the better second basemen in the game. He was named Rookie of the Year.

In 1963, Hubbs helped anchor the infield as the Cubs improved to 82–80 under Bob Kennedy.

Hubbs never made it to spring training the next year. He had conquered his fear of flying by earning a pilot's license. On February 13, 1964, Ken Hubbs and a close friend he was visiting, Dennis Doyle, took off from Provo Airport in Utah to return to Colton, California.

Utah can be brutally cold in mid-February. Outside the cockpit, temperatures were around one degree below zero. There were snow flurries and only three miles' visibility. Veteran pilots didn't like flying under these conditions.

Hubbs lifted the Cessna 172 into the air. Either ice was weighing down the plane or the plane flew into a front. Hubbs lost visibility and must have become disoriented, because the plane was in the air less than a minute when it dived and then crashed onto an ice-covered section of Utah Lake. The bodies of twenty-two-year-old Hubbs and Doyle, who was twenty-three, weren't found for two days, when a helicopter spotted the wreckage.

Hubbs's death was a blow that delayed the resurgence of the Chicago Cubs for several years. His teammates remembered Kenny not only for his great skill but for his religious beliefs and his character.

DON ELSTON: "Kenny was one of the to-be all-stars, Hall of Famers. That first year and a half was all he got.

"Kenny was built a lot like Ryne Sandberg. If you would stand them side by side, their backs to you, maybe he wasn't as big as Ryne, but he was built a lot like him.

"Kenny would have been one of the all-time greats. He wouldn't have hit like Sandberg, but with that glove, there was nobody I've ever seen who was any better. He made the turn well and he was so smooth. He was very very good at it, and hell, he was only twenty-two.

"I roomed with Kenny one trip in St. Louis. He was a different breed of cat than the rest of us. He had the Book of Mormon on the table. I read part of it that night. He was explaining some of the religion to me.

"The accident came before spring training started. I was in Arizona. The Cubs flew us out to Colton. Glen Hobbie, Ernie, Ron Santo, myself. I was one of the pall-bearers at Kenny's funeral.

"I've never seen faith like that family had. That was unbelievable. At that funeral it was as though Kenny was still there. That's the kind of faith they had.

"They moved the services from a church to a high school to get more people in, and they were still lined up all the way around the school, packed in there. It had to be the longest funeral there has ever been in California, I don't care who it was."

* * *

RON SANTO: "Kenny Hubbs was my roommate. He was about six foot three, very talented, moved like a gazelle, a great basketball player, stuffed the ball, a great athlete. He was a Mormon, deeply religious, never swore, never drank, played hard, played the game. He was talented. You knew this guy was going to be great.

"He would always go out with us. He wouldn't drink, but he'd have as much fun as we did.

"The Cubs always had a chartered DC-6. His rookie year, '62, he would always sit next to me on the plane. He was scared to fly. He always wanted me to save a seat for him.

"In '63 we were roommates in spring training. I happened to come in early every evening, because we were working hard and I was tired. He was coming in about ten o'clock every night. I started kidding him. 'What do you have going out there?' He said, 'I got a surprise for you.' I said, 'What is it?'

"'I can't tell you until spring training is over.'

"Spring training ended, and we got on a plane heading to Chicago. He was sitting next to me, and he seemed much more relaxed. He said, 'I have to show you something.' He pulled out his wallet and showed me his pilot's license. He had taken flying lessons after every game and got so many hours so he could fly his own plane.

"He told me, 'When I get up there, Ron, and I fly, it's like being next to God.' Kenny wasn't overreligious, but it was a wonderful thing he said. 'It's like I'm next to God.' That helped him get over the fear of flying.

Ken Hubbs

"He was in love with this girl in Los Angeles. He was in Colton, and he was going to marry her in February. I was going to be his best man. Then he broke it off, I think mainly because his family didn't think she was a devout Mormon. That was hard for him. That's when he ended up buying a plane. After he separated from her, he had to keep himself occupied, and he bought a Cessna. ·

"I flew in his plane at the end of the 1963 season on my way home to Seattle, Washington. He took me up. I was a nervous wreck. He didn't do instrument flying. It was a beautiful day. He could phone right to his house, where he stayed with his parents. His dad was in a wheelchair. He had twin brothers. He was his dad's legs.

"He flew me around, and we came down, had dinner, and went to the airport, where I headed to Seattle. He told me, 'I'm going to Salt Lake City to pick up my best buddy.' His friend Dennis had just gotten married. 'I'm going to fly him to Colton, and we're going to spend a couple days and fly back.' I guess he had done it before.

"I was home. I was in my mother's car the next day, and it came over the radio. 'Kenny Hubbs is missing.' I was on the road, so I had to wait until I got home, and when I called his dad, they had already found him.

"His dad told me what had happened: When he went to the airport, it was a nice day. He flew to Salt Lake City to pick up his buddy. He took off bringing him back to Colton, and his best buddy's wife got to the tower about fifteen minutes after they took off to tell him they forgot something. So the guy at the tower got on the radio to try to get ahold of him and couldn't reach him, but all of a sudden Kenny was radioing back, 'I've run into a front. I need a flight pattern. I'm in a front. I don't know where I am.'

"He wasn't instrument trained. If you run into a front, there's no visibility, and you don't know where the horizon is. You could think you're flying straight, and you could be flying straight down. Anyway, it ended up the last person to see him was a passenger on a train. The plane went straight down into a thick layer of ice on a lake, and they were both killed.

"The funeral was unbelievable. They shut the whole town down, the town of Colton, California, and it was unbelievable. It was hard to believe. He was twenty-two years old. Only twenty-two years old."

59

Leo

The College of Coaches had been an abject failure. The Cubs needed leadership, and they needed it desperately, so much so that Phil Wrigley did something he hadn't done since he took over the Cubs in the 1930s: He hired a strong-willed, autocratic baseball genius, a proven winner capable of leading the team to a pennant. The man's name was Leo Durocher, one of the most famous (and infamous) managers in the history of the game. To get him, Phil Wrigley had to sit back and let Leo make the decisions on trades and other roster moves. But by 1966, Phil Wrigley was embarrassed, and if he had to step back and let Leo take over, so be it.

Leo, unlike most every other manager Wrigley had ever hired, was *not* a nice guy. Leo had been the one who had declared in effect that "nice guys finish last." Leo had once been accused of stealing Babe Ruth's watch when they were teammates on the Yankees in the 1920s. He was one of the leaders of the raucous St. Louis Cardinals' Gas House Gang. As manager of the Brooklyn Dodgers in the 1940s, his teams were known for their guile and ruthlessness. While a Dodger, Leo made headlines when he carried on a love affair with actress Laraine Day when she was still married to someone else. He was suspended as manager for the entire 1947 season for consorting with gamblers. As both a player and a manager, Leo's morals were questioned, but never his will to win.

Durocher, who managed in the big leagues for twenty-four years, knew how to shape winning teams. His teams won three pennants, in 1941 with the Dodgers, and in 1951 and 1954 with the New York Giants. His '54 team had beaten the favored Cleveland Indians in the World Series in four straight.

Before coming to Chicago, Leo's last stint as manager, an eight-year run with the New York Giants, had ended in 1955. During that period he had won twice, finished second once, third twice, fourth once, and fifth twice. He then moved on to coach the Los Angeles Dodgers under manager Walter Alston. After causing dissension there, he was fired.

When Phil Wrigley hired him, Leo Durocher was sixty years old, an age too old for many men to manage. But Leo successfully ran the Cubs for six full seasons, and most of a seventh. After a first-year maiden voyage during which the Cubs finished tenth and last, the team under Leo never finished lower than third during the rest of his stay.

His Cubs never won a pennant, but they came damn close, and for almost seven years Cubs fans had the pleasure of being able to root for one of the most exciting teams in Chicago Cubs history.

Leo Durocher was elected into the Hall of Fame in 1994, almost three years after his death on October 7, 1991.

By the time Leo wore out his welcome with the Cubs in mid-1972, a substantial number of the Cubs players were relieved to see him go. But during those first few years, Leo made players' careers by teaching them how to win ball games and how to be pros.

One of Leo's favorites on the Cubs was an infielder named Glenn Beckert. Beckert, from the Pittsburgh area, was a Pirates fan, but at the time he left Allegheny College, the Pirates had Bill Mazeroski and Dick Groat playing in their infield. In 1962, Beckert fell in love with Fenway Park and signed with the Boston Red Sox for a $6,000 signing bonus.

Beckert played one season in the low minors and was promoted to Boston's Triple A team in Seattle. The way the draft rules worked back then, if a player wasn't on the forty-man roster, another team could draft him if it promoted him a level. The Cubs took Beckert and placed him on their forty-man roster.

Beckert played for Wenatchee, Washington, in the Northwest League and then at Salt Lake City in Triple A.

In February 1964 Kenny Hubbs was killed in a plane crash. One year later Glenn Beckert found himself with the Cubs in spring training. By the end of 1966, playing for Leo Durocher, he would be known among the players as Leo's Boy. Beckert became the starting second baseman for the Cubs, a spot he would hold for nine productive seasons.

GLENN BECKERT: "A lot of times in life a bad break for one individual becomes a big break for another. My break came when Ken Hubbs, the Cubs' outstanding second baseman, tragically got killed.

"I knew Kenny from spring training in '63. He was a super-nice gentleman, a tremendous athlete who never got a chance in life to see what he could do. Back then when you were a rookie, to a lot of players you were a piece of shit. We had to carry the veterans' bags when we came off a road trip in spring training. You had to wait until they took their hits in the cage. Nothing like today's game, where these guys sign for a million dollars and are treated like royalty. I don't want to get into that. I remember Kenny Hubbs just being a great individual. He said, 'Glenn, feel comfortable if you need anything, or if I can help you in any way.' And that winter he got killed in a plane accident.

"To that point I had always been a shortstop, but I didn't have the tools to play shortstop in the major leagues. The arm was missing. And then when Kenny Hubbs tragically got killed, the Cubs brought me to their Winter League and moved me to second base.

"In '64, Joey Amalfitano played at second base for the Cubs, and I played at Salt Lake City. The Cubs had a whole group of guys playing second, Amalfitano, Ron Campbell, Jimmy Stewart, and then after the Instructional League during the winter,

Leo Durocher

I started for the Cubs during spring training in '65—somebody must have liked me—and there I was.

"Nineteen sixty-five was a transition year. They were phasing out that College of Coaches, which was a bad experiment. You just can't have eight chiefs. Bob Kennedy was the manager that year, and in 1966, Leo Durocher came in. That was the big changing point in the Cubs thinking from the brass on down. Leo came in and took charge. He said, 'No more of this bullshit. I'm the manager. Mr. Wrigley's the owner. John Holland's the GM.'

"When Leo came I was scared of him. When you're a kid you read about him. My dad told me about him. And for some reason, he was great to me. In '65 I won Rookie of the Year in Chicago. There must have been a hell of a shortage of rookies. I only hit .239.

"After the season Leo and I went to a banquet together. I was a nervous country kid from western Pennsylvania. I looked up, and there was Willie Mays, Frank Robinson, and Mickey Mantle. I didn't know what to say, but I did know a little baseball history. I stood up and said, 'It's very unaccustomed that a .239 hitter gets to sit at the dais with such important people, and as I look around I see Mr. Durocher here, so I'm not alone.'

"And it brought down the house. Leo went crazy. He loved it. Maybe the way I played reminded him a lot of him, but he got the most out of my ability. I played hard-nosed. I knocked a lot of people down at second base. Everybody teases me today that I was Leo's pet.

"After I hit .239 that first year, Leo helped teach me to hit and run. I learned to keep the strikeouts down, put the ball in play, and hit behind the runner. Leo would talk to me about it.

"Leo wasn't scared to work with the GM, John Holland, to go out and gamble. We traded Larry Jackson and Bob Buhl, well-established pitchers, for unknown guys—Ferguson Jenkins and Adolfo Phillips. Leo and Holland went out and got Randy Hundley and Bill Hands. And some of the young kids were coming up from the minors: Kenny Holtzman. They already had Billy, Ernie and Ron. But it was Leo's leadership that put the team together.

"Don Kessinger and I became the double play combination. We were opposites in personalities. Kess was inward, quiet. He was very religious, highly religious, never swore. Never had a beer. I was flat-ass, bust-out, tell them what I think about them, and go for it. But Kess and I hit it off, playing together, communicating. We had a couple spats. I don't recall over what. We were fortunate to play together nine years. It is a rare thing.

"That first year under Leo, we finished tenth, but we started playing Leo's brand of baseball. He wanted to get that losing attitude out of there, that .500 attitude. And he made us believe in ourselves.

"He ran the team like we were men. He said, 'You're all mature guys. I'm not going to lay down any rules. I'll lay the rules at the ballpark. You're mature enough to learn what you should do on the outside.' He put the responsibility on the players for their conduct.

"Every now and then he'd run a room check, but it was a very loose room check, if you know what I mean. Spring training was great once the team got together. He said, 'OK, men.' He never called us boys—it was, 'Men, here's what we have to do individually to get in shape.' Back then, the money wasn't there and you had to get a job during the winter, so you used spring training to get in shape. And Leo gained your respect by doing this. Not some guy who said, 'I want you here, you'll wear this type of tie, you'll shave and wear your hair this way.' You can't do that and gain a man's respect. This isn't high school or the army. He taught us to be responsible. But he was tough on that field, man. You better play your ass off and give 120 percent on that field or you're history. Back up the truck. That's the way it was. Baseball's a business, and the business is winning. The more you win, the more money the owner makes.

"Leo knew the game of baseball. And he wasn't scared to gamble. He hated the press and the umpires. He took no BS from anybody. I'm sure he had his dislikes for some players, but under Leo I just kept getting better and better. I was maturing as a baseball player. I was learning things and picking up things, listening to the veterans from our team and other teams.

"On July 2, 1968, the Cubs went into first place. We changed the thinking about the Chicago Cubs. True, we never did end up winning, but if you go around and ask fans about the teams that they remember, our team would be one of them.

"If we faulted Leo for one thing, it was that he played the same guys every day. He never asked if you were hurt. There was no such thing as being hurt. He just put the same lineup out there. The first day of spring training he put the lineup card on the wall. He said, 'Kessinger leads off, Beckert bats second, Williams third, Santo fourth, Jim Hickman fifth, Joe Pepitone, et cetera.' And he'd list the extra men and tell them, 'This is the slot you're aiming for.' This was the first day of spring training. And it was the same with the pitching.

"Leo never asked us. He posted his lineup, and every day would be the same lineup, unless someone got banged up. He'd ask the trainer, and then he'd cross the name off and put another guy in. His lineup was always filled in with the same names. He didn't go around like today, 'Do you think he feels OK?' 'Is his wife OK?' None of that shit. That lineup was there, and you knew it when you went to the ballpark. That was it. Leo didn't care if you had a fever or what. Your name was on that card.

"A lot of times he pushed you across the line where, 'Well, I really shouldn't play,' and you'd play. You would say to yourself, 'God, if the man thinks I can play, I'll play.' And you'd be surprised. You'd have some good days when you were sicker than hell."

Another of the young players to benefit from the coming of Leo Durocher was twenty-three-year-old catcher Randy Hundley.

Hundley, who hails from Martinsville, Virginia, was seventeen years old in 1960 when he signed with the San Francisco Giants for $100,000. When Hundley started out, he discovered the Giants were stocked with catchers, including Tom Haller, John Orsino, Dick Dietz, and Bob Barton. The competition was brutal.

Hundley played two games with the Giants in '64 when Tom Haller got hurt, and then six games in '65. At the end of the season, the outspoken youngster told the Giants brass, "Play me, trade me, or release me. It looks like I'm not going to go anywhere in this organization."

Chub Feeney was the Giants general manager, and he obliged Hundley in the off-season. He traded him to the Cubs with pitcher Bill Hands for Lindy McDaniel, Don Landrum, and Jim Rittwage.

When Hundley showed up for spring training in '66, the Cubs had a new manager, Leo Durocher. Randy Hundley was about to receive the biggest break of his career.

RANDY HUNDLEY: "I was intimidated even before I got to spring training knowing I was going to be playing for Leo Durocher. It made me nervous, scared me. I knew what his reputation was as a manager, how tough he was. I knew baseball enough to know his reputation, and he turned out to be that tough, if not tougher.

"That first spring training, within a few days of his being there, Leo called a clubhouse meeting, and the first thing he did, he kept Charlie Grimm from coming into the clubhouse and being around the players. He reamed him out. And then he got all over Ernie Banks. The point was that he was showing everybody who was the boss. *He* was going to be the boss, and it was going to be his way, period, 'and don't fool with me because I'm serious about it, and this is the way it's going to be.' And that toughened the ball club up, and from there it began to go from a country club to 'Hey, we're going to play with a Leo Durocher–type attitude on this club or else we'll see you later.'

"What's interesting about it, it was one of those deals where I was at the right place at the right time, because at that time Leo went through a lot of catchers, but he stuck with me. Anybody else who came in to catch, essentially nobody could do anything right, and for a long time I didn't do anything right for him too, but maybe he felt I was the best pick of the litter.

"If the pitcher made a bad pitch, it was the 'dumb, no-good, SOB of a catcher' that called the pitch, and maybe that was his way of getting to the pitcher, but he absolutely wore my fanny out.

"I knew I was doing the best I could, that it wasn't all my fault. Maybe that was Leo's way of managing, and that was his prerogative. Guys would try to console me with 'Just stay tough and don't let it get you down.' It got to the point where the players felt sorry for me having to put up with the bull from him all the time that first year. They couldn't believe how he would chew me out all the time.

"After my first year in the big leagues, I thought, If this is major league baseball, I don't want it, and I don't need it.

"That first season we finished tenth. It was a combination of inexperience mixed in with veteran players, some of whom were at the tail end of their careers, others who really were kind of finishing up mediocre careers, with all due respect. Leo just started releasing a lot of guys, 'backing up the truck,' as he called it, and started molding the team that he wanted.

"That second year, 1967, we were a contender. Leo released some guys who didn't play the game the way he wanted it to be played. And some guys started to believe in him too. Pitching was always the major problem in Chicago. I don't care how far you go back, it's always been pitching. We started to get some pitching, made the trade for Fergie Jenkins, and Fergie became a starter. Bill Hands and Ken Holtzman came, though we always had a tough time out of the bullpen.

"But Leo made us believe that we could win, and it was fun. That second year, he turned me loose. Basically he said, 'You're my manager on the field,' and he depended on me to do that for him. That year he treated me a lot differently. He didn't blame me so much when guys made bad pitches, and he didn't rag on me so much.

"Leo and I had a love-hate relationship. You loved him one minute, you hated him the next, you loved him the next. He did a lot for me. He gave me the opportunity to play, and I can't say anything but good about the guy because in the long run I loved the guy. He was tough, but thinking back, he was good to play for. Being with him, I loved him. I wish he was still with us."

Under Leo Durocher, the men on the bench tended to rot from disuse. One of the Cubs bench players was Gene Oliver, once a productive catcher for St. Louis and Milwaukee. In 1965 he hit 21 home runs for the Braves.

Early in his career Oliver was traded for all-star pitcher Lew Burdette. Later he was traded even-up for Bob Uecker. With the Cubs, Oliver was relegated to pinch-hitting once a week and giving Randy Hundley an occasional rest. But he was one of those guys every great team must have, a comic and storyteller whose job it was to keep everyone loose. And with Leo Durocher at the helm, Oliver's role was an important one.

GENE OLIVER: "My best years with the Milwaukee Braves were when I played regularly under Bobby Bragan, but I was cast into a utility role because of an arm injury playing football in high school. I had been a catcher all my life. I had a shotgun arm. I had to go back to the outfield to strengthen and redevelop my throwing strength, and because it didn't come back real fast, they said, 'Let's play him at first base,' because I could hit. So here you are. You're caught in the syndrome of utilityism, and it's labeled. And there is nothing harder in playing the game than being an extra man.

"If you were an extra man who produced, Leo loved you, but if you were unproductive, he could bury you too. Leo could do it verbally. I have to be candid—he could embarrass his extra men.

"Leo liked veterans, didn't have patience with rookies, couldn't stand mediocrity. Leo is such an intimidating person, and he can belittle you so easily and make you feel so inferior, you learn to play in fear when you play for Leo Durocher. He was that intimidating. You knew he'd rip you behind your back. He'd rip you to your face. Leo couldn't tolerate mediocrity, and he couldn't stand mental mistakes.

"Leo was a bench manager who didn't rely much on his coaches. He made any decision made on that playing field. He'd even rip his coaches if they made mistakes.

"One time Pete Reiser was coaching third, and he sent somebody home from second base, and whoever it was was thrown out at the plate by twenty feet, and Leo stood up in front of everybody—and in Wrigley Field the third-base coach is almost in your dugout—and he yells out to Reiser, 'That is the *dumbest* fucking decision I have *ever* seen in all my years of baseball.' With that Reiser said, 'Thank you,' and walked right into the clubhouse and never worked another game for Leo. That's when Joe Amalfitano became the third-base coach. Unbelievable! Un-be-lie-vable!

"Johnny Callison wasn't afraid of Leo until he got there [in 1970]. John got caught up in this fear. He was out in right field this day. He had been rain delayed. Leo patrolled his outfielders with a towel, waving it to the right if he wanted you to move right, straight back for you to go back, left for left, and if he waved it toward himself, he wanted you in. Well, the rain delay had caused a lot of water to sit on top of the dugout, and Yosh Kawano, our equipment manager, happened to be down there, and the water was dripping where Leo sat, and no matter where Leo moved, the water was still dripping off the front of the roof of the dugout, and it just irritated Leo that this water was dripping, so here was Callison out in right field, the game had started, and Leo asked Yosh for the towel to wipe the rain away from the dugout so it would stop dripping. Leo stood up, and he waved the towel at the water dripping on him, sweeping it to his right, and Callison saw this, and he moved immediately to his left. After he settled there for one pitch, Leo now took the towel to wipe the water away and moved it to the left, which was Callison's right, and so Callison moved the other way.

"This went on for three or four times, back and forth, up and down, and it was just unreal. The players saw what was going on, and we were laughing, but nobody could tell Johnny out there because he didn't hear the conversation on the bench.

"One player said, 'Look at this. He's got Callison going nuts out there. He's wiping the water with that towel, and Callison thinks he's telling him to move.'

"Callison, who was afraid he was doing something wrong, finally called time and ran all the way across the field, and he said to Leo, 'Where in the fuck do you want me to play?'

"Leo said, 'What the hell are you doing in here? You're not in here for glasses, are you?' Because it was still overcast.

"John said, 'You got me going left. You got me going right.'

"And it just broke Leo up. He said, 'I was just wiping off the roof here.' It was unreal.

"And John did not have a good year for him at all, but I think it was because he was so intimidated and afraid of him.

"Another story. It's funny the things you remember about a manager that stick with you so long. I respected Leo as a manager. I respected his knowledge of the game, but what I didn't like was his habit of—I don't want to say he was two-faced, but he second-guessed a lot. It's the easiest thing in baseball.

"We were playing in Wrigley Field one day, and God love Lee Thomas. Lee and I played together with the Braves, and everybody knew that Lee was a first-ball, fast-ball hitter, a dead pull hitter with power. [Outfielder] Ted Savage and I were sitting next to each other down a little bit from Leo on the bench. I had come in from the bullpen for some reason or other, and we were trailing with Kess [Don Kessinger] coming up.

"Pete Reiser, one of our coaches, was sitting there, and Leo said to Pete, 'Get me Lee Thomas.' So Pete said, 'Lee, get a bat.' Lee got his helmet, his bat, his resin, the pine tar, and he went out to the on-deck circle. Here was Lee within earshot, and Leo said to Reiser, 'Why am I going to hit that fucker? He's going to go up there, and he's going to jerk the first two pitches foul, and the third one he's going to foul straight up on the goddamned infield.' Now Lee could hear this. As fate would have it, he stood in there, foul, strike one; foul, strike two; and Leo says, 'Heeeeeere it comes,' and just as Leo predicted, Lee hit it right up the shoot.

"So Mad Dog—we called Lee Mad Dog—came in, and he was hot because he had heard Leo second-guessing him, and our bats were right in front of Leo. Mad

Dog intended to take his bat and swing at the bats in the bat rack and break all the handles off the bats, and he swung and missed, and Leo said, 'Jesus Christ, you can't even hit anything that's sitting still.'

"Mad Dog was so mad he threw his skully [batting helmet].

"Leo turned to Ted Savage and said, 'Savage, grab a bat. You're hitting for the pitcher.' Savage said, 'There ain't no goddamned way *I'm* going up there. I know you're going to second-guess me too, Leo.' And he just wouldn't move.

"The whole bench was laughing like hell until Leo finally got Savage to bat.

"I had come over to the Cubs from Boston, after playing nine years in the National League. This one day Leo decided Randy would take a day off. Leo said to me, 'You're catching Fergie today.' Well, I knew Fergie's ability after hitting against him, and so Fergie and I talked about the hitters. We were playing Pittsburgh. I told him how I pitched and caught against these guys. He said, 'That's the book here too.'

"So the game started, and Matty Alou was the first hitter, and we wanted to crowd him. So I put an inside fastball sign down. Fergie acknowledged it, and he threw a fastball. Alou fouled off the ball, fought it off, and hit a cripple double over Santo's head down the left-field line.

"One pitch, and there's a runner on second base. So I looked out to Fergie and said, 'Let's go to the pump signs.' He said, 'OK.' The second hitter was Bill Mazeroski. Maz, we knew, was going to advance the runner, move him to third. He could hit the ball to the right side as good as anybody. And the ball he hit the best was the ball inside. I thought, Let's go with a hard slider, which still gave Maz the opportunity to go to right field. I put down three fingers, Fergie hung it, and he hit a shot right up the middle. Alou scored. Maz was on first base. This was after just two pitches.

"The next hitter was Roberto Clemente. And there is no safe place to pitch Clemente. He was a bad-ball hitter, a first-ball hitter. You just had to mix it up. So there again, I said, 'Let's start him out with a breaking ball,' and Fergie agreed. He hung it, and Clemente hit it out of the ballpark. And before Clemente hit home plate, Leo was already out of the dugout, and he was hollering, 'Ollie, come here.'

"We're going to go to the mound. We got to the rubber, and he looked to me—I had the reputation of being a comedian, of trying to take the pressure off the team. I was the kind of guy who kept them all loose. Leo turned to me and said, 'Has Fergie got anything?' And I said, 'How the fuck do I know? I haven't even caught one.'

"Leo said, 'This might be your last goddamned game if you don't start calling a better game.'

"I said, 'How 'bout Fergie throwing some better pitches?'

"That was my first confrontation with Leo, and I went right into the shithouse—it's either a castle or a shithouse when you're an extra man.

"I was sleeping on the bench one day, 'cause I knew Randy was going to catch, when we had another pinch-hit situation. I was kind of dozing, and we were trailing, and all of a sudden Leo yelled, 'Ollie, get a bat.' Christ almighty, I ran and got my helmet, and I started to walk up the steps to go to the on-deck circle, and I thought I was going to hit for Hundley. Leo said, 'Where are you going?' I said, 'Don't you want me to hit for Hundley?' He said, 'No. Hundley cracked his bat. He needs another one.'

"That's how cruel he was. Oh man."

60

Fergie

The last time the Cubs had won the pennant, 1945, they were tied for fifth in home runs but first in earned run average. That was perhaps the most important aspect of the game of baseball that Phil Wrigley never understood. You can have the greatest hitters in the world, but if you don't have quality arms to get the other side out, you don't win very many ball games.

To have a winning team, you need a great pitcher to lead the staff, with solid starters backing him up. In 1945 the Cubs had Hank Borowy, along with Hank Wyse, Paul Derringer, and Claude Passeau. In the next twenty years not a single pitching star emerged from the Cubs organization. Not one. Warren Hacker, Paul Minner, Bob Rush, Moe Drabowsky, Dick Drott, Glen Hobbie, Don Cardwell, Cal Koonce, Larry Jackson, and Bob Buhl were the best of a mediocre group of pitchers. Over this twenty-year period, they were the top starters. Good teams have four good starting pitchers at one time. More than any other weakness, the lack of solid starting pitching plagued the Cubs during the late '40s, the '50s, and the early '60s.

Because of the friendly confines of Wrigley Field, over the years the Cubs emphasized hitting. The more runs, the more fans. Outfielder Hank Sauer had an MVP year in 1952. The team still finished fifth. Even with Ernie Banks, the greatest slugger in the team's history, the Cubs couldn't reach the first division throughout the 1950s. Even the addition of all-stars Billy Williams and Ron Santo did not allow the Cubs to escape the second division.

The team's resurgence did not occur until Leo Durocher, a manager who could identify talent and nurture it, and John Holland rebuilt the Cubs pitching staff. In the team's very first move after Leo's arrival, on April 21, 1966, Holland and Durocher made one of the finest trades in Cubs history when they swapped two veteran pitchers, Larry Jackson and Bob Buhl, to the Phils for an exciting young outfielder named Adolfo Phillips, a first baseman named John Herrnstein, and a little-known relief pitcher named Ferguson Jenkins.

Holland made the trade only after Durocher and he were unable to acquire slugger Orlando Cepeda from the San Francisco Giants to replace Ernie Banks at first base. Leo had wanted to get rid of Banks, in part because he had been part of the Cubs tradition, and also because he felt Ernie's bad knees were affecting his play. The Cubs offered starter Dick Ellsworth to San Francisco for Cepeda. Giants owner Horace Stoneham said no, then traded Cepeda to St. Louis for pitcher Ray Sadecki two weeks later.

Unable to get Cepeda, the Cubs then turned to Philadelphia for John Herrnstein. When the Phils expanded the deal, they included Jenkins.

Herrnstein played nine games for the Cubs and was traded to Atlanta. Banks stayed on first, and Fergie became a star en route to a nineteen-year Hall of Fame career.

One Philly pitcher, Robin Roberts, a Hall of Famer nearing the end of his career, had seen Jenkins's talent. Roberts begged the Phils management to switch Jenkins from relief to a starting role and let him pitch every fifth day.

Fortunately for the Cubs, the masterminds of the Pathetic Phillies didn't listen to their pitching star. The Phils brass was convinced that Jenkins didn't throw hard enough and that he wasn't durable, a laughable assessment considering that in his career he would pitch 267 complete games. The Phils also felt that in Darold Knowles they had plenty of relief pitching. So they traded the expendable Jenkins. It is trades such as these—the sort of trades the Cubs had been making for twenty years—that change baseball history.

In 1966, Ferguson Jenkins won six games. Two were complete games. The following year Leo Durocher handed him the ball every fourth day, left him in to the end of ball games, and showed confidence in him. Under Leo's watchful eye and acid tongue, Fergie produced 20 victories, a feat he accomplished in six of the seven years between 1967 and 1973. Under Durocher, Jenkins flourished. He was a rock. When his career ended in 1983, he had accumulated 284 victories, striking out 3,192 batters, ninth-best in major league annals. He was elected to baseball's Hall of Fame in 1991.

Under Leo, Fergie Jenkins became the finest pitcher to wear a Cubs uniform since Mordecai "Three-Finger" Brown, who retired from the game in 1916.

Ferguson Jenkins, one of the gentlemen in the game, recalled his rise to greatness under Leo Durocher.

FERGUSON JENKINS: "My dad's family is from the Bahamas, and they settled in a little town, Windsor, Ontario, in Canada. My mother's family escaped from the South on the Underground Railroad, in the late 1800s, probably from Kentucky. They came up through Ohio, Michigan, and settled in Ontario.

"I never had any problems with prejudice in Canada. My family lived wherever it wanted. I went to an all-boys school called Chatham Vocational, where I played all the varsity sports, hockey, basketball, soccer, track and field, and football.

"Tony Lucadello, who was the Phils' area scout for Michigan, Ohio, Iowa, got word from Gene DeJure, who was the scout in Chatham, that there was a young fellow who was a pretty good athlete. I played all the high school sports but baseball, no high school baseball at all. There wasn't any, none whatsoever. We had different organized baseball through service clubs like JCs, Kiwanis, Kinsman, Rotary.

"Mr. Lucadello took a look at me when I was sixteen years old. I was a first baseman–outfielder at the time. My hero as a kid was Larry Doby, so I wanted to be a first baseman but never got an opportunity to play first base.

"The Phils said pitching would be a quicker way for me to sign professionally because I had a pretty good arm and I was the tallest kid on the team. They felt that pitching might be a position I could learn and adapt to and maybe I could sign professionally. So I started pitching at sixteen.

"Mr. Lucadello gave Gene DeJure, the area scout, an instruction book on how to pitch. Gene might have it at home. He got me to go out on the mound, and he caught me. He taught me the windup and the delivery, and I adapted, being a fairly good athlete. I watched television a lot, and my favorite teams were Cleveland and Detroit. Six teams were interested in me, Boston, the Chicago White Sox, the Pittsburgh Pirates, the Tigers, Cleveland, and Philadelphia.

"I signed with the Phils because they had worked with me for three years. I leaned toward them because they had taught me and 'cause I became real good friends with Tony Lucadello. He came down every weekend to watch me play. Gene was there too. He was a local high school teacher, and I had thought because they showed me so much, if I was going to sign, I would learn more in the Philly organization.

"I signed a bonus clause for $6,500, and I signed for $400 a month, and I went to Class D ball to pitch for the Miami Marlins. It was the Florida State League.

"And when I arrived in Florida, I found that being a black athlete, I couldn't eat and sleep at the same hotels with the white ballplayers. When I arrived, Freddie Mason, who was twenty-four, one of the older players in the organization, gave me an insight into what was happening. Alex Johnson was on that team. Reno Garcia from Cuba, a young fellow named Swanson from the Virgin Islands.

"We had to be billeted in private homes or a black motel. We would go to Tampa or St. Pete, and we couldn't stay in the white hotels. The team dropped us off, then picked us up before the game. But it was OK. Hey, I was down there to play baseball, and I was comfortable with that.

"In '63 I signed a major league contract, went to the big-league camp with the Phils, and during spring training Clearwater was another eye-opener. At the time Grant Jackson had made the major league roster, along with Alex Johnson and Pat Corrales, and we got embarrassed one afternoon.

"We went to eat at a restaurant and one of the young waitresses who was my age, nineteen, said, 'We can't serve you.' I knew what I heard, and I said, 'Why?' And then the owner came over and said, 'You black ballplayers can't eat here.' So we left. Pat Corrales, who is a Mexican American from California, stayed, but ten minutes later he walked out of the restaurant too because they asked him to leave. That was something in the South predominantly. We had forgotten where we were, and so we left and went to a Trailways bus station and ate.

"We were able to eat in the Clearwater hotel. Other than that, we came up against it. But like I said, I wasn't down there to be a crusader. I was down there to be an athlete.

"After we left spring training, I went to Little Rock, Arkansas. It was the first time I had seen where all the black fans could only sit down the right-field line. They had white washrooms, black washrooms. White fountains, black fountains. That was an eye-opener. And it was the first time they had black ballplayers—ever. The Phils never told us that. They just said, 'We have a Triple A affiliation at Little Rock, and this is where you young men are going to play.' I was nineteen years old. Dick Allen was on the team, Marcelino Lopez, Frank Barnes, Rich Karros, and myself. They just pummeled us with all kinds of signs. 'We don't want you here.'

"I got catcalls every so often. 'We don't want you here, nigger.' 'Why don't you go play someplace else?' I only stayed there a month and a half, and then I got sent to Chattanooga, and I was there with Frank Lucchesi, and I pitched there the rest of the season, and then when our season was over, I got pushed back up to Little Rock again.

"In '63 we didn't do much, but in '64 when I went back to Little Rock the next year, we won the championship. We had the best ball club in the minor leagues. The year at Chattanooga I was 12–5, and then at Little Rock I had won 8 games in relief before the Phillies brought me up.

"I got to play for Gene Mauch in Philadelphia in '65. I was a relief pitcher. I was 2–1 and pitched pretty good. I was only up about thirty-five days at the end of the season. It was a cup of coffee. And then the Phils traded me. Right after spring training was over in 1966, I went to the Cubs.

"At the time I heard a lot of conflicting stories. They thought I couldn't pitch in the big leagues. They said I didn't have a major league fastball. They said the only thing I had was good control. And they said that they had enough relief pitching and that they were going to go with some veteran players, so that this was going to be an opportunity for me.

"The Cubs were rebuilding under Durocher when I got over there. They said this might be a good opportunity for me to enhance my career, which ended up being true.

"I was twenty-two years old when I joined Durocher in '66. He didn't say much. He was a man who had a short fuse. 'Hey, this is what I want you to do.' And you tried to do it. When he put me in the bullpen and wanted me to pitch—I had a rubber arm, so boom, I pitched. I pitched in a lot of ball games [sixty] that year, '66, and at the end of the year he said, 'When you come to spring training, we're going to put you in the starting rotation, but you have to win the job.'

"So I came to Scottsdale, and they put me in the starting rotation. I won a job, and I was the opening day pitcher in '67. And that was the first year I won 20 games.

"We had an infield of Banks, Beckert, Kess, Santo. And Hundley was the catcher, and yet in '66 it was a terrible team. A *terrible* ball club.

"We were all fairly young, except Ernie was a veteran, along with Ronnie and Billy. We had Kenny Holtzman, Bill Hands, and our infield. We had Adolfo Phillips in the outfield, and George Altman, Ted Savage. And all of a sudden, in '67 we started winning ball games, and in '68 we became an even better ball club. We started playing well together, and then in '69 we started off the season winning, and we stayed in first place almost the whole year, until the Mets caught us.

"I can remember a game in early July in 1967. The Cubs had been a second-division team since 1947. That's twenty years of losing baseball. I beat the Reds to put the Cubs in first place. It was the first time the Cubs had been in first place in so long [since 1945]. Wrigley Field was packed, and after the game was over, the fans all stayed there to see what would happen on the East Coast, whether the Cardinals would lose, to see if our pennant would fly on the top of that pole in Wrigley Field. See, we had pennant flags to show the standings of the teams, and I can recall that when they announced we went into first place—the Mets had beaten St. Louis—there was a cheer for, man, ten minutes.

"A lot of us were in the dressing room, and when this cheer came up, we knew with all the excitement that something was happening. We said to each other, 'Hey, the fans are still in the ballpark.' And we were happy to hear we were in first place for the first time.

"We all rushed outside to see what the heck was going on. We stood in the doorway and we watched them put that Cubs flag up at the top of the pole. We were jubilant.

"The fans knew we had a ball club that was on the rise. We had good, young players, and Durocher was the type of guy who was leading us, and the fact he wasn't going to stand for a second-division ball club, because he had always managed teams that eventually got into first place, and this is what happened to us.

"I respected Leo. And because of that fact, I got a chance to play a lot. I went out and did my job, and he gave me the ball every fourth day, and I told him I could pitch and wasn't hurt, and I went out there and won some ball games.

"Randy Hundley was my catcher. Randy didn't get an opportunity to catch in the Giants organization, and he had come over to the Cubs, and it was a new life for him too. Kenny Holtzman and Bill Hands and I were young, and because Randy caught most of the games, we learned what he wanted us to throw, which pitch in what situation. We learned to play the game together.

"Leo called a lot of games for Kenny Holtzman and Bill Hands, but not that much for me. A lot of times you saw Randy looking into the dugout, but not very often when I pitched. Randy and I had full control of the ball game.

"We had a very close-knit ball club, and we're still friends. I see these guys all the time because of the Randy Hundley Fantasy Camps. We go to Upper Deck old-timers games. We've kept in contact over the years.

"We were close. A lot of times we used to all go out. I can recall the first time I ever got caught after curfew. There were a bunch of us out in St. Louis. We were staying at the Park Plaza Hotel. Leo was not one to check on everybody, but he gave the night elevator operator a ball. 'Hey, would you sign this ball for my kid?' And it was like signing your death warrant, because if you signed it you got caught out after curfew.

Fergie Jenkins

"We had a meeting the next day, and Leo said, 'We had eleven guys out after curfew. I know the eleven guys. The eleven guys know who you are. I don't need to say anything more. I want a check for a hundred bucks on my desk after the ball game.' And you asked yourself, How does he know? And everyone whispered, 'Did you sign that ball?' And boom, we knew we were caught. So you wrote your own death warrant.

"Every team goes through that kind of thing where the manager is smarter than the ballplayers.

"Guys would kid with each other, make jokes. On another road trip, I was the opening day pitcher in St. Louis. I got to the ballpark, and in my equipment bag all I had were left shoes. No right shoes. I called Yosh, the clubhouse man. 'Yosh, I threw two pairs of shoes in my bag, and I know I didn't just put two left shoes in there. How am I going to pitch? I don't have any spikes.'

"Twenty minutes before the game the guys said, 'Hey, Ferg, I think somebody at the door has a shoe for you.' I went outside there, and the security guard had my shoe. I said, 'Where did you get that?'

"I was always worried they would steal my away uniform pants. You don't like to pitch in somebody else's pants. It's like a phobia. You don't want to pitch in somebody else's uniform, or with somebody else's glove.

"I remember one other joke guys did with me. I fall asleep pretty easy. We flew into a city. The team bus picked us up at the airport, took us to the hotel. I fell asleep in the bus, but no one woke me. The players got off the bus. The guys let me sleep, and the bus driver took me to the bus terminal, where they dropped off the bus.

"At the terminal, the driver said, 'Mr. Jenkins, time for you to get off the bus.' I said, 'Where's everyone else?' He said, 'We dropped them off a half hour ago.'

"The team captain was Ronnie. The practical joker was Glenn Beckert. We called him Bruno. He'd always step on your feet. He was always bumming cigarettes. Little things. He'd say, 'Hold on to these cigarettes for me.' Because you were allowed to smoke then. I never smoked. I'd put the guy's cigarettes in my pocket, and some guy would ask for the cigarettes, and the guy who owned the cigarettes would put one of those exploding things in a cigarette, the guy bumming would light a cigarette between innings, and boom, it would blow up in his face. And since I had been holding them, the victim would blame me. I would say, 'Hey, man, I didn't do it. I don't even smoke.'

"Players like to stick matches in the keyhole of your hotel room. You can't get your key in, and you have to run back downstairs to the lobby and get another key. The coaches were always down there. 'What's wrong?' 'I can't get in my room.' 'Why? Somebody in your room with your roommate? He got a chick in your room?' 'Nah nah. I just can't get in the room.' So you had to alibi why you couldn't get in the room. You paid the price by having to go back to the lobby. Always some practical jokes.

"A lot of times when I pitched, I got the number one pitcher on the opposing team. Against the Dodgers, I didn't usually pitch against Koufax. I got Drysdale most of the time, or Don Sutton. Kenny Holtzman got Koufax a lot, and Bill Hands a few times. I got Juan Marichal a lot, Tom Seaver, Steve Carlton, and sometimes Gaylord Perry.

"I pitched a lot of times against Bob Gibson. I had some good games against him. We had some battles. If Gibson knocked our players back, hey, I was going to knock their players down. Brock, Flood, Shannon, Boyer, whoever they were. Bill White, hey, I was going right after them, because if I didn't get my teammates' respect, the guys wouldn't play for me.

"There are a lot of times I'd pitch against Seaver, and he might knock Santo back, or Ernie. If he didn't come up in that inning, I'd knock their leadoff hitter back. If Seaver came up, I'd let him know.

"One of the players I was privileged to play with was Ernie Banks. When he came up I loved to see him twiddle his thumbs, move those thumbs around.

"Ernie was a pretty good guy, didn't have a bad word to say about anybody, always wanted to play two. I roomed with him for a year and a half. I was rooming with a legend.

"Ernie was the type of guy, if he had someone call him for lunch or dinner, he'd say, 'Ferg, tell him I went out.' After a while I was kind of his secretary. He was a pretty even-keeled guy. He played hard, wanted to play. He loved the game, and the records stand for themselves.

"Ernie occasionally would say the odd thing, a little bullshit here, a little bullshit there, but other than that I can tell you he always wanted to play. He'd put that uniform on, and he'd play hard for you.

"He was one of the first shortstops who really did it all. He was the Most Valuable Player two years in a row in a losing organization, and then once we started to win, he then went to first base. He had pretty good hands, a good glove, and always a dangerous bat, even when he was in his forties. He was dangerous at the plate.

"I can remember Ernie and Leo were constantly feuding. Leo was always giving Ernie Banks's job away. Every spring he'd give it to John Boccabella or George Altman or [Willie] Smith or Lee Thomas, and Ernie would win it back again.

"Leo felt pressure in the respect that Ernie was more popular than he was. Leo had his charisma and his position but you couldn't take away the fact that Ernie *was* the Cubs organization. He had been there, done so much, and he was still there. When Leo came on the scene, two spots Leo wanted to improve was center field and first base. When he got me, he got Adolfo to play center and John Hernnstein to play first.

"John Herrnstein was a left-handed first baseman, and he hit well in Wrigley Field. Ernie won the job back again from him even. Ernie just kept playing and winning the job back. Ernie would get in there and get some hits and get back in the lineup, and you couldn't take him out. He was a hitter.

"Ernie knew that Leo didn't like him. There was no, 'Come over for tea and crumpets' with Ernie for Leo. Hey, you play hard for yourself, not for the manager. So Ernie was always going to spring training, and someone always had his job, and Ernie would always win it back.

"When we were roommates, Ernie would say to me, 'Oh, Boccabella's got my job.' Or 'Lee Thomas has got my job.' Shoot, Ernie would hit 25 home runs, and Lee Thomas would be on the bench. Boccabella got traded to Montreal. Because Leo knew Ernie's ability but didn't have the confidence in him. One year Ernie had a bad leg, and another year he had a bad hip, but he could still hit. He could flat out hit.

"Ken Holtzman didn't like Leo either. Kenny was a real competitor. Kenny and Leo played hearts against one another, and Leo was the type of guy, he didn't care who you were, he called you your ethnic background. Kike or Spook. Adolfo was a Panamanian, he called him a Cuban or Puerto Rican, and Adolfo would say, 'No, man, I'm Panamanian.' That's the way Leo was. He always called you Stupid. Guys would take it because he was Skip. Kenny disliked him. I don't know the real reason. Ask Kenny.

"Odd little things. Leo tried to play with your mind. I wasn't sensitive. But there were some odd things he would say. He'd ask me, 'Are you sure you're a Canadian?' I'd say, 'Of course I'm a Canadian.' I wouldn't get riled. I knew how to take him."

61

Flying High in '69

GENE OLIVER: "During my career I played with the game's greatest stars. I came up to the Cardinals with Stan Musial, Ken Boyer, Larry Jackson, Red Schoendienst. After three years there I went to Milwaukee and roomed with Eddie Mathews, played with Hank Aaron, Joe Torre, and Warren Spahn.

"Hank Aaron is the nicest man you'll ever meet in your life. I called two hundred of his home runs, and I watched at least three hundred of them. In his demeanor Hank Aaron went to the ballpark every day much like Stan Musial. He knew he had a job to do. He was all business on the field. He never jacked around on the field.

"I can remember catching behind Hank one night when I was with the Cardinals. I was the type of catcher to get your mind off what you're doing. I said, 'Hi, Hank, how are you doing?' He wouldn't talk. And I kept pushing him, and he finally stepped out and said, 'When you're done chirpin', let's get on with the game. I'm not in here to talk, I'm in here to hit.' And I thought, 'Well, goddamn.' But I knew right then that I wasn't going to get to this guy's head.

"There was no one set way to pitch Hank Aaron. The guys who got him out the most successfully pitched inside. When I joined the Braves from the Cardinals in '63, Hank came right to my locker, and he said, 'Tell me about your pitching staff. I want to know if a guy's got balls. Will he throw at me? Can he pitch inside? Can he get the breaking ball over when it's 2–0, 3–1?'

"I told him that there were only about two or three pitchers on that staff who could pitch inside, that from that staff Bob Gibson would and could. And Hank did not hit Gibson that good. If he knew a guy would not come inside on him, he owned you.

"See, Don Drysdale's theory of pitching was, 'The inside half of the plate is yours. The outside half is mine.' And that's the way Gibby pitched. Warren Spahn too. If you start leaning over that plate, they got to get you off the plate. The game today, if you throw six inches from a guy, it's a knockdown pitch. Modern-day players don't even know what a good knockdown pitch is anymore. If you go out there and you got shit in your veins, you aren't going to succeed in this game. Especially a pitcher. Because here you are as a pitcher, and they're beating your brains out. You got to say, 'Listen, you're not going to lean over the plate after me anymore. You keep that half, and I keep the other half.'

"Eddie Mathews was my roomie. We roomed together three years. I'll tell you something about Eddie Mathews that you've never heard. Eddie Mathews is shy. He's a country boy. He's very physical, strong but unpretentious. He was a beer drinker for years. Now he's graduated to other things, which I'm sad to say. Eddie had a reputation for being tough, and it would be a challenge for some guys to find out, 'Is he or is he not that tough?'

"I'll cite a story to show you how tough Eddie was. We were in West Palm Beach during spring training. Bob Sadowski, Bobby Teifenauer, myself, and Eddie were sitting at the Pelican Bar. All we wanted to do was have three or four beers after a hard day's workout. We were sitting there, and it was cool, air-conditioned, and ballplayers do have a way of becoming a little obnoxious. We can take over a bar. Because the owner wants us to. He wants us in there drinking. And so the next thing you know, the bar owner is asking you for pictures, and the pictures are on the wall, he buys you a drink occasionally, and you frequent the guy's place, and in a majority of times, people don't greenfly us. A greenfly is a guy who lays on your shoulder and wants to talk baseball. There is no privacy, and Eddie didn't have privacy because he was so recognizable.

"We were sitting there and four men who looked like longshoremen came in. They were right off the boat. They had tattoos and T-shirts, riggers.

"They couldn't get to the bar, and they were leaning over to get the beer, leaning between Eddie and whoever, and Eddie moved over. So they were standing behind us, and somebody said Eddie's name, and all of a sudden one of the bigger guys comes in between me and Eddie, spins Eddie around, and grabs him by the shoulders! And he says, 'You're the great Eddie Mathews.' And I thought, 'Aw fuck. Here we go.' And he says, 'Are you as tough as you think you are or are you a puss?' The guy is driving Eddie.

"Eddie just reached for his bottle and was going to drink when the longshoreman said, 'Hey, you chickenshit prick. Are you tough or aren't you?'

"Eddie said, 'I'll show you how tough I am,' and whoom. He took that bottle in his hand, and he hit him with his fist. The bottle splintered in his hand. Eddie just beat him to a pulp.

"We had a donnybrook! All of us four got into it with the four longshoremen.

"Finally, the bar owner called the cops. He said, 'You guys get out of here, and I'll handle the situation.' At this time it was like eight-thirty at night, getting dark. I went back to the room. Eddie said, 'I'm going to go out and get something to eat.'

"At five o'clock in the morning, Eddie still wasn't in the room. And all of a sudden I hear the key. And he comes in.

"I said, 'Roomie, where have you been?' He was pretty well smashed. He said, 'Roomie, you should have stayed with me. Goddamn, did I have a great time.'

"I said, 'Where did you go?' He said, 'You know those four guys we beat the fuck out of?' I said, 'Yeah, why?' He said, 'I went out on the boat with them.'

"I said, 'You dumb fuck, they could have put concrete shoes on you. You went out there with those four bastards?'

"He said, 'Yeah. I walked around the block a few times and went back into the bar, and son of a bitch if they didn't come back,' and they started loving Eddie, and they got into a conversation, and they invited him on the boat for dinner, and he was with them overnight sleeping on the boat.

"You wouldn't do that in your right mind. But this was the kind of guy Eddie is.

"And then there's the other Eddie Mathews: When you cross the lines he's there to play, like Santo.

"We were in Cincinnati playing a doubleheader on a Sunday. Roy McMillan was our shortstop and Frank Bolling our second baseman. I was catching that day and Joe Torre was playing first, and Eddie was at third base.

"Frank Robinson, who was another intense competitor, hit a ball to right-center field off the wall that Hank [Aaron] got a good hop on, and he threw a rocket to McMillan, who was making the throw on a sliding Robinson, and Robinson came in spikes high and cut the living shit out of McMillan. Forty-one stitches.

"We were in the dugout, and Roy was bleeding like a stuck pig. Well, it was not four innings later, and here comes Robbie to hit, and now he hits the ball just about the same place, hits the light tower inside old Crosley Field, bounces around a little bit, and it's a triple, but again Aaron hits Bolling with a perfect cutoff, and Bolling throws Eddie a strike, and here comes Robbie with another slide.

"Eddie stepped out of the way, and he slapped him in the face with it, and after Robbie was on the bag, Eddie jumped on top of him and has him by the throat, and he hit him four times with his fist dead in his face. You could hear him mashing meat. Boom. Boom. Boom. Boom. Just like rapid fire.

"Robbie said, 'Stop, stop. That's enough.' He knew it was retaliation for cutting Mac.

"At old Crosley Field there was a little runway that went through. You had to walk through the fans to get to the locker room. They took Robbie out. He had fourteen stitches under one eye, and the other one was closed.

"And in the second game Robinson hit two home runs against us. That's the way the game used to be played.

"After Milwaukee, I went to Philadelphia and I played with Richie Allen. We were like brothers. At Boston I got a taste of Carl Yastrzemski and Rico Petrocelli, and then I came to the Cubs for just one year, 1969. [He did play eight games with the Cubs in 1968, a year he started in Boston.] I am asked constantly, 'Why are you so close to the Cubs when you played the major portion of your career with the Cardinals and the Braves?'

"It's because on the Cubs it was, 'I for you, we're all in this together, win, lose, and draw.' There was a sense of camaraderie. We were brothers. We cared about each other.

"We were a *team*. And we were involved with the fans. In late April [1969], we traded for Dick Selma, and he and Hank Aguirre began their love affair with the Bleacher Bums, and during that season every game Selma got 40,000 people up and cheering by waving his hanky. They had this hanky thing going, and I'll be damned if we didn't rally every time we did it.

"There was a rejuvenation of fan appeal in Chicago that had begun the year before. The fans saw the way we played the game, and they said, 'This is it. We're going to win it.' It was just unbelievable to see a million seven in a ballpark that wouldn't draw 400,000 a year! It was the World Series every day.

"I can remember when I had played for the Braves, we would go into Wrigley Field and play in front of 500 people. And the scores would be 13–12 because we didn't have any pitching and the Cubs didn't have any pitching.

"Then all of a sudden Beck, Kess, Santo, Williams, they all started to come, and when I played with the opposition we recognized that these kids were going to be great ballplayers. And when I got to Chicago, I found out they are not only good baseball players but they are great guys. There wasn't a snitch or a stoolie. You could get off the elevator in any town we were playing in, and it didn't matter who was sitting in the lobby, it was 'Smitty, you have breakfast?' 'Kess, you want to go to a movie?' You'll never see that in a ball club again.

"Randy was very religious. He wouldn't say 'shit' if he had a mouthful. We went out after the game on the road—we didn't go back to our rooms—you have to go out and relax and eat and have a few beers. He never drank, but he was always with us. He was always involved in the things we did, even though some of it wasn't to his religious beliefs. Might be a strip joint—ballplayers are notorious for living in the neons—and he was always with us.

"Kess was the quiet one. He was the hardest one to get to know. We called Kess Milquetoast. He didn't drink, didn't smoke, doesn't cuss, much to the religious style and belief of Randy, but not nearly the intense competitor. Kess wasn't an aggressive type of person. He busted and gave his all, but he didn't show it in a flamboyant way like Santo and Randy, Beck or myself. Kess just did his job and run silent, run deep. That's all Ernie or Billy Williams ever did too.

"We were the extroverts. We would pop off to somebody else.

"By the time I left, Ron Santo and Beckert and Randy had become my greatest friends in the game. We have stayed close to each other. If I was ever in need, or they were ever in need or had a problem, they would pick up a phone, and I would be there in a minute, and vice versa. The *whole team* was that way.

"When Fergie lost his first wife, and later his second wife, a little bit of all of us died with him, and I'll tell you what, I guarantee you Fergie would say, 'I'd have never gotten through this ordeal without my '69 teammates.'

"And the memories . . . '69 was the greatest year I ever spent in baseball. It was the greatest. We finished second, and it broke our hearts, but by God, we were a hell of a good ball club."

RANDY HUNDLEY: "In '69 the Cubs led from April through August. Winning made being a major leaguer so much more satisfying. That's what the Sam Hill you play the game for. You don't play the game for the money. You play the game to win and to play in a World Series. That's every player's goal, dream, ambition when you strap that uniform on—it's to play in the World Series.

"We played for a ring. To be able to walk around and have the right that says, 'World champions.' Money? If I could have afforded it, I would have paid them to let me play. What the heck? Rather than getting paid, I'd pay them to let me play, if I could compete to be a world champion."

*   *   *

GLENN BECKERT: "It was fun, exciting. You knew you had the edge in Wrigley with the crowds there. It was a very emotional high, and you knew the odds of your winning was 90–10. And the confidence was just steamrolling. We'd say, 'St. Louis is coming. We'll take two out of three. Let's try to sweep.' And it would happen. It caught the town, because up until that point there was little interest. Usually the Cubs were out of it by July.

"We were winning, and everybody was getting along fine. The bench players would gripe. They always do. 'Why aren't I playing a little bit more?' 'Why aren't I pitching?' Not the regulars. We knew we were playing.

"Leo was on top, and he and the players were getting along. Kenny Holtzman and Leo would get on each other. Leo would play cards with Phil Regan and Kenny. Holtzman and Leo had a funny relationship. Holtzman would say anything. 'How the hell can you play that card, you old son of a bitch?'

"But once they played the national anthem, it was a different Leo. His attitude was 'Win,' and we knew it."

FERGUSON JENKINS: "We started the season in first place, and we kept on winning. It was enjoyable to go to the ballpark, because you knew that the ball club you had was going to score runs for you. That makes it easier for you, makes the game a lot more interesting, and the game becomes more fun.

"We had a good ball club. We scored four or five runs a game. We had good defense, and we played well. And we were all getting along.

"Leo was hard. He didn't let you lay back. If you had a good home stand, hey, you had to keep playing hard. If you got fifteen hits in thirty at bats, you didn't sit back and say, 'Hey, I'm hitting great.' You had to keep doing it because Leo was the type of guy who wouldn't let you sit back."

In 1969, the Cubs under manager Leo Durocher began the season 11–1 and by the end of April were 16–7. In May the team again won 16 games, as they began to distance themselves from the defending champion St. Louis Cardinals.

The Cubs had four fine starters in Fergie Jenkins (21–15, 3.21, 7 shutouts), Bill Hands (20–14, 2.49, 300 innings pitched), Ken Holtzman (17–13, 3.59), and Dick Selma (10–8, 3.62), a relief corps that included Phil Regan (12–6, 17 saves), Ted Abernathy, and Hank Aguirre, and in the field again was the infield of Banks, Beckert, Kessinger, and Santo, with Randy Hundley behind the plate, Billy Williams in left field, and Jim Hickman in right.

If the team had a weakness, it was center field. The regular was supposed to be Adolfo Phillips, the speedster acquired from the Phils along with Fergie Jenkins. But Adolfo was a worrier. He worried about how his stance was, how his outfield play was. He worried, Did I steal on the right count? And he developed an ulcer.

Adolfo needed a manager to pat him on the back. Leo Durocher was not that sort of man. Leo would say to him, "Come on, Dolfo, you got to be better. You're capable of playing better than that." And Dolfo's ulcer would flare.

In the spring of '69 in a game against the New York Mets, Adolfo Phillips got hit in the hand by a pitched ball thrown by one of the New York Mets' young pitchers. When he returned, he didn't play well, and on June 11, he was traded to the Montreal Expos for utility infielder Paul Popovich. In Phillips's place in center was a twenty-three-year-old outfielder named Don Young.

On July 8, with the Cubs in first place, Ferguson Jenkins was one inning away from his twelfth victory of the season. He was defeating the youthful New York Mets, 3–1. The Mets hadn't been rated highly by the sportswriters, but they were exhibiting some strong pitching from a group of kid pitchers. There was a hard-throwing righty named Tom Seaver, who two years in a row had won 16 games, and a hard-throwing lefty named Jerry Koosman, who as a rookie had won 19 games the year before. A rookie named Gary Gentry was the third starter, and a twenty-two-year-old fireballer named Nolan Ryan, a pitcher who had trouble with blisters, started when he could.

Other than the pitching, the Mets had an outstanding center fielder named Tommie Agee, a talented left fielder in Cleon Jones, a pretty good shortstop in Bud Harrelson, a solid catcher in Jerry Grote, and platoon players everywhere else.

The Mets had never won anything, and as this ball game was nearing its conclusion there was no reason to believe they ever would.

Ahead by two runs, the indomitable Jenkins pitched to Mets second baseman Ken Boswell, who took a half swing and lined a ball weakly into right-center field. The sun was bad in Shea Stadium at that time of day, and after center fielder Don Young got a slow break on the ball, it fell in front of him for a double.

The next batter fouled out. Mets manager Gil Hodges sent Donn Clendenon in to pinch-hit. Clendenon drove a ball toward the outfield fence in left center. Don Young raced back for it, got his glove on it, and as he hit the wall, dropped it. Boswell went to third, Clendenon to second.

Jenkins, shaken, was only able to get one more out. A double by Cleon Jones and a single by first baseman Ed Kranepool ended the game with the Mets victorious.

In the dugout afterward, a furious Leo Durocher told anyone within earshot, "It's tough to win when your center fielder can't catch a fucking fly ball. It's a disgrace."

Many managers believe that it is bad practice to humiliate a player in public. Leo wasn't one of those managers. In front of Young, Durocher shouted, "My son could have caught that ball. My three-year-old could have caught those balls."

Among the players upset by the loss was captain Ron Santo. Santo, who had befriended Young in spring training and had been an influence on the youngster, felt Young should have caught one or both of those balls. To win a pennant, the players must make the plays.

Santo, an emotional player, unleashed a stream of words that was picked up by a New York reporter. He blasted the Mets infield of Kranepool, Boswell, Al Weis, and Wayne Garrett, calling it "minor league." He even blasted Young, wondering aloud why he hadn't caught those balls. Santo was quoted as asking Young, "Why don't you get your head out of your ass?"

On any ball club, players tend to be vocal about teammates who don't make the plays. That's common. Santo's mistake was to allow himself to be overheard in the press. His words to Young—whether quoted correctly or not—were picked up in one of the New York papers and blasted in headlines. Ron Santo was vilified by many for not sticking up for a teammate.

This was the first in a series of odd, highly charged Cubs losses that would occur throughout the 1969 season. Cubs players would remember each loss the way players on other teams recall World Series victories.

FERGUSON JENKINS: "I can recall it like yesterday. Ken Boswell, the Mets second baseman, hit a swinging bunt, and it went over second. It was an afternoon game, and before the inning started Don Young had not taken his sunglasses out. The ball dropped in front of him, no problem. He said he didn't see it. OK? I got an out, and then Donn Clendenon hit a high fly ball to right center, and Young went back on it, and 'cause he couldn't see it, the ball dropped in, and that was the ball game. The score was 3–1, and I ended up losing 4–3. But I lost the ball game.

"There was a lot of rigamarole about his not coming in fast enough, this and that. See, back then the reporters could walk right in after the game was over to get stories, and then supposedly Ronnie said something, and everything got blown out of proportion where they blamed Ronnie for getting on Don Young, and that wasn't the case.

"It was Leo who was criticizing Don Young. Ronnie was always telling Donnie, 'Hey, don't ever get down. Keep your head up.' But the press blew it up and blamed it on Ronnie, which wasn't the case. I even said to myself, 'What the hell is going on here. I'm pitching a strong ball game, and balls are dropping in.' Being a pitcher, I wanted to win too. Everybody did. But the thing was, they played it up so big in the press, and Ronnie, the captain of the team, had to take the rap. Boom, that's the way it came out."

GENE OLIVER: "The Don Young controversy was ignited in a New York newspaper. The headline came out the next day in the New York paper. The writer was trying to stir up the Cubs. Keep in mind we had a hell of a lead at that time. When that New York writer overheard what Santo said, he wrote, SANTO RIPS YOUNG, DISSENSION ON BALL CLUB. That's all you needed to have a festering influence on a ball club.

"Ron was the backbone, the catalyst, for the Chicago Cubs the two years I was there. Billy Williams and Ernie were intricate parts, but Ron was the spokesman, not because Billy and Ernie were Afro-American—they knew the game and knew how to play it, but they were the silent type of guys, where Ron was more vocal. Ron took offense to everything that happened to one of us. If we got knocked down, he'd be the first one to go to the pitcher and say, 'Hey, we got to get this guy.' And Ron got knocked down and hit a lot for it. He'd say, 'We can't let them do that to our players.' And he was our captain. He would do that, where Billy and Ernie couldn't. So he was cast into the position of leader and he did a hell of a job.

"The next day Ronnie called a meeting, and he said, 'Don, you know what I said to you,' and there was no problem. It was nothing near what was said in the paper, where he supposedly said, 'Get your head out of your ass,' accused him of dogging, which was totally untrue.

"The Chicago writers supported Ron, because they came to Ronnie, and Ronnie told them what happened, and it was reported in the Chicago paper in a lighter vein, and I don't think much more was said. Don Young was sent back to the minors shortly after that. But as far as *we* were concerned, it was a nonincident."

* * *

RANDY HUNDLEY: "I remember Donn Clendenon pinch-hitting. He hit the ball into left-center field. I thought Don Young had made a great play just by getting to the ball. I thought he had caught the ball, but when he ran into the fence, the ball popped out of his glove. I didn't think too much about that one, though earlier that same inning there was a little flare hit to center field that he broke back on, and that ball should have been caught.

"If I was going to say anything about either play, that play would have been the one I was upset about. The one against the wall—I mean, what the heck, the guy didn't mean to drop the ball.

"Sure, Leo said, 'My kid is three years old, and he could have caught that ball,' but that's Leo. Maybe Don Young hadn't experienced the crap I had experienced with Leo, and maybe this was the first time he had had a tough time with Leo, but so what if Leo makes that blooming statement? Maybe that's the way Leo saw it. That's his prerogative to think that.

"The one I was upset with was the flare. I wasn't upset with the other ball.

"What was interesting to me was whenever we went on the road, they assigned the lockers based on your uniform numbers. I was 9, Santo 10, Kessinger 11, and after that game I was right there, and I didn't hear Santo saying anything.

"I came in the clubhouse the next day, and Santo called a clubhouse meeting, and he's apologizing for the headlines that came out in the paper in Chicago. I thought, What the crap is this all about? I didn't know anything about it. So what the Sam Hill, big stinking deal.

"As far as I'm concerned, those headlines didn't win or lose for us. That was a bunch of bull. I don't think it had anything to do with us winning or losing. All it did was cause Santo a lot of grief and aggravation when we got back to Chicago.

"Once we got back to Chicago, the fans got all over his case. I don't know if the media ever did him justice by getting on his case about it, because it wasn't that stinking big a deal that they made it out to be. Jiminy Cricket, are they a bunch of wusses, for crying out loud?

"Let me tell you something. I resent it, if that's the only thing they can resort to to sell those stinking newspapers. Plus, it did major damage to Santo. And there were times—he'd be the first one to tell you, 'I should keep my mouth shut.' But in that particular situation, it was ridiculous."

GLENN BECKERT: "*Everybody* was saying, 'Jesus Christ, the ball's got to be caught. He dogged after the ball.' Santo's name got associated with it. Not the other twenty-four guys who were saying the same thing. And then when Ron read something like that, it hurt him, 'cause 'that's not what I mean.' But once it's out, how do you correct the impression?"

GENE OLIVER: "My locker was right next to Ron's. My directive on the ball club, in addition to being a utility player, was to keep the ball club loose. I was the comedian, threw a lot of batting practice. Ron went through that Don Young thing, which was unbelievable.

"He'd say, 'Do me a favor. Go to the ballpark early and go through my mail.' You can tell the hate mail. There's no return address, 'Mr. Santo' scribbled on the envelope. And we'd go through it. He was dealing with it emotionally. It was an emotional setback for Santo, 'cause that story was written so out of context, it was not true, and he was really come down on by the fans. He needed emotional support. He didn't need to be knocked down."

Despite the turmoil caused by the press embarrassing Santo and humiliating Young, the Cubs continued to play championship baseball. In one of the finest games played that year, on July 16 at Wrigley Field, Bill Hands defeated Tom Seaver and the New York Mets 1–0.

The Mets won the second game and beat Fergie Jenkins in the third to take the series and cut the Cubs' lead to seven games. In the clubhouse afterward reserve catcher Gene Oliver sneered to Ron Santo, "If we lose to this club, we should jump off the Hancock Building."

Jerry Holtzman, the longtime columnist for the *Chicago Tribune*, overheard the remark and printed it the next day. The Mets seemed little threat.

RANDY HUNDLEY: "We were feeling pretty good about ourselves and the ball club and what was going on in Chicago for the Chicago Cubs, and it was a tremendous thrill for us. All we were trying to do was grind it out and concentrate on winning today's game and not looking ahead.

"Who would have ever thought the New York Mets would have been the team to beat? Their first year was '62. How could they win a division title in '69?

"We had a great pitching staff. Fergie was blessed with a tall, lean body, and at six foot six, he looked like he was standing right on top of you. If the guy on that mound is six feet tall or under, you have an advantage because it seems you have an extra three or four feet to wait on that ball. But with him, it looked like he was up closer on you, and that was an intimidating thought.

"Fergie had tremendous control. I could almost catch him with a pair of pliers. If I wanted the ball outside, he had the ability mentally not to overdo things. He stayed within himself. He didn't try to overpower the batter until he had to. If he got into a jam, he could reach back and literally throw the ball by you. But until then, he'd say, 'Here, I'm going to stay right out there, stay right out there. You're going to think I'm going to come in on you.' And he'd stay out there, stay out there. He and Bob Gibson had a lot of that going for them, although Bob Gibson was a little meaner than Fergie. Fergie was not a mean pitcher. He didn't have to be.

"Ken Holtzman had a lot of ability, and he learned to be real tough mentally too. In the beginning he and Leo had a love-hate relationship. Leo absolutely loved Kenny. Leo started to call him Hebe and called him everything you can imagine, and Kenny absolutely loved it. And to this day Ken Holtzman to all of us is Hebe. We don't know him any other way. If I were to say, 'Hey, Kenny,' he would think, 'Something is wrong. . .'

"Bill Hands was an intimidating pitcher. I've seen balls Hands threw whizzing past batters' throats that scared the pee out of me as a catcher. Bill knocked Tom Seaver down one day, and I'm telling you, it missed his chin by a half an inch, if not less. It just barely missed his chin. If it had hit his chin, the guy never would have made it to the Hall of Fame. It was that close. That's the way this crazy game is. It's an amazing game.

"Froggy [his teammates called Hands Froggy because he threw with the same delivery as the Yankees' Don Larsen, who loved to go frog hunting] finally developed a new windup style. He had Joe Becker as a pitching coach, and that's what Joe Becker worked out for him. And he had a real tough mental attitude about things. Froggy was tough. He was an intimidating pitcher. The opposing players knew if you knock one of our players down, this guy will get you.

"Nobody talks about Bill. He's kind of dropped out of sight, but he was very instrumental to our ball club. He had an attitude about him that was real important too. It was a big part of it. And it rubbed off on the other pitchers. You better believe it."

On offense the '69 Cubs featured a quartet of heavy hitters: Ernie Banks; Billy Williams; Jim Hickman, who got overlooked because he was so quiet; and Ron Santo, the emotional, spiritual leader of the team.

RANDY HUNDLEY: "For years I had heard about Ernie Banks, and then joining the ball club and being with him, needless to say, it was a real privilege to be able to play with him. Ernie had an innate ability to play the game. If you were to look at the guy, his talent, his body—you wouldn't think he was so great. From a personal and maybe a selfish point of view, it was very frustrating to see this little scrawny, bony guy knocking the pee out of the ball, hitting all these home runs. You just couldn't figure out how in the world he did it. He didn't know how he did it either, how he could get that ball to carry enough to get it over the fence.

"Ernie gave you 'Let's play two' and all that stuff, and we knew that a bunch of it was BS. You know what I mean. I mean, what the heck? Ernie actually got Leo in a lot of trouble a lot of times because if they'd ask him how he was feeling, he'd say, 'I feel fine.' Well, he was really hurting. And now Leo doesn't play him, and the media says to Leo, 'Ernie says he's fine.' Leo: 'Oh, really?' So he got Leo in a lot of trouble that way, and it caused a problem as far as Ernie and Leo were concerned. But you've got to know Ernie. You have to know what the heck he means when he opens his mouth. And no one could tell the writers what the heck was going on.

"Billy was the quiet, sweet-swinging Billy Williams. He analyzed what was going on on the field, and he just went about his job in a very professional way, and you just held a lot of respect for him. This guy was really a great hitter. Billy mixed in well with the players. I love the guy. He's a good person. But as far as the media, he didn't get much media attention, like Ernie did, because Ernie had all these quotes going on all the time.

"Billy played in Ernie's shadow. Everybody did. We all did. I don't care who was there. As far as Ernie Banks was concerned, anybody and everybody was in Ernie's shadow.

"Billy's still in the shadow of Ernie Banks. With all due respect, they don't call Ernie Banks Mr. Cub for nothing. Billy has never talked about that. Not a word. I don't know that Billy cared. As long as he got paid, it didn't bother Billy Williams. He just didn't let that stuff upset him. He knew what was going on, and he understood it. And he and Ernie are great friends. Billy will never say anything derogatory toward Ernie."

* * *

Billy Williams

FERGUSON JENKINS: "Hey, Billy Williams had the best swing I ever saw in base-ball. I played with him and against him a total of eleven years. He got traded to Oakland when I was in the American League. He was a dangerous hitter all the time. He generated power through his forearms and his wrists and hands. Very strong hands, similar to Ernie.

"Back then we didn't pick up a lot of weights. We weren't upper-body strong, where guys can bench-press 300 to 400 pounds. But Billy had strong hands and wrists and very good bat speed.

"Billy and I used to hunt and fish together. We lived close by on the South Side of Chicago. We bought a boat together and did a lot of fishing in the off-season. He had four daughters, and I had three. Our wives were close. Billy did most of his talking through his ability. He didn't talk much to the press. He wasn't flamboyant. He just went out and did his job day after day after day."

GLENN BECKERT: "Quiet Bill. Just write his name in the lineup and watch him swing the bat. I was very fortunate to bat in front of him, because the amount of fastballs I got was directly dependent on how Billy was hitting. Billy would go into a slump, and I'd say, 'Billy, goddamn, I'm getting more curve balls than I've ever seen. I like those fastballs. Start hitting, will ya?'

"In '69, Jim Hickman had a tremendous year. He hit 21 home runs, and every one he hit was a game winner, it seemed. He was unbelievable. He was Mr. Clutch for us in '69.

"The true fans who follow the game understand what Jim Hickman was. If it was the bottom of the eighth and we were losing by two runs, he'd hit a three-run homer. It was a big lift for a team. In extra innings he'd get the extra-base hit to start the rally, or he'd drive in the run."

RANDY HUNDLEY: "Ron Santo was a tremendous player. The thing I remember about him, I caught batting practice in spring training, and I never saw a bat as quick as his. He could wait and wait and wait, and the last second he would all but take the ball out of my mitt. He'd come through that strike zone and take that ball out of there so quick. He has a tremendously strong upper body, his hands and arms, and that bat was quick coming through there, and I can still picture it as if I was right there catching right now. And when you're playing with the guy, you don't have occasion to see that. That was interesting to me. Then I understood why he was such a good hitter.

"Once we discovered that Ron was not only a diabetic but a hypochondriac, he was fair game. With us, nothing was sacred. We'd walk in the clubhouse and say to him, 'Ron, you don't look too good today.' And he'd say, 'I don't feel too good today either.' That's the kind of stuff we would do. And some days he'd respond and say, 'Blank you.' We'd say, 'Why? What do you mean? What's wrong? You look a little pale.' He'd say, 'Yeah, you know, I don't feel too good.' We ragged on him unmercifully."

GLENN BECKERT: "Ron is highly emotional, the Italian side of his family. He was very outgoing, voiced his opinion, and the writers would write his opinion, and sometimes they didn't present it the way he meant it. It would come out to the fans wrong, so they'd say, 'Geez, if he's that way . . .' You'll find with Ron Santo there's no middle of the road with him. They either loved him or they hated him.

"Ronnie was the center of most of our stuff. When we got bored with something, he was so easy to agitate. We'd say, 'Let's create some excitement. Why don't we stir up Santo. Let's get him going.' And we all did it.

"We'd say, 'Jesus Christ, Ron, are you losing your hair?' Or 'Where did you get those shoes?' He prided himself on the way he dressed. 'Jesus Christ, those are ugly shoes.' Aw man, he'd go crazy. He'd say, 'Let me tell you something, you son of a bitch.' We had all the guys doing it. He was so easy to stir up. But he's a very sensitive man, and he's done so much for juvenile diabetes. I roomed with him for nine years on the road, and we're still very close friends.

"The funniest was when his life was threatened. It went on for two months. We don't know who was sending the letters and making the calls. And this went on, and we were in Montreal, and the Cubs called in the FBI.

"They sent two or three agents with us. I was rooming with him, and I said, 'I can't take this.' So in New York we were staying at the Waldorf; of course, there are four of us now, including Ron and myself and the two FBI guys. But everyone is asking me questions about how I feel about this whole thing. So I decide, Shit, let's have some fun. So I put a big sign over his bed, Santo Sleeps Here. And one over my bed, Beckert Sleeps Here. With the arrows pointing down.

"We went to Shea Stadium one night, and one of the telegrams that was sent said, 'Tonight you're history. Bye bye.' With all these cutout letters. So they sent him home. They had no idea who it was.

"So anyway, after we came off the road trip, I went to the ballpark, Wrigley Field. When we get back from a road trip, you get a big pack of fan mail. Our lockers were Billy, Ernie, myself, Santo. Billy was there when I arrived. Billy said, 'Let's have some fun with Santo. He's playing tight. We have to loosen him up.'

"People sent you balls to autograph in those little boxes. Billy and I cut with a razor blade one of these boxes addressed to Santo, took out the ball. We got a minute timer, which ticked louder than hell, and we put that in there and taped it back up and threw the box underneath the mail.

"Santo came in. He was hyper. We were just sitting there, and Billy said, 'You know, Beck, do you hear something ticking?' I said, 'Yeah, I heard that ever since we got here this morning.' Santo rooted through his pile, and he found the box. He said, 'It's a fucking bomb.' We lockered in the left-field area, and he took it out and threw it onto Waveland Avenue.

"A few minutes later Al Schoonmeir, our trainer, came out and said, 'What the hell happened to my timer?' I said, 'Doc, Santo just threw it onto Waveland Avenue.'

"You had to be nuts, right? But that was Santo, a good man. You had to have some fun, loosen up."

As proof positive of the Cubs' first-half-season dominance in '69, at the All-Star Game in late July the entire Cubs infield of Banks, Beckert, Kessinger, Santo, and Hundley made the lineup, as the National League won 9–3.

GLENN BECKERT: "All five of us, Kess, Ernie, Ronnie, Randy, and I. It was just like a regular game. And we went to the White House to see President Nixon. It was something to go in and see that. They treated us very nicely. I even called my parents to tell them about it."

No matter how smoothly things were sailing, life with Leo Durocher was always an adventure. Leo was the sort of man who didn't play by the rules. The players didn't mind, but his unconventional activities gave the newspapermen reams of paper to fill.

Leo's first serious controversy concerned his decision to skip two games against the Dodgers in late July. He had gotten married a month earlier to a woman who had a ten-year-old son who was attending summer camp.

It was Parents Weekend at Camp Ojibwa. Lynn Durocher asked him if he would go with her. Leo said no. Then she challenged him. She said, "Well, after all, you are the boss of the Cubs, aren't you? How serious could it be to miss one or two little old games?" At the time she brought it up, Lynn Durocher thought skipping games for Leo would be no different than if he were an accountant and missed a couple days behind the calculator. She had no idea how serious the consequences would be for him not to show up for ball games.

Part of Leo's charm was that he rarely considered the consequences of his words or deeds. Leo wanted to impress his bride, and so he agreed to go with her. After telling the press he wasn't feeling well, he headed for summer camp instead of going to the ballpark. Under coach Pete Reiser, the Cubs and Dodgers split the two games he missed.

The razor-tongued Durocher made enemies easily, and among those who despised him was Chicago reporter Jim Enright. Enright had co-written Ernie Banks's autobiography, *Mr. Cub*, and Enright resented the way Leo had treated Ernie.

As soon as Leo arrived in Chicago, one of his first pronouncements was that Ernie Banks should retire. "He's too old to play the game anymore," said Leo. Ernie disagreed, and proved him wrong. That Leo had been wrong made their relationship even worse. Leo belittled Banks whenever possible, and vice versa.

When Leo showed up at Camp Ojibwa, one of the other camp parents—either a White Sox fan, an Ernie Banks fan, or someone who knew Leo—called Enright at home and ratted on him. Enright then created the maximum amount of trouble for Leo by calling Phil Wrigley and telling him what Leo had done.

According to journalist Rick Talley, Phil Wrigley fired Durocher. Two hours later, after talking to Mrs. Wrigley, Wrigley decided to allow Durocher to explain. When Leo apologized, Wrigley let him keep his job.

The papers had a field day.

In the clubhouse the incident did not affect the players one whit. Said Ferguson Jenkins, "We heard rumors about where Leo was. We didn't care. Pete Reiser managed in his place. It wasn't played up that big until the press got ahold of it."

Said Gene Oliver, "It was a nonincident. Period."

According to Hank Aguirre, "The only guys upset were the writers."

The Chicago writers, who *were* the only guys upset, later awarded Durocher their Camper of the Year Award.

Going into August, the Cubs were still cruising. Their spirits were high, though the wear and tear from playing every game was beginning to affect the regulars.

Randy Hundley, who had played virtually every game, had been spiked in San Diego by Chris Cannizzaro. It was the beginning of a string of events that demon-

Randy Hundley

strated the dedication and intensity of Hundley and the rest of the Cubs players. Whenever Leo needed him, if Randy could walk, he'd be in the lineup.

RANDY HUNDLEY: "Chris Cannizzaro caught my finger and bent it all the way back, and it's a wonder it wasn't broken. I had to sit out a couple games for that, and in the meantime the trainer decided to clean my ears out with a syringe. He forced water into my ears, and I got this tremendous infection.

"We were on the West Coast, and flying home my ears were just hurting like crazy. After a couple days back in Chicago I had to go into the hospital. They fed me antibiotics and put wicks down my ears. My ears were hurting me so bad they gave me Demerol. I was in the hospital for a week.

"Finally they said, 'You're feeling better, you can go home. Would you like a shot of Demerol before you go to make the trip home?' I said, 'By all means. I don't need this pain.'

"My wife came to the hospital and picked me up. I said to her, 'Let's go by the ballpark. I just can't stand not being at the park. Let me just go and see what's going on.' I walked out of the hospital and went to the ballpark.

"I hadn't played in two weeks. When I walked in, Leo was having a meeting. He looked up and he said, 'Randy, can you play?' I felt my finger. It didn't hurt. I said, 'Well, skip, if you want me to, I'll go back there.'

"He said, 'Well, you're in the game.'

"I thought, Holy cow, what the crap have I gotten into?

"It was against Houston on national TV. I got the uniform on. My wife was still sitting out in the parking lot waiting on me. I forgot to tell her what was happening, and of course when she found out, she about hit the ceiling.

"As the game wore on, my blooming finger started killing me. Man. But they taped me up. They took a ball and put it in my hand, and they taped my hand so I could put the ball in there and play.

"I played the game, 'cause Leo counted on me to run the pitching staff. He said, 'I don't care if you take the bat and bunt every time you come to the plate.' There were a couple situations: I made a sacrifice bunt. I bunted for a base hit. I played a decent game, and we won. And I was back in the lineup from then on. I never came out again.

"When I think about it, it was unbelievable. I got hit once on a play at the plate. Lou Brock was on first base. There was a hit and run, and the ground ball went through to the outfield. I could tell that Brock was going to try to score. Sure enough, he did. The throw came in to Ernie at first, and Ernie was kind of slow getting the ball to me, and I could hear Brock bearing down on me. Ernie short-hopped me at the plate. The ball was laying right in front of the plate, and I knew I was going to get creamed. I went to pick the ball up, and whaaaack. I mean, Brock just flattened me.

"Speed will hurt. Size doesn't hurt. It's speed that will absolutely knock you into the next county. I have scars on my hand where Brock hit me, ripped my hand apart, and knocked the daylights out of my calf. I couldn't walk. I had to come out of the game because I was bleeding all over the place. He spiked me on my hand.

"The next day, we went to Cincinnati, and Leo said, 'Randy, can you play?' I could hardly walk to get on the airplane. I said, 'Skip, I don't know whether I can play or not. You see the condition I'm in. If you want me to play, I will play, but just know I'm limited to what the heck I can do.'

"He said, 'You're catching.' So again, they taped my blooming hand, put a ball in my hand, and taped it up so I could go behind the plate. I didn't realize that in '69 I still caught 150 some odd games that year [151]. All I missed were the two weeks because of an ear infection and a hand. It was hard to believe. And I wonder why my body hurts.

"But at the same time, I wouldn't have it any other way. I gave them every freaking thing I had, and they can never take that away from me. I never balked about never coming out of the lineup. I didn't think about myself. If Leo felt this was best for the ball club, then let's go strap it on.

"I became aggravated when I was managing in the minor leagues and somebody else from the outside [Dallas Green] came in and then says, 'We're going to build a new tradition. We're going to change . . .'

"You know what? I'm a freaking Chicago Cub. I'm the one who went on the field and gave it everything I had and literally and figuratively almost lost my life to knee surgery when I had a blood clot break loose and go through my heart and go into my lung, and then they want to tell me about building a new tradition and whatnot?

"To me, that '69 ball club was made up of guys who gave it every stinking thing they had. And I think we can all be comfortable with that. We did everything we could. It didn't work out, but when you fill that bucket up and you put one more drop in it, and it overflows, that's a hundred percent. That's not 110. It's a hundred percent, and I feel that's what the Sam Hill we gave them."

62

Freefall

GLENN BECKERT: "We were in front in early September by six or seven games. There was a game in Wrigley Field [on September 7] against the Pittsburgh Pirates where we had it locked. It was late in the game, and Phil Regan was on the mound. Regan had a great slider and a great spitball, and he was a real competitor. Willie Stargell, a left-handed batter, was up. Hank Aguirre, who was left-handed, was warming up in the bullpen, and Aguirre had had good luck against Stargell. Leo stuck with Regan, who had pitched great.

"And Willie Stargell hit a miracle home run, and we lost that game. I looked back at that one game, and I think, Jesus, did that change our attitude? I don't think so. I think the price we paid for playing every day was starting to show its effects.

"Leo had stuck with his horses, and maybe that hurt us the last month of that season. Who knows? That's second-guessing now. But there was no platooning with Leo. I knew I was somewhat tired, and I had an injury before that. Kess was getting a little weary, not only physically, but mentally. Ron and Randy were hurting.

"We were playing banged up, and maybe that was the time when we could have used a couple days' rest. We had a good bench. Papa [Paul Popovich] was the best utility infielder in baseball, the greatest hands, and he could have come in for a week. But that's looking back. It's history."

RANDY HUNDLEY: "Leo did the right thing keeping Regan in to pitch to Stargell. I never would have even thought of bringing in Aguirre, even to this day. The wind was blowing in about thirty-five miles an hour. You figure that nobody can hit the ball out. Regan was *the* pitcher for us. Stargell fouled off about eight consecutive spitters, and I mean great pitches. He got just enough of them to foul off.

"And finally, about the ninth one, he took it not only out of the ballpark but out onto Sheffield Avenue. And I mean no human should have been able to hit the ball that far on that particular day.

"We always had a tough time with the Pirates. They left that bench swinging, and we had a tough time getting them out. To this day, I haven't figured out how to pitch any of those hitters. You just have to be lucky and hope they hit it at somebody.

"That, to me, was one of the toughest defeats we had the whole year, because that *really* busted our bubble. That was a tough defeat for us because we lost that game on Sunday, and the next day we went to New York to play the Mets. And that's when the Tommie Agee incident occurred, and losing that game *really* took some momentum out of our sails."

GENE OLIVER: "I think the turning point for the Mets was when we went into New York three games ahead and lost the first game of the series to Koosman and the Mets.

"We held a clubhouse meeting before the game how we were going to pitch and defense them. Bill Hands was our starter. You wouldn't want any other pitcher on the mound for the game—'cause Bill Hands was an intense competitor. And Bill Hands made the decision in the meeting before we ever got to the field, he said, 'Agee is going on his ass the first pitch.' Because Agee was hitting him pretty good. When Hands said that, we *knew* Agee was going to go on his ass the first pitch.

"It was tense. It was the heat of a pennant race, and in the first inning, Jerry Koosman got us out one, two, three.

"Agee was the leadoff hitter. Everyone in the bullpen was up standing. Everyone was standing in the dugout 'cause we knew Agee was going down.

"I have never seen a better knockdown pitch. It was just right under the chin. Asshole, helmet, bat—that's all you could see of Agee.

"But Tommie Agee, being the professional he was, was not intimidated. He did not even make a face at Hands. He simply picked up the bat, and on the very next pitch, a low and away slider, he hit it over the center-field fence!

"And everybody went, 'Huh?' He let the air out of us. We were going to let the air out of him. He let the air out of us. He took an offensive situation we were trying to create, and he turned it into a negative for us. We thought we were going to intimidate them, and they were not about to be intimidated. And then they went on to get a couple runs that inning.

"In the top of the second, Santo was the leadoff hitter. Retaliation was inevitable. We *knew* Santo was going on his ass, and Koosman hit him right on the elbow. Ron was out for five days, and to me, that's when the Mets said, 'We're young, but we can compete, and baby, we're after ya. We're men now.'

"I thought the way Agee and the Mets reacted to the knockdown said, 'Hey, we're out here to play.'

"That was the night a black cat walked into our dugout prior to the game. Somebody had brought it, and it walked right in our dugout. We saw it. Nobody said anything, but there it was. Somebody knew it was coming, and it was great press to see this black cat coming into our dugout.

"That was also the game when the umpire blew the ball game by calling Agee safe on a call at the plate.

"Even if Agee had been called out at the plate, the score would have been tied. They might have gone on to win it anyway."

GLENN BECKERT: "I can remember Wayne Garrett got a base hit, and here comes Agee around third, and Jim Hickman, our center fielder, threw a strike to the plate. I said to myself, 'He's dead at home. We got him. OK, that's a big play.'

"If he's out, it changes the whole game. The game goes in our favor. And when he was called safe . . . I couldn't believe he was called safe. I thought, What the hell's going on now? I said, 'Jesus, is this going to happen all the time?'

"After mid-August, the Mets got strong. They came from fifteen back, and they had an .800 record. They won something like twenty-eight of thirty-five ball games. [Actually, they were 9½ back at their worst, then won 38 of 49 games.] They beat Pittsburgh in a doubleheader 1–0 both games! Unfortunately, Pittsburgh didn't score against them, and every time we went to another city like Philly or St. Louis or Cincinnati, we'd get beat, and our lead went from nine games down to one after the Agee game.

"Later Agee admitted, 'You guys had me,' but what are you going to do, go back twenty-five years and start again? But that happens in baseball. It's the nature of the game."

RANDY HUNDLEY: "I was thinking about the play before it ever developed. If Garrett got a base hit, we wanted to try to keep the ball in the infield. And then Garrett got a base hit to Hick. Hick came firing and threw a perfect strike.

"I tagged Agee about six feet up the line, and I tagged him so hard the ball almost popped out of my mitt. I thought nothing of it. I looked at first to make sure the runner didn't go, and then I was going to give the ball to Bill Hands, and we were going to work on the next hitter.

"And all of a sudden I heard this tremendous roar go up. And with my quick analytical mind, I figured something was wrong.

"Sure enough, I turned, and Satch Davidson's giving the 'safe' sign.

"And we lost that game, 3–2, and that was the winning run, and I . . . two days in a row to lose two ball games like that, it was a difference of four games in the standings for us.

"And then there was the Selma game."

GLENN BECKERT: "The Selma game was in Philadelphia [on September 11]. Selma had been outstanding. Dick was doing a hell of a job for us.

"Earlier in the year Selma had apparently worked out a trick play with Santo. With a full count and with two outs and runners on first and second going on the pitch, Selma was going to step off the mound and throw to third. The signal was something like, 'Hey, Dage.' They had not practiced this thing for months.

"Santo was over at third, and Selma said, 'Hey, Dage. Be alive.' That was the signal. Well, Ron said to himself, 'Hey, I'll be alive. I'm going to catch everything hit to me.'

"Selma put this play on, and he threw a perfect strike to third, except Santo was still down in his crouch, and the ball was rolling down the left-field line, and the runners were circling like a track meet.

"Leo jumped up in that old dugout and hit his head! Now, I really thought he was going to scream.

"We blew the game. And Leo was the most quiet guy in the world. He had a bandage on his head from jumping up. And I don't know if he should have ripped us apart at the time, but he didn't say a word.

"What do you say? What would you say in that situation?"

RANDY HUNDLEY: "I didn't hear about Selma's trick play until after the game was over. I guess he and Ronnie had been sitting around sometime and decided they were going to do this play. Now, months later, Selma gave the sign to Santo as if he was supposed to know the blooming play. Shucks, Santo didn't see it. I didn't see it. We just wanted to get the hitter out, and here comes this stupid play they scored two runs on.

"Actually the play was a balk, and the umpires didn't call it, so the play stood. I had never seen the play before in my life, but with runners on base, you cannot throw to an unoccupied base. He was throwing the ball to third base with nobody there.

"It must have been a high school play, because you would know in the big leagues you can't do that play because you're throwing to an unoccupied base.

"To lose a game that way was frustrating. Those kinds of things turn ball clubs around, and we could never get back on track, so that's why I said earlier, the Don Young incident, as far as I was concerned, was irrelevant. Forget it. *This* was the period that knocked the wind out of our sails.

"After [the Selma game] we just never could get the momentum back. The momentum had turned for the Mets when the Agee play developed, because we went from a three-and-a-half-game lead to two-and-a-half when it should have been four-and-a-half, a two-game swing for us, and a two-game swing on Sunday, and then another two-game swing when we got to Philly and the Mets won, and we had had that game won.

"Within that four- or five-day period, it was a six-game swing on three very strange plays.

"And that's when the Mets started believing. They said to themselves, 'Hey, you know what? We can catch these guys.'

"I can remember when we came off a road trip [reserve outfielder] Al Spangler made a statement, 'They have to win thirty-five out of forty ball games in order to catch us.' And shucks, they did. And I guarantee you, you would have bet the house that there was no way that ball club could do it. But they did it with pitching, they did it with starting to believe in themselves, and they got breaks.

"I mean, I don't give a confound what anybody says, every time you turned around, they were getting the breaks.

"Everybody wanted to whomp up on us 'cause we were the leaders, and when they went to play the Mets, they said, 'Ah, it's just the New York Mets, for crying out loud.'

"The Cardinals were the team that was supposed to win the pennant in '69. We played the Cardinals a series in Wrigley, and they beat us two out of three, and then they went to Shea Stadium and lost three to the Mets. What the crap, when they had just won the pennant the year before."

GLENN BECKERT: "You have to give the Mets credit. They came up with a hell of a pitching staff, guys nobody heard of. Who had heard of Tom Seaver? Or Jerry Koosman? I mean, they were good, but who knew they were that good? They won with pitching, and the ball just turned in their corner. When you saw Ron Swoboda make catches like he was, you knew something was up. I mean, I'm telling you, the way Swoboda ran out there, it was like putting a glove on a donkey and letting him loose. Nothing against his ability, but he was not noted for being a great defensive player, and he was making great plays, and of course Agee caught everything that was hit. They got hot at the right time, and we cooled off at the wrong time.

"We kept telling ourselves, 'We have to keep winning one game at a time and not look forward to another series against so-and-so and to keep playing hard,' and unfortunately we stopped scoring runs. Our offense dwindled, and then our defense was subjected to a lot of criticism.

"We began to feel the pressure. The pressure comes from trying to play hard to win. The writers put it on a lot of things: playing in the heat, day games in Chicago, that we didn't have much of a bench. We had four guys, Popovich, Nate Oliver, Gene Oliver, and Willie Smith. We weren't spelling a lot of the regulars, and unfortunately, guys were tired."

FERGUSON JENKINS: "We suffered a bit because the critics—the fans, the press, maybe even the front office—gave so many different reasons why we lost, and not the right reasons. The only true people who knew were the manager, Leo Durocher, the coaching staff, and the ballplayers.

"The real reason was that we had played out the string. We were tired. Leo played the regulars almost the whole season. Billy played 160 games, Santo 160, Ernie 150-some, Kessinger [157] and Beckert [129] played unless they were hurt, they played *all* the time. And Randy caught 150 games.

"In my opinion, when we knew we were faltering, we should have bought some pitchers. We had good defense. We should have bought some pitching, to take the pressure off the starting staff, but we never did it."

GENE OLIVER: "You hate to be called a *choke*. That's the one word in all sports, that you choked up, that you couldn't play under pressure. It wasn't that we couldn't play under pressure.

"Not long before Leo died, right here in Scottsdale, Arizona, we did Great Game '69, and Leo was invited. I don't think it's any secret, everybody knew that there was tremendous animosity between Santo and Leo, and Ernie and Leo.

"At the banquet after the Dream Game, Leo got up and spoke. He must have known he was dying because this was so unlike him. Leo was not one to ever admit he was wrong, and until then he was unforgiving.

"He said, 'This is my opportunity to apologize to the '69 Cubs, because I let them down. I should have won the pennant. They didn't lose it. I lost that pennant.' He explained that he had gotten caught up too much with what he was going to say to the writers after the game than being in the game. He saw us dissipating leads we shouldn't have lost. He saw errors that the team wasn't making in the early part of the season that we were making later. But what caused those errors . . . Leo said to me and he said it to Willie Smith, he said it to Nate and Papa and several guys in the bullpen, he said, 'If I'd only have given Beck and Kess a little rest, and Ollie, if I'da taken you and put you in there and given Randy a couple days off, spelled Billy in left field occasionally, and kept 'em strong, kept the pressure off them . . . but I didn't do it, and we would have won the pennant if I had done that.'

"One thing people forget: You don't have to be a mathematical genius. We had a thirteen-game lead with thirty games to play. All we had to do was play .500 ball. The Mets had to win a lot of games. And they did. They won twenty-seven out of thirty-five, and we didn't play .500 ball. That isn't choking. We didn't lose it. They *won* it.

"We failed to win the National League championship, and even though they didn't get their World Series, the fans of Chicago said, 'Baby, you gave us the best season we had since 1945.' And they have remembered our ball club more than the '84 Cubs, more than the division-winning Cubs of '89. I'll guarantee, you ask any Cubs fan who played on the '69 Cubs, they'll know. It was a love affair. I think winning that year would have been anticlimactic.

"What was more important for us as players was the overwhelming concern we have had for one another, respect that we as teammates had for one another.

"Randy Hundley and I had been rehired by the Cubs by Bob Kennedy. I was a minor league instructor and so was Randy, and as fate would have it, the game turns in funny ways, Dallas Green came over, and he fires Ernie Banks, fires Billy Williams, fires Randy Hundley, and fires myself, because we were the only people in the organization who were members of the '69 Cubs. And may he rest in peace, our farm director, C. V. Davis, was so maligned, he died of a heart attack two years later, because Dallas and Goldsbury, his farm director, came over in September, made a quick analysis of our farm system based only on team records, and said, 'It was the worst minor league system we have ever seen.' Having never seen it on the field! And he fired C. V. Davis.

"The next year or two this 'worst minor league system' was able to trade twenty-seven ballplayers to build the '84 club. Out of that system we gave away a lot of guys who started in the big leagues, and I'll name them: Joe Carter, Mel Hall, Oscar Gamble, Craig Lefferts, Mike Diaz, Henry Cotto, Scott Fletcher, Willie Hernandez, who won the Cy Young with Detroit [in 1984], and Pat Tabler.

"These guys were all playing regular in the big leagues for somebody, and they had been in our minor league system. Now you tell me another minor league system that can develop eleven starters in one year, and then to say they're horseshit?

"If Dallas Green hadn't come in, the likelihood was we would have developed all these players, and they would have stayed with the Cubs, but Dallas wanted to build his own domain.

"Anyway, Randy and I got fired. We're bullheaded, stubborn, but we're dedicated people, and we know the game, and that was when Randy and I became like brothers. He called me the following year and said, 'Ollie, I want to bounce something off of you. Dream camp, fantasy camp.' I told him to take a pill, lay down and call me when he felt better. Who in the hell is going to spend two thousand dollars to play ball with washed-up ball players? This is where the camaraderie of the '69 Cubs blossomed into one of the biggest businesses in baseball today. Randy couldn't patent or copyright it. Everybody's trying to copy him, but they can't touch him. We're surviving and others are falling by the wayside, and that's a compliment to Randy and his organization, and in a nutshell, when you do thirty-five percent repeat business, you're doing something right.

"All of us have had setbacks in our lives. We were there for Fergie. We were there for Randy when he had his knee problems. He has an artificial hip. Hank Aguirre has cancer. Myself, I have cancer. It's curable, we hope. We stay in touch, we love each other, we're concerned for each other, and they are always there for you.

"That is the lasting legacy of the '69 Cubs."

63

Leo's Demise

GLENN BECKERT: "We had a stronger team in 1970. We added Joe Pepitone and Milt Pappas, had a little more depth. We were in first place in early September, but we just couldn't beat out the Pirates. They had a lot of stars, Bill Mazeroski, Matty Alou, Willie Stargell, Manny Sanguillen, and of course they had Roberto Clemente.

"The Pirates never walked much. They always brought their bats to town. They were free swingers, and they were a hard-hitting team. They had such a balanced attack too, and they had good defense.

"Matty Alou was constantly on base against us, and Gene Alley and Mazeroski, and then you had the bombers coming up. They had a really complete ball team, and a lot of guys had good years.

"Clemente was an awesome talent. He was a right-handed hitter, but he would hit the ball to me at second as hard as any power-hitting left-hander. He used a very heavy bat, and he had an inside-out swing. He was very difficult to defense. He would hit shots at you, and the balls would come out of his uniform. The second baseman and first baseman really had to stay on their toes when he was hitting. He was gifted."

FERGUSON JENKINS: "Clemente was a nemesis for me. He'd come up with a big hit in the eighth or ninth inning to beat me 2–1 or 3–2 with a double. He had that knack. He beat a lot of people, but when the Cubs faced Pittsburgh—and I would get five or six starts against them—I just knew psychologically Pittsburgh was the team we had to beat, and unfortunately I didn't have a winning record against Pittsburgh.

"I can remember we had a game against the Pirates I was winning 1–0 in Chicago, and a short fly ball was hit to right field and Johnny Callison misjudged it, and it fell in for a single. It would have been the third out of the inning, and then Clemente came up and hit a home run. I can see it like yesterday. But hey, those things happen.

"Or, in another game I got taken out winning in the eighth or ninth inning, and Stargell was the hitter, and Phil Regan came in to pitch, and Regan gave up a shot to right field, a misjudged ball, and he ended up with a triple. And they put on a squeeze play and scored him, and we lost the ball game.

"I was something like 11–22 [lifetime] against Pittsburgh."

In 1970 the Pirates finished five games in front of the Cubs. In 1971 the difference widened to fourteen games as the Cubs players and Leo became more disenchanted with each other. Adding to the craziness on the Cubs was the addition of former New York Yankees star Joe Pepitone. Pepi was an individualist. He was like a little kid in school who hated to be reprimanded or lectured by the principal. That Leo was the Cubs' principal made for a volatile relationship.

GLENN BECKERT: "Joe is a very outward-going guy. Whenever people looked at Joe, they tended to see his crazy actions, his wild hairpieces, his off-field activities. At first the players thought, Who is this weirdo we have coming to our team? He had this hair dryer when hair dryers were unheard of. Crazy stuff he'd do.

"But let me tell you: Joe Pepitone had a great amount of ability, and Joe Pepitone got the respect of the players by what he did on the field. You don't care what a fellow does off the field. It's none of your business and shouldn't be any of anyone else's business but his own. It's what happens once he crosses that line and they play the national anthem. That's what counts to a player, and that's how you gain other players' respect, by what you do on the field, period.

"Joe was a tremendous defensive player, the most outstanding fielding first baseman I ever played with. I felt so good with Pepi at first, not to discredit other guys, Ernie or Jim Hickman, but with Joe at first I felt confident that if I made a wild throw in the dirt, Pepi was there. So that's a good feeling to have when you're an infielder.

"Off the field, Joe had a way of relaxing people.

"I remember the day that Joe came in and ran the hair dryer for the first time. It was the noisiest thing you ever heard. Leo's office was up two little flights of stairs, and he yelled to the clubhouse men, 'Yosh, what in the hell is that noise?' There had never been a hair dryer in our clubhouse before, and Yosh yelled up, 'Leo, it's Pepitone with his hair dryer.' And I remember Leo just scratching his head and closing his office door.

"Pepi was the type of guy who was open with any part of his life. There wasn't anything he wouldn't discuss. Pepi had had some marital problems. This one day he brought over his paycheck—we get paid every two weeks, and he showed it to everybody. He said, 'Take a look at this,' and he was making a good salary, and on the check it said, 'First wife, alimony,' and underneath was 'Child support,' and then 'Second wife, alimony,' and 'Child support.'

"He said, 'How the hell am I going to play in the big leagues on sixty-five dollars every two weeks?'

"Joe had a habit of buying clothes and just signing for it. This one time Leo went to Mr. Wrigley and asked him to bail Pepi out, to take care of the tabs. And he did.

"Leo had chewed him out saying, 'Pepi, I don't want you charging any more and just writing your name down at these clothing stores in the hotel.'

"We went to Cincinnati, it was our first road trip, we're in the ballpark, and we're sitting there in the clubhouse—a few of us, including Leo, were out there early, and here comes Pepi with four garment bags over his shoulder. Without the bat of an eye Pep said, 'Don't worry about it. It's just my laundry.'

"You have to love a guy like that."

Some of the funniest exchanges were between Pepi and Cubs icon Ernie Banks.

JOE PEPITONE: "There were mornings when I'd come dragging into the clubhouse, hung over, still half asleep. Ernie would be sitting there and he'd burst into a loud announcer's voice, 'Here comes Pepi! What's happening, man? Oh, *look* at those eyes! Open those eyes, Pepi, and see what a beautiful day it is to play baseball in beautiful, ivy-covered Wrigley Field. It's a great day to win two, Pepi! And we're gonna win two with you, Pepi! Two for the Cubs! We're gonna *win two* because we love baseball, don't we, Pepi? Now isn't this a great day to win two for the Cubs, Pepi?'

"'Ernie,' I'd say, 'it's a great day for two more hours' fucking sleep.'

"'Oh, Pepi's got his eyes open! He is *ready.*'"

RANDY HUNDLEY: "Some of the players had mixed emotions about Joe, but I absolutely love the guy. And some of the other guys did too. I also know some of them weren't too happy with him at times, and neither was Leo, but the guy was a tremendous talent. He could flat play. We thought also the fact he had been with the Yankees, had been on some pennant winners, he knew what that was, and that was the kind of player we were looking for. But I would say overall he had a good effect on the team.

"Pepi at times wanted to do things his way. We would get aggravated with it, but at the same time he had the type of personality we could deal with, and let him get by with it. He made you laugh, no question about it, and he could flat play. Sometimes you'd think if he took the game more seriously that he might have been a better player, but who the heck knows? It might have been just the opposite.

"Leo loved Pepi at first, but then Pepi got involved in a lounge in Chicago, and I think Leo felt that baseball might not have been his priority, and with Leo, you don't get by with that."

By midseason 1971 the relationship between Durocher and some of the players, especially the younger ones, was beginning to sour. Leo was hearing that players were talking behind his back to management. And after two years of going down to the wire and not winning a pennant, the pressure on Leo not to fail once more was making him even harder to live with than before.

FERGUSON JENKINS: "We *were* having some problems. Leo was too hard on some of the younger players, and they were playing tight all the time, and Leo was not comfortable with them being in ball games.

"At the same time Leo thought there was a clique to get rid of him. He had heard that players were grumbling to the front office, saying he had lost part of the game, the aspect of being a sharp manager, of not being on top of plays, ridiculing guys. He thought certain players were against him.

"In late August we had a team meeting. At the meeting we said, 'Let's talk and work this out.' At the start of the meeting he said he would stop shouting at players, that he was going to try to keep things on an even keel and not put all this pressure on these younger guys.

"By the end, it had turned into a shouting match."

RANDY HUNDLEY: "Leo called me up to his office that day. I didn't know why he called me. Whether he just assumed I was his leader or what the crap it was, I don't know. As soon as I got to the clubhouse, he called me up to his office. I went in his office, and I hadn't even paid any attention going in, and Leo said, 'Come here. I want to show you something.' He took me right outside the door, and a big motorcycle was right outside his blooming door.

"He said, 'Look at this. That's why Pepi's not hitting. He's out riding his motorcycle late at night, and his hands are tired and sore, and this is why he's not hitting.' He said, 'Now listen, I'm going to call a clubhouse meeting after batting practice. I want you to tell Pepi to just sit there and keep his mouth shut.' I said, 'OK, skip.' I would really like to have known why he called *me* in to go do this.

"I went to find Pepi. I said, 'Now, Pepi, listen. Leo's going to call a meeting. He's going to chew your fanny out about the motorcycle. He's just trying to shake up the ball club. I want you to sit and keep your freaking mouth shut and just go with it.'

"Pepi said, 'Uh-uh, he won't do that to me.' I said, 'Pep, listen to what the crap I'm telling you.' I finally calmed him down. He said, 'All right.'

"Now here comes the meeting. And just like he told me, Leo jumped on Pepi, and really not as bad as I thought he was going to, and of course Pepi had to say something to come back.

"The meeting was at the end when Leo said, 'Look at me as a player, not a manager. If you have something to say, say it.'"

GLENN BECKERT: "It was all over with until Leo said, 'Does anyone have anything else to say?' Pepi raised his hand and said, 'Leo, when I was with Ralph Houk . . .'

"And that was it. It set Leo off, and he went on a tirade. He said, 'Pepi, I brought you from the damn gutter. Nobody wanted you. I gave you a fresh start.' And then Pappas started on Leo. Milt was always known as a clubhouse lawyer with any team he was with. He was a hell of a pitcher, won a hundred games in each league, but he was always getting into the politics of the business. [Actually, Pappas won 110 in the American League and 99 in the National League.]

"And now Leo was *really* on the defensive, and so Leo got on Ron Santo for missing batting practice. Then Leo said, 'The only reason you're having a Ron Santo Day is that Billy and Ernie had one and you asked John Holland for one.'"

RANDY HUNDLEY: "I mean, Leo should not have said what he said to Santo. I don't give a confound. First of all, it wasn't true. The Cubs were giving Ronnie his day. John Holland had suggested it to him. But Leo was backed into a corner, and Leo and Ron hadn't gotten along, and that's how Leo responded."

GENE OLIVER: "That clubhouse meeting was absolutely unbelievable. Pepitone was there, and once you get him talking, he's like a psychic woodpecker. That was absolutely so unjust, what Leo did to Santo in front of all the players.

"Leo just didn't like Ron's approach to the game. Ron was a difficult guy to get along with. When you played against Santo, you knew he was a 190-percenter. I respected him as good a third baseman as anyone in the league. But Leo saw him as a self-centered 'I' and 'my' type of guy. Which Ron was not. He was totally a team man, but Leo wanted to bring down Santo. He wanted to be able to control Santo and Banks just like he controlled every other player he managed. His theory was, If you play in fear, I can get more out of you. Hate me, but you'll be a better ballplayer for it. It's what made Leo successful, but you don't have to go along with it.

"You knew Ronnie and Leo hated each other. You just knew it. It's like going to the dentist. You don't really want to go, but you have to. Or going to work for a boss who's an idiot, where you don't see things the same way he does.

"And that day Leo reduced Santo to wanting to choke him to death, and then to tears. If we'd have not pulled Ronnie off him, he'd have killed Leo. He would have absolutely killed him."

FERGUSON JENKINS: "Leo finally said, 'Shit, I'm taking this uniform off,' and he threw it down and went up to his office. It was kinda crazy."

RANDY HUNDLEY: "He quit. He took his jersey off and said, 'That's it. I resign.' And somebody talked him back into staying on, because we didn't want to look like a bunch of spoiled brats. We got to Leo and talked him into staying, and he did stay."

FERGUSON JENKINS: "We all wanted Leo to stay. It would have been embarrassing for the press to say, 'The players disliked Leo, and PK Wrigley is firing him.' And the fact was we were still playing good ball. We weren't out of it. Fortunately, cooler heads prevailed and he finished the season."

GLENN BECKERT: "I was lockering next to Billy Williams, and I said, 'I can't believe this is happening.'

"It was just a bad scene. But about ten years later Leo did come to one of the fantasy camps, and he actually apologized to Ron openly. But it was a matter of the pressure building up and Leo not liking to be put on the defensive."

* * *

RANDY HUNDLEY: "It was very ugly, the worst clubhouse meeting I had ever been in. A wedge started coming in there as far as Leo was concerned."

As bad as the Leo-Santo confrontation had been, it did nothing to morale compared to a thoughtless memo published in the Chicago papers written by owner PK Wrigley. In it Wrigley apologized to the fans for the mediocre performance of his ball club. That part the players could have lived with. But with just one line—a P.S. at the end—Wrigley ruined the morale of his ball club.

The line read: "If only we could find more players like Ernie Banks."

GLENN BECKERT: "He was talking about Ernie Banks, and it hurt me, because I was having a great year, and a lot of other guys were out there busting, playing for the team. That was a dumb move on Mr. Wrigley's part and the Cubs' part. It should never have been done. It was bad for him to go through the media and air it in the press instead of coming and sitting in a meeting and saying, 'I wish . . .'

"We could have said, 'Mr. Wrigley, I think you're wrong about this thing. There are a lot of other guys who are busting their tails too.' It was a bad scene. It took everything downhill."

RANDY HUNDLEY: "After that letter in the paper from Mr. Wrigley, Kenny Holtzman decided he wanted to be traded. Not till years later did we discuss it. He saw the handwriting on the wall and asked to be traded. The guy had won a lot of ball games. You knew he had talent."

Holtzman was traded to the Oakland A's for outfielder Rick Monday on November 29, 1971. In his next four seasons with the A's he would win 19, 21, 19, and 18 games. Those first three years he would help pitch Oakland to the world championship. In the fourth year the A's lost to Boston in the playoffs.

In the spring of 1972, Leo Durocher returned with his usual optimism. He told the press, "This is the best team I ever managed." He predicted that the Cubs would win the pennant.

But Phil Wrigley lost patience with and gave up on Durocher. The boo birds among the fans and the writers covering the Cubs wanted Leo's head, and after a 46–44 start, they got it; Leo was forced out in July.

FERGUSON JENKINS: "The biggest thing about Leo, the guys respected him, but he had lost the game. He wasn't that sharp anymore. In the past he would make the other manager make mistakes by substituting a pinch hitter early in the game or whenever. No more. I think the game was catching up to him. He was getting old."

RANDY HUNDLEY: "At that time Leo was slipping as a manager, and it didn't surprise me he did resign.

"We were in Philadelphia at the time. I don't remember much about it except that I sent Leo a telegram. I just told him I appreciated the opportunity he had given me to play major league baseball and wanted him to know I loved him and appreciated all he had done for me.

"We understood what Leo meant to our ball club. Most of us understood what he was to our club, but it's like anything else, there comes a time when you have to have change, and maybe it was that time. We never did know for sure whether he quit or was fired."

FERGUSON JENKINS: "Mr. Wrigley fired him. We let him go, and Whitey Lockman took over the team. We said good-bye to Leo, and he went to manage Houston."

Leo may have been slowing down, but even at age sixty-seven, he was still sharper than most managers. While Leo was managing the Cubs, he handled his players the way the Soviet Union had controlled its conquered countries. Once the Soviet Union broke up, there was chaos. After Leo left, the Cubs broke up the same way.

RANDY HUNDLEY: "We respected Leo all the way through, and we realize looking back after we were traded and went to other teams and the team was broken up that he was a player's manager. Sometimes it was good and sometimes it was bad, but the man deserved a lot of respect for what he did to change the thinking of the Chicago Cubs organization. Leo's critics were only able to see what sort of manager Leo was after Leo left.

"Whitey Lockman had been a coach for Leo in '66, and after that season Whitey left, and I never did understand it. I guess Whitey and Leo didn't get along, that Whitey couldn't stand Leo. Whitey had played for him in New York on the '54 Giants team. And I always thought they were buddies, but they weren't.

"Whitey didn't like me for whatever reason, and he was the manager, and it was his prerogative not to like me. But I didn't understand why and was very frustrated by it. Hey, that's life.

"Whitey hurt Fergie by not showing confidence in him. I didn't pay much attention to why Whitey did or didn't use Fergie. I just know the change in managers wasn't what we had hoped it would be.

"Leo was a manager who tried to build confidence in his players, and I'll tell you one thing, Leo Durocher created some ballplayers by doing that. Leo Durocher made Willie Mays. Leo Durocher made Fergie Jenkins. And whatever the Sam Hill Randy Hundley ever was, Leo Durocher helped make him, because if it hadn't been for him, I don't know if I would have ever played major league baseball. But Fergie won 20 games six consecutive years because Leo didn't go get Fergie out of the game and let somebody save it out of the bullpen. He let Fergie win the stinking game. He had that much confidence in him."

GLENN BECKERT: "Whitey was a very quiet man. From the time when Whitey took over to the end, we could see by the way he was using us that the writing was on the wall, that most of the vets were going to be gone. You could see it happening just by the way Whitey was using us.

"I was banged up. I wasn't getting to play quite as much. It's tough going from a manager who is totally outgoing to a manager who keeps everything inside, and . . . see, Leo would leave Fergie in if we were one run behind, and when Whitey became manager, if there was a game when we were winning by one run and Fergie gave up a base hit, Whitey took him out. With Leo, that would never happen. It was just a different managing philosophy.

"There was a total change of view at the top, not to say Whitey's view wasn't good, but we really didn't know what our status had become. You don't have to be a rocket scientist to see what was happening. And after '73, Santo went [to the White Sox], I went to San Diego. Don't ask me about it. It wasn't a pleasurable experience. I had rheumatoid arthritis. Wherever I would have gone, it would have been over. The Padres had the world's ugliest uniform, puke yellow and brown, and it was a bad experience, going from training in Scottsdale in spring training to Yuma, Arizona. You ever been to Yuma? Don't ever go. It was like where they filmed *Lawrence of Arabia*. The sand and the wind. It was like *Stalag 17*, big speakers on a pole. 'Would Beckert report, you have a phone call in the clubhouse.' And you'd run about twelve miles to get there.

"I was there a year and a half, and I was released in May of '75. I was banged up. When the arthritis hit my ankle and knee, it was over. But I went out with a good year batting in the few at bats I got. But the end was there.

"My memories will always be with the Cubs."

FERGUSON JENKINS: "Well, Lockman wasn't a nice guy to play for. Nobody understood him. As a starter with Leo, I knew I was going to get that ball every fourth day and I was going to pitch my ass off to win and I was going to give what I could to win, and with Whitey it didn't seem like things were happening for me. There were a lot of guys who didn't like Whitey's approach to doing a lot of things. But hey, you couldn't do much about it. He was the manager. One manager likes certain people, another one doesn't like certain people. I see that all the time.

"They accused me of having a bad arm. I told them, 'There's nothing wrong with me.' In '72 I finished the year 20–12. My ERA was a little higher. I went from 2.77 to 3.21. I still pitched 289 innings. I thought I still pitched well.

"And then the next year I was 14–16, and that's when the criticism really got heavy, when they again said I had a bad arm. I didn't have a bad arm. I had a manager who didn't show any confidence in me. Leo had left. Leo would give me the ball and say, 'This is your game to win or lose.' I pitched a lot of nine-inning ball games, eleven innings, twelve innings, whatever, to win a ball game under Leo. But with Whitey, he didn't show the same confidence in me.

"I remember in this one game Whitey took me out in the seventh inning with the score tied 2–2. After I came into the dugout, I threw the bats out on the field. I was angry.

"John Holland had me go to a therapist. He thought something was wrong. I had been holding a lot of things in about certain things. My mother had died during the season in 1970 from cancer, and I didn't miss a start. I went home for the funeral, and four days later I started in Montreal. But I played because I wanted to play.

"And at the end of '73 I ended up getting traded. The press pushed for it, and maybe it came from Lockman, but I got traded the next year. I was traded in November to Texas for Vic Harris and Bill Madlock. The next year I won 25 games for the Rangers. How bad could my arm have been?

"I thought I got cast aside. They were breaking up the team. They thought we were too old together. They were rebuilding. The year I got traded I was thirty.

"I spent eight seasons in Texas and Boston. I played for Billy Martin, Don Zimmer, Pat Corrales, Billy Hunter, and back with Dallas Green and the Cubs again, pitching for Lee Elia [in 1982–83].

"In '82, Dallas got ahold of me and asked point blank, 'Can you still pitch?' I said, 'Yeah, I can still pitch.' He said, 'We need a veteran right-handed pitcher.' So I signed with the Cubs. He gave me the money I wanted. I had second thoughts at first coming back. 'I'm thirty-nine. I wonder if I can catch the magic again?' And I did. I pitched well. I won 14 games, and I could have won more, but we didn't have much of a bullpen. And the next year we didn't have any bullpen at all, and I was in and out starting and relieving, and I was 6–9 and I had fifteen no-decisions that year.

"In '84 I came to spring training, and Dallas and I had talked about my winning a starting role, but I only pitched three innings in the spring, and they let me go. So I went home.

"Six teams phoned me. I said I didn't want to play for anybody else. If I was going to get to the 300 plateau, I wanted to do it with the Cubs. I wanted to win for the Cubs, and they ended up winning that year, they won their division. But unfortunately I wasn't on the team.

"I look back at it and say, 'Hey, I played as long as I could. I played well. I got nineteen years in.'

"Baseball is a game of 'What have you done for me lately.' I didn't want to be a hanger-on, to bounce from team to team. I said to myself, 'If I can do it in a Cubs uniform, I'll stay.'

"When they didn't give me a shot, I went home."

RANDY HUNDLEY: "At the end of the '73 season, they just upped and traded everybody, and we still had a good ball club. Shucks, I was one of the first to go. To this day I don't know why, and I don't care to know. I went to Minnesota for George Mitterwald. Part of that was that Bill Hands had gone to Minnesota, and he got up there and told them what a great catcher I am, a handler of pitchers, because he and I were roommates, and they traded for me.

"That was the beginning of breaking up that ball club. And I'll tell you what: I was devastated. Absolutely devastated. But what are you going to do? You do what you have to do and keep on trucking.

"One of the things that bothered me was that I heard it on the news before it ever got to me, and I wasn't pleased about that, the way it was handled.

"I came back to the Cubs in '76. I didn't get to be with them opening day. The next day they put me in as a pinch hitter, and I hit a triple to tie the ball game in the bottom of the eighth, and that was a highlight, a tremendous thrill, because the Cubs fans were glad to get me back.

"We got in a big fight in San Francisco in '76, and I snapped a disk in my neck, ended up having a cervical fusion. I had [Giants third baseman] Ken Reitz by the throat, and I had a hammerlock on him. He said, 'Randy, you're hurting my shoulder, man, let me go.' I said, 'Just don't try any funny stuff.' And as I said that, I starting easing up, and he tried to get away, and as he did I got ahold of him again, and when I got control of him I felt something had snapped in my neck, a terrible feeling. I got nauseous, and that night I was sick.

"We were in San Francisco, back in the hotel. I ordered room service and lay down. The muscle in my neck pulled the vertebrae out to put pressure on my nerve. I kept moving my neck. I felt sick. My head was all messed up.

"I didn't think too much about it, but every day I'd go to the ballpark and put the catcher's mitt on my hand, and I noticed every time I did it my arm ached like a toothache through my shoulder into my elbow all the way down my hand. After a while my fingers were getting tingly, and then after a while I held my arm up so it wouldn't hurt, and finally they did a test on me and saw I had a slipped disk that was putting pressure on the nerve. So I had to have a cervical fusion.

"I came back the next year from that. I had to. I don't know any other way to do it.

"I figured they would release me, but Bob Kennedy brought me back as a coach. In spring training I was throwing infield, 'cause I was in pretty good shape, and [Cubs manager] Herman Franks and [coach] Alvin Dark saw me throw and they say, 'We're going to keep you active.' Bob said, 'We want to keep you as a coach and we want you to stay in shape in case we want you to play.' I loved it. I was Herman Franks's bench coach, and I absolutely loved it. At the end of the season Herman told me that Bob Kennedy wanted me to go to the minor leagues and manage, so I went from the big leagues to rookie ball to start my career as a manager, when I thought I should have been and could have been with Herman, that I had done an excellent job for him. I told them I wanted to stay with Herman, but there was nothing I could do about it.

"I managed in the minor leagues and really had tremendous ambitions to be a big-league manager. I had a Triple A ball club, either real young players or guys who were over the hill, couldn't play. We couldn't play doodley.

"Joey Amalfitano was managing the big-league club, and they were struggling like crazy, and I was struggling at Triple A, so they couldn't make the change, and after that, I was really excited about the fact that Bill Wrigley Jr. was going to get involved with the ball club. We had meetings in August, calling all the field managers to Chicago. He was taking notes, evaluating players. I'm thinking, This is great. I want to be a part of this.

"We had the organization meeting in October 1981, and a couple weeks after that they announced they had sold the ball club to the Tribune Company. I thought, Holy cow.

"Dallas Green was put in charge, and he came in, and right out here at Hohocam Field he told me to find a job somewhere else. I went to the winter meetings to find a job. I was scheduled to be there three days. I went for a day and a half, put up with crap. They told me I was overqualified to do what they had to offer. I couldn't get a job, and I said, 'Forget this. I'll go dig ditches.'

"I decided I would start my fantasy camps, and I haven't regretted it since. There are times when I want to get back in the game. I think I have a lot to offer, but there is too much stinking politics. Getting a job depends on who you know or who you don't know. Ah, shucks, I don't have the personality for that crap. You go between the lines to play the game, the rules are set, you understand the rules, you play by the rules, and you bust your fanny, and after it's all over with, this team wins and that team loses. You don't have to do any finessing when you go between the lines, and you don't do any politicking or kissing fanny.

"I just didn't know how to do that stuff, and even to this day—I've been out of the game since '82—I still have a baseball-player mentality. I go between the lines, play the game, let's go strap it on, and then whoever has the best team, they win, and you pick up and come back tomorrow and strap it on again. But I'm honest, I don't know how to BS. I wish to Sam Hill I did. It bothers me. It's the only goal I have not fulfilled—to be a big-league manager. And at this day and time, I don't know, I still feel like I have a lot to offer a ball club. I think I'm a pretty good teacher, and as I tell a lot of guys, 'Hey, go check the freakin' record.'

"I wasn't a great hitter, but check out this thing." With his right pointer finger Randy Hundley, who during the interview at his fantasy camp was wearing his Cubs uniform, tapped repeatedly on the blue *C* in a circle over his heart.

64

Mad Dog and Bruce

Leo Durocher had been the glue holding the Cubs together. Soon after Whitey Lockman came in to replace him, the freefall began. With Lockman at the helm the Cubs got rid of anyone from the Leo Durocher era who hadn't already been traded. In 1974, Billy Williams was sent to Oakland for Manny Trillo, Bob Locker, and Darold Knowles. Ron Santo was traded across town to the White Sox for pitcher Steve Stone. Only shortstop Don Kessinger remained, and in '76 he would be dealt to the Cardinals.

After the Cubs sank to last place in midseason '74, Lockman, who had badly handled his players and destroyed the morale of the team, was fired as manager and promoted to the job as Cubs director of player development. Around the same time Phil Wrigley hired as his general manager Salty Saltwell, who previously had been in charge of the food concessions at Wrigley Field. To the end, with the exception of Durocher, who was the only manager to bring him a period of extended success, Phil Wrigley hired people he liked, not baseball executives who were talented. With Durocher gone, the old Cubs practice of trading future stars for damaged goods and lesser players resumed.

Replacing Lockman as manager was Jim Marshall, a mild-mannered man who said little and made no waves. The highlight of the Jim Marshall years was the emergence of two young stars, Bill Madlock, who won the National League batting titles in 1975 and 1976, and Bruce Sutter, who threw an unhittable pitch that headed for the strike zone and then dropped sharply as it reached the batter. The newfangled pitch, called a split-fingered fastball, was a sensation, and its master became one of the great relievers in the history of the game.

Darold Knowles, who had pitched for Gil Hodges and then Ted Williams with the Washington Senators and then helped the Oakland A's to three straight world championships, was one of the players sent to Chicago in exchange for Billy Williams.

Knowles, himself a fine relief pitcher, recalled his days with the Jim Marshall–led Cubs.

*   *   *

DAROLD KNOWLES: "The last year I was with the Oakland A's, which was 1974, we were flying to Los Angeles to play the Dodgers in the World Series. During the flight I went to Charlie Finley, the owner of the A's, and I said, 'Charlie, I know you're going to trade me when this is over.'

"He said, 'Why do you think that?'

"I said, 'Two reasons. [A's manager] Alvin [Dark] and I don't get along. You know that too. And if I'm here this year, I become a ten-and-five player, which means you can't trade me without my permission. So I can figure out that after the Series you're going to trade me.

"'All I'm doing is asking you, please, if you will, try to trade me to a contender.' After all, I had just played on three straight world champions.

"I said, 'I've enjoyed winning,' and I thanked him for having me.

"He said, 'Aaaah, you're not going anywhere. You're in our plans for next year. We've already sat down and talked about it.'

"It wasn't a week after the season was over, *not a week*, that Charlie traded me to the Cubs, who were in last place.

"I said, 'Jesus, Charlie, the Cubs?'

"He said, 'Great organization. You'll really enjoy it there.'

"That was the trade that sent Bob Locker, Manny Trillo, and me to Chicago for Billy Williams.

"Chicago turned out to be a great city. I love it. I hate New York, and I love Chicago. And I liked Wrigley Field. I like the old ballparks. You're always up. That's a good feeling. You go out there and play every day, and sometimes, I don't care what they say, sometimes you just feel down, but I never felt that way in Chicago. A great city. A great ballpark.

"When I arrived for spring training that first year in '75, one thing I noticed was that in comparison to the A's, the Cubs had a lack of talent. The talent was sparse. They had Bill Madlock, but I didn't see a lot of young guys in camp that you knew were knocking on the door. For years the Cubs didn't have the young kids coming up. Who knows why? They were in the minors somewhere. We did have Andre Thornton, but the Cubs traded him to Montreal for Larry Biittner and Steve Renko [in '76]. Andre didn't come into his own until he left the Cubs. He was a young kid with talent and pop.

"I can remember my first year with the Cubs, in May we traded Burt Hooton, a good young pitcher, for two kids, Eddie Solomon and Geoff Zahn.

"Hooton was what the Dodgers lacked. They had a good ball club, but they needed another pitcher, so they traded the young guys to get him, and they wound up winning the World Series [in 1981].

"The A's traded Rick Monday for one good pitcher, Kenny Holtzman, but they had somebody to fill Monday's role. Holtzman took them to the World Series. But you have to have the nucleus of that good ball club before you can afford to do that, and that's where the Cubs, and a lot of other organizations as well, have lacked.

"Why couldn't the Cubs do the same thing? Because they didn't have that nucleus, where one guy was going to get them over the hump.

"Solomon and Zahn never did pitch for the Cubs. Eddie was young, looked like he would become a good pitcher. I don't know what happened to him. Zahn didn't throw very hard. He was a junkballer with good control. If he was on, he could pitch, but if he was off, he didn't. [Zahn was 2–7 for Chicago in 1975, 0–1 for the Cubs in 1976, and then was traded to Minnesota, where he won 12, 14, 13, 14 the next four years. With California in '82 he won 18 games. Solomon was shipped out after '75, after appearing in six games, to St. Louis, which sent him to a bad Atlanta team. He was never more than a marginal player.]

"In '75, Jim Marshall was the manager, and we finished fifth. With what we had, Jim Marshall was all right. I always liked Jim. He's a good friend. You wouldn't say he was a great manager, but he wasn't a bad manager, either. We didn't have a great club, and he did as good as he could with it. He had a good coaching staff around him, but when you're lacking the horses, the manager gets the blame. We didn't have talent. We were run-of-the-mill. We were close to .500 [75–87].

"We *could* hit. I had come from Oakland, which had won three world championships in a row, and man-for-man the Cubs had a better-hitting ball club than Oakland. It didn't have a Reggie [Jackson], who could carry you, but I mean it was a phenomenal offensive club. We had Bill Madlock, Don Kessinger, Manny Trillo, a rookie, who hit well. At first base after Andre Thornton broke his wrist, Pete LaCock and George Mitterwald would platoon, but in the outfield we had Rick Monday, Jerry Morales, and Jose Cardenal. I mean, we scored runs, lots of runs. And of course, Wrigley Field had a lot to do with it too. 'Cause we also gave up a lot of runs.

"We didn't have enough pitching, but that's true of most teams. But the weakness in pitching is going to show up more in a place like Wrigley Field than it is in other places. You can make mistakes and get away with them in St. Louis. You can't make a mistake and get away with it in Chicago. That's the one thing that really hurts you. You can throw a fly ball, and if the wind is blowing out, it can go out of Wrigley Field, and does, a lot. The park is famous for that.

"It seemed like other ball clubs would come in there, and the hitters couldn't wait to get up. The first thing they look for is that flag in center field. I played there two years, and even playing against the Cubs, the first thing you did when you got to that ballpark was look at that flag. First thing.

"My second year I lived over on Lake Shore Drive. I used to walk to the ballpark every day. A lot of us did, half the club. The first thing we did was look at that flag. Every day. And not just me. Everybody.

"We had a young staff. Rick Reuschel was just coming into his own, Ray Burris too. Billy Bonham, Steve Stone. Turned out to be a good bunch. Reuschel had the most durability. Billy Bonham probably had the best stuff. Burris was a battler. He didn't have great stuff. Steve Stone at that time was so-so. He was coming up, and he went on to win the Cy Young Award one year with Baltimore [1980].

"I remember sitting in a bar one night talking to Stony about how to pitch. I was one of the older guys. He was very stubborn. I used to try to tell him to throw a backdoor slider. He didn't think it was a good idea. Why not? He was very stubborn. It eventually turned out to be one of his better pitches. It's only a good pitch if you have good control. That was my argument. I said, 'You have good enough control. You can do that.'

"That year or the next year Stony called his own pitches during the game. He went all year. I remember he was standing on the mound, and if he put his arm in one position, it was a fastball, and if he put it in front of his leg, it was another pitch. Nobody ever caught it. He called his own game all year.

"I thought, Goddamn, somebody has got to figure this out. 'Cause it was so obvious. When you knew it, it was obvious. You know how hitters study pitchers, but nobody ever figured it out.

"Stony went on to become a good pitcher. He had good control, good stuff. He had a bad arm, though, and it finally broke down.

"Ray Burris was a quiet guy, but a nice guy. A good guy. Loved to laugh. I like guys who like to laugh and have fun. He was a practical-joke guy.

"I was the anchor of the bullpen, and so you knew we were in trouble. I was going downhill fast, trying to hang on. And I didn't have a good year in '75. I had 15 saves that year. I didn't pitch well. The worst year I ever had. I had an ERA of 5.83. One goal I had in my career was to have a lifetime ERA under 3.00, and if it hadn't been for that year, I think I would have done it. [He finished his career with a 3.27 ERA.]

"I couldn't blame the park. I was a ground-ball pitcher. I gave up a few home runs, but not more than anywhere else. I was the reason. That town ate me up. I had a lot of fun. But you can't do that.

"I was married. My wife came up there, and she spent the summer. But I was in a habit of staying up late. I didn't go to bed until one or two in the morning. I'd go home, and my wife and I would sit up and watch TV and talk and have a cocktail. And then I would have to get up every morning and go to that ballpark. I was, and always have been, one of the first to go to that ballpark, and I was there at seven-thirty every morning and easily the first guy in the clubhouse. That part was a habit.

"I remember Don Kessinger telling me that first year in spring training, he said, 'In August and September, you're going to be more tired than you've ever been in your life.' I said, 'That's a cop-out.' And to this day, I think it is. But mentally, you're thinking, Man, that sun beats on me every day. And Don was right. Playing all day games *does* wear on you. But the main reason I didn't do well was because I didn't get my sleep. I didn't adjust to the lifestyle I needed to in Chicago for all the day games.

"The next year I set a curfew on myself. I was in bed every night by at least twelve o'clock. I came back and had a good year. My ERA was 2.88. So I figured that part of it out. 'Cause I still had enough pride and desire, and I wasn't going to let that happen to me again.

"During those years there were a couple of great-hitting clubs in the league, powerhouses: Pittsburgh, who had Willie Stargell, Dave Parker, Al Oliver, and Richie Zisk; and Cincinnati, the Big Red Machine.

"Leading off for the Reds was Pete Rose. I always liked Pete. I played against him in the minor leagues, and you could tell he was going to be a good player, and then he became one. He came up as a second baseman, never was a good defensive player, but he was better than what people gave him credit for. He made up for it in—pardon the expression—hustle.

"I remember whenever I faced him, it seemed like he always got a hit when he needed it. When you needed to get him out, it seemed like you never could. If it didn't mean anything, you'd get him out. He'd come up in a situation where they really needed a runner, I'll be a son of a buck, that guy would wind up on base. He was that type player. He got some hits off me. I got him out a few times.

"I recall Rick Reuschel had a streak when he was pitching good for the Cubs. It seemed that every game he'd hit somebody. He would *drill* somebody. Rick was not afraid to throw inside. He was a big guy.

"This one night he had warmed up in Cincinnati. He was sitting on the bench. I walked by and I said, 'Who you going to hit tonight, big boy?' He said, 'Who's leading off?' I said, 'Rose.' He said, 'He's good enough.' And the first pitch, he drilled him right in the back. I'll never forget it. And Pete was mad. Reuschel didn't care.

"Joe Morgan was a great hitter with a great eye. He would pride himself on knowing where the strike zone was, like Ted Williams used to do. I struck him out one night in Cincinnati on a borderline pitch. Borderline. It could have gone either way. But I wouldn't sit here today and swear it was a strike. It was so close, you can't take it. So they rung him up, and the next day he came to me and wanted to know where that pitch was. Of course, I said, 'It was right there. On the black.' I wanted him to swing at it the next time. He argued with me for ten minutes. 'That ball was a half inch outside.'

"I said, 'Your eyes are so goddamn good that you can see a half inch?' He said, 'Yesss. That ball was outside.' I said, 'Well, I thought it was right there.' I don't know whether it was or not. But Joe was tough.

"The third batter in the Reds lineup was Ken Griffey. I got Griffey out pretty good. He was left-handed. I got Griffey out better than I did Morgan. What kept me around as long as I did was that I could get left-handed hitters out. Morgan gave me trouble, but not a lot. Griffey I got out. But you get one guy out, and the next guy is just as good. You had [Johnny] Bench, and then [Tony] Perez.

"John Bench hit cleanup. He was as dangerous as anybody I ever faced. He was so strong. He was not that *good* a hitter, compared to those other guys, but in that lineup you didn't dare walk the guy—you didn't dare walk anybody. You couldn't pitch around anybody, 'cause they always had somebody better coming up. Bench was a great mistake hitter. On 2–0, 3–1, he was tough. You better put it where you want it or you were in trouble. And what power he had. But he would swing and miss a lot of times and strike out. He was a dead fastball hitter. If you got in a 2–0, 3–1 situation with someone on, you were in trouble. He wasn't a great hitter, but he was a dangerous, strong hitter. He was very durable, played every day, a hell of a catcher, a Hall of Famer.

"Tony Perez was next. He got lost on that team. Doggie was like Bench. He'd strike out a hundred times a year, but he was a great clutch hitter. He drove in so many runs. You have to realize they did that because they always had men on base on that club. But you still got to knock them in. He did get lost a little bit. He was just a class act. You never got mad at Dog. Bench you might get mad at. But Doggie, 'Ah, he got his hit.' Nobody showed you up on that club. The great players don't show you up. And he was definitely a great player. He ought to be in the Hall of Fame. Might be, eventually.

"Then there was George Foster. Foster hit a home run off me one day in Cincinnati. This was how strong he was. I remember I threw him a change-up. He was a great off-speed hitter. I threw a change-up, which obviously was a mistake. It was low and away, and he was out front, and he hit a fly ball to center field, and I went,

'Ooh, thanks. I got away with it.' The ball hit off the facade in straight center field. I mean, it just did not come down. I could not believe how far that ball went. One year he hit 52 home runs.

"The only other ball hit that far off me Mickey Mantle hit. His 508th. I was with Gil Hodges, playing for Washington in '67. I had started a game in Baltimore and got beat. I came in in relief the next day in Baltimore and got beat. And then we went to New York. We were in the bottom of the eighth inning, and he brings me in. I got the first two batters out, and Mantle pinch-hit for the pitcher. Mickey had hobbled up there on that bad leg. He was about done then.

"I remember to this day I said to myself, 'This guy is not going to beat me. I don't care if I walk him.' They always drill it in your mind, 'Don't let the big boys beat you.' I threw him a ball two feet outside and ankle high, and he went, 'Ugh,' slapped at it, and I said to myself, 'Oh, thanks. Got him out.' And the crowd kept roaring. And I got to looking at the ball, and it just kept going. And going. And going.

"It went into the right-center-field bleachers. How in the hell? And I ended up losing that game, lost three games in four days.

"A few years later Mickey and I went duck hunting together. I told him, 'You hit your 508th off me.'

"He said, 'I was probably drunk.'

"I'll always remember that home run and the one Foster hit off me—the strength those guys had.

"Bob Verdi, a writer in Chicago, a beat writer then, followed the club, and I remember his opening paragraph one day. We played Cincinnati, and they killed us. And his opening paragraph was, 'Yesterday at Wrigley Field the Big Red Machine ran over the Little Blue Bicycle.' You gotta laugh. He's a witty writer anyway, and I always liked to read his stuff.

"One day I came in to pitch late in the game. I started the inning. I got two out, and a couple guys were on, and [Reds pitcher] Pedro Borbon was the hitter. He couldn't hit, but Pedro hit it on the handle and he hit a little flare. The next thing I knew, I had given up nine runs!

"After giving up six runs, I had the bases loaded and two out. Jim Marshall came to the mound. It had been base hit after base hit. They weren't all hitting them hard, but that lineup. . . .

"Marshall said, 'I better get you out of here.' I said, 'Hell no, it's a goddamn challenge now. The game is over. Leave me in here. Rather me than one of them kids.' We had young pitchers down there in the bullpen. I had already got the shit kicked out of me.

"He didn't even get in the dugout when the next batter hit a double to clear the bases.

"When I finally got out of the inning, I had bases loaded again, and someone caught one in the vines.

"The next day, I was out at the park shagging flies in the outfield. The gates weren't even open yet. There was a little old lady sitting up there. I heard, 'You gotta lot of nerve.' I didn't see her. She repeated it. 'You gotta lot of nerve.'

"I said, 'Are you talking to me, lady?'

"She said, 'You gotta lot of nerve just showing up here today!' And she wasn't being nice. She was mad.

"As a rule the Cubs fans were very supportive. They are *great* fans in Chicago. They will boo you when you do bad, but they are not like Philly fans. Philly fans have the reputation of waiting for you to do something wrong so they can jump on you. In Chicago they *want* you to win. They *root* for you, and if you're bad, they'll boo you, but they will turn right around and cheer you. Chicago fans will cheer the opposing team if they do something good, and that's great, they are baseball people.

"During the time I was with the Cubs, Bill Madlock was a highlight. And Bruce Sutter was a highlight.

"Madlock—we called him Mad Dog—won the batting championship in '75 and '76. He played the game the way it was supposed to be played. Obviously, he could hit. He was a better defensive player than people gave him credit for. He didn't have the greatest range, but he had decent hands, and his arm was OK. He played a long time [1973–87], and did a great job with the bat.

"They called him Mad Dog, which came more from Mad-lock than because of his volatile nature, though he *was* a volatile player. Why he was that way, I don't know. He was angry, always had a chip on his shoulder. He could play. He liked to laugh, was a fun-loving guy too, but when he got on the field—one of the things I really remember about him that you don't see too much anymore, he slid into bases as hard as anybody I've ever seen. He could run. This guy could run. On double play balls, he was always on top of that fielder, and he always took him out. You don't see that. He took them out clean, but he took them out hard. He always was right on top of them because he could run.

"And Mad Dog would charge the mound in a minute. And did a couple times. That caused some excitement. I miss that. They are not allowed to do that in the

Bill Madlock

minor leagues anymore. Now you can't charge the mound. You can't even leave the bench or you get a hundred-dollar fine. No bench clearing anymore. And I miss it. It takes away that element. But the hitter can't charge the pitcher anymore either. He's automatically fined, and in the minors these kids don't have any money.

"Anyway, Madlock was a great player, a good, young kid, but really developing as a hitter. He had the shortest successful stroke I've ever seen. It's something hard to teach.

"He didn't have the best body. We teased him. That's the nature of the game. They used to call him Buddha Body. He was a little squatty guy. Some guys love the game more than others, and Bill really loved the game. Which I liked him for, because I loved it too. Some are just playing to play. They're trying to make some money. Some of us played it because we loved it, along with trying to make a living. Bill was one.

"Bill made '76 unique because he went to the last day of the season and went 4 for 4 to overtake Ken Griffey and win the batting title.

"We were rooting for him. Everybody knew he could hit. They had it in the newspaper that if Griffey didn't play—and he didn't, because the game didn't mean anything to Cincinnati—Bill had to go 3 for 4 to overtake him. Well, 3 for 4 is a good day.

"We were playing Montreal, and the first time up, Bill got a hit. The second time up, Bill got a hit. And Cincinnati was listening too. The third time up Bill got a hit, and now Griffey has to hit. So they pinch-hit him, and he didn't get a hit.

"After Bill went 4 for 4, it didn't matter what Griffey did. Madlock had it won. It was very exciting. We knew what he needed to do while it was happening, and he did it.

"We were happy for him because it was a long year, and he had done extremely well. He hit .339, and everyone knew he was going to be around for a while as a hitter.

"The other player who sticks out on my mind was Bruce Sutter. He was in spring training with us in '76. He had pitched in Double A the year before.

"I was the oldest guy on the club, after they traded Don Kessinger. The last week of spring training Jim Marshall came up to me in the outfield and he said, 'What do you think about our staff?'

"I said, 'You going to take that kid?' I pointed to Sutter. He said, 'No. He needs more seasoning.' I said, 'He'll be here in a month.' He said, 'Nah.' I said, 'You'll see.'

"Well, he was back in about three weeks. And when he came up, Jim Marshall would pitch me against the lefties and him against the righties. That was all right.

"And I remember one night in Cincinnati, late in the game, he's got us both warming up. Something happened, boom, a couple hits, and Joe Morgan was the hitter. Marshall went out to the mound. Morgan was left-handed. I was ready.

"Jim signaled, 'Give me Sutter.' And I remember standing there thinking, It's time. Because Jim Marshall had figured out that it didn't matter whether you hit left-hander or right-hander, Bruce Sutter would get you out.

"I thought, Marshall has figured this out, and he's right. I had to give Jim credit, and that started Bruce Sutter. He came on, and there was no contest. What a few great years he had.

"Bruce was one of the nicest guys I've ever met in the game. Most thoughtful. He doesn't even know how to spell *ego*. He just wanted to pitch, wanted to win, and if he didn't do the job he was the most apologetic guy you ever saw, but he usually did, so he didn't have to apologize very much.

"He did what he had to do, gave credit where credit was due. He credited Fred Martin with teaching him the splitter. Anybody wanted to know how to throw it, he'd show you. A lot of guys don't want to do that if they have a specialty pitch.

"Bruce had freak hands, huge hands and long fingers, which was one of the keys to why he had such a good splitter. I can't throw it. I've tried to teach it to a few guys, even though I don't like to teach it too much because of the arm problems that go with it. I only teach it to guys with big hands. And it's helped a few. Most guys throw it like a change-up. Bruce threw it *hard*. He didn't have a great arm, threw it in the mid-80s, but I never saw so many guys swing at balls that wound up in the dirt. It always looked so good.

"Guys *hated* to hit off him. He was very, very successful. He had nerve. He knew he had that great pitch.

"Bruce came up in '76, and he was outstanding until they traded him to the Cardinals in '80 [for Leon Durham, Ken Reitz, and Ty Waller], and he was great over there.

"Understand, if you don't win with your star, then you have to make changes. Bruce was a star, but with the Cubs they didn't get to him enough. They weren't going to win with just Bruce Sutter. They got two or three players they thought might put them over the hump. If you're losing, you get rid of him. Get somebody else.

"The other incident I remember occurred in April of 1976 at Dodger Stadium. Two young guys jumped on the field, and one guy was running around, and the other guy was trying to light this big American flag. At first I didn't know what those guys were doing. But everyone was in shock for a moment when they noticed, 'What the hell? He's going to burn the flag.'

"The guy was in left center, and Rick Monday was in center, and Rick went over, grabbed the flag, and took it into the dugout. The cops came out and grabbed the guy.

"That put Rick on the map. At Oakland, Rick had played in the shadow of Reggie and Sal Bando. He was a young player. In Chicago, you had Madlock, Kessinger. Rick got some recognition, but we were losing. You don't get much recognition when you lose. And he wasn't putting up great numbers. He didn't hit a lot of home runs. He didn't steal a lot of bases. He just played hard, did a good job. He wasn't great, but he was good.

"Rick was your all-American-boy type. He was rather quiet, your astute-acting guy. He was always perfectly groomed, his hair was always right. Not to a fault. Clean cut, good looking. He just went about his job. He would talk. He always had a great voice. Now he does radio and TV. We used to laugh at him because he'd talk in a normal voice, and somebody would put that camera in front of him, and his voice would go down about nine octaves. 'Cause he had visions then of someday being in radio and TV. He didn't have that outgoing, pat-himself-on-the-back attitude like Reggie.

"Rick got more recognition out of the flag incident than he got as a player. He was getting letters from all over the country all the time, from VFWs and American Legions, organizations. Every place we'd go somebody would honor him with a plaque. He let us read some of the letters, people thanking him.

"Anyone who would have done that would have gotten the same recognition. It just happened to be him.

"Bob Kennedy came in to run the Cubs in the winter of 1976. I had come off a good year [58 appearances, 5 wins, 9 saves, 2.88 ERA]. I lived in Kansas City at the time, and the Cubs called me, asked me to fly in and talk contract. I said, 'Fine.' So they flew me in, put me up, and I went in and talked to Kennedy, and he offered me the same $65,000 I had made the year before. I said, 'You flew me all the way up here to offer me the same money? No. I had a good year.'

"He said, 'Then I'll trade you, because I can't give you any more money.' Just like that, I said, 'All right.'

"He said, 'Who do you want to go to?'

"I said, 'Let me tell you where I don't want to go.' I didn't want to go to Canada, didn't want to go to Cleveland.

"He said, 'Fine. I'll try as hard as I can to trade you to one of these other clubs.'

"He called me in a week, and he said he could trade me to two or three places, and he told me, and I said, 'That's fine. You do what you can. Make the best deal you can make.'

"But at least he was honest with me.

"He didn't think I fit into his plans. Even if I had accepted his offer, he still might have traded me. He knew I wasn't going to settle for that. He was rebuilding and re-shaping. Of course, they had Bruce Sutter. They didn't really need me.

"And he traded me down to Texas, and I signed a two-year deal at $90,000 a year. Back then, five or ten thousand dollars was a pretty good raise, so I got what I thought was a hell of a deal, especially considering that the Cubs weren't going to give me anything."

65

The Death of the Reserve Clause and PK Wrigley

The death of baseball's reserve clause and that of Philip Knight Wrigley occurred around the same time. The coincidence was more than symbolic. The reserve clause had been the brainchild of Albert Spalding, who had founded the National League and owned the Chicago franchise more than a hundred years earlier. Because of this clause, which provided that at the end of a season a player's contract would auto-matically be renewed, owners did not have to pay their players a fair wage. Because of it, players were indentured servants—famous but still bound—with most made to feel grateful they were making the money the owners deigned to pay them. The better players, of course, had more leverage than the lesser ones, but under the system even the greatest player had no weapon in his salary struggle other than a hollow threat not to play unless he got what he felt he deserved.

Glenn Beckert, who for nine years starred at second base for the Cubs, was typical. He was treated paternally and was offered crumbs for raises.

GLENN BECKERT: "Back then, without free agency, if you got a $4,000 raise, you really robbed the bank. And if you sent your contract back without signing it, you might get a letter saying, 'Fine. We got two other guys who are ready to break in.'

"As players we didn't have anything to stand on. Fortunately, as far as treating the players, Mr. Wrigley was very good to us. If you had a problem, you'd go to him and say, 'I need to rent an apartment, and I'm a little short,' and it would just be taken care of. He took care of a lot of problems on the Q.T. with players. At that time a lot of other owners would say, 'Fuck you, you signed it.'

"As far as negotiating our contracts, it was a one-way street. The problem was, we were ballplayers. Even though several of us went to college, our courses were not in labor management, and a guy like John Holland was a professional in that area. He'd say, 'Here's the figure.'

"He would write a figure down, and he knew what he was going to sign you for. He would always win.

"John would call you. 'Why don't you come in and straighten out next year's contract?' He would always like to get you in there around Christmas. Everybody was in a good spirit. You wanted to get signed. So you would go in, drive to Wrigley Field.

"This one time I had had a good year. I was making $33,500, and the new contract was for $35,000. I walked into his office. He gave you, 'How's the family? The folks in Pittsburgh? . . .' You know the bullshit.

"Then he said, 'Let's be fair.'

"I said, 'John, there is no way I'm going to play for that contract that you sent me.'

"He said, 'What do you really think you deserve?' I said, 'John, $37,500 is a fair figure.'

"He calls his secretary out, Linda Dillman. He said, 'Linda, write out a contract for Glenn for $37,500, and bring me a check for $1,500.' So he handed me the check for $1,500.

He said, 'We're going to pay you $1,500 to get you through Christmas. Have a nice holiday.'

"So I had my contract for $37,500, but when I left, now I was pissed off. I was thinking, 'If I knew it would be that easy, I should have gone for $45,000.'

"Every year I would tell Mr. Holland the salary I wanted, and if it was more than he wanted to pay me, he would say, 'I talked to Mr. Wrigley, and Mr. Wrigley and I have gone over our budget, and Mr. Wrigley says we absolutely cannot go any higher with your contract. If you don't believe me, here's the phone. Call Mr. Wrigley.'

"Now, Mr. Wrigley *always* answered his own phone calls. I said, 'No, John, I don't want to call Mr. Wrigley.'

"Finally, this one year I called his bluff. I said, 'Give me the phone. I want to talk to Mr. Wrigley.'

"John said, 'Let's wait a minute. Let's talk some more.' I said no.

"Four years I had been doing this. I had probably left about twenty grand in pay raises out on the board. But we weren't professional enough to negotiate for ourselves. We weren't astute as to market value. We had no way of knowing.

"Agents now are paid professionals to do a job they are trained and educated to do. Our job was playing baseball."

It was a system that perfectly fitted the needs of an owner like Phil Wrigley. So long as he kept salaries low, attendance would cover expenses. For owners who didn't care about building winning teams, the reserve clause was a necessity.

And then, one month after the World Series of 1975, the world of Phil Wrigley, and the other baseball owners, was tumbled topsy-turvy. Two pitchers, Andy Messersmith and Dave McNally, decided to play the 1975 season without a contract. When the season was over they argued that because they were not playing under a binding contract they were free agents. They took their grievance to arbitrator Peter Seitz, as provided in the 1970 Basic Agreement with the players.

The owners were confident. Baseball had weathered challenges to the reserve clause in the past and won.

Few contemplated what would happen next. Arbitrator Seitz declared that the end of a contract meant just that, the *end* of the contract. Now for the owners it was panic time, as they had to negotiate de novo with Marvin Miller, the brilliant head of the players union.

Before the spring training of '76 could begin, the owners locked out the players. Who knows what would have happened had Commissioner Bowie Kuhn not stepped in and ordered the camps to open? Because of Kuhn's action, his most important decision during his reign as commissioner, the owners were deprived of their most powerful bargaining chip: The players could eat while Miller and the owners hammered out a new Basic Agreement.

Miller, in a stroke of genius, chose not to insist that every player be freed immediately. To do that, he knew, would not have raised salaries dramatically because so much talent would have been available for the choosing.

Instead, he negotiated a new players agreement that provided for only a handful of quality players to be freed: Any player with six years of major league experience could opt for free agency and put himself on the open market.

The money the players began making was staggering.

After the arbitrator ruled that Andy Messersmith was a free agent, the Dodgers pitcher, who had been making $100,000, signed a four-year deal with the New York Yankees for $1.5 million. The quixotic Messersmith then decided he didn't want to go to New York, and his contract was nullified by Commissioner Bowie Kuhn. The pitcher then signed a similar agreement with the Atlanta Braves.

Reggie Jackson, one of the premier hitters in the game, had hit 36 homers in 1975. He had helped A's owner Charlie Finley's team win five divisional championships, three pennants, and two world championships.

Finley offered him a $140,000 contract for the 1976 season, and when Reggie didn't accept it, the quarrelsome A's owner threatened to cut his salary 20 percent to $112,000, then traded him to Baltimore.

At the end of the '76 season Reggie was a free agent. Owners rushed at Reggie with bags of money. The greatest players in the game, Joe DiMaggio, Ted Williams, Mickey Mantle, and Willie Mays, had led their peers with salaries of around $125,000 a year.

Ray Kroc in San Diego was offering Reggie five years for $3.4 million. Charles Bronfman in Montreal was offering a contract that amounted to as much as $5 million. The Orioles offered several million. Walter O'Malley was offering the big bucks too.

In the end Jackson signed a five-year contract with the New York Yankees for $2.96 million. Plus a Rolls-Royce. Suddenly those former stars were looking like paupers in comparison.

For men like PK Wrigley and Calvin Griffith of the Minnesota Twins, the days of the gravy train were over. Like the reserve clause, Calvin and PK had become relics of the past.

Two of the Cubs players who had played six years and were opting for free agency were Rick Monday and Bill Madlock. Monday in '76 had hit 32 home runs and scored 107 runs. He was a productive member of the team. He asked for a salary just over $100,000 for 1977.

Wrigley responded by saying, "No player is worth more than $100,000 a year."

On January 11, 1977, Phil Wrigley traded Rick Monday to the Los Angeles Dodgers for Bill Buckner and Ivan DeJesus.

At the same time the Cubs' Bill Madlock, the league's batting champion the past two seasons, was demanding a five-year contract at $200,000 a year. Wrigley's answer was to get rid of him, and on February 11, he traded Madlock to the San Francisco Giants for outfielder Bobby Murcer, the former Yankees star, and third baseman Steve Ontiveros.

The era of free agency had arrived. Phil Wrigley, who would not put up lights, also would not put up cash for his players.

Said Wrigley, who in his dotage could not comprehend the changes that were coming, "I have outlived my usefulness. Everything has changed."

On April 12, 1977, Philip K. Wrigley died. He was eighty-two years old. And with his death, the era of player servitude begun by Albert Spalding back in 1872 died as well. The time when star players would have to beg for a $4,000 raise was over.

66

Big $$$, Low Morale

The player who would come to embody the difference between the olden days of baseball (before the Seitz decision in 1975) and the new was the Cubs' sensational relief pitcher, Bruce Sutter. Rarely had baseball seen a more dominating pitcher.

In the low minor leagues Sutter had learned from roving pitching instructor Fred Martin a newfangled pitch called the split-fingered fastball. The ball would come up to the plate like a fastball, and then as the batter was swinging, suddenly it would drop six inches. In 1977, Sutter had a 1.35 earned run average. He was so effective that by himself he elevated a mediocre team to a pennant contender.

Sutter was a sensation, but because of the new pay system, his salary also bordered on the sensational. His first season he earned $19,000. After he was named Cy Young Award winner in 1979, he took the Cubs to arbitration, and he was awarded a pasha's salary of $700,000 for the year.

Having to pay such a grand salary fell to Phil Wrigley's son, William, who inherited the team. William, who evinced little love for the game, quickly saw that he would not have the finances necessary to continue running the Cubs.

The problem for Bill Wrigley was not just that salaries were escalating at an alarming rate. His major problem was that his father, Phil, had screwed up when in his will he had left half of his estate to his wife, Helen, who unfortunately had died before he did. As a result, the estate was taxed twice, first when she died, and again with PK Wrigley's death, to the tune of $50 million.

William thus was faced with the choice of having to sell a large block of Wrigley Co. stock—or the Chicago Cubs. And selling a large block of the Wrigley Co. was very risky. A company called American Home Products owned 9.6 percent of Wrigley Co. stock. If PK Wrigley's 20 percent were to go on the block, and if American Home Products were to snap it up, the Wrigleys risked losing control of the company.

Bill Wrigley had little choice. Until he could find a buyer for the Cubs, life for the Cubs would be a struggle. The Cubs' star pitcher, Bruce Sutter, was one who experienced the Cubs' fall in those few short years under Wrigley *fils*. With the Cubs, Sutter, the master of the split-fingered fastball, saved 31 games in 1977, 27 in '78, 37 in '79, and 28 in '80.

The shame for Cubs fans was that Sutter, who was one of the greatest relievers in the history of the game, had some of his best years for the St. Louis Cardinals and the Atlanta Braves. In 1982 he led St. Louis to the world championship, and with the Cards in 1984 he saved 45 games—tying Dan Quisenberry's all-time single-season record for saves, set in '83 with the Royals. At the end of the season the Atlanta Braves reportedly paid him $10 million for six years.

BRUCE SUTTER: "I graduated from high school in June 1970 and was drafted in the tenth round by the Washington Senators. I chose not to sign with them.

"At that time it was, 'Go to college, go to college, go to college.' I hadn't liked high school. I went to Old Dominion University for about six weeks, and I decided I didn't want school, either. Looking back, I probably should have signed with the Senators.

"In the summer of 1971 I was pitching for a semipro team in Lancaster, Pennsylvania. It was mostly made up of guys who had graduated from high school, a lot of college players. That's when Cubs scout Ralph DiLullo came to some games, and he offered me a contract. I signed for $500. He was the only scout interested in me. I knew nothing about the Cubs organization.

"I reported in '72. I was with Bradenton. At the time we were a co-op team with the Red Sox, half Cubs and half Red Sox. I was a reliever. That's a little bit of the politics of the game. The higher draft picks are thought to be better pitchers, so they get to start. The lower draft picks come in as relief pitchers. I was just happy to have a chance. As long as I could remember, I wanted to be a major league ballplayer, and this was my chance. So it didn't bother me. But I didn't pitch all that much. I hurt my elbow pretty quick. I popped something in my elbow, and I rested for a while, and I came back and tried to pitch and went through that whole season unable to do a lot of things.

"I was real young. I graduated from high school, had just turned seventeen, so even when I signed with the Cubs, I was just eighteen. Usually when they sign a kid out of high school, they stick with him for three or four years. A lot of it is trying to forecast what you're going to do, and there is no way of knowing.

"That winter I came home, and I rested my elbow until January and started throwing again. I had a pinched nerve, and it was still bothering me, so I had an elbow operation in the winter, and I didn't tell anybody. I didn't even tell the Cubs. I went to a doctor back in Lancaster, Pennsylvania, and had it done, came to spring training and didn't say a word.

"I was pitching and pitching, and finally this one day I had short sleeves on, and the pitching coach noticed the big scar on my elbow. He asked me about it, and so I told him what I did, and evidently he went to the Cubs higher-ups and told them, 'Let's give this kid a little bit more chance.'

"They liked the way I went about getting ready for the game, being tough and wanting to play and not complaining, just doing the work and taking whatever comes your way and trying to work harder at it. Plus they didn't have a whole lot of money invested in me. So what would it hurt to keep me on for another year, and as it turned out, that's when I started to turn my career around.

"I was at Quincy, Illinois, when I met Fred Martin, the roving pitching coach for the Cubs.

"Today a lot of clubs have a manager and a pitching coach at every level, and they have some rovers who go around. When I was playing, we had one pitching coach for the entire minor leagues! We'd see him five days—he'd try to see all the starting pitchers once and see the relievers pitch and go on to the next team, and we might not see him for another three weeks.

"After I had my elbow operation, I was reluctant to throw the slider and try to snap off curve balls, so he said, 'Why don't you try this,' meaning the split-fingered fastball. And the rest speaks for itself. I learned it real quick.

"It was Fred Martin who made the pitch popular. It wasn't Roger Craig. It was all Fred. Fred and I showed Roger Craig how to throw it. I know Roger likes to think he did it. But it was Fred.

"Right off the bat I could make it break. I had no problems with it. I mean, it bounced half a foot in front of the plate, and the batter was still swinging at it. And all of a sudden I started pitching more. That was the biggest difference that I noticed. I only used it the last two months of that season.

"The next year I went to Key West, Florida, which was A ball, and I started right out throwing real good with the split finger. I had it going right off the bat. And fielding a bunt, I tore up my knee, so I had to miss about six weeks in the middle of that season, because I went home for a knee operation. But then I came back and picked right up.

"After that season I went to the Instructional League. It was me and a left-handed pitcher by the name of Buddy Schultz. Relief pitchers were starting to become prominent in the big leagues, and they were trying to groom us to see if we could pitch day after day. We pitched in thirty games apiece out of fifty, just an inning at a time. They wanted to see if we could bounce back.

"So I got invited to the major league spring training in '75. I didn't get to pitch much in A games. I pitched a little bit in B games, and they sent me down to Double A Midland, and I had a real good year. We won the Texas League that year.

"We played Shreveport, Louisiana, for the championship. We were at two games apiece, and it started raining, and it rained for three or four days. There were kids on each team who had been called to the big leagues, and they said, 'The big-league teams want these kids to come up. We're just sitting here watching it rain. We'll have co-winners.'

"So they made us co-winners.

"I didn't get called up. I thought I would. I didn't. That's the way it goes.

"At the end of the season, the arbitrator, Peter Seitz, declared the reserve clause illegal. I saw it, but I wasn't really that concerned about it. It was one of those things that was part of the big leagues, and I wasn't in the big leagues. It didn't affect us one way or the other in the minor leagues.

"I went to spring training in '76, and we had the lockout that year. What most major league teams did was to send their younger pitchers down to keep pitching, and so I got sent to Wichita, Kansas, and I think I only pitched ten or twelve innings down there, and on May 8, when the lockout ended, I got called right up to the big leagues.

"Jim Marshall was the manager. When you got called up from the minor leagues, he liked to get you in a game as soon as he could, just to get it over with, get rid of the butterflies, get those feelings out of the way.

"I got there in the morning, and I pitched that afternoon against Cincinnati. They were beating us pretty bad, and most of the big boys were out by the time I got in. I pitched to Dave Concepcion and Joel Youngblood and Doug Flynn and some of the guys on the team who weren't necessarily the starters. I got 'em out. I gave up a walk and a base hit, but I got 'em out.

"Darold Knowles and Mike Garman were the relief pitchers for the Cubs then. I was pitching pretty good, and one of the turning points was one game against the Cincinnati Reds. Garman was struggling a little bit, and Knowlzie was struggling, and I had been pitching pretty good in the middle.

"Knowlzie and I were both warming up to come in the game, we were winning, and Joe Morgan was coming in to hit. Morgan bats lefty, Darold is a lefty, and I'm a righty.

"Even so, Marshall went out and brought me in to face the left-hander, and I got him out, got a save, and from then I became the closer, and Knowlzie and Garman were the middle guys. That happened my first year.

"At the end of the year the Cubs traded Bill Madlock, Rick Monday. At the time I didn't think it was all money oriented. I was making $19,000, which was more money than I ever made. I was pretty naive about all that. Monday wanted $100,000, and to me then, I wasn't very familiar with anything, and when you're talking about a hundred thousand dollars, I mean, you're talking like ten million dollars to me. And when Phil Wrigley died, sure, you feel grief, but as far as it making any difference, no.

"In 1977 the Cubs fired Marshall and hired Herman Franks. They did that because we didn't win. It's easier to make a change with the manager, to appease the people, than it is to fire twenty-five ballplayers.

"In 1977 I had 31 saves, and I missed six weeks of the season. I tore muscles off my rib cage. You know, I pitched an awful lot. I had 25 saves in seventy-five innings at the All-Star break. We didn't have the middle men then. I was pitching two and three innings at a time. If we had the lead after the sixth, I was the pitcher. I got selected to the All-Star Game, but I couldn't go. I hurt my arm a day or two before the game, and then I really didn't pitch again until September. I missed half of July and all of August. I couldn't do anything for a while, and then I came back in September and pitched pretty well. I ended up with a 1.35 ERA. I think if I had stayed healthy that year, it would have been one of my best years ever.

"And we were in first place until I got hurt. The fans were really great. Cubs fans are exceptional, whether you're in first place or last place. They are one hundred percent Cubs fans. They are the most loyal fans in the United States. When we went on road trips, there would always be a bunch of Cubs fans there. They love their ball team. You know how Chicago is. You love the Cubs or you love the White Sox. You don't like them both. It's one team or the other. And you're a diehard for that one team. It's something special. I enjoyed Chicago a lot.

"The workhorse on the team was Rick Reuschel. Rick is a good friend of mine. Rick helped me a lot coming up. He's just so even-keeled. Rick was the same whether he won the game or if he got knocked out in the first inning. He was steady. He worked at his game all the time, worked and worked, and when the games came, he did the same thing.

"Rick was the enforcer of the team. If the other team was mouthing off or if they were hitting some of our players, Rick was the one who took care of that. And he made no bones about it. I remember Pete Rose said something negative about our pitching staff one time, and Rick was pitching the next day. The first pitch of the game, Rick buried one right in his ribs. I mean, that was the old school. Pete just went down to first base. He had read the paper, and he probably figured it was coming anyhow.

"The next year, 1978, we had a good team. We had Bobby Murcer and Dave Kingman. I liked Dave. I did. He wasn't the most graceful outfielder, but Dave gave you what he had. He'd run through a wall to try to catch the ball. He came to play every day. I don't remember him ever saying he was hurt, that kind of stuff, to sit out. He just played, and he hit a lot of long home runs. He had a big swing, and he'd strike out a bunch too. If you wanted those three-run homers, you had to live with those strikeouts, and that's the way it goes.

"I found that sometimes Dave was a little bit moody. Some days he'd want to joke around, and some days he'd sit quietly in his locker, for whatever reason. That was the way Dave was, and it was all right.

"Kingman hit them as high as he did far. He didn't watch his home runs in batting practice. A lot of times he'd hit them, and with the wind in Wrigley Field, there would be two up in the air at the same time. He was a strong man.

"That year Billy Buck hit over .300 [.323], and I had Ivan DeJesus at short and Manny Trillo at second behind me, and they were fantastic. Manny was the best second baseman I ever played with. Of course, later I played with Ozzie Smith, so

Dave Kingman

Ivan is not going to be at the top of the list, but both of those guys were the same way. They came to play every day. We had a lot of good guys on the Cubs teams. We might not have won, but we didn't have guys who complained or sat out. They came to play every day.

"The Phils won in '78. If you made a mistake with that lineup, they were going to hit it over the fence. Their star was Mike Schmidt. Schmitty was a great player, and he hit a bunch of home runs off me. Four or five. Schmitty was a smart player. He'd stay back, wouldn't try to pull it all the time. Actually, as he got older, he got to be a better hitter. 'Cause he was so strong, he started hitting balls to right-center, more like the players today, where the power is all over. Not the big pull hitters like Richie Zisk or Willie Stargell and Greg Luzinski, Dave Kingman, who tried to pull it all the time.

"In '79 the Cubs again had a shot at winning a pennant. That year Dave Kingman hit 48 homers, drove in more than a hundred runs [111]. In his prime, Dave was one of the most exciting hitters in the league to watch. He might hit it six hundred feet, or he might swing three times and fall down striking out. But something was going to happen when he was up. When Kingman came up, you didn't get a drink of water. You stayed there and watched.

"They put those cement dugouts in that year in Wrigley Field, and they had the benches way up high, and hell, I don't know how many times we stood up trying to watch a Kingman home run go over the left-field fence and jammed those buttons on the top of your cap against the top of your head by hitting the cement roof.

"That was the year, by the way, we lost a game to the Phils 23–22. You're going to ask who gave up the last run, aren't you? It was a Mike Schmidt home run—off me.

"That ball game was just crazy. Dennis Lamp started the game, and Randy Lerch started for the Phillies, and the first inning Lerch hit a home run off Lamp. The wind was blowing out as hard as it can blow there. Lamp gave up six or seven runs in the first inning. We said, 'Shit, man, they are going to beat us 50 to nothing.'

"Then that quick, we started pounding Lerch, and it just went back and forth. I think Schmidt hit three home runs that day. And we had some guys hit a couple. It was one of those games when after the first inning, I thought, I'll take a shower and go home. I'm not going to be in this one.

"And then I'm right in there.

"In '79 I won the Cy Young Award. Now it's starting to come to light what Peter Seitz's ruling four years before meant.

"Back in '76 everybody could have been a free agent. Anybody. Didn't matter how much service you had. At the end of '76, go ahead and play your option out. Well, I couldn't do anything at that time. I was just one year in the big leagues, where am I going? I'm going back to the minor leagues. It wasn't anything to take a chance on.

"And then the next year, '77, I made $50,000, and then in '78 I made $75,000, and so now I win the Cy Young.

"I talked to Bob Kennedy, the general manager. He wanted to hook me up with a long-term contract. I hired Rick Reuschel's agents, Jim Bronner and Bob Gilhooley.

"We had a deal just about worked out. I was going to get $400,000 a year for four years. At the time that's what the big players were getting. Guys like Steve Garvey, he was making $350,000 a year. Rollie Fingers was making $350,000 a year locked into a six-year deal with San Diego. That was the figure. The Cubs were talking to me about four years at $400,000 a year.

"Well, that sounded real good, because I was making more than these other guys, and these other guys had eight, nine, ten years in, and I only had four.

"Well, Bob Kennedy said we needed to go down to the Wrigley Building to speak with Bill Wrigley, who had taken over the team when his dad died. My attorneys and I went down, and we met up in the Wrigley Building, and Bill Wrigley just overruled what Bob Kennedy said. He acted like Bob had been talking out of turn, making a deal without talking to him first.

"His biggest thing was deferred money. By not taking all the money in the four years, I was going to get paid for a long time, twenty years. It was a big tax advantage to me. I wanted to put it away, because you don't know how long you're going to play. I wanted to put it away for my kids.

"Bill Wrigley said he didn't like the deferred money deal. It was something Jim and Bob thought was the best for players to do, to put money away. You're not going to play forever. That's one thing: My attorneys, and they are my friends, were a little ahead of the rest of the guys, who went after the big money and then they would make investments for tax breaks, and a lot of them lost their money. This way I was guaranteed some income for a long time, whether I played baseball or not.

"He wasn't paying me any more. The money was on his side. He could have put it in the bank and made interest on it. But he didn't choose to do that. I don't know if it was the $400,000 a year he didn't like, but he said he didn't like the deferred money. He said he didn't want to pay me for twenty years, when I wasn't going to be playing. So the deal was off.

"So then I went to arbitration. The Cubs went in at $350,000. The contract with Kennedy had been for $400,000, so even if I lost, all I had gambled was $50,000.

"We went in at $700,000. Just the one year. Whatever the arbitrator decides, that's what you get. The decision is binding.

"When you go in to do arbitration, there are two contracts there. One was for $350,000, the other for $700,000. Bob Kennedy signed them both, and I signed them both. Remember, only a few years ago, I was making $19,000.

"Gilhooley and Brooner argued my case. The hearing was pretty mild. It wasn't ugly. The Cubs were basing their case on the argument that I didn't have enough time of service to make that much, and our whole case was, Should I be penalized because I had good years too soon? Is the system saying you aren't supposed to have a good year until your sixth year? And that was the whole thing, that you might not make ten years in the big leagues.

"You're talking about one year, and he didn't have to decide whether I was worth $350 or $700. The break-even was $525? If he thought I was worth $524, then he could pick the $350,000 figure. He had to decide whether I was worth $526. And once he decided that, he had to go to the $700,000 figure. That's the way the process works.

"I had just had a banner year. He picked the $700,000 figure. It's just crazy, isn't it?

"I don't know what happened to us in 1980. When Herman Franks resigned at the end of 1979, a lot of people thought Joey Amalfitano was going to be the manager the next year. Joey was the third-base coach, a little bit younger, and we related to

Bruce Sutter

him a little bit. And a real nice guy. He knew all the players, and he thought he'd get the job the following year. Well, they didn't hire him. They brought in Preston Gomez, and Preston was a good manager. But you can only push so many buttons after they trade your good players away. Mike Krukow was traded, and some of the other guys started getting traded or going elsewhere. Bobby Murcer left in 1979, and Ivan DeJesus left after '81. Our defense up the middle was gone, and they just started filling in with utility players from other teams.

"And when you trade a good player and get two or three mediocre players back, when you're not getting a starting player in return, then you're getting numbers and not quality.

"The other thing that happened, we traded for players who were disgruntled somewhere else, and then they came here, and they were still disgruntled. Sometimes things don't work out.

"When I was with the Cubs we never did have a team you could say on paper at the beginning of the year, 'We're going to be in contention.'

"In '80 we didn't have the leads a lot in the eighth. We just didn't play very good as a team. Also, that year Dave Kingman got hurt, and he was two-thirds of our offense. We just weren't very good.

"Preston was fired on July 25, and that's when Amalfitano took over. And when Dave Kingman finally came back, the fans gave him a terrible booing.

"Fans are the same way all over. They read how much money you're making, and if you're not performing well, they are going to be on you. We won the Series in '82 with the Cardinals, and the next year, '83, I didn't start off real well, and they were booing me. That's when I was glad my name was Bruce, so you couldn't tell the difference.

"Fans pay a lot of money to come into the games. It's not so much personal. They are disappointed, and if somebody boos, everybody just kind of joins in.

"Dave took it personally. Like I say, he was moody. And there are a lot of times a player will be hurt, something is nagging you, and you don't say anything, and you're playing, and when people boo you, you just want to say, 'Jesus Christ, I'm out here and I can't hardly walk. I can't get out of bed in the morning, and I'm playing, doing the best I can, but I'm not going to say anything.' And after you get booed a bunch, you can't say, 'I'm hurt,' because that doesn't make you look too good either.

"So Dave was hurt, and there was no way he could defend himself.

"You get your feelings hurt sometimes. You're out there. Never, ever have I ever seen a player go out and try to do badly. You're trying the best you can, and it's such a fine line. You make a pitch, and it's a pretty good pitch, and the guy is a good hitter, and it hits the chalk line down the opposite-field line, and it goes for a double and two runs score, and you get a loss, and the people boo you. You say, 'Jesus Christ, you don't even know baseball. What else can I do? I jammed the shit out of him, and he hit a quail down the right-field line on the chalk line.' 'Cause two inches the other way, and it's a foul ball. What are you going to do? That's the game. You have to stay on an even keel. Especially if you play every day. You take your ten best games and throw them out and the ten worst and throw them out, and let's see how you fare.

"By the end of the year the players who could become free agents wanted out. Jerry Martin, I recall, was one of them. There is one thing every player wants to do: He wants to play in October in that World Series. If you are on a team you don't think is going to get there, you want to leave. And for the first time, the players had a way to do it, and it was fantastic.

"We had gotten Billy Buckner from the Dodgers, and he was leading the league in hitting, and he wanted out. It's what happens when you trade for players from winning organizations.

"Jerry Martin had come from the Phillies. Buckner had come from the Dodgers, and the Dodgers were always in contention, always in the playoffs. They were unhappy with how far they had dropped.

"We'd have been OK if we could have played three-inning games. We were strong in the bullpen, as strong as anybody who was playing, any team in the major leagues, we were as strong as anybody. We had a bullpen of Dick Tidrow, Bill Caudill, Willie Hernandez, Lee Smith, and me. Pretty strong, huh? And we finished last.

"After the 1980 season I got traded. I had no warning. I was up hunting in Pennsylvania, and it was on the TV. December 9. Nobody called my house to tell me or anything. I heard about it on the news. The Cubs traded me for Ken Reitz, Ty Waller, and Leon Durham.

"The Cards and the Cubs always were big rivals. The Cardinals weren't a winning team, and neither were we. They played a little bit better than we did. We finished last, and they finished next to last or fourth. They weren't at the top.

"But in terms of salary, they sure were different. At the time of the trade I was close to getting six years in, after which I was going to be a free agent. The Cardinals wanted to make sure when they traded three players for me that they were going to have me for a while.

"The Cards offered me $3.5 million plus incentives for four years. When you're making money like that, it gives you an opportunity to help your family, your *whole* family, not just my wife and kids, but her family and my family, and it gives us security to put money away, that we know we are going to be able to take care of our kids if I get hurt and can't play, and once I'm done playing, I don't have to go punch a clock if I choose to, and the security of it means an awful lot to you.

"When you're actually playing, you don't think about what you're making or what the other guy is making next to you. You don't think about it. There isn't much talk about it in the locker room or on the plane. I don't think anyone holds hard feelings toward another guy for what he makes. You think, That's great, because if I can have that kind of year, I can make that kind of money.

"But just because you're making more money, it doesn't make you a better player. And you don't try less hard. You aren't playing against a clock, you're playing against other great players, and it's a game of inches. The ball hits the foul pole, and it's a three-run homer. There are a lot of ifs, ands, or buts. The game is real fine.

"There are guys who deep down feel they have to justify what they are making, and that's not good. You can't do any more than you are already doing. You get out there and press, tighten up and try harder, and that's just going to make it worse.

"That never happened to me and I've never seen it happen to a teammate, but I know it does happen.

"The money never changed the way I played the game. Not at all. It never changed the way I approached the game. It just changed the way I lived. You're buying a bigger house, a different car. It gives you some luxury. But as far as playing the game, that was the same.

"Looking back on my years with the Cubs, I shall always remember best the first time I stepped out on the mound. They gave me a standing ovation. Which is what they do to every new player. They welcome you right in, and you're right there.

"Everyone is cheering real loud and pulling for you. And that takes place right off the bat. It's fantastic that they do that.

"The saddest part was leaving. I had a lot of friends on that team, had come up through the minor leagues, never played for a different team. We lived in Arlington Heights, liked where we lived. We had neighbors as friends. Two of our kids were born there. That's where I thought I would be for a long time.

"I can't say for sure the Cubs traded me because of my high salary. Nothing was ever said. There was a lot of speculation that that was the reason, that they traded me because I was making more money than the rest of the guys, by far. They wanted to keep their pay scale within the $300,000 to $400,000 range, and then when someone comes in at $700,000, it kind of throws a whack into everything.

"Right now [November 1994], the strike, what they are doing right now, it's over money. Everybody can say what they want, but it's over money. Nobody really knows how much money the owners are making. And I don't think anybody will ever really know.

"Take the guys who own teams. Why do they own teams? They are all multi-millionaires in other businesses. So why do they own a team? Because they like the prestige and the publicity. You're in the news all the time. You're doing interviews, and I think they are making a lot of money. I don't know for sure, but I *think* they are. Why would someone put up $120 million to buy an expansion franchise if they weren't making money?

"So then you get a guy like Bill Wrigley, whose dad owned the team. Maybe Bill Wrigley didn't like baseball. Maybe he didn't like the exposure, being in the limelight, having to make decisions, or taking calls from the press and media. 'Why didn't you sign this player?' Maybe he didn't like it."

After shedding most of the team's talent, in February 1981, Bill Wrigley got rid of his last high-salaried player, Dave Kingman, trading him to the Mets for low-profile outfielder Steve Henderson.

The Cubs began the 1981 season 1–13. By May the team's record was 5–27, the worst in Cubs history. When the players went on strike June 12, their record was 15–37. They trailed the Phillies by a full seventeen-and-a-half games.

On the eve of the strike, Bill Wrigley sold the Cubs' best pitcher, Rick Reuschel, to the Yankees for Doug Bird, Mike Griffin, and $400,000. It was one last chance for Wrigley to make some money before selling the team.

Four days later, on June 16, 1981, William Wrigley sold the team to the Chicago Tribune Company for $20.5 million.

67

Harry

Every decade or so a team owner, a man highly successful in another field, will make an error in judgment so disastrous that it affects the course of a franchise. Under PK Wrigley it often was the Cubs who screwed up, as when they traded talented youngsters such as Dolph Camilli and Lou Brock. But in 1981 it was the Cubs who benefited from such a misjudgment. Even though the person involved wasn't a player, every baseball fan in Chicago was affected. The Cubs have benefited ever since.

The gargantuan snafu was made by Jerry Reinsdorf and Eddie Einhorn, the new owners of the Chicago White Sox. They had just bought the White Sox from Bill Veeck, who no longer could afford to pay the salaries demanded in the free agency age. Though they had inherited a team of no-names, the White Sox had one great asset, a gravelly, bubbling presence, the bleacher fans' favorite announcer, Harry Caray, who even back then was known as the Mayor of Rush Street.

Caray, whose given name was Harry Christopher Carabina, was orphaned at an early age. He had begun his broadcasting career in Joliet, Illinois, in 1943, moved to Kalamazoo, Michigan, then in 1945 went to St. Louis to enlist in the army. When his eyesight kept him out, he talked himself into a radio sports talk show.

He didn't read the scores like everyone else. He gave his opinion. Quickly he became a popular figure in St. Louis.

When in early 1945 one of the two stations carrying Cardinals games had an opening for play-by-play announcer, Caray applied for the job, pleading with the president of Griesedieck Brothers, the brewery sponsoring the games. The president told him the company was looking for a big name. One of the brewery executives mentioned who he had in mind and told Caray, "I can listen to him and read the paper at the same time."

Caray, whose strength was the power of his words, told him, "That's your problem. You're paying hundreds of thousands of dollars and what are you getting for it? People are reading the damn paper while your commercials are on."

Caray got the job.

He took to the air on April 17, 1945, broadcasting the St. Louis Cardinals against the Chicago Cubs. His partner for this first baseball broadcast was Gabby Street, Walter Johnson's catcher at Washington.

By early 1947, Cards owner Sam Breadon liked Harry so much he awarded the Griesedieck Brothers an exclusive contract, even though his station was weaker than the competition, which featured Dizzy Dean. Breadon figured if Caray was the only announcer the fans could listen to, Harry would sell them all.

In 1954, Breadon sold the Cardinals to August Busch Jr., the scion of Budweiser beer, and Caray had to sell himself all over again. Busch was wary of hiring Caray for fear that when he mentioned Budweiser, his listeners would think Griesedieck.

Caray told August Busch, "Just give me six months to show what I can do—that's all." It was all Caray needed.

From 1953 to 1969, Caray was the voice of the Cardinals on KMOX, the Cardinals' flagship station that reached 124 stations in fourteen states in the Midwest. For fifteen years Cardinals fans thrilled to Harry's jubilant home run scream, "Way back . . . There it goes. It might be outta here. It could be. It iiiiiiissssss. A home run. Holy cow!"

Harry was the complete broadcaster. He was an actor whose words created excitement. He was also an accurate reporter. Like Howard Cosell, he told it like it was. If a player made an error, Harry would say, "Right at him. Muffs it. Should have made the play."

Harry liked to think of himself as the fan's alter ego.

HARRY CARAY: "My whole philosophy has always been to broadcast the way a fan would broadcast. I'm so tough on my guys because I want them to win so much. I've often thought that if you gave the microphone to a fan, he'd sound a lot like me. The disappointment, the hurt, the anger, the bitterness, the love, the ecstasy—they'd all be there."

Rather than lying to the fans and kissing the asses of the players, he chose honest reporting.

HARRY CARAY: "I just report what they do, and if they do badly, then they get a bad report. If they're horseshit, there's nothing I can do about it. The way I broadcast—I sound the way I do because I'm just an inveterate fan who happens to be behind the mike."

The players, to be sure, didn't always like it.

JIM BROSNAN: "When I played for the Cardinals, Harry expected every Cardinals player to hit 1.000 and never give up a base hit. With the Cubs he is much less strident, but still sounding like the typical fan, which is what he called himself. This is what fans say in the bars. He maintains that reputation. He goes into a lot of bars and talks the way people talk in bars.

"Anyway, the year I was with the Cardinals [1958–59]—he got on my ass several times. My wife resented the hell out of him. The year after that I was with Cincinnati, still living in the same place and went to the same restaurant where Harry went every night. It was one of the better restaurants on Gulf Boulevard, and there was Harry. He wanted to buy us a drink, and my wife said, 'I wouldn't take a drink from you if you were the last man on earth.' And he couldn't understand that. He wanted to know why. So he sat down.

"We were there two and a half hours later talking about it, and he explained himself to us. I never resented it as much as my wife did. But I still wondered, Why did he have to do it that way? Red Barber doesn't do it, Vin Scully doesn't do it.

"Harry said, 'I'm the fan. I talk like a fan.'

"I said, 'Neither Red Barber nor Vin Scully talks like a fan. They talk like poets.'

"He said, 'That's true. I ain't no poet.'"

* * *

Though the players at times resented his criticism, the fans loved him. Caray was one of them. Said Bob Broeg of the *St. Louis Post-Dispatch*, "Harry was a god."

Everyone thought Harry Caray would broadcast St. Louis Cardinals games until he died, which almost happened on November 3, 1968, when he was struck down by the car of a reckless Vietnam veteran as he tried to cross the street in front of the Chase Park Plaza Hotel.

Caray recovered, but less than a year later he was fired by the Cardinals. Detectives hired by the Busch family discovered a string of telephone calls from Harry to the wife of August Busch III, Gussie's son. They intuited that Harry, whose reputation for drinking and partying was legendary, was having an affair with this woman.

Harry never denied it. All he said was, "I never raped anyone in my life." Jack Buck replaced him in St. Louis.

His reputation either sullied or enhanced (depending on who was doing the judging), Harry found a job with the pragmatic, unpredictable Charlie Finley, the owner of the Oakland A's. Finley brought him in to boost attendance. But Harry's rah-rah Midwest style did not appeal to the laid-back San Francisco Bay Area fans. The A's drew only a few more fans to the park than the year before.

Unhappy with his reception, Harry went to the 1970 World Series, the traditional site for job seekers. At the Series he learned from writer Jim Enright that the Chicago White Sox had an opening in their announcing booth. A month later Caray fled sunny California to return to his Midwest roots. Chicago White Sox owner John Allyn signed him to replace another Chicago legend, Bob Elson, who himself was going to Oakland to work for Charlie Finley.

When Caray arrived in Chicago, he found he had aligned himself with a team that had lost 106 games and had drawn but 495,000 diehards. The White Sox, moreover, were carried only on suburban stations. No major station would carry the games.

Through the sheer force of Caray's personality, he became the symbol for the team, as he created a whole new following for the White Sox from 1971 through 1981.

The White Sox that first year gave him a base salary of $50,000 plus ten grand for every hundred thousand fans drawn over the total of the year before. The increase was 338,000. The next two years it kept climbing and climbing. By 1973 the Sox had drawn an incredible 1,316,527.

Caray's drawing power helped the White Sox put together a radio and TV network, and along with slugger Richie Allen, he proved his ability to bring fans out to watch bad teams. Even with Allen, who was a crowd pleaser, it was Harry who became the major attraction of the team.

BILL VEECK (who bought the White Sox from Allyn in December 1975): "There have been great announcers who've brought people to the park to watch good teams, or when their teams have gone bad, who've kept people listening to the radio and TV even when attendance slips. But Caray had mostly lousy teams, had especially lousy stations for a while, and not only were the ratings great—far better than the clubs deserved—but attendance was far higher than the standings warranted. Whether we won or lost, folks followed the White Sox—even when they shouldn't have. Why? With rare, brief exceptions, the Sox didn't have stars people could identify—it wasn't the players. It wasn't the marketing. God knows, we didn't have dough to market. It was Caray."

* * *

The team of Bill Veeck and Harry Caray was a natural. Since Caray first began broadcasting in St. Louis, he had always sung "Take Me Out to the Ball Game" during the seventh-inning stretch. On opening day, 1976, Veeck's first day as owner, Harry was singing, and the fans directly below him in the stands sang along. It had been that way for years. No one had ever noticed until Veeck. A few days later Veeck secretly installed a PA system mike in the broadcast booth and had it turned on for the seventh-inning stretch. Harry began singing, and his voice boomed throughout the park. One of America's greatest traditions had begun.

By 1981 free agency had made it too expensive for Veeck to continue, so early that year Veeck sold the White Sox to Reinsdorf, who had made a fortune syndicating real estate deals, and Einhorn, who made his money syndicating sports events.

The 1981 season, which had been interrupted by a long midseason strike, was not a happy one for Harry.

From the first Caray had reservations about Reinsdorf, who when he bought the team had vowed to clean up Comiskey Park and make baseball a "family affair." Reinsdorf told the press, "Baseball is more than one guy, more than a park full of drunks." Reinsdorf could have been talking about Bill Veeck, who loved to sit in the stands and drink beer. But Harry was convinced Reinsdorf was talking about him, and it was Harry's feeling that Reinsdorf had said this because he resented Harry's popularity.

Said Harry, "What it really came down to was they were jealous of me 'cause my picture was in the paper more than theirs."

And toward the end of '81, Reinsdorf kept telling Harry that manager Tony La Russa wanted him to be more supportive. At the same time, whenever La Russa saw Harry he would tell him how great his broadcasts were. Harry began to feel someone was lying to him. Maybe, Harry told himself, Reinsdorf, not La Russa, was the one who wanted him to be more supportive and he was pinning it on his manager.

At the end of the 1981 season Caray met with Reinsdorf and Einhorn. The two new owners had great plans. Their central vision combined the ownership of cable television with that of a baseball team. Their plan was for every home to be hooked into a cable network and for White Sox fans to pay for the privilege of watching the team. Games offered on free TV would be cut drastically. If the White Sox fans wanted to watch their team play on TV, they would have to subscribe to SportsVision Cable.

After stating their intentions, they asked Caray if he would re-sign with them to broadcast the games. Caray, a bright man who was very protective of his career, was not looking long-term the way Einhorn and Reinsdorf were. He asked around and learned that only 50,000 homes in the Chicago area were wired for Sports Vision Cable service. To Caray, this was akin to being invisible.

Said Caray, "I figured at the end of '82 I might be Harry Who?" He asked for a long-term contract for more money than they were willing to pay. When the two balked, Harry began to look across town to the Cubs, who had just been purchased by the Tribune Corporation, owners of superstation WGN. The Cubs had 28 million viewers who watched for free.

Timing is everything. At the end of the 1981 season Jack Brickhouse retired. The Cubs were looking for a replacement. Harry called the Cubs. He had the job in five minutes.

Instead of holding a press conference and announcing he was re-signing with the White Sox, at his press conference crosstown he announced he was taking over as the voice of the Cubs.

When the 1982 season began, Harry Caray began a career with the Cubs that would make him not just the most famous baseball personality in Chicago but in the entire country, as the white-haired announcer with thick black glasses came to Wrigley Field, one institution, and became a second institution.

At first it was a shock for Cubs fans. Cubs fans were more genteel and prim and respectable than White Sox fans. White Sox fans were working class, beer guzzlers. Like Harry.

Some Cubs fans would never accept Harry as the voice of the Cubs because of their loyalty to their childhood announcer, Jack Brickhouse, and because Harry's association with the rival Cardinals and the White Sox had been too strong.

CUBS FAN BRUCE LADD: "The guy is nothing but a lowly son of a bitch St. Louis Cardinals announcer. I don't like the sound of his voice. It makes me want to clear my throat all the time. The guy should have retired. If you can retire Brickhouse, how the hell can you turn and pick the St. Louis Cardinals, White Sox guy and put him in there?

"I grew up with Jack Brickhouse. Why do you love your mother? You grew up with her. Come on. Brickhouse was *it*. He was what you were accustomed to. It was familiar, all that good stuff. At least Jack has been prudent enough to step aside. Jesus, Caray keeps going and going.

"I haven't run into anybody yet who has ever said, 'Ah boy, that Harry Caray is a hell of a guy.' I don't hate him. But he ain't Cubs. He's *Cardinals*. There was some competition in the olden days. How in the world can you look at the guy all of a sudden as the great spokesman and mouthpiece and epitome of Chicago Cubdom?

"With cable, the advance of WGN, sure. But when you look at people who picked this up forty-eight years ago, a different ball game."

For the grand majority of Cubs fans, however, in no time Harry won them over. They loved him on the air, and they loved him at the ballpark.

RON SHAPIRO: "Harry adds great color, great spirit, and great knowledge to the game. He's an unabashed supporter of the team, and he has become very much a part of the Chicago scene. He's a colorful guy, tells great stories, and he has added a dimension of magic.

"When we go to the game at Wrigley Field, I tell my daughter, 'Wait till we get to the seventh inning and we have to sing.' It's a magic moment, not just for Cubs fans, or baseball fans, but it's a magic moment for the country. It gives me goose bumps just thinking about it.

"I have to tell you, if somebody would say, 'What is the absolute essence of America? The inner heart of America?' It would be an afternoon ball game at Wrigley Field, it's in the high seventies, 38,000 people at the ballpark—the Cubs winning or losing is immaterial—it's the last of the seventh, and without any flicker or any clue, 38,000 people stand up, and they are all looking at this little white-haired guy.

"And they are looking as though he is a beacon, a kind of guru, which I suppose he is, and every head in that ballpark is turned to Harry, and then people—absolute strangers—are joining hands and swaying and singing, 'Take Me Out to the Ball Game.'

"If that isn't the absolute essence of America."

When Harry Caray joined WGN to broadcast Cubs games, what he accomplished for the Cubs far outdistanced what Reinsdorf and Einhorn had envisioned for their White Sox. While their local pay cable plan failed, WGN began broadcasting nationally over cable networks, reaching more than 30 million homes. Harry Caray entertained Cubs fans not just in Chicago but made millions of new Cubs rooters all over North America and as far south as Mexico and the Caribbean islands.

On March 9, 1982, Harry began his road to national fame with the Cubs, as he announced the opening spring training game in Phoenix. His partners were Milo Hamilton, Vince Lloyd, and Lou Boudreau.

Said Harry, "The Chicago Cubs are on the air. Good afternoon, everybody."

68

Dallas Green Takes Over

The three men who made the decisions for the Tribune Company, Stanton Cook, John Madigan, and Andrew McKenna, decided that they needed to find a man to run their new acquisition, the Cubs. They wanted a man with experience and a track record.

The man they selected, Dallas Green, had fashioned the Philadelphia Phils into a team that won its first world championship in 1980, when they defeated the Kansas City Royals in the World Series. Green, who ruled with an iron fist, tended to polarize people. He was loved or hated. He was not a politician, and he cared little what others thought of him. He was the first such Cubs leader since Leo Durocher, and in the end he came even closer to winning a pennant than Leo did.

Because of fortuitous timing, Green was available. Phils owner Bob Carpenter, the man who had hired Green to run the Phils, was in the process of selling to Bill Giles, the son of former National League president Warren Giles. Green well knew that new owners often wanted to choose their own general managers. Green decided to jump before he was pushed.

Two weeks before the Phils sale was completed, Green signed with the Tribune Company to run the Cubs in 1982. A week later, he hired a tough-minded Lee Elia to replace Joey Amalfitano.

Dallas Green came in and announced his goal to rebuild the Cubs. He fired everyone from the '69 Cubs and derided Cubs tradition, calling the team losers. Green had barely arrived, and a lot of people quickly resented his arrogance.

For forty years, the Cubs general managers had been reluctant to trade, for fear of criticism of both management and the fans. Trading is a very risky business, especially when pitchers are involved. Every time a pitcher goes to the mound, it can be the last time. A pitcher who wins the year before doesn't necessarily continue his success. Trading pitching is the single most difficult task for a general manager.

And so it took a man who was willing to roll the dice, a man willing to take great risks, to attempt what Green was seeking to do. He made a series of trades, several with his old team, the Phillies. With each trade, he was lambasted by both the press and the fans. In the post–Richard Nixon era, when no one in power can ever do anything right, Dallas Green was pilloried like no Cubs executive had been in the past.

The reason: In the past the Cubs fans had been promised a beautiful afternoon at Wrigley Field. This new man, from the Phils no less, came to town and was not only deriding the Wrigley era but actually promising the fans a winning team.

The first move Green made was to trade away the Cubs' best pitcher, Mike Krukow. In a deal with his old team, the Phillies, on December 8, 1981, he acquired a young catcher-outfielder, Keith Moreland, and pitchers Dickie Noles and Dan Larson for their ace. In the press Green took a pounding.

It was the beginning of a rocky rebuilding process that would not bear fruit for another three years. In the meantime, though some Cubs fans derided the team for being the Phillies West, Green was building a strong nucleus.

Then he made a second trade with the Phils. He knew veteran shortstop Larry Bowa, then thirty-six, was fighting with Bill Giles and Paul Owens in Philly. He traded Ivan DeJesus, a fine player seven years younger, for Bowa. The press howled. But Green wanted Bowa for his feistiness and his leadership. More, Green had received as a throw-in a young infielder named Ryne Sandberg. Because the Phils had two other talented second basemen, Julio Franco and Juan Samuel, in their farm system, they could afford to let Sandberg go.

On January 20, 1983, after trading two minor leaguers for Ron Cey, Dallas Green signed him to play third base. More over-the-hill players for the team, the writers carped.

Six days later Green traded pitchers Dick Tidrow and Randy Martz, shortstop Scott Fletcher and infielder Pat Tabler to the White Sox for starting pitcher Steve Trout and reliever Warren Brusstar. The writers howled that Green had been taken. But by the next year, only Fletcher remained on the Sox.

Even with these trades, the team hadn't improved significantly in '82 and '83, and the fans were becoming restless and contemptuous about Green. They didn't like his trades, didn't particularly like his manager.

Lee Elia had managed the Cubs to a fifth-place finish in 1982 and fifth again in 1983. In April 1983, the Cubs began their season 2–10, the worst in their history. The record was 5–13 when the Cubs went up against the Los Angeles Dodgers at Wrigley Field.

During the game the boo birds in the bleachers made their feelings heard. At the end the Cubs lost the game on a wild pitch by young reliever Lee Smith.

After the game a reporter asked Elia a question, and Elia cracked under the strain. Elia let loose with an outburst that contained forty-six expletives, aimed at the Cubs bleacher fans. He included the memorable appraisal of Cubs fans' employment status.

*   *   *

LEE ELIA: "Eighty-five percent of the people in this country work. The other fifteen percent come here and boo my players. They oughta go out and get a fucking job and find out what it's like to go out and earn a fucking living. Eight-five percent of the fucking world is working. The other fifteen percent come out here. A fucking playground for the cocksuckers."

These were not the sort of words to endear him to Cubs fans, and according to observers, Elia was never the same again, becoming too cautious. Soon afterward, the Cubs fell out of the race completely.

Elia sealed his doom in late August when the Atlanta Braves came to town. A reporter asked him about the scouting report on rookie Gerald Perry. Elia said he hadn't been given one. On August 22, Green fired Elia, his best friend. Charlie Fox, another longtime baseball career man, replaced him on an interim basis.

On October 6, 1983, Green changed managers again. He opted for the mild-mannered Jim Frey, who had been Earl Weaver's assistant for ten years in Baltimore. Frey had played fourteen years in the minor leagues but never played in the majors. He had led the Royals to the World Series in '80. After his firing during the '81 season, Frey coached with the Mets in '82 and '83. Only those Mets had finished lower than the Cubs.

At the end of the 1983 season, the Cubs pitching staff was in disarray. The four starters were Chuck Rainey, Steve Trout, an over-the-hill Fergie Jenkins, Dickie Noles, and Dick Ruthven. The staff had a 4.08 earned run average, by far the highest in the National League.

Dallas Green went after quality pitching with a vengeance. He traded a talked-about rookie, Carmelo Martinez, to San Diego for a talented but colorless starting pitcher, Scott Sanderson.

Dallas Green

Unfortunately for Green and the Cubs, nothing seemed to be working. In 1984 spring training, the Cubs' record was 3–18. After he released Ferguson Jenkins, a legend in Chicago, Dallas Green's stock could not have been lower.

And yet despite all the criticism, he would not be deterred from his course. He traded two minor leaguers for pitcher Tim Stoddard. He then traded young promising catcher Mike Diaz and relief pitcher Bill Campbell to the Phils for an outfielder, Bob Dernier, whom the Phils intended to send to the minors, veteran outfielder Gary Matthews, the key man in the deal, and a minor league pitcher.

Green moved Leon Durham to first base and ordered Jim Frey to sit one of his best hitters, Bill Buckner, on the bench.

Almost magically the team began the regular season 16–4 at home, the best record in their history. The New York Mets, led by sensational rookie Dwight Gooden, were snapping at their heels.

With Ron Cey at third, Larry Bowa at short, youngster Ryne Sandberg showing signs of being able to play at second, and Leon Durham at first, the team had a mix of youth and vets. In the outfield Dernier and Matthews played well alongside Keith Moreland, who had begun to hit.

The biggest problem still was pitching. Dick Ruthven's arm was sore, and he couldn't pitch. Green went back to the trading table. On May 25, he traded the disgruntled Buckner and young infielder Mike Brumley to the Boston Red Sox for starting pitcher Dennis Eckersley in a deal that would change history for both teams.

Green would not stop there. On June 14, he made one of the most important trades of his career when he sent two of his most promising young players, Joe Carter and Mel Hall, along with two minor league pitchers, to the Cleveland Indians for pitching ace Rick Sutcliffe, catcher Ron Hassey, and relief pitcher George Frazier. When the reporters learned that Dallas Green had given up two exciting prospects for Sutcliffe, and that Sutcliffe's contract was to run out at the end of the season and he would become a free agent, their derision of Dallas Green never was greater.

Dickie Noles, a favorite of Green's, began on the Phillies with Dallas Green. Soon after Green came to the Cubs, he traded for Noles, who saw firsthand Green's rebuilding process. Noles had a world of talent, but he didn't have the emotional stability to make full use of his talent. Noles had suffered from the disease of alcoholism since he was a teenager, and it seemed that whenever he began pitching well, he would get drunk and injure himself in a brawl. Noles would pitch for the Cubs through July 1984. While the Cubs were on their way to a division championship, Dickie Noles was on his way to last-place Texas and sobriety.

DICKIE NOLES: "I grew up in Charlotte, North Carolina. I signed with the Phillies out of high school in 1975. Wes Livengood was the scout. I was drafted as a pitcher-outfielder. From the very beginning, I was always getting into trouble.

"I was playing in Clearwater, my first year out of high school. Jim Wright, the Phils' Triple A pitching coach, was trying to take a young boy under his wing and teach him the right things. Wright, who was a big, strong guy, wanted to get to the big leagues and was doing all the right things.

"Jimbo said to himself, 'This kid needs some direction, and I'm six foot six, 245 pounds, a big guy, and I'll give him some direction.' Jimbo wasn't a drinker, fighter, or brawler like I was. He was just trying to give me some positive input. The only thing was, he made the mistake of getting into my car with me.

"I was driving my Z-28, and he was in the passenger seat, and on the street beside me this guy revved his engine. Boom, we were racing down Mandalay Boulevard, flying through Clearwater, with Jimbo sitting in the passenger side saying, 'Man, are you nuts?'

"The next thing you know, the other car outran me, but the cops got after me and I tried to outrun them. I was flying through the city of Seminole going toward St. Pete, down that big stretch, and finally I decided to take a couple turns and lose them, and I did.

"I ended up in somebody's backyard, flying off the back of their driveway. My car set down, and I said to Jimbo, 'Let's stay right here. We'll lose them.' He was looking at me in shock like, This guy's nuts.

"The next thing you know, these cops come flying around, and they got us. Jimbo got out of the car and hid behind a bush. He was wearing a big sombrero.

"The cops came running over, ready to arrest me with their dogs, and I grabbed my left arm, because in high school I had ripped up my left arm, had 211 stitches in it. So I grabbed my left arm and went, 'You don't understand. I'm trying to get to the hospital. My arm is messed up.'

"And one police officer bought it.

"He said, 'Come on. I'll take you to the hospital.' The other cop said, 'Hold it. Where is that big old fella who was with you? I said, 'There was nobody with me.' He said, 'I saw a big old fellow in this car.' Finally I said, 'Jimbo, come out behind that bush.' He didn't move. I said, 'Wright, get out from behind that bush.' He finally came out. He said, 'Are you looking for me?'

"He was mad at me because I said his first name and I said his last name. He said, 'I don't want to get in trouble. The only thing I did was get in the car with you.'

"We went over to the hospital, and Jimbo was paranoid. He said, 'What are you going to do?' I said, 'Don't worry about it. I'll let them look at my arm.' So the police officer set there with us for about twenty minutes, and then when he left, boom, we were out the door, gone.

"Some of us like to do kid things. This also took place in Clearwater: In one of the craziest things I remember doing in the minor leagues, on Halloween night we spent all our money to buy a bunch of wine and a grocery carton of eggs. We drank the wine and threw the eggs at everybody. It got so out of hand that we were throwing them at cop cars. We'd run right up to the cop and blast his windshield so bad, by the time he got out of the car the six of us had gone our own separate ways. They couldn't catch us.

"Then I got really carried away. Our rivals were the Dunedin Blue Jays. One of the Blue Jays, Boomer Wells, had a fight with us in spring training, so we had some stuff going back and forth with them.

"They had a really nice van, and on this same Halloween night it was driving up the road, and I said, 'Let's get that van.' We all went out and just bammed this van, covered it with eggs.

"Before you know it, I stayed a little bit longer. I *always* pressured things a little bit longer. So they stopped, and six or seven of the Blue Jays players started running after us.

"Some of the Philly players I was with, Kevin Saucier was one, he took off running, and he hid in the woods. Marty Bystrom took off running, and he hid. Bobby Walk took off running, and he hid. And I stood out there all alone.

"I'm this tough guy, see. Shoot, I was tired of running. All of a sudden I saw these guys get out of the van, and I said to myself, 'Aw, man, these are ballplayers!' So I didn't run.

"I stood where I was, and for some reason a drunk can think pretty quickly, and of course I *was* drunk that night. I grabbed a water hose and I said, 'Did you guys throw eggs at *my* car?' They all stopped. They were ready to kick my rear end. They went, 'Throw eggs at your car?' I said, 'Yeah. Did you guys throw eggs at *my* car?' Now they looked at me and said, 'Hell no. Somebody was throwing eggs at *our* van.' I said, 'Bring it over here. I'll wash it off.' I washed their van off and sent them on their way.

"Now my teammates were hiding in the bushes, laughing their rear ends off. Joe Charboneau was five feet behind me, and they're going, 'What's he doing?' The Blue Jays brought the van over, and I washed it for them.

"After they left, Charboneau said he was dying. He said, 'Dickie, there isn't another car around you.' You're saying they egged your car, and all one of them had to say was, 'Where is your car?'

"I came up to the big leagues on July 4, 1979. I was in the starting rotation every fifth day. Danny Ozark was the manager, and late in the season he was fired and Dallas Green replaced him.

"At that moment, Dallas brought uncertainty. Danny was very popular with the players, allowed the players to do whatever they wanted to, and when Dallas showed up, here was this big huffy guy showing up with this talk of this 'We, not I' attitude and 'We're going to do things this way,' and everybody was going, 'Shoot. This guy is full of crap coming in here with this minor league bull crap.'

"Dallas brought in a no-nonsense attitude to say, 'Hey, we're going to get aggressive. We're going to get excited. We're going to play every game and have fun.' Even at the end of the season some guys—Greg Luzinski, Garry Maddox, Larry Bowa—were still going around with that attitude, though all three turned out to love him. But Dallas had dropped a few seeds, and he had some of the younger players, myself, Lonnie Smith, Keith Moreland, guys like that. No matter what he did, he had us.

"When spring training came the next year, players started walking around and saying, 'We're going to do it the Dallas Green way.' People decided to jump on his side when they saw he was consistent. He didn't change. Every day he showed them his desire to win, and in spring training he won over Larry Bowa. 'Cause Larry is a lot like Dallas. A whole lot like him. He won Larry over, and then he won Pete Rose over.

"The thing with Pete Rose, he is going to play hard. You don't ever have to worry about Pete Rose. If you love baseball and you show you want to win, you got Pete. So Pete was one of the easiest to win over. And after he won Pete over, the rest of it fell into place.

"Put it this way: Dallas Green is one of the greatest motivators. He has a single-mindedness in his approach to get where he wants to go, and he believes in his own concept, his way, one hundred percent.

"And in 1980 I pitched consistently the whole year, and we won the world championship, beat the Kansas City Royals. Every player on the team had to perform in order to win. A lot of people give me credit for throwing a pitch that knocked George Brett down, but I think the biggest thing I did, I helped down the stretch in August and September pitching very well, and also pitching in middle relief.

"In 1981 I showed up for spring training out of shape, and Dallas sent me back to the minors. A lot of it had to do with the fact my behavior [the alcoholism] was starting to affect the way I was performing. Dallas had given me every opportunity to perform, to make the club, and all season I didn't really work out, and he sent me down for the betterment of the team and of me.

"And when I came to camp out of shape, he didn't say a word. He didn't have to. The way Dallas was, all he had to do was look at me, and I knew. And in spring training that year, I did a couple things that were not nice.

"One time Marty Bystrom was talking to a reporter, and I went up to talk to Marty, and the reporter said, 'Excuse me. I'm talking to him.' And I spit tobacco juice on him. I don't think that was a feather in my cap. So it was the little things that kept adding up, and [Dallas] sent me to the minor leagues. That was the year of the strike, and after it was over I rejoined the Phillies.

"At the end of the season Dallas went over to the Cubs. I didn't see anything coming. I was too stupid to see. I'm a recovering person now, so I live one day at a time, but back then I lived for the moment, and I remember when I heard it and I went in to say good-bye to him in the office, I felt like somebody was taking a piece of me away.

"I said, 'Dallas, good luck in Chicago.' And I said to him, 'But I'm going to kick your rear end when we play you.' That's the way Dallas would have wanted it. And he made a little joke. He said, 'What makes you think you're not coming with me?' And he laughed. And I got traded over here with Keith Moreland and Danny Larson.

"I joined the Cubs. Lee Elia was the manager. He was our manager in '82 and '83. Lee was the person who was there for me the most and made the biggest impact on me, the guy I really idolized. At times I even tried to walk like him and act like him. Lee to me was one of the greatest men I ever met, because he's an unbelievable motivator.

"And the thing about Lee was, even though he was always trying to help me, I stepped on his toes so much, constantly got into trouble, constantly wrecked his team, constantly bickered with him. One time I even tried to punch him out. But after we got into something, there was always crying on my part—I didn't cry for very many people, and that shows how much I thought of Lee Elia. Here was a guy who, I think, we loved each other.

"In my first year in Chicago, 1982, I won 10 games. Now that I look back and see the talent that I wasted, that I only won 36 games in the major leagues—hell, I could win 36 games in two years in the major leagues right now, if someone were stupid enough to give me the ball. But looking back at that time, I had some great stuff. I just didn't know how to use it.

"My mental attitude was great. It was just that the disease that I had wouldn't allow me to be positive or to focus on things that I needed to. I kept focusing on things that made me feel good. I can't believe how much I was pulled to that nightlife, where I couldn't wait until the game was over.

"I was at peace at the ballpark, and being at peace at the ballpark, it was the only place I was at peace in my life, but I couldn't wait for the game to get over. I wanted to get out there. And after I got in a street fight in Montreal with some guys, I missed a month and a half of a season. It wasn't even my fight. Another teammate had said something to some guys, and I ended up fighting six or seven guys, and finally I come back to my hotel room and I'm all torn up. The room service guy came to the door to see if I was OK. My knee was ripped up so bad, the calf muscle was pulled away from the knee, so I couldn't perform for a month.

"The next day I went to the ballpark fearful of Dallas, of getting in trouble again. I went and told Dallas I fell in a bathtub. When I told him that morning, I had a big knot in the head where they had beat me up in the street.

"I tried to start. Billy Connors, our pitching coach, walked to the bullpen mound with me. My first pitch sailed completely into the stands. Billy said, 'That's it, man. You're messed up.'

"I could have won 15, 16 games that year just by being as dumb as I was and by the fact he was giving me the ball every fifth day, but I ended up screwing that up too.

"That year we finished fifth. We were improving as a team, but the fans were hard on us. They didn't like the Philly way. Dallas had come over with all this Philly stuff, Philly players, new tradition talk. They didn't like that for some particular reason. Hell, some of the Cubs players, Bill Buckner was one of them—they didn't accept him right away, either. Green's coming over to Chicago, to a last-place team, and saying, 'We're going to start doing things a little different here. If we lose, we're going to lose trying our best.' And they were like, 'Who are you?'

"They soon found out. Right after I came he traded Ivan DeJesus to the Phils and got Larry Bowa. He wanted a fiery general, and he got one, and in that trade he got a pretty good throw-in, too, one of the greatest second basemen who ever played the game, a kid by the name of Sandberg.

"I had played with Ryno in the minors. He never said a word. Just smiled. A great guy. He just went out and played. He was playing with a bunch of idiots, guys like me and Joe Charboneau, who played hard, who liked to have some fun and do some crazy things off the field, and here he was, doing things the right way, looking around him and going, 'Wow, these guys are nuts.'

"One of the things I remember was the positive impact Larry Bowa had on Ryno when he came to Chicago, how he took to Ryne Sandberg. I hadn't seen that in Larry Bowa before. I had seen the fiery guy with all the veterans. But the way he took to some of the younger players in Chicago and was still able to perform himself, that was very impressive, because he really took Sandberg under his wing. Without Larry I don't know if Ryno would have turned out to be as great as he did—the ability was there, but Larry took him out of his shell. I had known Ryno longer than I knew Larry. And what Larry did for Ryno, he made him laugh, made him a little more vocal—we called him Gabby—he made him get a little bit more aggressive. He rubbed off on Ryno in a most positive way.

"Bowa was such a great competitor. I remember I was a young kid when I joined the Phillies. He came up to me in the dugout just before I was scheduled to pitch on the national *Game of the Week*. He said, 'Are you scared?' I looked at him and said, 'No, I ain't scared of nothing, man.' He said, 'Are you scared to pitch?' I said, 'No,

I'm not scared to pitch.' He said, 'The last rookie we had pitch on national TV threw up.' I looked at him and said, 'I'm going to kick your little ass if you don't get out of my face.'

"At that moment I watched him walk off, strutting, saying, 'I like this guy.' It's one of my fondest memories, because I thought I had insulted someone I had looked up to so much. But when he walked off, I realized I had said the right thing.

"The other thing about Larry Bowa: After the 1983 season I went into alcohol rehab. Larry said, 'Why don't you come down to Florida and stay for the winter?' So me and my wife did. We went down and looked around for a home, and me and him and Sheena, Larry's wife, we all started to hang out. Now Larry had talked to Billy Connors, my pitching coach, who also lived down there, and Billy had told Larry about the [alcohol] rehab program. Billy told him, 'You've got to keep him busy.'

"Larry would show up at my door at nine o'clock wanting to do aerobics every morning. He'd have a golf game set up in the afternoon. He would take me to lunch, and me and him and Sheena would be together in the evening for dinner.

"Finally, I said, 'Hey, Larry, I'm going to be all right.' But it was incredible that a person would extend himself that much for me.

"I thought the next year, 1983, would be a real big season for me, but it just didn't turn out that way. Dallas had told me to quit my drinking. But then when I got arrested the first week of the season, it put a damper on the whole thing.

"That's when I beat up the police officer in Cincinnati.

"I pitched the second game of the year and lost 1–0 to Bill Gullickson of Montreal. After that game Ferguson Jenkins, who had rejoined the team, told me and Dallas repeated it, 'The way you threw in spring training, the way you're throwing now, you've quit drinking down to just drinking beer'—which is the most absurd thing to do, but it was what I tried to do, because Dallas was trying everything . . . and I tried to take care of myself. I made up my mind to get my life in order, and in spring training I threw the ball unbelievable, and the season started, when I pitched that first game, people said, 'Damn, he's got it together.'

"I never made it to the mound to pitch my second game that year. I went out to drink with a friend named Scott Moneyhoff. I had talked Dallas into giving him a job in Triple A, and Scotty and I went out to celebrate, and we got into a big brawl, which I can't tell you a lot about, other than the fact the story goes that I beat up a police officer.

"It started with me fighting in a bar and then leaving that bar and going to another bar and starting a big fight in that bar, and when the police officer was called, apparently—it's hard for me to remember, because I was in a blackout—I kicked the bouncer I was fighting in the nuts and ruptured him, and he came over, and the police officer too, and they tell me I hit the police officer and apparently whooped up on him pretty good.

"Of course, the bouncer and the police officer tore up the ligaments in my knee so bad it took me two years to get the strength back in my knee.

"I got sued for $800,000 and sentenced to 180 days in jail and fined. I went to jail immediately and got out of jail on bail and went into the drug and alcohol rehab center in Chicago, and I had to serve my jail time at the end of the season. I was 5–10 that year.

"When I came back to pitch, I didn't tell anyone about my knee. No one knew it was that hurt, but after I got traded to Texas the following year, I had a physical, and when they looked at my knee they went, 'Man, your knee has no strength at all.'

"Nineteen eight-three wasn't a complete loss. I got to play with Ferguson Jenkins. Fergie was the best man at my wedding, and that goes to show how I appreciated him. I don't think there is anybody in baseball who can teach the slider better than Ferguson Jenkins. I'm appalled that some major league team hasn't taken Ferguson Jenkins and made him a major league pitching instructor or at least the head of the pitching in the minor leagues. [On November 17, 1994, one day after this interview, the Cubs hired Jenkins to be pitching coach.]

"I will say one thing about Fergie, he was a perfect person in my life at that moment, because Fergie's so compassionate. He took me and my wife under his wing and tried to talk to us in so many ways. He was one of the few people in my life who could say some words and calm me down. He was like a father figure to many of us. For everything Fergie did for me, he did the same thing for everyone on that ball club, especially some of the young black players. Fergie's a positive guy. Fergie never gets into negativity.

"One of the things Fergie did real good, Lee Smith had a little anger on him by the fact that when he'd do bad, the press would come in—I don't think Smitty ever totally got rid of that—but Smitty is a wonderful person who doesn't like to be blamed for things. The writers would come in and say, 'Hey, big boy. You got a 1.65 ERA but you're 4–10.' And it never was his fault that year [1983] that he lost those games. He'd come into a tie game and there'd be two errors, and all of a sudden the game would be over.

"That season Smitty was the most dominating relief pitcher that I have ever seen. I've never seen anybody come into a game and make guys look like Little Leaguers. Of course, he had some terrible luck. I'd never seen a guy come into a ball game to get losses when he wouldn't give up a hit.

"Smitty was a great person to have on a team. He is very quiet. We called him Peashooter. He was very compassionate. He gave himself to his teammates. He was very private but great around his teammates, and a good family man. As big and strong as he is, thank God he turned out to be this way, because if he had ever thrown at a guy, he would have hurt somebody. Basically, Smitty is as compassionate a guy as you'll see, and he doesn't get rattled by very many things. He's very into his performance and baseball and doing his job the right way, and if you look at his walks and strikeouts and his longevity, it shows. But Fergie had a unique way of helping guys like Smitty—or Mel Hall.

"When Mel Hall first joined the ball club, he was trying to fight everybody. Fergie, who was a quiet leader, got him to calm down.

"We had two pretty good leaders there. Fergie led by example, a quiet leader, and Larry Bowa led by example and let you know about it.

"In April 1983, I remember we lost a game at Wrigley Field, and we were walking from our dugout to the clubhouse, which was still in the left-field corner. As we were walking, a fan really got on us, and then another fan threw a beer into Keith Moreland's face. Moreland tried to get into the stands after the fan, and I remember while Lee Elia was trying to contain Moreland, trying to get into that clubhouse, many other fans were hollering at us. Elia was very hot over the fact that his team was being treated that way. And that was the day he threw that tantrum, which one of the reporters filmed, where he said some nasty things about the Cubs fans.

"If you remember, the fans were down on us because they didn't feel it was totally a Cubs team, that Dallas was trying to turn us into a Phillies second-division ball club. And the only reason they felt that way, the media hype had built it up to where they were saying that. The fans were fueled by that media coverage.

"I do remember one thing Lee Elia said afterward to some of us. He said, 'Sometimes I wish we had some time to cool off before we have to address the press, because any human is going to be mad at that situation.'

"He said, 'I really like the Chicago fans, and I like baseball fans. I'm a baseball fan.' I remember him saying, 'Lord knows, this is going to haunt me.' And it did.

"Dallas had to fire him in August. It was the result of pressure from his employers. I know Dallas. Dallas Green would *never* have let Lee Elia go unless he thought Lee was doing a bad job. And Lee was doing a very good job. When you're a general manager, and the owner doesn't like the way things are going, and he tells you to fire your manager, you've got to do it.

"Lee was replaced by Charlie Fox. Unlike Lee, he was mild-mannered, to say the least. It was a huge turn to have Charlie Fox to come in after that. We as a team had formed an unbelievable respect for Lee Elia. When Lee went, a lot of us were angry, and so Charlie came into an angry clubhouse. There was a lot of resentment, not at Charlie personally, but toward whoever was going to come down there. And we played worse under Charlie.

"Then in 1984, Dallas hired Jim Frey as manager. Why him? You got me. Dallas must have liked what he did in Kansas City.

"I don't think Jimmy liked me. I was coming back from the alcohol center, ready to pick up the pieces. I had earned the fifth starting job. Billy Connors had told me, 'You're not going to get one of the top three jobs.' We had picked up Scott Sanderson. We had Chuck Rainey and Steve Trout. 'You can battle for that fifth job or be in relief.'

"I more than won the fifth starter's job, but instead I became Scott Sanderson's caddy. I'd sit in the bullpen and never start. In '84, in my only start, I only gave up one run, and it was 1–1 after seven or eight.

"I would come in for Scott Sanderson every time Scott couldn't make it to the mound because Scotty was having back troubles. He'd go out and throw a couple of pitches, and I'd be in his game. And then my start would be given to Rich Bordi. I was looking at this whole thing and becoming angry and concerned. I put a ton of pressure on myself for the first time in my life to perform, not just for myself but for all the alcoholics out there. I was trying to do everything. I thought just because I was sober that everything was going to pan out. And this guy was not giving me the opportunity to perform.

"It got to the point where every time I gave up a couple of runs, I'd say, 'Here we go again.' I just didn't think for me that he used me the right way, and I was very angry. I took it as an insult to be in the bullpen, and I was a terrible pitcher when I came into games when we were losing 8–3. I would come into those ball games and get whacked.

"It got to the point where I asked Dallas to trade me. I didn't want to leave the Cubs, but I felt I needed a change for my recovery. And also I wasn't stupid. I realized the minor leagues were around the corner if I continued playing for this guy.

"What I remember best about the time I spent with the Cubs in '84 was the performance of Ryne Sandberg. It was incredible to watch Ryno play because it was like watching a guy like Joe DiMaggio—he did it so smoothly. Ryne would be beating hits out, and it would look like he wasn't even running. He'd steal a base, and it would look like he wasn't even running. He'd make plays where it would look like he wasn't moving, and yet he would make a play nobody else could get to. His consistency was unbelievable. He was a shortstop playing second base.

"One of the things about Ryno that was so incredible was the fact he didn't just hit home runs, for the first time in his life he hit *big* home runs. The thing about Ryno also was the fact that when you get into a ball game with a guy like him and you need a base runner, he might look bad on the first two sliders, and then with his speed—he had *great* speed, he could run as good as Bobby Dernier—he'd top a ball off the plate, and you got him on first. He'd steal second, the throw goes into center, he's at third, and the next thing you know, he's beating the throw to home, you've got a tie game, and if you'd look it up, he did that so many times.

"The other thing I remember about Ryno that year was the fans. Ryno grabbed them. The way he grabbed the fans elevated that whole team's performance of play.

"Another highlight for me was our getting Dennis Eckersley in late May. As a kid, though he's only a couple years older than me, he was my favorite player in the minor leagues. Myself and Marty Bystrom, it used to be that Eckersley was our man. I used to wear my socks like him, wore Pumas like him. He had charisma, Bubba. He's got it.

Ryne Sandberg

"And then I got to play with him in '84 for a couple months, and it was wonderful. His attitude and personality are just special. He's a unique person. He's got his own lingo for balls and strikes and hits. Eckisms. 'Throw some gas.' 'That man ain't taking me bye-bye.' He would say, 'I got the slide Johnson going and threw some gas.'

"One thing about Dennis Eckersley, I never saw anyone work as hard as this guy, and it shows. Having him on the ball club, it was like, 'God, Eckersley is here.'

"And then Sutcliffe came in June. Rick Sutcliffe is the most intense competitor that I have ever played with outside of Pete Rose. People laugh when I say that, but I say, 'Listen, that man went about his business in a way, when it was game day, he got prepared in a way that would *scare* you. He'd sit in his locker, and he didn't want anybody to talk to him. He listened to his headphones, his Alabama tapes, and he'd sit over there. Then he went out to warm up, and he'd put the towel on his shoulder, and Billy Connors had to have the towel, and he would start warming up, and Glenn Brummer would catch him, and if Brummer would start talking, boy, he would glare at him. Brummer had to be silent. But with Sutt it was, I'm pitching to every hitter right now. You set down there and move in and move out, and when I take that towel from Billy Connors to wipe my forehead off, you keep your rear end setting down, 'cause I may want to throw a pitch. That's Sutt.

"So we were playing with Sandberg, the best player in the game, and now they've added some players around Sandberg, especially some pitching iike Eckersley and Sutcliffe, and now all of a sudden, you're starting to fill in the pieces. And Sandberg just seemed to elevate everybody to a new level. It was like he was Wonderkid for that whole year.

"The man behind the success of that team was Dallas Green. I respected him so much. He was the one who rebuilt the Cubs. It was his ship, his crew. Those were his scouts. When you go out and get a guy like Gary Matthews, you know what you're doing. He fit on that ball club. When he got Rick Sutcliffe, he knew what he was getting. When you pick up a Dennis Eckersley, you know you're getting some quality pitching. Eckersley is going to take the ball for you forever. That guy is going to *be* there. You don't have to worry about a young guy coming out in the fifth or sixth inning because he's mad at the umpire or whatever. You have a professional guy who's been through it. Eck is going to let it fly and be there for eight.

"Dallas put Scott Sanderson in a good place, protected him. Scott was our fourth or fifth starter, and he had Steve Trout as our third starter. Nobody could get more out of Rainbow than Billy Connors. Billy was another part of Dallas's ship. Billy Connors knew how to get Rainbow to pitch. He understood Steve Trout. Steve Trout was a mechanical pitcher. There were times when he wanted to do things so perfectly and analyze it, and there is nothing in the world wrong with that, but sometimes he wanted to be too perfect, and Billy knew how to loosen him up and talk to him. 'That's it, that's it, go get them. That's what you're looking for.' And Steve was one of our better pitchers that season. [Trout finished 13–7.]

"On July 1, 1984, I got my wish to be traded. Jimmy Frey wasn't using me the way I felt I needed to be used, and I didn't fit in well helping this team get to where they wanted to go. Even though I hated to leave my teammates in Chicago, I was traded to Texas. Those players had been very protective of me. Those guys were so tight. Dallas never would have traded me if I hadn't asked him. But even though I felt I had to leave, nobody wanted to see the Cubs win more than I did."

The Red Baron

The modern era of the Chicago Cubs, today the most popular baseball team in the country, began in 1984. The elements at the start of the season were in place: There was Beautiful Wrigley Field, America's most cherished ballpark. There was WGN, a superstation connected to 20 million homes, broadcasting the games. There was Harry Caray, the voice of the Cubs, who was about to become a national icon, thanks to his talent and the growing power of cable television.

"Cubs win. Cubs win. The Good Lord wants the Cubs to win!" Harry would chant.

All that was missing was a winning team.

Dallas Green had promised a pennant when he took over before the '82 season, and coming off his early performance, few believed or had faith in him.

When on June 14, 1984, Green traded for Cleveland pitching ace Rick Sutcliffe, few Cubs fans could imagine the impact the tall pitcher with the red beard would have on the team.

When the six-foot-seven-inch Sutcliffe arrived, his record with the Indians had been 4–5. With the Cubs, however, he was virtually unbeatable, winning fourteen games in a row and compiling a 16–1 record as he became lionized more than any Cubs pitcher within recent memory.

The fans saw his toughness on the mound and were impressed that he was a battler who was not afraid to throw inside. It wasn't greatly publicized, but Sutcliffe was a man who always insisted on giving something back to the community, and he started a foundation that donated tickets to the needy for every home game. In his spare time he visited sick kids in hospitals, and for hours wherever he was he would stand and sign autographs.

In '84, Rick Sutcliffe and the rest of Jim Frey's Cubs gave Harry Caray a top-rated show every day. Not only did the Cubs draw more fans than any year in their history—2,108,055 in tiny Wrigley Field—but the Cubs were the top-rated show every day of the season from mid-June on—regardless of the time they played.

As Curt Smith described, "It was striking, the emergence of the eighties' most popular baseball team, the persevering naif buoyed by hope and natural greenery, like America itself."

RICK SUTCLIFFE: "At the end of '83 in Cleveland, I demanded to be traded. I wanted out. We had had two straight years of losing, and I was willing to sacrifice my free agency to do that. I gave them a list of six teams where I wouldn't let them trade me. One of the teams was the Cubs. The reason for that was the Cubs had a terrible year in '83, and I wanted to go somewhere where I could win.

"I had held my request through late January, but the Indians refused to deal me. This was all Gabe Paul. Mr. Paul. He wasn't going to let me go.

"So I signed back with him, and in June I got the phone call from Dallas Green. 'We want you to come over to the Cubs, but we can't make the deal until you sign an extension.'

"I had wanted to leave Cleveland, but when I found out they had traded me, my first reaction was, How come Cleveland doesn't want me anymore? Cleveland had given me an opportunity to be in the big leagues when I came over in 1982 from the Dodgers after Tom Lasorda said that I didn't even belong in the big leagues.

"Cleveland gave me the baseball, and I won the ERA title in '82, won 18 games and made the All-Star team in '83. At that point in mid-June 1984 we weren't playing well as a team, but like everyone else in baseball, I still felt the Indians could make a run at it, we could get back in it.

"So that was the first emotion that I had. I remember Phil Segui, the Indians general manager, telling me for the deal to be completed, I needed to sign a three-year extension. Cleveland emphasized to me what a great opportunity it was, but I knew in my heart I was going to be a free agent at the end of the '84 year. My whole life I dreamed of playing baseball in my hometown in Kansas City, and I wasn't going to sign that extension because I knew at the end of the year I was going to go home and play. At first they said that my refusal to sign the extension was going to throw the deal off, and [the Cubs] might have taken Bert Blyleven at that time.

"In the end I became a Cub because of Dallas Green. He said that he wanted me. I was the guy he *had* to have. Even though I wouldn't sign the extension, he still insisted that I was the pitcher who was in there. Bert Blyleven actually *wanted* to be traded. He had been there longer than I had, was frustrated by not winning. He was ready to go. But Dallas wanted me.

"I wasn't that excited about it when it first happened because I believe you sleep in the bed you make, and someone else was deciding what bed that was for me. I had made that bed in Cleveland, and I wanted to try to straighten it out.

"But once I got on the plane and got to Chicago, immediately I felt the excitement that was in the air.

"There was a waiver wire with Joe Carter that got messed up, and because of that I didn't get to pitch for the first four games. I saw the Cubs lose four straight games, and at the end of the fourth one, Billy Connors, the pitching coach, brought all the pitchers and catchers into the weight room for a little meeting, and I mean he m-f'ed everybody. 'You fucking guys are horseshit.' Lee Smith had thrown a sidearm breaking ball to Mike Schmidt, and he had hit it about 500 feet. He said, 'You big son of a bitch. What the fuck are you doing dropping down. You stay over the top and you blow people away.' He went right down the line and aired on everybody.

"It's kind of funny looking back, but I was in the group, and when he got to me, I thought, What the hell can he say to me? And I'll never forget, he said, 'You big motherfucker, when the fuck are you going to do something around here, you lazy so-and-so. When are you going to get somebody out?'

"I thought, Holy shit. He meant it too. His eyes were big, and he was sweatin' and spittin' and it lit a fire under all of us, and I got to pitch the next night in Pittsburgh, and we won the game 2–1. And Lee Smith came in and got the save and blew them away.

"We were off and running. I can remember as the season went on, we were winning, and everybody enjoyed it so much. On the buses and planes, the music was loud and everybody had fun. The one thing that team really shared was the desire to win. We'd get on a plane after losing two out of three, and there wouldn't

Rick Sutcliffe

be anything going on. No one would play cards. Everybody was just pissed because we didn't win. That team was so focused on winning.

"That year we had one of the best coaching staffs in the history of baseball. We had Billy Connors, Johnny Oates, John Vukovich, Ruben Amaro, Don Zimmer— what a great third-base coach he was. Jim Frey just orchestrated it all. He had surrounded himself with a great cast. Billy ran the pitching staff, and everybody had his role. Jim ultimately made the final decisions. The MVP of the team had to be Dallas Green. He brought Ryno over there. He brought me there. He's the one who created the Cubs that we have today, and the tremendous following.

"We never played on the road that year. We might not have hit in the bottom of the ninth, but everywhere we went we had more fans than the home teams did. I had played in Dodger Stadium for three years. That year against the Dodgers in L.A., [Cubs catcher] Jody Davis came up in the bottom of the seventh, and the crowd began chanting, 'Jody, Jody, Jody.' I saw the Reds come to town in L.A. in the late '70s, all the great teams, and that *never* happened at Dodger Stadium, but that did in 1984.

"There's no question that Harry Caray was more popular than any five players that we ever had. When he would come on the field, you didn't have to see him. You could hear it. You knew that he was in the area somewhere. Just the excitement that he brought to a game. Harry didn't broadcast from his mind. It always came from his heart. I don't know that anybody in the history of baseball ever had more fun than Harry Caray did, both on and off the field.

"And I can remember in one of the biggest weekends that year, we came home and played the Cardinals. The Saturday game, on June 23, was one of the top-ten all-time games. Because of the importance, the Cardinals-Cubs rivalry. Because there were 38,000 people at Wrigley Field. Because the guy on the mound for the

Cardinals was Bruce Sutter, probably the best reliever in the game at that time. Because at that point Ryno was an unknown middle infielder.

"I had never heard Ryne Sandberg's name before I came to the Cubs. He reminded me that I had faced him in spring training in Arizona when I was with Cleveland, that I only faced him once, and I drilled him. I hit a lot of people back then. My control wasn't real good, and being a little bit wild helped me. But I didn't remember that. We kidded about it.

"The game seemed real uneventful until the ninth. Ryno had some hits, but we were getting our butts kicked. And then Ryno took Sutter deep to tie it up.

"And then in the eleventh, we were losing again, and Sutter had Bobby Dernier 0–2, and he battled back to get a walk. Ryne came up against Sutter, and we thought, There is no way, and I'll be damned. He did it again, hit another home run, tied it up again, and if I remember right, in the twelfth or thirteenth he led off with a double and actually scored the winning run to win 12–11."

HARRY CARAY: "The first pitch to Sandberg [in the tenth] is low, ball one. One ball, no strikes, two out, a runner at first, 11–9 in favor of the Cardinals. The pitch. Strike on the outside corner. They give Sandberg the entire right-field section. Now the stretch, the pitch, there's a drive, way back, it might be out of here, it IIIIIIS. He did it again. He did it again. Oh. The game is tied. Un-believable. How about that! Listen to this crowd. Everybody has gone bananas. Holy cow! What would the odds be if I told you that twice Sandberg would hit home runs off Bruce Sutter? Come on, you guys. He can't do it all himself.

"An 11–11 tie. We're now lining up for the extra point. This is baseball, the Cardinals and the Cubs. The pitch to Dave Owen. Base hit! The Cubs win, the Cubs win. Holy cow. The Cubs win. Listen to the crowd. I never saw a game like this in my life, and I've been around a long life. Holy cow! Down 7–1. How 'bout the kid, hit a line drive like a bullet.

"Everybody up, high-fiving each other. Whoa, what a victory. What a victory! Listen to that crowd."

RICK SUTCLIFFE: "It was my wife's first game at Wrigley Field as a member of the Cubs, and after the game she looked at me and said, 'Are all the games like this?' We had come from Cleveland with 800 people in the stands. This was incredible, and my thought was, I got to pitch the next day. Gee, how do you follow this act? And that was probably the best game of the year for me. In front of 40,000 fans I threw a four-hit shutout, struck out 14 guys, against St. Louis. The win put us a half a game behind the Phils and the Mets.

"We didn't put them away at that point, but we certainly got their attention.

"My next start was against the Dodgers, where I started my career. With the exception of one man, everyone there had been so good to me. Peter O'Malley, Walter O'Malley before he passed away, was just wonderful. Ron Perranoski, the pitching coach, was like a second father to me. I knew more of the Dodgers teammates than I did the Cubs.

"When I went out to pitch that day, I really wanted to prove that Tommy Lasorda was wrong, to show the Dodgers they had made a mistake getting rid of me.

"It all started in '81, after we came back from the strike. For about a week or so I didn't pitch at all. I was in the bullpen and didn't really know what my role was. We were in San Diego, and I went to Ron Perranoski, the pitching coach, and asked him, and he said, 'I don't know. Go ask Tommy.'

"He went with me, and we sat down in Tommy's office, and I said, 'Tommy, I know I'm not pitching great, but I've done everything you've ever asked of me. When I've come in games, I've protected our players. I'm the first one out in a fight. I'm here early every day, running extra. I know you don't think I'm doing a whole lot, but if you'd just start me one more game, let me pitch four or five innings, maybe somebody else would see something they liked and I might get a chance.

"He almost had tears in his eyes. Tommy said, 'You've done everything we've ever asked of you.' He promised me another start.

"The next to the last day of the season we were at home. I had pitched one inning. I went to Ron Perranoski and said, 'Perry, am I starting today or tomorrow?' He said, 'No.' I said, 'What did Tommy have to say?' He said, 'You'll have to go ask him.'

"It took all the nerve I had just to walk in. There were reporters around him. I said, 'Tommy, excuse me. Can I talk to you.' He said, 'No, I don't have time.' I said, 'Tommy, I really need to talk to you.' He said, 'Listen, I have important things to take care of. It's going to have to wait.'

"I said, 'I'm sorry, but you guys are going to have to leave. I need to talk to him.'

"I escorted the writers out and shut the door, and I walked back to him and said, 'Tommy, you gave me your word I was going to get to pitch. How come I can't pitch?'

"He said, 'The opportunity didn't present itself.' We had already won the first half. If we win the second half, we play the team that finishes second. It didn't matter whether we won or lost.

"I said, 'Tommy, that's not going to fly.'

"He said, 'I wanted to look at the younger guys.' He was talking about Bob Welch and Dave Stewart and Joe Beckwith and Ted Power. I mean, some of them were *older* than I was.

"I said, 'Tommy, that ain't gonna work.' He said, 'Look, you don't even belong in the big leagues. I don't know what you're doing bothering me.'

"And I lost it. I said, 'You lied to me. You can do anything you want to me, but you can't lie to me.' And I cleaned things off his desk, and I grabbed his desk and slammed it.

"I grabbed a chair, and I was going to throw it through his wall. He had all these pictures signed by Frank Sinatra. I had met Mr. Sinatra a couple of times. He always came in with a big entourage. I swear it's amazing what goes through your mind in a short period of time, 'cause I had that chair, and I rared back to throw it through those pictures, and all that went through my mind, and I stopped. I thought, I'm in enough trouble. I don't need Frank Sinatra after me.

"So I slammed the chair on the ground, turned around, grabbed Tommy, and I lifted him. I didn't hit him. I picked him up in the air, told him if he wasn't so old . . . and I dropped him.

"When you get excited, you get carried away.

"And I left. We went upstairs and told Mr. O'Malley and Mr. Campanis that I couldn't stay. My agent, Barry Axelrod, was with me, and so was my wife. We got on a plane that evening and flew back to Kansas City.

"The next day I read in the paper the reason it happened was that I was upset because I wasn't on the World Series roster. That had nothing to do with it. I had pitched one inning since the strike. I knew I wasn't going to be on the roster.

"But Tommy had the power of the press, and it really wasn't until 1984 that my side of the story even came out, and with all that was going on in '84, nobody really cared to hear it.

"No question, the biggest mistake I made in my career. That was immaturity. I didn't know how the game was played. I didn't know the manager-player relationship. I grew up in the Midwest, I'm a country boy. And people were honest back there. They may not tell you what you want, but they are going to tell you the truth.

"It was a tough lesson for me to learn. I found myself a few months later in Cleveland as a player-to-be-named-later in a trade.

"Anyway, this was my first chance to pitch against the Dodgers. I didn't want them to get to me, but I guess they did. About the third or fourth inning, as I came off the mound, Jody Davis said, 'Hey, are you going to throw anything besides fastballs?' We had gotten to the third or fourth inning, and I hadn't thrown a breaking ball. I was so determined to beat them the only thing I threw was fastballs. And I just ran out of gas. There was too much emotion. That was my only loss that year, when they got to me.

"I did get even with them later on during the year, and several times after that. But I learned a lesson that night. I learned it's tough enough to win when you've got your mind together, let alone adding all that pressure and all the emotions to it.

"The Mets were the team we had to beat. In early August at Wrigley we had a series against them. After we scored a bunch of runs off Ed Lynch, he drilled Keith Moreland. Eddie was a big competitor.

"Keith, who we called Zonk, went out to the mound, and when Lee Smith and I got to the pile, I don't think they wanted anything to do with us. We had a huge team, with Tim Stoddard, Jody Davis, Gary Matthews, Leon Durham, a big club. They didn't want *anything* to do with us.

"In the ninth inning Lee Smith was on the mound, and I remember the biggest pitch he threw was the one he threw at George Foster's head. We had all been warned not to throw at another batter. But Lee didn't care about the save. He knew we had the bullpen who could come in and get the out before they scored four runs. And I mean Lee threw it a hundred, in the shadows. I'm sure George Foster thought it went in one ear and came out the other. He doesn't know how it missed him.

"They knew it was coming. And everybody thought, George Foster is going to go get him. Here we go again. And George Foster didn't want anything to do with him. And nobody on that Mets bench moved. We felt, 'We got their attention and maybe a little bit more.'

"Lee set it in stone, 'Look, boys, there's a new sheriff in town.'

"It was ironic that the guy who started the fight in the first game, Eddie Lynch, is now the general manager of the Cubs. Eddie was just doing what a lot of people would have done. They were getting their butt kicked. If you're going to go, take somebody with you.

"All through the summer we battled the Mets. We had a pretty good lead going into September. It seemed that every series was so big. There was all of the talk of the '69 team and the collapse, and the fans not wanting us to do it again. The media wrote, 'It's not going to last. It never does. Never will.'

"I remember on a Friday night at Shea Stadium in early September, Dwight Gooden threw a one-hit shutout against us. Dwight was a rookie, and he was unhittable. He had one flaw—that you could run on him. But how do you get on first to do it? Once we got to first, it was pretty easy to get to third, and that's the only way he got beat that year. But every series, you hoped that he pitched the night before and you didn't have to face him.

"I remember he and I filmed a cover for *Sports Illustrated* and we never talked. We never even said hello. Don Drysdale had taken me under his wing when I was with the Dodgers, and he told me that unless it was somebody I had played with, I should never talk to an opponent. I didn't care who you were. I was going to have to get you out or beat you at one time, and I didn't want to be your friend. So we shot that cover and never talked. I think Dwight felt the same way. They were trying to win the division, and let's get this thing over with so I can kick your ass.

"So Dwight threw that one-hitter, and I was scheduled to pitch the next game. I had lunch with Jody and Keith Moreland that day, and they looked at me and said, 'Hey, Bigun, we need you tonight. We really need you tonight.' When my teammates told you that, that filled me with confidence, and I threw a shutout, and we beat them 6–0.

"I remember as I was warming up in the bullpen, the fans were hollering things at me, like they can in New York. From the second deck a guy threw a black cat at me. It landed right next to the mound in the bullpen, and Billy Connors's eyes looked like silver dollars when he saw that cat. It landed, didn't miss me by a foot, and it waddled off right there beside me.

"Billy said, 'Oh no.' I looked at him, and I thought, I feel sorry for the cat too. I said, 'I think it's all right.'

"Billy was worried about the cat. He knew the history of the black cat and the Cubs in '69. He was figuring, 'Here we go again.'

"I had never heard of it before. I had followed the Kansas City Royals and the Kansas City Athletics. I didn't know much about the Chicago Cubs. Probably a good thing. I couldn't have cared less about the black cat and the bad luck it was supposed to bring.

"I remember after the last out—this was my twelfth win in a row—Billy came running out, and Billy is a big man, and he hugged me. 'Yeah, yeah, yeah. That cat didn't bother you at all, did it?' He was so excited. I would have thought he would have been used to it, because we had been playing pretty well. But he was worried about the effect of the black cat.

"The next day we laughed about it. First of all he had to explain the history to me."

JIM SHAPIRO: "Even when the Cubs were ahead in September, you didn't really believe they would do anything. Early September of 1969 wasn't that far away for Cubs fans. It's like a no-hitter. We weren't even going to talk about it. But you got to the second week in September, maybe September 10, and the Cubs did not unravel, they were still kicking butt, and it really began to dawn on me, 'I don't believe it. Something magic could happen this year.' It was really, really exciting.

"Every year you said, 'They have a good team but the pitching stinks,' but this year the pitching was great. Rick Sutcliffe is a very imposing guy, no matter how you call it. And the team clicked, and there was a spirit. It was as if I was watching something new—which it was. It was a winning team and a winning spirit. I was impressed with the way the Cubs would win on the road, not just at Wrigley Field."

RICK SUTCLIFFE: "Beginning in mid-June things started to get crazy. I lived downtown. I rented an apartment with my wife and daughter. I couldn't even go out and put gas in my car. The next thing you knew, there'd be a huge traffic jam, with everybody wanting autographs. For a guy who had just come from Cleveland . . . I couldn't believe it. It was an honor to be recognized, but you learned you had to eat dinner at home, and you couldn't go anywhere because things would get out of control.

"Some players resented it a little, but they should have played in Cleveland for a couple of years. I couldn't give away Indians tickets, and in Chicago I could have gotten cars and houses for those tickets, they were just so tough to come by.

"I lived downtown at Lake Point Tower, and I'd come down to get in a cab to go to the park, and there were all these people there waiting on me. They knew I was going to come out eventually every day. I'd sign autographs there. I'd get in the cab and get to the park, and I'd sign more autographs. And then during batting practice, I'd sign autographs. And after the game there'd be people there and I'd sign autographs. And then I'd get in the cab to go home, and once I got back there, the people who didn't get your autograph at the park would be waiting there. It was just a lot of fun.

"Through September we kept winning. I don't recall there was tension. The best team that ever played baseball is going to lose one out of three, and the worst team is going to win one of three. There was concern as to whether the Mets could catch us, but everyone was so focused on winning. It helped having a veteran team too, because I had gone through three pennant races in L.A., and Bowa and Matthews and Eckersley had all been there, and because of that I don't think there was ever any tension or panic, just a lot of emotion and desire. Pat Riley, the basketball coach, got credit for the word *focus*. We might not have called it *focus* back then, but that team certainly had it.

"Probably the one moment that stands out in my mind that season was the night we clinched the pennant in Pittsburgh. There were 5,000 fans that night.

"As I walked to the bullpen to warm up, I'll never forget looking over and seeing about thirty people holding this big banner that said, 39 Years of Suffering Is Enough. I just remember the look in those people's eyes, the little kids. You could tell they had come a long ways to watch that game. In the back of my mind, I thought, We can end that tonight.

"We got a run in the top of the first. Ryno got on, and Gary Matthews drove him in. I remember when we got that first run it seemed like a big run, because I had things going, everything felt good, and normally when my control is there, at that point in my career it was tough to score on me. And we ended up beating them 4–1. I threw a two-hitter.

"As I went out to take the mound in the ninth, all I could think of was, Three outs. I remember Jody Davis running up to me, and he said, 'I want to catch the last out. I want that ball on the last out.'

"As I was warming up, it hit me what he meant. We got the first two out, and I thought, Golly, he not only wants me to get him out, he wants me to strike this guy out. The batter's name was Joe Orsulak. He was real tough to strike out. The funny part was I threw a two-hitter and Joe had both hits and actually scored the run.

"Well, I struck him out, and Jody came running out, and everybody was hugging, and Jody handed me the baseball and he said, 'Here, man, you deserve this more than anybody.' I said, 'I don't know who deserves it, but I want you to have it.' And he still has it today. I imagine he could retire on that baseball if he ever wanted to sell it."

HARRY CARAY: "One more and it's over! The Chicago Cubs will be the new Eastern Division champs! They're getting security on the field. These Cubs fans are going to explode. . . . Who's excited? Listen to this crowd! Might as well join 'em. . . . Hey, it's in there! Cubs are the champions! The Cubs are the champions! The Cubs win! Look at that mob scene. Orsulak down on strikes! Rick Sutcliffe— his fourteenth in a row, 16–1 for the year! He faced only twenty-eight men! He pitched a two-hitter! Let's just watch it. The fans are getting on the field! Now our lives are complete! The Cubs are number one! The Cubs have clinched the Eastern Division title!"

JIM SHAPIRO: "It was an incredible thrill. I still see one of the great images: There were two outs in the ninth, the Cubs were ahead, and there was a group of a few thousand Cubs fans out in Three Rivers Stadium, and they began unfurling a huge banner, maybe three hundred feet long, with letters three or four feet high, that said '39 Years of Suffering Is Enough.'

"There was another out, and they clinched it. It was a great euphoria. It was simply unbelievable, almost like you couldn't absorb it."

RICK SUTCLIFFE: "All season long the Cubs fans were just so great. They love ya. You're like family to them, more than just a ballplayer. Being part of that family, being with people like Harry Caray . . . those people created me. I had done some things in L.A. and Cleveland, but there weren't many people who even heard my name, could even spell it. Harry Caray called me the Red Baron. The next thing I knew, it was unbelievable. I get goose bumps just talking about it."

70

So Close

RICK SUTCLIFFE: "I was the pitcher for the Cubs in the opening game of the division championships. It was really hectic, because tickets were so hard to come by, and I had to come up with twenty of them.

"I threw a fastball in the low nineties, had a good slider, but my main asset was my location and ability to pitch in. If a guy took a good swing at me, I was going to come in and come in hard to try to get the outer half, where I could throw it out there and not get hurt. Don Drysdale taught me that early. And having that good location on the outer half, when you pitched in, it was a good combination.

"San Diego had a great team. Tony Gwynn was always tough. You don't walk him. You gotta make him hit the ball. Alan Wiggins was the same way. Then came the power. Garv [Steve Garvey] and [Kevin] McReynolds, Graig Nettles and Terry Kennedy. They had Garry Templeton hitting eighth, so you knew they were solid all the way through."

PAUL BUCHBINDER: "I was trying to muster up everything I could to believe we were going to win. I was confident at the beginning of that series. When Bob Dernier stepped up to the plate and hit a home run, the first batter for the Cubs, I said, 'This is it.' The poetry happening. Sutcliffe hit a home run, the Cubs won 13–0. It was a breeze, a cakewalk."

HARRY CARAY: "We're in the bottom of the third. Here's Rick Sutcliffe getting a big hand. A good hitter batting .250 for the year. With six RBIs. Here's the pitch by [Eric] Show. There's a drive, way back, it might be, it could be, it IIIIS, Holy cow, out onto Sheffield Avenue, his first National League home run.

"Rick Sutcliffe, his cup overfloweth now. His first home run in the National League. That's the third home run of the day. For the Cubs the twenty-first off Show this year. Everybody's running down the stairway from the rooftops to see if they can locate the ball."

RICK SUTCLIFFE: "I have no idea how that happened. I've always swung hard, in case I hit it. I couldn't believe it. He basically hit my bat. I hadn't hit one all year. I had been swinging the same way. The next thing you know, it was out in the middle of the street somewhere. That was neat. It was probably the biggest thrill of the day, because the game was over with early.

"Rainbow [Steve Trout] pitched beautifully in the second game. Lee came in in the ninth to nail it down.

"We knew we were going to win. That's the way I felt but I don't think any more so than the way we felt the whole year. We knew going into every series we were going to win."

PAUL BUCHBINDER: "Three games to go. You can't win one out of three games? It's a lock. Except that what is this deal, there should have been three games at Wrigley Field. But because Wrigley Field didn't have lights, the league cheated us. There should have been three games in Chicago. TV wanted the weekend games at night. So something was happening here. Wait a second! It's our home field advantage, and the league has taken it away."

RICK SUTCLIFFE: "I don't think that plane trip to San Diego was any different from any other. There was some celebrating, but we did that when we took two out of three from Montreal. I didn't see any difference. We knew what we had to do. And we weren't just looking at the Padres. We were looking at the Detroit–Kansas

City series too, wondering who we were going to beat in the Series. Not that we looked past anyone. We felt like we were going to win.

"In the third game Garry Templeton hit a big bases loaded, opposite field double. Eck threw something down and away, and Templeton went with it, and the game was over at that point.

"Originally I was going to pitch Game 4. I got taken out of the first one, saved some innings so I could do that. Then Frey changed his mind and started Sanderson instead. The score was 5–5 in the ninth inning. Lee was on the mound. There was a runner on, and Steve Garvey was up."

PAUL BUCHBINDER: "Anybody, anybody but Steve Garvey. I pitied Cindy. Garvey always seemed like a politician from the get-go, the way he looked, his demeanor, his all-American image, and I just hated Garvey. And I certainly don't like him any more today.

"And sure enough, Garvey comes up in the situation.

"I was watching it on TV at my house. We had champagne in the refrigerator. I had about fifteen friends. Friends who weren't even baseball fans were there because they wanted to be there. They wanted to see what it would be like for me after all this time to finally celebrate winning a pennant.

"I paced and I paced. In the early parts of the game I watched a little bit. Went into the kitchen, prepared some food and drinks for everybody.

"And then we just got engulfed in this television thing, and my stomach sunk.

"I was more certain that the Cubs were going to win at the point where Lee Smith came in than I was at any time during the playoffs. My pacing stopped, and I was frozen, and I couldn't believe it. My whole body slumped.

"Steve Garvey punching his right fist into the air. He's rounding first base, clapping his hands, and I'm seeing Lee Smith walking off the mound, he's sort of slumped, hands on his hips at first, and then he slumped off. It's like watching Ruby shoot Oswald, you know. You see it in slow motion.

"I recorded that series. I have it on tape, and I can watch the first two games, and I can even watch the fifth game. I can watch the ball go through Durham's legs. But I can't watch Steve Garvey circle the bases and listen to the commentators talk about him and Cindy and something about their little girl. It was just terrible.

"Durham is a Cub. I can criticize Durham, and I can forgive him. But *not Steve Garvey*. It's like the way Indiana Jones feels about snakes. Aw, not the snakes."

RICK SUTCLIFFE: "When Garvey hit the home run, I got pissed. 'Son of a bitch.' We wanted to get on to Detroit and get it going. I never overlooked them, but when he hit it, I was pissed that we didn't win that game, and then I thought, It doesn't matter. Everybody felt, Oh well, we should have won it today. I wish I could have pitched the opener in the series. Now we got to beat their butts tomorrow. We'll get that done and start Rainbow against Detroit. I remember San Diego tried to sign me later that winter. I went to dinner with Joan Kroc and Garv and [manager] Dick Williams. She was talking about seeing me going out to warm up, and she said she had just hated me so much because she knew they had no chance of beating me. She said, 'If there is any way something would happen to him, we would have a chance.' I felt that way. I thought, No matter what it takes, we're going to get it done."

PAUL BUCHBINDER: "I have a friend, Warren Mullen, who lives out in San Francisco. He's a Cubs fan. When the Cubs come to town, Warren goes to Candlestick Park with a Cubs uniform jersey on. That's a fan. He called me Saturday night about one in the morning, Sunday morning really, and he said, 'Paul, we have to go to the fifth game.' He had a business where he brokered airplane frequent flier mileage, so he was encouraging me to come out, and I wouldn't have to even pay for the airfare. But I didn't know whether I should actually be there. I didn't know whether it was better to have that many Cub fans together in one place or to send our vibes out to San Diego.

"All through the night I was going back and forth. I eventually decided I could not go, even though he was pleading with me. I just felt it was better to remain in Chicago—this sort of strange psychological phenomenon of unity, we must be together, and that there would be fewer of us in Chicago out there if I went.

"For the fifth game, contrary to what I should have done, I was still at my house. I should have learned from the night before that my house was unlucky. But I watched it at my house. Not a big crowd. I couldn't go through that again. I called all my friends who I knew to make sure they would be watching too.

"'Cause I could see in Game 5, it's happening. It's happening *again*. It's like this is fate. We're *not* going to win now. We're going to find some way *not* to win.

"By the beginning of the fifth game, I was back in the position of thinking, Boy, we *are* the Second City. These players may have no relations to previous Cubs teams, but they are wearing the same uniform. Dallas Green, the New Tradition—doesn't matter. I don't know that *new* goes with the word *tradition*. I don't know if you can modify it.

"Sutcliffe was going again. Should he be going again? My brother and I argued about it. 'Nah, Frey should start Trout.' 'Ah, well, Sutcliffe is really incredible. Maybe he's meant to win.' 'Nah, Trout . . .'

"Finally, my brother and I sent a telegram to Larry Bowa. He was the Cubs captain. We addressed it to 'Captain Larry Bowa.' Essentially it said, 'We Must Believe. We Are the Cubs.' There again is a contradiction. We're the Cubs. You *can't* believe we're going to win! But I didn't realize that when I was writing it. I felt 'All the bad stuff is behind us. We're the Cubs.' And it was signed by me and my brother. We were sending our spirit out there. We wanted Bowa to know we believed in them, because we were feeling what the Cubs were feeling."

RICK SUTCLIFFE: "We got the early lead. When I got three runs in the first couple of innings, that game should have been over. That whole season, when that happened, that was it. I felt like that was going to be it.

"I remember it was hot, as hot as it could be, and they got a couple runs off me in the sixth, and then [Tim] Flannery hit a bullshit ground ball.

"Oh man. You know, on that ground ball [through Leon Durham's legs], I don't know what happened, because I was breaking to the bag. I had my head down and was going to cover first. I don't recall what all was said. After that . . . I took the blame. I remember sportswriter Bob Verdi coming up to me the next year and saying, 'In all these years of sports, it would have been so easy for you to hide and blame somebody else.' I didn't.

"The tying run was on second. If Leon could have knocked it down, then the tying run wouldn't have scored. And when the tying run scored, I'm telling you, it seemed like that whole place erupted. Then everything started going their way. The crowd doesn't bother you, but it seemed they were really motivated.

"The rest was freakish—Alan Wiggins, the count was 0–2, and he hit a bloop single over the third baseman's head. And then Tony Gwynn hit the ball up the middle, and it hit something on the infield and bounced over Sandberg's head, and then Garv hit the shit out of it. He hit a ground ball up the middle, and it was just disbelief.

"I remember thinking, I cannot believe that this has happened.

"I sat there on the bench as the game was winding down and I thought, There is no way, no way this thing could get away from us.

"We had chances to get more runs. Things could have been different. But when they gave me three runs early in the game, that should have put us in the World Series, and because of that, I felt, it's my fault. It's not anyone else's fault. I should have been able to take care of it then. Forget Templeton's hit. Forget Garvey's home run. I should have been able to take care of it then.

"Wiggins did a great job putting it in play, Gwynn battled his ass off . . . you know. I give them all the credit. Sometimes you have to tip your hat to people. It's just unfortunate that it happened to be the fifth game of the series."

PAUL BUCHBINDER: "I remember watching as the ball went through Leon Durham's legs. Tim Flannery was the batter. It is so clear in my mind. It was an almost identical play to what an ex-Cub would do in the Series a couple years later.

"As soon as the ball went through his legs, I remember yelling, 'Oh no.' Whether that means 'Oh no, I can't believe it' or 'Oh no, they've done it again' or 'Oh no, it's not going to happen,' I'm not sure. Maybe it expresses all those things. But it may be something about the world just not being fair. Why don't we get a chance somehow?

"And then, you just saw Padres players crossing the plate. For all effect, that was the ball game. The game was lost. The series was lost. The Cubs were—the Cubs—again."

JIM SHAPIRO: "I remember watching the final game on television at home. As I recall, the Cubs were ahead. I remember when that ball was hit and went through Durham's legs, and the tying run scored, at that moment it was the end. I remember yelling out a bloodcurdling scream. My wife came running in, thought something had happened to me, that I was having some kind of attack, and of course, I was having an attack, a Cub attack.

"I have to tell you, and for a year or so I was ashamed to say it, but I actually got physically very sick. I'm a big fan, and I'm into the Cubs, but if they lose, OK, we get on with our lives. I'm a reasonable guy, I have my life. I have my family. I have my job. But I can clearly remember in 1984, I actually got physically ill. I went into the bathroom and I vomited. And I was sick for two days. I kept saying, 'Wait a minute. I'm a grown man. This is ridiculous. This shouldn't be me. It's just a baseball game.'

"I was wiped out for that day, and I was very sick the next day. I didn't eat. I simply couldn't eat for the balance of the day of the game, and for the entire next day I couldn't get any food down. And I do remember clearly saying to myself, 'It's a baseball game. What is this? It's crazy. I'm an adult.'

"But I couldn't get over it, and I still can't get over it."

NED BUCHBINDER, PAUL'S BROTHER: "My brother-in-law, Bob, is a family therapist, a Ph.D., a really good baseball fan. During the '84 playoffs, he had one patient, a nurse, a really great Cubs fan, who told him, 'I've been so depressed, I'm suicidal, but the Cubs winning has lifted my spirit.'

"My brother-in-law came up to West Bend to watch the San Diego series. After it was over he returned to Chicago for an appointment with her.

"She walked in, and he actually said, 'I know this doesn't sound professional, forgive me, but because the Cubs lost, I thought I might not ever see you again. It doesn't sound right, I shouldn't say this, but I'm so happy to see you!'"

RICK SUTCLIFFE: "After the game there were eight hundred reporters around me. I didn't have any players to talk to. Everyone wanted a story. I had no reason to ice my arm. There was no tomorrow. All I did was stand there and talk to them. I remember taking a real quick shower to get on the bus. As we pulled out, the Padres fans were holding ten thousand little Cubbie bears that were hanging from ropes, nooses, and they were throwing things at the bus. It was pretty tough getting out of there, what with the traffic. It was probably the longest day of my life.

"When I first arrived in Chicago in the spring, I began a foundation. I didn't do it because of the fans, I did it because it was important to my wife and me. I donated $100,000 a year from my salary to the foundation, donated all my appearance money, all my endorsements, my glove contract, my shoe contract, all that money went to it.

"We bought fifty tickets for each Cubs game and gave them out. We had an unbelievable number of requests and gave them out. We gave out T-shirts. Kids, elderly, handicapped. The only criteria is that normally you wouldn't be able to go. We serviced all those people. I had ten college scholarships I gave away each year. We would go through the inner city and process requests, and we've got doctors and lawyers who graduated from all over the country now. It's been a real neat thing.

"We visit the children's hospitals at least once a month, bring gifts and souvenirs, hats, baseballs.

"The neatest thing we did was the IOU program, where every time I visited the hospital, there always would be some kid who wasn't motivated, wasn't taking his medicine, had kind of given up. I'd go in there knowing his background and I'd say, 'Hey, I'm Rick Sutcliffe. I'm here to offer you some tickets to the Cubs games. Look, when you get well, I know you have a brother and a couple of buddies, and your favorite teacher in school and Mom and Dad want to go. Here's my home number. All you have to do is call me.' And I had a separate line just for the foundation.

"It was remarkable the responses we got, the letters and calls from doctors and nurses, that overnight these kids got better. It wasn't a cure, but it gave them hope to get out, to get well. We had so many great stories. They all bring tears to my eyes.

"After the visits to the hospitals and getting to meet all those wonderful people, it all came back to me with letters that winter. After we lost that final game to San Diego, I should have gotten letters like, 'You bum. You cost us the series.' Instead, people wrote, 'We wouldn't have been there without you. You were the only reason we got there.'

"I was a free agent at the end of the '84 season, and the reason I went back to Chicago was because the people took me into their hearts. I knew those fans deserved an opportunity to win. Sure, I could have gotten a lot more money than the Cubs gave me, and a couple more years too, but it was more money than I was ever going to need the rest of my life [$9.5 million for five years].

"I got offers from Ted Turner, Steinbrenner, millions of dollars. San Diego offered condos and money. When Kansas City tried to sign me back, I went to dinner with Ewing Kauffman. We were at a restaurant at the Kansas City Men's Club, and all of a sudden the mayor walked in. 'Just happened to be in the area,' he said. He had a drink with us. 'Hope you sign.' He left and five minutes later, Governor Kip Bond walked in. 'Just happened to be in the building. Heard you were here, and I wanted to come by. Happy you're going to be a Royal.'

"I said, 'I haven't signed yet.'

"He said, 'We know you're going to.'

"I remember, my agent looked at Mr. Kauffman after the governor left that night and said, 'I'll tell you what. If Ronald Reagan walks in, that's it, we'll sign.' And Mr. Kauffman looked at him and said, 'If you want that, we can have that arranged.' He was serious.

"I thought, This is crazy.

"But it was those Cubs fans who wrote their letters. And the things that they said. I got letters saying, 'Sorry you can't read this, but I can't stop crying while I'm writing it. Please come back to the Cubs.'

"I know the city of Chicago had a blast when the Bears won the championship in '85, and the last three years with the Bulls before this year, but I don't know that that city ever had more fun than they had the summer of 1984. Everybody had a ball.

"Those fans were crazy. To walk around the ballpark, to take batting practice at Wrigley and have the fans in bleachers hollering encouragement at you. I'd always throw baseballs up to them, play games with them. We had a blast that year.

"And since then we have had a special relationship. I had up and down years, went from Cy Young [in '84] to 8–8, 5–14 back to leading the league in wins [with 18 in '87], then 13–14. A lot of players have ups and downs after signing for lots of money, and the fans have been hard on them. I tell you what, after some of the worst times I had coming off those fields, I got some of the biggest ovations that I have ever got in my whole life. They took me into their hearts. We have a *real* special relationship.

"Players don't get treated like that very often. But the Cubs fans have been unbelievable to me. I don't know if any player was ever treated any better than I was."

71

The Demise of Dallas

In 1984 the Cubs constructed by Dallas Green had been eight outs away from winning the first pennant since 1945. Though Chicago didn't get a championship banner, Cubs personnel won most of the top awards. Rick Sutcliffe, who finished the year 20–6 [4–5 with Cleveland, 16–1 with the Cubs], won the Cy Young Award. Second baseman Ryne Sandberg, in his third year with the Cubs, hit .314 with 200 hits, 19 homers, 84 RBIs, and 32 stolen bases and was named the league's Most Valuable Player. Jim Frey was named the Manager of the Year, and Dallas Green was named the Executive of the Year.

After finishing first in 1984, the Cubs finished fourth and then fifth. In 1985, all five of Chicago's starting pitchers were injured. Midway through the 1986 season Dallas Green fired Jim Frey and replaced him with Gene Michael.

Green had made the Cubs, trading for Ryne Sandberg, Keith Moreland, Gary Matthews, Larry Bowa, Ron Cey, Dennis Eckersley, Steve Trout, Scott Sanderson, Dick Ruthven, Bob Dernier, and Rick Sutcliffe.

After the '86 season Green acquired Andre Dawson from Montreal. Seven times the Hawk had hit 20 homers, he had won six Gold Gloves, he had been named Rookie of the Year [in 1977], and he was the best player in Montreal history. One of his most impressive stats was a .346 average during day games.

In the spring of 1987, he announced he wanted to go to the Cubs. Dallas Green had a problem: The owners secretly had agreed not to sign any free agents from other clubs. How they thought they could get away with this is hard to imagine, but they did. Later an arbitrator would find them all guilty of collusion, and the penalties they would have to pay would be astronomical.

But while the collusion agreement was in force, no one could sign anyone else's free agents. Dawson put pressure on the Cubs when said he would sign a blank contract to play for them. Cubs pitcher Rick Sutcliffe increased the pressure when he said he'd chip in $100,000 of his own salary.

Dallas Green, a hard-liner against signing free agents, was in a bind. But getting a potential Hall of Famer such as Andre Dawson at a bargain-basement price was too much to turn down. By the end of the week, Dawson was a Cub. He had been offered $2 million for two years by the Expos. He signed with the Cubs for $500,000.

RICK SUTCLIFFE: "I got in a lot of trouble in '87. I came out at the end of '86 and said I'd give $100,000 of my salary to sign Andre Dawson. I got a pretty nasty phone call from Dallas saying, 'Look, you just pitch and I'll run the ball club.' That was the end of that. I told him, 'I'm not trying to do your job. If the Tribune Company doesn't have the money to pay him, I'll help. I know this: We got no chance to win without him. And it would be worth it to me to get him on our club, if that will help.' And a lot of people say that's the reason he showed up that day. He was standing outside the fence, just trying to get a contract. I don't know. Hawk told me that had a big part, to be wanted and for me to make a gesture like that. . . . Hawk always wanted that $100,000 from me. Doing what was best for the team, that's all I cared about."

In 1987, Cubs right fielder Andre Dawson was named the league's MVP. He was the first player ever to win the award while playing on a last-place team. That year Rick Sutcliffe almost won the Cy Young, just losing to Steve Bedrosian of the Phillies. The vote was 57–55. Another ex-Cub, Rick Reuschel [then with the Giants], finished third with 54 votes.

Though many Cubs fans continued to voice their dislike for Dallas Green, they were not noticing that Green had been rebuilding the farm system from top to bottom.

Since the 1960s the Cubs had received only paltry benefits from the players they raised themselves—particularly everyday players. Some of their most accomplished farm prospects—Joe Carter, Mike Krukow, and Willie Hernandez—went on to star for other teams.

The three most productive farm clubbers had been pitchers—Rick Reuschel, Bruce Sutter, and Lee Smith.

When Shawon Dunston became a regular in 1986, he became the first product of the Cubs farm system to win a full-time place in the team's lineup since Don Kessinger in 1966.

Andre Dawson

Coming up in 1986 were farm system prospects Jamie Moyer, Rafael Palmeiro, Greg Maddux, and Dave Martinez.

Unfortunately for Dallas Green, his relationship with the Tribune Company soured. Perhaps it was the disappointment over not winning the pennant in 1984. Perhaps it was his abrasive personality. Perhaps it was a lack of patience on the owners' part.

As the Cubs were finishing sixth (and last) in 1987, Dallas Green decided he would fire Gene Michael as manager and take over the job himself. This would have made him president, general manager, and field manager. After reconsidering, he decided that becoming manager would spread himself too thin, and he was planning to hire John Vukovich as manager when the Tribune Company decided it would step in and have a little chat with Green. Suddenly, unexpectedly, Dallas Green resigned from the Cubs entirely.

DICKIE NOLES: "In 1987 we finished last, but Dallas was putting things back together again. He's the one who went out and got Mark Grace. He went out and put together these scouts to draft all these young players who ended up making that such a good ball club in '88.

"I came back to the Cubs in '87, and the unique thing about coming back was the fact Chicago was my favorite place I ever played. I just loved that place.

"Andre Dawson had joined the club. I got to play with one of the greatest baseball players I've ever seen. Dallas had been through some rough times and had been told obviously, 'You can't sign a free agent,' and finally when Hawk said, 'I'll play for nothing. I'll sign a blank contract,' Dallas took him. The following year in the winter Dallas wanted to name Vukovich manager, which was the smart move, and why the owners in Chicago didn't want to do that I'll never know. But I do believe they wanted to take some of his power away. So he resigned."

Under Green the Cubs had won a division title, rebuilt their farm system, and made money. But like Leo Durocher, Green was too forceful, too threatening to the tranquillity of Cubdom.

Jim Frey, who had managed under Green from 1984 to 1986, took over as general manager. Frey hired old pro Don Zimmer to manage the Cubs. The Dallas Green era was over.

A funny thing happens when talented team builders depart. The team falls apart. The Cubs that Green built won another division title in '89, but after Jim Frey got finished, the Cubs would once again fall back into the cellar.

The start of the Cubs' decline came with one of Jim Frey's first player transactions, a deal that bewildered even his players. In 1988, Frey traded his dominating relief pitcher, Lee Smith, to the Boston Red Sox for two lesser pitchers, Calvin Schiraldi and Al Nipper. The reason Frey traded him? He didn't like that Lee Smith trained differently than the other pitchers.

RICK SUTCLIFFE: "Lee *knew* what it took for him to do his job. And that's what he did. Just running so many sprints a day. He did all the throwing that was needed. A lot of programs, pitching coaches throw everybody in spring training and say, 'I

Lee Smith

want everyone to run three miles.' Lee knew he was only going to pitch an inning or two. He could get that done by running fifteen to twenty sprints a day. He had his program when I got there in '84. My first spring training of '85, he knew what he had to do. A lot of people might not like that. But I'll tell you what, he ran those sprints every day, and he did his throwing every time. He was always available. To me, the game . . . people look at too many things that go on outside the lines. If we focus on what people do between the lines, then we've got a chance to put together a much better ball club. I don't care what they do off the field, as long as it's not il-legal or doesn't hurt anybody.

"I don't know how it came down, but once Frey became general manager and Zim was manager, they made the deal to get rid of him. You'd have to ask them. Maybe they thought Schiraldi and Nipper were going to be great players. I don't know."

FERGUSON JENKINS: "The bullpen became a significant part of baseball from the mid-'70s right through to now. The bullpen is a predominant part of a ball club now. They are the force that the manager works on all the time, and they influence the ball game.

"From 1985 to the present, all the strategy revolves around the bullpen. And the Cubs haven't understood that. They have a terrible bullpen. They had Bruce Sutter, and they traded him to St. Louis. They traded Lee Smith. He has 400 saves [471 at the end of the 1995 season]. He could have had 400 saves with the Cubs.

"They had some people, but unfortunately people get traded."

72

Let There Be Lights

The first night baseball game was played in Des Moines, Iowa, in the Class A Western League on April 28, 1930. When attendance soared, other minor league team owners, including William Wrigley, took notice and followed along. Wrigley installed lights in Wrigley Field—his minor league park by that name in Los Angeles.

The major league owners balked. Only Sam Breadon of the St. Louis Cardinals campaigned for night games. His Cards weren't drawing, and he needed help. He was given permission starting in 1932, but Philip Ball, who owned Sportsman's Park, where the Cards played, refused.

Larry MacPhail was the first major league owner to use lights, in 1935, at Crosley Field in Cincinnati. The American League granted its members the right to play night baseball in 1937, and lighting systems began popping up everywhere. Shibe Park in Philadelphia, Municipal Stadium in Cleveland, and Comiskey Park in Chicago first turned on their lights in 1939. The Polo Grounds in New York, Forbes Field in Pittsburgh, and Sportsman's Park in St. Louis lit up in 1940. Griffith Stadium in Washington, D.C., did it in 1941. Until 1942, only seven night games per team per year were permitted.

Braves Field and Yankee Stadium had lights in 1946, Fenway Park in 1947, and Briggs Stadium in Detroit in 1948.

The only holdout was PK Wrigley in Chicago. The Cubs had purchased a lighting system after the 1941 season, intending to begin construction on December 8, 1941. When the Japanese bombed Pearl Harbor, Phil Wrigley donated the steel for the light towers to the war effort.

By war's end, nearly every other major league stadium except Wrigley Field had lights. For the rest of his life, Phil Wrigley contended that night games would disturb the neighborhood around the park. Day games at Wrigley became part of the Cubs mystique.

When the Tribune Company bought the team, the talk about installing lights began. Lights were not the only tradition the Tribune Company changed.

Since William Wrigley bought the team, bleacher tickets had been sold only on the day of the game. It was a democratic system. Whoever showed up got to watch. The practice was what added the spontaneity to the decision to leave work and go to the ballpark at the spur of the moment.

In 1985 the Tribune Company changed the system and began selling bleacher tickets in advance. They argued that the fans in the long lines waiting to buy tickets on the day of the game were becoming rowdy. In terms of economics, one reason to sell tickets in advance is that the income from the tickets had to be invested, and interest can be made on the money from the time of purchase until game day.

One of the negative side effects of changing the system was that scalpers ended up buying many of the tickets. When the Cubs became the rage starting in 1984, many of the old regulars found they couldn't get into the ballpark.

The Cubs' success in 1984 also led to the installation of lights at Wrigley Field. When the Cubs made the playoffs that year, baseball commissioner Peter Ueberroth issued a statement that future postseason games involving the Cubs might not be played at Wrigley Field if they could not be played there at night. The reason, of course, was national television. Ueberroth told the Cubs that their home games might not even be played in Chicago—might, in fact, be played in St. Louis, of all places.

The Tribune Company had seen the economic benefit of playing night games but was hesitant for fear of alienating their fans. When Ueberroth threatened them with moving any playoff games to another ballpark, the Tribune Company began making plans for lights.

First, though, the Tribune Company had to overturn city and state ordinances that prohibited night games in residential neighborhoods. The Tribune Company filed a lawsuit declaring that the legislation was restricting their right to conduct business. Their petition, however, was met with derision by Circuit Court Judge Richard Curry, who cited the hallowed tradition of playing hooky from work and taking long lunches at Wrigley.

"The real litmus test for Cub loyalty," wrote Judge Curry, "is the willingness to blow off the job and flirt with unemployment to attend a game starting in the early afternoon."

By 1987 the city suggested that the Cubs might be able to get the ordinances suspended for postseason games. The Tribune Company wasn't satisfied with that, however. They wanted a partial schedule—eighteen night games, in order to justify the cost of installing the lights.

Opponents argued that they could use temporary lights at far less expense, but the Cubs didn't want to talk about temporary lights. They wanted real lights, like every other major league baseball team had used since 1946—which, it turned out, was when the Cubs' pennant drought began. The Tribune Company began whispering that if they could not erect permanent lights—and soon—they would have to consider the option of moving the team from Wrigley Field.

In May 1987 the Cubs asked Chicago mayor Harold Washington to lift the local laws so they could install lights. In conjunction with installing the lights, the Tribune Company promised they would also refurbish the ballpark, installing sky boxes and adding ten thousand seats to the upper deck of the grandstand.

When the residents of Wrigleyville protested, Mayor Washington polled the entire city. To everyone's surprise, the results showed that a majority favored lights.

Four conditions were imposed: only eight night games, no games would start after 7:05, no beer would be sold after the seventh inning, and there would be fewer 3:05 games.

On the day before Thanksgiving, 1987, Mayor Washington keeled over in his City Hall office and died. Would there still be lights?

On February 25, 1988, the city council passed an ordinance by a 29–19 vote allowing lights and scheduling night games.

The first night game was scheduled for August 8, 1988, against the Philadelphia Phillies. Under the glow of the 540 individual lamps, Morganna the Kissing Bandit brought the first roar when she was thrown out for planting a soggy kiss on the face of an embarrassed Ryne Sandberg. After three and a half innings, the rains came, and the traditionalists were able to spout on about Cubdom and God's will.

The next evening the game was played, and the Cubs beat the Mets 6–4. Many fans were grateful they could see a ball game without having to skip work or school to do so.

73

Departures

By 1988, baseball had entered a new age—it had become *big* business. Entrepreneurs like Phil Wrigley one by one were being replaced by corporate entities like the Tribune Company, which owned not only the Cubs but television station WGN and the *Chicago Tribune.*

Players, now free to go to the highest bidder, all had agents to do their negotiating, sophisticated men who could talk to the general manager on equal—and sometimes superior—footing. With the arrival of the agent–big corporation relationship, the players no longer had a personal relationship with the ball club. Owners like William Wrigley and Tom Yawkey in Boston had known every player personally and treated some of them as sons. Under the new system, paternalism was dead. As the salaries grew, more and more team executives stopped seeing their performers as people. Much as kids stopped trading bubblegum cards and began only to look at the value of the cards, so the team owners saw only the cost of their players. More and more the owners became disillusioned and bitter with how much they had to pay the players.

An owner would dangle millions of dollars in front of a free agent, and after the player would accept the money, the owner would then grumble that the player was getting too much money. Few asked who had put the shotgun to the owner's head.

The most important skill in the new age of checkbook competition was to know whom to pay and keep happy and whom to discard. The new Cubs, unfortunately, have consistently allowed their brightest stars, including potential Hall of Famers Lee Smith, Greg Maddux, Andre Dawson, Rafael Palmeiro, and Rick Sutcliffe, to get away.

The one exception was Ryne Sandberg. Ryno was handsome, white, and wholesome, and in the history of the game few performed more valuably at second base.

In 1993 the Cubs surprised a lot of people, including their fans, when they and Sandberg agreed to a four-year, $28-million contract. Ryne was to receive an astonishing $7 million a year, becoming the highest-paid ballplayer in the history of the game.

Had the Cubs kept their other superstars, especially pitchers Lee Smith—with Oakland's Dennis Eckersley one of the two dominating relief pitchers of the period—and Greg Maddux, *the* best starter of the age, who knows how much better the Cubs would have fared?

In 1989 starting pitcher Greg Maddux helped lead the Cubs to a division championship. With one start to go, Maddux had 19 victories. Like every pitcher, his goal was to win 20. But manager Don Zimmer asked Maddux *not* to pitch that final game so he would be better rested for the playoffs against the San Francisco Giants. Maddux agreed. This act was a measure of Maddux's character. Always, he wanted what was best for the team.

The Cubs took a beating from the Giants, but that year, Maddux, with a 19–12 record and a 2.95 earned run average, moved into the upper echelon of major league pitchers.

Maddux in 1992 won the Cy Young Award, compiling a 20–11 record with a 2.18 earned run average. Of all the players on the roster, Greg Maddux was the one the Cubs most desperately needed to remain. But inexplicably, the Tribune Company chose to make Greg Maddux an example.

Maddux shunned both the Cubs and the New York Yankees and signed with the Atlanta Braves, with whom the gritty right-hander did something no other pitcher in the game has ever accomplished—with the Braves in 1993 and 1994 and 1995 he won three more Cy Young Awards, for a total of four in a row.

JIM BROSNAN: "The first time I saw him, [clubhouse man] Yosh [Kawano] said, 'I want you to meet Greg Maddux,' and this kid, who looked like he was about sixteen, wearing cutoffs and a tank top, he looked like a junior in high school at best. 'Yes, sir. How are you, sir? Nice to talk to you.' I glance at Yosh. I say to Yosh, 'Isn't he nice? A nice, sweet guy?' And I watched him on the pitching mound, and he's a hell of a lot meaner than I ever was. He's as mean as Don Drysdale. 'Cause he knows how much his fastball and slider move, and yet he'll pitch inside all day. He doesn't

Greg Maddux

hit many batters, but it looks like the batters are scared to death of him. He has an eighty-three-mile-an-hour fastball. I threw harder. Of course, I've never seen him throw a ball straight. It's always going to do something, even if he's just laying it over the plate. Then when he wants to put something on it, he can make it go inside or outside a couple inches with his fastball. It's a cut fastball. When you let it go, there's a movement, a break of a couple inches, but his will break six inches. And he knows how to pitch. He changes speeds so beautifully. It's a pure delight to watch him. Tom Seaver was like that, Dwight Gooden when he was pitching very well.

"The Cubs could have kept Greg Maddux. All they had to do was treat his agent with some respect, to return a phone call. They have backed off that story and said there was no phone call. He was willing to sign with the Cubs for less money than he got with Atlanta, because he wanted to stay here. He has the loyalty to the people he knows that you might expect out of an army brat.

"How can you let a guy like this go? And yet, it was Stanton Cook, the big guy, who did it. He was the one in charge. He was CEO of the Cubs. 'Let's get Maddux at our price.' And his hatchet man insulted the agent, and the agent told Maddux, who was insulted. Until then, Maddux had been willing to sign with the Cubs for less, and then he got a hard-on about it.

"And after it was announced he was leaving, he and Ryne Sandberg had some well-publicized moments. Sandberg said that Maddux promised him he would sign with the Cubs, and then when he didn't, Sandberg said, 'He ran out on us.' Which really pissed Maddux off, because Sandberg hadn't known about the insults."

After winning the division in 1989, the Cubs fell apart when the entire outfield of Andre Dawson, Jerome Walton, and Dwight Smith went on the disabled list at the same time. Pitching, as usual, was another of the biggest reasons. Without Maddux, the staff was shaky.

By 1994, Cubs players and some vocal fans had replaced the Wrigley-era philosophy that winning didn't matter. Dallas Green had brought in a new bottom-line win, win, win attitude, but unfortunately, Green was gone, the Cubs were losing once again, and the fans were left feeling frustrated and angry.

The fans apparently weren't alone. This frustration led to one of the more remarkable events in recent Cubs history: the midseason retirement of Cubs Hall of Famer Ryne Sandberg. When the Quiet Hero retired on June 13, 1994—Sandberg, only thirty-four, hadn't given anyone, not even his teammates, a clue. Cubs fans were stunned.

CHICAGOAN JACK WIERS: "This is the craziest thing. I'm a very sound sleeper, but this night I woke up in the middle of the night, I'm in Honolulu, five hours' difference from Chicago, three A.M. with this overwhelming sense of dread that something terrible had happened. I've never had something like this occur before. I woke up the next day and found out that nine A.M. Chicago time, which would have corresponded with the time I woke up, Ryne Sandberg had announced his retirement. Figure that out.

"I grew up a Chicago fan, living with the trials and tribulations of both the White Sox and the Cubs, and have been an avid baseball fan all my life. I can't think of anything as a Chicago fan that would have been more shocking."

* * *

At the time he quit the game, Ryne Sandberg, the ten-time all-star, had been in a 1 for 28 slump. His batting average was but .238, far below his .290 lifetime average, and he had hit but 5 home runs in fifty-seven games, not very many for the second baseman who started the season with the fourth-highest career total in home runs, 240. Also depressing him was that the Cubs were wallowing in last place. The Cubs had let both Andre Dawson and Greg Maddux go after the '92 season, and Ryne was said to have been "upset."

In his thirteen years with the Cubs, Sandberg had played for eleven different managers—Joey Amalfitano, Lee Elia, Charlie Fox, Jim Frey, John Vukovich, Gene Michael, Frank Lucchesi, Don Zimmer, Jim Essian, Jim Lefebvre, and Tom Trebelhorn—but on only three winning teams, and after the Cubs lost their first twelve games at Wrigley Field in '94, Sandberg once again found himself playing on a loser. All those factors led him to walk off the field in midseason.

Most shocking to a public used to societal greed and salaries that far outrun performance, Sandberg walked away in the second year of his four-year, $28-million contract. He was waving good-bye to millions.

Said Sandberg, "I didn't have what I felt I needed to go on the field every day, give my very best and live up to the standards I set for myself."

About the money he was losing, Sandberg told reporters, "It's never been a big part of my thinking or why I played the game. It's not the thing that motivated me."

JIM BROSNAN: "Ryne quit because it was a matter of pride. Right from the start this year he was feeling about himself how less of a player he was, against the possibility of the club doing better if he did not play.

"As a matter of fact Rey Sanchez took over at second base and actually played better this year. Two years ago, Sanchez couldn't carry his glove. And not his bat.

"But Sandberg would be excoriating himself, saying, 'Look, you have Rey Sanchez, who can play better than I can right now, because I can't play up to my standards. I can't get to the ball. I can't pick up the ball.' He got to the point where it was like the very first year when he came up, swinging at pitches he couldn't handle at all. All discipline was gone.

"And when he quit, I understood it, and I respected him for it. I don't know if you're going to find a single ballplayer who thought it was a negative thing. Because every player, anyone who has been around for a while, has seen the aging process start and understands. Players usually know when they can't do as well as they did at their best.

"Aging is what causes you to lose a half a step, a quarter of a step, and I don't think Ryne lost more than a quarter of a step, but he was less able, his range was down, and he played with less confidence. At his best he never seemed to play with a lot of spirit, but he was always confident in what he was doing, and occasionally he would make a difficult play, and he'd have just a little smile on his face, just a little grin, knowing maybe he was the only one who could make that play, that everyone ought to appreciate that. I would go to the ballpark to watch him play.

"Tenure players have seen players play beyond the time they should have quit. They become aware themselves that they are aging, that they are not quite able to do what they did before, and you can't think of a way to do better: Get in better shape? rest more? Secretly they know. Not even secretly. They *know* they are losing it.

"So when do you say, 'I'm losing it. I can't play up to what I used to be. Should I quit on top?' Not many of them can do it. Ryne was still capable of playing better than ninety percent of the second basemen. But that something else that maybe only he would put into the equation was how much money he was making and how little Sanchez was making and some of the other players, who were very good players, so he felt he was taking money from them if it were divided up more equitably. He figured if he quit, then Sanchez wouldn't be playing for $109,000.' "

CHICAGO COLUMNIST MIKE ROYKO: "Maybe that's what they should put on his plaque when he goes into the Hall of Fame: 'Ryne Sandberg, who walked away from one of the biggest paychecks in baseball, because he didn't think he was earning it.'"

When the 1994 season ended, the Cubs were still in last place. The *Chicago Tribune* had promised Cubs fans a winner, but after Dallas Green was let go, no one seemed to be able to lead the Cubs to a fulfillment of that promise.

After Green quit, his successors were Jim Finks, a football executive who then left to run the New Orleans Saints, John Madigan, Jim Frey, Don Grenesko, Stanton Cook, and Larry Himes, who didn't seem to be getting anywhere when in September 1994 the Tribune Company hired Andy McPhail. MacPhail had started in the Cubs organization in 1976 as the business manager of the Bradenton Cubs in the Gulf Coast Rookie League. He left after Green came.

Since 1986, MacPhail had run the Minnesota Twins, bringing the franchise two world championships. Andy is the grandson of Larry MacPhail, who was one of the geniuses in the game, and the son of Lee MacPhail, the highly respected former New York Yankees executive and American League president. Andy MacPhail has bloodlines. He has a track record. All of Cubdom awaits his magic.

74

Semper Harry

In February 1987, Harry Caray sat playing gin at a country club in Palm Springs when the cards fell from his hand. He had suffered a mild stroke. While he was recovering, famous Cubs fans like Bill Murray, Jim Belushi, and Dan Aykroyd filled in at the microphone. They were a hoot, everyone agreed, but it wasn't the same without Harry.

Following a three-month recuperation, the voice of the Cubs returned to the booth. Upon his return, he was welcomed back by his partner, Steve Stone, and also a former Cubs announcer, movie star, and president.

* * *

STEVE STONE: "I'm happy you're here. The cigars have been piling up at the house. You look terrific, and it sounds like you've never been away."

Artie, his producer: "I have a special phone call for you on the line. I'm in the truck. Here's your phone call, Harry."

Harry: "OK, Artie."

Ronald Reagan: "Hello, Harry."

Harry: "Hello."

Reagan: "This is Ronald Reagan."

Harry: "Well, Mr. President, what a pleasant surprise."

Reagan: "I'm just joining all your other fans across the country in welcoming you back on the air today."

Harry: "That's awfully, awfully nice. I don't know what to say. I certainly appreciate it, sir."

Reagan: "I know it's Harry Caray Day in the Chicago area, and it's great to have you back. I'm a little familiar with Wrigley Field myself. I broadcast a lot of Cubs games."

Harry: "I remember you, Mr. President, coming through St. Louis when I was broadcasting there. You played the role of Grover Cleveland Alexander in *The Winning Team*, and you were on the air with me then."

Reagan: "Yes. You've had a lot of big-name celebrities fill in during your recovery, but there is no substitute for the real thing."

Harry: "You're awfully nice. Thank you so much, sir. I know how busy, you have a lot of things on your mind, to take time and call me up, I just can't get over it."

Reagan: "Well, listen, I know I have to let you get back to that game and start telling them what's happening, but it was never the same without the *real* voice of the Chicago Cubs."

Caray: "Thank you, sir, very much."

Reagan: "OK."

Caray: "Bye-bye."

Reagan: "Bye-bye."

Caray: "Boy oh boy. How about that. And in the excitement, Bobby Dernier beat out a bunt down the third-base line, and he was safe when the throw got away. We have Dernier on base.

"I can't get over that."

With the return of Harry Caray, Cubs fans once again had the thrill of stretching during the seventh inning and singing along with his gravelly voice to "Take Me Out to the Ball Game."

Everyone knows he sings it with the wrong words. He sings, "Take me out *to* the crowd," when it's "*with* the crowd," and he sings, "I don't care if I *ever* get back," when it's supposed to be "*never* get back." But as writer Lonnie Wheeler so aptly put it, "At Wrigley Field it isn't the lyrics that matter, it's the experience."

On July 23, 1989, Harry Caray earned the Ford C. Frick Award for excellence in broadcasting. It was an honor long overdue. In front of the Baseball Hall of Fame in Cooperstown, where Abner Doubleday *didn't* invent baseball but everyone pretends he did, Harry Caray recounted his career.

*   *   *

HARRY CARAY: "I look back on forty-five years of broadcasting, the thrills of the wonderful game of baseball, which we all love so passionately, and then I think of the fans, and perhaps that's who I represent here today. You, the fans. We are all fans of the world's greatest game, baseball. And I know that it is the fans who are responsible for my being here. I've always tried in each and every broadcast to serve the fans to the best of my ability. In my mind, they are the unsung heroes of our great game. The baseball players come and go, but the game goes on forever. The players, the writers, the broadcasters, no matter how great, all are temporary actors on the stage. It's a game. It's baseball. It moves ahead, reaching new heights all the time, generation after generation, and I'm very, very proud of being some part of this important piece of Americana."

Harry, who has enriched the national pastime so much, has no retirement plans. Ask most any Cub fan: Harry is not allowed to retire. But even after the inevitable occurs and he does step down, his spirit and his love of the game will live on.

For now and forevermore, if there is a time when we are feeling blue, we can think upon a sunny afternoon at Wrigley Field, 38,000 fans buzzing in the stands, and it's the seventh-inning stretch. Harry has the mike, and as his voice booms through the loudspeaker, we can sing along.

HARRY CARAY: "Take me out to the ball game, take me out to the crowd, buy me some peanuts and Cracker Jack, I don't care if I ever get back, so it's root, root, root for the Cubs team, if they don't win it's a shame, for it's one, two, three strikes you're out at the old ball game."

Win or lose, we're in heaven.

Harry Caray

Bibliography

Alexander, Charles. *Our Game: An American Baseball History.* New York: Holt, 1991.

Allen, Lee. *The Hot Stove League.* Ithaca: Barnes, 1955.

————. *The National League Story.* New York: Hill & Wang, 1961.

————. *The American League Story.* New York: Hill & Wang, 1962.

Allen, Maury. *Baseball: The Lives Behind the Seams.* New York: Macmillan, 1990.

Angle, Paul. *PK Wrigley: A Memoir of a Modest Man.* Skokie, IL: Rand McNally, 1975.

Anson, Adrian. *A Ball Player's Career.* Chicago: Era, 1900.

Appel, Marty, and Burt Goldblatt. *Baseball's Best.* New York: McGraw-Hill, 1977.

Banks, Ernie, and Jim Enright. *Mr. Cub.* Chicago: Follett, 1971.

Bartell, Dick, and Norman Macht. *Rowdy Richard.* Berkeley, CA: North Atlantic Books, 1987.

Bartlett, Arthur. *Baseball and Mr. Spalding.* New York: Farrar, Straus and Young, 1951.

Brown, Warren. *The Chicago Cubs.* New York: Putnam, 1946.

Carmichael, John. *My Greatest Day in Baseball.* New York: Grosset & Dunlap, 1963.

Cleveland, Charles B. *The Great Baseball Managers.* New York: Crowell, 1950.

Coffin, Tristan. *The Old Ball Game.* Herder and Herder, 1971.

Coletti, Ned. *You Gotta Have Heart: Dallas Green's Rebuilding of the Cubs.* South Bend, IN: Diamond Communications, 1985.

Condon, Dave. *The Go Go Chicago White Sox.* New York: Coward-McCann, 1960.

Connor, Anthony J. *Baseball for the Love of It.* New York: Macmillan, 1982.

Cromie, Robert. *A Short History of Chicago.* Lagunitas, CA: Lexikos, 1984.

Daley, Arthur. *Times at Bat.* New York: Random House, 1950.

Dedmon, Emmett. *Fabulous Chicago.* New York: Atheneum, 1981.

Durant, John. *The Story of Baseball in Words and Pictures.* New York: Hastings House, 1947.

————. *Highlights of the World Series.* New York: Hastings House, 1971.

Ellis, William T. *Billy Sunday: The Man and His Message.* Myers, 1914.

Eskenazi, Gerald. *Bill Veeck: A Baseball Legend.* New York: McGraw-Hill, 1988.

Evers, John J., and Hugh Fullerton. *Touching Second.* Reilly and Britton, 1910.

Fleming, G. H. *The Unforgettable Season*. New York: Holt, 1981.

Frisch, Frank, and J. Roy Stockton. *Frank Frisch: The Fordham Flash*. New York: Doubleday, 1962.

Frommer, Harvey. *Primitive Baseball*. New York: Atheneum, 1988.

———. *Shoeless Joe and Ragtime Baseball*. Dallas: Taylor, 1992.

Gallen, David, ed. *The Baseball Chronicles*. New York: Carroll & Graf, 1991.

Gifford, Barry. *The Neighborhood of Baseball*. New York: Dutton, 1981.

Gilbert, Bill. *They Also Served: Baseball and the Home Front 1941–1945*. New York: Crown, 1992.

Gold, Eddie, and Art Ahrens. *The Golden Era Cubs*. Chicago: Bonus Books, 1985.

———. *The New Era Cubs*. Chicago: Bonus Books, 1985.

———. *The Renewal Era Cubs*. Chicago: Bonus Books, 1990.

Goldstein, Richard. *Spartan Seasons: How Baseball Survived the Second World War*. New York: Macmillan, 1980.

Graham, Frank. *McGraw of the Giants*. New York: Putnam, 1945.

———. *The Brooklyn Dodgers*. New York: Putnam, 1948.

Grimm, Charlie, and Edward Prell. *Jolly Cholly's Story*. Chicago: Regnery, 1968.

Honig, Donald. *Baseball When the Grass Was Real*. New York: Coward-McCann, 1975.

———. *The Man in the Dugout*. Chicago: Follett, 1977.

———. *The October Heroes*. New York: Simon & Schuster, 1979.

Hornsby, Rogers, and Bill Surface. *My War with Baseball*. New York: Coward-McCann, 1962.

Kaese, Harold. *The Boston Braves*. New York: Putnam, 1948.

Kelly, Mike. *"Play Ball," Stories of the Diamond Field*. Emery & Hughes, 1888.

Koppett, Leonard. *The Man in the Dugout*. New York: Crown, 1993.

Kowet, Don. *The Rich Who Own Sport*. New York: Random House, 1977.

Krueger, Joseph. *Baseball's Greatest Drama*. Classic, 1943.

Kupcinet, Irv. *Kup's Chicago*. Chicago: World, 1962.

Langford, Jim. *The Game Is Never Over*. South Bend, IN: Icarus Press, 1980.

Lansche, Jerry. *Glory Fades Away: The Nineteenth Century World Series Rediscovered*. Dallas: Taylor, 1991.

Leitner, Irving A. *Baseball: Diamond in the Rough*. Criterion, 1972.

Lieb, Fred. *The St. Louis Cardinals*. New York: Putnam, 1945.

———. *The Detroit Tigers*. New York: Putnam, 1946.

———. *The Pittsburgh Pirates*. New York: Putnam, 1948.

———. *The Story of the World Series*. New York: Putnam, 1949.

———. *The Baseball Story*. New York: Putnam, 1950.

———. *Connie Mack*. New York: Putnam, 1950.

Lindberg, Richard. *Who's on Third*. South Bend, IN: Icarus Press, 1983.

Mathewson, Christy. *Pitching in a Pinch*. New York: Putnam, 1912.

Mead, William. *Two Spectacular Seasons*. New York: Macmillan, 1990.

Meany, Tom. *Baseball's Greatest Pitchers*. Barnes, 1951.

Meeker, Arthur. *Chicago with Love*. New York: Knopf, 1955.

Pepitone, Joe, and Barry Stainbeck. *Joe, You Coulda Made Us Proud*. New York: Playboy Press, 1975.

Phalen, Rick. *Our Chicago Cubs*. South Bend, IN: Diamond Communications, 1992.

Rader, Benjamin. *Baseball: A History of America's Game*. Champaign, IL: University of Illinois Press, 1992.

Ritter, Lawrence. *The Glory of Their Times*. New York: Macmillan, 1966.

Rosenburg, John. *They Gave Us Baseball*. Harrisburg, PA: Stackpole, 1989.

Royko, Mike. *Up Against It*. Chicago: Regnery, 1967.

———. *The Boss*. New York: Signet, 1972.

Seymour, Harold. *Baseball: The Early Years*. New York: Oxford University Press, 1960.

———. Baseball: *The Golden Age*. New York: Oxford University Press, 1971.

Shecter, Leonard. *The Jocks*. New York: Bobbs-Merrill, 1961.

Smith, Curt. *America's Dizzy Dean*. New York: Bethany Press, 1978.

———. *Voices of the Game*. South Bend, IN: Diamond Communications, 1987.

Smith, Ira, and H. Allen Smith. *Low and Inside*. New York: Doubleday, 1949.

Smith, Red. *To Absent Friends*. New York: Atheneum, 1982.

Smith, Robert. *Baseball*. New York: Simon & Schuster, 1947.

———. *Baseball in America*. New York: Holt, 1961.

———. *Pioneers of Baseball*. New York: Little, Brown, 1978.

———. *Baseball in the Afternoon*. New York: Simon & Schuster, 1993.

Spalding, A. G. *Base Ball*. New York: American Sports, 1911.

Sugar, Bex. *Hit the Sign and Win a Suit from Harry Finklestein*. Chicago: Contemporary Books, 1978.

Sullivan, Neil. *The Minors*. New York: St. Martin's Press, 1990.

Talley, Rick. *The Cubs of 1969*. Chicago: Contemporary Books, 1989.

Terkel, Studs. *Chicago*. New York: Pantheon, 1985.

Thorn, John. *A Century of Baseball Lore*. Hart, 1974.

Veeck, Bill, with Ed Linn. *Veeck as in Wreck*. New York: Putnam, 1969.

Wagenknecht, Edward. *Chicago*. Tulsa, OK: University of Oklahoma Press, 1964.

Wallop, Douglas. *Baseball: An Informal History*. New York: Norton, 1969.

Wheeler, Lonnie. *Bleachers: A Summer in Wrigley Field*. Chicago: Contemporary Books, 1988.

Wrigley, William Jr. *The Man and His Business*. Self-published, 1935.

Notes

Chapter 1. Chikagou

2: "I remember one little occurrence . . ." *A Ball Player's Career*, by Adrian Anson, 1900, pages 10–11.

3: . . . they celebrated every rebel victory. *A Short History of Chicago*, by Robert Cromie.

4: ". . . fast horses, faster men . . ." Cromie. *Ibid.*

5: . . . common for a keg of beer and a dipper. *Low and Inside*, by Ira Smith and H. Allen Smith, page 194.

5: ". . . liquor vendors went through the stands . . ." *The Baseball Story*, by Fred Lieb, 1950, page 52.

6: "the city of the big idea." *Fabulous Chicago*, by Emmett Dedmon.

Chapter 2. Albert Spalding

All Spalding quotes from *Base Ball: America's National Game*, by Albert Spalding, American Sports Publishing Company, 1911, pages 109–192.

See also *They Gave Us Baseball*, by John Rosenburg.

Chapter 3. Spalding's Revolution

12: "He has sense enough to know that fair and manly play . . ." *They Gave Us Baseball*, by John Rosenburg, page 13.

12: "a schemer and promoter to his very core." *Baseball in America*, by Robert Smith, page 45.

13: . . . the need for bringing baseball to the Mother Country. *Ibid.*, page 45.

13: Spalding used to spend "most of his idle hours working out schemes for reforming the organized game." *Pioneers of Baseball*, by Robert Smith, pages 18–29.

14: . . . club owners would relieve "the players of all care and responsibility . . ." *Base Ball*, by Albert Spalding, page 194.

15: "I was greatly impressed by the personality of Mr. Hulbert . . ." Spalding, pages 200–203.

16: "The Monday morning when the announcement . . ." Spalding, page 204.

17: "I discussed this phase of the question [of expulsion] with Mr. Hulbert . . ." *Ibid.*, pages 207–8.

19: "There have been other forceful men . . ." *Ibid.*, page 214.

See also *Baseball: Diamond in the Rough*, by Irving A. Leitner.

Chapter 4. The Great Anson

21: "Now, Anse, come tomorrow in uniform." *Baseball and Mr. Spalding*, by Arthur Bartlett, page 92.

21: "The first game that we played on the Boston Grounds . . ." *A Ball Player's Career*, by Adrian Anson, pages 95–6.

23: . . . that "rule" in the book was "an unmitigated falsehood . . ." *Baseball: The Early Years*, by Harold Seymour, page 358.

24: "I knew that I was slipping before anybody else did . . ." Bartlett, page 118.

24: "There are more loose timbers around the Chicago ball park and Spalding's store . . ." pages 86–87.

26: "often ending in a comprehensive summary of his views . . ." page 127.

26: "Unlike the majority of the clubs the Chicago Club . . ." Anson, page 104.

27: "The color line has been . . ." *Base Ball: Diamond in the Rough*, by Irving A. Leitner, page 200.

28: "[In Omaha,] we were met with another great reception . . ." Anson, pages 148–50.

29: "Clarence Duval, our colored mascot . . ." *Ibid.*, page 219.

See also *Baseball's Best*, by Marty Appel and Burt Goldblatt; *Primitive Baseball*, by Harvey Frommer; *Glory Fades Away*, by Jerry Lansche; *Baseball*, by Robert Smith; *Baseball in the Afternoon*, by Robert Smith.

Chapter 5. Mike Kelly

30: "Anson became a bit interested in my playing . . ." *"Play Ball," Stories of the Diamond Field*, by Mike Kelly, pages 19–20.

31: "I think that a pitcher would rather face Wagner . . ." *The Boston Braves*, by Harold Kaese, page 43.

31: "King Kel was the greatest player I ever knew . . ." *Ibid.*, page 43.

32: Kelly fooled Mack with a feint and then made a curving slide . . . *Ibid.*, page 43.

32: "Like Cobb, Kelly never gave an infielder or catcher . . ." *Baseball and Mr. Spalding*, by Arthur Bartlett, page 134.

32: "To many, King Kelly and baseball were synonymous . . ." *The Baseball Story*, by Fred Lieb, page 79.

32: "Unless I am very much mistaken, I was the first one to introduce signs to the pitcher . . ." Kelly.

33: "Swat on, most admirable paragon . . ." Bartlett, page 134.

33: "Kelly at the plate never failed to bring a bubbling of cheers . . ." *Baseball*, by Robert Smith, page 88.

33: "Keep hold of it, Ed. Nothing wrong with it . . ." *Low and Inside*, by Ira Smith and H. Allen Smith, pages 36–37.

34: "Kelly had a better trick for the other corner of the diamond . . ." Smith, page 89.

34: "In an exhibition game played at Austin, Texas . . ." Kaese, page 41.

35: "So yer Kerry Patchers, eh? . . ." *Ibid.*, page 44.

35: "How a Boston audience would shout and roar . . ." Kelly, page 44.

35: "Had he been possessed of good habits . . ." *A Ball Player's Career*, by Adrian Anson, page 116.

35: "It depends on the length of the game." *Glory Fades Away*, by Jerry Lansche, page 7.

35: "[Kelly] knew how to enjoy every minute of his life . . ." Smith, page 87.

36: "Slide, Kelly, Slide." For the complete lyrics of the parody, written by J. W. Kelly, the Rolling Mill Man, sung by popular singer Maggie Cline, see Kaese, page 45.

Chapter 6. Spalding's Dynasty

36: "We wore silk stockings . . ." *"Play Ball," Stories of the Diamond Field*, by Mike Kelly, page 46.
36: "You haven't any idea what Anson meant by training . . ." *Ibid.*, pages 25–6.
37: "Anson took more long chances to win a game . . ." *Ibid.*, page 35.
37: "It's a comparatively easy matter to answer the question . . ." *Ibid.*, page 36.
38: "Round up the strongest men who can knock a baseball . . ." *Primitive Baseball*, by Harvey Frommer, page 99.
38: "The team that brought the pennant back to Chicago in the early '80s . . ." *A Ball Player's Career*, by Adrian Anson, pages 109–11.
39: "indisputably the finest in the world in respect of seating accommodations and conveniences." *Baseball: The Early Years,* by Harold Seymour, pages 192–93.
40: "The only fault that could be found . . ." Anson, page 106.
40: "All in all, it was the best ball team ever put together . . ." *Baseball and Mr. Spalding,* by Arthur Bartlett, page 143.
40: "Both the Wrights were confident that Chicago would drop three straight games to the Providence boys . . ." *Ibid.*, pages 78–79.
42: "This fellow came to me in the corridor of the United States Hotel . . ." Kelly, pages 40–41.
43: "A great many people in this lovely country of ours . . ." *Ibid.*, page 41.
43: "It takes just nine healthy, peaceable men . . ." *Ibid.*, pages 38–40.
44: "He was as fine a pitcher as ever crawled into a uniform . . ." *Billy Sunday: The Man and His Message*, by William T. Ellis, page 35.
45: "John Clarkson is the star pitcher of the Chicago club . . ." Kelly, page 61.
46: "[Clarkson] was the possessor of a remarkable drop curve . . ." Anson, pages 130–31.
46: "Ed was, in my opinion, the greatest all-around ballplayer the country ever saw . . ." *The Boston Braves*, by Harold Kaese, pages 113–29.
47: "The team that brought the pennant back to Chicago in the years 1885 and 1886 . . ." *Ibid.*, pages 128–30.
48: "The Chicago team of 1880, which reached its fullest development five years later . . ." *Touching Second,* by John J. Evers and Hugh Fullerton, page 200.
48: "'The Old Gag,' a play christened and used by Anson's infield . . ." *Ibid.*, pages 214–15.
49: "There were a good many funny stories told about those closing games . . ." Anson, pages 123–24.

Chapter 7. World Series Failure

50: "Comiskey won pennants at St. Louis by his inventiveness . . ." *Touching Second*, by John J. Evers and Hugh Fullerton, page 201.
50: "The games were played after the regular season was over . . ." *A Ballplayer's Career,* by Adrian Anson, page 136.
51: "It was the speed that he showed on that occasion that opened my eyes . . ." *Ibid.*, page 133.
53: "Perhaps the most exciting games of ball played in late years were the games between the Detroits and Chicagos . . ." *"Play Ball," Stories of the Diamond Field*, by Mike Kelly, page 54.
54: "That afternoon we played the old Detroit club . . ." *Billy Sunday: The Man and His Message*, by William T. Ellis, pages 35–36.
55: . . . a grateful Cap Anson bought each Philadelphia player a suit of clothes. *The Boston Braves*, by Harold Kaese, page 40.
55: "A notable incident of the campaign was the fact that . . ." Anson, pages 126–27.
56: "Bobby's got the heart disease bad." *Glory Fades Away*, by Jerry Lansche, page 77.
57: "the White Stockings, with the exception of Cap Anson, seemed strangely undisturbed by their loss . . ." *Ibid.*, page 84.
57: "Admitting that base ball is a business conducted for pecuniary profit . . ." *Ibid.*, page 87.

58: "on a warm, cloudy day before a grandstand full of men in high-crowned derbies . . ." *Baseball in the Afternoon*, by Robert Smith, page 96.

58: "Arlie was oddly silent . . ." *Ibid.*, page 96.

59: "[Clarkson] took his stance again and, as he did . . ." *Ibid.*, pages 96–97.

61: "We were beaten, and fairly beaten . . ." Adrian Anson, page 137.

See also *The Baseball Story*, by Fred Lieb

Chapter 8. Stars for Sale

61: "Wealth, the Protestant churches and the Yankee aristocracy . . ." *Fabulous Chicago*, by Emmett Dedmon.

62: "The two great obstacles in the way of success . . ." *The Baseball Story*, by Fred Lieb, page 77.

63: "were too awful for patient considerations . . ." *Ibid.*, page 137.

63: "It was straight whiskey. I never drank a lemonade at that hour in my life." *Ibid.*, page 137.

64: "The Chicago management will aim to secure the highest standard of baseball efficiency obtainable . . ." *Ibid.*, pages 170–71.

65: Anson later learned he had been at the racetrack. *Baseball: The Early Years*, by Harold Seymour, page 175.

65: "He was a whole-souled, genial fellow . . ." *A Ball Player's Career*, by Adrian Anson, page 115.

65: "Sure, spare anybody." *Glory Fades Away*, by Jerry Lansche, page 20.

65: "the cause of that sale never was made public . . ." *Touching Second*, by John J. Evers and Hugh Fullerton, page 59.

65: "At the close of the season of 1886 . . ." *"Play Ball," Stories of the Diamond Field*, by Mike Kelly, page 45.

67: "So, they began a philosophical discussion . . ." *The Boston Braves*, by Harold Kaese, page 43.

67: "The sensation of the year was the sale of Mike Kelly . . ." Anson, page 137.

68: "He can make nine poor players go on the field and make them play a stiffer game of ball than any man living . . ." Kelly, page 37.

69: "Clarkson himself wanted to play in Boston . . ." *Ibid.*, page 64.

69: "Tom Daly added gray hairs to the heads of many managers . . ." Evers and Fullerton, pages 82–83.

70: "Every new man or reporter, who sojourned with the team risked not only limb but life." *Ibid.*, pages 80–82.

See also *Baseball: The Early Years*, by Harold Seymour.

Chapter 9. The Players Revolt

71: Under Spalding's system, the players . . . were forced to accept a salary cap of $2,000 a year. *Baseball in the Afternoon,* by Robert Smith, page 75.

72: . . . ballplayers often made a little money on the side by selling baseballs . . . *Low and Inside*, by Ira Smith and H. Allen Smith, page 140.

72: Several Chicago players were arrested for incurring debts in different cities. Smith, pages 78–80.

72: To make extra money, players also took part in games in the off-season. Smith and Smith, pages 224–5.

73: Spalding deducted $1,000 from his $2,500 salary. *Baseball: The Early Years*, by Harold Seymour, pages 192–93.

73: "In Paris on March 8, 1889, it was in the second inning of the game . . ." *A Ball Player's Career*, by Adrian Anson, pages 256–57.

73: Spalding . . . and the press libeled Ward, calling him "greedy, self-seeking . . ." Seymour, page 106.
74: "graded like so many cattle . . ." *Baseball: A History of America's Game*, by Benjamin Rader, page 58.
74: "We've got to get more money out of this game . . ." *The Baseball Story*, by Fred Lieb.
74: Ward demanded that Spalding meet with him as he had promised. Spalding refused. Smith, page 75.
75: The only famous player in the National League not to jump to the new league was Cap Anson . . . *Ibid.*, pages 78–80.
75: "It was a proposal that I declined with thanks . . ." Anson, page 287.
75: Anson criticized the Chicago players who had "deserted" him as "men of low principle." Lieb, page 77.
75: Writer Oliver Hazard Perry Caylor of Cincinnati . . . Seymour, pages 192–93.
76: "It is wonderful that these poor oppressed souls do not organize a procession under a red flag . . ." Smith, page 76.
76: [Mills] gave Spalding a choice: Put Morton out of business or get out of baseball. *Baseball*, by Robert Smith, page 35. According to John Rosenburg in *They Gave Us Baseball*, when Mills learned what Spalding was doing he vowed to give him "a piece of my mind," page 35.
77: "I'm going to take a walk." *Baseball in the Afternoon*, by Robert Smith, page 80.
78: "The defection of Tener, Williamson . . ." Anson, page 292–93.
78: Hart [said] the cuts were "only the natural consequence of baseball history." Seymour, page 268.
79: "[We] would have landed the pennant had it not been for the fact that the jealousy of the old players in the East . . ." Ibid., page 295.
80: "With the downfall of the Brotherhood . . ." *Ibid.,* page 294.
80: Story of Anson's attempt to buy Cy Young from Cleveland, Lieb, page 130.
See also *Glory Fades Away*, by Jerry Lansche; *The Hot Stove League,* by Lee Allen.

Chapter 10. Anson's Demise

81: "Anson was one of the most tireless runners . . ." *Touching Second*, by John J. Evers and Hugh Fullerton, pages 238–40.
82: "If the ball so much as ruffles these whiskers . . ." *Low and Inside*, by Ira Smith and H. Allen Smith, page 19.
82: "[The 1893 club] was a team of great promises . . ." *A Ball Player's Career*, by Adrian Anson, page 299.
83: "We'll win the flag this year for sure, and I'm betting on it, boys." *Baseball and Mr. Spalding*, by Arthur Bartlett, page 243.
83: ". . . sometime in the next 1,500 years." *Ibid.*, page 244.
83: "The team with which I started out in 1897 was certainly good enough to win the pennant . . ." *Ibid.*, page 302.
84: "It is a poor plan for any man not to look closely after his own business interests." Anson, page 314.
85: "After I had been released by the club Mr. Spalding still posed as my best friend . . ." *Ibid.*, page 310.
85: "Good morning, Captain Anson." *Hit the Sign and Win a Suit from Harry Finklestein*, by Bert Sugar, pages 322–23.
85: . . . he cried, "YER OUT!" Smith and Smith, page 19.
86: "We're Ten Chubelin [Shoveling] Tipperary Turks." *Baseball*, by Robert Smith, page 93.
86: "Base-ball as at present conducted is a gigantic monopoly . . ." *Ibid.*, page 329.
86: "He was often accompanied at night by a Japanese valet and a monkey." *Glory Fades Away*, by Jerry Lansche, page 21.

86: "This was the day Boston lost the pennant . . ." *The Boston Braves*, by Harold Kaese, pages 52–53.
87: "He played good ball for a time, but his bad habits . . ." Anson, page 116.
87: "This is me last slide." Smith, page 93.
88: Clarkson cradled him in his arms. *Primitive Baseball*, by Harvey Frommer, page 73.
88: "Ed Williamson came back to Chicago and started a saloon . . ." *Billy Sunday: The Man and his Message*, by William T. Ellis, pages 43–44.
89: "Over the graves of three of them . . ." Anson, page 134.

Chapter 11. Al Spalding: Savior

90: "The least talented laborers [would be] dumped on the vineyards where the picking was poorest." *Baseball in the Afternoon*, by Robert Smith, page 157.
91: Baseball, wrote Spalding, was "the exponent of American courage, Confidence . . ." *Baseball and Mr. Spalding*, by Arthur Bartlett, pages 2–3.
93: Spalding . . . "pretended he really believed it though privately he thought it was nonsense." *Pioneers of Baseball*, by Robert Smith, page 29.
See also *Baseball*, by Robert Smith; *They Gave Us Baseball*, by John Rosenburg

Chapter 12. Selee's Genius

94: "Why, you old gray-headed stiff . . ." *Touching Second*, by John J. Evers and Hugh Fullerton, page 76.
95: "If I make things pleasant for the players . . ." *The Boston Braves*, by Harold Kaese, pages 55–56.
95: "He was a good judge of players . . ." *Ibid.*, page 55.
96: "The real beginning of the Chicago Cubs was in March 1898 . . ." *Touching Second*, Evers and Fullerton, page 60.
96: "Frank Chance, the 'Peerless Leader' of the Chicago Cubs, was a catcher . . ." *Ibid.*, pages 39–40.
97: "There was not much sign of promise of a championship team in Chicago then . . ." *Ibid.*, page 61.
97: "Selee and Hart reached an agreement as to the management in the fall of 1901 . . ." *Ibid.*, pages 61–62.
98: "Joe Tinker refused to play shortstop . . ." *Ibid.*, page 40.
98: "As I climbed aboard . . ." *Literary Digest*, May 31, 1913.
98: "All there is to Evers is a bundle of nerves . . ." Evers and Fullerton, page 64.
99: "Prospects for getting a winning team improved . . ." *Ibid.*, page 65.

Chapter 13. The Cubs Grow Claws

99: . . . the Chicago Spuds. *Baseball in the Afternoon*, by Robert Smith, page 174.
99: ". . . bear-like strength and a playful disposition." *This Week* magazine, Frank C. True, 1957.
99: For the story of Charles Sensabaugh, see the *Chicago Daily News*, June 29, 1972.
100: "Chance, although only advisor to Selee . . ." *Touching Second*, by John J. Evers and Hugh Fullerton, pages 65–66.
102: "[By 1905] Selee was sick . . ." *Ibid.*, page 69.
102: "In the middle of the season Selee's illness forced him to surrender . . ." *Ibid.*, pages 69–71.

Chapter 14. The Peerless Leader

104: "One of the Chicago pitchers, at the start of his career . . ." *Touching Second,* by John J. Evers and Hugh Fullerton, page 92.

105: ". . . if two players didn't get along together, he'd knock their heads together." *The Great Baseball Managers,* by Charles B. Cleveland, page 85.

105: He immediately wrote Fraser's unconditional release. *The National League Story,* by Lee Allen, page 128.

106: Chase very suddenly found himself traded away. *Baseball in the Afternoon,* by Robert Smith, page 164.

106: Zimmerman . . . foolishly accepted Chance's challenge. The manager beat him. Cleveland, page 85.

106: For the account of the Egan-Tinker fight, see *Low and Inside,* by Ira Smith and H. Allen Smith, page 31.

106: "When we'd get rained out, we'd be sitting around the clubhouse . . ." Cleveland, page 86.

107: "I figure that a little bet now and then results in moderate excitement . . ." Smith and Smith, page 155.

107: "Chance never has dabbled in psychological experimentation . . ." Evers and Fullerton, page 250.

107: "That will cost each of you $25 . . ." *Ibid.,* page 85.

107: "Chance was great on balls in the dirt." Cleveland, page 88.

108: "The Chicago Cubs used the force bunt during all their championship term . . ." Evers and Fullerton, pages 162–63.

108: "I was picking up a bat one day . . ." Cleveland, page 89.

108: "No man can think for nine players . . ." *Ibid.,* page 89.

108: "There was an odd play introduced on the Polo Grounds . . ." Evers and Fullerton, pages 207–8.

109: "When [Cubs catcher Pat] Moran knelt down he put the index finger of his right hand straight down . . ." *Ibid.,* pages 124–25.

109: "In one game Evers and Kling analyzed and discovered every hit and run signal . . ." *Ibid.,* page 255.

110: "To show how closely the two teams watched each other . . ." *Ibid.,* page 134.

110: "Chance is a great believer in the waiting game. . . ." *Ibid.,* page 156.

110: "One time we won thirteen straight games . . ." Cleveland, page 86.

110: ". . . many a time this afternoon I'd have traded you for a base hit." *Times at Bat,* by Arthur Daley, pages 47–48.

Chapter 15. 116–36

112: "Mordecai Brown's 'hook' curve is the highest present development of the fast overhand curve pitch . . ." *Touching Second,* by John J. Evers and Hugh Fullerton, page 104.

113: "Pitchers were pitchers in those days . . ." *The Great Baseball Managers,* by Charles B. Cleveland, page 78.

113: "Three-Fingered Brown, gee, he was one of the wonders of baseball . . ." *The Glory of Their Times,* by Larry Ritter, pages 123–24.

113: . . . and so it was Kling who introduced the snap throw to the National League, where it soon became standard practice. *Baseball in the Afternoon,* by Robert Smith.

113: When Johnny Evers was asked to list the "great" players . . . Evers and Fullerton, page 38.

113: "In this particular of catching runners in the crucial moments of games . . ." *Ibid.,* page 97, page 218.

114: "Late [one year] Boston presented a new outfielder who never had played in a major league before . . ." *Ibid.,* pages 248–50.

115: His constant stream of heckling was so irritating that Frank Chance once admitted he would have preferred that Evers played the outfield. *Baseball's Best*, by Marty Appel and Burt Goldblatt, page 141.

116: For the story of the Klem-Evers bet, see *The National League Story*, by Lee Allen, page 128.

117: "In giving his signs from the bench to the players, McGraw depends on a gesture or catch word." *Pitching in a Pinch*, by Christy Mathewson.

117: "That just seems to indicate that there is something unusual . . ." *Low and Inside*, by Ira Smith and H. Allen Smith, page 157.

118: "The Cubs that day had dressed at a local hotel and were supposed to ride out to the ball park in hacks . . ." Allen, page 106.

118: "Tinker and [I] plotted a play a few years ago that caught many men and furnished the spectators much joy . . ." Evers and Fullerton, page 205.

119: The Franklin P. Adams poem can be found in many a history of the game, including *The Story of Baseball in Words and Pictures*, by John Durant.

Chapter 16. A Fine Bunch of Stiffs

119: "All the honors worth winning in the most sensational . . ." *Chicago Tribune*, May 8, 1906.

120: "It must be admitted that [manager] Fielder [Jones] won his pennant with mirrors." *The World Series*, by Fred Lieb, page 44.

121: "It's hitting that wins . . ." *The American League Story*, by Lee Allen.

122: "So the lucky stiff is up again . . ." Lieb, page 48.

122: "When the gates were thrown open for the game, long lines that extended in every direction from the park . . ." *Baseball's Greatest Drama*, by Joseph Kreuger, page 26.

123: "Issy, you're a white-livered so-and-so . . ." Lieb, pages 48–49.

123: "We're relying on you. You've got to keep us in this thing . . ." *Ibid.*, page 49.

Chapter 17. World Champs

125: "It's a wonder they wouldn't be carting you off to the Old Woman's Home . . ." and the rejoinder. *The Detroit Tigers*, by Fred Lieb, page 76.

126: "Forget that tie. That's gone, and I don't want to hear any more about it . . ." *Ibid.*, page 99.

126: "What are you going to do with that, Hughie? Eat it?" *Ibid.*, page 100.

127: "I'll finish it today." *The Story of the World Series*, by Fred Lieb, page 56.

Chapter 18. The Warren Gill Affair

129: "Chicago presents the spectacle of a great city positively raving over baseball . . ." *New York Herald*, August 27, 1908.

130: "We went into Chicago at a time when we were neck and neck . . ." *The Pittsburgh Pirates*, by Fred Lieb, page 124.

130: "Mordecai Brown was pitching for the Cubs and he'd shut out the Bucs three straight times earlier in the season . . ." *My Greatest Day in Baseball*, by John Carmichael, page 68.

130: "We had the bases full and two out with the score tied in the ninth . . ." Lieb, page 127.

131: "Gill didn't go to second. He ran off the field . . ." Carmichael, page 68.

131: "It long has been a wonder that the crafty John McGraw, who never missed a trick . . ." Lieb, page 127.

Chapter 19. September 23, 1908

132: "The race was close, and to Chicago even one defeat . . ." *Touching Second*, by John J. Evers and Hugh Fullerton, pages 83–84.

133: "Pitching from angles consists in angling the ball from high overhand . . ." *Ibid.*, page 115.

134: "To show you what a pitcher's battle it was . . ." *My Greatest Day in Baseball*, by John Carmichael, page 69.

134: "I had my eye on [Merkle], saw him stop . . ." *Ibid.*, page 69.

135: "I don't know where Evers got the ball that he used . . ." *Baseball's Pitchers*, by Tom Meany.

135: "I can see the fellow who caught it yet . . ." Carmichael, pages 69–70.

136: "There was hell a-poppin' . . ."*Ibid.*, page 70.

136: ". . . one of the greatest examples of individual heroism the game has known." Evers and Fullerton, page 187.

136: "Even after New York claimed the game and the entire country was aroused . . ." *Ibid.*, pages 187–88.

Chapter 20. A Tie

139: Dooin claimed that he . . . and other Philly players were offered more to throw their 1908 series games to the Giants than the White Sox were promised in 1919. *Baseball: The Golden Age*, by Harold Seymour, pages 283–85.

140: The location chart revealed that her seat had been in *fair* territory. *Times at Bat*, by Arthur Daley, page 37.

140: Mr. Ebbets: "Why did you declare Merkle out?" Transcript of Proceedings of the Board of Directors of the National League, October 5, 1908.

141: "The Giants protested so vigorously and long that the board of directors finally had to settle matters . . ." *My Greatest Day in Baseball*, by John Carmichael, pages 70–71.

142: "If you didn't honestly and furiously hate the Giants, you weren't a real Cub." *Ibid.*, page 224.

Chapter 21. Four to Two

143: "I want to tell you about this playoff game . . ." *My Greatest Day in Baseball*, by John Carmichael, page 23.

144: "When manager Frank Chance led the Chicago Cub team into New York the morning of October 8, 1908 . . ." *Ibid.*, 23–24.

145: "On the afternoon that New York and Chicago played off their tie for the National League Championship of 1908 . . ." *Touching Second*, by John J. Evers and Hugh Fullerton, pages 192–93.

145: "Here's $2,500. It's yours if you will give all the close decisions to the Giants and see that they win sure . . ." *The National League Story*, by Lee Allen, page 119.

146: "We tried to get Frank Chance thrown out of the game, but didn't succeed . . ." *The Glory of Their Times*, by Larry Ritter, pages 99–101.

146: "We had just come out onto the field and were getting settled . . ." Carmichael, page 26.

147: "Mathewson put us down quick in our first time at bat . . ." *Ibid.*, page 26.

147: "A throw of that kind made by Kling that caught Herzog off first base . . ." Evers and Fullerton, page 94.

147: "Turkey Mike Donlin doubled, scoring Tenney . . ." Carmichael, pages 26–27.

148: "Who lost the game? It was 'Cy' Seymour . . ." Evers and Fullerton, pages 247–48.

148: "Kling singled Tinker home. I sacrificed Johnny to second . . ." Carmichael, pages 27–28.

149: "As the ninth ended with the Giants going out . . ." *Ibid.*, pages 28–29.

Chapter 22. Champs Again

150: "One day during the off season I ran into Roger Bresnahan . . ." *My Greatest Day in Baseball*, by John Carmichael, page 71.

151: "You can do it, Eddie . . ." *The Detroit Tigers*, by Fred Lieb, page 111.

152: "Why is it a homer?" *The Story of the World Series*, by Fred Lieb, page 59.

152: "Chicago had made two runs in the third inning and with Brown pitching, appeared to be winning easily . . ." *Touching Second*, by John J. Evers and Hugh Fullerton, pages 256–58.

153: "There are many players, among them members of the Detroit team . . ." *Ibid.*, page 105.

153: "Don't feel too badly about it . . ." *The Detroit Tigers*, by Fred Lieb, page 117.

154: "Could a soothsayer have told the happy Chicago fans what World Series cards fate would deal them . . ." *The Story of the World Series*, by Fred Lieb, page 61.

Chapter 23. Continued Success

154: "It was in 1910, late in the season . . ." *Literary Digest*, March 5, 1921.

155: "The Cubs seemed to have lost the confidence and dash that was theirs in the days of 1906 to 1908." *Baseball's Greatest Drama*, by Joseph Krueger, page 57.

155: "One evening after Frank Chance had won two World Series Championships, he sat gloomily silent for a long time . . ." *Touching Second*, by John J. Evers and Hugh Fullerton, page 79.

156: "My greatest day? You might know it was against the Giants . . ." *My Greatest Day in Baseball*, by John Carmichael, pages 223–27.

Chapter 24. Murphy's Law

159: ". . . a public benefactor, a friend of the anti-tuberculosis league . . ." *Baseball: The Golden Age*, by Harold Seymour, page 20.

159: "Fogel, a former Philadelphia baseball writer . . ." *The St. Louis Cardinals*, by Fred Lieb, page 47. The Cardinals released Bresnahan at the end of the season despite his four-year contract. He ended up signing with the Cubs in June 1913.

159: "Murphy turned out to be a growing trial to his fellow owners . . ." Seymour, pages 31–32.

160: For the Herrmann and Dreyfuss comments on Murphy, see *Ibid.*, page 34.

160: "At the request of the *Chicago Tribune* I have consented to write articles about what may be my last series of games as manager of the Chicago Cubs . . ." *Chicago Tribune*, October 6, 1912.

161: Murphy was so furious he came down from his box seat to the bench and fired Chance as manager. *The Baseball Story*, by Fred Lieb, page 196.

161: "No manager can be a success without competent players, and some of these I have are anything but skilled . . ." *The Chicago Cubs*, by Warren Brown, pages 64–65.

161: "I'll bet $1,000 he never does," said Chance. *Ibid.*, page 65.

161: "Ignoring the fact that these men had helped him toward very considerable profits . . ." Seymour, page 35.

162: According to Sam Weller in the *Chicago Tribune* . . . This account was described in the *Literary Digest*, February 28, 1914.

163: "The reaction was electric, not only in Chicago but all over the National League . . ." *The National League Story*, by Lee Allen, page 135.

Chapter 25. Charles Weeghman

164: For an account of the Ebbets-Murphy contretemps, see *The Brooklyn Dodgers*, by Frank Graham, pages 41–43.

165: "Weeghman Weeghman Federal man . . ." See *Baseball: The Golden Age*, by Harold Seymour, page 204.

165: "You are invited to come to the Federal league quarters in Chicago and discuss terms . . ." *Ibid.*, page 205.

167: He was a close friend of Monte Tennes's . . . *Ibid.*, page 300. Weeghman testified after he was out of baseball that Tennes told him in August 1919 that the Series was fixed. Tennes denied ever having that conversation.

Chapter 26. Hippo Loses a No-Hitter

168: "I don't believe there has been another game in the history of baseball like the one I'm going to talk about . . ." "My Biggest Baseball Day," *Chicago Daily News*, as cited in *The Fireside Book of Baseball*, edited by Charles Einstein, page 356–57.

See also *Times at Bat*, by Arthur Daley, page 289; *The Chicago Cubs*, by Warren Brown, page 71.

Chapter 27. Transitions

172: The agreement was never put in writing, but Wrigley kept his word. See the "Ups and Downs of Old Pete," by Jack Sher, *Sport*, April 1950, as reprinted in *The Baseball Chronicle*, edited by David Gallen, page 133.

172: For an account of the short players' strike during the 1918 Series, see *The National League Story*, by Lee Allen, page 150.

173: For the life of William Wrigley, see "The Case of the Moving Jaws," in *Readers' Digest*, December 1947.

174: "Nothing great was ever achieved without enthusiasm." *The Man and His Business*, by William Wrigley Jr., page 282.

174: . . . he looked . . . "like a jolly bartender . . ." *Fortune*, January 1943, pages 98–100.

177: "We'll tie up the entire city." *Voices of the Game*, by Curt Smith, page 14.

178: "With the exception of the immortal Honus [Wagner] . . ." *The Pittsburgh Pirates*, by Fred Lieb, page 188.

178: . . . he regaled a large Boston audience with the comment that the Braves had won the Series because of prayer. *Baseball: The Golden Age*, by Harold Seymour, page 118.

178: . . . he took out a pair of glasses, polished them . . . *The Boston Braves*, by Harold Kaese, page 132.

179: "You can't sing your way through this league." Lieb, page 192.

179: "Go over there and see what the hell is wrong . . ." *Jolly Cholly's Story*, by Charlie Grimm with Ed Prell, pages 17–18.

180: "I suppose you realize you have a couple of wild Indians on your club . . ." Lieb, page 195.

180: "Mine are in that one over there!" *Ibid.*, page 196.

180: "But at least you knew that I was safe and sound in jail." Kaese, page 132.

180: "The first drunken ballplayer I was really aware of was Rabbit Maranville. Maranville was always loaded . . ." *Veeck as in Wreck*, by Bill Veeck, with Ed Linn, pages 30–31.

181: [Lardner's] all-drinking team, see "The Baseball Playboy, Past and Present," by John Lardner, as reprinted in *The Third Fireside Book of Baseball*, edited by Charles Einstein, pages 248–49.

181: "We were playing a game in Chicago . . ." *The Chicago Cubs*, by Warren Brown, pages 90–91.

Chapter 28. Tales from the Visiting Clubhouse

Interview with Ed Froelich.

Chapter 29. Alex

Interview with Ed Froelich.

185: "Sometimes a fit would strike him while he was out on the mound . . ." "The Ups and Downs of Old Pete," by Jack Sher, *Sport*, April 1950, as reprinted in *The Baseball Chronicles*, edited by David Gallen, page 143.

186: "Sometimes he'd have one of those spells . . ." *Two Spectacular Seasons*, by Bill Mead.

186: "Alex always thought he could pitch better with a hangover . . ." Gallen, page 143.

Chapter 30. Marse Joe Arrives

Interview with Ed Froelich.

191: "The trouble was, he was right. I was only hitting about .252 at the time . . ." *The Great Baseball Managers*, by Charles B. Cleveland, page 119. See also "Nobody's Neutral About McCarthy," by Ed Fitzgerald, *Sport*.

191: . . . you can do that when you're an eighth-place team. *The Chicago Cubs*, by Warren Brown, page 93.

191: "They tell me we don't look very good on paper. Well, we don't play on paper." *The National League Story*, by Lee Allen, page 196.

193: "Grover Cleveland Alexander was with the Cubs when I took over in 1926." *The Man in the Dugout*, by Donald Honig, page 84.

193: "In June of 1926 Joe McCarthy thought that Grover Cleveland Alexander was dissipated, drank too much, and was finished as a major-league pitcher . . ." *My War with Baseball*, by Rogers Hornsby and Bill Surface, page 152–53.

194: The great pitcher looked the young manager in the eye, smiled, tipped his cap, and kept walking. *The Baseball Chronicles*, edited by David Gallen, page 145.

195: "Hack Wilson was a wonderful little fellow . . ." Fitzgerald.

196: " . . . if I keep on drinking liquor, I ain't gonna have no worms!" *Ibid.*

Chapter 31. Mr. Wrigley

Interviews with Woody English and Ed Froelich.

199: "Outside of school hours, when I was a boy in Philadelphia, I worked for my father . . ." "Owning a Big League Ball Team," by William Wrigley Jr., as told to Forest Crissey, in the *Saturday Evening Post*, September 13, 1930.

Chapter 32. A Powerhouse

Interview with Woody English.

207: "I'm a married man with a family." *Times at Bat*, by Arthur Daley, pages 72–73.

207: Les Bell quote from *The October Heroes*, by Donald Honig, page 90.

209: "Once you put down that bat of yours . . ." Daley, page 157.

209: "I don't care what you thought . . ." *McGraw of the Giants,* by Frank Graham, page 225.

209: "They did everything but yawn in his face." *The Boston Braves*, by Harold Kaese, page 206.

209: " . . . It would help everybody concerned." *Ibid.*, page 207.

209: "I really enjoyed playing for the Braves . . ." *My War with Baseball*, by Rogers Hornsby and Bill Surface, page 141.

210: It was only after Wrigley promised that he would never interfere again that he was able to get Veeck to come back. *Veeck as in Wreck*, by Bill Veeck, with Ed Linn, page 25.

210: "I hated to leave the Braves . . ." Hornsby and Surface, page 141.

Chapter 33. When Eight Runs Weren't Enough

Interview with Woody English.

213: "Not only are the admissions to Wrigley Field . . ." "Owning a Big League Ball Team," by William Wrigley Jr., as told to Forest Crissey, in the *Saturday Evening Post*, September 13, 1930.

215: Mack's intention was to give the fourteen-year veteran his unconditional release. *Connie Mack*, by Fred Lieb, page 223.

215: "He looked at me . . ." *To Absent Friends*, by Red Smith, page 330.

216: "Ring Lardner was writing fiction and plays by 1929 . . ." *Ibid.*, page 331.

216: "None of us figured on batting against Ehmke . . ." *My War with Baseball*, by Rogers Hornsby and Bill Surface, page 203.

217: "It was my intention at that stage of the game to send in substitutes . . ." "Mr. Mack," by Bob Considine, in *Life*, August 9, 1948.

217: "I was sitting beside Joe McCarthy . . ." "Gabby Likes 'Em Hot," by Warren Brown, in *Saturday Evening Post,* February 11, 1939.

217: "While Art Nehf was taking his warm-up pitches . . ." *The Chicago Cubs*, by Warren Brown, page 115.

217: "[Haas] banged a kind of a line drive right out at Hack Wilson . . ." "Gabby Likes 'Em Hot," by Warren Brown.

217: "Two A's got on base . . ." Hornsby and Surface, page 199.

218: "Pat Malone, our pitcher, got pinch hitter Walter French out . . ." Hornsby and Surface, pages 199–200.

218: "The poor kid simply lost the ball in the sun . . ." *Sporting News*, by Sam Murphy of the *New York Sun*.

Chapter 34. One Firing Too Many

Interview with Woody English.

220: "I go to his place of business. Why shouldn't he come to mine?" *Two Spectacular Seasons*, by William Mead, page 74.

220: "Hack could hit a ball with his eyes shut . . ." *Ibid.*, page 82.

220: "Sheriff, it seems like things always happen to you . . ." *Ibid.*, 85.

221: "He made the money for us . . ." to sportswriter Ed Wilks, *Ibid.*, page 85.

221: "Hack was small, but he was powerful . . ." *The Man in the Dugout*, by Donald Honig, page 85.

221: "We had a little fellow named Clyde Beck on our club . . ." "Gabby Likes 'Em Hot," by Warren Brown, *Saturday Evening Post*, February 11, 1939.

222: "What am I supposed to do? Tell him to live a clean life and he'll hit better?" Mead, page 85.

222: "Hack, one of the idols of my youth . . ." *Veeck as in Wreck*, by Bill Veeck with Ed Linn, pages 31–32.

223: "Pitching to Hack." *Sporting News*, September 4, 1930.

224: "Oh, that O'Doul . . . my O'Doul." *The Chicago Cubs*, by Fred Lieb, page 99.

224: "I want a man who can bring me a world championship." *The Baseball Story*, by Fred Lieb, page 263.

225: ". . . I am not sure that Joe McCarthy is the man to give me that kind of a team." Mead, page 113.

225: "I think McCarthy knew more baseball than any other manager I ever saw . . ." "Gabby Likes 'Em Hot," by Warren Brown.

Chapter 35. The Death of William Wrigley

Interview with Woody English.

225: "I broke in with the Cubs under Hornsby in 1931." *The Man in the Dugout*, by Donald Honig, page 245.

227: "It just seemed that every time that situation came along . . ." *Two Spectacular Seasons*, by William Mead, page 115.

227: "It killed Hack Wilson . . ." *Ibid.*, page 113.

228: "Shhh. Not so loud. I wouldn't want Max to hear you . . ." *The Brooklyn Dodgers*, by Frank Graham, pages 126–27.

228: "It must have been a combination of things . . ." to J. Roy Stockton. Mead, pages 114–15.

228: "When [Wilson] heard the ball rattle off the fence . . ." *Ibid.*, page 116.

Chapter 36. Scandal—and Victory

Interviews with Woody English and Billy Jurges.

231: "Billy Jurges was living at the Carliss Hotel in Chicago . . ." *Rowdy Richard,* by Dick Bartell and Norman Macht, page 223.

Chapter 37. The Mythical Called Shot

Interview with Woody English, Billy Jurges, and Ed Froelich.

235: "We had a lot of fire and spirit on the Cubs . . ." *Baseball When the Grass Was Real*, by Donald Honig, pages 138–39.

235: "All this time a noisy battle of words was mounting from the rival dugouts . . ." *Jolly Cholly's Story,* by Charlie Grimm and Edward Prell, page 90.

236: "That's the Series where they say he called his home run . . ." "Nobody's Neutral About McCarthy," by Ed Fitzgerald, in *Sport*.

236: "Babe waved his hand toward our bench on the third-base side . . ." *Baseball for the Love of It*, by Anthony Connor, pages 196–97.

237: "Sure, Babe gestured to me . . ." *The Old Ball Game*, by Tristram Coffin, page 33.

237: "For years nothing made Root madder than hearing about how Ruth called his shot . . ." *Rowdy Richard*, by Dick Bartell and Norman Macht, page 224.

Chapter 38. The Death of William Veeck

Interview with Woody English.

239: "I probably would have ended up a garage mechanic." *Chicago Sun-Times*, May 17, 1975.

239: "Spend all of it or get nothing." *PK Wrigley: A Memoir of a Modest Man*, by Paul Angle, page 16.

240: "I'm not sure I'm succeeding solely on my own merits . . ." *The Rich Who Own Sport*, by Don Kowet, page 16.

240: "The club and the park stand as memorials to my father . . ." Angle, page 60.

240: "And so Phil Wrigley assumed the burden out of his sense of loyalty and duty . . ." *Veeck as in Wreck*, by Bill Veeck, with Ed Linn, page 39.

242: "A few weeks after school started, I was told that my father had been stricken with leukemia . . ." Veeck, with Linn, pages 35–36.

243: "Klein had two things going for him . . ." *Jolly Cholly's Story*, by Charlie Grimm and Edward Prell, page 103.

245: "If you own the club, you get the blame . . ." Kowet, page 17.

Chapter 39. Philibuck

Interview with Phil Cavarretta.

Chapter 40. Twenty-one in a Row

Interview with Phil Cavarretta.

Chapter 41. Stan Hack Stands on Third

Interview with Phil Cavarretta.

Chapter 42. The Home Run in the Gloaming

Interview with Phil Cavarretta.

Chapter 43. Diz's Last Stand

Interview with Phil Cavarretta.

Chapter 44. The Crazy World of PK Wrigley

Interviews with Woody English and Phil Cavarretta.

266: "That chewing gum is not an unessential is proven . . ." "Chewing Gum Is a War Material," *Fortune*, January 1943.

267: "Then just sit back and see what the people call it." *Chicago Sun-Times Midwest*, March 6, 1977, excerpted from *The Great American Chewing Gum Book*, by Robert Hendrickson.

268: ". . . the public had been conditioned to demand a winning team." *PK Wrigley: A Memoir of a Modest Man*, by Paul Angle, page 63.

268: "His solution was to sell 'Beautiful Wrigley Field' . . ." *Veeck as in Wreck*, by Bill Veeck, with Ed Linn, pages 40–41.

269: "Phil Wrigley has one overriding flaw . . ." *Ibid.*, page 39.

269: . . . he admitted to making two speeches. *Chicago Sun-Times Magazine*, November 26, 1972.

269: "My ambition is to go hide in a cave somewhere . . ." *Chicago Tribune Magazine*, October 12, 1969.

269: "We could have turned the Grand Canyon into a forest with all the trees we planted . . ." Veeck, with Linn, page 42.

270: "There are a great many stockholders in the Wrigley Gum Company . . ." *The Chicago Cubs*, by Warren Brown, page 133.

271: Wrigley asserted he had approved every trade . . . *PK Wrigley: A Memoir of a Modest Man*, by Paul Angle, page 59.

272: "We figured if we could measure the physical characteristics and reflexes of an established ballplayer . . ." William Barry Furlong, in the *Chicago Tribune Magazine*, October 1, 1969.

273: "One afternoon, I was called to Mr. Wrigley's office . . ." Veeck with Linn, pages 45–46.

275: "One night in New York Dizzy and his wife Pat went to an Italian restaurant . . ." *Rowdy Richard*, by Dick Bartell and Norman Macht, page 221.

275: "Throughout the 1938 season Hartnett's future was rumored to be in doubt . . ." *Ibid.*, page 230.

276: "I came to Chicago respecting [Hartnett] as a player . . ." *Ibid.*, page 231.

277: "Because [PK Wrigley] is such a shy man . . ." Veeck with Linn, page 39.

277: "There was one thing I was unable to persuade Mr. Wrigley to do, even for the park . . ."
    Ibid., pages 44–45.
279: "He was the most honest man I ever knew . . ." *Jolly Cholly's Story*, by Charlie Grimm
    and Edward Prell, page 177.
See also "The Case of the Moving Jaws: Why Millions Chew Gum," by Don Wharton, in the
    Baltimore Sunday Sun, October 26, 1947; "Wrigley: Chews All He Bit Off," in *Business
    Week*, November 17, 1945.
According to the article in *Fortune*, "Twice a day, when a cutie comes around the office with
    a tray of gum, Phil selects a stick and chews it gravely."
According to the *Sun-Times Magazine* of November 26, 1972, Phil Wrigley had to give up
    chewing gum after losing all his teeth.

Chapter 45. Wartime Ball

Interview with Don Johnson.

Chapter 46. The Workhorse

Interview with Hank Wyse.

Chapter 47. Jolly Cholly

Interview with Len Merullo.

Chapter 48. Roomies

Interviews with Len Merullo and Phil Cavarretta.

Chapter 49. The War Pennant

Interviews with Dewey Williams, Phil Cavarretta, Len Merullo, Hank Wyse, Bill Nicholson,
    and Don Johnson.
306: "Just take him out." *They Also Served: Baseball and the Homefront, 1941–45*, by Bill
    Gilbert.
307: "How about it, Gallagher, do you want Borowy or not?" "The Upside Down Man," in
    Collier's, October 6, 1945.
310: "I'll always think we would have brought the Wrigleys their first world champion-
    ship . . ." *Jolly Cholly's Story*, by Charlie Grimm and Edward Prell, pages 171–72.

Chapter 50. The Depths

Interviews with Hank Wyse and Phil Cavarretta.
313: "In 1945, we had been fortunate that many of our regulars were not acceptable for
    military service . . ." *Jolly Cholly's Story*, by Charlie Grimm and Edward Prell,
    page 175.
317: "Early in June 1949, while I was enjoying a most pleasant job as coach . . ." *Frank
    Frisch: The Fordham Flash*, by Frank Frisch and J. Roy Stockton, page 232.

Chapter 51. The Minor Leagues

Interview with Jim Brosnan.

Chapter 52. Boyhood Memories

Interviews with Jim Shapiro, Paul Buchbinder, and Bruce Ladd.

Chapter 53. Mr. Cub

Interviews with Hank Wyse, Len Merullo, Phil Cavarretta, Jim Brosnan, Glenn Beckert, Paul
  Buchbinder, and Jim Shapiro.
346: "Most Chicago whites hated blacks . . ." *The Boss*, by Mike Royko, page 139.
347: "See if you can find a history book . . ." Robert Hendrickson, in the *Chicago Sun-Times
  Midwest Magazine*, March 6, 1977.
347: ". . . we had to have a roommate for the one we've got." *Fabulous Chicago*, by Emmett
  Dedmon, pages 391–92.
349: "I'd never sat down next to a white man, and I wasn't sure what to do." *Mr. Cub*, by
  Ernie Banks and Jim Enright, page 56.
349: [Blades gave Ernie] a book called *How to Play Baseball.* "Ernie Banks," by Bill Furlong in the *Saturday Evening Post.*
350: "The sudden association with so many white people often left me speechless and wondering why they were so kind." Banks and Enright, pages 80–81.
351: "Some people feel that because you are black you will never be treated fairly . . ." *Ibid.*,
  page 84.

Chapter 54. The Professor

Interview with Jim Brosnan.
357: "They had budgets."
During the hearings held by the House of Representatives Antitrust Subcommittee chaired
  by Emmanuel Celler, the ball clubs were asked to open their books and reveal how
  much they were paying for salaries for the years 1952–56.
This is what Cubs players received those years, according to the committee records:

Chicago	Total Salaries	Average	Median
1952	$263,000	$10,520	$9,000
1953	404,500	16,180	13,000
1954	362,000	14,480	13,000
1955	303,000	12,120	12,000
1956	283,625	11,340	10,000

In 1956, Brooklyn spent $472,000; Cincy, $305,500; Milwaukee, $437,500; New York,
$396,500; Philly, $409,000; Pittsburgh, $248,500, and St. Louis, $403,000.

Chapter 55. The Kid from Garlic Gulch

Interviews with Len Merullo and Ron Santo.

Chapter 56. The College of Coaches

Interviews with Don Elston and Ron Santo.
365: "Phil Wrigley called me in . . ." *Voices of the Game*, by Curt Smith, page 93.
366: "You're making too many changes . . ." *Our Chicago Cubs*, by Rick Phalen, page 125.
375: "The great unknown of the Banks-Williams-Santo . . ." *Bleachers: A Summer in Wrigley Field*, by Lonnie Wheeler, page 175.
375: "To this day, the Cubs do not view baseball as a battle of foot soldiers . . ." *Ibid.*

Chapter 57. The Cornerstone

Interview with Ron Santo.

Chapter 58. Kenny Hubbs

Interviews with Don Elston and Ron Santo.
See also *The New Era Cubs*, by Eddie Gold and Art Ahrens, pages 112–14.

Chapter 59. Leo

Interviews with Glenn Beckert, Randy Hundley, and Gene Oliver.

Chapter 60. Fergie

Interview wtih Ferguson Jenkins.

Chapter 61. Flying High in '69

Interviews with Gene Oliver, Randy Hundley, Glenn Beckert, Ferguson Jenkins, and Billy Williams.
412: "How serious could it be to miss one or two little old games?" *The Cubs of '69,* by Rick Talley, page 80.

Chapter 62. Freefall

Interviews with Glenn Beckert, Randy Hundley, Gene Oliver, and Ferguson Jenkins.

Chapter 63. Leo's Demise

Interviews with Glenn Beckert, Ferguson Jenkins, Randy Hundley, and Gene Oliver.
423: "There were mornings when I'd come dragging into the clubhouse, hung over, still half asleep . . ." *Joe, You Coulda Made Us Proud*, by Joe Pepitone, with Barry Steinbeck, page 194.

Chapter 64. Mad Dog and Bruce

Interview with Darold Knowles.

Chapter 65. The Death of the Reserve Clause and PK Wrigley

Interview with Glenn Beckert.

Chapter 66. Big $$$, Low Morale

Interview with Bruce Sutter.
444: . . . the Wrigleys risked losing control of the company. *Chicago Sun-Times,* July 10, 1977.

Chapter 67. Harry

Interviews with Jim Brosnan, Bruce Ladd, and Ron Shapiro.
455: "My whole philosophy has always been to broadcast the way a fan would broadcast . . ." *Voices of the Game*, by Curt Smith, page 459.
455: "I just report what they do . . ." *Ibid.,* pages 459–60.
456: "There have been great announcers who've brought people to the park to watch good teams . . ." *Ibid.,* page 468.
457: "What it really came down to was they were jealous of me . . ." *Ibid.,* page 471.
457: "I figured at the end of '82 I might be Harry Who?" *Holy Cow!* by Harry Caray and Bob Verdi, page 213.
Note: After the Cubs began telecasting over WGN cable in 1982, Harry Caray and Steve Stone became so popular in Phoenix that they opened two restaurants there.

Chapter 68. Dallas Green Takes Over

Interview with Dickie Noles.

Chapter 69. The Red Baron

Interview with Rick Sutcliffe.

Chapter 70. So Close

Interviews with Rick Sutcliffe, Paul and Ned Buchbinder, and Jim Shapiro.

Chapter 71. The Demise of Dallas

Interviews with Rick Sutcliffe, Dickie Noles, and Ferguson Jenkins.

Chapter 73. Departures

Interviews with Jim Brosnan and Jack Wiers.

Chapter 74. Semper Harry

498: "At Wrigley Field it isn't the lyrics that matter, it's the experience." *Bleachers: A Summer in Wrigley Field*, by Lonnie Wheeler, page 68.

Index

Aaron, Hank, 356, 368, 377, 400, 402
Abbaticchio, Ed, 140
Abernathy, Ted, 404
Adams, Bobby, 366
Adams, C. F., 209, 210
Adams, Franklin P., 119, 163
Adams, Sparky, 187, 220, 330
Adcock, Joe, 374
Addy, Bob, 7
Agee, Tommie, 405, 416–17, 418, 419
Agents, professional, 442, 493
Aguirre, Hank, 402, 404, 413, 415, 421
Alcohol, *see* Drinking
Aldridge, Vic, 182
Alexander, Aimee, 171, 185–86, 192
Alexander, Grover Cleveland, 171–72, 181,
    183, 185–90
  death of, 190
  Joe McCarthy and, 192–93
Algren, Nelson, 1
Allen, Dick, 395
Allen, Lee, 116, 118, 163
Allen, Richie, 402, 456
Alley, Gene, 421
Allison, Doug, 23
All-Star Game, first, 241–42
Allyn, John, 456
Alou, Matty, 392, 421
Alston, Walter, 367, 385
Altman, George, 368, 369, 372, 396, 399
Altrock, Nick, 121
Amalfitano, Joey, 386, 390, 430, 450–51, 459,
    496
Amaro, Ruben, 474
American Association, 41–42, 71, 195, 278
  demise of, 77
American Athletic Union, 92

American Home Products, 444
American League, 99, 120, 294, 346
  first season of, 91, 96
  name change from Western League, 120
  night games, 491
  see also Western League
American Sports Publishing Company, 92
Ames, Red, 132
Amoros, Sandy, 346
Anderlick, Bob, 329
Anderson, Bob, 355, 370, 376
Anderson, Bull, 74
Andrews, Nate, 292–93
Angle, Paul, 271
Anson, Adrian "Cap," 2, 15–16, 20–22, 24–29,
    42, 43, 46–49, 51, 52, 53, 73, 81–90, 87,
    89, 90, 104, 342
  death of, 86
  Hart and, 82, 83, 84
  home runs, 40
  as manager, 24, 25–30, 32, 35, 36–38, 44,
    50–59, 61, 63, 64–65, 67–70, 78–84, 133
  Players League and, 74, 75, 80
  retirement, 84–86
Antonelli, Johnny, 329
Appolonio, Nathaniel, 20
Archer, Jimmy, 105, 106–7, 108, 110, 112–13,
    127, 156
Armour, Bill, 125
Armour, J. Ogden, 174, 175
Armour, Philip, 4
Arnovich, Maury, 328, 329
Atchley, Jim, 327
Athletics, *see* Oakland A's; Philadelphia
    Athletics
Atlanta Braves, 393, 444, 461, 494
Averill, Earl, 260

Axelrod, Barry, 476
Aykroyd, Dan, 497

Bailey, Ed, 362, 376
Baird, Tom, 349
Baker, Frank, 155
Baker, Gene, 321, 322, 347, 348
Baker, William, 171–72, 243
Baldwin, Lady, 53
Baldwin, Mark "Fido," 57
Ball, Philip, 166–67, 491
Baltimore Orioles, 69, 142, 443
Bancroft, Davey, 184
Bando, Sal, 439
Banks, Ernie, 321, 322, 339, 342–43, 347–54,
    355, 362, 368, 372, 376, 379, 381, 382,
    396, 399, 404, 406, 412, 414, 419, 422,
    423, 426
  autobiography, 413
  career achievements, 349, 352
  Leo Durocher and, 389, 393, 399, 409
  fired by Dallas Green, 420
Barber, Red, 455
Barnes, Frank, 395
Barnes, Ross, 6, 7, 10, 15, 16, 20, 21, 22, 73
Barrett, Red, 287
Barrow, Ed, 176
Barry, Jack, 155
Bartell, Dick, 231, 237, 253, 275–76
Bartlett, Arthur, 25–26
Barton, Bob, 388
Baseball, 228
Baseball Hall of Fame, 20, 46, 48, 96, 111,
    113, 145, 155, 182, 195, 206, 215,
    229, 256, 349, 352, 385, 393, 394,
    435
  Spalding and, 19, 93
Baseball magazine, 76
Baseballs, selling of, 72
"Baseball's Sad Lexicon," 119
Baseball Writers Association of America, 159,
    223
Batting order, instituting of prepared, 26
Baumholtz, Frank, 321, 339
Beck, Clyde, 221
Beck, Walter, 228
Becker, Beals, 157
Becker, Heinz, 305
Becker, Joe, 409
Beckert, Glenn, 351–52, 385–88, 388, 396, 403,
    404, 407, 410–12, 415–19, 420, 421–28,
    441–42
  traded to San Diego, 428
Beckley, Jake, 74
Beckwith, Joe, 476
Bedrosian, Steve, 488
Bell, Cool Papa, 345
Bell, Les, 207
Belushi, Jim, 497
Bench, Johnny, 435
Bender, Albert "Chief," 44, 125, 155
Bennett, Charlie, 31, 33, 53, 54–55, 88, 95

Benswanger, William, 301
Benz, Joe, 162
Bergen, Marty, 94
Berry, Edwin, 346
Bertell, Dick, 363, 369, 372
"Between You and Me," 128
Biittner, Larry, 432
Bilko, Steve, 333
Billings, J. B., 66–67
Bird, Doug, 453
Bishop, Max, 217, 218
Bishop, Orick, 18
Black, Joe, 346
Blacks in baseball, 342–54, 395
  bigotry against, 26–29, 342–46, 395
  see also names of individuals
Black Sox scandal, *see* World Series, 1919
Blackwell, Ewell, 302
Blades, Ray, 348, 349
Blake, Sheriff, 213, 217, 220
Bluff bunt, 108
Blyleven, Bert, 473
Boccabella, John, 399
Boley, Joe, 217
Bolling, Frank, 402
Bond, Kip, 486
Bonham, Billy, 433
Bonham, Ernie, 306
Boone, Levi, 3
Borbon, Pedro, 436
Borowy, Hank, 286–87, 288, 293, 294, 301,
    306–8, 313, 340, 393
  1945 World Series, pitching in, 310–12
Bortz, Bob, 328, 329
Boston Braves, 74–75, 79, 86–87, 95–96, 114,
    141, 142, 155, 162, 163, 171, 178, 209–10,
    249, 306, 340
  move to Milwaukee, 91
Boston Globe, 76, 87, 139
Boston Herald, 63, 249
Boston Red Sox, 96, 253, 385, 402, 462
  World Series play, 172–73
Boston Red Stockings, 4, 5–6, 10–11, 13, 14,
    15, 16, 21–22, 35, 42–44, 69
  Mike Kelly traded to, 64–68
Boswell, Ken, 405, 406
Bouchee, Ed, 369
Boudreau, Lou, 365, 366, 369, 370–71, 379–80,
    459
Bowa, Larry, 460, 462, 464, 466–67, 468, 483,
    487
Boyer, Ken, 400
Bragan, Bob, 390
Bransfield, Kitty, 139
Braves, *see* Atlanta Braves; Boston Braves;
    Milwaukee Braves
Braves Field, 491
Breadon, Sam, 208, 454, 491
Brecheen, Harry, 287
Bresnahan, Roger, 108, 109, 129, 150, 159
Brett, George, 465
Brewer, Jim, 339

Brewers, *see* Milwaukee Brewers
Brickhouse, Jack, 337, 338, 339, 365, 372, 457, 458
Bridges, Tommy, 256, 257
Bridwell, Al, 113, 115, 134, 149
Briggs, Herbert Buttons, 103
Briggs, Johnny, 355
Briggs Stadium, 491
Bright, Harry, 376, 377
Brinkopf, Leon, 327
Brock, Lou, 372, 373, 374–75, 414, 454
Broeg, Bob, 456
Broglio, Ernie, 374, 375
Bronfman, Charles, 443
Bronner, Jim, 449–50
Brooklyn Atlantics, 4
Brooklyn Dodgers, 138, 156, 164, 227–28, 241, 272, 274, 284–85, 299, 300, 305, 307, 313, 314, 319, 323, 340, 355–56, 365, 367, 368, 373, 377, 385
    first black players, 343–46, 349
    Jackie Robinson's first season with, 343–45
    see also Los Angeles Dodgers
Brooks, George, 139
Brosnan, Jim, 325–34, 347, 348–49, 352–53, 355–58, 455, 494–95, 496–97
    as minor league player, 325–34
Brotherhood of Professional Baseball Players, 73–78, 80, 84
Brouthers, Dan, 53, 55, 74, 82
Brown, Big Bill, 72
Brown, Mace, 261, 262, 263
Brown, Mordecai, 100, 111–13, 114, 120, 124, 129, 130, 132, 138, 139, 140, 153–54, 157, 160, 163, 394
    with Chicago Whales, 164, 165
    elected to Hall of Fame, 111
    nicknames, 111
    playoff game against New York Giants in 1908, 142, 143–49
    sent to minor leagues, 161
    World Series, pitching in, 121, 122, 123, 127, 152–53, 155
Brown, Warren, 119, 173, 182, 191, 217, 219, 224, 316
Brumley, Mike, 462
Brummer, Glenn, 471
Brush, John T., 76, 91, 102, 137, 141, 142, 145, 150
Brusstar, Warren, 460
Bruton, Billy, 356
Buchbinder, Ned, 483, 485
Buchbinder, Paul, 338–40, 353, 481–84
Buck, Billy, 447
Buck, Jack, 456
Buckner, Bill, 443, 452, 462, 466
Buhl, Bob, 372, 387, 393
Bulkeley, Morgan, 19, 92
Burdette, Lew, 390
Burgess, Smoky, 376
Burke, Frank, 122
Burkett, Jesse, 34

Burkhart, Ken, 287
Burns, George, 217
Burns, Tommy, 28, 40, 41, 46, 47, 48, 52, 53, 74, 78, 96
    as manager, 84, 94
Burris, Ray, 433, 434
Busch, August, Jr., 454
Bush, Donie, 184, 205
Bush, Guy, 195, 213, 216, 229, 231, 235, 236, 244
Bush, Joe, 173
Bushong, Doc, 58, 59, 60
Bystrom, Marty, 464, 465, 470

Callahan, Nixey, 162
Callison, Johnny, 390–91, 422
Camilli, Dolph, 244, 454
Campanella, Roy, 346, 355, 367
Campbell, Bill, 462
Campbell, Ron, 386
Cannizzaro, Chris, 413, 414
Capone, Al, 184, 219–20, 242–43
Caray, Harry, v, 454–59
    comes back after illness, 497–98
    Ford C. Frick Award, 498
    as voice of the Cubs, 457–59, 472, 474, 475, 480, 481, 497–99
Cardenal, Jose, 433
Cardinals, *see* St. Louis Cardinals
Cardwell, Don, 370, 372, 393
Carey, Max, 188, 228
Carlson, Hal, 213
Carlton, Steve, 398
Carmichael, John P., 134
Carpenter, Bob, 459
Carroll, Fred, 72
Carter, Joe, 420, 462, 473, 488
Cartwright, Alexander, 24, 93
Caruthers, Bob, 49, 50, 51, 56
Casey, Doc, 102, 103
"Casey at the Bat," 36
Caudill, Bill, 452
Cavarretta, Phil, 245–65, 285, 297, 299, 300–304, 308, 309, 312–16, 318–19, 375–76
    in 1935 World Series, 256–58
    1945 season, 245, 308
    as manager of the Cubs, 319–25, 331, 367
    Jackie Robinson and, 343, 345
Caylor, Oliver Hazard Perry, 75
Cepeda, Orlando, 393
Cey, Ron, 460, 462, 487
Chadwick, Henry, 12, 13, 76, 77, 92, 93, 150
Chambers, Cliff, 314
Champion, A. B., 4
Chance, Frank Leroy, 96, 99, 104, 113, 124, 127, 138, 139–40, 151, 153, 154
    building of team and, 100, 101, 102–4
    death of, 156
    as fighter, 104–5, 128–29, 135

Chance, Frank Leroy (continued)
  leadership skills, 96, 102
  as manager, 102, 105–11, 123, 124, 126–29,
    132, 135–37, 139, 147, 151–57, 160–61,
    162
  move to first base from catcher, 96, 98, 99
  playoff game against New York Giants in
    1908, 142, 144–50
  stolen base records, 107, 111
  Tinker, Evers, Chance double plays, 98, 119,
    129
Chance, Mrs. Frank Leroy, 150
Chandler, Happy, 343
Chapman, Ray, 188
Charboneau, Joe, 464
Chase, Hal, 105–6, 168, 170
Chesbro, Jack, 168
Chicago, 61–62
  history of, 1–6
  segregation in, 27–28
Chicago Cubs:
  attendance records, 213, 219
  College of Coaches, 327, 365–67, 371–73,
    375, 376, 380, 384, 387
  disputed game with New York Giants, 1908
    pennant and, 132–44, 146, 150–51, 156,
    162–63
  managers, *see names of individuals*
  in 1900s, 99–154
  1906 season and, 111–19
  1906 World Series, 119–24
  1907 season and World Series, 124–28
  1908 season, 128–51, 160
  1908 World Series, 151–54
  1910–1911, 154–57
  in 1920s, 175–220
  in 1930s, 220–76
  in 1940s, 276–318
  1945 World Series, 309–12
  in 1950s, 318–65
  in 1960s, 365–421
  1969 season, 396, 400–421
  in 1970s, 421–51
  in 1980s, 451–93
  1984 division playoffs, 480–86
  in 1990s, 493–99
  naming of, 99
  owners, *see names of individuals*
  purchased by Weeghman and merged with
    Chicago Whales, 166
  see also Chicago White Stockings
Chicago Daily News, 99
Chicago Excelsiors, 8–10
Chicago Herald-American, 316
Chicago Journal, 115
Chicago News, 57–58, 132
Chicago Onions, 77
Chicago Pirates, 74
Chicago Post, 159
Chicago Tribune, 3, 4, 16, 19–20, 119,
    120–21, 123, 124, 131, 137–38, 141,
    149–50, 162, 219–20, 242, 408, 493, 497

Chicago Tribune Company, 199, 430, 453,
    457, 459, 487, 489, 491, 493, 494, 497
Chicago Whales, 162, 163, 164–65
Chicago White Sox, 50, 151, 161, 162, 280,
    335, 338–39, 428, 431, 460
  1906 World Series, 120–24
  1919 World Series, 139, 166, 167
  Harry Caray and, 454, 456–57
Chicago White Stockings, 15–17, 20, 21–99
  of the 1880s, 4, 5, 26, 30–69, 90
  in 1890s, 69–96
  in 1900s, 98–99
  Anson as manager of, *see* Anson, Adrian
    "Cap," as manager
  name changes, 80, 99
  organizing of, 4
  photograph of the team, 54
  Players League, effect of, 74–75, 78–80
  Selee as manager of, *see* Selee, Frank, as
    manager
  see also Chicago Cubs
Chikagou, 2
Chipman, Bob, 281, 284, 299
Church, Bubba, 332, 334
Cincinnati Buckeyes, 30
Cincinnati Enquirer, 24–25, 42, 102, 141
Cincinnati Reds, 41–42, 91, 109, 158, 163, 164,
    167–70, 278, 288–89, 293, 325, 361–62,
    434–36, 446
Cincinnati Red Stockings, 4, 6, 10
Clarke, Fred, 99, 130, 131, 154, 161
Clarkson, Arthur "Dad," 44
Clarkson, John G., 63
  death of, 88
  as pitcher, 32, 44–46, 52, 53, 54, 56–60, 68,
    69
  traded to Boston, 65, 68–69, 71
Clarkson, Walter, 44
Clemente, Roberto, 392, 421
Clendenon, Donn, 405, 406, 407
Cleveland, Charles, 119
Cleveland Indians, 278, 346, 360–61, 385, 462,
    472–73, 479
Cleveland Naps, 151
Clinton, Hillary, 341, 342
Cloninger, Tony, 358
Coates, Bob, 333
Cobb, Ty, 31, 32, 113, 125, 126, 127, 151, 152,
    153, 207, 281
  records held by, 125
Cochrane, Mickey, 215, 217, 218, 256–57
Cole, Dave, 367
Collins, Eddie, 155
Collins, Jimmy, 94, 96
Collins, Rip, 259, 366
Collum, Jackie, 365
Comiskey, Charles, 58, 60, 74, 108, 158
  as manager, 50–53
  as owner of Chicago White Sox, 50, 120, 121,
    123, 165
Comiskey Park, 491
Concepcion, Dave, 446

Cone, Fred, 10
Congress Street Grounds (later West Side Park),
     39–40, 50, 166
Conlan, Jocko, 262, 368
Connor, Roger, 48, 74, 79
Connors, Billy, 466, 469, 471, 473, 474, 478
Cook, Stanton, 459, 495, 497
Coombs, Colby Jack, 155
Cooney, Jimmy, 187, 204
Cooper, Mort, 288
Cooper, Walker, 305, 332
Corbett, James J., 105
Corcoran, Larry, 38–39, 42–45, 48
Corrales, Pat, 395, 429
Corriden, Red, 299
Cotto, Henry, 420
Coveleski, Harry, 138, 139
Craft, Harry, 366, 370, 371
Craig, Roger, 445
Crandall, James "Doc," 132
Crane, Sam, 137, 141
Crawford, Wahoo Sam, 125, 151, 152, 153
Creamer, Joseph, 145
Crocker, Thomas, 139
Crosetti, Frank, 263, 264
Crosley Field, 491
Cubs, *see* Chicago Cubs
Cueto, Manuel, 169
Cummings, Arthur "Candy," 38
Cunningham, Bruce, 210
Current Literature, 150
Curry, Richard, 492
Cuyler, Kiki, 184, 189, 198, 204, 205, 212, 213,
     216, 220, 244, 248

Dahlen, Bill, 81
Daley, Arthur, 150, 207
Dallessandro, Dim Dom, 248, 259, 305, 314–15
Dalrymple, Abner, 40, 47, 50, 52, 59, 60
     traded to Pittsburgh, 64
Daly, Tom, 69, 70
Dark, Alvin, 324, 376, 432
Davidson, Satch, 417
Davis, C. V., 420
Davis, Curt, 274
Davis, George, 120, 122, 123
Davis, Harry, 155
Davis, Jody, 474, 477, 479–80
Davis, Spud, 321
Davis, Zachary Taylor, 165
Dawson, Andre, 487–88, 489, 493, 495, 496
Day, John, 79, 80
Deal, Charlie, 169
Dean, Dizzy, 253, 255–56, 260–61, 272,
     274–75, 281–82
     as announcer, 275, 454
     1938 World Series, 263, 264
Dean, Paul, 253, 255, 282
Decker, George, 81
DeJesus, Ivan, 443, 447–48, 451, 460, 466
DeJure, Gene, 394
Delahanty, Ed, 74, 181

Demaree, Frank, 258, 265, 303
Denny, Jerry, 72
Dernier, Bob, 462, 470, 475, 481, 487
Derringer, Paul, 286, 288, 292, 301–2, 305, 306,
     310, 311, 313, 393
Detroit baseball club (1880s), 53–55, 68
Detroit Tigers, 125–28, 154, 155, 253, 484–85
     1908 World Series, 151–54
     1935 World Series, 256–58
     1945 World Series, 309–12
Devlin, Arthur, 129, 134, 147, 149
Devore, John, 157
Diaz, Mike, 420, 462
Dickey, Bill, 263, 264, 349
Dietz, Dick, 388
Dillhoefer, Pickles, 171
Dillinger, John, 220
DiLullo, Ralph, 444
DiMaggio, Joe, 263, 264, 442
Dobernic, Jess, 315
Doby, Larry, 346, 394
Dodgers, *see* Brooklyn Dodgers; Los Angeles
     Dodgers
Doerr, Bobby, 382
Donahue, Jiggs, 120
Donlin, Mike, 129, 133, 134
     playoff game against the Cubs in 1908, 142,
     146, 147, 148
Donohue, P. J., 49
Donohue, Pete, 221
Donovan, Wild Bill, 125, 127, 151, 152
Dooin, Red, 139
Doolan, Mickey, 108, 139
Doubleday, Abner, 20, 92, 93, 498
Dougherty, Patsy, 120, 121
Douglas, Phil, 181
Douglas, Stephen, 3
Dovey, George, 141
Doyle, Dennis, 382, 384
Doyle, Jack, 250–51
Doyle, Jimmy, 160
Doyle, Larry, 129, 149, 157, 168
Drabowsky, Moe, 354–55, 356, 376, 393
Draft of players, 358
Drake, Charles, 268
Drake, Sammy, 376
Drake, Solly, 365
Dressen, Charlie, 296, 299
Dreyfuss, Barney, 101, 160, 163, 179, 180
Drinking, 61–62, 292
     by players and fans, 5, 11, 35, 41, 50, 53,
     56, 57, 61, 62–65, 67, 69–70, 86–87, 88,
     106–7, 160, 179–80, 181, 184, 185,
     186, 190, 194–96, 198, 209, 213,
     221–22, 228, 297, 333–34, 401,
     462–70
Drott, Dick, 355, 356, 376, 393
Dryden, Charles, 123, 124
Drysdale, Don, 368, 377, 398, 400, 478, 481
Duffy, Hugh, 31, 74–75, 94, 96, 108
Dunlap, Fred, 54
Dunston, Shawon, 488

Durham, Leon, 439, 452, 462, 477, 482, 483, 484
Durocher, Leo, 253, 277, 281, 285, 299, 300, 305, 317, 341–42
  Ernie Banks and, *see* Banks, Ernie, Leo Durocher and
  described, 385
  election to Hall of Fame, 385
  fired as Cubs manager, 426–27
  as manager of the Cubs, 384–94, 396–400, 404, 405, 406, 407, 412–15, 416, 418–20, 422, 423–28, 431
Duval, Clarence, 28–29
Dykes, Jimmy, 217, 349

Earnshaw, George, 215, 216
Easter, Luke, 346
Ebbets, Charlie, 140, 158, 164
Ebbets Field, 299
Eckersley, Dennis, 462, 470–71, 487, 493
Edwards, Bruce, 323, 330
Egan, Dick, 106
Ehmke, Howard, 215–16, 218
Eighteenth Amendment, 62
Einhorn, Eddie, 454, 457
Elia, Lee, 429, 459, 460–61, 465, 468–69, 496
Ellsworth, Dick, 370, 372, 376, 393
Elson, Bob, 177, 456
Elston, Don, 365, 367–75, 382
Emil Verban Memorial Society, 341–42
Emslie, Bob, 132, 136, 137, 140–41, 157
Endorsements, 32, 485
English, Elwood "Woody," 184, 195, 198, 201–2, 204–6, 216, 218, 219–20, 225, 226, 227, 229–35, 240–44, 257, 271
  All-Star Game of 1933, 241–42
  Rogers Hornsby and, 210–12
Enright, Jim, 413, 456
Erickson, Paul, 312, 343
Ernaga, Frank, 339
Essian, Jim, 496
Essick, Bill, 288–89
Evers, Johnny, 48, 50, 65, 69, 70, 81, 96–99, 100–104, 107–8, 109, 110, 112, 113–19, 124, 128, 129, 140, 152–53, 154
  with Boston Braves, 163
  described, 98, 115–16, 117
  disputed game with New York Giants in 1908 and, 132, 133–34, 136, 137, 138, 141, 150
  Warren Gill affair and, 130–31
  as manager, 161–62, 175, 224
  nervous breakdown, 155
  1910, misfortunes of, 154–55
  playoff game against New York Giants in 1908, 142, 145, 147, 182
  Tinker, Evers, Chance double plays, 98, 119, 129
  Tinker's relationship with, 117–19
  World Series play, 122, 151, 153, 178
Ewing, Buck, 31, 48, 74
Ewing, John, 79
Expos, *see* Montreal Expos

Fanning, Jim, 369
Fans, memories of lifetime, 334–42, 353–54
Fantasy baseball camps, 421, 425, 430, 431
Farm system (minor leagues), 270–71, 272, 281, 283–84, 287, 294, 315, 322, 325–34, 358, 395–96, 420, 445, 488–89
  see also names of specific teams
Farrell, Duke, 74
Federal League, 93, 163–67, 280
Feeney, Chub, 389
Fenway Park, 299, 385, 491
Ferguson, Bob, 24
Ferrell, Rick, 211
Field, Eugene, 32–33
Field, Marshall, 5
Fielding innovations, 26, 32, 50
Fingers, Rollie, 449
Finks, Jim, 497
Finley, Charlie, 432, 456
Finneran, Bill, 178
Fitzgerald, Honey, 173
Fitzsimmons, Freddie, 370
Fixing of games, *see* Throwing or fixing of games
Flack, Max, 172, 173
Flammini, Umberto, 327
Flannery, Tim, 483, 484
Fletcher, Art, 187
Fletcher, Scott, 420, 460
Flint, Frank "Old Silver," 40, 43, 47, 48, 63
  death of, 88, 89
Floyd, George, 66
Flynn, Doug, 446
Flynn, John "Jocko," 53, 57
Fogarty, Jim, 74
Fogel, Horace, 139, 159
Fondy, Dee, 321, 322, 357–58
Fonseca, Lew, 189
Forbes Field, 491
Force bunt, 108
Ford, Whitey, 173
Forman, G. F., 159
Fortune, 174, 266–67
Foster, Elmer, 69, 70
Foster, George, 435–36, 477
Foster, John, 191
Fournier, Jack, 207
Foutz, Dave, 50, 60
Fox, Charlie, 461, 469, 496
Foxx, Jimmie, 215, 217, 218, 283
Frain, Andy, 202–3
Franco, Julio, 460
Franks, Herman, 447, 450
Fraser, Chick, 105
Frazee, Harry, 173
Frazier, George, 462
Free agents, 442–43, 449, 452, 457, 486, 489, 493
Freedman, Andrew, 84, 90–91
French, Larry, 244, 253, 254–55, 257, 258, 303
French, Walter, 218
Frey, Jim, 312, 461, 462, 469, 471, 474, 482, 487, 489, 490, 496, 497

Frey, Lonny, 291, 293
Frick, Ford, 228
Friend, Bob, 379
Frisch, Frankie, 223, 242, 253, 260, 317–19
Froelich, Ed, 182–85, 186–90, 192–93, 196–99, 202–3, 237–39
Fuchs, Emil, 209, 229
Fullerton, Hugh, 48, 98, 109, 120–21, 139–40
Fulmer, Chick, 42

Gaedel, Eddie, 278
Gaffney, James, 162
Galan, Augie, 244, 250, 253, 255, 257, 265, 303
Gallagher, Jim, 278–79, 284, 291, 294, 296–97, 301, 304, 306–7, 314, 316, 318, 325–27
Galvin, Pud, 74
Gamble, Oscar, 420
Gambling, 11, 18, 19, 49, 56, 57, 61, 72, 107, 123, 145, 167, 210, 212, 226, 229–30, 282, 385
    throwing or fixing of games, 42–43, 56, 57–58
Ganzel, Charlie, 31
Ganzel, John, 109
Garcia, Reno, 395
Garman, Mike, 446
Garrett, Wayne, 417
Garver, Ned, 226
Garvey, Steve, 449, 481, 482, 484
Gehrig, Lou, 232, 233, 234, 263–65
Gehringer, Charlie, 256, 257
Gentry, Gary, 405
Gernert, Dick, 380
Gessler, Doc, 151
Getz, Gus, 170
Giants, *see* New York Giants; Philadelphia Giants; San Francisco Giants
Gibson, Bob, 351, 399, 400
Gibson, George, 179–80, 224
Gibson, Josh, 288, 345, 349
Gilbert, Charlie, 279
Giles, Bill, 459, 460
Giles, Warren, 345–46
Gilhooley, Bob, 449–50
Gill, Warren, 130–31, 134, 136
Gillespie, Paul, 292
Gilliam, Junior, 346
Gleason, Bill, 57
Gleason, Kid, 162
Glenn, John, 15
Gloves, baseball, 23
Goldsmith, Fred, 38, 39, 40, 42, 43, 44, 45
Gomez, Preston, 451
Gonzalez, Mike, 289
Gooch, Johnny, 184
Gooden, Dwight, 462, 478, 495
Goodwin, Nat, 66
Gordon, Joe, 263
Gore, George "Piano Legs," 37, 40, 42, 48, 50, 51, 63
    traded to New York Giants, 64, 66
Gorman, Arthur, 92
Goryl, Johnny, 377

Goslin, Goose, 257, 258
Grace, Mark, 489
Grant, Ulysses S., 5
Grantham, George, 184
Gravel Gertie, 336
Graves, Abner, 92, 93
Green, Dallas, 415, 420, 429, 430, 459–71, 472, 473, 474, 483, 487, 488, 495, 497
    resigns as coach of the Cubs, 489
Greenberg, Hank, 256, 309, 311
Grenesko, Don, 497
Griesedieck Brothers, 454
Griffey, Ken, 435, 438
Griffin, Mike, 453
Griffith, Calvin, 443
Griffith, Charles, 165
Griffith, Clark, 72, 82, 96
Griffith, Coleman, 272, 273
Griffith Stadium, 491
Grim, Jack, 98
Grimes, Burleigh, 227, 235
Grimm, Charlie, 33, 179–81, 198, 201–2, 211, 213, 221, 232, 235–36, 243, 244, 275, 279, 366, 389
    as manager of the Cubs, 230–31, 246, 248, 251, 252, 254, 257, 259, 271, 280, 284, 291, 293–301, 306, 307, 309–14, 316, 317, 365, 369, 376, 377
    as Milwaukee Brewers' manager, 280, 282–83
    switches jobs with broadcaster Boudreau, 365, 369, 379
Groat, Dick, 385
Grote, Jerry, 405
Grove, Lefty, 215, 216, 242
Gullickson, Bill, 467
Gwynn, Tony, 481, 484

Haas, Mule, 217, 218
Hack, Stan, 27, 244, 251, 255, 257, 275, 285, 296, 299, 301, 303, 308, 309, 311
    as manager of the Cubs, 324, 331, 354, 355, 367
Hacker, Warren, 393
Hafey, Chick, 184, 187, 189
Hahn, Eddie, 120
Hall, Mel, 420, 462, 468
Haller, Tom, 388
Hall of Fame, *see* Baseball Hall of Fame
Hamilton, Billy, 96, 374–75
Hamilton, Milo, 459
Handley, Gene, 381
Handley, Lee, 377
Hands, Bill, 387, 389, 390, 396, 397, 398, 404, 408–9, 416, 429
Hanlon, Ned, 54, 69, 82, 103
Hardin, Bud, 333, 334
Harper, Jack, 104
Harper's, 39
Harrelson, Bud, 405
Harris, Jim, 184
Harris, Vic, 428
Harrison, Carter Henry, 61–62

Hart, Bob, 178
Hart, James A., 79–80, 87
    Anson and, 82, 83, 84
    as owner, 91, 94, 97, 99, 100, 101, 102, 120
    as president of Chicago team, 78, 82
Hartman, J. C., 376
Hartnett, Gabby, 184, 188, 189, 195, 198, 204,
        206, 212, 213, 216, 217, 219–20, 221, 226,
        231, 236, 239, 241, 250, 258, 303
    famous home run, 261–63
    as manager, 259–60, 265, 274–77, 294
Hassey, Ron, 462
Hatten, Joe, 323
Hatton, Grady, 376
Hayworth, Ray, 327
Hempel, H. R., 128
Hemsley, Rollie, 181, 231
Henderson, Ricky, 375
Henderson, Steve, 453
Hendrix, Claude, 172
Henry, Bill, 372
Herman, Babe, 241, 244, 245, 272
Herman, Billy, 225–26, 231, 233, 235, 243–44,
        250–53, 256–59, 265, 275
    traded, 278, 279, 307
Hermanski, Gene, 323, 340
Hernandez, Willie, 420, 452, 488
Herrmann, August "Garry," 91, 160, 164, 166
Herrnstein, John, 393, 399
Herzog, Buck, 129, 133, 147, 149
Hickman, Jim, 388, 404, 409, 410–11, 417,
        422
Himes, Larry, 497
Himsl, Vedie, 348, 366, 371
Hines, Paul, 15
Hippodroming, *see* Throwing or fixing of games
Hit-and-run play, 32, 387
Hoak, Don, 357
Hobbie, Glen, 355, 370, 372, 376, 382, 393
Hodges, Gil, 355, 367, 405, 431, 436
Hofman, Artie, 130
Hofman, Solly, 100, 101, 105, 120, 134, 147,
        151
Holland, John, 355, 358, 370, 372, 374, 375,
        377–79, 387, 393, 428, 441
Hollis, Red, 332
Holt, Goldie, 366
Holtzman, Jerome, 326, 352, 408, 432
Holtzman, Kenny, 390, 396, 397, 398, 400, 404,
        408
    traded to Oakland, 426
Home run records, 40, 376
Hooks, Gene, 330
Hooper, Harry, 173
Hooton, Burt, 432
Hoover, Joe, 310
Hornsby, Rogers, 184, 193–94, 198, 207–13,
        216, 217–18, 241, 359–60, 363–64
    firing of, 229–31
    as manager, 224–26, 229, 327
Houston Colt 45s, 372
Houtteman, Art, 312

Howard, Del, 126, 148, 149
Howard, Elston, 349
Hubbell, Carl, 241, 258–59
Hubbs, Kenny, 372, 381–84, 386
Huff, George, 99–101, 103–4
Huggins, Miller, 32, 110
Huhn, Hap, 169
Hulbert, William, 15–21, 30, 36, 39
Humphries, Rolfe, vii
Hundley, Randy, 387, 388–90, 392, 396, 397,
        403, 404, 407, 408–9, 411–21, 423–26,
        429–31
    fantasy baseball camps, 421, 430, 431
    traded to Minnesota, 429
Hunter, Billy, 429
Hurst, Don, 243, 244, 245
Hurst, Tim, 85
Hutchinson, Freddie, 361, 362

Indians of Chikagou, 2
International League, 329
Irish players, discrimination against, 26–27
Irvin, Monte, 346
Isbell, Frank "Bald Eagle," 120, 121, 122,
        123

Jackson, Grant, 395
Jackson, Larry, 370, 374, 387, 393, 400
Jackson, Randy, 330
Jackson, Ransom, 320, 322–23, 365
Jackson, Reggie, 433, 439, 442–43
Jackson, Travis, 195
Jarbeau, Mlle., 28
Jeffcoat, Hal, 314, 315, 321
Jenkins, Ferguson, 387, 390, 392–400, 403–6,
        408, 410, 413, 419, 421–22, 424–29, 461,
        490
    as Hall of Famer, 393, 394
    as pitching coach for the Cubs, 468
    return to the Cubs, 429, 467
    traded to Texas, 428, 462
Jennings, Hughie, 82, 125, 126, 152, 153
Jewish players, discrimination against, 27
John, Tommy, 258
Johnson, Alex, 395
Johnson, Ban, 91, 120, 127, 163, 173
Johnson, Don, 280–87, 292, 296, 297, 303, 306,
        308, 312, 315
Johnson, Ernie, 280
Johnson, Roy, 284, 290, 291–92, 313, 321, 359,
        362–63
Johnson, Tom, 55
Johnson, Walter, 44, 165, 186, 187
Johnston, Jimmy, 162
Johnstone, Johnny, 145
Jones, Cleon, 405
Jones, Fielder, 120, 121, 122, 123
Jones, Col. Frank, 7–8
Jones, Percy, 210
Jones, Sam, 173
Jorgensen, Spider, 333
Joss, Addie, 151

Jurges, Billy, 231–33, 236, 244, 251–53, 255, 257, 259
  shot by jilted lover, 229, 231, 232, 252–53
  traded, 253, 265, 275–76

Kaese, Harold, 34–35, 55, 86–87, 178, 209
Kansas City Monarchs, 346–49
Kansas City Royals, 459, 465, 484–85, 486
Karros, Rich, 395
Kauffman, Ewing, 486
Kawano, Yosh, 391, 398, 422, 494
Keane, Johnny, 375
Keefe, Tim, 48, 74
Keeler, Willie, 82, 168
Kelley, Joe, 82, 142
Kelly, George, 237–38
Kelly, John, 52, 87
Kelly, Mike, 29–48, 51–55, 57–60, 63, 69, 72, 74, 76–77, 94, 108, 181, 198, 342
  death of, 86–87
  traded to Boston, 64–68, 71, 81
Kennedy, Bob, 366, 373, 374, 382, 387, 420, 430, 440, 449, 450
Kennedy, Terry, 481
Kerins, Jack, 45
Kessinger, Don, 351–52, 387, 388, 391, 396, 403, 404, 412, 415, 419, 420, 433, 439, 488
  traded to Cardinals, 431
Killefer, Bill, 165, 171, 172, 181, 188, 193, 194, 224
Kiner, Ralph, 320, 321
Kingman, Dave, 447, 448, 451, 453
Kirk, William, 129
Kittredge, Malachi, 81
Klein, Chuck, 243–44, 245, 257, 272
Klein, Lou, 366, 371, 372
Klem, Bill, 113, 116, 145, 147, 152
Kling, Johnny (nee Kline), 97, 99, 102, 108, 109, 113–14, 120, 121, 122, 124, 151–54
  playoff game against New York Giants in 1908, 146–149
  traded to Boston Braves, 155
Kluszewski, Ted, 332
Knabe, Otto, 139
Knowles, Darold, 394, 431–40, 446
Knowles, Fred, 91
Koenig, Mark, 231–34
Koonce, Cal, 372, 393
Koosman, Jerry, 405, 416, 419
Kopf, Larry, 168, 170
Koscher, Dave, 359–60, 362–63
Koufax, Sandy, 367, 398
Kranepool, Ed, 405
Kroc, Joan, 482–83
Kroc, Ray, 443
Kroh, Floyd, 135, 136
Krueger, Joseph, 122
Krukow, Mike, 451, 460, 488
Kuhn, Bowie, 442
Kupcinet, Irv, 1

Labine, Clem, 367
LaCock, Pete, 433
Ladd, Bruce, 340–42, 458
Lade, Doyle, 332
Lajoie, Napoleon, 31, 151
Lamp, Dennis, 448–49
Lampton, W. J., 146
Landis, Kenesaw M., 122, 166, 210, 220, 233, 234, 346
Landrum, Don, 389
Lange, Bill, 81, 96
Lanier, Max, 305, 332
Lansche, Jerry, 57, 86
Lardner, John, 181
Lardner, Ring, 216
Larsen, Don, 409
Larson, Dan, 460, 465
La Russa, Tony, 457
Lasker, A. D., 175
Lasorda, Tommy, 473, 475–77
Latham, Arlie, 50, 51, 58, 59, 60, 74
Lavagetto, Cookie, 299
Law, Vernon, 379
Lawrence, Brooks, 352
Lazzeri, Tony, 233
Leach, Tommy, 113, 117, 130, 140, 162
Lee, Bill, 238, 254, 255, 344
Lefebvre, Jim, 496
Lefferts, Craig, 420
Legett, Doc, 210
Leibold, Nemo, 247–48
Lemon, Jim, 339
Leonard, A. J., 21
Leonard, Buck, 345
Leonard, Dutch, 370
Lerch, Randy, 448
Lewis, Bob, 230, 231, 295, 309, 322, 323
Lewis, Llody, 61
Lewis, Ted, 94
Lieb, Fred, 4, 18, 32, 46, 74, 80, 120, 126, 131, 154, 159, 178, 180, 192
Lincoln, Abraham, 3–4
Lindstrom, Freddie, 209, 244, 253
"Line-up for Yesterday: An ABC of Baseball Immortals," 117, 207
Liquor, *see* Drinking
Literary Digest, 154–55
Livengood, Wes, 462
Livingston, Mickey, 292, 297, 332
Lloyd, Vince, 459
Locker, Bob, 431, 432
Lockman, Whitey, 427–28, 431
Loftus, Tom, 94, 96
Logan, Jimmy, 356
Lombardi, Ernie, 185, 204, 205, 278
Long, Dale, 368
Long, Herman "Dutch," 33, 94
Long Season, The (Brosnan), 325
Lopez, Al, 227
Lopez, Marcelino, 395
Los Angeles Angels, 175, 251, 272, 315, 325, 332–34, 347, 348

Los Angeles Dodgers, 385, 398, 443, 452, 460, 473, 475
see also Brooklyn Dodgers
Lotshaw, Andy, 206, 222, 248–49, 261, 294, 303, 305
Louisville Cardinals, 191
Lovejoy, Elijah, 27
Lowe, Robert Lincoln, 94, 95, 96, 98, 102
Lowrey, Peanuts, 285, 286, 296–98, 299, 309, 315
Lowshaw, Arty, 275
Lucadello, Tony, 325, 365, 394, 395
Lucchesi, Frank, 395, 496
Lundgren, Carl, 99, 100, 111, 124
Luque, Adolpho, 237
Luzinski, Greg, 448, 464
Lynch, Ed, 477
Lynch, Thomas, 82, 159
Lyons, Teddy, 313

McCaffery, Harry, 52
McCarthy, Jack, 98, 103
McCarthy, Joe:
  as New York Yankees manager, 225, 232, 236
  as player and/or manager of Cubs, 94, 182, 189, 190, 191–99, 204, 207, 210, 212, 213, 216, 217, 218, 221, 222, 227–28
  replaced as Cubs manager, 224–25
McCarthy, Tommy, 31, 94
McChesney, Harry, 101
McCloskey, John, 97–98
McCormick, Cyrus, 2
McCormick, Frank, 292
McCormick, Jim, 46, 50, 52, 53, 56, 57, 63
  traded to Pittsburgh, 64
McCormick, John, 30
McCormick, Moose, 134, 149
McCullough, Clyde, 292, 295–97, 323, 343
McDaniel, Lindy, 374, 389
McDonald, George, 154
McGinnity, Joe, 132, 134–35, 146
McGraw, John, 30, 82, 91, 99, 104, 111, 113, 117, 121, 129, 131, 134, 136, 137, 150, 154, 155, 156, 157, 161, 167, 172, 182, 183–84, 195, 196, 208–9
  playoff game against the Cubs in 1908, 141, 142, 145, 146, 147, 149
McIntyre, Matty, 153
Mack, Connie, 31–32, 74, 94, 154, 155, 215–17
McKechnie, Bill, 180, 259
McKenna, Andrew, 459
McKnight, Denny, 42
McLean, Larry, 100, 120
McMillan, Norm, 217, 218
McMillan, Roy, 402
McNally, Dave, 442
McNamee, Graham, 177
MacPhail, Andy, 497
MacPhail, Larry, 238, 277, 306–8, 491, 497
MacPhail, Lee, 497
McPhee, John Alexander "Biddy," 41, 42
McQuaid, Umpire, 87
McReynolds, Kevin, 481

McVey, Cal, 11, 15, 16, 20, 21, 22
Maddern, Clarence, 314
Maddox, Garry, 464
Maddux, Greg, 489, 493–95, 496
Madigan, John, 459, 497
Madlock, Bill, 428, 431, 432, 433, 437–38, 439, 443, 446
Magee, Sherwood, 118, 139
Maguire, Freddie, 207, 210
Malone, Pat, 195–99, 204, 205, 213, 217, 218, 222–23, 226, 227, 229, 231, 246, 276, 303, 327
Maloney, Billy, 102, 103
Mann, Les, 173
Mantle, Mickey, 387, 436, 442
Maranville, Rabbit, 163, 178–82, 191, 224
Marichal, Juan, 398
Marion, Marty, 286, 287, 342
Marquard, Rube, 44, 132
Marshall, Bruce, 438
Marshall, Jim, 431, 433, 436, 446, 447
Marshall, Joe, 98
Martin, Billy, 429
Martin, Fred, 366, 370, 439, 443, 445
Martin, Jerry, 452
Martin, Pepper, 181, 206, 253
Martinez, Carmelo, 461
Martinez, Dave, 489
Marty, Joe, 303
Martz, Randy, 460
Mason, Freddie, 395
Mathews, Eddie, 376, 400, 401–2
Mathewson, Christy, 44, 111, 113, 115, 117, 129, 132, 134, 136, 137, 139, 150, 156, 157, 173, 186
  playoff game against the Cubs in 1908, 141, 142, 144–49
Matthews, Ed, 356
Matthews, Gary, 462, 471, 477, 479, 487
Matthews, Wid, 318, 319, 320, 323–24, 327, 330, 340, 347, 349, 355
Mauch, Gene, 333, 348, 396
Mayo, Eddie, 310
Mays, Carl, 172, 173, 188
Mays, Willie, 346, 368, 376, 387, 427, 442
Mays, Willy, 356
Mazeroski, Bill, 385, 392, 421
Meany, Tom, 137
Medart, Harry, 52
Medill, Joseph, 3, 61
Medwick, Joe, 253
Merkle, Fred, 129, 133–36, 137–39, 140–41, 143, 144, 146, 150, 151, 156, 157, 168, 172
Merullo, Lennie, 281, 285, 295–301, 302–4, 306, 308, 309, 310, 311–12, 343–45, 347, 358–59
Messersmith, Andy, 442
Metkovich, George, 333
Metro, Charlie, 366, 371, 372
Mets, *see* New York Mets
Meyer, Russell Charles, 314–15
Meyerhoff, Art, 356
Michael, Gene, 487, 489, 496

Miksis, Eddie, 323, 349
Miller, Bing, 217, 218
Miller, Eddie, 292
Miller, Henry, vii
Miller, Marvin, 357, 442
Mills, A. G., 23, 76, 92–93
Milwaukee Braves, 355, 356, 377, 400
Milwaukee Brewers, 278, 280, 282–83, 294
Minner, Paul, 339–40, 393
Minnesota Twins, 429, 443, 497
Minor leagues, *see* Farm system (minor league);
    names of specific teams
Minoso, Minnie, 339
Mitchell, Clarence, 215
Mitchell, Fred, 171, 172, 175
Mitchell, Mike, 101, 109
Mitterwald, George, 429, 433
Monday, Rick, 426, 432, 433, 439–40, 443, 446
Moneyhoff, Scott, 467
Montreal Expos, 404–5, 443, 467, 487
Moore, Frank, 210
Moore, Percy, 246
Morales, Jerry, 433
Moran, Pat, 103, 109
Moreland, Keith, 460, 462, 464, 465, 468, 477,
    478, 487
Morgan, Cy, 155
Morgan, Joe, 435, 438, 446
Moriority, George, 257
Morrill, John, 21
Morse, Jacob, 76
Morton, Samuel, 76
Moryn, Walt, 357, 368
Moyer, Jamie, 489
Mr. Cub (Banks and Enright), 413
Mullen, Warren, 483
Municipal Stadium, Cleveland, 491
Murcer, Bobby, 443, 447, 451
Murnane, Tim, 76, 87
Murphy, Bob, 247
Murphy, C. Webb "Charlie," 102, 104, 111, 121,
    127, 131, 137, 139, 150–51, 156
    playoff game against New York Giants in
        1908, 141, 142, 144
    practices enraging fans, players, and other
        owners, 151, 155, 158–63, 167
Murphy, Sam, 219
Murray, Bill, 497
Murray, Red, 157
Musial, Stan, 287, 292, 293, 300–301, 305, 339,
    368, 400
My Greatest Day in Baseball (Carmichael), 134

Nash, Ogden, 117, 207
National Association of Base Ball Players, 4–5,
    8–10
National Association of Professional Ball
    Players, 11
National Commission, 125–26, 158, 164, 173
National League Guide, 23
National League of Professional Baseball Clubs,
    23, 41–42, 97, 163, 164, 166–67
    American Association teams joining, 77

Board of Directors, 137, 140–41
    constitution of, 18, 19, 20
    creation of, 6, 12–20
    Andrew Freedman and, 90–91
    players defection over salary, 71–80
Navin, Frank, 128
Neale, Earle "Greasy," 168, 169, 170
Needham, Tom, 146
Neeman, Cal, 369
Negro Leagues, 113, 345, 349
Nehf, Art, 217
Nettles, Graig, 376, 481
Newcombe, Don, 346, 361–62, 373
Newhouser, Hal, 309, 311–12
Newton, Jack, 168
New York All-Stars, 360
New York American, 129, 139–40
New York Evening Journal, 137, 139, 141,
    148
New York Evening Mail, 119
New York Giants, 27, 48–49, 64, 66, 69, 75, 79,
    82, 84, 87, 99, 111, 113, 117, 119, 129–36,
    154–57, 159, 172, 177, 183–84, 195, 201,
    208–9, 213, 241, 253, 255, 258, 355, 385
    disputed game with Chicago Cubs, 1908
        pennant and, 132–44, 146, 150–51, 156,
        162–63
    first black players for, 346
    Spalding's ownership interest in, 80, 82
New York Globe, 128–29, 131, 141
New York Herald, 129, 133, 135, 138, 142
New York Highlanders, 155
New York Mets, 372, 453, 462, 477–78, 479
    1969 season, 396, 404, 405, 408–9, 416–17,
        418–19, 420
New York Sun, 137, 145, 146, 219
New York Times, 133, 134, 146, 150, 207
New York Tribune, 149
New York World, 130, 132, 135
New York Yankees, 40, 173, 177, 220, 225, 272,
    288, 360, 442, 443, 453, 494
    Borowy traded by, 286, 293, 294, 301, 306–8
    1932 World Series, 231–39
    1938 World Series, 263–65
Nice Guys Finish Last (Durocher), 341
Nichol, Hugh, 38–39
Nicholds, A. N., 9
Nichols, Kid, 94, 96
Nicholson, Bill, 285, 295, 296, 297, 301, 306,
    311–15, 320, 340
Night games, 491–93
Nipper, Al, 489, 490
Noles, Dickie, 460, 461, 462–71, 489
Noren, Irv, 368
Norman, Bill, 286
Northey, Ron, 330
Northwest League, 71

Oakland A's, 426, 431, 432, 439, 442, 456
Oates, Johnny, 474
O'Day, Hank, 31, 131, 132, 134–36, 137–39,
    140–41, 162, 178
    as manager, 162–63

O'Dea, Ken, 265
O'Doul, Lefty, 224
Official Baseball Guide, 91
O'Hara, Johnny, 177
Old Gag play, 48
O'Leary, Charley, 127, 152, 153
Oliver, Al, 434
Oliver, Gene, 390–92, 400–403, 406, 407–8,
    413, 419–21, 425
Oliver, Nate, 419, 420
O'Malley, Peter, 475
O'Malley, Walter, 443, 475
O'Neil, Buck, 349
O'Neil, Jack, 100
O'Neill, Bill, 120
O'Neill, Tip, 57, 58
Ontiveros, Steve, 443
O'Rourke, Jim, 21, 48, 74
Orsino, John, 388
Orsulak, Joe, 480
Osborn, Don, 326, 327, 330
O'Toole, Marty, 44
Ott, Mel, 258
Outen, Chick, 281
Outlaw, Jimmy, 309
Overall, Orval, 102, 103–4, 111, 124, 127, 132,
    153–54
    retirement of, 155
    World Series play, 123, 151, 153
Overmire, Stubby, 312
Owen, Marv, 253
Owens, Paul, 460
Owens, Steve, 310
Ozark, Danny, 464

Pacific Coast League, 155, 175, 224, 281, 325,
    347
Pafko, Andy, 285, 306, 308, 315, 323, 340
Paige, Satchel, 288, 345, 346, 349
Palmeiro, Rafael, 489, 493
Palmer, Potter, 5
Pappas, Milt, 421, 424
Parker, Dave, 434
Passeau, Claude, 286, 288, 291–92, 294, 296,
    297, 305, 306, 310, 313, 340, 344, 393
Paterson Keystones, 30
Paul, Gabe, 259, 472
Payne, Freddie, 126
Pearce, Dickey, 58, 59
Pearce, George, 162
Peck & Snyder, 24
Pegler, Westbrook, 234
Peiper, Pat, 183, 263, 336
Pennant Race, The (Brosnan), 325
Pennant races, 94
    in 1880s, 38, 46, 47, 48–49, 53, 55, 67
    in 1890s, 79, 82, 83, 95
    in 1900s, 101, 118, 124, 125, 128, 132
    in 1908, 132–51, 156, 160
    in 1910, 154
    in 1914, 163, 178
    in 1918, 172

    in 1927, 193, 194
    in 1929, 212, 213
    in 1930, 223, 224
    in 1932, 229, 231, 232
    in 1934, 253
    in 1935, 229, 245, 253, 255–56
    in 1938, 245, 261–63
    in 1945, 172, 229, 245, 294, 295, 301–9
Penn State League, 87
Pepitone, Joe, 388, 421–25
Perez, Tony, 435
Perranoski, Ron, 376, 377, 475, 476
Perry, Gaylord, 398
Perry, Gerald, 461
Peters, Johnny, 15
Peterson, Bob, 325–26
Petrocelli, Rico, 402
Petway, Buddy, 113
Pfeffer, Fred, 40, 46, 47, 48, 51, 52, 53, 56, 57,
    58, 74, 78
Pfiester, Jack, 103, 111, 120, 124, 129, 132,
    133–34, 137, 153–54
    playoff game against New York Giants in
        1908, 144, 147, 149
    World Series play, 122, 123, 126
Phelan, Art, 162
Phelon, W. A., 115
Philadelphia Athletics, 31, 55, 68, 125, 138,
    139, 155, 178
    1910 World Series, 154, 155
    1929 World Series, 215–19
Philadelphia Centennial Club, 68
Philadelphia Phillies, 159, 171–72, 177, 224,
    243, 314, 345–46, 393–95, 402, 437,
    448–49, 452, 459, 460, 462, 466
Phillips, Adolfo, 387, 393, 396, 399, 400,
    404–5
Phillips, Taylor, 370
Pinkerton Agency, 63
Pinson, Vada, 361
Pirates, *see* Pittsburgh Pirates
Pittsburgh baseball club (1880s), 64
Pittsburgh Pirates, 74, 75, 96, 99, 124, 129, 130,
    132, 139–40, 154, 177, 179–80, 182, 184,
    213, 231, 232, 244, 261, 301, 308, 392,
    415–16, 417, 421–22, 434, 479–80
PK Wrigley: A Memoir of a Modest Man
    (Angle), 271
Plank, Eddie, 155
Players League, 71, 74–77, 80
Pollet, Howie, 325, 331
Polo Grounds, 491
Popovich, Paul, 405, 415–16, 419, 420
Power, Ted, 476
Powers, John, 175, 369
Prendergast, Mike, 171
Providence baseball club, 40–41, 45
Pulliam, Harry, 131, 136, 138–39, 145, 158
Push bunt, 127

Quest, Joe, 48
Quinlan, Jack, 339

Quinn, John Picus, 215, 217
Quisenberry, Dan, 444

Radbourn, Hoss, 40, 44, 45, 74
Radio, baseball broadcast on, 177–78, 200,
 213, 337
 rights for, 357
 see also names of announcers, e.g. Boudreau,
  Lou; Caray, Harry
Rainey, Chuck, 461, 469
Reach, A. J., 23, 24, 92
Reach Company, A. J., 24
Reagan, Ronald, 341, 498
Red Sox, *see* Boston Red Sox
Red Stockings, *see* Boston Red Stockings;
 Cincinnati Red Stockings
Reed, Thomas, 91
Reese, Pee Wee, 279, 300
Regan, Phil, 404, 415, 416, 422
Reinsdorf, Jerry, 454, 457
Reiser, Pete, 279, 390, 391, 412
Reitz, Ken, 429, 439, 452
Renko, Steve, 432
Reserve clause, 18, 71, 73, 76, 90, 93
 death of, 440, 442–43, 446
Reulbach, Ed, 99–101, 109, 111, 114, 120, 124,
 138, 153–54, 164
 traded to Brooklyn, 161
 two shutouts in a doubleheader, pitching of,
  138
 World Series play, 121–22, 123, 126, 138
Reuschel, Rick, 433, 435, 447, 449, 453,
 488
Rhem, Flint, 181
Rice, Grantland, 234, 238
Rice, Hal, 333, 334
Richards, Paul, 312
Richardson, Hardy, 53, 54
Rickey, Branch, 194, 208, 227, 270–71, 272,
 279, 280, 340, 346
Riggs, Lew, 299
Rigler, Cy, 238
Riley, Pat, 479
Ripken, Cal, Jr., 350
Risberg, Swede, 280
Rittwage, Jim, 389
Rivera, Jim, 339
Roberts, Robin, 319, 355, 393
Robinson, Frank, 330, 352, 387, 402
Robinson, Jackie, 343–46, 347, 355
Robinson, Wilbert, 82, 164
Robinson, Yank, 60
Rockford Forest Citys, 6–9, 20–21
Rockford Mercantiles, 6–7
Rockford Pioneers, 6–7
Roebuck, Alva, 5
Roebuck, Ed, 367
Rogell, Billy, 257
Rogers, Andre, 372
Rogers, Colonel John, 91
Rohe, George, 121, 122, 123
Roosevelt, Franklin D., 284

Root, Charlie, 195, 204, 205, 213, 216, 231,
 234–39, 255, 321, 327, 328, 370
Rose, Pete, 354, 434–35, 447, 464
Rossman, Claude, 127, 153
Roth, Frank, 110
Rothstein, Arnold, 167
Roush, Edd, 169, 189
Rowe, Jack, 54
Rowe, Schoolboy, 256
Rowland, Pants, 247, 278
Royko, Mike, 346, 497
Ruffing, Red, 264
Ruppert, Colonel Jacob, 176, 224
Rush, Bob, 314, 331, 356, 393
Rusie, Amos, 79, 90
Russell, Alan, 332
Ruth, Babe, 32, 40, 181, 207, 223, 232, 233,
 242, 248–49, 274, 280
 Called Shot, 231, 234–39
 death of, 228
 World Series play, 172, 173, 231, 234–39
Ruthven, Dick, 461, 462, 487
Ryan, Connie, 298
Ryan, Jimmy, 69, 70, 74, 78, 81, 83
Ryan, Nolan, 405
Ryder, Jack, 141

Sadecki, Ray, 393
Sadowski, Bob, 401
Saier, Vic, 156
St. Louis Browns, 49–53, 55–61, 63, 64, 151,
 166–67, 226, 275
St. Louis Cardinals, 159, 177, 188–89, 193–94,
 223, 224, 227, 253, 255, 260, 270–71,
 272, 275, 286, 287, 288, 294, 300,
 308, 313, 325, 358, 374, 375, 400, 404,
 419, 431, 439, 444, 452, 474–75, 490,
 491
 Harry Caray and, 454–56
 1945 pennant race, 305–9
St. Louis Democrat, 4
St. Louis Dispatch, 12
St. Louis Post-Dispatch, 456
St. Louis Republican, 61
Salaries, player, 71–80, 93, 129, 161, 208, 227,
 240–41, 251, 273, 279, 289, 290, 297, 331,
 355–56, 358, 374, 440–43
 after death of reserve clause, 440, 442–43,
  444, 446, 449–50, 452–53, 454, 486, 493,
  496
 baseball-related income in addition to, 72,
  485
 cap on, 71, 72, 73–74, 291
 rules about, 8–10, 42
 see also Reserve clause
Saltwell, Salty, 431
Saltzgaver, Jack, 288
Samuel, Juan, 460
Sanborn, E. I., 131, 137–38
Sanchez, Rey, 496
Sandberg, Ryne, 460, 462, 466, 470, 471, 474,
 475, 479, 484, 487, 492, 493

Sandberg, Ryne (continued)
 retirement of, 495–97
Sanders, Roy, 288
Sanderson, Scott, 461, 469, 471, 482, 487
San Diego Padres, 428, 443, 486
 1984 divisional playoffs, 480–85
Sanford, Jack, 379
San Francisco Giants, 388–89, 393, 429, 443,
 488, 494
Sanguillen, Manny, 421
Santo, Ron, 359–64, 369, 372, 375–81, 388,
 393, 396, 399, 403, 404, 409, 411–12, 415,
 416, 417–18, 419, 425
 home runs, career, 376
 Kenny Hubbs and, 382–84
 signing with the Cubs, 359–63
 traded to White Sox, 428, 431
 Don Young incident and, 405–8
Saperstein, Abe, 349
Saucier, Kevin, 464
Sauer, Ed, 315
Sauer, Hank, 320, 321, 339, 393
Savage, Ted, 391, 392, 396
Scalzi, Frank "Skeeter," 326
Schaefer, Herman "Germany," 125–26, 153, 181
Schang, Wally, 173
Scheffing, Bob, 292, 315, 331, 333–34, 344, 350
 as manager, 355, 356, 365, 367–69
Schenz, Hank, 315
Schiraldi, Calvin, 489, 490
Schmidt, Boss, 125
Schmidt, Charlie, 126
Schmidt, Mike, 376, 449, 473
Schmitz, Johnny, 315
Schoendienst, Red, 382, 400
Schoonmeir, Al, 412
Schriver, Bill, 81
Schulte, Frank, 100, 101, 103, 120, 123, 126,
 127, 148, 151, 153
Schultz, Buddy, 445–46
Schuster, Billy, 315
Schwartz, Manny, 336
Scott, Everett, 173
Scully, Vin, 455
Sears, Richard, 5
Seaver, Tom, 398, 399, 405, 408, 419, 495
Segui, Phil, 473
Seibold, Harry, 210
Seitz, Peter, 442, 446, 449
Selee, Frank:
 death of, 102
 as manager, 94–102, 191
Selma, Dick, 402, 404, 417–18
Senators, *see* Washington Senators
Sensabaugh, Charles, 99
Serena, Bill, 319, 320, 322
Seward, William, 3
Seymour, Cy, 146, 147, 148, 149
Seymour, Harold, 26, 159, 161
Seys, John, 181
Shapiro, Jim, 334–38, 354, 478–79, 480,
 484–85
Shapiro, Ron, 458–59

Shea Stadium, 405
Sheckard, Jimmy, 102, 103, 108, 109, 126, 127,
 148, 149, 156, 157
 near blinding of, 128–29
Shibe Park, 491
Shires, Art, 181
Signals, 48, 417–18
 to batters, 26
 by catcher to pitcher, 32, 189, 328
 Chance's team's reading and relaying of,
 109–10, 117, 118, 153
 stealing of, 295–96, 299, 305, 310
Simmons, Al, 215, 216, 217, 218
Simmons, Curt, 319–20
Sinatra, Frank, 476
Sinclair, Harry, 166
Slagle, Jimmy, 97, 99, 101, 126, 127
Slattery, Jack, 209
Slaughter, Enos, 287, 379
"Slide, Kelly, Slide," 36
Smalley, Roy, 37, 304, 315, 320, 347, 348
Smith, Curt, 472
Smith, Dwight, 495
Smith, Earl, 184
Smith, H. Allen, 106, 117
Smith, Ira, 106, 117
Smith, Lee, 123, 452, 461, 468, 473, 477, 482,
 488, 493
 traded to Boston Red Sox, 489–90
Smith, Lonnie, 464
Smith, Ozzie, 447
Smith, Red, 216, 295
Smith, Robert, 13, 19, 33, 34, 35–36, 56, 58, 59,
 60, 65, 90, 93
Smith, Willie, 399, 420
Snap throw, introduction of, 113
Snider, Duke, 355
Snodgrass, Fred, 129, 146, 157
Snyder, Pancho, 211
Soden, Arthur, 76, 79, 80
Solomon, Eddie, 432
Soriano, Dewey, 361, 362
Southworth, Billy, 285, 313
Spahn, Warren, 355, 368, 400
Spalding, Albert Goodwill, vii, 5–24, 90–94,
 143
 Anson's last years with Chicago and,
 83–86
 Baseball Hall of Fame and, 19, 20
 bigotry of, 27, 29
 death of, 93
 employment agency for ballplayers, 76
 first professional baseball league and, 6, 11,
 12–20, 23
 as manager, 17, 22
 National League presidency and, 90–91
 origins of baseball and, 92–93
 as owner, 17, 21, 27, 36, 39, 49, 50, 53, 56,
 58, 60–69
 ownership interest in New York Giants, 80,
 82
 as pitcher, 5–6, 7, 10, 12, 16, 22
 Players League and, 76, 77, 80

as president of Chicago White Stockings, 17, 78

salaries of players and, 71–73, 75, 77–78, 440, 443

sale of Chicago team, 91

sporting goods business, 13, 15, 17, 19–20, 22–24

trading of players by, 64–69, 71, 81

Spalding, J. Walter, 19

Spalding, Keith, 24

Spalding & Bros., A. G., 76, *see* Spalding, Albert Goodwill, sporting goods business

Spalding Guide, 62, 92, 93

Spalding Score Book, 24

Spangler, Al, 418

Speaker, Tris, 113

Spicer, Bob, 327

Spink, Al, 76

Sporting Life, 163

Sporting News, 76, 82, 131, 223

Sports Illustrated, 478

Sportsman's Park, 491

Stahl, Chick, 94

Stainback, Tuck, 257

Stallings, George, 171

Stanky, Eddie, 281, 284–85, 298–99, 305, 339

Stargell, Willie, 415, 416, 421, 422, 434, 448

Steinbrenner, George, 486

Steinfeldt, Harry, 102, 103, 113, 114, 120, 126, 133, 135, 148, 151, 152, 156

Stengel, Casey, 195, 306

Stephenson, Riggs, 184, 189, 195, 198, 204, 206, 212, 213, 216, 218

Stewart, Dave, 476

Stewart, Jimmy, 386

Stock, Milt, 298, 310

Stockton, J. Roy, 228

Stoddard, Tim, 462, 477

Stolen base records, 107, 111, 374–75

Stone, Steve, 431, 433–34, 497–98

Stoneham, Charles, 167, 208, 209

Stoneham, Horace, 346, 393

Storke, Alan, 140

Stovey, George, 27

Strang, Sam, 97

Street, Gabby, 454

Strikes, player, 71–80, 172–73, 453, 457

Stringer, Lou, 278

Stuart, Dick, 356

Stuart, Don, 290

Suhr, Gus, 261

Sullivan, Billy, 120

Sullivan, Dave, 51, 52

Sullivan, James E., 92

Sullivan, Ted, 31, 66–67, 97

Sullivan Award, 92

Summers, Ed, 151

Sunday, Billy, 44, 51, 52, 54–55

as evangelist, 88–89

Sutcliffe, Rick, 462, 471, 472–86, 480–90, 493

Andre Dawson's signing with the Cubs and, 487–88

foundation started by, 485–86

as free agent, 486

1984 division playoffs, 480–85

records and achievements, 486, 487

Sutter, Bruce, 431, 437, 438–39, 440, 443–53, 475, 488

records and accomplishments, 443, 444, 449

salary of, 444, 446, 449–50, 452–53

traded to Cardinals, 439, 444, 452, 453, 490

Suttergren, Gus, 269

Sutton, Don, 398

Sutton, Ezra, 15, 20, 21, 42

Sweeney, Bill, 162, 332–33

Swift, Gustav, 4

Swoboda, Ron, 419

Tabler, Pat, 420, 460

Taft, Charles P., 102, 159, 163, 167

"Take Me Out to the Ball Game," 128

Talley, Rick, 413

Tannehill, Lee, 120, 122

Tappe, Elvin, 363, 364, 366, 369, 371, 372, 380

Taylor, Ben, 332

Taylor, "Dummy," 117

Taylor, Jack, 100, 111, 120

Taylor, Sammy, 363, 369–70

Taylor, Zack, 206, 217

Teachout, Bud, 227

Teifenauer, Bobby, 401

Television, baseball broadcast on, 337–38

rights to, 357

see also names of announcers, e.g. Boudreau, Lou; Caray, Harry

Templeton, Garry, 481, 482, 484

Tener, John, 74, 78, 163, 173

Tennes, Monte, 167

Tenney, Fred, 94, 95, 134, 147, 149

Terkel, Studs, 1

Terry, Bill, 183–84, 187, 223, 258

Texas Rangers, 428, 429, 462, 471

Thacker, Moe, 363, 369

Thayer, Fred, 24

Third-base coach, 22, 26

"Third batter," 101

Thomas, Frank, 376, 377

Thomas, Lee, 391–92, 399

Thompson, Hank, 346

Thompson, Sam, 53, 54

Thompson, William Hale, 163

Thomson, Bobby, 368

Thorner, Justus, 41

Thornton, Andre, 432, 433

Thorpe, Jim, 168, 170

Throwing or fixing of games, 42–43, 56, 57–58, 100, 139

Thurlby, Birdie, 328

Tidrow, Dick, 452, 460

Tierney, Cotton, 179, 180

Tigers, *see* Detroit Tigers

Tinker, Joe, 97–98, 99, 106–9, 113, 114–15, 124, 126–30, 132–35, 137, 140, 151, 152, 154, 156–57, 163

Tinker, Joe (continued)
  with Chicago Whales, 164–65
  Evers's relationship with, 117–19
  move to shortstop from third base, 98
  playoff game against New York Giants in
    1908, 142, 145, 148, 149
  Tinker, Evers, Chance double plays, 98, 119,
    129
  traded to Cincinnati, 161, 164
Tinker, Mrs. Joe, 150
Tobin, Jim, 310
Todd, Al, 263
Toney, Fred, 167–70
Torre, Joe, 360, 400, 402
Traynor, Pie, 182, 184–85, 261
Trebelhorn, Tom, 496
Trillo, Manny, 431, 432, 433, 447–48
Tripartite Agreement, 71
Trout, Dizzy, 310, 312
Trout, Steve, 460, 461, 469, 471, 481, 487
Troy Haymakers, 30
Trucks, Virgil, 309
Tuohey, George, 86
Turley, Bob, 329
Turner, Ted, 486
Tyler, Lefty, 172, 173

Ueberroth, Peter, 492
Uecker, Bob, 390
Union League, 71
United States All-Stars, 360
United States League, 164
Ushering system, 202–3

Valentinetti, Vito, 365
Valli, Violet, 231, 232, 252–53
Vance, Dazzy, 221
Vandenberg, Hy, 305, 311, 312
Vander Meer, Johnny, 288–89, 291
Van Haltren, George, 74, 75
Vaughn, Jim "Hippo," 162, 167–70, 172
Veeck, Bill, Jr., 167, 180–81, 222–23, 240,
    242–43, 268–70, 272, 273–74, 276–78,
    294, 454
  black players and, 345–46, 349
  Harry Caray and, 456–57
  success as owner and promoter after leaving
    Cubs, 278, 280, 282, 457–58
Veeck, William, 175–78, 185, 191, 195, 208,
    209–10, 213, 214, 219, 224, 229, 230, 232,
    240–41, 272, 276
  death of, 177, 242–43
Verban, Emil, 287, 341–42
Verdi, Bill, 436
Verdi, Bob, 484
Von der Ahe, Chris, 49, 53, 56, 58, 60, 61
Vukovich, John, 474, 489, 496

Waddell, Rube, 151, 181
Wade, Gale, 333
Wagner, Honus, 31, 96, 113, 129, 130, 154, 350
Waitkus, Eddie, 315
Walberg, Rube, 215

Waldo, Hiram H., 9
Walker, Dixie, 293, 299, 300
Walker, Rube, 314
Walker, Verlon, 366
Walker, William, 174, 243–45, 253, 272
Waller, Judith, 177
Waller, Ty, 439, 452
Walls, Lee, 368
Walsh, Ed, 120, 121, 122, 123, 151
Walters, Bucky, 288–89
Walton, Jerome, 495
Waner, Lloyd, 184, 204, 220, 261
Waner, Paul, 184, 204, 207–8, 242, 261
Ward, Arch, 242
Ward, John Montgomery, 5, 27, 40, 87
  players union and, 73, 74, 75, 77
Ward, Robert, 166
Warneke, Lon, 226, 231, 242, 253–54, 255,
    258
Washington, Harold, 492
Washington Nationals, 7–8
Washington Senators, 125, 165, 177, 431, 444
Weaver, Jim, 244
Webb, Earl, 195, 204
Weber, Boots, 272, 274, 276, 277
Webster, Charles, 277, 278
Weeghman, Charles, 164–67, 170–71, 174–75,
    336
Weeghman Park, 165–66, 167
Weimer, Jake, 103
Welch, Bob, 476
Welch, Curt, 50, 58, 59, 60
Welch, Johnny, 188
Welch, Smiling Mickey, 48
Weller, Sam, 162
Wells, Boomer, 463
Western Association, 120
Western League, 85
  see also American League
Westlake, Wally, 333
West Side Park, *see* Congress Street Grounds
    (later West Side Park)
WGN, 337, 457–59, 472
Wheeler, Henry, 42
Wheeler, Lonnie, 375, 498
Whistler, Lew, 79
White, Bob, 399
White, Jim "Deacon," 15, 16, 20, 21, 22
White, Sol, 27
White, Will, 41, 42
White Sox, *see* Chicago White Sox
White Stockings, *see* Chicago White Stockings
Whitlow, Colonel Bob, 366, 373, 380
Whitney, Pinky, 186
Whitted, George, 179
Wicker, Bob, 104
Wiers, Jack, 495
Wiggins, Alan, 481, 484
Willard, Frances, 62
Williams, Billy, 364, 369, 372, 376, 388, 393,
    403, 404, 406, 409–10, 419, 420, 425, 431,
    432
Williams, Cy, 168, 169, 170

Williams, Dewey, 286, 292, 305–6, 310–11, 312, 344
Williams, Dick, 482
Williams, Stan, 377
Williams, Ted, 207, 281, 367, 431, 435, 442
Williamson, Ed (Ned), 33, 40, 42, 43, 46–47, 50, 52, 53, 57, 60, 63, 73, 74, 78
    death of, 88, 89
Willis, Vic, 130, 139
Wilson, Art, 168, 170
Wilson, Bert, 337
Wilson, Hack, 327
Wilson, Jimmie, 278, 284, 290, 291, 294, 295, 306
Wilson, Lewis Robert "Hack," 184–85, 195–99, 204, 212, 213, 220–24, 226–29, 241
    death of, 228
    elected to Hall of Fame, 229
    1930 season, 220–24, 229
    traded, 227–28
    in World Series of 1929, 216–19, 220, 221
Wilson, Owen "Chief," 130, 140
Wilson, Rube, 358
Wiltse, Hooks, 129, 138
Wistert, Whitey, 255
Women's Christian Temperance Movement, 62
Wood, Smokey Joe, 44
World Series:
    1885, 49–53, 62
    1886, 55–61, 63
    1906, 119–24, 138
    1907, 124–28
    1908, 151–54, 158, 159
    1909, 154
    1910, 154, 155
    1914, 178
    1918, 172–73
    1919, 139, 166, 167
    1921, 177
    1929, 215–19, 220, 221, 224, 225
    1932, 231–39
    1935, 256–58
    1938, 263–65
    1945, 309–12, 334
    precursor to, 41–42
World War I, 170–72, 185
World War II, 266, 280, 283–84, 290, 329
Wright, George, 4, 5, 6, 7, 11, 13, 21, 40–41, 92
Wright, Glenn, 184, 228
Wright, Harry, 4, 5, 6, 10–11, 13, 14, 16, 18–21, 24, 40, 41, 55, 76
Wright, Jim, 462–63
Wright & Ditson, 20, 24

Wrigley, Bill, Jr., 430, 444, 449, 453
Wrigley, Philip K., 182, 199, 229, 259–60, 265–80, 284, 294, 314, 318, 320, 322–23, 370–71, 393, 413, 423, 426, 454, 491
    black players and, 346, 347
    College of Coaches, 327, 365–67, 371–73, 375, 376, 380, 384, 387
    death of, 440, 443, 446
    described, 239–40, 265–69, 271
    estate of, 444
    as final decision maker, 271, 358, 374, 384–85
    managers selected by, 243, 244–45, 276–79, 295, 317, 326, 330, 331, 365–66, 384–85, 427, 431
    salaries of players and, 273, 279, 306, 307, 356–57, 358, 374, 440–42, 443
    unconventional methods of, 272–74, 373, 374
    Wrigley Field's importance to, 268, 269–70, 277, 280, 315, 337
Wrigley, William, Jr., 172–78, 182, 185, 190, 195, 199–203, 207, 209–10, 212, 213–15, 224–25, 242, 268, 491
    death of, 229, 239, 240
Wrigley Field, 202–3, 213–15, 219, 242, 243, 246, 261–63, 268–70, 277, 280, 315, 335–38, 393, 403, 432, 433, 443, 472, 481
    blocking off of center field bleachers, 319–20
    lights at, 491–93
    sale of bleacher tickets, 491
Wyatt, Whitlow, 272
Wyse, Hank, 286, 287–94, 297, 306, 309–10, 310, 312, 313–14, 343, 344, 393

Yankees, *see* New York Yankees
Yankee Stadium, 491
Yastrzemski, Carl, 402
Yawkey, William, 125, 127, 128
Yellowhorse, Chief Moses, 179, 180
York, Rudy, 310
Young, Dentin True "Cy," 80, 125, 186, 187
Young, Don, 405–8
Young, N. E., 92
Youngblood, Joel, 446

Zahn, Geoff, 432–33
Zimmer, Don, 374, 376, 377, 380–81, 429, 474, 489, 490, 494, 496
Zimmerman, Heinie, 106, 128–29, 156, 157
Zisk, Richie, 434, 448